The Hospitaller Knights of Saint John 1565–1623

The Hospitaller Knights of Saint John 1565-1623

Gordon Ellyson Abercrombie

Grosvenor House
Publishing Limited

This book is published by
Grosvenor House Publishing Ltd
Link House
140 The Broadway, Tolworth, Surrey, KT6 7HT.
www.grosvenorhousepublishing.co.uk

A CIP record for this book
is available from the British Library

ISBN 978-1-78623-735-4
eBook ISBN 978-1-80381-083-6

Table of Contents

Kos is subdued while in 1606 three of five galleys are storm lost. Finally, 1606 pay-back at Hammamet. All the while enrichment of Papal nephews reaches a new extreme.

Chapter IX years 1606-1613 under Grand Master Alof de Wignacourt includes a sixteen-month visit to Malta during which Caravaggio paints five masterpieces. It also includes 1609 destruction by four Hospitaller galleons of the Ottoman fortress at Lajazzo/Laiazzo in the Gulf of Alexandretta, one of the galleons the 80-gun *Galion Rouge* belonging to corsair Jean-Jacques d'Isnard de Fraisinet. This chapter further includes the consequence at the Battle of Kara Djahannum which marked the appearance in history of Khalil Pasha son of Piri His, three times Ottoman Kapudan Pasha and twice Grand Vizier. The chapter continues with a succession of Hospitaller assaults at Ottoman Navarin, Corinth, and Tunisian Cherchene.

Chapter X years 1613-1617 under Grand Master Alof de Wignacourt opens with a failed Hospitaller assault on Ottoman Phocaea (Foça), a 1613 Tuscan assault on the Karamanian fortress at Agha Liman, the port for ancient Seleucia, and destruction at the Battle of Cape Corvo of eight Ottoman galleys with freedom of 1,200 chained Christian oarsmen. There follows a 1614 Ottoman raid on Malta, payback for the year-earlier raid on Phocaea. During 1615 the 26.5 kilometer Wignacourt Aqueduct was inaugurated, each day bringing 49,000 cubic feet of water from elevated springs near Dingli and Rabat to Valletta and consumers in between. Finally, there is the 1616 Naval Battle of Cape Gelidonia depicted on the dust jacket.

Chapter XI years 1617-1622 under Grand Master Alof de Wignacourt includes the 1617 Battle of Mljet between Neapolitans and Venetians as well as 1618 and 1619 Christian assaults on Susa (Sousse), a fortified port on eastern Tunisia's Gulf of Hammamet harboring English renegade Sampson Denball. There follows the Spanish Conspiracy against Venice and the 1620 Ottoman sack of Manfredonia, a devastating pay-back for the Catholic Armada's assaults on Susa. And more.

Introduction

The author came to the writing of *The Hospitaller Knights of Saint John* with an unflagging interest in history and decades of residence and travel in the Near East. A former naval officer and sailing-yacht owner, he also brought to the undertaking a deep respect for seamen of the age of sail. As importantly, he brought tens of thousands of sea miles to the undertaking, including thousands of miles of solo sailing leaving him with a profound awareness of weather at sea and its impact on maritime history. He in addition brought hundreds of personal explorations of Mediterranean arenas of history a number of which were of those remarkable redoubts called Rhodes and Malta, not to overlook multiple inspections of most other Hospitaller facilities in the Mediterranean.

The author is deeply indebted to Giacomo Bosio who has already written an unsurpassable *Istoria della Sacra Religione et Illustria Militia di San Giovanni Gierosolimitano*. And Bosio did it without the World Wide Library available today. The author is also deeply indebted to Bosio's 1571 successor Bartolomeo dal Pozzo, an Hospitaller who participated in some of the history he describes, an history as detailed as that of his predecessor.

For many readers and students of history, however, the Renaissance Italian of Giacomo Bosio and Bartolomeo dal Pozzo is a difficult read as it was for this author. It is this author's hope he has nevertheless transcribed some of the wealth of Bosio and Dal Pozzo content and complemented it with truths revealed in the nearly 400 years of scholarship since Bosio's death in 1627. These complementary truths are the work of scores of learned historians too numerous to name here but who are named in notes to the text. One standing out among others, however, is linguist and historian Kenneth M. Setton whose four-volume *The Papacy and the Levant 1204-1571* and *Venice, Austria, and the Turks in the Seventeenth Century* are must-reading for anyone with an interest in the Hospitaller Knights of Saint John, or with an interest in the Levant, or simply with an interest in history.

The Hospitaller Knights of Saint John comes in four volumes, the first volume encompassing the Order's years at Rhodes between 1306 and 1522, including the three great sieges of Rhodes Town the last of which resulted in the Order's eviction by Ottoman Sultan Suleiman. This period also witnessed the Order's transition from Hospitallers on horseback to Hospitallers at sea, and it gave rise to the Barbarossa Brothers and other corsairs both Christian and Muslim. The second volume deals first with the seven years 1523 into 1530 during which the Hospitallers with 4,000 displaced Rhodians in train searched for a new home and finally found it at Malta. For the next 35 years the Order transformed this bare rock without a tree into a promised land, ending when the same sultan failed to evict the Order from its new home. This the third volume covers the years 1565 into 1623, while the fourth volume will cover the years 1623 into 1688. By intention all four volumes focus on individuals, not only on popes and royalty but also on properly identified lieutenants as well as on properly identified allies and opponents. But not at the expense of history itself. The author hopes the reader finds *The Hospitaller Knights of Saint John* as instructive and interesting as did he.

List of Illustrations

Chapter I

1565–1568

On 6 September 1565 the Spanish Relief Armada or Grand Soccorso at Sicily set off for Malta in three squadrons, vanguard, battle, and rear guard. The vanguard consisting of 19 galleys was commanded by Sancho de Leyva aboard a royal capitana flanked by the capitanas of Genovese entrepreneurs Stefano di Mare and Giorgio Grimaldi. The battle group of 20 galleys was commanded by Garcia de Toledo and consisted of 8 royal galleys and 12 others. Juan de Cardona commanded the rear guard of 17 galleys, 7 of Sicily, 7 of Gian Andrea Doria, and 3 of the Genovese Marco Centurione.[1] Early the next morning these landed on the north shore of Malta 8,000 infantry under Alvaro de Sande and 1,600 adventurers under various commanders[2] before returning to Sicily for a second embarkation, first, however, sailing past Grand Harbor to announce their arrival.[3]

Upon sighting of reinforcements from Sicily on 7 September, the Ottoman siege of Malta was lifted beginning that day and ending 11 September, after which Mathurin Romegas led a company of soldiers to the remains of Fort Saint Elmo where he raised the white-cross-on-red-field banner of the Religion in honor of the fort's 1,200 dead defenders.[4] A contemporary source asserts the Turks lost 30,000 dead during the failed Siege of Malta.[5] Participant Francisco Balbi di Correggio puts the number at 35,000.[6] But as only 30,000 arrived and 10,000 departed, a better estimate is 20,000, most of them as innocent of evil as their Christian counterparts. Among defenders three thousand died.[7] Of the 470 Hospitallers mustering in May joined by 47 others of the Piccolo Soccorso, 212 are known to have lost their lives. One of these not mentioned elsewhere was François de Bouliers dit Tour-d'Aigues of the Langue of Provence. One of eleven children of Jean Louis de Bouliers, Baron de la Tour-d'Aigues, only the tragedy of his death earned him a place in history though his death was mourned by family and those who knew him as deeply as any other.

The grief-stricken included non-combatant Maltese who lost both family and home while distraught widows and parents populated every corner of the Mediterranean. Truly, the 1565 Ottoman Siege of Malta was the work of the devil and his minions who brought it about. Hospitallers lost to family and friends may be found listed in the final pages of *The Hospitaller Knights of Saint John 1523-1565* under Elmo Dead with the balance listed under Other Dead. Dead combatants other than Hospitallers consisted of hired soldiers, Maltese militia, and a handful of adventurers. For three consecutive days last offices were conducted in the Church of San Lorenzo honoring those gone.

Garcia de Toledo arrived at Malta with 48 galleys during the evening of 15 September 1565 to embark some of the Spanish soldiers assigned to defense of Malta and to then go in pursuit of the Ottoman armada which only days earlier had taken course for the Levant from Sicily's Cape Murro di Porco, sailing ships towed by oared galleys in an absence of wind. Toledo's arrival was accompanied by the Hospitaller galleys of Pierre de Roquelaure-Saint-Aubin and Jean de la Valette-Cornusson laden with foodstuffs, refreshments, and material supplies. The Spanish armada entered Grand Harbor with flags flying and an artillery salute. Upon debarking Toledo was met at the port by Grand Master, Council, and leaders of earlier rescue missions. Grandmaster and Viceroy greeted each other with an embrace. Following their verbal exchange, Gian Andrea Doria was also greeted by Grand Master Parisot de la Valette with open arms. And then Don Juan de Cardona. Others similarly greeted included Andrea Provana, Alvaro de Bazán, Sancho de Leyva, and Juan de Bivero y Mercado, Count of Altamira, among many others. Valette also greeted returning Grand Hospitaller Jacques d'Arquinvillier de Tourville, Grand Conservator Pedro de Iunient, the venerable Bailiff of Mallorca Onofre de Monsuar, Commander Niccolò Orsino di Rivalta, and others whom Toledo had physically restrained from joining the Grand Soccorso for reasons of age or debility.

Following a celebratory dinner that evening, and having embarked Don Alvaro de Sande with the tercios of Sicily and Naples, and Chiappino di Vitelli with his volunteers, the Spanish armada departed Malta on 16 September and sailed in good time to the Strivali Islands south of Zante. Learning at the Strivalis the Turks were still ahead. Toledo then proceeded to Cerigo (Kithera) arriving on the 23rd.

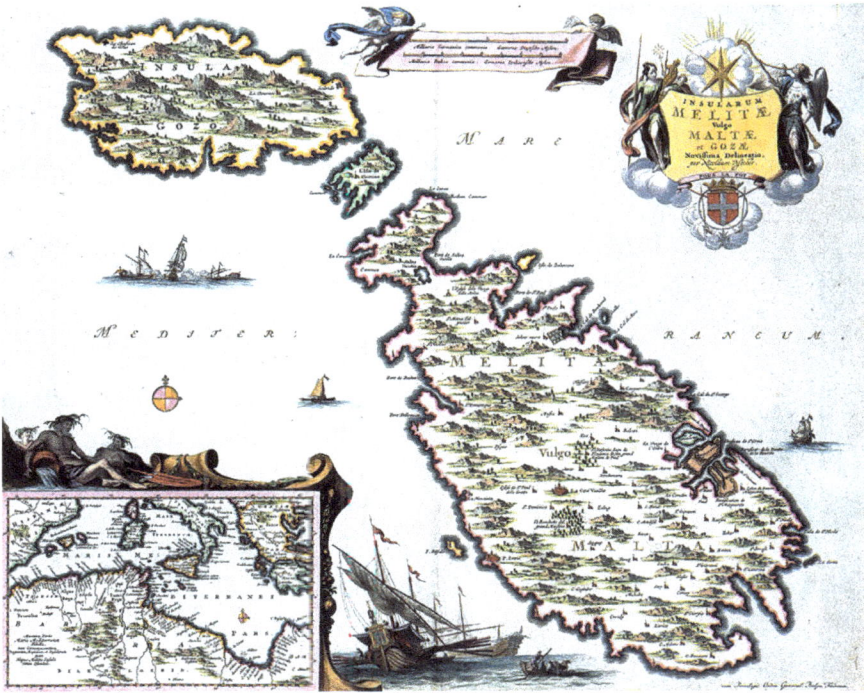

Atlas van der Hagen's Malta Map.

By then the enemy were in the Turkish Aegean. On 1 October he abandoned his quest and on 7 October was back at Messina.[8]

At the October Council meeting following the end to hostilities, Hospitaller Don Diego Enríquez y Guzmán was appointed Bailiff of Negroponte in succession of the deceased Juan de Eguaras. Enríquez y Guzman went by the same name as and is believed to have been a nephew of the 5th Count of Alba de Liste and future Viceroy of Sicily (1585–1591). Grand Hospitaller Jacques d'Arquinvillier de Tourville and Don Ernando de Alarcón were appointed Procurators of the Common Treasury while the latter was also appointed Lieutenant Grand Chancellor. Magistral Receiver Giovan Francesco de la Motta was appointed Conventual Conservator succeeding the deceased Luis Cortit, and was succeeded as Magistral Receiver by Olivier d'Aux de Bourneuf of the Priory of Aquitaine. Provision was made for ransom of Adrien de là Rivière Sainte-Geneviève of Paris and Don Girolamo di Gravina of Catania, both taken captive by the Turks during the Siege. It was soon discovered, however, that

Geneviève, captured on the first day of hostilities, had either been killed during capture or had died in captivity, while Gravina, a part of June's Piccolo Soccorso, was captured at the Rinella Bay rendezvous with small boats transporting the Soccorso to Birgu. He had made a wondrous escape by means of one of his father's ships. No provision was made for Elmo captives as no such captives had yet to be revealed. The Sacred Council also appointed Jacques-Philippe de Ligneville de Tantonville of the Priory of Champagne a Curator at the Church of the Madonna of Picciana in Apulia; Ligneville had been taken captive during the Grand Soccorso but escaped and wished to give proper thanks to the Madonna. Given his personal family losses during the Siege the Grand Master reassigned Jean de la Valette Cornusson from command of *San Iacomo* to his Magistral staff. Commander Jean de Viry de la Forest of Auvergne succeeded to command of *San Iacomo*. Appointed Treasurer at the same time was Guillaume de Malain de Lux, Commander of Bellecroix and Pontaubert of the Priory of Champagne. The Dignity of Treasurer had been vacant since the July 1564 promotion of incumbent Pierre Pelloquin de la Plesse to Bailiff of the Morea.[9]

Having first paused at Gallipoli to obtain license to return to port from Sultan Suleiman, the Ottoman Armada reached Constantinople on 9 November 1565. No heads rolled, and Piali Pasha remained Armada Commander. Siege commander Kizilahmedli Mustafa Pasha would serve under Suleiman during 1566's Hungarian campaign, would lose his position as 4th Vizier following the sultan's death, and would then retire.[10]

For the remainder of the year at Malta and well into the next the Infirmary remained full of those wounded during the Siege, besieged and besieger. Overflow was accommodated in individual houses of Birgu and Senglea. Over the same period burial of cadavers, especially of besiegers, seemed never-ending. Fields had become fallow and beasts of burden had been eaten. There was little food and the little was rationed. Special ambassadors were sent begging. Commander Paolo Fiamberto of Pavia was dispatched to Pius IV's Holy See, Captain Rodrigo Maldonado of Castile to Holy Roman Emperor Maximilian II, Commander Antoine Flotte de la Roche to his Christian Majesty King Charles IX of France, and Commander Pedro Boninseña of Castile to his Catholic Majesty Philip II of Spain. And then there was destruction, massive destruction as 35 years of improvements had been wasted by combat. All of the trees planted by Hospitallers on the once barren island had been cut down for gun platforms and cooking fires. Commissioners of re-construction were appointed. Pierre de la Chastre of Auvergne and Vasino Malabaila of Asti found only a single piece of artillery at Fort Saint Elmo, all of the rest earlier shipped to Constantinople. Orders were placed for both re-construction materials and munitions, stretching the Order's already suspect credit.

During the Siege of Malta Captain of Reserves Pedro de Mendoza had succeeded Lieutenant Grand Chancellor and Pilier of the Langue of Castile and Portugal Don Luis de Paz, killed in action at Birgu.[11] In Mendoza's place, Pedro Boninseña had been appointed Captain of Reserves. Following departure of the Ottomans, Mendoza and others received the thanks of Grand Master Valette, Mendoza as Captain of the Post of Castile (the section of wall at the SW corner of Birgu) where he had also succeeded De Paz. By year-end Mendoza had replaced Pierre de Gioù as General of the Galleys.[12] The (Magistral) Great Galleon or captured Sultana which had become an Ottoman target late in the Siege was repaired and re-fitted at the Arsenal; Guion de Saugniac de Belcastel of Provence was appointed to her command in succession of the deceased Gaspard de la Motte, his lieutenant Andrea Magnasco of Genoa, called Captain Fantone. First appearing at Malta in 1550 as an established mariner, Fantone's own Genovese-flag sailing vessel had been trapped at Malta by the Great Siege during which he took Holy Orders as a combat novice and was knighted only following Ottoman withdrawal. The Great Galleon sailed outbound with discharged combatants and inbound filled to capacity with foodstuffs, construction materials, and munitions, the latter as the Grand Master believed there was every chance the Ottomans would return in 1566. This time with Suleiman![13]

Upon pleas of Ambassador Boninseña, of Ascanio della Corgnia, and of Don Alvaro de Sande, late in 1565 King Philip II granted the Order 30,000 gold scudos toward construction of the new city of Valletta.[14] On 5 January 1566 the Grand Master and Council, in apprehension of a second assault by the Turks, appointed ten of the Order's knights most experienced in war each to enlist a company of 300 soldiers in Rome, Tuscany, Naples, Calabria, and Sicily. Additionally, a General Summons was sent to all priories and commanderies ordering assembly at Malta in April. On the same date Guillaume de la Fontaine (Captain Champagne) was dispatched as ambassadeur extraordinaire to the court of French King Charles IX to plead the Order's impoverished circumstances as well as the continuing Ottoman threat to Malta.[15] On 7 January Antonio Ghislieri of the Piedmont was elected Pope as Pius V, succeeding Pius IV who died on 9 December.[16]

Special ambassadors to local viceroys and princes were appointed, Seneschal Pierre de Gioù to the Viceregency of Sicily, Pietro Giustiniani of Venice to other Italian states, and senior Hospitaller at the Convent Francisco Borguès to Spanish nations. These departed Malta on 14 January aboard the Magistral capitana temporarily commanded by Pierre de Saint-Aubin and aboard San Giovanni commanded by Francisco Guiral. Each ambassador was seeking immediate assistance in terms of food supplies and reconstruction assistance.

All three were returned to Malta by Garcia de Toledo in the company of Vincenzo del Bosco Agliata, Sicilian Count of Vicari and Minister of Justice in Toledo's viceregency. Vicari was charged with approving plans for the new city of Valletta, a prerequisite for the 30,000 scudo Royal grant, and he had reservations concerning what came first, reconstruction or the new city. This interference in the business of the Order by Garcia Alvarez de Toledo did not sit well with Parisot de la Valette, adding to the latter's distress with death and destruction caused by late arrival of Toledo's Grand Soccorso.[16]

It might be noted in defense of Toledo, however, he had only nominal experience commanding at sea, his armada was smaller than the Ottoman Armada surrounding Malta, the numbers manning and conveyed by his ships to be risked were greater than the number of besieged to be succored, and as importantly, he would have been haunted by Spain's dismal record of combat at sea. Finally, it is probable that King Philip himself, not Toledo, demanded oversight of the expenditure of his 30,000 scudos. These issues among so many others seemed to have escaped Parisot de la Valette.

Meanwhile Prior of Capua and future Grand Master Pietro del Monte had been appointed Ambassador to the Holy See with brief to render the Order of Jerusalem's obeisance to new Pope Pius V. He and the Count of Vicari with advisers departed Malta on 3 February as passengers aboard four galleys under command of General of the

Galleys Pedro de Mendoza. Mendoza's capitana was then commanded by nephew Don Garcia de Mendoza in succession of Thomas de la Tour de Murat. The other three galleys were the Magistral padrona commanded by Pierre de Saint-Aubin, *San Iacomo* commanded by Jean de Viry de la Forest in succession of Jean de la Valette Cornusson, and *San Giovanni* commanded by Francisco de Guiral, the latter returning from Rome with ambassadeurs extraordinaire Antonio Maldonado and Guillaume de la Fontaine. While at Rome the two ambassadors obtained from new Pope Pius V promises of coin as well as maintenance of 3,000 Italian infantry at Malta. The same four galleys on orders of the Grand Master then proceeded to Sicily and Italy in a quest for munitions, transporting, as well, six of the ten captains appointed to hire soldiers for service at Malta.

On 10 February 1566 the Grand Master's oft-postponed 2nd Chapter General convened at Malta's Church of San Lorenzo with a Pontifical Mass, the sermon delivered by Prior of the Church Antoine Cressin, a Greek chaplain of the Latin Church received into the Langue of Auvergne. Following Mass the Convent proceeded in procession to the Great Hall of the Magistral Palace where Bailiff of Santa Eufemia Don Fabrizio Pignatelli 40 years an Hospitaller delivered a sermon noteworthy not for Christian zeal but rather for prudence, justice, religion, and the rule of law. Following Pignatelli's sermon the Grand Master summarized Malta's present state of affairs, listing its urgent needs. Bearers of the Grand Cross present were recognized. These were Bishop of Malta Dominico Cubelles of Aragon, Prior of the Church Antoine Cressin of Auvergne, both chaplains, Marshal Guillaume Coppier of Auvergne, Grand Hospitaller Jacques d'Arquinvillier de Tourville of France, Admiral Luigi Broglia of Chieri, Grand Conservator Pedro de Iunient of Junyent 195km NNW of Barcelona, Prior of Saint-Gilles Louis du Pont, Prior of Champagne Jean Audebert de l'Aubuge, Prior of Auvergne Louis de Lastic, Prior of Messina Signorino della Gattinara, and Bailiff of Caspe Luis de Salcedo of Aragon, the latter a veteran of 1522's Great Siege of Rhodes as well as of 1565's Great Siege of Malta.

Recognition of Bearers of the Grand Cross was succeeded by incorporation of the Chapter General with election of Sixteen *Capitolari* or legislators, as follow: Bertrand de Vintimille d'Ollioules and Mathurin d'Aux de Lescout-Romegas for Provence; Marshal

Guillaume de Coppier, pre-eminent among the others as President of the Chapter General, and Prior of Auvergne Louis de Lastic for Auvergne; Jacques d'Arquinvillier de Tourville and Jean Audebert de l'Aubuge for France; Pedro de Iunient and Luis de Salcedo for Aragon; Signorino della Gattinara and Conventual Conservator Giovan Francesco Langosco de Conti della Motta for Italy; Lieutenant Turcopolier Oliver Starkey and, there being only one English knight at the Convent, Jacques de Vieuxpont of the Langue of France for England; Lieutenant Grand Bailiff Konrad II von Schwalbach and, there being only one eligible German voter at the Convent, Jean de Viry de la Forest of Auvergne for Germany; and Don Fernando de Alarcón and Commander Pedro de Mesquite for Castile. These Sixteen Legislators then took an oath to deliberate in the best interests of the entire Republic. In their company representing the Grand Master but not voting were Seneschal Pierre de Gioù and Vice Chancellor Martín Rojas de Portalrubio as financial advisor, as well as Treasury Scribe Augustin de Sainte-Maure to record proceedings. These nineteen individuals retired to the house of Jean de la Valette Cornusson to deliberate motions put before them. Because Procurators of the Common Treasury were among the Sixteen, Pietro Giustiniani of Venice and Geronimo de Guete were elected as advocates to assist the Chapter in defending its motions. Other than extending annual levies on priories and commanderies at a level insufficient to please the Grand Master, however, there were no significant motions adopted.[17]

The Chapter General was still in session when the galleys of the Religion and the padrona of the Grand Master returned to Malta from Sicily with news that in Constantinople preparation of the Ottoman Armada for deployment was again proceeding at a steady pace, and that among Turks throughout the Levant there was talk of another strike at Malta. This report moved Grand Master and Council to press ahead with ambassadorial solicitations of assistance, particularly for re-construction and re-armament of Fort Saint Elmo and for strengthening Castle Saint Angelo and the city of Notabile. A dry moat or fosse was planned for Fort Saint Elmo stretching from Grand Harbor to Marsamuscietto. Initial hires of soldiery arrived at Malta on 22 February. Four new Captains were dispatched to Italy each to hire 300 more soldiers. For this and other purposes the Order's Receiver in

Naples Giorgio Vercelli was authorized to borrow 20,000 scudos at interest. Giuseppe Cambiano of Turin, Resident Ambassador and Procurator General to the Holy See, was directed to assist Vercelli in raising necessary funds. Cambiano was also to solicit from the Holy Father declaration of a Jubilee against Turks during which contributors would be forgiven their sins. The Jubilee was subsequently declared for July through December. (This Jubilee was also presented to Elizabeth I, Queen of England and Ireland, as an opportunity to restore the Order of Saint John in her dominions. The Queen failed to avail herself of this means of expiating her sins.) Grand Master and Sacred Council considered establishment of a permanent home guard of 1,000 soldiers divided into three or four companies, a proposal tabled for further study.[18]

The Chapter General convened on 10 February 1566 concluded on 6 March. The following day Grand Master and Council determined that solicitation of princes would best be effected by the Grand Master himself, and not by his ambassadors. Marshal Guillaume Coppier was appointed Lieutenant to the Grand Master and Captain-General of the defense of Malta should the Grand Master be absent in Sicily or elsewhere with the galleys. Coppier had at his disposal all other Hospitallers at Malta as well as 4,000 hired soldiers, all of whom had the ability to retire to Notabile should defenses at the ports fail. That same day, 7 March, Don Francesco di Guevara of Naples and Geronimo Sagra of Aragon began to stock Castle Saint Angelo with water, grinding wheels, artillery and other arms, munitions, artificial fire, hardware, timber, earth, medicines, foodstuffs, and especially with grain, biscuit, wine, vinegar, and salted meat. Fort Saint Elmo was provided with the same items at the same time.

Hospitaller Rafaello Salvago, lyric poet and historian, returned to Malta from Genoa without succor for the Order. He had acted as courier between Malta and Sicily for much of the Great Siege before returning to his home city following Ottoman withdrawal. Robert des Guillaumanches of Auvergne similarly returned empty-handed. Bailiff of Negroponte Don Diego de Guzman died at Barcelona. Appointed his successor was Commander of Novillas and Aliaga Luis de Talavera. Still on 7 March three galleys of the Malta Squadron under command of General Pedro de Mendoza departed Malta for Sicily transporting

Catalan Francisco Borguès to meetings with Viceroy Garcia de Toledo for the purpose of accelerating the hire of 3,000 infantry.

Departing with squadron galleys was the Magistral capitana commanded by Mathurin Romegas. Romegas was bound for Syracuse to place orders for certain necessities after which he was to proceed into the Levant to ascertain movement of the Ottoman Armada. He was also to put ashore in Turkish territory Hospitaller Knight of Grace Yiannis Bareles, a native of Constantinople, as well as a second unnamed agent. During the passage from Malta to Sicily the four Maltese encountered the Genovese galley *Lomellina* en route Malta with the Order's Prior of Hungary Gabrio Serbellone embarked. A cousin of deceased Pope Pius IV who had in 1562 force-fed Serbellone into the Order of Jerusalem with the dignity of Prior of Hungary and attendant Grand Cross, Serbellone was also a highly regarded condottiero, a veteran of combat in Hungary against Suleiman's 1543 Ottoman Siege of Esztergom, and a respected fortifications engineer. He had been dispatched by King Philip II of Spain to help design the new city of Valletta.[19]

With agreement between Grand Master, Council, and Serbellone, foundation blocks for the new city of Valletta were laid on 14 March 1566 under immediate supervision of the Order's engineering lieutenant and non-Hospitaller, Captain Francesco Laparelli. As Serbellone had reached Malta only three days earlier, it cannot be said, as it is sometimes said, that Serbellone designed the new city of Valletta. It can be said he approved the design, perhaps with modifications. It may be said in addition that he endeavored to repair relations between the Grand Master and the Viceroy, a relationship soured by the tardy arrival of the Grand Succorso and further exacerbated by Viceregal interference in planning for the city of Valletta. On 22 March the three galleys of the Religion were again dispatched to Sicily transporting to safety many Maltese families. Serbellone departed with them aboard the same galley *Lomellina*. After meeting with Serbellone, Viceroy Garcia de Toledo penned a long letter to and concerning his respect for the Grand Master. Support in the way of foodstuff availability suddenly improved. There was a promise of laborers to assist in construction and re-construction. Pierre de Saint-Aubin was loading the Magistral padrona *Santa Marta* with the Order's Sacred Relics brought from Jerusalem and Rhodes for transport to safety in Sicily when news was received at

Malta that Sultan Suleiman had decided to personally lead another campaign through Hungary to Vienna departing Constantinople at April-end.

A second siege of Malta suddenly seemed improbable. The anticipated departure of Valette to seek succor from surrounding heads of state was indefinitely postponed. Sacred Relics were off-loaded, and *Santa Marta* was ordered to the Barbary Coast to ascertain preparation of Ottoman corsairs, if at all, for a joint undertaking with the Ottoman Armada. Saint-Aubin, however, found unseasonal winds so daunting he was unable to approach Uluç Ali's Tripoli and Djerba. Meanwhile hired infantry was assembling in the thousands at Palermo, Messina, Calabria, Naples, Rome, Perugia, and Florence. Assembling at Hospital expense. Arms shipments were enroute Malta from Italy, France, Spain, Germany, and all the provinces of Europe. Adventurers were gathering. Arriving Malta on 27 March was a ship belonging to Jean la Belle of Marseille full of war munitions and provisions ordered by François de Moreton Chabrillan, Receiver at the Priory of Saint-Gilles. The galleon of Pierre Chanaud, also of Marseille, was the same day ordered to embark 14 pieces of bronze artillery from Avignon. Commander Marc de la Goutte, Receiver for the Langue of Auvergne at Lyons, was readying for shipment 12 pieces of artillery comprised of four serpentines, four medium cannon, and four basilisks. Foundries at Messina and Syracuse were furiously producing artillery to orders from Malta.[20]

Unbeknownst to the Grand Master, Sultan Suleiman departed Constantinople on the first day of May 1566 on campaign into Hungary. Within days the Grand Master was informed Captains Don Juan Pereiro de La Roca, Pierre de Montauban de Voguedemar, Esteban de Claramonte, Don Costantino Castriota of Naples, and Nicolas de Mirè of Pays de la Loire had completed hire and equipping of their companies of 300 infantry each. Tomás Coronel of Aragon had his company ready a few days later. On 7 May the Grand Master sent the three galleys of the Religion, the capitana *San Giovan Battista*, *San Giovanni*, and *San Iacomo*, to Messina where they were joined by the refitted *Santa Maria della Corona* which had earlier been raised from the bottom of Dockyard Creek and placed under command of Pietro Giustiniani of Venice in succession of the deceased Carlo Ruffo and, nominally, of Naples' Ercole Caraccioli. These galleys were to tow to Malta ships chartered to transport hired soldiers.

Suddenly rumors of Ottoman intent began to vacillate between an assault on Malta and a campaign into Hungary. The Grand Master was still caught between a need to be prepared at Malta and a need to preserve every penny for construction and reconstruction. He sent his Secretary Laurent Raymond to Pozzalo, Sicily, with orders to pour through every piece of captured correspondence for clues. Not much later he received from Ambassador Antonio Maldonado at Madrid the promise of King Philip II to send a large number of soldiers to the defense of Malta over and above 2,000 coming from Sicily under command of Ascanio della Corgnia, those coming from Spain comprised of 3,000 veteran Spanish soldiers under command of Don Pedro de Padilla plus 3,000 Germans under command of Paris Graf von Lodrone of Trentino Alto Adige. This advice was followed by another from Maldonado that the same troops were being diverted to a siege of Algiers, a siege which did not take place. Finally came advice from Emperor Maximilian II of a major Ottoman incursion into his territory by forces under command of Sultan Suleiman. Hospitaller Grand Prior of Germany Georg Bombast von Hohenheim led a contingent of knights and hired infantry to the emperor's aid. Saint-Aubin and Rafaello Salvago returned to Malta with certain news of Ottoman occupation of Scio (Chios) but without news of Ottoman intention to send an Armada west. On 20 May[22] the two galley captains were sent yet again into the Levant, heading for the Arms of Maina (the Morea's Mani Peninsula), and from there headed in the direction of Candia (Crete). From a Ragusan ship coming from the Black Sea they learned on 27 May Piali, having occupied Scio, was then collecting tribute from various islands in the Greek Archipelago. Two galliots of Piali's armada were then in Candian waters for that purpose. Saint-Aubin, sailing at dawn near Garbuse (Gramvousa Islands) at the NW corner of Candia, soon encountered the smaller (18 banks) of the two galliots, and his faster and more powerful *Santa Marta* quickly subdued the enemy vessel; her Christian oarsmen became her crew, her Turkish complement became her oarsmen, and soldiers from *Santa Marta* were added. Five miles later the two ships sighted the second, 20-bank, galliot. Both oncoming vessels grappled and the second Ottoman was also subdued.[22]

While 36 Turks lost their lives in the two engagements, 90 Turks were taken captive and most would be sent to the oars. Having re-armed the larger galliot with items from the smaller, and manned her with liberated Christians, *Santa Marta* started for Malta with the larger galliot, arriving 2 June; the smaller was donated to Candia's Church of San Giovanni of Garbuse. Re-furbished, the larger galliot would be presented as a gift to the Pope in May 1567. Meanwhile not only were companies of hired infantry beginning to reach Malta, but so too were hundreds of adventurers dispatched from France by and with Guillaume de la Fontaine. These included Timoleone de Cossé, Count of Brissac; Philippe Strozzi, son of deceased Florentine Marshal of France Pietro Strozzi and a principal Captain of the Royal Guard; Roger de Saint-Lary, Lord of Bellegarde and favorite of Kings Henry III and Henry IV; Jean de Vivonne, Lord of Sangatte, Marquis de Pisani, and French Ambassador to the Holy See; Jacques de Villiers de la Riviere, of the family of Grand Master Philippe Villiers de l'Isle-Adam; 19 year-old novitiate Alof de Wignacourt who took the Habit in August with other nobles of Provence, and who in 1601 would be elected 54th Grand Master of the Order of Jerusalem. There were in addition many other lords of France with retinue. They had all come to lock horns with the Ottomans of Sultan Suleiman. And for glory, sole raison d'etre of nobility's warrior class. After tarrying at Scio and collecting tribute in the Aegean for six weeks, Piali Pasha at end-May 1566 turned the prows of his galleys further west.[23]

Early in June Pierre de Saint-Aubin and Rafaello Salvago voiced their view Piali Pasha's armada was bound for the Venetian Gulf or Adriatic in support of Suleiman's Campaign in Hungary. Parisot de la Valette remained unconvinced. On 8 June Gian Andrea Doria appeared at Malta to alert the Grand Master to the imminent arrival of Spanish, German, and Italian infantry. On 14 June there was still no concrete news of Ottoman intent. A few days later Grand Bailiff of Germany Adam von Schwalbach arrived at Malta with a company of German knights and German adventurers, the knights stocking a near-empty German auberge and donating 3,000 scudos to the Common Treasury. On 24 June the Ottoman Galley Armada was sighted near the Strofadi Islands south of Venetian Zante and 385 nautical miles east of Malta, 106 galleys and seven galliots strong.

Importantly, there were no support vessels; this could not be a siege fleet without siege artillery, munitions, ground forces, and provisions. Rather the galley armada appeared to be headed into the Adriatic, probably to Austrian locales in the north which could be shelled from the sea. The Grand Master received this information on 29 June. Meanwhile, on 17 June, 8,000 Spanish, German, and Italian infantry had been put ashore at Malta. As many more had been hired by the Order and by the Church or had accompanied French commanders. And that did not include the Maltese themselves. Nor did it include the hundreds of Hospitallers arriving from mainland Europe in response to the Grand Master's summons. At its peak the total was 18,000 visiting infantry and 300 horse. It was not just a financial disaster, but a feeding disaster, and a housing disaster, and a potential medical disaster. In Rome, Pope Pius V pled by letter for Viceroy Garcia de Toledo who commanded an armada equivalent to that of Piali to trap and destroy the Ottomans in the Adriatic. To no avail. Spain had no love for Venice, and no record of successful war at sea. Piali sailed all the way to the top of the "Venetian Gulf" to assail the Empire's Fiume (Rijeka) and Trieste in support of Suleiman's campaign. There was neither siege of Malta nor nearby naval engagement. Six months of hires and preparation had been for naught.[24]

Finding no glory in their Maltese circumstances, French adventurers were the first to depart, embarking aboard three squadron galleys and Saint-Aubin's Magistrale padrona on 12 July to be transported to the vicinity of Rome. At the feet of Pope Pius V these penitents were granted 10,000 scudos to cover their travel expenses. Accompanying the French at Rome was Pierre de Rocquelaure Saint-Aubin on the Grand Master's errand to thank His Holiness for his support, and particularly for his support financing the new city of Valletta at 5,000 scudos per month from Jubilee income. The Pope thanked Saint-Aubin for liberating Christian oarsmen from the two Ottoman galliots captured in May.[25]

In mid-July Bailiff of Venosa Ardicino Barba of Turin came to the end of his life, 53 years of which had been as an Hospitaller. Barba was succeeded as Bailiff of Venosa by Antonio Peletta of Asti. Peletta was in turn succeeded as Admiral by Pietro Giustiniani of Venice on a split vote going against Niccolò Rivalta of Turin. The Ottoman Galley Armada, meanwhile, found Fiume and Trieste well-armed and ready, and retired to Valona (Vlorë) in Ottoman Albania without firing a shot in anger. At Malta 18 galleys under command of Don Alvaro de Bazán put into the pratique port (crews normally not permitted ashore) of Marsamuscietto on 22 July to embark 2,000 Italians commanded by Ascanio della Corgnia and 3,000 Germans commanded by Count Lodrone. As soldiers departed, construction workers arrived.[25]

François Salviati of the Langue of France was dispatched in August 1566 to the Court of French King Charles IX and Queen Regent Catherine de Medici as Ambassadeur Extraordinaire, his first order of business to thank the crown for assistance rendered the past two years. Antonio Maldonado was continued as Resident Ambassador to the Court of Spanish King Philip II. On 10 August Commander Diego de Solis of Asturias sailed aboard the Grand Master's personal galleon in company with Grand Conservator (Draper) Pedro de Iunient (Pere de Junyent in Catalan), departing Malta bound for Mallorca and thence by brigantine to Barcelona. Solis was charged with collecting all due responsions in Spain and returning with them to Malta. Old and said to be infirm, Iunient had permission to return to his commandery in Spain from whence he had arrived with the Grand Soccorso 11 months earlier; he would live another twelve years, ten of them as Prior of Catalonia. The galleon itself was accompanied by the Magistral capitana commanded by Mathurin Romegas as far as Agrigento, Sicily, where Hospitaller Captain Guion de Saugniac de Belcastel of Provence embarked. (This entry clarifies Bosio's confusing references to the sultana captured in June 1564. The ship belonged to Parisot de la Valette and not to the Order of Jerusalem. Similarly, credit (or blame) for her capture went to the overall Magistral commander at her capture, Romegas, and not to General of the Galleys Pierre de Gioù. An old conflict sustained and a pre-existing angst amplified.

On 12 August Alvaro de Bazán's 18 galleys departed Malta with embarked Italian and German infantry. On the same date 15 other galleys under command of Don Juan de Cardona reached Malta to embark Spanish infantry commanded by Pedro de Padilla for transport to Messina, departing on 14 August. At Messina Viceroy Garcia Alvarez de Toledo was assembling a Catholic Armada to proceed into the Adriatic in pursuit of Ottoman galleys which had been raiding possessions of the Spanish Kingdom of Naples. By letter he requested participation of Malta's galleys. Toledo's 80 galleys departed Messina for the Adriatic on 20 August but returned two days later having learned the Ottomans were no longer there. Malta's four galleys commanded by Pedro de Mendoza arrived too late for the departure.[26]

The Malta galleys departed Malta on 20 August with both Prior of Auvergne Louis de Lastic and Prior of Champagne Jean Audibert de l'Aubuge embarked, both too old for duty at the Convent, but returned to Malta from Italy with Francisco Borguès embarked. Borguès had in his possession 50,000 scudos contributed by Italian princes including Duke of Florence Cosimo I de'Medici and his son Francesco de'Medici. Also embarked was 53 year-old Grand Prior of England Richard Shelley.[27] Shelley was a student of the classical arts and a diplomat fluent in Latin and its derivative languages. He was also independently wealthy and on familiar terms with aristocracy having spent time in Constantinople, Venice, Paris, and Madrid but had never before been to Malta and, thus, had never attended a meeting of the Sacred Council of which he was a member. Neither had he ever seen combat. Upon arrival he knelt at the feet of the Grand Master and took an oath, apparently the oath all Hospitallers took of chastity and obedience. Days later the Sacred Council of which Shelley by virtue of position was a member discharged those companies of 300 infantry each excepting that of Pierre de Montauban de Voguedemar of Provence, most capable of the lot.[28]

On the Danube Hospitaller Philipp Flach von Schwarzenberg commanded Holy Roman Empire naval units during the Empire's war with Suleiman's Ottomans. Suleiman the Magnificent died on 6 September 1566 during the Siege of Szigetvár, then a part of the Kingdom of Hungary. He was in his 72nd year and ruled the largest empire in Ottoman history. He was survived by Gülbahar, chief consort of his early years, but not by Hürrem Sultan known as Roxelana and his legal wife after Gulbahar. He was also survived by son Selim, soon to take the throne as Selim II, and by daughter Mihrimah Sultan. Also known as Suleiman the Law Giver, he is said by many historians to have been the greatest of all Ottoman Sultans.

The four Malta galleys were released by Alvarez de Toledo in time to return to Malta on 14 September 1566 having loaded provisions enroute. Eight thousand workers were laboring on the new city of Valletta. These labored under the supervision of Bailiff of Venosa Antonio Peletta and his staff which included Ramón Fortuyn of Mallorca, Pierre de la Chèrines, Pier Filippo della Corgnia, and Juan

Antonio Fuster. Fortuitously, a fountain flowing sweet fresh water was tapped on the Sciberras Peninsula at what would be the heart of the new city. In need of funds to support construction, Grand Master and Council on 25 September deputized Grand Hospitaller Jacques d'Arquinvillier de Tourville with Commanders Christophe le Boulleur de Montgaudry the Younger and Nicolas Durand de Villegagnon to return to France to audit each of the Order's six priories in that country, to recapture any shortage of responsions uncovered, to locate the estate of Louis de Vallée-Passy who in July 1564 bequeathed the Common Treasury the largest single estate in living memory excepting those of certain Grand Masters, and to value for possible sale forest land owned by the Priory of France. Toward the end of September Commander of Germendorf Ulrich von Sternenfels died at Malta. He left the Common Treasury an estate valued at 7,000 gold florins.[29]

On 2 October Mathurin Romegas returned to Malta from the Levant with the two Magistral galleys. He brought news from a Ragusan Argosy bound from Constantinople of accession in Constantinople of Sultan Selim II on 22 September 1566.[30] On 3 November Melchor de Eguaras, Secretary to the Grand Master, returned to the Magistral Palace at night guided by a lighted torch. An ember from the torch ignited his arquebus fuze, the weapon fired, and he collapsed dead on the floor. On 22 November Bishop of Malta Domenico Cubelles died of natural causes. Pursuant to the Grant of Malta to the Order in 1530, the Order nominated three candidates as successor, Prior of the Church of Saint John Antoine de Cressin of Auvergne, Vice Chancellor Martín Rojas de Portalrubio, and Jean Pierre Mosquet, Under Prior of the Church. King Philip II so appointed Martín Rojas de Portalrubio subject to Papal ratification. Dying at Rome was Commander of San Giovanni in Selva di Montefalcone Annibal Caro, a knight of belle lettres renowned for his poetry as well as for translations from Latin and ancient Greek. He was 59 years of age. While best known for his translations of Virgil's Aenid and Longos's Daphnis and Chloe into rhythmically seductive Italian, his Gli Straccioni (The Scruffy Scoundrels) translated to English has been described as a masterpiece. It is available from bookstores today.

By authority delegated at the recent Chapter General, the Grand Master appointed his Seneschal Pierre de Gioù to the Lango vacancy and awarded Gioù the attendant Grand Cross, these actions not without resentment on the part of the more senior Jean l'Evésque de la Cassiere who would become Grand Master in 1572. Throughout the winter Royal galleys present at Malta contributed their oarsmen to the new city's labor force. Cavaliers, bastions, and curtain wall rose. New cisterns captured the flow of the recently discovered sweet-water spring. Plots of land were allocated among citizenry by a commission of three knights in consultation with three citizens. The knights were Catalan Rafa Xatmar, Denis Guiran of France, and Raffaello Salvago of Genoa. An earthquake destroying Randazzo in Sicily did not damage Malta.[31]

Early in the year 1567 the Grand Master convened his Sacred Council during which he reviewed information from east and west concerning the considerable peril in which the Christian Commonwealth survived 1566. He termed then-current circumstances a truce in a continuing war, an interregnum which could only be considered temporary. He referred to Ottoman pacts with Hungary and Persia relieving pressure on the Ottoman Empire from those quarters in the context of each new sultan's practice of mending fences here in order to prove himself there. He cited information from agents at Constantinople concerning new Sultan Selim's shipyards on the Black Sea coast and the number of new galley hulls on skids. Meanwhile Piali Pasha on his return to Constantinople had set the Golden Horn Arsenal to work reconditioning and refitting older galleys. In the Grand Master's view these developments pointed to the likelihood Selim intended a maritime thrust.[32] The Venetian Senate came to the same conclusion.[33]

Venetian concern, of course, was focused on Cyprus, Crete, and Corfu. Parisot de la Valette's concern was always Malta. He saw the Catholic King's attention veering to Flanders and feared for an unprotected Malta and destruction of the Convent. The Council agreed prudence was warranted and approved borrowings with interest at Genoa, Florence, Rome, Naples, and anywhere loans might have been obtained. Ten new captains of infantry companies to be hired were appointed as follow: Alonso de Tejada of Castile, Nicolas de Blanchelayne of Auvergne, Giulio Malvicino of Naples, Don Rodrigo Maldonado of Castile, Cencio Guasconi of Florence, Pier Filippo della Corgnia of Perugia, Charles de Saint-Belin of Vaudrémont, France, Marcello Mastrillo of Nola (Naples), Jean de Barbeziers de Boisberthon of Aquitaine, and Don Jorge de Rebolledo of Valencia.

Captain Pierre de Montauban de Voguedemar and his existing company of infantry were to be retained as defenders of the new city of Valletta. Each new company of 300 was to consist of 50 pikemen with corselets and 250 arquebusiers with morion helmets. Each company was to have a flagbearer, a sergeant, nine corporals, a paymaster, a tambourine player, and a fife player. The estimated cost was 50,000 scudos at five percent interest. Because most of the Order's cannoneers had lost their lives during the Great Siege, Pierre de Grammont of Burgundy was to seek expert replacements among mountaineering Grisons of eastern Switzerland.[34]

Early in 1567 Grand Master Valette obtained Council approval for the Order to purchase the Malta estates of former Prince of Malta Ludovico Spadafora and wife Margarita. These estates which at the time were wastelands without trees, agriculturally unproductive, and with no redeeming feature became Magistral trappings. Within months of the transaction's completion Spadafora divorced Margarita and married Leonora Vassallo, heiress to additional wasteland on the island. It is not clear whether Spadafora again became a seller.[35]

The *Great Galleon* of the Grand Master, which had departed Malta in August bound for Mallorca under command of Guion de Saugniac de Belcastel of Provence, eventually reached Roses, a port in northern Catalonia. There she collected a large amount of responsions due the Convent from priories and commanderies in Spain before proceeding to Marseille. At Marseille she collected a comparable amount of French responsions as well as 16 pieces of artillery, a large supply of saltpeter and sulfur for the manufacture of gunpowder, munitions, and cloth for clothing and other uses. Coin and merchandise were valued at 150,000 scudos. Embarked as well were 300 passengers, mostly gentlemen expected to take the Habit on arrival at Malta. Too large to enter the port of Marseille, the ship sailed from the Pomegue Islands a bit offshore on the last Sunday of Carnival bound directly to Malta. A full day along her way, however, she was hit by a Tramontana storm coming off mountains to the north with icy wind. By Wednesday she was taking on water and down at the poop. That night a great leak was discovered with water pouring into the ship. The sixteen new cannons were jettisoned. The captain was advised to take to a ships boat, but damaged by the storm, the boats were useless. For five days and five nights the ship was in danger of foundering. Both passengers and crew bailed 24 hours a day before coming in sight of the Galite Islands off the north coast of Tunisia. The galleon was beached in good shelter at 2:00 in the morning. Having made repairs, the galleon two days later took course for Trapani and enroute Belcastel sent his lieutenant Rostaing de Laudun by frigate to Malta to advise the Grand Master of his circumstances and of his pending arrival at Trapani. Believing the galleon unserviceable, the Grand Master sent Romegas with both Magistral galleys to take off valuables and passengers. Romegas, however, found the galleon ready for sea and the three vessels departed for Malta. During the return to Malta two brigantines were seized near the island of Favignana while in pursuit of two Christian vessels transporting supplies to the Spanish garrison at La Goletta. Both crews were enslaved while Christian oarsmen were liberated. The galleon and Magistral galleys reached Malta at the beginning of March. Days earlier Pietro Giustiniani had been appointed Prior of Messina upon the death of Signorino della Gattinara, in turn relinquishing the dignity of Admiral to which Niccolò Orsini di Rivalta had been appointed.[36]

Not much after return of Romegas and the galleon, news was received of the death in Germany of Hospitaller Grand Prior of Germany Georg Bombast von Hohenheim. The last of the Hohenheims, Georg Bombast is believed to have died of wounds suffered at the 1566 Ottoman Siege of Szigetvár. On 12 March 1567 the Priory was conferred on Grand Bailiff Adam von Schwalbach who in turn was succeeded as Grand Bailiff by Commander Konrad von Schwalbach the Younger. By special grant the new Grand Prior and his successors were conceded the engraved silverware a part of the deceased's estate, apparently to compensate for losses at the Priory during periods of Protestant unrest.[37]

At the March Council meeting a difference concerning precedence arose between Grand Prior of England Richard Shelley and Prior of Messina Pietro Giustiniani which was argued with considerable vigor. Referred to a committee for study, the difference was eventually resolved in Shelley's favor. Appearing at Malta in March was an ambassador of King Charles IX of France, son of Henry II and Catherine de Medici, who made it known the King would like his 16 year-old half-brother Henri d'Angouleme, illegitimate son of Henry II of France and Lady Janet Stewart, received into the Order of Jerusalem with award of a Grand Cross anticipating appointment as

Grand Prior of France. Received forthwith, Henri de Valois, duc d'Angoulême, would succeed Pierre de la Fontaine as Grand Prior of France in November 1573. He would remain Grand Prior until June 1586 when in a pistol duel both parties were killed.[38]

Pierre de Grammont of Burgundy returned to Malta with 50 practiced cannoneers while Ambassador Giuseppe Cambiano at Rome had added twelve more. Meanwhile all of the new city's posts had been equipped with artillery thanks in large part to Hospitaller Cesare Rusca, Superintendant of the Foundries at Messina and Syracuse. Toward the end of March the Grand Master had news from Ragusa, Otranto, and Venice as well as from his agents in Constantinople all of which pointed to no Ottoman campaign by land or sea in 1567 while Sultan Selim consolidated his hold on power. Consequently only 80 galleys were expected to put to sea in the Spring for the purpose of transporting new beylerbeys to and between stations, for the purpose of collecting tribute from the sancaks (sanjaks) of Greece and the Morea, and to guard the Archipelago. Pedro Enriquez Afan de Ribera, 1st Duke of Alcalá and Viceroy of Naples, separately came to the same conclusion. All infantry but for the company of Pierre de Montauban de Voguedemar were released.[39]

Not able to sit back and reflect but having an opposite need for initiative in the war on Islam, even at age 72, Grand Master Valette decided to activate the galiot seized from Kuçuk Yusuf by Saint-Aubin and his Magistral galley in July 1562, and to refit her as a fast galley-sottile of 22-banks. Valette had a weakness for proprietary operations with his own proprietary assets, profit from which accrued to his own purse. This weakness stole from his ability to lead the entire Order of Malta. Proprietary operations, moreover, were seen by many as having prompted Suleiman's 1565 Great Siege of Malta. Antonio Martelli of Florence was assigned as the new galley's captain while her crew was raised at Malta. She was sent to Messina, however, for embarked soldiers, marines, and paid oarsmen. Not finding the soldiers needed at Messina, Martelli took his galley to Reggio di Calabria with intent to hire mountain bandits instead. One of these mountain bandits carelessly wounded Martelli with an arquebus round, and he remained gravely wounded for an extended period.

The galley-sottile was returned to Malta under command of Jorge de Rebolledo of Valencia, but at Malta was reassigned to Pierre d'Esparbez de Lussan of Provence. She was then incorporated into the Magistral squadron commanded by Romegas which departed Malta on 24 April for the Barbary Coast, the squadron's inglorious mission to encircle, sack, and return with captive laborers from the hostile port of Zuaga (Marsa Zuaga) 50 miles west of Tripoli. Embarked were 500 infantry between hired soldiers, knights, and seamen. Saint-Aubin commanded the ground force, Lussan his lieutenant, Raymond de Gozon-Mélac his Standard Bearer. A Moor led the Maltese into the city. There was no report of resistance or of Hospitaller casualties. The sack proved fruitless. Sixty persons were enslaved, for the most part women and children who later were all baptized Christians. During the return voyage a garbo was seized in the shallows of Palo with a cargo of barracan and other Moorish merchandise. The squadron returned to Malta at end-April with the garbo in tow. By order of the Grand Master, the captives were put ashore while the three ships were re-provisioned and departed the same day, the two galleys for the Strofadi Islands west of the Morea and the galliot for Libya's eastern Cape Buonandrea. At about the same time as Martelli had taken the galley-sottile to Messina, General of the Galleys Pedro de Mendoza with three galleys of the Malta squadron had been escorting to the mouth of the Tiber below Rome as a gift to Pope Pius V the refitted and elaborately decorated 20-bank galliot captured by Saint-Aubin off the Gramvousa Islands of Crete eleven months earlier.[40]

Prior of Navarre Juan Cerdan de las Cortes died at Malta in May. He was succeeded as Prior by León de Peralta. Charles de Saint-Belin of Vaudrémont and the Priory of Champagne died of unreported cause; he had been appointed a new Captain of Infantry only four months earlier. For the past three years the Convent had been expanding primarily in consequence of the General Summons to Hospitallers each of those years, and in spite of losses during the Great Siege. So, too, had the Convent consequently become younger and more unruly with the indiscipline and disrespect of youth. The Sacred Council was forced to mandate more severe punishments for infractions, including privation of the Habit.

Charles III called *The Great*, Duke of Lorraine, donated to the new city of Valletta by way of his Hospitaller General of Artillery, Jean d'Anglure Bourlemont, a serpentine or basilisk cannon and two great culverins.[41]

Romegas had weeks earlier been ordered to the south of Zante with both Magistral galleys, that is, the never-named capitana originally a galliot which he commanded, and *Santa Marta* commanded by Pierre de Saint-Aubin. From there the two galleys proceeded further under the Morea to Cerigo where Andrea Magnasco (acclaimed in 1565 for his chain-linked piles driven into the sea off Senglea to prevent Ottoman boats and barges from reaching the shore) was sent ahead in a caique to ascertain whether in a regularly frequented cove of Cerigotto (Antikithera) there might have been Turkish galliots. Two were sighted, one of 18 banks and one of 20 banks. As bait, Magnasco lured the larger ship out of the cove which ran up against the waiting galleys and fled with Romegas in pursuit. Saint-Aubin's padrona took the smaller galliot still in the cove. She was commanded by Kara Borno who in 1560 had with Uluç Ali and Pilot Kara Mustafa sailed among the Christian force anchored off Djerba Island correctly determining the Christians ill-prepared for battle. This time it was Kara Borno who was ill-prepared, his crew fleeing ashore. Most were eventually captured. The larger galliot meanwhile fled in the direction of Monemvasia (Malvasia); when overhauled by Romegas her 150 Azaps resisted with fusillades of arquebus and crossbow fire. Sixty of Romegas's men were killed among whom was the same Andrea Magnasco, João d'Azevedo of Portugal and the Langue of Castile, and two other knights. Romegas himself was wounded in the face by a crossbow bolt.[42]

Tayx Mami commanding the larger galliot took advantage of fire aboard the Magistral capitana and sought, in turn, to take the offensive. Saint-Aubin, however, having the faster of the two galleys, as his *Santa Marta* had no ramming spur, intervened and invested the Ottoman galliot. Romegas returned to Malta on 27 May; pursuant to his wishes, the two galliots were towed into port by Saint-Aubin alone. From the two galliots only 94 Turks remained alive; the remainder fell in combat or evaded capture at Cerigotto. Three hundred Christians were freed from the oars. There was unhappiness with Romegas at the amount of blood spilled for which some deemed him culpable. Because of his wound he became overly careless in readying his soldiers, it is said, and in his estimation of enemy strength. Valette was critically angry at the loss of so many soldiers and at the loss of Fantone, a merchant captain who took his Hospitaller vows after the Great Siege. A few days following return of Romegas, Pierre de Lussan also returned to Malta accompanied by a captured galliot of 18 banks and a captured caramussal loaded with a variety of merchandise.[43]

In belated awareness of Cyprus's vulnerability to Ottoman expansion the Grand Master ordered sale of Malta's's three commanderies and other assets on the island with removal to Sicily of monies and other portable items. Amounts received might have been expected to right the Hospitaller ship-of-state. Kolossi alone was a major producer of wine grapes, cotton, corn, olive oil, and sugar which was refined in-house, refining, as well, sugar produced at nearby Phoinike. As the Order continued on shaky financial footings following sale, it may be assumed the sale or sales came too late.[43]

Doctor Francesco Mego, a noble Rhodiot, in July succeeded Martín Rojas de Portalrubio as non-Hospitaller Vice Chancellor. Portalrubio, Bishop of Malta in-waiting, had failed to be endorsed by Pope Pius V and would not be appointed Bishop of Malta until the Papacy of Gregory XIII.[43] Antonio Maldonado, the Order's Resident Ambassador at the Spanish Court of Philip II, requested permission to return to the Convent. Grand Master and Council agreed to seek the King's permission for Pedro Boninseña to be named Maldonado's successor. With the King's permission, Boninseña made his way to Spain, travelling in company with Geronimo de Guete and Ernando de Zuniga, Receivers-designate for Aragon and Castile in respective succession of Martín de Duero and Don Luis de Talavera.[44]

Construction of the new city of Valletta was consuming incredible quantities of wood and metal. Because the Great Galleon (Sultana) had been disarmed during and following her storm-tossed February passage from Marseille to Malta, Grand Master and Council with assistance of Cesare Chierigati, Receiver at Venice, had been able to charter the Venetian galleon *La Barbara* with a gross capacity of 4,000 salmi (1,160 metric tons). In August *La Barbara* reached Syracuse with the Order's cargo of wood and metal plus other provisions, but refused to proceed further for fear of angering the Ottomans with whom Venice was at peace. Only with intercession of the President of Sicily could *La Barbara* be forced to continue on to Malta.

During this hot summer month Marshal Guillaume de Coppier fell ill and died. Nothing exists in the public record concerning his roots or family, not even his date of reception into the Order. First mention by

Bosio is as Standard Bearer at 1535's conquest of Tunis. He may have been a native of Haute-Savoie. On 23 August Pierre de Gioù was appointed Marshal succeeding the deceased while vacating the dignity of Bailiff of Lango to which Jean l'Evésque de la Cassière succeeded.[44]

Continually suspicious of Ottoman intentions respecting Malta, the Grand Master on 28 September visited the Castle of Gozo in company with Captain Francesco Laparelli, his Fortifications Engineer. They remained at the Castle for four days itemizing repairs and improvements needed and taking necessary action.[45] At about this time King Philip II of Spain accepted the resignation of Garcia de Toledo and appointed his own half-brother Don Juan of Austria as Captain-General of the Mediterranean Galley Fleet.[46] Soon thereafter Don Juan appointed Don Luis de Zuniga y Requesens of Castile his Lieutenant-General. Don Juan de Zuniga, Requesens' brother, was appointed Spain's successor Ambassador to the Holy See.[47]

Resident at Malta with the Grand Master's permission was Don Galceran de Finogliet of Mallorca, captain of his own galliot. Early in October the Grand Master sent Finogliet to the Barbary Coast in company with the Grand Master's galliot/galley-sottile commanded by Lussan. Within a few days Finogliet returned to Malta with 36 Moors taken captive from a garbo. Not content with his share of the spoils, Lussan had continued east to Syrian waters where in the Cypriot Channel he encountered a Greek vessel carrying 116 Jewish Italians to the Holy Land, both men and women, whom Pope Pius V had exiled from the Papal States at large and ordered made resident of Rome and Ancona only. Lussan made captive all 116 as they were traveling with no safe-conduct, and the Pope upheld the Grand Master's (not the Order's) right to demand ransoms.[48]

Jubilee contributions to Malta having ceased, the Grand Master appointed Prior of Messina Pietro de Giustiniani Ambassadeur Extraordinaire to the Holy See seeking funds from other sources. Marshal Pierre de Gioù was similarly appointed to solicit French King Charles IX, while Commander Don Pedro de Mendoza who would shortly be relieved as General of the Galleys was appointed to solicit Spanish King Philip II. Mendoza was in fact succeeded by Niccolò Orsini di Rivalta on 24 October. Another General Summons was issued for Hospitallers to gather at Rhodes in April of 1568.[49]

Because of contrary winds, the three ambassadors did not depart Malta until November 1567 by which time reports of Turkish shipyard activity could not be ignored. Again. Similarly, appointment of ten infantry captains could not be postponed. These were Alonso de Tejada of Castile, Nicolas de Blanchelayne of Auvergne, Giulio Cesare Malvicino of Naples, Jean de Barbeziers de Boisberthon of Aquitaine, Pier Filippo della Corgnia of Perugia, Don Rodrigo Maldonado of Castile, Tomás Coronel of Aragon, Marcello Mastrilla of Nola, Don Jorge Giron de Rebolledo of Aragon, and Pierre de Montauban de Voguedemar of Provence. These ten departed Malta with the three ambassadors on 11 November aboard the galley *San Iacomo* bound for Messina and from Messina to more distant points. Embarked as well was Hospitaller Gaspare Bruni of Budua, Albania (now Budva, Montenegro) who was to take up residence in Ragusa (Dubrovnik) to collect mail addressed to "Magnifico Domino Victorio Belforte," mail coming from the Grand Master's agents at Constantinople. Bruni was under order to employ a fast frigate to forward missives of imminent importance.[50]

The Venetian galleon *La Barbara* was by then in relatively permanent service between Marseille and Barcelona on the one hand and Malta on the other with a complement of one knight and 50 soldiers in addition to crew. Garcia de Toledo had been retired as Viceroy of Sicily at end-1566 and had since been succeeded by President of Sicily Carlo d'Aragona Tagliavia. Toledo had also been retired as Commander of the Mediterranean Galley Fleet and had been succeeded by Don Juan of Austria, son of former Emperor Charles V and half-brother of King Philip II of Spain. Francisco de San Clemente was Receiver of the Order in Catalonia and had transported to Naples 50,000 scudos which had been delivered to him in September at Barcelona by Francisco Borgès, the Order's Depositor-General at Barcelona. San Clemente (Francesc de Santcliment i de Santcliment in Catalan) had been escorted from Barcelona by two Spanish galleys commanded by Gil de Andrade. In a misunderstanding the ships had been diverted from Sicily to Naples. San Clemente eventually reached Sicily by other means and at December-end arrived at Malta with the transported monies. Also at December-end post arrived from Pierre de Gioù in France suggesting the charter of *La Barbara* be terminated as all cannon, munitions, and other items of war contracted to Malta had been seized by order of His Most Christian Majesty for war against the Huguenots.[50]

At Rome the Order's ambassadors were pleading with Pope Pius V for funds with which to complete construction of the defences of Valletta. A lot of funds. They were given jewels confiscated from Matteo Minali, former Treasurer for Pope Pius IV, which when sold yielded 10,000 scudos. Pius V also promised support payments for 1,500 infantry. Finally, the Pope authorized mortgaging of Hospitaller assets to the tune of 150,000 scudos. From the Spanish Court a loan of 50,000 scudos was obtained, interest-free for the first two years. In February the Grand Master carried out a second inspection of the Castle of Gozo, this one over six days, ensuring everything had been provided for the castle's defense. One hundred fifty infantry of the companies being raised by Hospitallers Don Jorge Giron de Rebolledo of Aragon and Pierre de Montauban de Voguedemar of Provence for Valletta were re-assigned in advance to Gozo under command of Captain Vincenzo Ventura with his Flag Bearer as lieutenant.[51]

In April 1568 Juan Miguel de Castellar died in Spain. Castellan of Amposta for eight years, he left the Order a rich estate including 10,000 Maltese scudos and was succeeded as Castellan by Luis de Talavera who in consequence renounced the Bailiwick of Negroponte which was ceded to Luis Rengifo of Castile. Ambassador Pierre de Gioù died in France of unreported cause. Thirty-four years an Hospitaller, Seneschal to two Grand Masters, General of the Galleys, veteran of the Great Siege, Bailiff of Lango, Knight of the Grand Cross, Marshal, and Resident Ambassador to the Court of France, he was only 51 years of age and should have gone further. Giù was not immediately succeeded as Ambassador or as Marshal out of respect.[52]

Hoping to learn of Ottoman Armada intentions, the Grand Master dispatched Pierre de Lussan and his Galley-sottile to the Spanish fortress of La Goletta outside of Tunis. During the return voyage Lussan ran ashore a Barbary brigantine which he towed back to Malta with a cargo of some value. Because Lussan reported no sign of an imminent Armada arrival along the North African coast, Mathurin Romegas and his Magistral capitana were dispatched into the Levant, also seeking information. The infantry companies of Don Jorge Giron de Rebolledo and Pierre de Montauban de Voguedemar were embarked at Licata aboard *La Barbara* and reached Malta on 20 April.[53]

General of the Galleys Niccolò Orsini di Rivalta was ordered to take three squadron galleys to Palermo in company with

Saint-Aubin's *Santa Marta* to embark Cardinal Alessandro Farnese and retinue for transport to Terracina. During their return they were again to put into Palermo to take on board artillery cast at Barcelona to Order specifications. These departed Malta on 29 April. En route Malta returning from the Levant Romegas paused at Syracuse where he embarked Prior of Hungary (in waiting) Vincenzo Carafa. Carafa was carrying briefs concerning mortgage aid for construction available against Priory assets. Romegas reported the Ottomans were building a huge armada with many galleys and the items galleys need, so huge it would be capable of separating into several parts and deploying in several directions. Because there were 50,000 sappers escorted by 40,000 Turkish cavalry then intending to dig a navigable canal between the Volga and the Don in order to connect the Caspian Sea to the Sea of Azov, speculation concerned war against the Persians or the Tartars, the Muskovites or the Poles, and not against Malta. Because Ivan IV was moving against the Ottomans in concern for his borders, it appeared to be war with the new Russian state, and war with Russia would require at least a part of the Ottoman Armada to be sent to Caffa (Feodosia) in the Black Sea. There was also rebellion at the mouth of the Persian Gulf and a need for security in the Greek Archipelago where 80 Turkish galleys had been immobilized at Scio infested by plague. The eight captains yet to hire infantry companies were ordered to stand-down. The four galleys with embarked artillery returned to Malta on 25 May. Returning with the galleys were the eight captains of infantry as well as Prior of Capua Pietro del Monte, the latter for the purpose of escaping the foul air of Rome and Naples.[54]

In June 1568 Grand Commander Antoine de Rodez-Montalègre died at Malta. Forty-two years of age, his cause of death was not reported. He was succeeded as Grand Commander by Jean-Claude de Glandevèz. The vacant Bailiwick of Lango was conferred on Commander of Marseille Balthazard de Vintimille of Provence together with its attendant Grand Cross. Sultan Selim meanwhile, on learning of the appointment of 21 year-old Don Juan of Austria to command of Spain's Mediterranean Galley Armada, recalled 70 Turkish galleys sent to Caffa and sent them out into the Aegean under command of Müezzinzade Ali Pasha, so called because as a young man at a mosque outside the sultan's palace in Adrianople (or

Hadrian's city, modern Edirne) he would recite the call to prayer from the mosque's minaret, his cantor's voice soon attracting palace attention, so much attention that at a young age he had been wed to a member of the sultan's family. As 4th Vizier in Sokollu Mehmed Pasha's government he was in June 1568 appointed Piali Pasha's successor as Commander-in-Chief of the Ottoman Armada. His 70 galleys were soon joined by 30 more galleys coming up from Alexandria and suddenly posed a threat to the Christian world. Eight of these galleys were sent to Antalya on Anatolia's south coast where they posed a threat to Cyprus. The others exited the Aegean on patrol of the western Morea and the coast of Albania and all points in between, including Venetian Zante and Corfu and the Venetian Adriatic. In Spain Don Juan was preoccupied with expulsion of Spanish Moors leaving only Malta in between. The Grand Master revoked his order for the eight infantry companies to stand-down, and on 19 June dispatched Saint-Aubin to locate the Great Galleon (Sultana) commanded by Rostaing des Essards-Laudun in succession of Guion de Saugniac de Belcastel, and to return her to Malta with her complement of gentleman adventurers. Saint-Aubin was then sent east to ascertain Müezzinzade Ali's movements. Commanders Scipione Ajazza of Vercelli, Jeronimo da Cunha of Portugal, and Clemente d'Aoiz of Navarre were appointed city-sector wardens responsible for ensuring readiness for siege in respective sectors of Birgu as well as for civil obedience in the event of hostilities.[55]

Early in July Saint-Aubin returned to Malta with advice the Ottoman galleys were not accompanied by a siege train and thus posed little threat to Malta though detachments were conducting raids on southern Calabria. From this information the Grand Master concluded that only Gozo was at risk and accordingly reinforced the presidio with additional knights and soldiers. Women and children living on Gozo were relocated to Malta. During the month news was received at Malta of the death in Germany of Grand Bailiff Konrad II von Schwalbach. Schwalbach was succeeded by Commander Joachim Sparr. Also in July there was a rebellion among young Castillian knights unacquainted with discipline and unacquainted with religious observances perhaps in consequence of tales of conquistadors coming from the New World. Some were so rebellious they were stripped of their Habits and punished. They were also unacquainted with punishment, and some of them fled to Sicily. Giovan Battista Caprona of Palermo was sent in pursuit and the young rebels were imprisoned. Much to the disgust of the Grand Master, Pope Pius V awarded the commanderies of Prato and San Sepolcro in Florence, vacated by recent death of incumbents, to a non-Hospitaller nephew of Guglielmo Sangalletti, the Pope's Treasurer. The Priory of Rome was vacated by death of much-loved Hospitaller Cardinal Bernardo Salviati. The Pope on his own recognizance awarded the Priory to non-Hospitaller Michele Bonelli, Dominican Cardinal Alessandrino, the son of his niece. The strained relationships with Rome and with younger knights of Castile weighed heavily on an aging Grand Master. At Cape Passero, Sicily's SE tip, a Barbary corsair brigantine captured a Messinese cargo ship with numerous Christians embarked and then flaunted the capture by towing her through the Freo Channel between Malta and Gozo. Saint-Aubin's padrona went in pursuit and seized both brigantine and tow within sight of Tripoli, returning both to Malta. The disdain for Malta exhibited by the brigantine commander also weighed heavily on the Grand Master.[56]

Unbeknownst to Malta, Müezzinzade Ali's Armada had been recalled to Constantinople in early August for fear of rebellion in Egypt or Arabia or both. Or so it was reported.[57] By 10 September 64 of these galleys would appear off Cyprus's Cape Greco on false pretenses. On 10 August the Grand Master appointed Grand Commander Jean-Claude de Glandevèz his Lieutenant in the event of his incapacity. Before that the Grand Master was advised in code by agents at Constantinople that Ottoman officers in North Africa were to whisper the Armada would soon be sent to relief of the Moors of Spain. At about this time a difference concerning precedence arose in Council between Prior of England Richard Shelley and Prior of Capua Pietro del Monte.

On 16 August Grand Master Valette fell ill with fever following a serious fall on stone inside the Magistral chapel. Having liberated fifty of his galley slaves, pardoned all those deprived of the Habit, separately provided for his two offspring and their mothers, and willed his remaining 160,000 scudo estate (principally the two galleys and galleon) to the Order, Jean Parisot de la Valette confessed his sins and died on the 20th day of August 1568 at the age of 73 years. He was presently interred in the Chapel of Santa Maria della Vittoria in the

Conventual Church of Saint John at Valletta. The inscription on his tomb, composed by Oliver Starkey, states in Latin: //Here lies La Valette. Worthy of eternal honor, He who was once the scourge of Africa and Asia, And the shield of Europe, Whence he expelled the barbarians by his Holy Arms, Is the first to be buried in this beloved city, Whose founder he was.// Said by some without attribution to have been Valette's Latin Secretary, Starkey is described by Bosio simply as an English knight of "belle lettere ornato."[58]

Chapter II

1568–1572

Following a 23 August requiem Mass for deceased Grand Master Jean Parisot de la Valette at the Church of San Lorenzo, a General Assembly of all Hospitallers present and eligible to vote was convened by Magistral Lieutenant Jean-Claude de Glandevèz for the purpose of electing a new Grand Master. Glandevèz had earlier that day rolled back magistral salary from 8,000 to 6,000 Maltese scudos per year, said salary to fund all expenses of the Magistral Palace as well as personal expenses. This step was taken in the context of a Valette estate comprised of little more than three corsair vessels, of an estate which throughout Valette's Malta years had reaped the gains of a personal corsair enterprise operating at the expense of the Order's own marine assets, and of an estate not known to have ever advanced monies to a cash-starved Treasury. It must have been an open secret that Valette had by virtue of his children two greater families to fund in his time and later. It may be hoped that was the explanation.

Once the General Assembly had convened eight initial electors were selected in camera, one by each langue. These eight retired into private chambers to select four election officials. These were Niccolò di Rivalta of Italy as non-voting President of Elections, Giovan Francesco Langosco de Conti della Motta of Italy as Knight of Elections, Prior of the Infirmary Louis Floury of France as Chaplain of Elections, and Serving Brother Laurent Raymond of Provence as Sergeant-at-Arms of Elections.[1]

The initial eight electors having then retired, Knight, Chaplain and Sergeant selected a fourth elector from the Assembly, the four selected a fifth, the five selected a sixth in diminishing weight of individual preference until there were Sixteen Electors at two per langue. The final Sixteen Electors were: Serving Brother Laurent Raymond and Commander of Selve Antoine Flotte de la Roche for Provence; Lieutenant Marshal Jean de Viry de la Forest and Commander of l'Aumusse Germain de Bridiers-Gardanne for Auvergne; Chaplain

Louis Floury and Lieutenant Treasurer Louis de Mailloc Sacquenville for France; Francisco Martinez de Marcilla and Juanito Torreglias for Aragon; Giovan Francesco Langosco de Conti della Motta and Commander of San Guglielmo di Pavia Scipione Ajazza for Italy; Lieutenant Turcopolier Oliver Starkey and, there being no other eligible English Hospitaller, Giulio Cesare Malvicino of Naples for England; Commander of Dobel Walter von Helfenstein and Commander of Ueterser Englebert Flach for Germany; and, last, in lieu of Antonio Maldonado his unnamed squire and Commander of Algoso (Portugal) Pedro Mesquite for Castile. During the election said electors were presented with three candidates by the President of the General Assembly each needing nine votes to secure the nomination. Two candidates were one vote short, the third two votes short. These candidates are said to have been Pietro del Monte, Niccolò di Rivalta, and Antonio Maldonado with the two Italian electors splitting their votes. Finally, though, Prior of Capua Pietro del Monte secured the nine votes necessary and was elected 50th Grand Master of the Order of Jerusalem. The absence of a second English Hospitaller given the presence of Grand Prior Richard Shelley was attributable to a by-law prohibiting Knights of the Grand Cross from influencing voting outcomes.[2]

Pietro or Pierino del Monte was 73 years of age at the time of his election as Grand Master, the same age as the deceased Parisot de la Valette. First born of Margherita del Monte and of Checco di Cristofano Guidalotti at Monte San Savino, Tuscany, he was by his mother cousin to future Pope Julius III, nephew of Cardinal Antonio Del Monte, and uncle of Hospitallers Carlo Sforza and Antonio del Monte. Received into the Order in 1516, he is said by several sources notably excluding Giacomo Bosio to have been present at 1522's Great Siege of Rhodes and would have likely been assigned to the Langue of Italy's sector of the city wall adjacent to Valette's sector. With the exception of dignities unique to each langue, Del Monte and Valette followed similar career paths for the remainder of their lives. Del Monte was successively Castellan of Rome's Castel Sant'Angelo (1550-1555), Admiral (1555-1565), Knight of the Grand Cross (1555), General of the Galleys (1558), Prior of Capua (1565-1568), and Ambassador to the Holy See (1566-1568). He was in all probability a candidate for Grand Master at the 1557 election of Parisot de la Valette and he served under Valette in defense of 1565's Great Siege of Malta when as Pilier or senior knight of the Langue of Italy he commanded defense of the island/peninsula of Senglea until collapsing from exhaustion at end-July.

At a 27 August meeting of the Sacred Council following election Del Monte appointed Giovan Francesco della Motta his Seneschal, the dignity acting as executive of the Grand-Master in all cases where his eminence did not choose to act or appear personally.[3] Motta was also appointed Commander of Polizzi Generosa in the hills above Palermo, a commandery of grace attending his appointment as Seneschal. The Priory of Capua having been vacated by Del Monte's election, it was awarded to Scipione Ajazza of Vercelli. Another Council appointment was of Bailiff of Lango Bertrand de Vintimille d'Ollioules of Provence to the additional position of Lieutenant-Governor of the new city of Valletta.[3]

On 3 September news reached Malta of the death in France from unreported cause of Marshal and Resident Ambassador Pierre de Gioù. A native of Occitan Aveyron 51 years of age, a former General of the Galleys and Seneschal to two Grand Masters, he had been on track to become Grand Master. Commander of Rosières Jean l'Evésque de la Cassière who does become Grand Master was appointed his successor as Marshal. Nicolas Durand de Villagagnon was at royal request appointed Giou's successor as Resident Ambassador to the Court of France. Villegagnon was a student of rhetoric, the classics and languages, fluent in ancient and modern Greek, Latin, Italian, and Spanish, a friend and contemporary of John Calvin, both studying law at the University of Orleans, and had been a Hospitaller for thirty-two years.[4] Ambassadors were also appointed to notify European leaders of the death of Valette and election of Del Monte. These were Filippo Corgna to the Pope and other Italian princes, Don Juan de La Rocha Pereira to the Emperor and German princes, Don Rodrigo Maldonado to the Court of Spain, and Jerónimo Botello to the Court of Portugal.

These ambassadors departed Malta on 9 September aboard the four galleys of the Religion under General Niccolò di Rivalta, the squadron capitana which Rivalta commanded himself in succession of Don Garcia de Mendoza, *San Iacomo* commanded by an unidentified skipper in succession of Jean de Viry de la Forest, *San Giovanni* commanded by René le Cirier de Semeur of Aquitaine in succession of

Francisco Guiral, and the former Magistral capitana re-named *Santa Anna* commanded by Catalan Salvador la Batta in succession of Mathurin Romegas. The former Magistral padrona *Santa Marta* commanded by Pierre de Saint-Aubin had been hauled and her crew and equipment distributed among the remaining four galleys. *Santa Maria della Corona* commanded by Pietro Giustiniani had proved unseaworthy and had been scrapped. Also embarked aboard *Santa Anna* was the new Magistral Receiver Bernabo della Marra ordered to pay the Order's respects to Francesco Ferdinando II d'Avalos, 5th Marchese of Pescara and new Viceroy of Sicily. Embarked aboard all four of the galleys were the infantry companies commanded by Pierre de Montauban Voguedemar and Don Jorge de Rebolledo hired in April but never employed.

Left behind within the city of Valletta were 150 infantry under Captain Vicenzo Ventura representing the entire garrison; this because having done considerable damage to southern Calabria, the Ottoman Armada had retired into the Archipelago. On 10 September 64 Ottoman galleys appeared off Cyprus's Cape Greco on false pretenses. It was not a courtesy call; Müezzinzade Ali's true purpose was to inspect Venetian fortifications at Famagusta and elsewhere on the island.

Because envy and infighting among electors and favorites of Grand Master Del Monte began almost immediately following his election,[3] because Antonio Maldonado, for example, could not abide Giovan Francesco della Motta's dictatorial rule and decided to leave Malta, because Giulio Cesare Malvicino, unable to obtain an audience with the Grand Master, became violent, because Seneschal Motta was unable to quiet discord he was in October promoted to Resident Ambassador to the Holy See, succeeding Giuseppe Cambiano, while remaining Seneschal-in-Absentia.[5]

On a subsequent passage of the Galley Squadron departing Malta on 25 November Seneschal and Ambassador Giovan Francesco della Motta embarked bound for Rome. Louis de Mailloc Saquenville who had been Master of Valette's House left for a new assignment as the Order's Receiver in France. Commanders Mathurin de Lescut Romegas and Jean de la Valette Cornusson were also embarked destined to assume management of their commanderies in France. Prior to departure Antonio Maldonado was able to wangle re-assignment as

Resident Ambassador to the Court of Spain in apparent return for having delivered his vote to Del Monte in the latter's successful bid for the dignity of Grand Master (the earlier appointment of Don Rodrigo Maldonado was as ambassadeur extraordinaire and not as resident ambassador). To be truly effective at the Court of Spain, with the necessary wherewithal, Antonio Maldonado needed to also be appointed to a Commandery of Grace in Castile, and to take with him to Spain the Magisterial Bull making it so. (A Commandery of Grace is one granted by the Grand Master within a number of limitations.) Wishing to be free of Maldonado, the Grand Master and new Seneschal Bernardino Scaglia quickly agreed to Maldonado's proposition. Before departing with the others on 25 November, Maldonado counseled Giulio Malvicino, elector for the Langue of England, he too should apply for a Commandery of Grace, one permitting Malvicino to retire in comfort to Naples. With departure of the former Seneschal two others quickly became the Grand Master's favorites. These were Commander Bernardino Scaglia of the Piedmont appointed Master of the House, and Federico Sangiorgio of Casale Monferrato appointed Cup Bearer, the latter soon to also be appointed Commander of Forli. Returning from this passage on 6 December, the galleys brought to Malta Signor Eustachio di Monte, beloved nephew of the Grand Master. Contemplating permanent residence, he, too, would find an influential position within the Magistral household.[6]

Grand Master Valette had earlier ordered two new capitanas from the arsenal at Marseille, one for the squadron and one as the new Magistral capitana, both of 152 feet LOA with 28 oar-banks requiring 250 oarsmen. These compared with others in the squadron of 137 feet LOA, 25 banks, and 200 oarsmen. Scheduled for Spring completion, Signor di Monte intended to take delivery of both, one of which would be his uncle's personal property manned at Order expense. Speaking for his uncle the nephew made it known both galleons were to be overhauled and improved while an order would be placed for a very large cargo carrier. A new galleon to be constructed in the fosse of the Posts of France and Aragon, she would be christened *San Pietro* in honor of his uncle and would be commanded by Hospitaller Pirro Melzi of Milan. Melzi and his Hospitaller First Officer Davide Serra of Genoa would oversee construction. There seemed little need for a Sacred Council.[7]

Twenty-eight Bench Hospitaller Galley.

The year 1569 commenced with little or no suspicion of Ottoman threat because of Sultan Selim's preoccupation with the Volga-Don Canal and Muscovite resistance. During the first few months of the year, in fact, a part of the Ottoman Galley Armada deployed to Caffa and elsewhere in the Black Sea. The Grand Master early-on concluded 1569 would be a break with the past, a break with the annual rush to arms and the annual regret of funds wasted. Prior of Catalonia Don Dimes de Requesens died in January. A veteran of the 1522 Siege of Rhodes, his arrival that year in October from Spain by way of Venetian Candia was cause for much skepticism at the time concerning inability of the Messina relief armada to overcome adverse weather. A saintly knight, he left the Order a substantial estate and on 10 January was succeeded as Prior by Don Pedro de Iunient. Iunient vacated the dignity of Grand Conservator (Draper) to which Francisco de San Clemente succeeded. San Clemente in turn vacated the Commandery of Barcelona which was conveyed to the City of Valletta, thus providing Valletta with an irregular annuity. Because this last transfer left San Clemente without an income, the Commandery of Acquaviva was ceded to him by Ramón Fortuyn who was the senior

Commissioner of the new City of Valletta. Following the death of Prior of Saint-Gilles Louis du Pont in France, Grand Commander Jean-Claude de Glandevèz was on 21 January appointed his successor. Glandevez was in turn succeeded as Grand Commander by Bailiff of Lango Balthazard de Vintimille who renounced the latter dignity which would remain vacant eleven months until awarded to Christophe le Boulleur de Montgaudry.[8]

During February 1569 Grand Master Del Monte ordered Engineer Francesco Laparelli to begin construction of residential housing and public buildings at Valletta under supervision of Commissioners Ramón Fortuyn, Nicolas de Miré, Cesare Roero, and Bernabò delle Donne. Antonio Maldonado abruptly returned to Malta no longer wishing to take up the position of Resident Ambassador to the Court of Spain, finding Naples more to his taste. The Grand Master publicly lamented Maldonado's ingratitude while the Sacred Council on 21 February revoked Maldonado's credentials and re-appointed Pedro Boninseña to the position. Neither was the choleric Grand Master yet satisfied; he also revoked the Commandery of Grace conveyed with the ambassadorship. Further, he directed his Receiver in Naples to let it be known Maldonado no longer had commandery income. Undeterred, Maldonado importuned Viceroy of Naples and fellow-Spaniard Pedro Afán de Ribera who provided Maldonado access to all Malta correspondence routed through Naples. In this way Maldonado learned of the death of Castilian Bailiff of Negroponte Luis Rengifo and the consequent vacancy at Rengifo's Commandery of Rubiales. Maldonado immediately petitioned the Grand Master who after additional choler appointed Maldonado Commander of Bamba in Maldonado's Castile rather than of Rubiales in Aragon. But because Maldonado had withheld correspondence addressed to Malta, the deceased Rengifo had recently been advanced to the dignity of Grand Chancellor in succession of the deceased Cristobal Sarnach. That promotion had to be unwound and the dignity instead awarded to Don Fernando de Alarcón while the Bailiwick of Negroponte was awarded to Salvador de Sin.[9]

Not much later advice was received at Malta of corsairs pillaging the south coast of Sicily. Niccolò di Rivalta and his four galleys were dispatched to Xacca (Sciacca) on the southwestern coast of Sicily and thence to Trapani. Within a few days the galleys returned to

Malta with five corsair brigantines taken at the island of Marettimo off Trapani. These were rowed to Malta by their captive crews, while a comparable number of Christians had been released from the oars and liberated.[10]

While making his ceremonial first visit to Notabile, the Grand Master received a report a large number of Ottoman galleys had exited the Dardanelles into the Aegean. On 9 May 1569 Juan Vasquez de Coronado of Castile, Francesco Caccia of Novara, and Antoine Flotte de la Roche of Provence were appointed Sector Wardens with requisite authority to ensure adequate munitions, water, and provisions in the event of a siege. The number of Ottoman galleys in the Aegean was later reported by Venice to be eighty.[11] Because reports of Ottoman activity were so varied, Rivalta on 18 May dispatched the galley *San Iacomo* to the Levant under recently-appointed Captain Guion de Saugniac Belcastel to ascertain Ottoman strength and intentions with respect to Malta. Rivalta's remaining galleys meanwhile captured two Turkish corsair brigantines off Syracuse, one commanded by Cassan Nebi Ogli of Sovrassari (Skyros) and the other by Peri Ali Ogli of Gallipoli.

Returned with these to Malta, the Viceroy of Sicily requested the three galleys proceed to Pantelleria 45 nautical miles east of Tunisia's Cape Bon where a storm-damaged Genovese galley had washed up on the island's shore. This galley had been a part of a squadron bound from Pomègues Island off Marseille across the Gulf of Lyon with 14 companies of Spanish veterans embarked. Commanded by Luis de Requesens, Lieutenant-General of the Spanish Galley Fleet under Don Juan of Austria, the crossing was undertaken against the advice of his captains. Hit by a severe storm, many of the galleys went to the bottom including five of Florence, several of the Kingdom, and others of Genoa. Thanks to a miracle, Requesens' capitana was blown all the way to Mallorca, severely damaged but few deaths, those attributable to hunger. Having towed the Genovese galley to Palermo, Rivalta and his galleys took three additional brigantines off Favignana liberating numerous Christian oarsmen. *San Iacomo* meanwhile returned to Malta on 3 June with some dead and many wounded Maltese. She had encountered a Turkish galliot in the waters of Zante which put up a stubborn resistance; of a crew of 60 only 20 survived and the galliot went to the bottom. Belcastel reported the Ottoman fleet numbered no more than sixty galleys, all assigned to the Archipelago Guard, and did not appear to have intent to leave the Aegean.

The squadron was accordingly sent to Marseille on 27 June 1569 to take delivery of two new capitanas which were in danger of being requisitioned by the Crown for war against Huguenots at New Rochelle. There was also a pregnant request from Viceroy of Sicily d'Avalos that one of the new galleys be donated to Spain in view of that country's latest disaster at sea (above). Rivalta commanded his capitana, Saugniac de Belcastel commanded *San Iacomo*, Salvador la Batta commanded *Santa Anna*, and René le Cirier de Semeur commanded *San Giovanni*. Embarked among others were Prior of Saint-Gilles Glandevèz, Prior of England Richard Shelley, and Bailiff of Venosa Antonio Peletta headed for Spain, as well as Antoine Flotte de la Roche headed for France as Receiver. Shelley would never return to Malta. Enroute the four galleys were emptied of passengers and baggage at Messina, proceeded to Palermo where the Viceroy was embarked with court for transport back to Messina, after which passengers and baggage were re-embarked. The four galleys then proceeded by way of Naples and Genoa to their destination. At Marseille one new galley would replace *San Giovanni* which would be hauled for possible transfer to Sicily. The other new galley would become the new squadron capitana commanded by Rivalta. Belcastel moved from *San Iacomo* to the old capitana, while *San Iacomo* was also hauled for possible transfer to Sicily.[12]

Pierre Roquelaure de Saint-Aubin equipped the Lussan galliot inherited from Grand Master Valette, and together with a smaller galliot belonging to Hospitaller Ferrante Coiro of Milan, sailed from Malta bound for Cape Buonandrea. There they took on fresh water and headed past the Arab's Tower waypoint at Abousir for Alexandria. At the mouth of the Nile questioned Moors told them that a convoy had recently sailed from the port of Alexandria bound for Greece and Constantinople which had been escorted by Şuluk Bey, Sancakbey of Alexandria known in the west as Mehmet Scirocco, the convoy supported by the Rhodes Guard. The Hospitallers turned in pursuit and below the Gulf of Antalya captured a germa which had become separated from the convoy. Rated at 2,000 salmi (580 tons), she was heavily laden with a cargo of carpets. Even so the crew of 40 Turks supplemented by 50 janissaries put up a determined resistance before yielding. The two corsairs a bit later took a second convoy-germa carrying flax and rice, and ransacked yet other vessels. Among the latter was a large ship bound from Lindos aboard which was embarked Scirocco's treasurer together with family and staff sent by Scirocco to Constantinople to render an accounting of his administration. Aboard this ship they also found twenty-four Turkish thoroughbred horses and four white mules, many pieces of woven cloth, as well as fur pelts of martens and sables. The plunder was taken aboard the two Maltese galliots, new captives bringing the total to three hundred. The Hospitallers released this vessel with horses and mules, and on 28 June returned to Malta. Sale of the plunder made Saint-Aubin so wealthy he quit the corsair war and gave his galliot to Hospitaller brother Bernard Roquelaure de Saint-Aubin.[13]

Bernard Roquelaure de Saint-Aubin seeking in 1569 to enjoy his brother's good fortune took the Saint-Aubin galliot together with two other large galliots and departed Malta for the Levant, the others la Maiorchina belonging to Don Alonso de Castelui, and the third jointly owned by Cesare Rusca (Superintendant of the Foundry of Messina) and Petrachi Caloriti. These set upon and took a germa, cargo of spices and opiates, bound from the mouth of the Nile to Alexandria in order to join a caravan to be escorted by seven galleys. While the three galliots were turning toward Malta with their rich plunder they were set upon in turn by Scirocco's seven-galley squadron which had heard the clamor of their artillery. La Maiorchina carried most of the plunder and shook out her sail to run before the wind. So, too, did the others, but the fastening affixing the antennae to the mast snapped on Rusca's galliot, and she was overhauled and taken by Scirocco. Enslaved were Cesare Rusca, Giovan Battista Alciati, Francesco Isnardo, and all of the crew. The other two galliots, following a long, strained, and perilous chase arrived safely at Malta with fifty Turkish and Moorish captives. With the proceeds from sale of the spices and opiates they were just able to ransom their shipmates. Partly compensating for the foregoing disappointment, the Mallorcan galliot of corsair Fino de Galceran took in combat a Turkish galliot of 18 banks, and while returning to Malta with the captive galliot in tow took near Malta a Turkish germa bound from the Levant to Barbary, cargo of various merchandise, the prize exceedingly rich. Various other corsairs were successful during the year, including the galliot of Hospitaller Marcantonio de Marchesi di Busca, that of Hospitaller Basilio Basilico of Messina, that of Hospitaller Giovan Battista Vivaldo of the Piedmont, the brigantines of Hospitaller Pierre de Noe and of the corsair Paolo Micciola of Malta, and the fusta of corsair Martino Mula of Gozo.[14]

During the year Niccolò di Rivalta succeeded the deceased Lamberto Doria as Bailiff of Naples and was himself succeeded as Admiral by Giuseppe Cambiano.[14] Lieutenant Turcopolier Oliver Starkey was advanced to Bailiff of Eagle entitled to wear the Grand Cross having first warranted he would not pretend to precedence over the Bailiffs of Manosque and Caspe who were present in the Convent before his arrival, said declaration without prejudice to subsequent Bailiffs of Eagle.[16] At Florence Duke of Florence Cosimo I de Medici was crowned by Pope Pius V Grand Duke of Tuscany.[15]

The four active galleys of the Squadron returned to Malta early in November 1569. Without the wherewithal to properly man and equip *San Iacomo*, she had been hauled-out and parked on the hard at Marseille. The four were the new capitana commanded by Niccolò di Rivalta as General, the new *Santa Maria della Vittoria* commanded by René le Cirier de Semeur, the old capitana commanded by Guion de Saugniac de Belcastel, and *Santa Anna* commanded by Salvador la Batta. Embarked aboard the galleys were, among others returning for the November Chapter General, Marshal Jean l'Evésque de la Cassière and Commander Giorgio Vercelli, the latter leaving Giulio Bravo of Verona as successor Receiver at Naples. On 7 November Don Juan Vasquez de Coronado of Castile was appointed to succeed Rivalta as Regent in command of the galleys because as Bailiff of Naples, Rivalta's presence was required at the Chapter General. In order to avoid disturbance at the Chapter General, Coronado was ordered to embark younger members of the Convent and to go on patrol. He departed Malta on 15 November with three of the four galleys bound for the Barbary Coast where he hoped to intercept enemy vessels. The three galleys were the new capitana, the new *Santa Maria della Vittoria*, and *Santa Anna*. Sailing in company were the galliot of Bernard de Saint-Aubin, the galliot of Don Pietro la Rocca of Messina commanded by Hospitaller Basilio Basilico of Messina, the brigantine of non-Hospitaller Giuseppe of Messina and that of non-Hospitaller Gamba di Bosco of Alba in the Piedmont, plus two frigates. Reaching

Lampedusa midway between Malta and the Tunisian coast all were forced to hide from adverse winds in lee coves. Conditions worsened on a wind shift, and in attempting to find new shelter the capitana and padrona *Vittoria* ran aground while *Santa Anna* anchored. That night and the following 72-hours were perilous, the wind at the same time blowing from Malta and Trapani and toward Cape Passero. The three squadron galleys eventually managed to reach Syracuse, and when the winds abated, returned to Malta. The accompanying vessels abandoned at Lampedusa were later able to reach the Barbary Coast where they were put to the chase by eight Algiers galliots. Only the two galliots of Saint-Aubin and Basilico and the brigantine of Gamba da Bosco managed to save themselves.[17]

The Priory of Aquitaine of the Langue of France commemorated its dead and missing in defense of Poitiers under siege by French Huguenots. So, too, did the Langue of Germany recognize its fallen in that country's religious wars. At Brandenburg Martin Graf von Hohenstein succeeded Franz von Naumann as Bailiff. Hohenstein would later renounce Catholicism and the Bailiwick of Brandenburg would become a Protestant arm of the Order of Jerusalem.

On Sunday 20 November 1569, the first and only Chapter General during the magistracy of Pietro del Monte and the eighth Chapter General since the Order's 1530 settlement at Malta convened in the Church of San Lorenzo at Birgu where a Mass of the Holy Spirit was heard. Mass was followed by a procession to the Great Hall of the Magistral Palace. There the Grand Master asked all attendees to unite for the common good. Under the Grand Master and Prior of the Church Antoine de Cressin of Auvergne there were five of eight Conventual Bailiffs attending, Grand Commander Balthazard de Vintimille d'Ollioules of Provence, Marshal Jean l'Evésque de la Cassière of Auvergne, Grand Conservator (Draper) Francisco de San Clemente of Barcelona, Admiral Giuseppe Cambiano of Ruffia in the Piedmont, and Chancellor Fernando de Alarcón of Alarcón SE of Madrid, the other three dignities of Turcopolier (England), Grand Bailiff (Germany), and Grand Hospitaller (France) either vacant or absent. Two priors attended, Prior of Messina Pietro Giustiniani and Prior of Capua Scipione Ajazza. There were five Capitulary Bailiffs present, Bailiff of Negroponte Salvador Sin, Bailiff of Naples Niccolò Orsini di Rivalta, Bailiff of Manosque François de Gozon-Mélac, Bailiff of Caspe Luis de Salcedo, and Bailiff of Eagle

Oliver Starkey. There were three lieutenants to Conventual Bailiffs, Christophe le Boulleur de Montgaudry of France, Walter von Hauenstein of Germany, and Olivier d'Aux de Bourneuf of the Priory of Aquitaine.

On 25 November 1569 the eight langues selected Sixteen *capitolari* or legislators to consider matters brought before the Chapter General not settled by acclimation. These were the Grand Commander and Bailiff of Manosque for Provence, the Marshal and Antoine de Villemontel for Auvergne, Montgaudry and Bourneuf for France, the Grand Conservator and Bailiff of Negroponte for Aragon, the Admiral and Prior of Capua for Italy, Hauenstein and Lieutenant Grand Bailiff Heinz von Metternich for Germany, Procurators Don Pedro Hurtado de Mendoza and Pedro de Mesquite for Castile, and with Starkey the only eligible representative of England at the Convent, Ubertino Solaro of Turin was appointed. These sixteen retired to the house of Eustachio di Monte, secular nephew of the Grand Master, where they were joined by non-voting Procurator of the Grand Master Giorgio Vercelli, Vice Chancellor Francesco Mego, and Treasury Scribe Augustin de Sainte-Maure. On 2 December the Grand Master requested and obtained from the Sixteen authorization to confer the Bailiwick of Lango on Montgaudry, Montgaudry abstaining. That day the Grand Master also requested and received authority to extend tenure of Giovan Francesco Langosco de Conti della Motta as Seneschal for the remainder of his Magistracy. The Sacred Council chaired by the Grand Master met in conjunction with the Chapter General on 3 December and appointed Francisco de San Clemente General of the Galleys, and on the latter's nomination also appointed Catalan Don Federico Meca to command of the capitana. This action seemed incongruous as during other Chapter Generals this particular appointment had been the prerogative of the Sixteen. The appointment was also unusual as San Clemente had never commanded a galley and had no experience at sea. None whatsoever, as several Grand Crosses observed.[18]

Because the Chapter General was ever so aware of the strength of the Ottoman Armada and embarked soldiery, the Grand Master was authorized by the Sixteen to borrow at interest 70,000 scudos. Ten thousand additional scudos were contributed by attendees at the Chapter General. For three years there would also be a levy on commanderies of 30,000 scudos per year over and above normal responsions. The Chapter General adjourned on 12 December not without some disgruntlement that Pedro Hurtado de Mendoza, a knight of the small cross (albeit a knight with a university education in church and civil law as well as in the classics), had exercised the authority of a Knight of the Grand Cross, whereas Fernando de Alarcón, a Knight of the Grand Cross and senior knight of the Langue of Castile had been overlooked. Alarcón believed this incongruity was somehow attributable to Don Bernardino de Mendoza, 13 year-old nephew of Pedro Hurtado currently a page to the Grand Master. Without further cause, Bernardino de Mendoza and two young friends, Rodrigo de Ribera and Francisco Briceño, bastinadoed the 70 year-old Alarcón on the steps of the Magistral Palace, drawing considerable blood. On his recovery Alarcón concluded the guilty party was not Bernardino but rather Bernardino's uncle Don Pedro Hurtado de Mendoza. Bernardino had meanwhile been deprived of his Habit. As the Convent divided into two factions and took to the streets, Bernardino and his de-frocked accomplices were imprisoned in Castle Saint Angelo. For life. And for their own safety. This incomprehensible and shameful conflict within the Convent would endure for months with many injured or wounded and with Don Juan de Villegas, a Mendoza partisan, torn to pieces by people in the street. The blame rested with Grand Master Pietro del Monte.[19]

While discord continued in the streets of Malta Grand Master Del Monte notified the Sacred Council he had replaced René le Cirier de Semeur in command of the new *Santa Maria della Vittoria* with Prospero di Pignone of Naples, while replacing Guion de Saugniac de Belcastel in command of *San Giovanni* with Pierre de Montauban de Voguedemar of Provence. In light of the perceived threat posed by an Ottoman Armada of record proportions, San Clemente on 29 December took the four galleys directly to Palermo to obtain from Viceroy and Marchese del Vasto Ferdinando d'Ávalos agreed consignments of grain, meat, and other foodstuffs as well as license to transport to Malta foreign soldiery. Francisco de San Clemente had secret orders from the Grand Master to also seize any grain carrier encountered at sea and to force her into port at Malta.[20]

On the first day of January 1570 San Clemente encountered ashore the Viceroy returning from Trapani where he had received a communication from Don Alonso Pimentel, Governor of La Goletta outside of Tunis, with an astounding report concerning Uluç Ali, Ottoman Viceroy of Algiers. Uluç Ali had in the heart of Winter marched from his realm by land with remarkable speed over swollen rivers and streams with all of his janissaries and azaps and hired Moors, five or six thousand infantry in number, and suddenly fallen on Tunis. And, furthermore, by treachery of resident Moors unhappy with the King, had seized the fortress and then the walled city in the name of Sultan Selim. Nothing remained to be conquered but La Goletta to which the Hafsid Bedouin (Beni Haf) King Ahmad III had fled. The same Uluç Ali had, furthermore, laid siege to La Goletta both by land and by lagoon-boat. Meanwhile he had the vessels and resources of Algiers, nearby Bizerta, Bone, Djerba, and Tripoli at his disposal. The Governor's communication requested relief in the form of men, munitions, and foodstuffs. The Viceroy had eleven galleys of Naples commanded by Alvaro de Bazan at his disposal plus nine of Sicily under command of Don Juan de Cardona together with cargo vessels and troop carriers. He requested the four galleys of Malta, as well, and to overcome San Clemente's reservations on 19 January dispatched an aide by frigate to Malta who promised the Grand Master the same relief force upon return from La Goletta. The Grand Master agreed, and there ensued the annual frantic race to ready Malta with hired infantry and to take other defensive measures absent the four galleys. These measures included appointment of four more captains of hired infantry, Antoine de Villemontet of Auvergne, Nicolas de Mirè of France, and both Jerónimo de Foçes and Alonso de Tejada of Castile.[21]

In Venice at 1570 March-end an Ottoman ambassador delivered a note to Doge Pietro Loredan demanding immediate cession of Cyprus. This note followed a verbal notification in January by Grand Vizier Sokollu Mehmet to Marcantonio Barbaro, Venetian Ambassador at Constantinople, that Sultan Selim considered Cyprus a part of the Ottoman Empire. Girolamo Zane at age 79 was appointed Venetian Captain-General of the Sea commanding 70 galleys under order to prevent the loss of Cyprus. He immediately departed Venice for Zara (Zadar) in the Gulf (Adriatic). Marco Querini, Captain-General of the Gulf, proceeded with 25 galleys to Candia for the purpose of activating 20 more currently laid-up on that island.[22] Defensive measures earlier initiated at Malta, the corsair galliot of Hospitaller

Giovan Battista Vivaldi of Mondovi was sent in late-March to the Levant to ascertain movement of the Ottoman Armada. Vivaldi would return on 11 May with certain advice the Ottoman Armada was bound for Cyprus and not for Malta or La Goletta, as it was known by then an Ottoman envoy had at March-end delivered an ultimatum to Venice demanding immediate cession of the island or war.[23]

The La Goletta relief force including the four galleys of Malta had meanwhile been waiting at Trapani in western Sicily for a break in the weather before proceeding the 135 nautical miles to Tunis. While waiting a brigantine of Susa had been taken by the capitana of Naples, the captive crew divided among the participants, five captives to the four galleys of the Religion. They brought disease. During the transit to La Goletta Hospitallers Bartolomeo Castigleone of Milan and Jean de Romain de Fontaines of Senlis died of the disease. Dying a bit later was Strozzo Strozzi of Florence, only two years a Hospitaller. Others were laid low. The relief force reached La Goletta at end-April to find circumstances there much better than predicted. Governor Pimentel had at end-February destroyed the small craft besieging La Goletta from the Lagoon, and there had been no further attempt against the fortress.[24]

Francisco de San Clemente's four galleys returned to Malta early in May to not a little dissatisfaction; it was increasingly clear the Order of Malta had become an extension of the Spanish Empire. The Convent, moreover, now recognized neither Malta nor La Goletta was to sight the Ottoman Armada this year. A General Summons announced in January had been rescinded. Five companies of hired infantry had been released. A letter even so had been received from Pietro Loredan, Doge of Venice, seeking assistance from Malta in Venice's war with the Ottomans. While Venice had never come to the aid of Hospitallers in conflict with the Ottomans, by the same token Venice had never failed to seek and receive aid from Hospitallers during its own conflicts with the Ottomans. On 11 May Grand Master and Council resolved to send the galleys as well as an embarked ground force of knights and soldiers under command of Pietro Giustiniani of Venice. Bernardino Scaglia of Jurea was appointed Giustiniani's lieutenant. With the embarked ground force, San Clemente and the galleys were dispatched on 31 May to Syracuse and then to Messina with expectation of proceeding to Venetian Corfu to join the Venetian Armada.[25]

At Malta Grand Master Pietro del Monte was sick and tired of governing the Convent and was on the verge of renouncing the Magistracy. He sent his Secretary Lorenzo Ramondo to Rome to seek permission of the Holy Father. His four galleys meanwhile encountered off Pozzalo three Turkish brigantines one of which led the galleys on a 30-mile chase while the other two beached 15 miles west of Cape Passero, their crews fleeing. The remaining brigantine was overhauled by Voguedemar's *San Giovanni* while the Christian oarsmen of all three were liberated. San Clemente again returned to Malta, this time on 13 June with 80 captive Turks but without the three Hospitallers taken by disease. At Pozzalo Antonio Maldonado took possession of the three captured brigantines.[26]

At Rome Pope Pius V had little time for tired Grand Masters. He had fostered formation of a Holy League to combat enemies of Christendom and had agreed to contribute to the war against the Ottomans. Because the Church had had no fleet of its own since the 1560 disaster at Djerba when her three galleys had been entrapped by Piali Pasha and lost with most of the rest of the Holy League fleet, he had acquired 12 galley hulls from Venice, equipped and manned them, and placed them under the command of Duke of Tagliacozzo and Prince of Paliano Marcantonio Colonna. By virtue of his position at the Vatican, Colonna became Holy League Commander-in-Chief.[27]

San Clemente was again sent to Messina, this time on 26 June 1570 to rendezvous with Gian Andrea Doria. Commanding his capitana was Don Federico Meca of Catalonia. The padrona *Santa Maria della Vittoria* was commanded by Prospero Pignone of Naples, *San Giovanni* by Pierre de Montauban de Voguedemar of Occitanie, and *Santa Anna* by Salvador de Labata of Huesca. Each galley was reinforced with additional oarsmen and carried forty or fifty knights under command of Pietro Giustiniani. The balance of the Hospitaller ground force intended to go to the aid of Venice in its war with the Ottomans was embarked on other convoyed vessels. En route Messina Salvador de Labata died of a fever, and Gerónimo de Foçes of Aragon was plucked from the caravan and appointed to command *Santa Anna* in his place. Convoyed vessels were left at Messina as were Prior of Messina Pietro Giustinani and Lieutenant Bernardino Scaglia to await rendezvous with Doria. These missed events to follow.[28]

Doria had meanwhile deployed to the African coast hoping to surprise Uluç Ali, but came away with a single Ottoman vessel captured. While Doria was on the African Coast upward of 60,000 Ottoman janissaries, Spahi cavalry, and artillery plus support units, transported from Phineka (modern Finike) on the south coast of Anatolia by naval units under command of Piale Pasha, made an unopposed landing on the Venetian island of Cyprus. Also during Doria's absence the Viceroy of Sicily ordered the Malta Squadron to Trapani to escort several vessels loaded with mortar and other building materials needed to build a castle on the island of Marettimo. From Palermo the squadron sailed to Ustica; and then to Trapani; from that port the galleys towed loaded barges to Marettimo. Meanwhile at Malta Hospitaller Ippolito Malaspina, Marchese di Fosdinova in Tuscany and cousin of Gian Andrea Doria, had been appointed successor to the deceased Salvador de Labata, and the squadron had been ordered back to Malta to embark the new captain.[29]

The squadron returned to Trapani and from there headed for Malta by way of Licata. At Licata San Clemente was visited by Malta-flag corsair Gamba da Bosco who informed him four of Uluç Ali's galliots in the area had attempted to capture his brigantine. San Clemente was counseled not to leave for the time being due to presence of the Barbary corsairs. He paid Bosco little heed and decided to return to Malta, imprudently loading on the decks of his ships meats, barrels of wine, bovine and other cattle, timber in bulk, iron, and other items rendering his ships unstable. The Bishop of Mazara del Vallo and the government of Licata also advised him not to leave because Uluç Ali (Occhiali) was in the vicinity with 18/20 sails. Convening a council of his captains and pilots, San Clemente finally overrode council advice not to risk an immediate passage to Malta but rather to wait. Clemente announced his intention to sail the following morning of 15 July. Leaving some ashore who expected departure the following morning, San Clemente on impulse to obtain a head start instead sailed from Licata in the evening of 14 July with trumpet blasts and saluting-cannon fire heard by Uluç Ali at Cape Passero less than 35 nautical miles distant.[29]

Hopeful of an offshore wind which was slow to materialize, for five hours the four heavily-laden galleys and squadron frigate struggled along the shore of the Gulf of Terranova (modern Gila) before altering course to reach Malta. At first-light they had a point of land in sight believed to be Cape San Demetrio at the NW end of Malta's Gozo 20 miles distant. Astounded by their progress, they were due to be disappointed. The point of land was not Cape San Demetrio but rather Sicily's Cape Passero which soon became evident with a rising sun for backdrop. The Maltese had been steering ninety degrees to the left of intended course, the capitana and *San Giovanni* out ahead, the capitana's pilot and navigator error-prone in spite of a moon three days short of full. The rising sun also made clear a squadron of 19 oared vessels, 12 of them single-masted galliots of 22 and 23 banks comparable to galleys which some Maltese initially took for the vanguard of Gian Andrea Doria's double-masted galley armada returning from the Barbary Coast. They were again due to be disappointed. Francisco de San Clemente had encountered not the Doria vanguard but the Algiers squadron of Uluç Ali, a former Dominican novitiate then Beylerbey or Viceroy of Algiers, 19 vessels strong looking for prey along the shipping corridor between East and West.[30]

The enemy capitana along with 11 others set off in pursuit of San Clemente's capitana and Voguedemar's *San Giovanni*; the other seven Barbary vessels at the same time set off in pursuit of Prospero Pignone's *Santa Maria delle Vittoria* and Gerónimo de Foçes' *Santa Anna*. Reinforced corsair vessels were rowing northwest with light wind on the starboard bow. Over-burdened galleys were attempting to aid their oarsmen by pointing as close to the same wind as possible while still filling their sails, heading northwest on the starboard tack back where they came from. *Santa Anna* was overhauled by five enemy vessels but captured only after four hours of intense combat. Initially boarded at the poop by the galliot crew of Kara Peri, Gerónimo de Foçes's crew gave more than it got and the Peri galliot withdrew with two mortar hits and large numbers of dead and disabled. The galliot crew of Mad Deli Mami was next aboard and then the crews of Mami Gancio and Kara Memi. Foçes would be among the dead and missing. So, too, would be Francesco Girolamo Bertio of Pavia barely in his 20's, gravely wounded in three places when last seen. Other young caravan knights lost during those four hours included a wounded Diego Enriquez de Guzmán two years an Hospitaller thought to be a nephew of the 5th Count of Alba de Liste of the same name, Gentile Sassetti of Florence, Pier Antonio Leopardi of Recanati in the Apennines, Oratio

Maggio of Urbino, Giovanni Francesco Gondi of Florence, Galeazzo Carretto of Turin and of a Carretto family contributing a full score of knights to the Order of Saint John, and Diego de Brochero of Salamanca, the same Diego Brochero who would rise to become Admiral-General of the Spanish Ocean Armada. Others were missing never to reappear. Galeazzo Carretto, though, would be rescued with other oarsmen from a drifting Ottoman galliot at the Battle of Lepanto and would thus regain his freedom. Voguedemar's *San Giovanni* was captured by Uluç Ali without a shot fired, Voguedemar and his crew contemptuously sent to North African slave markets without an audience. Pignone's *Santa Maria delle Vittoria* equivalent in size to the capitana managed to escape danger courtesy of *Santa Anna*'s resistance, eventually reaching safety under the guns of Girgenti (Agrigento) twenty miles beyond her Licata starting point.[31]

San Clemente aboard the capitana commanded by Federico Meca was pursued by Uluç Ali's principal lieutenant Caragiali born at Lepanto in modern Greece's Gulf of Corinth who would reappear there at the Battle of Lepanto in October 1571. Casting off the towed frigate of Bernardino Rispolo while also pointing toward Girgenti, the Maltese capitana ran aground on a sandbank off La Torre di Montechiaro (Torre di Gaffe) fifteen miles short of the guns of Girgenti. San Clemente and the crew fled ashore, the first aboard a tender or ship's boat having abandoned a warship still afloat as well as with the Standard of the Religion still at mast-head, but not the gold and silver coin which he carried with him. It was left to Bongiani Gianfigliazzi of Florence, still a novitiate, to lower the Standard, place it within his corselet, and later to present it to Grand Master del Monte. A severely wounded Gianfigliazzi would be taken captive at the Battle of Lepanto 15 months later, a captive of the same Uluç Ali.[32] But it would not be his end, and he would appear yet again in these pages. Note: the Standard of the Religion was a squared flag denoting command of more than one vessel or command of more than one military unit, in this instance a white 8-pointed Maltese Cross centered in a squared red field.

Captain Federico Meca was also still aboard the capitana, and with First Officer Claude de la Salle de Colombière of Auvergne and Emilio Pucci of Florence attempted to blow the magazine to prevent the ship's capture. The oarsmen seeing their own unhappy end, however, frantically summoned Caragiali. Caragiali quickly took possession of the galley and her oarsmen were liberated. Meca and Colombière made it ashore in the confusion, Emilio Pucci did not. And thus Uluç Ali came into possession of the finest galley capitana in the Mediterranean aboard which to hang his own stern lanterns a symbol of rank. Those making it ashore, and not all did, took refuge within La Torre di Gaffe, a small fortress without garrison. Cavalry came to the rescue and the corsairs departed.[32]

Upon completion of the engagement, nine knights from the Langue of Provence were dead or missing including Voguedemar commanding *San Giovanni*, four from the Langue of Auvergne, ten from the Langue of France, twenty-seven from the Langue of Italy, seven from the Langue of Aragon including Gerónimo de Foçes, three from the Langue of Germany, and five from the Langue of Castile. Nine missing knights would die in slavery. Voguedemar would be among those ransomed. He would next appear in 1572 as Seigneur and Commander of Moussoulens near Carcassonne, would be appointed Grand Commander in 1594 at the advanced age of 64, and would die of natural causes three years later. The bearer of his ransom, Hospitaller François de Claveson acting for Bishop of Apt François de Simiane, was subsequently captured at the Battle of Lepanto and detained at Algiers by the same Uluç Ali. He would die nine years later at the age of 31 still awaiting his own ransom.[33]

Two of those from the Langue of France, Jean le Cirier de Semeur received into the Priory of Aquitaine but a year earlier and Pierre de Bertaucourt of Villes de l'Oise received four years earlier, forcibly circumcised and appearing to have disavowed Christianity, survived captivity in relative freedom for a number of years. Semeur became attracted to personally improved Epicurean circumstances and would never return. Pierre de Bertaucourt's circumstances would also improve thanks to a benevolent patrone, and he would become owner of a timar or landholding in Epirus not far from Corfu. Even so, he remained Christian at heart, and with his patrone's blessing would eventually return bringing with him some of his new wealth. This caused him to be accused of Turning Turk. He would be exonerated by an Hospitaller board of inquiry, his knighthood restored, and later would be advanced to Knight Commander and assigned a commandery. Future Grand Master Alof de Wignacourt and Bertaucourt had served overlapping novitiates at Beauvais, and one of the former's sisters would marry into the Bertaucourt family.[34]

Bernardino Rispolo commanding the frigate made it back to Malta with his crew, not aboard the frigate but aboard a commandeered brigantine reaching Malta two days after the engagement. At about the same time a galliot was dispatched to Constantinople from Collo (ancient Chullu) in Algeria to inform the Grand Vizier and Sultan of the victory. Hospitallers Ferrante Maggiolini of Milan and Giovan Battista Somaia of Florence were embarked captives. *Santa Anna* would be towed to Constantinople as a battle trophy, arriving at the Ottoman capital with Michel de Barthélemy-Sainte-Croix of Provence and Miguel Cruzat of Navarre in magnificent Christian battle dress, one at the poop and the other at the prow. *Santa Anna*'s remaining crew received the best medical care available at Algiers as befitting admired warriors.[35]

San Clemente meanwhile hid at Licata, Sicily, dressed as a monk, then made his way to Rome to complain of his lot to Spanish Ambassador Fernández de Córdoba. Later he wrote repentantly to the Grand Master and asked permission to dedicate himself to a life of atonement. In formal proceedings at Malta San Clemente's hired Pilot Orlando Magro and Navigator Scarmuri, enchained aboard *Santa Maria de la Vittoria,* were found culpable, but San Clemente was found most culpable as well as negligent and cowardly. All three were sentenced to death by judge and jury. San Clemente would shortly be executed by weighted sack at Malta. Magro and Scarmuri would be hung. The severity of these penalties in spite of impossible odds suggests the capitana was indeed equipped with a working magnetic compass and/or that navigational stars were visible and/or that bulk iron should have been stowed on the bow and not proximate to the compass binnacle. There was no reported review of San Clemente's 3 December 1969 appointment to squadron command despite vocal objections concerning his dearth of galley command experience. Given vocal objections, this was an appointment which could have only been approved at behest of Grand Master Pietro del Monte.[36]

Pietro Giustiniani was appointed General of the Galleys succeeding San Clemente who was then appearing before a jury of his peers. The squadron consisted of the former padrona *Santa Maria delle Vittoria* which then became the capitana and which Giustiniani commanded himself, Prospero Pignone's resignation asked for and received.

There were in addition two new hulls at the Arsenal of Messina donated by the Marchese de Pescara, Viceroy of Sicily. The first of these hulls was christened *San Giovanni* and placed under the command of Ippolito Malaspina. The second was called *San Pietro* and at the time of San Clemente's disaster was already being outfitted by Pierre de Saint-Aubin for employment as a corsair sailing under the flag of Sicily. She was turned over to the Order and placed under command of the same Saint-Aubin who, to equip her, had disarmed his own galliot commanded by Bernard de Saint-Aubin, donating everything to the Religion. Meanwhile more than two hundred Maltese oarsmen had been levied into paid service while crew and other survivors from the former squadron capitana run aground by San Clemente had been returned to Malta together with forty-five captive oarsmen donated by the Duke of Terranuova. Upon outfitting of the three-galley squadron, Giustiniani stepped down as skipper of the capitana and was succeeded by Michele Montauto of Syracuse, Montauto's First Officer Davide Serra of Genoa.[37]

Meanwhile the 12-galley Papal Squadron under Marcantonio Colonna was waiting at Otranto on the Adriatic coast of Italy while the 49-galley Spanish Armada under Gian Andrea Doria remained at Messina until 12 August and did not reach Otranto two days distant for another eight days. Neither did Doria mask his resentment of Colonna nor his Genovese distaste for Venetians. He had no interest in going to the assistance of Ottoman-beleaguered Cyprus. Colonna's lieutenant was Duke of Zagarolo Pompeo Colonna while his captains included Prospero Colonna, Domenico di Massimi, Giovan Matteo Paravicino, each of Rome, Hospitaller Alphonso Malaguzzi of the Lombard, and commanding the capitana (Papal "generale") was Hospitaller Gaspare Bruni of Dulcigno (Ulcinj), a prudent and practiced commander. Doria lieutenants included both Alvaro de Bazan commanding Neapolitan galleys and Juan de Cardona commanding Sicilian galleys. Once at Otranto Doria ignored Holy League Commander Colonna, prevaricated and obstructed, and only reluctantly agreed to proceed in company as far as Suda Bay, Candia (Crete), and a rendezvous with Venetians under Girolamo Zane. Zane had 127 galley-sottiles, eleven large merchant galleys armed as galleasses, a large galleon, and 14 warships among other support vessels. The battle-crippled Malta Squadron of three galleys, however, remained at Syracuse not yet ready for sea.[38]

The rendezvous was effected on 1 September 1570 when Doria immediately voiced his belief Venetian galleys were undermanned and unseaworthy. Girolamo Zane, however, was under orders to proceed to Cyprus with or without allies, and Colonna had agreed to accompany him. Doria then objected on the basis of weather so late in the season. While Doria tarried inspecting Venetian galleys for seaworthiness, Nicosia fell to the Ottomans on 9 September following 45 days of siege and was sacked by Lala Mustafa Pasha, Commander of Ottoman ground forces and future Grand Vizier. Unaware of Nicosia's fall, the combined fleet moved from Suda to Sitia at the other end of Candia where it arrived on 13 September. Four days later the Holy League Fleet sailed from Sitia and reached Vathi (modern Kas Marina, Turkey) on 22 September. There the news of Nicosia's fall was received as well as advice besieging Ottomans had moved on to Famagusta, last redoubt of Venice on the island of Cyprus. A further council was called at which it was recognized Famagusta could not accommodate the Holy League Armada and at which all but one commander agreed the Holy League campaign to disrupt or relieve the Siege of Cyprus had failed. The Holy League Armada immediately took course back to Candia. Reaching Porto Figa (Pigada) and Tristomo on the island of Scarpanto (Karpathos) on 26 September, Gian Andrea Doria was licensed to depart and did so. At end-September the three Malta galleys at Syracuse were still not ready for sea.[39]

The three galleys of the Religion when fully ready sailed for the Levant on 17 October. Gian Andrea Doria and his 49 galleys reached Messina one day later on 13 October, their campaign ended. At Cyprus only Famagusta remained under the Venetian flag. The Maltese reached Chania at the western end of Crete on 26 October where after an exchange of salutes they were in time for the final dispersion of the Holy League on 7 November. On that date the Maltese and Papal galleys took course for Corfu accompanied by ten galleys of Venice where on 10 November the squadrons intended separating, Colonna headed for refit and repair at Venice with the ten Venetians, and Giustiniani headed for Malta. On the same date a Venetian relief squadron of 13 galleys and four support ships under command of Marco Querini sailed to the relief of Famagusta. In addition to ships company, troops, munitions, and food supplies were an unspecified number of transhipped Hospitaller volunteers. Upon reaching Corfu Giustiniani's three glleys were beset by north winds, icy boras, that forced a retreat all the way to Porto Fiscardo in Keffalinia 85 miles to the south. At Fiscardo they were further beset by contagious disease taking the life of Hospitaller Guido de Conti della Torre of Naples, nephew of future Cardinal Michele della Torre.

By 18 November, however, one day following Zane's arrival at Corfu with shiploads of the afflicted including Zane himself, the Malta Squadron was able to depart Corfu and by way of Otranto safely reach Syracuse on 11 December. Because of disease and contrary winds, though, the three galleys would not reach Malta until 22 January. Among scores of oarsmen and soldiery, knights Don Sancho de Lodosa of Navarre, Muzio Raspa of Vercelli, Ferdinando Guidi and Bernardo Ridolfi both of Florence, Flaminio della Torre of Forlano, Tuscany, Giovan Battista Mombretto of Pavia, Vespesiano Antinori of Florence, and Luis de Torres of Castile, none of them yet the age of 30 years, were all dead of typhus. Luis de Torres was the son of Fernando Torres de Portugal y Mesia Venegas y Ponce de León who would in 1584 become Spanish Viceroy of Peru.

Still at Corfu was Marcantonio Colonna's Papal Squadron now reduced by storm-loss and disease from twelve to three galleys.[40] These departed Corfu Town on 28 November 1570 but were stymied on the north of the island by contrary winds which kept them at Porto Casopo (Kassiopi) for another month, able to reach Kotor City in the Gulf of Kotor only on 31 December where days later lightning struck the capitana, ignited the magazine, and sank the flagship under the walls of Kotor's Venetian fortress. Thanks to quick thinking by Hospitaller Gaspare Bruni of Dulcigno (Ulcinj), there were no fatalities but the ship was lost. Colonna trans-shipped to a Venetian galley which exited the Gulf of Kotor but was herself lost off Ragusa 25 miles further up the Adriatic coast. Eventually Colonna reached Rome by way of Ancona and carriage where he was immediately plunged into planning for the new year. Back at Corfu Girolamo Zane had been arrested by order of the Doge and imprisoned. He would die still incarcerated in October 1572. At Genoa Gian Andrea Doria remained a Spanish Admiral but his reputation was souring, even with King Philip II. At Malta a decision had been reached to re-activate *San Iacomo* parked on the hard at Marseille by Niccolò Orsini di Rivalta one year earlier. She was to be commanded by François de Moreton de Chabrillan of Chabrillan in Dauphiné, 14 years enslaved following 1552's failed raid on Zuara. Also at Malta the Grand Master licensed Mathurin d'Aux de Lescout-Romegas to be the Pope's counselor on naval matters. Romegas took with him his own lieutenant, Gabriel d'Abzac la Douze of Provence.

At about the same time came reports to Malta of the passing of Prior of Navarre Leon de Peralta; the Priory was conferred on Luis de Cruzat. Dying at the same time was Bailiff of Venosa Antonio Peletta of Asti; he was succeeded by Admiral Giuseppe Cambiano who would be succeeded in turn as Admiral by Antonio Bologna. Alonso de Solis of Asturias was appointed Bailiff of Negroponte upon the death of incumbent Salvador de Sin. And Geronimo de Guete was appointed Grand Conservator (Draper) by deprivation of Francisco de San Clemente. The Priory of Toulouse was vacated by death of incumbent Pierre de Beaulac-Trebors, one of the few remaining veterans of 1522's Great Siege of Rhodes. He was succeeded as Prior of Toulouse by Balthazard de Vintimille d'Ollioules, the latter renouncing the dignity of Grand Commander to which François de Panisse, Receiver at Avignon, succeeded. Also passing away was the saintly Bailiff of Mallorca Onofre de Montsuar. Nineteen years bailiff, he left the Common Treasury a rich estate and was succeeded by Catalan Francisco de Borguès (Francesc de Borguès). In order to reduce expense while the Ottomans were preoccupied in the East the company of soldiers commanded by Captain Vincenzo Ventura garrisoning Valletta was discharged and replaced by a company of knights commanded by Christophe le Boulleur de Montgaudry, his Lieutenant future Grand Master Alof de Wignacourt. Engineer Francesco Laparelli of Venice, wishing to go to the defense of Cyprus, was licensed to depart the Convent, proceeded from Malta to Corfu where he died from the same typhus earlier afflicting Maltese and Venetian crews.[41]

At the turn of the year 1570-1571 the Galleon of the Religion called *San Pietro* commanded by Pirro Melzi, bound from Licata, Sicily, to Malta with a cargo of grain, was forced by a terrible storm to drop anchor off a lee shore and appeared lost. Her crew abandoned ship to save themselves. Weeks later the ship was discovered 300-odd miles to the northeast near Otranto but barely afloat. She was towed half submerged into the port where at a careening facility her artillery and other armaments were off-loaded. Miraculously, without this weight the ship began to shed water, rose to the surface, and was resurrected.[42]

Marco Querini's mini flotilla then consisting of 12 galleys and four sailing ships carrying troops, munitions, and food supplies to Famagusta forced an Ottoman blockade and entered the port of that besieged city on 26 January 1571. Prior to entry three of seven blockading Ottoman galleys were sent to the bottom, while the following day a large Ottoman mahon was discovered and captured off the port full of soldiers, munitions, and foodstuffs. Days later a second heavily-loaded vessel was brought into Famagusta, and then a third. These developments prolonged survival of the city by months. Hospitallers Aloisio Lippomani of Venice, Giovanni Maggio of Urbino, and a score of other Hospitaller volunteers accompanying Marco Querini's Venetians sacrificed their lives doing so.[40]

The foregoing successes on the part of Marco Querini were said to infuriate Sultan Selim who summoned Piali Pasha from his winter quarters near Constantinople and replaced him as Area Fleet Commander with Pertev Mehmed Pasha.[43] As Selim's son-in-law Piali did not lose his head but rather dropped down a rung. The next time Piali's capitana was sighted it was carrying one less fanale or stern lantern than the two displayed theretofore. Pertev Mehmed Pasha, a Herzegovinian product of the devsirme draft of Christian youth, later Janissary Aga and still later Beylerbey of Rumelia, moved up from Number Three in Ottoman Fleet hierarchy and commanded the Cyprus force during its relocation from Cyprus to the Morea. Pertev would be succeeded as Area Fleet Commander by Kapudan Ali Pasha known as Müezzinzade Ali Pasha.[44]

In March 1571 the entire Convent relocated from Birgu to Valletta effective for administrative and ceremonial purposes on Sunday 18 March.[45] Laying down his pen in 1602, Giacomo Bosio with this relocation completed the third and final part of his *History of the Sacred Religion and Illustrious Militia of Saint John of Jerusalem* with the same incredible detail concerning relocation from Birgu to Valletta typifying his entire account. No one yet has given readers more information on the subject than has Bosio. He would pass away 25 years later at the age of eighty-three. Henceforth this transcription will be *Mostly Bartolomeo dal Pozzo*, a professed Hospitaller knight present at the scene of some of his *Historia della Sacra Religione militare di S. Giovanni Gerosolimitano*.

An agreement was reached on 11 May 1571 between Pope Pius V and Cosimo I de Medici, Grand Duke of Tuscany, pursuant to which the Grand Duke would lease to the Church 12 galleys, 10 of them skippered by Tuscans, all fully-armed and crewed with 60 officers and sailors per galley. Eleven would have three rowers per oar with at least 24 banks per galley. The capitana was to have five rowers per oar from stern to mainmast, with four per oar forward of the mainmast. The Holy League Treaty was signed on 25 May. Its clauses provided that a fleet of 200 galleys, 100 warships, 50,000 embarked infantry, and 4,000 cavalry was to be ready by 1 April each year the expense of which was to be shared in the proportions of 3/6th's by Spain, 2/6th's by Venice, and 1/6th by the Church, and that Don Juan of Austria, the Spanish Captain-General, was to be Commander in Chief, Colonna his number two.[46] Rendezvous of the several components was set for 10 August 1571 at Messina.[47]

On 13 June 1571 Marcantonio Colonna left Rome for Civitavecchia where he spent a week inspecting assembled forces including Papal infantry commanded by Hospitaller Pirro Malvezzi of Bologna. There were also numerous volunteers many of whom as noble offspring of Church dignitaries necessarily had to be accommodated, some aboard the Papal capitana. The most notable person embarked aboard the capitana, however, was Mathurin de Lescout-Romegas as Superintendant or Governor of the Papal Squadron. He was not skipper of the capitana as some suggest; this position was occupied by Hospitaller Gaspare Bruni of Dulcigno (Ulcinj) who previously commanded the Papal capitana lost to lightning at Kotor City in January.[48]

Hospitaller Gil de Andrade was similarly embarked aboard Don Juan's capitana *Real* commanded by Hospitaller Juan Vasquez de Coronado. On 21 June the Papal Squadron departed Civitavecchia for Naples where it waited almost a full month. Leaving Naples in company with the three galleys of Malta, Colonna reached Messina on 20 July. Three days later the Corfu Squadron of the Venetian Fleet arrived with 50-odd galleys commanded by Sebastiano Venier. There they waited another month.[49] Also on 21 June came the first of seven great Ottoman assaults on the walls of Famagusta. For five hours the Ottomans failed to penetrate the city's defenses. A mine dug into the ravelin shattered everything within sight on 29 June preceding the second great assault. This second failure led the Ottoman command to undertake a prolonged artillery battering of the fortress's south wall where on 8 July alone 5,000 cannon blasts were reportedly counted.[50]

When out of gunpowder and with nothing left to eat, the garrison and residents of Famagusta agreed on 5 August to yield to Ottoman besiegers on honorable terms. The terms were violated by both besieged and besieger. The garrison murdered captives with knowledge of other Christian atrocities. The same garrison as well as many residents were slaughtered and worse on revalation of Venetian atrocities. Marcantonio Bragadin was flayed alive, his skin stuffed with straw and paraded on a donkey.[51]

Pietro Giustiniani sailed from Malta on 10 August, his capitana the 28-bank galley *Santa Maria delle Vittoria*. The padrona *San Giovanni* was commanded by Alonso de Tejada of Castile in succession of Ippolito Malaspina, while *San Pietro* remained under command of Pierre de Rocquelaure Saint-Aubin of Provence. Embarked ground forces were commanded by Grand Bailiff Joachim von Sparr aboard *Santa Maria*. The latter's three sergeants-major were Tomás Coronel of Aragon, Vasino Malabaila of Asti, and Hubert Hambrecht of Baden-Württemberg. There were 190 volunteers embarked, knights and serving brothers, and they rendezvoused with other components of Don Juan's Armada at Messina. Giustiniani's capitana would be inserted in the line of battle immediately to the right of Papal Captain-General Marcantonio Colonna, at the expense of Count of Leini Andrea Provana who commanded the galleys of the Duke of Savoy. This was the cause of a seniority dispute which would fester for years.[52]

Don Juan of Austria and his mistress Maria de Mendoza (Maria la Bailadora) arrived at Messina on 23 August with 44 galleys having spent time enroute from Barcelona at Genoa and Naples. In addition to his mistress, the Holy League commander was accompanied by an Executive Council of nine individuals hand-picked by King Philip II. Three of these were Hospitallers and Spanish commodores: Prior of Hungary Gabrio Serbellone, Juan Vasquez de Coronado, and Gil de Andrade. Just over a week later the balance of 70 Venetian galleys arrived from Candia as did the Genovese galleys of Gian Andrea Doria and as did the Naples Squadron of 30 galleys under Alvaro de Bazan, Marqués de Santa Cruz. Embarked aboard the Doria flagship were Hospitaller Prince of Padua Alessandro Farnese and his

Hospitaller Aide Alessandro Berzio of the same Diocese. On 8 September Don Juan held a review of the entire fleet comprised of 209 galleys and six galleasses plus innumerable transports. His Holy League Armada departed Messina nine days later bound for Lepanto by way of Corfu.[53]

There was yet another review of the Holy League Armada prior to its arrival at Lepanto, this one conducted by an enterprising lieutenant of Uluç Ali, his name Kara Ogia, among Turks "Karagoz" or "Black Eye," perhaps because of an eyepatch, perhaps because of his black-hulled, black-sailed, 60-oared galley. It may have even been a name corrupted from that of his place of birth, Chioggia in the Venetian Lagoon. But that latter was some time ago, before *devsirme* conscription as a youth into the standing Ottoman Navy, before seven long years of janissary training including the most menial of shipboard assignments. At the time his galley carried a lantern at the stern signifying his status as Sancakbey or Governor of Valona (modern Vlorë) in Albania. He was also a Captain of Janissaries and a veteran both of 1565's unsuccessful siege of Malta and of 1570's successful invasion of Venetian Cyprus. In between he had guided his galley squadron as far north as Venice itself, razing the islands of Hvar, Brac, and Lissa among Venetian communes ashore and merchant traffic at sea. He was an enterprising able seaman, and late in September 1571

Twenty-eight Bench Ottoman Sultana.

he transferred from his galley to a frigate equipped for deep-sea fishing and took his frigate among Holy League ships at anchor off Corfu and in the approaches to mainland Igoumenitza, counting. It was a reprise of Uluç Ali's own survey of the Holy League Armada before 1560's Battle of Djerba, and Kara Ogia took his count of enemy vessels back to Ottoman Kapudan Müezzinzade Ali Pasha.

Ali Pasha flew his flag from a two-masted 28-bench sultana such as that depicted, and not from a 24-bench single-masted galliot as some suggest. His command sultana would in addition to his personal flag have flown the Banner of the Caliphs, a great green banner embroidered in gold with text from the Qur'an and with the name of Allah inscribed 28,900 times. It should be noted as well that Ali Pasha had made a name for himself at a time when former Christians dominated the Ottoman civil service and army, rising through military ranks as an exceptional archer, Aga of Janissaries, and then vizier (minister) to a position as Beylerbey or Viceroy of Egypt. In 1566 he was appointed Fourth Vizier in the government of Serbian Grand Vizier Sokollu Mehmed Pasha and in 1568 succeeded Piali as Kapudan Pasha or Commander-in-Chief of the Ottoman Navy. It was as commander-in-chief that he led the largest Ottoman Armada in history to the Battle of Lepanto. Reportedly a sensitive and humane individual as well as a patron of the arts, he promised the Armada's Christian oarsmen freedom should he prevail. Don Juan, the opposing Holy League commander, also promised freedom to his oarsmen should the League prevail, but Don Juan went one step further and armed his Christian conscript and convict oarsmen for combat. As this bloodiest of all naval engagements would be one of hand-to-hand combat, and therefore of numbers, the armed oarsmen making up two-thirds of most galley complements were a crucial addition. Ali Pasha's flagship was at the center of the slaughter, and he with bow in hand took a fatal musket ball in the forehead at a critical moment. He had with him his two sons aged 13 and 17, captured, as well as 150,000 Venetian gold ducats believed by some to have been his entire personal fortune. He is presumed to have been more afraid of the Sultan than of Don Juan, and was thus prepared to buy his family's freedom in the event of defeat.

The Holy League Armada sailed from Corfu on 3 October, and with brief pauses at Keffalonia and in the approaches to the Gulf of Patras, formed a line of battle across the latter on 7 October 1571 as the

Ottoman Armada approached from the east in a similar formation. Giustiniani's three Maltese galleys were a part of the Holy League center-right opposite Uluç Ali and Caragiali (Bicheno's Uluch Ali and Kara Djaly). His capitana carried a large number of knights a part of the shore combat unit, including Grand Bailiff of Germany Joachim von Sparr, as well as a large proportion of the 190 volunteers and most of the Maltese oarsmen hired following the disaster at Cape Passero. She moved in support of Tuscan/Papal galleys immediately to her left, and for much of the day was engaged in fierce combat.[54] Uluç Ali meanwhile had seized upon an opening in Gian Andrea Doria's ranks, the Christian right wing, rolling up Doria's left and temporarily capturing 12 Christian galleys. The thirteenth galley was the 28-bank Malta capitana *Santa Maria delle Vittoria* also overrun. Most of those on board including the Grand Bailiff were killed in combat, among them 30 knights and officers who had their throats slit by boarding enemy. One of these was 18 year-old Alexandre de Saint-Vital of Savoy and the Langue of Auvergne, another 19 year-old Jean Tiercelin of Roche du Mayne and the Priory of Aquitaine. The first was still in his novitiate, the second not long out of his. Others included first officer Davide Serra of Genoa, Raymond de Loubières of the Priory of Toulouse, Giulio Cesar Peletta of Asti, Alessandro Fava of Bologna, and Arrigo Arrighi of Florence, none but the first more than 20 years of age. Three knights were enslaved, Giovan Battista Mastrillo of Nola with others enslaved later overcame the crew of a Turkish galliot and sailed her to safety. The additional two enslaved from Giustiniani's capitana would be ransomed. These were Pietro Guadagni and Bongiani Gianfigliazzi, both taken to Constantinople by Uluç Ali himself. Guadagni, it should be noted, had in 1565 been taken captive to Algiers following the fall of Fort Saint Elmo. He was ransomed by his family on both occasions. A fourth enslaved Hospitaller was also taken by another of Uluç Ali's galliots to Algiers. This unfortunate, 21 year-old François de Claveson of the Dauphiné and the Langue of Auvergne, refused to abjure his faith and died a slave. While it is frequently reported the Order's Standard flying at the capitana's main truck was captured and later presented to Sultan Selim, author Pozzo asserts on page 1-28 of his history that Don Martin de Ferrera in mortal combat with the Standard's Ottoman captor recaptured the symbolically important symbol which soon flew again from the capitana's main truck. In spite of debilitating wounds, Ferrera survived to

Fernando Bertelli's Lepanto Battle Formation Poised/Joined.

later earn a Grand Cross as Castellan of Amposta, reaching his end in 1620. Wounded by seven Turkish arrows, Giustiniani was carried by a Turkish slave to his cabin and here was saved from death both by the slave and by bribing with a large sum of money Algerian corsairs who had overrun his ship. Severely wounded but surviving with Giustiniani were *Vittoria*'s Captain Rinaldo Naro of Syracuse, Angelo Martellini of Florence, Ferrante Coiro of Milan as well as Martin de Ferrera. The capitana was reached and freed by the *Guzmana* of Francisco Ojeda of Spain who found 500 corpses on board, 150 of them boarders including those with the Giustiniani bribe; *Guzmana*, too, would suffer heavily. A deceased Ojeda would later receive the Grand Cross of the Order of Malta as a sign of gratitude, plus an annuity for his family. The overall total of Hospitaller knights lost at Lepanto was more than sixty, more than forty from the capitana, others the aforementioned sergeants-major

Vasino Malabaila and Hubert Hambrecht. Despite extensive damage, most of it was superficial and the capitana would survive to fight another day; so, too, would Saint-Aubin's *San Pietro,* relatively unscathed. Only Tejada's *San Giovanni* would be scrapped.[55]

Another galley prominent at Lepanto was *La Marchesa*, the personal property of Gian Andrea Doria, great-nephew of Andrea Doria. On board was Miguel de Cervantes Saavedra. Born 24 years earlier, Cervantes had fled his native Spain following a street brawl in which one of the participants had been killed. Arriving in Spanish Naples at the age of 22 Cervantes soon enlisted in a local detachment of marines which in 1571 was assigned to Doria's *La Marchesa* then lying at Genoa. Doria commanded the Holy League right wing rather than his own galley squadron distributed along the line of battle. *La Marchesa* was assigned to the Holy League left wing as the two fleets collided, a left wing very nearly enveloped by the Turkish right under Mehmed Scirocco, Sancakbey of Alexandria with a commendable record at sea. The fighting was hand-to-hand and furious. Seriously ill at the time, Cervantes rose from his sickbed to command the detachment of marines and armed oarsmen fighting in the ship's waist. While the sea ran red with blood, Cervantes took two arquebus balls in his chest and a third in his left hand, crippled for life, but held his post. He survived this the most deadly naval battle in history, and armed Christian oarsmen likely swung the tide, more than doubling the number of Christian combatants. Among others in the Christian left, Venice's *la Trinita* commanded by Giovanni Contarini sent Mehmed Scirocco's capitana to the bottom. Contarini's crew pulled a mortally wounded Scirocco from the sea. He would not survive. Scirocco's wife was recovered uninjured. She would later be described by Historian Mathieu de Goussancourt as "la plus belle creature de son temps."

Mathurin Romegas took part in the Battle of Lepanto on board the Papal capitana, Hospitaller Gaspare Bruni commanding, Holy League Lieutenant-General Marcantonio Colonna embarked. She was inserted in the blue squadron or command center to starboard of Don Juan's *Real* and during the battle was boarded by janissaries from the galley on which the sons of Ali Pasha were embarked, but Romegas's personal ferocity is said to have turned them away.[56]

Real commanded by Hospitaller and Spanish Commodore Juan Vasquez de Coronado later took and abandoned the corpse-littered capitana of 2nd Vizier and Deputy Armada Commander Pertev Pasha, the latter escaping by skiff. Of others in Colonna's Papal contingent, *La Elbigina* under Knight of Santo Stefano Fabio Galerati of Cremona was placed in the left wing under Sebastiano Venier, later Doge of Venice. She took the Rhodes capitana, Bey of Rhodes Hassan Veneziano (born Andretta) also fleeing in a skiff. *La Toscana* under Metello Caraccioli of Naples was placed in the left wing, as well, as were *La Vittoria* under Baccio Guirte of Pisa and *La Pace* under Giacomo Perpignano of Sicily's Barcellona Pozzo di Gotto (near Milazzo). *La Grifona* under Tuscan Alessandro Negrone was placed in the Christian right wing under Gian Andrea Doria confronting Uluç Ali where it has been credited with conquest of Kara Ogia's large black-hulled sultana resulting in death of the latter. In the right wing with *La Grifona* were *La Pisana* and *La Fiorenza* respectively under Tuscans Ercole Balotta and Tomasso dei Medici, *La Fiorenza* temporarily seized by Uluç Ali and suffering severe casualties. Also in the right wing were the Church's *Santa Maria* under Pandolfo Strozzi of Florence and the Church's *San Giovanni* under Angelo Biffoli of Florence, the latter killed with his entire crew, his galley scuttled. Held in reserve under Alvaro de Bazan y Guzman, Marqués de Santa Cruz, were *La Soberana* under Ercole Carafa of Naples and *La Serena* under Alphonso Appiano of Piombino, fragments from the latter's bow chasers wounding Ottoman commander Müezzinzade Ali Pasha prior to his terminal wound received while his sultana was entangled at the bows with Don Juan's La Real.[57]

An overwhelming Holy League victory, relations between Venetians and Spaniards soon soured, however, with Venetian commander Venier filing his own self-serving battle report without clearing it with the fleet commander. Following the victory Romegas was sent by Marcantonio Colonna to convey the news to Pope Pius V at Rome.[58] Lepanto was one of the largest and by far the most deadly naval battle in history, before or since. On one side were arrayed 208 Holy League galleys and galleasses as well as additional support vessels, and on the other side there were 251 Ottoman galleys and galliots as well as smaller vessels. These 459 vessels were manned by 141,000 sailors, marines, and oarsmen. Forty thousand of them lost their lives, the single most deadly toll in the history of naval warfare. One hundred forty Ottoman galleys were captured as well as seventeen galliots. Eighty more oared vessels were destroyed or sent to the bottom. The key to victory was number of combatants. Müezzinzade Ali promised his fleet's Christian oarsmen freedom should he prevail. Don Juan also promised freedom to his oarsmen should the Holy League prevail, but Don Juan went one step further and armed his Christian oarsmen for combat. As this bloodiest of all naval engagements was one of hand-to-hand combat, and therefore of numbers, the armed oarsmen making up two-thirds of each galley's normal complement were the decisive factor.

Giustiniani with Tejada's *San Giovanni* and Saint-Aubin's *San Pietro* each towing an Ottoman galley the Order's share of spoils returned to Malta on 3 November having first deposited critically wounded at the Priory's infirmary in Messina. Tejada's battle-damaged *San Giovanni* would be scrapped in favor of *San Iacomo* brought from Marseille by François de Moreton Chabrillan. A *San Giovanni* survivor in his fourth year as an Hospitaller, Pedro de Acuña of Castile, would in 1602 become Eleventh Governor-General of the Philippines.[59]

Returning Hospitallers found the Convent in a state of agitation reflecting a Papal Brief from Pope Pius V directing that Mathurin Romegas, Superintendant or Governor of the Church Squadron at the Battle of Lepanto, be elevated to the dignity of Turcopolier and awarded the accompanying Grand Cross. Chabrillan was one of three ambassadors selected by the Council and dispatched to the Holy See to discuss this conflict between Papal and Convent authority involving appointment of senior knights to positions of honor, authority, and income. The other ambassadors were Prospero Pignone of the Langue of Italy and Don Juan de Tello y Guzman of Castile.[60]

The remainder of the battered Ottoman Armada commanded by Uluç Ali reached Constantinople 80 to 90 oared vessels strong including additions acquired in the Archipelago enroute. The long-time corsair was immediately appointed Kapudan Pasha or Commander-in-Chief of the Ottoman Navy. His name, moreover, was ordered by decree changed from Uluç Ali or Occhiali to Kiliç Ali, meaning *Ali The Sword*.

San Iacomo returned from Civitavecchia and Messina with the Hospitaller ambassadors having presented to the Holy See the Order's position with respect to the dignity of Turcopolier, to wit, the dignity of Turcopolier was a dignity of the Langue of England, and there were more than 20 knights in the Langue of Provence alone not only senior to Romegas but more worthy of the honor. The capitana and *San Pietro* paused at both Messina and Licata to take on board cloth and coin destined for the Order's Common Treasury at Malta.[61]

During 1571 Grand Hospitaller Jacques d'Arquinvillier de Tourville succeeded the deceased Jean Audebert de l'Aubuge as Prior of Champagne and was succeeded himself as Grand Hospitaller by Pierre Pelloquin de la Plesse, Pelloquin in turn renouncing the Bailiwick of the Morea to which Guillaume de Malain de Lux was appointed. Malain de Lux renounced the dignity of Treasurer to which Christophe le Boulleur de Montgaudry the Younger was appointed. Upon review by the French Court, however, Arquinvillier de Tourville's elevation to Prior of Champagne was rescinded in favor of Hospitaller courtier and royal ambassador Michel de Seurre de Lumigny in culmination of a process initiated by the Crown early in 1563. Pedro de Mesquite of Castile, respected for his valor in combat, was elevated to the Bailiwick of Lango vacated by Montgaudry. Admiral Antonio di Bologna was elevated to Bailiff of Santo Stefano near Monopole, renouncing the dignity of Admiral to which the Piemontese Baldassar Begiamo, 42 years a Hospitaller, was advanced. Philipp Flach von Schwarzenberg was appointed Grand Bailiff in succession of Joachim Sparr von Trampe killed at Lepanto. François Salviati of a Florentine banking family which had immigrated to France was appointed Resident Ambassador to the Court of France in succession of the deceased Nicolas Durand de Villegagnon. Salviati was a cousin of Queen-Mother Marie de Medici.[62]

Without warning Grand Master Pietro del Monte passed away at dawn on 27 January 1572 at the age of 76. He was initially interred in the Chapel of Santa Maria della Vittoria, but upon completion of the Conventual Church of Saint John in Valletta was transferred to a subterranean chapel intended as the final resting place of Grand Masters.[63]

Chapter III

1572–1575

Following interment of former Grand Master Pietro del Monte, the Sacred Council appointed Grand Commander Jean-François de Panisse to the vacant position of Magistral Lieutenant with power to act on Magistral matters during the absence or incapacity of the Grand Master. A fifth son of Jean de Panisse, co-Seigneur de Vedènes 12 kilometers east of Avignon, Panisse's first act was to reduce the annual compensation paid the Grand Master from 6,000 to 4,000 Maltese scudos reflecting impoverishment and debt of the Common Treasury. This level of compensation was precisely half that of Del Monte's predecessor Jean Parisot de la Valette. Panisse's second act was to convene a General Assembly of Hospitallers at Malta eligible to vote for the purpose of electing a new Grand Master. The General Assembly convened on 30 January 1572 in the Church of Santa Maria della Vittoria where a Mass of the Holy Spirit was intoned before Knights of the Grand Cross and ancients of the Convent standing at the front of the congregation. This was followed by a eulogy and then by selection of electors representing each of the eight langues. These Eight Electors retired to the Sacristy where from assembled Hospitallers they selected Prior of Messina Pietro Giustiniani as non-voting President of the General Assembly. They then selected Martín Duero Monroy as Knight of Elections, Pierre Mosquet of Provence as Chaplain of Elections, and Serving Brother Jacques Marete of France as Sergeant-at-Arms of Elections. With these three new Electors the Eight original Electors retired.[1]

Duero, Mosquet, and Marete selected a fourth elector from among assembled Hospitallers, and the four selected a fifth, and the five a sixth, and so on to bring the total to Sixteen at two per langue who would by secret ballot select the next Grand Master of the Order of Jerusalem. The Sixteen Electors were: Chaplain Pierre Mosquet and Jean de Soubiran-d'Arifat (acclaimed veteran of 1557's Battle of Ierepetra) for Provence, Marc de la Goutte and Jacques de Dyo for

Auvergne, Serving Brother Jacques Marete and René le Cirier de Semeur for France, Galceran Ros and Ramón Fortuyn for Aragon, Giorgio Vercelli and Ubertino Solaro for Italy, Francisco de Remolons (of a Catalan family originally from Remoulins, France) of Aragon and Jean de Castellane d'Aluis of Provence were selected for England which had no eligible elector, Philipp Lesch and Weipert von Rosenbach for Germany, and Martín Duero Monroy and Jorge Correa for Castile. While some electors favored the Order's Treasurer and former Sengle-lieutenant Christophe le Boulleur de Montgaudry of the Langue of France and others favored Prior of Toulouse Bertrand de Vintimille d'Ollioules of Provence, in an exclusively French competition Marshal Jean l'Evésque de la Cassière of Auvergne was elected 51st Grand Master of the Order of Jerusalem.[2]

James Shelley of England, impoverished and unwelcome in Britain, was resident at the Convent much more often than not from August 1558 until after May 1587. On this Assembly date he was Preceptor of Templecombe, though the preceptory no longer existed. If present, he would have been deemed ineligible to vote by virtue of indebtedness (support allowance) to the Common Treasury.[3]

Jean l'Evêsque de La Cassière was born in 1502 at La Cassière 18 kilometers SW of Clermont-Ferrand in the modern Puy-de-Dôme Department of Auvergne the son of Jehan l'Evêsque, himself a younger son of Jehan l'Evêsque, Squire and Lord of La Cassière, and of the latter's wife Marie de Montfoulloux. As offspring of the dispossessed, but with proofs of nobility, the future Grand Master is believed to have been received into the Order of Jerusalem as early as 1519, thereafter heeding a 1522 summons for Hospitallers to repair to Rhodes for the expected Ottoman siege which was evident by May of that year. According to Pozzo I-46, Jean l'Evêsque de La Cassière survived loss of the three larger French vessels sent to Messina in response to the summons and there awaited favorable sailing conditions which never materialized. He thus was forced to do his minimum of five years at the Convent in Italy much of the time fleeing disease. These were the same years in which he completed his galley caravans. Early in the Malta years from 1530 he was appointed Commander of La Racherie 75 kilometers north of La Cassière. He bore one of the Order's Standards at 1552's ill-conceived and ill-fated raid on Mourad Aga's Zuara for the ignoble purposes of employing paid soldiery and of acquiring slave labour, emerging unscathed even though a choice target for enemy marksmen. By 1567 he had been awarded the Grand Cross in conjunction with assignment as Titular Bailiff of Ottoman-occupied Lango (Kos). Two years later he was elevated to the Dignity of Marshal, senior knight and conventual bailiff of Auvergne resident at the Convent.

The day following his election, Cassiere as Grand Master selected in accordance with customary practice the first of eight individuals, one per langue, for his household or official staff. As Seneschal he selected Panisse. Also selected was the Conventual Conservator who had circa 1475 replaced the Grand Treasurer as Chief Financial Officer. Treasury Secretary Augustin de Sainte-Maure meanwhile took an inventory of the former Grand Master's estate. The aforementioned Pierre Mosquet had been Pietro del Monte's Confessor, and Mosquet informed the Sacred Council that Grand Master Del Monte had on his death bed pardoned all Hospitallers deprived of their Habit. Commander Giorgio Vercelli was appointed Ambassadeur Extraordinaire to notify the Holy See of death and election. He would donate to the Papal Squadron the two Ottoman galleys the Order's share of Lepanto-captures in consideration of repair costs and incompatibility with squadron galleys. Recognizing need to have a responsible Hospitaller liaising at Messina with Holy League Commander Don Juan of Austria, Pedro Pardo de Villamarin of Castile was so appointed. Don Juan in turn dispatched to Malta from his staff Hospitaller Don Diego de Maldonado to congratulate Cassière on his accession and to also solicit the Order's participation in an Armada undertaking on the coast of North Africa. While Maldonado's solicitation loses something in translation, Pietro Giustiniani was directed to ready the galleys immediately. Treasurer Montgaudry was appointed to command of the embarked landing force with Don Juan de Villavicencio of Valladolid as lieutenant and with Jean de Lannoy Molyneux of France, Miguel de Sese of Castile, and Marcello Mastrillo of Nola as sergeants-major. Because Rinaldo Naro had been slow to recover from wounds received at the Battle of Lepanto, he was replaced in command of the capitana by Fabrizio Giustiniani, a Venetian patrician and relative of the General received into the Order of Malta weeks earlier.[4]

The three galleys with embarked caravans and soldiery departed Malta on 8 March 1572 bound for Trapani at the western end of Sicily, jumping-off port for traffic headed to Tunis and points west. At Trapani and environs search failed to locate Don Juan and his armada as both Church and Venetian units suspicious of a North African venture had been recalled until assembly of the Holy League Armada at Messina sometime in the Summer. Don Juan himself was wintering at Messina without venturing beyond the breakwater. Arriving meanwhile at Malta from Marseille was the Galleon of the Religion with a number of *forcé* or forced laborers, petty criminals dispatched by the King of France. These arrived just in time to replace conscripted Maltese oarsmen completing their term of paid service. Thus re-manned the galleys made a second trip to Sicily, this time to take on foodstuffs required at Malta, and to embark Antoine d'Espinay Saint-Luc, an Hospitaller since 1536 recently appointed to represent the Langue of France on the Sacred Council. Also embarked was Hospitaller Don Ferrante d'Aragona, son of Duke of Terranova and Prince of Castelvetrano Don Carlo d'Aragona, President and acting Viceroy of Sicily. Don Ferrante was soon awarded the Commandery of Guilla di Palermo.[5]

During the Order's 42 years at Malta the quality of local medical care had declined. At Rhodes the Order's Hospital had been said to offer the finest medical care in Europe (sic). At Malta the Order's Infirmary at Manoel, the pratique island in Marsamuscietto, concerned itself primarily with ensuring contagious disease remained on board incoming vessels, while a second Infirmary at Birgu was insufficient to accommodate a professional staff. Wounded returning from Lepanto were all put ashore at Messina. When Admiral and General of the Galleys Pietro del Monte began to suffer from kidney stones in December 1558 he did not seek help at Manoel but returned to Italy for treatment. The new Grand Master wished to restore local medical care to its status quo ante, and took a personal interest in construction of a new Sacred Infirmary at Valletta which would be commissioned in 1574 and which still stands today as an exhibit.[6]

Pope Pius V passed away on 1 May, thus depriving the Holy League of its single sincere and disinterested member. The second member, Venice, remained interested only in what assistance in the Levant she might receive from the remaining member, while the remaining member, Spain, was interested only in what assistance she might receive from Venice in extending Spanish North Africa.[7] Pope Pius V was succeeded on 13 May by Ugo Boncompagni of Bologna as Pope Gregory XIII following perhaps the shortest Conclave on record, 12-13 hours. The new Pope confirmed Marcantonio Colonna as Captain-General of the Papal Squadron, now fourteen galleys with gift of Malta's two prizes. Venice's Captain-General Sebastiano Venier had been recalled as disruptive to Holy League relations and replaced by Giacomo Foscarini. Kılıç Ali had meanwhile ordered construction over the Winter of 150 new galleys, and by Spring 1572 had 222 galleys under his command. But he did not have the seasoned hulls, experienced crews, and practiced oarsmen lost at Lepanto.[8]

Colonna reached Messina on 2 June with 14 galleys followed a few days later by Santa Cruz with 36 Neapolitan galleys, by Iacopo Soranzo with 24 Venetians, and by 3 Maltese under Giustiniani. Don Juan, however, soon received orders from Spain not to depart Messina without the Genovese of Gian Andrea Doria who had separately been directed to take his time reaching Messina. In the end Don Juan permitted Papal and Venetian galleys to leave for Corfu without him and sent 18 Spanish-Italians with them under Hospitaller Gil de Andrade, all with Colonna in command. These enlisted four Santa Cruz galleys en route and reached Corfu on 15 July. Awaiting Colonna at Corfu and Zante were 43 additional Venetian galleys, six galleasses, and 24 armed merchantmen. Kılıç Ali meanwhile exited Constantinople with his re-built Ottoman Armada which wasted the defenseless Venetian islands of Tinos and Cerigo enroute Modone (Modon in Venetian Italian) and Navarin.[9]

Colonna's armada of 139 galleys, 6 galleasses, and 24 ships headed for Cerigo off the foot of the Morea where it encountered the 222 Ottoman galleys on several occasions but without significant consequence. This was mostly attributable to the vagaries of wind which immobilized Christian sailing vessels as well as their galley screens. Pertinently, without the sailing vessels Colonna had a whopping disadvantage in all-important numbers.[10]

Pietro Giustiniani commanded the six-galley mixed vanguard of the Holy League armada. These included the three Maltese galleys, the capitana under Fabrizio Giustiniani, *San Pietro* under Saint-Aubin, and *San Iacomo* under Alonso Tejada. The vanguard, however, had been left with Don Juan and 58 additional galleys at Messina until August, then proceeding from Messina to Corfu, and in September from

Corfu as far as Cerigo without contact with the enemy. Following rendezvous with Colonna the allies proposed to attack the Ottoman Armada which then had most of its units in the Bay of Modone with some few units at Navarin eight miles distant. At Navarin Kiliç Ali was building a new fortress between Pylos and the entrance to Navarin Bay able to command both. The Ottoman Armada, however, refused combat and remained snug behind fortifications at both bays. At Constantinople Venice's Resident Ambassador Marc Antonio Barbaro received secret instructions on 19 September from the Council of Ten to negotiate peace.[11]

Threatened by weather in October, Don Juan tired of Kiliç Ali's refusal to come out from behind the guns of Navarin. He put 3,000 Italian and 1,000 Spanish infantry plus a battery of 12 pieces of field artillery ashore, augmented by the Order of Malta's Christophe le Boulleur de Montgaudry and embarked soldiery. These were dissuaded by a fierce storm which prevented re-supply, and the debarked force was recalled.[12]

A squadron of Ottoman galleys exited Modone in pursuit of a Venetian vessel enroute from Zante with Holy League supplies. Himself enroute Modone from Navarin, Don Juan ordered Marqués de Santa Cruz Alvaro de Bazan's Naples Squadron to intercept the Ottomans, causing the Ottomans to abandon pursuit of the Venetian. Trailing behind the rest of the squadron fleeing back to the safety of Modone, the Ottoman flagship was assailed by Bazan's capitana of Naples. While the Ottoman capitana animatedly resisted the enemy vessel, the Ottoman commander was in the end killed by a galley slave and the galley was taken. Two hundred twenty Christians were freed from the oars[13] while an equal number of janissaries and crew were captured. The slain Ottoman captain was Mohammad Barbarossa, Hassan Barbarossa's son and Kheir-ed-Din Barbarossa's grandson. Mohammad Barbarossa was wed to the deceased Dragut's only daughter and by her had a son. Mohammad had been scheduled to succeed Kiliç Ali as Beylerbey of Algiers. This was the final engagement of the Holy League which soon ceased to exist, and, shades of Barbarossa himself, its most notable action of 1572. The fleet dispersed, the Maltese returning to Malta in November.[14]

The year just ending was another year of personal success for corsairs flying the flag of Malta. Among these were two galliots the property of

Cosimo I de' Medici, Grand Duke of Tuscany, and one of Giangirolamo Acquaviva d'Aragona, 10th Duke of Astri. Three others belonged to Hospitallers Scipione Orsino of Barletta, Ferrante Coiro of the Piedmont, and Giovanni Barutto of Venice. These and a number of brigantines raided into the Levant and came away with significant reward. Gerónimo de Foçes commanding *Santa Anna* when the Malta squadron was overwhelmed by Uluç Ali in July 1570 had then gone missing with many others. He was ransomed in 1572 but returned to the Convent under suspicion of parties not present at the battle. He appealed to the Sacred Council and witnesses attested to his valiant defense of *Santa Anna* even though wounded, the Council finding Foçes neither negligent nor culpable. Receiver Niccolò Valori of Florence and *Santa Anna* returning under similar circumstances was also cleared. Commander Marc de la Goutte had earlier in the year been elevated to the dignity of Marshal vacated by election of the new Grand Master. Commander Ubertino Solaro had been appointed Lieutenant Admiral and then elevated to Prior of Lombardia in an apparent attempt to recover the Priory's income and unseat exiled incumbent Carlo Sforza who had been so appointed by grandfather Pope Paul III 27 years earlier. If so, the attempt failed. At year-end Pietro Giustiniani was succeeded as General of the Galleys by Grand Bailiff Philipp Flach von Schwarzenberg upon whose nomination François de Puget of Provence succeeded Fabrizio Giustiniani in command of the squadron capitana *Santa Maria delle Vittoria*. Pompeo Soardo of Bergamo was appointed to command of *San Pietro* succeeding Pierre de Saint-Aubin.[15]

Grand Conservator Geronimo de Guete was in February 1573 appointed Ambassadeur Extraordinaire to the Holy See to render the Order's obeisance to new Pope Gregory XIII and to obtain from the Pope confirmation of the Order's pre-existing privileges. While at Rome De Guete succeeded Giovan Francesco Langosco de Conti della Motta as Resident Ambassador, apparently at Vatican request. This was the same Della Motta who as Seneschal to Grand Master Pietro del Monte in 1568 had been the source of dissension among Del Monte's official Household. He would retire to his Commandery at Polizzi Generosa near Palermo. During his early tenure De Guete discussed with the Pope the end of financial support from the Church to Venice as no longer necessary given reports of peace negotiations.

By the same token there was no longer need for support of the hospital established at Corfu for sick and wounded veterans of the Battle of Lepanto. In that context he also discussed Malta's continuing need for external support, including a bankrupt Common Treasury and the yet incomplete City of Valletta.[16]

Having delivered De Guete to Rome by means of the capitana which put him ashore at Gaeta, Captain François de Puget and the capitana continued to Marseille where Receiver-General Ramón Fortuyn as well as Fulcrand de la Roque, Receiver at Avignon, and François du Broc, Receiver at the Priory of Saint-Gilles, were embarked, the latter two transporting coin, gold, silver, and jewels due the Common Treasury. From Marseille the capitana continued to Barcelona where Bailiff of Mallorca Francisco de Borguès with responsions from Aragon failed to make the rendezvous. Hospitaller Don Cosmo de Luna was dispatched to the Court of Spain to locate both Borguès and the Receiver for Castile. This process of locating Receivers and gathering responsions took an inordinate amount of time, and *Santa Maria* did not return home until 12 September when the Order was at wits-end begging and borrowing its needs.[17]

The Grand Master on 11 March 1573 requested of the Sacred Council and received authority to extend for another two years the 30,000-scudo annual imposition on commanderies previously authorized by the November 1569 Chapter General. Bailiff of Negroponte Alonso de Solis, Bailiff of Naples Niccolò Orsini di Rivalta, and Treasurer Christophe le Boulleur de Montgaudry were tasked to audit and reconcile Common Treasury accounts since the death of Pietro del Monte. This was a task which normally would be assigned to the Conventual Conservator or Chief Financial Officer. Should the audit prove it necessary, a special tax of another 30,000 gold scudos was to be levied on Langue of France woodlands. Prior of Champagne Michel de Seurre de Lumigny and Commander Louis le Bouteiller de Sainte-Geneviève were to investigate feasibility. With these measures and the late-1572 return from Spain of the capitana, immediate financial crisis was averted.[18]

Venice and the Ottoman Empire executed a treaty of peace on 7 March 1573 ending hostilities between the two parties and formally disbanding the Holy League. Piali Pasha celebrated in July by sailing Barbarossa's 1535 wake and torching Castro south of Otranto on the

Adriatic coast of the Kingdom of Naples. While commanding a fleet of
155 galleys, five galleasses, and 30 other vessels, Piali was soon forced by
bad weather to retire to the environs of Ottoman Valona on the opposite
shore of the Adriatic. He did not return to Italy but later re-fortified
the Bay of Navarin in the western Morea opposite if some distance
from Malta, leaving there a detachment of galleys and returning to
Constantinople.[19] Note: Kiliç Ali remained Kapudan Pasha while Piali
was a subordinate, though a son-in-law of Sultan Selim.

Returning to Malta in May was Prior of Ireland Mathurin Romegas
having obtained this lesser dignity in negotiations with the Order's
emissaries and by the hand of Pope Gregory, foregoing an initial Papal
award of the dignity of Turcopolier, the latter a dignity also Pilier of
the Langue of England and senior to more than a score of other Grand
Crosses. Resented by more senior Hospitallers for his aggressive
ambition and admired by younger aspiring warriors, Romegas without
the umbrella of Grand Master Parisot de la Valette patronage was
proving to be of more trouble than value.[20]

Don Juan of Austria meanwhile continued to plan re-conquest of
Tunis seized by Uluç Ali from Spain and her tributary King of Tunis
in January 1570, and for this purpose requested participation of the
Order of Saint John. The request was hand-delivered by Hospitaller
Don Juan de Abalos Ayala of Castile. Suspicious of Ottoman
intentions, the Order dispatched Commander of Argentens Pierre
d'Esparbez de Lussan with a galley to ascertain Ottoman movements,
Lussan having authority to proceed all the way into the Aegean.
Lussan departed Malta early in May and returned with a report the
Ottoman armada was still at Constantinople but in numbers of more
than one hundred galleys and many mahons or galleasses. Lussan's
report confirmed news brought several days earlier by *San Iacomo*
returning from a corsair excursion into the Levant. Under command of
Jean-Philibert de Foissy-Chamesson, *San Iacomo* had been newly
armed and equipped at the expense of the Grand Master himself, and
returned with a captured caramussal. Fearful of Malta's own exposure
to Ottoman ambition, lacking one of her four galleys and impoverished,
the Grand Master following consultation with the Council respectfully
declined to participate in the Tunis excursion, dispatching his own
emissary Don Diego de Solis of Castile to Naples to deliver the
declination. Sympathetic to Order circumstances, Don Juan dispatched

to Malta aboard five galleys 1,000 Spanish and German infantry under command of Hospitaller Gil de Andrade which reached Malta at mid-month. Another seven galleys were dispatched by the Holy See under command of Hospitaller Commander Juan Vasquez de Coronado with 1,000 Italian infantry embarked, Coronado Don Juan's skipper at Lepanto. These with 400 infantry hired by Vercelli's Centorio Cagnolo at Palermo relieved Maltese concern, but not enough to do without galleys.[21]

The Ottoman Armada under Piali departed Constantinople on 1 June 1573 with 155 galleys, five mahons, and 25 or more other vessels. At Malta Bernardino Scaglia of the Piedmont, Antonio Fuster of Aragon, and Hugues de Nagu dit Varènes of Auvergne were appointed Sector Wardens with authority to take such action as they felt appropriate to provide for Sector defense. Pietro Giustiniani was appointed Governor of Vittoriosa (Birgu and Castle Saint Angelo) and of adjacent Senglea, while Pompeo Pignone of Naples was appointed Governor of Cita Vecchia or Notabile (modern and ancient Mdina). Not long after the Ottoman departure from Constantinople a frigate arrived at Malta with wives and sweethearts of German infantry sent by Don Juan weeks earlier. This was not something with which the Convent had experience. Finding living quarters in a male habitat while preparing for siege was among the problems, this one solved by placing the visitors with Malta's non-combatant population.[22]

The new city of Valletta was defended by a ring wall with bastions and other defensive features. The Langue of Provence was assigned to the Bastion of Saint John the Baptist and half of the ring wall leading to Auvergne's Bastion of Saint Michael including the western gate. Moving clockwise, the Langue of Auvergne extended beyond the Bastion of Saint Michael to the tenaille of Saint Andrew. Then came the Langues of France, Germany, and England defending the entire sea wall portion of the ring wall from the tenaille of Saint Andrew including its cavalier along Marsamuscietto around Fort Saint Elmo and along Grand Harbor as far as the Bastion of Saints Peter and Paul at the southern corner of Valletta. The Langue of Aragon was responsible for the Bastion of Saints Peter and Paul while Castile defended ring wall beyond the latter bastion. The Langue of Italy was responsible for fortresses adjacent to the Bastions of Saint Michael and Saint Andrew.[23]

With the Turkish fleet having retired to Constantinople in September, Don Juan of Austria gathered at Sicily's westernmost port of Marsala an armada of 104 galleys, forty-four sailing ships, and fifty-nine small craft plus an embarked force of infantry including those previously assigned to Malta. While there were no Maltese or Papal galleys in the assembled fleet, Hospitaller Gil de Andrade commanded a squadron of Spanish galleys. The armada proceeded to the outer harbor at Tunis where the fortress of La Goletta was still in Spanish hands and where Don Juan put 12,000 men ashore on 9 October complementing the La Goletta garrison of 3,000 Spaniards commanded by Pedro Portocarrero. Tunis was entered without opposition the following day, the city's defenders said to number 40,000 Moors and 4,000 Turks having fled at the mere name of the Christian commander. Don Juan re-fortified and garrisoned the city with 3,000 Italians under immediate command of Hospitaller Pagano Doria (one of at least eight Genovese Dorias to become Hospitallers) as well as 3,000 Spaniards under command of Andrés Salazar, both reporting to Hospitaller Prior of Hungary and new Viceroy of Tunis Gabrio Serbellone. Similarly Muhammad VI was enthroned in place of his cousin Ahmad III who 30 years earlier had blinded and wrested the throne from his father Muhammad V and who on seizure was removed with family to Naples where he would soon expire as a fish out of water.

Neither did Tunis long survive as a Christian enclave, remaining in Spanish hands for a mere nine months in spite of a new fort constructed on the north shore of the inner harbor under direction of Serbellone, an engineer of distinction as well as a soldier and diplomat of considerable repute. Having assured Serbellone of ongoing Spanish support, Don Juan's armada departed Tunis on 22 October 1573 for Bizerta 25 nautical miles distant.[24] At that port city the inhabitants had risen against the Turks and were ready to turn the city and a Turkish galley present in the harbor over to the Spanish. Don Juan garrisoned Bizerta as he had Tunis albeit with fewer numbers, re-embarked his remaining troops, and departed on 30 October. He was back at Naples fourteen days later. Don Juan of Austria and half-brother Philip II never again gave more than passing thought to thousands of Spanish and Italian soldiers marooned on the coast of a hostile continent within 120 nautical miles of the Spanish Kingdom of Sicily.[25]

Philipp Flach von Schwarzenberg was in December 1573 appointed 25th Grand Prior of Germany succeeding Adam von Schwalbach upon the latter's death, and soon departed for Germany. Christophe le Boulleur de Montgaudry was appointed successor General of the Galleys, and upon his nomination Louis de la Roche la Boullaye was appointed to command of the squadron flagship succeeding François de Puget. Six days before Flach's departure Montgaudry took three galleys to succor at Syracuse the *Great Galleon* commanded by Rostaing des Essards-Laudun de Goût which had returned there in bad weather from Girgenti (Agrigento) with a cargo of grain and been blown onto the harbor shore. The hull was found to be holed in several places, and Laudon was adjudged responsible and deprived of his Habit. Returning to Malta with the galleys was former Vice Chancellor Martín Rojas de Portalrubio recently anointed by Pope Gregory as Bishop of Malta. Portalrubio was accompanied by Maltese Father Antonio Zahara of the Dominican Order whose missionary labors in the East Indies had earned him the Bishopric of Vico Equense in the Kingdom of Naples.[26]

Seventy-one years an Hospitaller, Grand Prior of France Pierre de la Fontaine passed away in France at the age of 83 years, a veteran of the Great Siege of Rhodes as well as the Great Siege of Malta. In between Great Sieges he had been a source of profound counsel opposed to corsair operations as well as to the 1560 expedition to Djerba, among other wisdom. He was interred with due ceremony at Moisy-le-Temple 100 kilometers northeast of Paris. Almost before the news reached Malta came a reminder from the French Crown the dignity of Grand Prior of France had been promised in 1551 to then 8 month-old Henri de Valois, Duke of Angoulême and illegitimate son of King Henry II and Janet Stewart, herself illegitimate daughter of Scots King James IV. In his Magistral munificence the Grand Master not only conceded the dignity of Grand Prior of France but the Commandery of Hainault, as well, Hainault a source of substantial income which would be greatly missed by the Convent and little noticed by the recipient.[27]

During 1573 the Priory of Saint-Gilles was awarded to Grand Commander François de Panisse in succession of the deceased Jean-Claude de Glandevèz, and the consequently vacant dignity of Grand Commander was assigned to Pierre d'Hérail-Rivière. Cristóbal Briceño de Valdoviño of Castile was appointed Resident Ambassador to the Spanish Court in succession of Antonio Maldonado. At year-end Don Diego de Copones was appointed to command of the new galley *San Giovanni* replacing the older galley *San Iacomo* commanded by Alonso de Tejada, this upon nomination by the Lieutenant Grand Conservator as the nomination was the turn of the Langue of Aragon.[28] Pier Filippo Corgnia of Perugia succeeded Pompeo Soardo in command of *San Pietro*.[29] The Grand Master appointed as a lieutenant Prioress Donna Caterina Torreglias of the Royal Monastery of Santa María de Sigena, and pursuant to a Papal Bull licensed the nuns to exit the monastery for medical care and for other urgent matters. Castellan of Amposta Luis de Talavera was ordered to visit the monastery as the Grand Master's emissary.[30]

The sting of Don Juan's seizure of Tunis sorely aggravated Sultan Selim at Constantinople, as did enthronement of a puppet-King within the Ottoman realm. Early in the new year he began assembling an Ottoman Armada even larger than those seen in the recent past. While Tunis may have been the Armada's eventual destination, as usual no one could have been certain. If Tunis, moreover, the Armada would in certainty pass within hailing distance of Malta and might well have been tempted to put troops ashore. Toward the end of March General of the Galleys Christophe de Montgaudry took the four galleys to Messina to acquire foodstuffs, munitions, particularly cannon balls and kegs of artillery powder, as well as lumber and earth-moving tools. Pier Filippo della Corgnia and *San Pietro*, though, were ordered to proceed by way of Syracuse to Zante and Cerigo where Corgnia was to present letters from the Grand Master to Venetian governors seeking information concerning the Armada. Corgnia was then to proceed into the Aegean as far as Negroponte or Candia and nearby islands of the Archipelago for the same purpose.

At Malta Commander Baldassar Imperatore of Palermo was appointed Captain-at-Arms and Governor of Citta Vecchia (modern Mdina) while Gabriel Vasco of Turin, François de Moreton de Chabrillan of Provence, and Catalan Francisco Gort (Francesc del Gort) were appointed Sector Wardens for Birgu and Senglea. Diego de Solis of Asturias was dispatched to Naples to raise 1,000 infantry, Onofrio Acciajoli of Florence to Palermo for 500 infantry, Tomás Coronel of Aragon and Claudio de Ortan of Castile to the same city for 300 each, and Alonso de Tejada of Castile to Messina for

300 more. These actions gave meaning to the word "perennial." But because it was impossible for so few soldiers to defend the expanded fortifications at Malta without assistance from the resident population, Prior of Messina Giustiniani, Prior of Ireland Romegas, Bailiff of Lango Pedro Mesquite, and Lieutenant Grand Bailiff Engelbert Flach von Schwarzenberg were deputized to organize a permanent militia of 1,000 Rhodiots and Maltese.[31]

The galley *San Pietro* under command of Corgnia returned from the Levant in April with recent news the Armada assembled at Constantinople had been delayed in sailing for North Africa by peste (plague) appearing at the end of 1573 but since controlled. Meanwhile the Spanish Armada had been delayed in even assembling by the absence of Don Juan of Austria in northern Italy. Also meanwhile the Spanish garrisons at Tunis and Bizerta had been forgotten, neither re-supplied nor relieved nor in receipt of mail or news.[32] When the Ottomans did sail the Armada was commanded by Kiliç (Uluç) Ali Pasha. Commanding embarked soldiery was Sinan Pasha, later Grand Vizier of the Ottoman Empire as Koca (the Great) Sinan Pasha. With them, according to misinformed sources, was Sultan Selim himself. Informed sources put the count of Ottoman galleys at 240 and accompanying mahons (galleasses) at 16, while these warships and others carried 8,000 jannisaries and 4,000 sipahis smong 58,000 less credentialed others. On this news the four Hospitaller galleys were sent to Licata on Sicily's south coast to embark 630 of the 2,400 infantry sought and to transport them to Malta. At Messina Diego de Solis had 350 more while a Captain Morales had a company of 400 Spanish arquebusiers hired as a unit. Seeking additional news of the Ottoman Armada the Grand Master dispatched into the Levant Federico Cenami of Lucca and Marcello Mastrillo of Nola together with non-Hospitaller Dimitris (Dimo) of Corfu, said to be an accomplished mariner. These three had orders to proceed to and remain within visual range of the Ottomans and to observe and report fleet movements. Mastrillo departed Malta at end-April 1574 aboard Dimo's frigate and returned 40 days later on 7 June with news the Ottomans appeared about to sail.[33]

Grand Master Cassière relayed his new information to Don Carlo d'Aragona Tagliavia, President and acting Viceroy of Sicily, to Don Juan of Austria, and to the Burgundian Viceroy of Spanish Naples

Cardinal Antoine Perrenot de Granvelle. Grand Conservator Juan de
Sangorrin had meanwhile hired 500 infantry in the Kingdom of
Naples commanded by Melchor de Morales and by Juan de Velasco
which embarked aboard eight galleys of Naples commanded by
Marqués of Santa Cruz Alvaro de Bazan together with 200 more
infantry contributed by Royal ministries. The Naples squadron was
detached by Don Juan and ordered to proceed to defense of Malta
at which the eight galleys arrived on 25 June. Also embarked
were Sangorrin, Marshal Étienne de Fraigne, and numerous other
Hospitallers responding to a General Summons. Still more Hospitallers
arrived in company with the aforementioned Federico Cenami
returning from the Levant with news the Ottoman Armada had sailed
from Constantinople. By Bazan's arrival at Malta the enemy Armada
had already been sighted off Cape Colonna on the sole of the Italian
boot. Among the Armada were 280 galleys, 15 galleasses or mahons,
15 galliots, and 19 sailing vessels all under command of the Calabrian
Kapudan Pasha Kiliç Ali. Seventy thousand embarked troops
were under Albanian ground force commander Sinan Pasha, a
former Sancakbey of Tripoli and former Beylerbey of Egypt. Both
commanders were born Roman Catholic, but the first matured on a
corsair rowing bench, the latter within Topkapi Palace's elite Endurun
Kolej. The Grand Master relayed the information to Tunis with two
messengers traveling separately. After Cape Colonna the Armada was
next sighted at Augusta just north of Syracuse taking on fresh water,
locals helpless to do anything about it. At Malta Martín Rojas de
Portalrubio, Bishop of Malta, evacuated the monasteries of Saint Peter
at Citta Vecchia and of Saint Scholastica at Birgu. Knights Costantino
Castriota of Naples, François de Puget of Provence, and Juan Vargas
Girón of Castile were appointed sergeants-major of ground forces,
each a veteran of the Great Siege of Malta.[34]

But the Armada was next sighted at Licata well up the south coast
of Sicily moving toward a fair wind at or near Trapani; Tunis was
clearly the Ottoman destination. On 18 July the Grand Master sped to
La Goletta the galliot of Pierre de Saint-Aubin commanded by his
younger brother Bernard to give yet another warning. The galliot
returned at month-end with 23 captives taken off various vessels and
with a fallacious report Kiliç Ali had departed La Goletta for Sicily in
order to carry out the remainder of his plans. The capitana *Santa Maria*

delle Vittoria, *San Giovanni*, and *San Pietro* were dispatched to Messina to alert acting Viceroy Don Carlo d'Aragona Tagliavia. In fact the Ottoman Armada reached the Gulf of Tunis on 12 July, its embarked force of 70,000 comparing with 2,000 Spanish at La Goletta and another 4,000 at Tunis itself. La Goletta succumbed on 23 August and Tunis on 13 September. At September-end the Ottoman Armada weighed anchor and headed for home, pausing in the Freo Channel between Malta and Gozo to take on fresh drinking water. King of Tunis Muhammad VI very nearly disappeared from the pages of history as the last Hafsid ruler of Tunis. Prior of Hungary Gabrio Serbellone was taken captive to Constantinople and imprisoned in one of the Seven Towers (*Yedikule Hısarı*) abutting the original walls of the ancient city. He would be part of a prisoner exchange in July 1575 brokered by neutral Venice. Hospitaller Pagano (Paganino) Doria, nephew of Gian Andrea Doria, was captured with Serbellone, but rather than treat his mortal wound he was immediately put out of his misery.[35]

Meanwhile Pope Gregory XIII had granted deceased French King Charles IX the right to sell Church assets to fund his war against Huguenots, and the French Court had interpreted this right to include Hospitaller assets in France. Commander Jacques de Dyo, Master of the Grand Master's House, was appointed Ambassadeur Extraordinaire to the new Court of King Henry III to persuade the Court this was never the Pope's intent. En route Dyo paused at Rome to coordinate with the Holy See, and then by way of Florence and Turin obtained the support of the Grand Duke of Tuscany and the Duke of Savoy protesting that the sale of Hospitaller assets in France would cripple Christian defenses against the Ottoman advance. Dyo was further assisted in obtaining an audience with the King by Prior of France Henri d'Angouleme, Prior of Champagne Michel de Seurre de Lumigny, and Prior of Saint-Gilles François de Panisse.[36]

The first Chapter General to convene in the new city of Valletta did so on the first Sunday of November 1574 the seventh day of the month (Julian calendar) in the Church of Santa Maria della Vittoria where Prior of the Church Antoine Cressin of Auvergne recited the Mass of the Holy Spirit before leading a procession of Hospitallers to the Great Hall of the recently completed Magistral Palace. There Michele Cimino, Chaplain of the Langue of Italy, read a devotional concerning well-being and harmony, after which the Grand Master addressed regulations and statutes and reasons for them. With presentation of colors and other ceremonials, it was not until Thursday the Chapter General turned to the business for which it had been convened. Six Conventual Bailiffs were recognized: Grand Commander Pierre d'Hérail-Rivière of Provence, Marshal Étienne de Fraigne of Auvergne, Grand Conservator-in-waiting Juan de Sangorrin of Aragon, Admiral Ubertino Solaro of Italy, Grand Bailiff Georg von Schönborn of Germany, and Grand Chancellor Alonso de Solis of Castile. Priors present were Prior of Saint-Gilles François de Panisse of Provence, Prior of Toulouse Bertrand de Vintimille des comtes de Marseilles d'Ollioules of Provence, Prior of Messina Pietro Giustinian of Venice, Prior of Ireland Mathurin Romegas of Gascony, and interim Prior of Hungary Don Vincenzo Carafa of Naples, interim while unaware of Serbelloni's fate. Capitulary Bailiffs in attendance were Bailiff of Santo Stefano Don Antonio di Bologna, Bailiff of Negroponte Juan de Ortiz, Bailiff of Naples Niccolò Orsini di Rivalta, Bailiff of Lyon Marc de la Goutte, Bailiff of Caspe Luis de Salcedo, Bailiff of Eagle Oliver Starkey, Treasurer Christophe le Boulleur de Montgaudry, and Bailiff of Lango Pedro de Mesquite. Thirty-six procurators of langues, priories, commanderies, and individuals were listed including James Shelley as Procurator for the Langue of England.[37]

The Sixteen Legislators selected two per langue to reach agreement or compromise on motions not approved or disapproved by acclimation of the Chapter were Grand Commander Hérail-Rivière and Prior of Toulouse Vintimille for Provence, Prior of the Church Cressin and Bailiff of Lyon Marc de la Goutte for Auvergne, Treasurer Christophe de Montgaudry and Lieutenant Grand Hospitaller Jean de Gaillardbois-Marconville for France, Grand Conservator-in-waiting Juan de Sangorrin and Bailiff of Negroponte Juan de Ortiz for Aragon, Prior of Messina Pietro Giustiniani and Bailiff of Naples Niccolò Orsini di Rivalta for Italy, Prior of Ireland Mathurin de Lescut Romegas and Bailiff of Eagle Oliver Starkey for England, Grand Bailiff Georg von Schönborn and Engelbert Flach for Germany, and Chancellor Solis and Bailiff of Lango Mesquite for Castile. The Sixteen retired to a remote section of the Great Hall where they were joined by non-voting designees Master of the Grand Master's House Jacques du Blot Viviers, Vice Chancellor Tomás Gargallo, and Treasury

Secretary Jacques de Sainte-Maure. The first order of business concerned authorization for and funding of a new Hospital within the walls of Valletta to have sufficient space to minister to the infirm as well as facilities supporting a permanent medical staff. The Hospital was approved and the cornerstone laid before year-end. Past due German responsions were among other items of business. So, too, were galley manning levels. Thenceforth the 28-bank capitana was to have 250 oarsmen, the 13 after-banks at 5 oarsmen per oar and the 15 forward-banks at 4 oarsmen per oar. Remaining 25-bank galleys were to be assigned 200 oarsmen at four oarsmen per oar. The capitana was set at 122 crew plus knights, the other galleys at 112 crew plus knights. Responsions payable by priories and commanderies were doubled for a period of two years. An impost on wealth of the German priories of 40,000 scudos was agreed. The Grand Master's support was increased from four to six thousand scudos per year. Duels were forbidden, violators to be stripped of the Habit and referred to a secular court.[38]

Grand Conservator Geronimo de Guete having completed two years as the Order's Resident Ambassador to the Holy See was succeeded by Bailiff of Santo Stefano Don Antonio di Bologna on authority vested in the Grand Master by the Chapter General. Bologna solicited and his lieutenant at Rome, Historian Giacomo Bosio, was awarded an honorarium of 200 scudos per year. De Guete was appointed to the dignity of Castellan of Amposta succeeding Luis de Talavera and was himself succeeded as Grand Conservator by Juan de Sangorrin. Jérôme de Bridiers-Gardanne was appointed Resident Ambassador to the French Court in succession of François de Salviati of Chateau de Talcy. At year-end Pietro Guadagni of Florence was appointed to command of *San Pietro* succeeding Pier Filippo Corgnia. Guadagni had in his youth accompanied elder brother Giovanbattista to the French court of Catherine de Medici where he had been known as Pierre de Gadagne. Sent to Florence a half-dozen years later to study languages and law, he preferred military science and was by age 19 received into the Order of Jerusalem at the Order's local commandery. He in 1565 appeared at Malta to assist in defense of that year's Great Siege, and was among nine wounded survivors of the fall of Fort Saint Elmo taken to Algiers and held for ransom. Four would survive. He was one of them.[39]

During 1574 Grand Chancellor Don Ernando de Alarcón succeeded to the Bailiwick of Lora and was himself succeeded as Grand Chancellor by Bailiff of Negroponte Don Alonso de Solis, the latter in turn succeeded as Bailiff of Negroponte by Catalan Don Juan de Ortiz. Also during the year Giovanni Battista Mastrillo of Nola constructed a galliot to his own specifications without prior authority of the Grand Master and Council. Pursuant to the Order's statutes, the galliot was confiscated and assigned to the Order's Treasury. The galliot of Pierre de Saint-Aubin commanded by brother Bernard, sailing in company with two other galliots, one the property of the Marqués de Santa Cruz and the second the property of Petrachi Caloriti of Malta, returned to Malta with 135 Turkish and Moorish captives removed from five vessels in the Levant. Two brigantines were armed and equipped at Malta, one belonging to Calabrian Count of Sinopoli Francesco Fabrizio Ruffo, and the other to Francesco Platamone of Catania, Sicily, which had numerous successes in the Levant.[40]

Toward year-end 1574 suspicion of the Ottomans heated up, fed by the Order's agents at Constantinople: what would the Ottomans be doing in the new year with such a large armada? The Sacred Council ordered a General Summons for all Hospitallers, and authorized the borrowing at interest of 100,000 scudos to purchase those items needed to be ready in the event of a siege. To effect the latter a commission of four knights was deputized, Castellan of Amposta Geronimo de Guete, Grand Conservator Juan de Sangorrin, Commander Francisco Martinez de Marcilla of Navarre, and Amposta Receiver Geronimo Coronel who were given wide-ranging authority to commit to loan terms and to acquire necessary supplies in Spain. A second similar commission composed of Ambassador Antonio di Bologna and Commanders Filippo della Corgnia, Lorenzo Guasconi, and Vincenzo Anastagi was sent to Rome.[41]

At Constantinople Ottoman Sultan Selim II died on 12 December 1574; he was survived by consort Nurbanu Sultan née Cecilia Venier Baffo of Venetian Paros, and by their son Murad III who took as his consort Sofia Baffo of Venetian Corfu. Sofia Baffo, later Safiye Sultan, would be the mother of future sultan Mehmet III. By then there would be a lot of Baffo at the top of the Empire.

General Montgaudry was ordered to Barcelona departing Malta on 19 January 1575 with the capitana *Santa Maria delle Vittoria* transporting Prior of León Don Antonio de Toledo (the Elder) and Resident Ambassador to the Court of Spain Cristóbal de Briceño who smoothed the way for the first of the two aforementioned commissions. These commissioners separately pled for a doubling from 12,000 to 25,000 salma at 9.77 bushels per salma of Malta's grain allotment from Sicily based upon growth of Malta's population, and requested assignment at Malta of a Spanish tercio of 3,000 infantry. While at Barcelona they ran up credits of 50,000 scudos for munitions, foodstuffs, and other items, credits guaranteed by appropriate Spanish ministries. Toledo and Briceño also placed orders at Barcelona for two bastarda galleys with stern deck-house, the priories and commanderies of the Langue of Castile donating 15,000 ducats for galley armament.[42]

A similar or duplicate plea submitted to Interim Viceroy and President of Sicily Carlo d'Aragona Tagliavia by special emissary Juan Ruiz de Bergara (*Vergara*) largely fell on deaf ears as Sicily itself was experiencing a grain shortage. The galleys *San Giovanni* and *San Pietro* respectively commanded by Don Diego de Copones and Pietro Guadagni were ordered to intercept grain carriers in the Malta Channel between Gozo and Sicily, and to force them into Maltese ports against payment for cargo. In this way between four and five thousand salma of grain made it into the Maltese food chain. There was also the perennial rush to hire soldiery, this year under overall supervision of Ferrante d'Aragona Terranuova with rank of Colonel who was to hire 600 infantry at Palermo. Two hundred fifty each were to be hired by Ferrante Averoldi of Brescia, Paolo Guasconi of Florence, Cataneo Tolomei of Siena, Don Girolamo Sanchez of Naples, and Lorenzo Guasconi of Rome. These took passage to Sicily on the aforementioned two galleys. Traveling with them was Pirro Melzi of Milan enroute to the Court of Spain to discuss matters having to do with the Langue of Italy. Also embarked was Catalan Onofre Belver to rendezvous at Messina with the frigate of non-Hospitaller Bernardino Rispolo hired to proceed to the Levant and seek information concerning the Ottoman Armada. Arriving at Malta soon after these departures was a Neapolitan galley commanded by Catalan Gutiérrez de Cardona dispatched by new Viceroy of Naples and 3rd Marqués of Mondejar Íñigo López de Mendoza y Mendoza. The latter proposed to come to the aid of Malta in the event of siege, but only in exchange for a Maltese commitment to respond to summonses from the Court of Spain for Maltese galleys and other armed vessels to join the Spanish Armada. Grand Master Cassière accepted the first offer but refused to commit Malta to respond to a fleet summons at a time of threat to Malta itself. Grand Commander d'Hérail-Rivière had in February 1574 been appointed the Order's ground-force lieutenant-general. He was in 1575 to be assisted as Captain-at-Arms and Governor of Notabile (Mdina) by Commander François de Lange de la Chenault of Alsace and the Langue of Auvergne, and assisted as Governor of Vittoriosa (Birgu) and Senglea by Prior of Toulouse Bertrand de Vintimille d'Ollioules. Sector Wardens were Commanders Don Alonso de Solis of Asturias, Centorio Cagnolo of Vercelli, and Guion de Saugniac de Belcastel of Provence. And because of the importance of completing Valletta fortifications, Prior of Saint-Gilles François de Panisse was appointed to coordinate allocation of resources. To interface with Regent ministries in Sicily the Grand Master appointed Spanish Commodore Gil de Andrade of Galicia and Giuseppe d'Aragona, another son of Prince of Castelvetrano (Trapani) and Viceroy of Sicily Carlo d'Aragona Tagliavia.[43]

With Montgaudry and the capitana absent in Spain, senior captain Don Diego de Copones in 1575 took *San Giovanni*, *San Pietro*, and a new or re-fitted *San Michele Arcangelo* to Syracuse and other Sicilian ports to embark newly-hired soldiers and war materials. Montgaudry shortly returned from Barcelona after four months in Spain to report the aforementioned ambassadorial and commission requests to the Crown had largely been satisfied. The same could not be said, however, of Sicilian and Neapolitan ministries where there was widespread belief Malta was crying wolf. Returning to Malta with Montgaudry's capitana was Commander Jacques de Dyo of Auvergne who had completed a similar embassy to France seeking arms with an endorsement from Pope Gregory XIII. Dyo also reported some success with the Crown and, moreover, returned with responsions from various receivers in France. At Constantinople Kiliç (Uluç) Ali was confirmed as Kapudan Pasha by new Sultan Murat III, but the Ottoman Armada suffered another onslaught of peste or plague and famine as did the city's resident population. Black Death, it was termed. While Pozzo ascribed onset of Black Death at Infidel Constantinople as Divine Justice, 50,000 died of the disease in Christian Venice over the next three years, one third of the population; 40,000 at nearby Messina. All three cities were terminals on east-west trade routes. Onofre Belver brought news of the disease at Constantinople and was immediately ordered to Messina to reverse infantry hires. There was to be no Ottoman assault in 1575.[44]

While at Messina the galley squadron transported the Viceroy and court from Messina to Palermo, but this activity was cause for concern on return to Malta; the squadron was quarantined at the pratique Infirmary at Manoel Island, the pratique island in Marsamuscietto. Following pratique the squadron was dispatched on 13 August to the Levant, initially taking course for Cape Buonandrea beyond modern Libya's Gulf of Sidra where it re-filled drinking water kegs. From there Montgaudry was ordered to raid parts of Anatolian Karamania, or alternatively take another course of action having the support of galley captains, senior officers, navigators, and pilots. The squadron returned to Malta in a bit less than two months having taken 44 captives from several small Turkish vessels. The squadron had also detained a Venetian galleonetto in the Gulf of Antalya and removed a rich cargo of cinnamon, indigo, and other items alleged to be the property of citizens of the Ottoman Empire. Hence Montgaudry had been unwilling to pay the Venetian captain for the confiscated merchandise which when sold by procurators of the Common Treasury brought 15,000 scudos. These funds were then used to pay down balances due on costs of Valletta fortification. The Republic of Venice immediately sought restitution in the name of its citizens. This incident was not the first of its kind all of which had ended up at a net cost to the Hospital. Neither would Venetian angst this time be remedied by Papal-ordered restitution.

The two galliots of Pierre de Saint-Aubin and the Marqués of Santa Cruz respectively captained by Rostaing des Essards-Laudun de Goût and by non-Hospitaller Nicolò Costa removed from various caramussals 100 Turks and Moors, while non-Hospitaller Pietro Caloriti later commanding the Aubin galliot in a single voyage to the Barbary Coast took from a garbo 50 Moors accompanying a *chiaus* or emissary, the latter yielding a significant ransom. The same galliot on the same excursion plundered another five vessels for an extraordinarily rich haul.[45]

Absent fear of the Turk as a unifying force a squabble ensued between the langues of Aragon and Italy concerning precedence only resolved by the Holy See. Of more consequence was a second confrontation between Mathurin Romegas, recently ascended to the dignity of Grand Commander upon death of his predecessor Pierre d'Hérail-Rivière, and Prior of Toulouse Bertrand de Vintimille d'Ollioules. This head-to-head was symptomatic of a major split across all langues which would reach crisis proportions in 1581. Upon obtaining the dignity of Grand Commander, Romegas attached for means of financial support the vacant commandery of La Cavalerie, a part of the Priory of Toulouse. Senior in rank, Prior of Toulouse Bertrand de Vintimille objected. This contretemps, too, required resolution by the Holy See. Who if either would be awarded the commandery was unknown, but it was clear the Convent was already dividing into pro and anti-Romegas factions. In a related matter, the Sacred Council deprived sixteen knights of their Habit, ten of them for speaking contemptuously of Grand Master Cassière, crux of troubles to come.[46]

Chapter IV

1575–1581

In September 1575 Greco-Albanian Admiral of Algiers Memi Arnaud commanding three large galliots comparable to galleys waylaid in the Gulf of Lyon south of Marseille the Spanish ship *El Sol* aboard which Lepanto (1571) and Tunis (1573) veteran Miguel de Cervantes Saavedra was returning from Naples to Spain. The future author, captured with brother Rodrigo, was taken a slave to Algiers and held for ransom not soon in coming. A second veteran of the Battle of Lepanto was also on board but failed to survive the contest. Castellan of Vallodolid 28 years an Hospitaller, he was Juan Bautista Ruiz de Vergara, a native of Basque Bergara, not Vallodolid. There is a sepulcher or elaborate sarcophagus upon which rests in repose a detailed lifelike sculpture of an Hospitaller knight, armored with a Grand Cross on the breastplate, presently lying in the Church of Saint John at Clerkenwell, London. Retrieved from Vallodolid, this sepulcher identified as that of Vergara is, however, more likely that of Bailiff of Lora Martín Duero Monroy, a native of Vallodolid who died of natural causes in 1584. This theory has been persuasively postulated by others. The clinching evidence is there for all to see. Fifty-three years an Hospitaller, Monroy was a knight of the Grand Cross, Vergara a knight of the small cross.

During 1575 Prior of Ireland and Grand Commander Mathurin Romegas was appointed General of the Galleys succeeding Christophe le Boulleur de Montgaudry. Upon the former's nomination, longtime lieutenant Gabriel d'Abzac la Douze was appointed to command of the capitana *Santa Maria delle Vittoria* succeeding Louis de la Roche la Boullaye. Juan de Ortiz succeeded to the Bailiwick of Mallorca upon death of incumbent Francisco de Borguès, thus vacating the Bailiwick of Negroponte and accompanying Grand Cross to which the aforementioned Martín Duero Monroy succeeded. Grand Conservator Juan de Sangorrin advanced to Castellan of Amposta, again apparently upon death of incumbent Geronimo de Guete. Don Vicente de Vallès

Martin Duero Monroy Sarcophagus.

became Grand Conservator while Enrique de l'Eltempore advanced to Prior of Dacia at Antvorskov, Zeeland, Denmark, succeeding Henrik af Helsingborg. Pursuant to authority granted by the Chapter General, Grand Master Cassière appointed Jacques de Virieu-Pupetières Resident Ambassador and Receiver at Rome succeeding Bailiff of Santo Stefano Antonio di Bologna who returned to his bailiwick.[1]

Because of plague and famine devastating the Ottoman capital city in early 1576, not to mention a reported storm-loss in the Black Sea of about 200 caramussals and accompanying galleys, cargoes of grain, agents at Constantinople continued to report pressure from Sultan Murat on Kiliç Ali to divert public attention and take the Ottoman Armada west in the coming year. These reports forced Grand Master and Council to again gird for assault. Peg-legged Lepanto-veteran Alonso de Tejada of Castile was selected to proceed to Sicily for the purpose of making Malta concerns known to Regency ministries and to treat with Prince of Castelvetrano and Viceroy of Sicily Carlo d'Aragona Tagliavia for quotas of grain and munitions approved by the Crown. These quotas included 25,000 salmas of grain, 4,000 casks of wine, 4,000 cantara (quintals at 112 pounds each) of biscuit, and 500 cantara of saltpeter or gunpowder. Tejada was also to seek authority to hire 500 local infantry. In the event of recalcitrance on the part of the Viceroy, Tejada was to continue on to Naples where he was to solicit the support of Don Juan of Austria by reminding the fleet commander Malta was the first line of defense for Spanish regencies in Italy. Tejada was graciously received by Aragona who agreed to what was possible.[2]

Various vessels as well as the four galleys under Romegas were soon dispatched to Sicilian ports including Syracuse where Michele Montalto of Syracuse had passed away of unknown cause. An Hospitaller since 1543 who briefly commanded *Santa Maria delle Vittoria* following the squadron's loss to Uluç Ali in 1570, Montalto left a rich estate to the Common Treasury. Off Cape Passero en route Syracuse for the purpose of claiming the estate, Romegas and the four galleys forced four grain carriers bound for Messina into port at Syracuse, greatly irritating the Viceroy who sent a blistering letter to Grand Master Cassière. The Grand Master attempted to justify Romegas's action in terms of University (Università of Gozo, or civil authority of Gozo) need, but the squadron commander appeared to the Viceroy a bull with hubris in a china shop. At the same time Bailiff of Santo Stefano Antonio di Bologna was appointed Governor of Birgu and Senglea while Commander Jean de Lugny of Burgundy was appointed Governor and Captain-at-Arms of Notabile (Mdina). Sector Wardens were Diego de Solis of Castile, Cesare Rovero of Savona, and Aimond de Beaumont du Boulay of France. Neither was there failure to notify the Holy See, the Court of Spain, and especially Don Juan of Austria of measures adopted and expectations of assistance should there be an assault on Malta. Castilian Don Antonio de Enriquez of Salamanca was appointed ambassadeur-extraordinare to keep Pope, King, and Fleet Commander informed.[3]

The Protestant Reformation in Germany and Bohemia had contributed to maladministration of Hospitaller priories and commanderies in those areas of the Holy Roman Empire resulting in substantial past-due responsions amounting to tens of thousands of gold scudos. Grand Bailiff Georg von Schönborn was in May appointed Procurator-General of the Religion representing Receivers and other administrators of the Common Treasury seeking to recover past-due amounts. In France there were also past-due responsions if not in such large amounts. The Council appointed recently returned Ambassador Jacques de Dyo of Auvergne to again make his way to the Court of France seeking not merely past-due amounts but also various munitions as well as forced-labor to man galley oars. New difficulties arose concerning grain shipments from Sicily to Malta, some having to do with weather and some having to do with Infidel corsairs but most having to do with cross purposes. Veteran diplomat Antonio Maldonado of Castile was dispatched to the Vice Regal court then at Syracuse where he was cordially received and where he obtained promises.[4]

Beginning in early June 1576 reports and rumor concerning movement of the Ottoman Armada began to be more skeptical of deployment toward the western Mediterranean during that year, while suspicion and apprehension on the part of Christians began to wane. Alvaro de Bazan, Marqués de Santa Cruz and General of Neapolitan Galleys, seizing the moment planned a Christian initiative along the Barbary Coast. Three Neapolitan galleys under command of Hospitaller Don Juan d'Aragona accompanied by Don Diego Vaneguas of the Santa Cruz staff arrived at Malta. Vaneguas was well known to the Grand Master as staff advocating a more aggressive Christian posture. The plan they had come to espouse contemplated a siege of Cherchene (Kerkenna Islands, Tunisia) with a good number of galleys and soldiers, thus diverting Turkish attention from Malta. The two emissaries proposed a siege force consisting of 33 galleys of the Kingdom of Naples, 12 reinforced galleys of Sicily, four of Malta, plus six thousand embarked Spanish infantry. In addition to four galleys, Malta was expected to provide 50 knights and essential pilots, especially Tomeo Cassia, Royal Pilot of the Religion, as the Kerkenna Islands were surrounded by shallow water. Should this first siege be successful, the expeditionary force would be expected to move on to Bône (Annaba) in NE Algeria. Grand Master and Council agreed.

Santa Cruz with 31 Neapolitan galleys arrived Malta on 14 June 1576 where he was joined by the four-galley Malta squadron.[5] Two days earlier a brigantine had arrived at Malta dispatched by Juan IV Coloma y Cardona, 1st Count of Elda and Viceroy of Sardinia. The brigantine brought a report several Ottoman galleys and galliots had appeared in Sardinian waters transporting "King of Algiers" and Beylerbey Ramadan Pasha from Constantinople to North Africa. This report had been obtained from a Turk captured on the beach who asserted the ultimate Ottoman objective was Malta. Unaware of Ramadan's Sardinian roots, Grand Master and Council chose to ignore the Sardinian report as an unlikely route. Pierre de

Saint-Aubin, Francesco Lanfreducci of Pisa, and Don Francisco Meca of Aragon were appointed sergeants-major for the embarked Maltese ground force. The Moors of Cherchene, however, had been forewarned by capture of a Maltese galliot and fled to the mainland not ten miles distant. Troops put ashore on the islands found no one and nothing of value left behind. The Marqués, seeing little prospect of success, abandoned the siege and returned to Malta 15 days later. From there he was recalled to Naples by Don Juan of Austria.

Meanwhile, Christian oarsmen of a galliot sent by Kiliç Ali to spy on the Spanish armada rebelled and overcame the Turkish crew, repairing to Naples. They reported the Turkish armada was expected in local waters at any time. Acting on the Christian oarsmen's report, Viceroy of Naples Iñigo López de Mendoza y Mendoza and Don Juan dispatched to Malta under command of the former's son Don Pedro Gonzales de Mendoza ten Neapolitan galleys transporting 2,000 Spanish infantry. The Marqués de Santa Cruz, having noticed during his visit to Malta several defects in the island's defenses, dispatched an additional two galleys transporting his fortifications engineer Captain Scipione Campi to suggest improvements. Given this level of Neapolitan concern, Grand Master and Council ordered Romegas with three galleys to the Levant for 15 days to obtain more certain news of the Ottoman Armada. Departing Malta on 7 August, Romegas encountered not far from the island a large Barbary germa bound from Tripoli to Alexandria which he plundered with little resistance, taking captive 95 Turks and Moors. These captives informed Romegas of reports the Ottoman Armada had raided the coast of Italian Apulia, taken large amounts of plunder, and was already returning to the Archipelago. Neither did the Armada have with it support vessels for any siege of Malta. While returning to Malta with this advice, Romegas following an obstinate defense took a second maona with a rich yield of captives and merchandise bound from the Levant to Tripoli. The first germa report, whether true or false, proved convincing, and given an approaching end to the sailing season, Malta was relieved of siege concern.[6] This report, however, apparently dealt with a corsair raid rather than Armada activity. Two thousand corsairs had been put ashore on the beach fronting the walled town of Calabrian Trebisacce north of Crotone and laid siege to the town's resident population of five hundred. These ordinary citizens held out for the better part of three days until succor arrived in the form of 300 infantry and 60 horse commanded by Prince of Bisignano Cola Antonio Sanseverino. The corsairs withdrew leaving behind 200 or more dead and captured.[7]

The Grand Master wished to make known Maltese appreciation of the 1576 support arriving at Malta when under apparent threat. He sent Hospitaller Pedro Hurtado de Mendoza to the Fleet Commander and to the two Marchéses conveying appreciation of Hospitallers and resident population. At about the same time 12 galleys of the Sardinian Count of Villatores reached Malta to embark 1,000 of the 2,000 Spanish infantry arriving with Pedro Gonzales de Mendoza in June. Three days following departure of the Sardinian galleys accompanied by a galley of Naples, Pedro Gonzales de Mendoza returned to Malta from Rome. *Not yet a professed Hospitaller*, he sought the dignity of Turcopolier and accompanying Grand Cross. An apparent quid pro quo, this intolerable request had to be denied without offending Don Pedro's father and Viceroy of Naples Iñigo López de Mendoza y Mendoza. Three ambassadors were appointed to bring the Order's case before the Holy See: Baldassar Imperatore of Palermo, Diego de Solis of Castile, and Louis de la Roche la Boullaye of Aquitaine. These departed Malta aboard the squadron capitana.

Meanwhile the continuing squabble between Mathurin Romegas and Prior of Toulouse Balthazard des Comtes de Vintimille d'Ollioules over the former's attachment of the Commandery of La Cavalerie remained more than a distraction, but pended resolution by the Holy See as well. This latter matter consumed as much Magistral time as recent military preparations, pitting the strong-willed and angry Vintimille against Romegas whom the Grand Master was inclined to favor. Vintimille became allied with Christophe le Boulleur de Montgaudry who resented having been deprived of the Priory of France in 1573 on its "sale" by the Grand Master to Prince Henri d'Angouleme. From Vintimille's quarters in Valletta issued streams of slander aimed at both the Grand Master and Romegas. On occasion of a request by the Magistral Procurator for a past-due responsion within one month, Vintimille appeared to go berserk, and in his fury finally provoked the Grand Master to demand resolution of the dispute by the parties themselves. As for the past-due responsion, Vintimille must pay it down within one month or be sequestered in his house while the Priory of Toulouse and its commanderies were re-possessed. Vintimille, failing to pay, was incarcerated on order of the Sacred Council not in his quarters but in Castle Saint Angelo. Unexplained charges were also filed against Vintimille's doctor and chaplain Grimaldo Marmarà which presumably had to do with Vintimille's failure to pay down past-due amounts and/or Marmarà having taken up arms in support of French Huguenots. Marmarà fled Malta. Vintimille's continuing recalcitrance resulted in deprivation of his Habit as well as deprivation of priory and commanderies. These consequences plus incarceration proved mortal and he died in Castle Saint Angelo. And so the fratricidal dispute resolved itself; Romegas ended up with the commandery as well as with the Priory of Toulouse but remained a source of friction. He was succeeded as Grand Commander by the senior Provencal knight François de Moreton de Chabrillan.[8]

Note the foregoing Mendoza matter was amplified at Mifsud 215 as follows: The Viceroy of Naples had recourse to Rome and applied for and obtained the Turcopoliership for his son, Don Pedro Gonzales de Mendoza, who had not as yet received the habit and whose proofs of nobility were at that moment (24th September 1576) being entered in the Priory of his nation, Castile and León. Don Pedro, on his way to Malta, was vested with the *insigna* of the acquired Grand Cross by a bishop of Calabria designated by the Sovereign Pontiff for the purpose. But upon his arrival the Knights did not permit him ashore. The Commanders Baldassare Imperatori, Diego de Solis and Louis de la Roche la Boullaye, then repeated to the Holy Father, on behalf of the Grand Master and Council, what had been submitted by their colleagues in the case of Romegas, that the Turcopolier would have to take precedence over the chiefs of the Langues of Germany and Castile in Council and public sessions, and not only over these but over thirty other Grand Crosses, Priors and Bailiffs of all the other Langues; and as this would touch to the quick a point of honor made so much of among so many noblemen, it might be the cause, as in times past, of some revolution or scandal. The stand made by the Knights, and their expostulations, got them nothing from the Pope but led to (interim) renunciation by Gonzales of the Turcopoliership (15th April 1578) upon his receiving in exchange a Grand Cross with the last place in Council. In spite of his presumption and the jump-start to his Hospitaller career, Pedro Gonzales de Mendoza would prove a valuable addition to Hospitaller ranks. Like most Mendozas, *the* leading family of Guadalajara, he had been educated in the classics, law, and languages, and would bring a sophisticated perspective to the Sacred Council of which he was already a youthful member.

In October 1576 reports began to be received from agents at Constantinople of Ottoman intent to assail Malta during the coming Spring. As ever, Malta could not afford to take these notices lightly. Antonio Maldonado was appointed Ambassadeur Extraordinaire to the Court of Philip II to explain the annual threat, the annual expense, and that were it not Malta it would be Sicily or Naples. Maldonado departed Malta on 20 October with the galleys *San Iacomo* and *Santa Maria* under senior captain Tomás Coronel. Also embarked was Dom Diego de Solis bound for Portugal to demand payment of certain debits, particularly 35,649 scudos due from Prior of Crato Dom Antonio of Portugal, Dom Antonio a claimant to the Portuguese throne. The two galleys carried the entire armament for the new galley *San Paolo* nearing construction-completion at Barcelona. Embarked bound for Barcelona was Commander Dom Jerónimo Botello of Portugal who had been appointed captain of *San Paolo*. Botello was under orders to arm and equip *San Paolo*, to conduct sea trials and then to accompany the other two galleys to Palamos to take delivery of a cargo of oars and additional equipment, several stone-firing petraras, and cases of arms. From Palamos Maldonado made his way to the Royal Court at Madrid while the three galleys proceeded to Marseille where they took delivery of coin, jewels, and cloth for the Common Treasury from Receivers Charles de Grasse-Briançon and Hugues Loubenx de Verdalle as well as received a consignment of forced-oarsmen contributed by the French Crown. In an additional precaution, Giulio Beccaria of Pavia was dispatched to the Grand Ducal Court at Florence to successfully request an allocation of Tuscan grain to supplement Sicilian shipments reduced by plague. Six hundred cantara of saltpeter was also forthcoming. During the past fifteen months the matter of the confiscation in July 1575 of Turkish cargo from a Venetian galleonetto had festered, infecting relations between the two parties as well as with the Holy See. A Papal Brief finally ended the dispute in Venice's favor, but mandated restitution by Malta left a bad taste in the mouths of Cassière detractors.[9]

Treasurer Christophe le Boulleur de Montgaudry was at year-end appointed Grand Hospitaller upon death of Pierre Pelloquin de la

Plesse received into the Order of Jerusalem in 1528. Jacques de Gaillardbois-Marconville succeeded to the dignity of Treasurer. In the Langue of Auvergne, Marshal Marc de la Goutte had succeeded to the Bailiwick of Lyon in 1574 upon the death of incumbent Annet de Varax[10] and had been succeeded as Marshal by Étienne de Fraigne. De Fraigne in 1576 was appointed Prior of Auvergne upon the death of incumbent Louis de Lastic and was succeeded as Marshal by Antoine de Villars.

The Convent entered the year 1577 somewhat fearfully given earlier reports of Ottoman intent, but soon found the Turkish war machine focused to the East where the Persian Shah Tahmasp I's death had ended a long and capable reign in May 1576, and where successor Shah Ismail II appeared vulnerable. In addition, a treaty with the Holy Roman Empire executed in 1576 for the time being secured Ottoman borders at the other end of the Empire. On the other hand, Catholic King Philip II of Spain, never eager to risk his Spanish Armada, was preoccupied with rebellion in Flanders where only two months earlier his Spanish tercios had turned on their officers over back-pay and sacked Antwerp, leading discontented Flemish to take up arms yet again. Philip could not be depended upon to quickly succor Malta in the event of an assault by the Sultan's naval arm, a naval arm for which the Sultan would have had little use in a war with Persia. Quite the opposite, the King was soliciting use of the cannon guarding Malta's harbor mouth.[11]

Don Vincenzo Carafa of Terra di Lavoro in the north of the Kingdom of Naples was commissioned a colonel and ordered to raise at Naples a regiment of 1,200 infantry and 40 cannoneers subject to license of Iñigo López de Mendoza y Mendoza, Viceroy of Naples and Marqués of Mondéjar. Several days following Carafa's departure there arrived at Malta with two galleys Don Tiberio Ottaviano of the Viceroy's official household, come to discuss several matters with the Grand Master. Ottaviano brought with him the new Inquisitor of Malta Monsignor Rinaldo Corso of Correggio in the Po Valley. Upon departure Ottaviano took with him the old Inquisitor Monsignor Sant'Humano as well as Bailiff of Santo Stefano Don Antonio di Bologna, appointed Lieutenant for Administration to Prior of Barletta Don Giovan Vincenzo Gonzaga of the Duchy of Guastalla who with his predecessors had let the Priory become run-down and ruined.

Also departing aboard the visiting galleys was Hospitaller Don Francisco de Coloma of Aragon to take up residence within the Viceregency of Naples as an adviser to the Marqués of Mondéjar concerning Malta affairs.[11]

As Spring brought fairer weather the Grand Master's concern about a 1577 Ottoman assault on Malta waned. Irrespective of assault it appeared to the Grand Master his destiny was to be continually beset by internal unrest. There was so much disquiet no one was above the fray. Hugues Loubenx de Verdalle who would succeed Cassière as Grand Master took sword in hand to threaten Commander Pierre de Vintimille d'Ollières (not the deceased Prior of Toulouse Bertram de Vintimille des comtes de Marseilles d'Ollioules) over an imagined slur, both of the Langue of Provence. Italians fought Aragonese in the streets of Valletta and no one remembered why. Bailiff of Negroponte Martín Duero Monroy was called before a panel of his peers for confronting Francisco Guiral with drawn sword and wounding him with a club. Punishing these infractions with confinement, or quarantine, or loss of residence, or loss of seniority, or loss of Habit was of little deterrent to other than the punished individual. Outbreak followed outbreak, and within the Convent it was the Grand Master's indecisive leadership or absence of leadership most often fingered as culprit by those looking for a scapegoat. Of all the excesses in this horrible year, that involving the Portuguese Knight Jorge Correa was most extreme. Forced to retire into his quarters by hostility of other knights of his Langue of Castile, he during the night was summoned to his doorway by the same individuals hiding behind false beards who clubbed him to death. Seven culprits were identified and convicted by a secular court. Each was bound in a sack with two iron cannon balls and dropped alive in the Malta Channel, but Jorge Correa could not have cared less.[12]

Arriving at Malta in May 1577 was Don Diego de Salas dispatched by the Spanish Ambassador at Rome with a letter from His Catholic Majesty King Philip II. The letter requested the Grand Master receive in his Magistral Palace the King's two nephews Archdukes of Austria Albert and Wenceslaus respectively 17 and 16 years of age. These were the two youngest of nine sons of the King's sister, Archduchess Maria of Austria, Holy Roman Empress, and Queen Consort of Bohemia and Hungary as the spouse of Maximilian II, Holy Roman Emperor and King of Bohemia and Hungary. King Philip asked that Wenceslaus be received into the Langue of Castile as Bailiff of Lora and that he be awarded the Grand Cross attending that dignity. He should further be recognized as imminent successor to the dignity of Prior of Castile and León. The King thanked the Order in advance for its courtesy. Salas also brought with him a letter addressed to the Grand Master from Pope Gregory XIII dated two months earlier endorsing the King's request. Grand Chancellor Alonso de Solis, heir apparent to the Bailiwick of Lora, expressed his unhappiness when the requests were brought before the Sacred Council. Beyond the Council other Castilian knights visualizing a detour in the paths of their own advancement were similarly unhappy. And beyond these latter knights there were many others who saw in the Grand Master's inevitable acquiescence to these joint requests evidence of his personal weakness. Most unhappy, of course, were Prior of León Don Antonio de Toledo (the Elder), Prior of Castile Don Fernando de Toledo, and Bailiff of Lora Don Ernando de Alarcón.[13]

In the jumble of misfortune besetting Grand Master and Convent the new galley *San Paolo* commanded by Dom Jerónimo Botello had been accepted following sea trials, but during the transit from Barcelona to Palamos had become separated from *San Iacomo* and *Santa Maria* under senior captain Tomás Coronel. Rather than continue alone to Palamos to take on a cargo of oars which would inhibit *San Paolo*'s ability to defend herself without company, Botello elected to take course for Malta. Toward the beginning of May *San Paolo* had Sardinia in sight when she was herself sighted by several galliots of Algiers a part of the squadron of Memi Arnaud, Admiral of Algiers and two years earlier captor of Miguel de Cervantes Saavedra. *San Paolo* was invested and, following the death of Botello and many others, was subdued and captured. At Malta the Order's reputation suffered another blow amid calls for a board of inquiry. A Board of Inquiry investigated but found no culpability. *San Paolo* next appeared in August conveying Sardinian-born Beylerbey Ramadan Pasha and Corsican wife from Algiers to Constantinople. Back at Algiers Spaniard Miguel de Cervantes had been joined by Hospitaller Spaniards Don Antonio de Toledo (the Younger) and Don Francisco de Valencia.[14]

The galleys *Santa Maria* and *San Iacomo* commanded by senior captain Tomás Coronel of Aragon returned to Malta early in July with collected responsions and bales of cloth after more than eight months at Barcelona and Palamos, and after a long voyage home in company with four galleys of Tuscany (not of the Tuscan Order of Santo Stefano) commanded by their General Prospero Colonna who had nominal command of Venetian infantry at the Battle of Lepanto. Colonna remained at Malta no more than two days before setting sail on a corsair voyage to the Levant. Prior to departure he requested of the Grand Master on behalf of Grand Duke Francesco I de' Medici permission to send Hospitaller Bongiani Gianfiliazzi (or Gianfigliazzi) of Florence as the Grand Duke's emissary to the Porte in Constantinople. This was the same Bongianni Gianfiliazzi who had rescued the Order's Standard from the Malta capitana abandoned by General of the Galleys Francisco de San Clemente at 1570's Battle of Cape Passero, and it was the same Gianfiliazzi who had been captured by the Ottomans at 1571's Battle of Lepanto. As a ransom could not be agreed and arranged by his family until early 1577, Gianfiliazzi had almost six years to become fluent in Turkish and to develop a useful familiarity with both Constantinople and captor Kiliç Ali. The Grand Master gave his permission, and Gianfiliazzi would proceed to Constantinople in 1578 where he would be well received by Sultan Murad III though unsuccessful in establishing a Tuscan-Ottoman trade agreement. In a perhaps apocryphal postscript, Gianfiliazzi would in 1583 be appointed the Grand Duke's resident ambassador to Spain. There he would incur large debts to finance a Spanish Court presence, debts not reimbursed by the Tuscan Court. He would spend sixteen years in part-time debtors prison before his commandery income was sufficient to make up the balance owed.[15]

Returning to Malta with Tomás Coronel and the two Maltese galleys was Ambassador Antonio Maldonado who reported favorable outcomes of his ambassadorial discussions with the Spanish Crown, discussions which included information supporting appointment of former Deputy Holy League Commander Marcantonio Colonna as Viceroy of Sicily. Upon arrival at Sicily Colonna immediately released shipments of grain to Malta sequestered by his predecessor. Maldonado had also made known to Philip II as former King of England award of the English dignity of Turcopolier to Don Pedro

Gonzales de Mendoza, much to the disgust of the remainder of the Convent. The King had accordingly written to Don Juan de Zuniga, his Ambassador at Rome, expressing his displeasure at the award and ordering the Ambassador to make his displeasure known to Pope Gregory XIII.[16]

As these unhappy developments unfolded with respect to Spain there arrived a similar dictat from the Court of France. Toward the end of October 1576 and reflecting his seniority, Marshal Étienne de Fraigne had been appointed Prior of Auvergne upon the death of incumbent Louis de Lastic. But Fraigne had so far been unable to take physical possession of the Priory by order of the French Court's Valet de Chambre, violinist, composer, and choreographer Balthasar de Beaujoyeulx. An individual of considerable power, Beaujoyeulx believed appointments to the six French Priories should be a prerogative of the Crown as should all other elective Hospitaller offices in France. This much-more serious assault on dignities of the Convent shook it to its foundations. The Order's Resident Ambassador to the Holy See Jacques de Virieu-Pupetières put the matter to Pope Gregory XIII who immediately sped two Briefs dated 12 August, one addressed to 26 year-old King Henry III and the second to Queen Mother Catherine de Medici exhorting both to desist from this dangerous expropriation. The briefs were first delivered to Malta by historian Giacomo Bosio and from Malta to the Court of France by Resident Hospitaller Ambassador Jacques de Dyo with endorsements by various princes including Marquis de Chaussin Francis of Lorraine, brother of Queen consort Louise of Lorraine. There was a face-saving retreat by the Crown.[17]

Following release from sequestration of Malta grain shipments from Sicily, the Grand Master dispatched his Master of the House, Commander Pons de la Porte of Auvergne, to pay the Order's compliments and to thank the new Viceroy who asked in turn for Porte to take under his wing the Viceroy's young nephew Giorgio Gaetano as a page to the Grand Master. That done, the new relationship between Sicily and Malta, however, could not long survive an epidemic of plague severely restricting Sicily's grain production. 1577 was the year more than 40,000 residents of Messina died of the disease also rampant in Lombardia and the Veneto. The Grand Master was forced to turn to the Kingdom of Naples where Viceroy Iñigo López de Mendoza y Mendoza remained unhappy over the Turcopolier business. The Grand Master dispatched Hospitaller Juan de Aragona to Naples to join with Receiver Pompeo Pignone to both ensure the Viceroy had every intention of doing what he could to relieve hunger at Malta. The Viceroy agreed to shipments in 1577 totaling 20,000 salmes of grain, and appeared to let bygones be bygones. One brother, one nephew, two sons, and two grandsons were, after all, Hospitallers.[18]

The four Tuscan galleys commanded by Prospero Colonna returned to Malta where they joined the three Hospitaller galleys. All seven galleys under command of General Romegas departed Malta on 14 August looking for opportunity in the Levant. In less than a month and a half these returned to Malta with an Ottoman galliot of Antalya seized while headed to Alexandria yielding 190 captive Turks, as well as with two caramussals laden with rice, flax, and other items of value.

For their part Grand Master and Council could no longer suffer the Malta Squadron absent a fourth galley since loss of *San Paolo*. (At Malta were the relatively new *San Giovanni* last commanded by Don Diego de Copones in June 1575, and *San Pietro* last commanded by Pietro Guadagni in January 1575, both of which were either retired or unsuitable.) Commander Charles de Grasse-Briançon was directed to place an order with the Marseille arsenal for construction of a new hull and to plead before the French Court for oarsmen. Briançon was able to hire a crew, purchase armament locally, and to soon deliver the new galley to Malta, but she was not ready for service for another two years.[19]

Following the French Court's face-saving retreat on power to appoint Hospitaller priors, bailiffs, and commanders in France, Etienne de Fraigne in 1577 finally assumed the dignity of Prior of Auvergne to which he had been advanced in 1576 and was succeeded as Marshal by Antoine de Villars. Admiral Ubertino di Solaro was appointed Bailiff of Santa Eufemia succeeding the deceased Don Fabrizio Pignatello, an Hospitaller for 52 years and Bailiff of Santa Eufemia for the last twelve of those years. Located 5 kilometers behind the mainland coast east of the Strait of Messina, it is not clear whether unpotable drinking water or fetid air killed Pignatello.

Solaro was succeeded as Admiral by his Lieutenant Bartolomeo Vasco. The deceased Christophe le Boulleur de Montgaudry was succeeded as Grand Hospitaller by Treasurer Jean de Gaillardbois-Marconville, while Antoine des Hayes d'Espinay Saint-Luc succeeded to the Dignity of Treasurer. Prior of Toulouse Romegas completed his term as General of the Galleys and was succeeded by former Ambassador to Spain Antonio Maldonado who nominated Francisco de Reinoso of Castile to command the capitana *Santa Maria della Vittoria*. Maldonado was also appointed Grand Chancellor succeeding Don Alonso de Solis. Coming to the end of his life at Rome was Bishop of Malta and former Vice Chancellor Martín Rojas de Portalrubio. Pursuant to terms of the gift of Malta to the Order, Grand Master and Council nominated three candidates as successor. These were Prior of the Church and native of Rhodes Antoine Cressin of Auvergne, Deputy Prior Pierre Mosquet of Provence, and Vice Chancellor Tomás Gargallo of Barcelona. These names were then submitted to King Philip II for nomination of the new Bishop to be approved by the Pope.[20]

Early in 1578 King Philip II nominated Tomás Gargallo of Barcelona Bishop of Malta. The appointment, however, was not immediately approved by Pope Gregory XIII who instead appointed Archbishop Don Luis de Torres of Monreale (Sicily) to additional duties as Bishop of Malta. The Grand Master dispatched two galleys to Syracuse to embark the Archbishop who arrived Malta on 5 February and was consecrated in the new Conventual Church of Saint John in Valletta on the 20th of the same month. Arriving Malta from Syracuse with the two galleys transporting Archbishop Monreale was Francesco Montauto, emissary of Viceroy Marcantonio Colonna, seeking possession of the estate of deceased Bishop of Malta Martín Rojas de Portalrubio. But Montauto was opposed by the Religion citing vague indulgences of Pope Gregory XIII as well as the Order's own requirement for Hospitallers to leave at least 80% of an estate to the Order, citing the latter as practice since before 1530 arrival of the Order at Malta, a practice applicable to all Hospitallers including serving brothers and chaplains up to and including bishops, and a practice recognized by the absence of previous challenge. Thus was born yet another dispute between the Viceregency of Sicily and the Order of Malta damaging other relationships between the two mutually-dependent neighbors. Meanwhile the aforementioned unrest among Hospitallers continued apace, particularly within the Langue of Castile affected by the advent of Archduke Wenceslaus and assignment of requested dignities. Tragically, Wenceslaus came to the end of his young life in October before much damage was done by discontented Castilians.[21]

While this particular cause of unrest still festered, eight Castilian malcontents came to the attention of the Holy See and by Papal Brief dated 28 March were summoned to appear within sixty days before the Auditor of the Camera to whom Pope Gregory had consigned the matter. Suddenly conscious of danger, the eight pled their error before Grand Master and Council and elected house-bound penance in lieu of appearing before the Holy Father. Elsewhere within the Convent brawls and destruction continued frequent with general rebellion against Grand Master and Sacred Council and even incidents of revenge killing. The Hospitaller Order of Saint John of Jerusalem was writing its own epitaph.[22]

Given the opposition of King Philip II to award of the dignity of Turcopolier to Don Pedro Gonzales Mendoza, the latter renounced the dignity on condition he could expect future award of the English dignity of Bailiff of Eagle with both attendant Grand Cross and place on the Sacred Council. This arrangement which was neither prejudicial to Bailiff of Eagle Oliver Starkey nor damaged relationships with Don Pedro's father the Viceroy of Naples, satisfied Grand Master and Council if not the Convent.

Receiver Bartholomäus Lauck reported from Germany that Prior of Bohemia Wenceslaus von Hasenberg had passed away. In danger of losing both priory and the deceased's estate, the Grand Master dispatched Grand Bailiff Georg von Schönborn to Bohemia. Proceeding by way of Prague Schönborn collected Christoph von Werdenberg enroute, the latter Lieutenant to the deceased Prior. With Imperial approval as well as approval of commanders and knights of the Priory, Werdenberg became Prior of Bohemia. Receiver Lauck was made responsible for estate and interment.[23]

Bernard Roquelaure de Saint-Aubin's well-equipped galliot in 1578 raided mostly in the Levant where he captured a richly-laden germa and took sixty Turks captive. Grand Master Cassière meanwhile planned with Marcantonio Colonna, Viceroy of Sicily, an excursion of combined galley squadrons into the Levant. Maldonado accordingly took to Messina the capitana *Santa Maria de la Vittoria* commanded by Francisco de Reinoso, *San Iacomo* commanded by Jean-Philibert de Foissy-Chamesson, and *San Giovanni* commanded by Don Diego de Copones. The combined excursion did not take place, however, as the Sicilian squadron was summoned to another undertaking by the

Spanish Crown. The Malta squadron therefore limited itself to a local search for Barbary corsairs among Sicily's deserted islands which was fruitless. The squadron was subsequently employed in transporting Barcelona fabrics from Palermo to Malta, reaching Malta in early September. The squadron was there joined by a Magistral galley built to the Grand Master's order at Taranto and equipped at his expense. She was commanded by Cassière's Master of the House Pons de la Porte. A planned excursion to the Levant by the four galleys was then aborted by bad weather, but the two galleys *San Giovanni* and *Magistrale* a bit later undertook the same excursion and returned from the Levant with a captured caramussal rich in cargo having a crew of fifty-two.[24]

August 1578 was the month the most enlightened and inspiring monarch in Europe went to war and did not return. Dom Sebastian I, grandson of Holy Roman Emperor Charles V, King of Portugal and of a global colonial empire for 21 of his 24 years, marched 17,000 Portuguese soldiers and adventurers into Africa over unfamiliar terrain on request of a deposed King of Morocco. All but a handful of the 17,000 failed to return from an encounter with an Ottoman-backed successor King of Morocco waiting on familiar terrain with 60,000 of his own soldiers and adventurers. Prior to this disastrous undertaking King Sebastian had liberated Indian slaves in Portuguese Brazil, brought in doctors from outside his country to help fight plague decimating Portugal's population, established shelters and food programs for widows and orphans, created university scholarships for those lacking means to aspire to higher education, created a code of conduct for the Portuguese military, created lending institutions to enhance agricultural production, increased the speed of civil litigation, and among other initiatives had become wildly popular with the people he ruled. Sebastian unmarried and childless, a principal claimant to the throne was Hospitaller Don Antonio de Crato a prisoner of the Moroccans until ransoming himself. In the interim Sebastian was succeeded by his uncle Henry, only surviving brother of Sebastian's predecessor King John III. By 1581, however, his kingdom and empire had become appendages of Philip II's Spain and Don Antonio had become a king in exile. In the meanwhile Philip II considered it prudent to ink the first of several consecutive truces with the Ottoman Empire.[25]

Grand Master Cassière's second Chapter General convened in the Magistral Palace at Malta on the first Sunday of September 1578 before proceeding to the Conventual Church of Saint John where a Mass of the Holy Spirit was intoned. Then it was back to the Magistral Palace where in the Great Hall preliminary steps such as incorporation of the Chapter General and election of the Sixteen *Capitolari* or Legislators, two per langue, were taken. The Sixteen elected by members of their respective langues were Grand Commander François de Moreton de Chabrillan and Prior of Saint-Gilles François de Panisse for Provence, Lieutenant Marshal Pierre de Sacconyn de Bourbon and Jacques de Virieu-Pupetières for Auvergne, Lieutenant Grand Hospitaller Charles de la Bama du Plessis-Hérault and Lieutenant Treasurer Louis le Bouteiller de Sainte-Geneviève for France, Bailiff of Mallorca Don Agustín Argençola and Don Lupe de Híjar of Aragon, Prior of Messina Pietro Giustiniani and Bailiff of Naples Niccolò Orsini di Rivalta for Italy, Prior of Ireland Mathurin Romegas and Bailiff of Eagle Oliver Starkey for England, Lieutenant Grand Bailiff Philipp von Groendorf and Augustin Baron von Meersburg (of the continuously occupied castle of the same name on the shore of the Bodensee/Lake Constance 80 kilometers NE of Zurich) for Germany, and Grand Chancellor Antonio Maldonado and Don Gundisalvo Pereira for Castile. These Sixteen would retire to their own chamber to take up matters brought before the Chapter General and to review rules and statutes of the Order. Among more notable items to be taken up was the Common Treasury expense of communal quarters adjacent to the Conventual Church of Saint John for chaplains, deacons, prior and under-prior, a college for priests, and so forth. A support allowance of 40,000 Maltese scudos was continued. A second matter addressed concerned return to Germany of the Priory of Hungary at the time occupied by Italian Gabrio Serbellone. A decision to reassign the priory to Germany was postponed. Bishop of Malta Gargallo (belatedly confirmed 11 August 1578), Prior of the Church Cressin, Bailiff of Naples Rivalta, Bailiff of Eagle Starkey, and prospective Vice Chancellor Diego de Ovando were commissioned to reduce the statutes of the Religion to a single volume in the Italian Language. There was no report of any attempt to quiet dissension in the ranks.[26]

During the year the office of Vice Chancellor, normally a secular office, had been vacated by elevation of Chaplain Tomás Gargallo to Bishop of Malta. In Gargallo's stead Diego de Ovando of Castile who for many years had been a consultant to the Holy Office (Inquisition) was appointed Vice Chancellor. Bernhard IV von Angelach-Angelach advanced to Prior of Dacia succeeding Swede Henrik af Helsingborg. Don Agustín Argençola was appointed Bailiff of Mallorca succeeding Juan de Ortiz, and Don Francisco Martinez de Marcilla was appointed Grand Conservator in succession of Don Vicente de Vallès.[27]

In April of 1579 Lepanto veteran Pietro Giustiniani was dispatched to Spain and Portugal to deliver the Order's official condolences, in the case of Spain for the untimely death of King Philip II's half-brother Don Juan of Austria, brought down by an unspecified fever on the first day of October at Namur (Belgium) where he was Governor-General of the Netherlands, and for the equally untimely death of Philip's nephew Archduke Wenceslaus at Madrid later the same month. At Lisbon he brought the Order's condolences amid national mourning over the death of King Sebastian, an extraordinarily popular monarch 24 years of age at his disappearance during combat. While in Spain Giustiniani obtained a commitment for delivery of 25,000 salme of grain in the event of an Ottoman threat to Malta. He also raised 2,000 infantry of the 4,000 he sought. Weeks later the Grand Master dispatched Giorgio Berzetti of Vercelli and Don Miguel de Alentorn of Castile to Rome for the purpose of obtaining approval of Hugues Loubenx de Verdalle as resident ambassador and procurator-general at the Holy See. New Bishop of Malta Tomás Gargallo had meanwhile expounded views of the scriptures differing from those embodied in the conduct of Hospitallers. Gargallo was supported in his views by some citizenry of Malta represented by civil servant Matteo Brisa. These two were licensed to travel to Rome to obtain support for their interpretations. Pope Gregory appointed the aforementioned Archbishop and interim Bishop of Malta Don Luis de Torres de Monreale to hear the two sides and make recommendations. Grand Master and Council appointed Prior of Ireland Mathurin Romegas, Bailiff of Santo Stefano Antonio di Bologna, Bailiff of Mallorca Don Agustin de Argençola, and Lieutenant Grand Bailiff Philipp von Groendorf to expound the Order's interpretation. These differences could not soon be resolved.[28]

The four galleys of the Religion during the month of April scoured the coast of North Africa, returning to Malta early in May towing a large germa seized in the waters of Tripoli with a crew of 52 and a cargo of various merchandise. But the germa was also suspected of carrying peste or plague. She was placed in quarantine at the Marsamuscietto pratique station while the four galleys were ordered back to North Africa rather than themselves remain idle in quarantine, this to the great displeasure of caravan knights. Some caravan knights went ashore without pratique and, in the latest manifestation of disregard for authority, proceeded to their auberges in Valletta and Birgu careless of the health of others in their auberges, while embarked soldiery absent supervision of those same knights sacked the captured germa. To the great disgust of General of the Galleys Antonio Maldonado, Grand Master and Council appointed a committee to study the matter, and the committee recommended placing a new caravan aboard the capitana on pain of defrocking should they disregard orders. This recommendation further infuriated Maldonado because he was also Grand Chancellor of the Langue of Castile responsible for proper conduct of the langue's Hospitallers, and should any of these be defrocked then he, too, might have been defrocked. Belatedly, three of the four galleys again put to sea with the capitana remaining in port because of a fractured mainmast antenna. During Maldonado's absence, Bailiff of Negroponte and former Lieutenant Grand Chancellor Martín Duero Monroy acted in his stead, accepting the committee's findings which included critical references to Maldonado. Presupposing the Grand Master favored Duero in this matter, Maldonado flying his flag from *San Giovanni* penned a letter addressed to Mathurin Romegas venting his anger and denigrating the Grand Master.[29]

Meanwhile the new caravan aboard the capitana still at Marsamuscietto was also quarantined. At sea the three deployed galleys encountered three Barbary corsair brigantines in Sicilian waters off Terranova (Gela). These fled with the galleys in pursuit. One brigantine beached and the crew of 36 escaped ashore. The other two brigantines lighter and faster presumably escaped while the beached brigantine's oarsmen were liberated and the brigantine destroyed. Attempting to return to the coast of Africa the three galleys were forced to fall off by contrary weather and returned to Malta either with fractured antenna or other damage, this time clearing pratique.[30]

With damage repaired all four galleys responded to a summons from the Viceroy of Sicily and proceeded first to Messina and then to

Palermo for a gathering of the Catholic Armada. Anticipating a siege of some Ottoman redoubt, the Catholic Armada appeared rudderless without Don Juan and did nothing but sail to Naples until dismissed late in October. The Hospitaller Squadron returned to Malta at end-October 1579 having been away from home for three consecutive months. Arriving Malta with the squadron was Castellan of Syracuse Don Alonso de San Martín dispatched by Viceroy Marcantonio Colonna to assess readiness of the island's fortresses as well as its stocks of foodstuffs.[31]

On the 1579 biennial anniversary of his predecessor's appointment, François de Moreton de Chabrillan was appointed General of the Galleys succeeding Antonio Maldonado, and upon Chabrillan's nomination Boniface de Puget Chastuel was appointed to command of the squadron capitana *Santa Maria de la Vittoria* succeeding Francisco de Reinoso. This was the same 28-bank *Santa Maria* delivered in November 1569 and very nearly lost 23 months later at the Battle of Lepanto. Chabrillan was also advanced to Bailiff of Manosque upon death of incumbent François de Gozon-Mélac 58 years an Hospitaller. Younger brother of the also deceased Pierre de Gozon-Mélac, both had together contributed 104 years to the Order of Hospitallers.[32]

The Germa of the Religion was dispatched to Trapani and Palermo to take on Barcelona cloth destined for Malta. The Council believed it prudent to place on board a number of serving-brothers from various langues under command of Hospitaller Knight Giovanni Citrone appointed Captain of Reserves for the occasion. Why prudent is not reported. Resident Ambassador to the Holy See Hugues Loubenx de Verdalle was appointed Grand Commander succeeding Chabrillan. He sought authority to return to France between assignments to attend to personal matters, such license denied. Instead he was dispatched to the Priories of Saint-Gilles and Toulouse on Hospitaller business enabling him to complete his personal affairs at Order expense.[33]

Penury of the Common Treasury at end-1579 brought an increasing fear of famine to the Maltese islands, while the Grand Master and Council were aware that inefficient distribution of available food supplies could only make it worse. Prior of Toulouse Romegas, Bailiff of Santo Stefano Don Antonio di Bologna, and Commander Francisco de Guiral were deputized to visit storehouses and to implement controls.

The galleys of the squadron commanded by Chabrillan spent November and December in a frantic search for wheat and corn to relieve the shortage. In December a Venetian cargo vessel bound from Girgenti (Agrigento) to Messina with 1,500 salme of grain was forced into Malta. Hunger was so extreme the grain was seized against payment. Commander Don Miguel de Alentorn was appointed Ambassadeur Extraordinaire to the Court of Spain to explain the extreme need for such activity. This was the Alentorn who in 1562 lost a hand and two brother knights to a swarm of Genovese galley crew at Messina.[34] (Pozzo I-168)

Dom Jerónimo da Cunha obtained the Bailiwick of Lango in 1579 succeeding the deceased Pedro de Mesquite. Bailiff of Negroponte Martín Duero Monroy acceded to the new Bailiwick of Noveville and was himself succeeded as Bailiff of Negroponte by Commander Raimundo de Veri (Ramon de Veri y Despuig in Catalan). Finally, Charles de la Bama du Plessis-Hérault succeeded Jean de Gaillardbois-Marconville as Grand Hospitaller upon retirement of the latter.[35]

Famine at Malta persisted into 1580. General Chabrillan continued to seek out vessels laden with foodstuffs while Bailiff of Santo Stefano Antonio di Bologna was ordered to Sicily to lay before Viceroy Marcantonio Colonna Malta's urgent needs and explain the squadron's conduct at sea. While Bologna was expounding the Order's circumstances at Palermo, and while the Viceroy was urging non-violence, Chabrillan intercepted a Ragusan vessel off Agrigento with a cargo of Sicilian grain and diverted her to Malta. Days later a second Ragusan was intercepted in the Strait of Messina bound for Naples with grain from Apulia, also diverted to Malta. A Venetian carrier with Apulian grain bound for Genoa soon followed. With these three diverted cargoes famine at Malta was sufficiently relieved to recall the galleys. While the galleys were still at sea advice reached Malta of two cargo ships loading various merchandise at Djerba to soon sail for the Levant. Chabrillan was ordered to investigate, proceeding by way of Lampedusa to the Gulf of Gabes where the squadron frigate might close Djerba over the shallows of Beit and Palo and return with more information. The two cargo vessels proved too small to be of interest, and the squadron took course for home 190 nautical miles distant on 11 March. Because of storms, however, it was not until 27 March the galleys safely reached Malta. They brought with them captives from a ship of Scio (Chios) who had disclosed the Ottoman Armada at Constantinople was preparing to sail for the western Mediterranean. It was during the Scio skirmish that François d'Arques du Lys of Arques in the Pas-de-Calais was lost. He was the youngest of four sons and five daughters of Didier d'Arques du Lys and of Nicole de Brixey de Gombervaux. He was also a first cousin thrice removed of Jeanne d'Arques, Maid of Orleans.[36]

Commander Pirro Melzi of Milan was dispatched to Palermo with this latest Armada advice under orders to discuss with Viceroy Colonna the need for Sicilian support should Malta be the Armada's destination. Melzi was also carrying for further dissemination a General Summons authorized by the Sacred Council for Hospitallers to rally to defense of the Convent. Two of the four galleys proceeded to Sicilian waters off shipping ports under orders to resume interception of grain carriers. The other two galleys and the squadron frigate departed Malta on 15 April 1580 under command of Don Federico Meca of Aragon and Pierre de Mayreville-Perles of Provence with orders to proceed into the Levant by way of Stanfane (Stamfani) south of Zante or by way of Cerigo (Kithera) under Cape Sant'Angelo (Cape Maleo) seeking further information concerning Ottoman intentions. Proceeding as far as Karamanian waters over the course of a month during which a large Turkish merchantman with a rich cargo and crew of 61 was taken, the two galleys returned to Malta in May with advice the Ottoman Armada was in fact quite large in suspicion the Venetians had solicited Hungary to take up arms against the Empire, and the Armada was therefore planning an assault on Venetian Corfu. Even so, the advice continued, the Ottomans did not wish a western war while at war with Persia in the east.[37]

With two galleys lurking in Ottoman waters, the other two plus a new galley just delivered at end-April carried out another raid on the coast of North Africa where some few captives were taken from several Moorish garbos. The three otherwise commuted between Malta on the one hand, and Messina, Palermo, and Naples on the other transporting items for the Common Treasury. Antonio Maldonado took passage on an outbound leg returning to Madrid again as resident ambassador succeeding Cristóbal Briceño de Valdoviño. Also taking passage outbound was Bernabò della Marra of Terra di Lavoro in the Kingdom of Naples having completed his tour as galley captain. He was en route Rome succeeding Grand Commander Verdalle as Ambassador in Residence at the Holy See.[38]

Reports reached Malta asserting Martin Graf von Hohenstein, Hospitaller Bailiff of Brandenburg, together with a number of commanders and knights of the Mark Brandenburg, had renounced the Church of Rome in favor of Lutheranism. This joint action was said to have been taken not merely in the names of the individuals but in the name of the Order of Saint John. A commission under date of 6 September was sped to Prior of Germany Philipp Flach ordering the heretics if any to appear at Malta within four months time on pain of losing their Habit. No heretics would appear, nor would anyone else. By far the largest of all Hospitaller bailiwicks, Brandenburg in northeastern Germany had since the 1382 Accord of Heimbach been almost an independent entity selecting its own bailiffs or herrenmeisters. By 1589 the Order would be appointing its own titular Bailiffs of Brandenburg while the herrenmeisters would continue to rule, would continue to wear the habit, and would continue to submit responsions, if irregularly.[33]

The Viceroy of Sicily graciously thanked the Malta Squadron for transporting from Naples to Palermo his sister Donna Girolama Colonna together with her family, that of Duke of Terranova Camillo Pignatelli. During the same voyage the new Inquisitor Monsignor Federico Cefalotto arrived at Malta in succession of Monsignor Domenico Petrucci. A bit later Commander (non-Hospitaller) d'Ugnac, the Grand Master's nephew, arrived at Malta from Rome in company with François de Puget and Doctor Melchiorre Cagliares in deep suspicion of a plot against the Grand Master's life, a scandalous and insulting insinuation absent evidence of which there was none. While no evidence of a plot against the Grand Master's life was uncovered, considerable dissatisfaction was found particularly among the langues of Aragon, Castile, and Italy. The Grand Master was accused, for example, of awarding Grand Crosses among his favorites. On the other hand there were assertions this crisis was manufactured at Rome, and the Council appointed three ambassadors to voice its position before the Holy See. These were Prior of Auvergne Antoine de Villars, Bailiff of Negroponte Francisco de Guiral, and Bailiff of Santo Stefano Antonio di Bologna, each of undisputed stature within the Convent. But instructions given the three ambassadors emphasizing the need for reform at Malta by their nature were critical of the Grand Master, and each ambassador resigned his charge. Two surrogates were appointed,

Otto Torreglias of Mallorca and Girolamo Avogadro of Vercelli. But while these two readied to depart, the Grand Master's nephew Commander d'Ugnac returned with a report Pope Gregory wished dissension resolved at Malta and not at Rome.[40]

Early in the Autumn of 1580 Trinitarian father Juan Gil arrived Algiers intending to ransom captives Miguel and Rodrigo Cervantes. At that time both were slaves of Beylerbey or Viceroy Hassan Veneziano born Andretta at Venice and, like Cervantes, a Lepanto-veteran.

Gustave Dore's Tilting at Windmills.

Veneziano would later be described by Cervantes as "large, lean, pale, skimpy red beard, moist and blood-shot eyes, haughty and cruel." Upon Gil's arrival Veneziano was on the verge of sailing for Constantinople expecting to obtain a new kaftan and thence to Tripoli as Beylerbey with his seraglio, accoutrements, and slaves including Cervantes. Had Gil not arrived that day it is likely Cervantes would have disappeared forever. Instead posterity was rewarded and both captives were released for an earlier agreed and relatively modest sum of 500 ducats equivalent to Maltese scudos. By way of contrast, the 1577 enslavement at Algiers of Spanish Hospitallers Francisco de Valencia and Antonio de Toledo that same year of 1580 brought the magnificent sum of 7,000 Venetian ducats. Veneziano was the loser; it would be three years before Tripoli would be elevated to a beylik, and rather than settle for a sancak he remained idle at considerable personal cost. Literature was the winner.[41]

During the year Bailiff of Negroponte Ramón de Veri was appointed Grand Conservator succeeding Francisco Martinez de Marcilla. Commander Francisco de Guiral was appointed Bailiff of Negroponte in Veri's stead. Veri a bit later succeeded to the dignity of Prior of Catalonia with Francisco de Pomar succeeding to Grand Conservator. Marshal Antoine de Villars was appointed Prior of Auvergne succeeding the deceased Étienne de Fraigne 48 years an Hospitaller, while Pierre de Sacconyn succeeded to Marshal. Treasurer Antoine d'Espinay Saint-Luc was appointed Resident Ambassador to the Court of France while Bailiff of Lango Dom Jerónimo da Cunha Pimentel was appointed Procurator-General and Ambassador to the Court of Portugal. Emilio Pucci of Florence was appointed to command of the 25-bank galley *San Iacomo*.[42]

The year 1581 commenced with the unvarying and perennial fear of an onslaught by the Ottoman Armada even though the Turkish Empire remained entangled in war with Persia, and even though the Armada had not made an appearance in strength in the west since its 1574 re-conquest of Tunis, and even though its commander, 62 year-old Calabrian Kiliç Ali, like his Sultan, appeared infinitely content immersed in his own seraglio. The new year also commenced with another constant, a paucity of funds and foodstuffs often bringing famine. And there was always the danger of plague and typhus. It was a vicious cycle wearing on the citizenry and fraying relationships within the Convent. The first Hospitaller action of the year was borrowing at interest. Forty thousand scudos worth of borrowing. The Order's Ambassador at Rome Bernabò della Marra and Receiver Giovanni Otto Bosio were its agents. It's not clear when these advances would be repaid; they too were perennial.[43]

Reports of Ottoman Armada strength and direction soon began to lose some of their urgency. Not so famine and hunger. One area of persistent concern was Gozo and its neighbor islet Comino in the Freo Channel between Gozo and Malta, both sources of drinking water for Ottoman Armadas, corsair squadrons, and even individual corsair vessels. While Comino had no population, that of Gozo had bounced back from Dragut's 1551 removal of essentially everyone to its previous level of 5,000 mostly farmers plus a rotating garrison at the citadel or walled city of Rabat. This year the garrison commander was Geronimo Valenzuela of Cordoba, and he had a solid supply of men and munitions sufficient to protect the island from sudden assault. Not so food stocks. Both Gozo and Malta were suffering from famine and hunger. On the final day of February 1581 General Chabrillan and four galleys were dispatched to Palermo to plead for grain from the Viceroy. Fortuitously, three grain carriers were encountered en route, and Hospitaller guests placed on board guided their reluctant hosts to Valletta. The local grain crisis eased. Pausing at Palermo, Chabrillan agreed to a commission on his grain acquisitions in the form of an escort for deposed King of Tunis Amida (Hafsid Ahmad III) seeking a return to his throne. Nominally under absentee control of the Venetian renegade Hassan Veneziano, former Beylerbey of Algiers, there had been no effective government at Tunis since reassignment of the Sardinian renegade Ramadan Pasha in October 1579. In the absence of outreach from Algiers, Tunis citizenry had ousted their un-empowered Ottoman overlords. It was this temporary vacuum Amida (Morgan's Hamida) hoped to fill.[44]

Amida, one son, and five retainers were embarked at Palermo and transported to Malta where the King was cordially received while Chabrillan and the galleys prepared to deploy from Tunis to the Levant by way of Libya's Capes Misurata and Buonandrea on either side of the Gulf of Sidra, both sources of drinking water. From Buonandrea the galleys intended climbing the vertical axis of the Cross of Rhodes and Cyprus for the purpose of putting raiding parties ashore in Karamania, upper reach of the vertical axis. Six days following arrival at Malta the galleys sailed for the Gulf of Tunis where the King and retinue were greeted by a welcoming party waiting on the beach. While any Ottoman deployment to reclaim Tunis would have likely appeared in the same waters of NW wind on the return voyage, it was unseasonal wind which forced the four galleys back to Malta on 14 April. Two days beyond Malta returning to the coast of Africa the squadron was hit by such a fierce storm the squadron frigate commanded by non-Hospitaller Giacomo Rispolo went to the bottom. It was a miracle everyone onboard was rescued by the galleys, but the deployment was aborted. Good fortune amid such adversity enabled *San Iacomo* under Emilio Pucci to take a suspicious vessel sighted from Valletta. She was one of three Barbary cargo galliots reported earlier at Cape Colonne on the sole of the Italian boot laden with grain and olive-oil. With a crew of only 21 Infidels plus several renegades, she was easily forced into port.[45]

Catalan Onofre Belver was in May 1581 dispatched as Ambassadeur Extraordinaire by way of the Holy See to various Imperial courts of Germany including those of Bohemia and Poland. He was to press for past-due payments of responsions and to assess the state of Lutheran affairs. He would remain in the Empire for two years in effect becoming Resident Ambassador.[46]

Early in July 1581 the four galleys again departed Malta bound for Messina and Palermo to replace masts and antennas and then to investigate Sicily's uninhabited western islands where three Barbary brigantines were discovered and taken on 14 July yielding 70 captive crew and liberating a near-equal number of Christian oarsmen. This fortunate development followed two disturbing developments, one coincident with rebellion at Malta and the other during the morning of 27 June when sixty Ottoman galleys passed within sight of several Maltese ports quite unconcerned with the consequences. The galleys were commanded by Kiliç Ali who had been ordered to install Hassan Veneziano as Governor of Tunis. In Kiliç Ali's current indolence, this assignment failed of completion. He reported back that Amida's force of poorly-armed Moors and Berbers was too strong for his embarked shore party and, that being the case, he chose to proceed to Algiers where he was still considered king in spite of the Sultan and in spite of resident Beylerbey Jafer Aga Pasha or Jafer Aga Magyar, a renegade Hungarian eunuch who had replaced Hassan Veneziano in

1580 as a sunny day follows a tormented night. In April Jafer had deposed his haughty Aga of Janissaries after which the janissaries rose in revolt. For this reason Kiliç Ali also avoided Algiers and pointed his galleys even further west where he was of a mind to take on the King of Fez. Fez was the forerunner of Spanish Morocco which became part of the Kingdom of Morocco in 1912, and when Kiliç Ali arrived on the scene he was reminded that Spain and Fez were allies and both had a truce with the Ottoman Porte. At that time he reversed course for Constantinople, but he still holds the record for taking a Turkish fleet further west than any other Turkish Admiral. One of few exceptional Ottoman sea commanders, he then returned to his seraglio.[47]

The same day Kiliç Ali's armada passed disdainfully by Malta, Commanders Pirro Melzi, Bernard de Gozon-Mélac, and Pedro Hurtado de Mendoza were appointed Sector Wardens with near unlimited power to ready their respective sectors for war. Don Gabriel Frias y Lara of Castile was appointed Captain-at-Arms at Notabile (Mdina). Prior of Lombardia Carlo Sforza reached the end of his life and was succeeded by Lieutenant Admiral Don Girolamo Gravina of Catania. The Priory of Hungary was vacated by death of Gabrio Serbellone, and Don Vincenzo Carafa was expected to take up the charge.

On 6 July the Council of State convened in the quarters of Prior of the Church Antoine Cressin and elected Mathurin de Lescout Romegas Lieutenant to the Grand Master with power to act in the Grand Master's incapacity. This act deprived the Grand Master of authority and was greeted with applause by all in attendance. Exiting the Council of State Romegas was accompanied to his quarters as if a newly elected Grand Master by more than 300 of his brethren including many knights of the Grand Cross among whom were Prior of the Church Cressin, Bailiffs Niccolò Rivalta and Martín Duero Monroy, and Commander of La Croix-en-Brie Mailloc Sacquenville. These four were considered by many to have been the principal authors of the insurrection, Duero Monroy the Knight of the Grand Cross with his sarcophagus lid proudly displayed in the Church of Saint John at Clerkenwell, London. Beyond the Council of State, however, there remained a considerable body of Hospitallers disturbed by this development. Among the opposition were several Knights of the

Grand Cross, all Captains of the Palace Guard, a substantial number if a minority of ordinary Hospitallers, and about 2,000 ordinary citizens under arms who considered Cassière's deposition to be sedition. On 12 July the Grand Master was placed under house arrest in Castle Saint Angelo where he was consigned to the care of Governor Pierre de Montauban de Voguedemar.[48]

François de Moreton de Chabrillan and the four galleys of the squadron returned to Malta on 14 July 1581. Upon being apprised of developments, Chabrillan led a committee of caravan knights and others to Castle Saint Angelo where he offered to re-install the Grand Master in the Magistral Palace. The Grand Master refused in order to not spark conflict within the Convent between those with opposing views on the matter. Romegas and the Council, for their part, hastened departure of Sacquenville, their ambassador to Rome, to present their version of developments to Pope Gregory XIII.[49]

Upon learning of the Grand Master's deposition and house arrest, Pope Gregory XIII immediately sent a special nuncio, Gaspare Visconte, as Apostolic Vicar to investigate developments and administer the Order until the matter was resolved. Visconte reached Malta on 8 September. The knights were ordered to obey him as a representative of the Holy See. Romegas resigned and the Grand Master was released from confinement. At Rome Historian Giacomo Bosio and his brother Giovanni Otto Bosio pled the cause of the Grand Master while Commander Francisco de Guevara pled the rebel cause. Cassière and Romegas were both summoned to Rome to themselves explain their conduct and to plead their own case. Chabrillan assigned three galleys to escort the Grand Master to either Terracina or Civitavecchia, the capitana, *San Pietro*, and *San Giovanni* aboard which he, three other knights of the Grand Cross (Marshal Antoine de Villars, Prior of Messina Pietro Giustiniani, and Bailiff of Santo Stefano Antonio di Bologna) plus 200 others embarked on 20 September. *San Iacomo* was left to transport Romegas. Waylaid by storm at Saint Paul's Bay with subsequent pauses at Augusta, Messina, Pozzuolo (Naples), Gaeta, and Civitavecchia, Cassière arrived at Rome on 26 October and, on orders of the Pope, was treated with deference and ceremony. Romegas embarked on 28 September without many of his earlier sponsors and adherents, had a speedier voyage, and arrived prior to the Grand Master. He was received at Rome with little fanfare, in fact with coldness and disdain. Following a private audience with the Pope, Romegas was ordered to publicly request a pardon from the Grand Master as were his principal adherents Louis de Mailloc Sacquenville, Gabriel d'Abzac la Douze, and René de Pins, among others. Romegas died on 4 November within a week of his audience and before requesting a pardon, alone and with broken spirit. Dead at the age of 53, Romegas was ceremonially interred in the Church of the Trinity of the Mountain at Rome in a ceremony attended at the Grand Master's request by all Hospitallers at Rome necessarily including the Grand Master himself. Jean l'Evesque de la Cassière was honorably acquitted of all charges against him and resumed his office. He did not live long enough, however, to enjoy his vindication, dying at Rome on 21 December 1581 at the age of seventy-eight. His remains would be transferred to Malta and interred within St. John's Co-Cathedral at Valletta.[50]

Chapter V

1582–1587

One day following the death of Grand Master Jean l'Evésque de la Cassière a Papal Brief was issued addressed to the Council and Convent at Malta and dispatched with Hospitallers Ferrante Maggiolini of Milan and Giorgio Nibbia of Novaro aboard *San Iacomo* lying at Naples. Reaching Malta on 3 January 1582 the Brief announced the deaths of Cassière and Mathurin Romegas *and* prohibited immediate election of a successor Grand Master. The balance of the Brief contained secret instructions for the Sixteen Electors in conclave at the next General Assembly.[1]

Viceroy of Sicily Marcantonio Colonna recalled three Sicilian galleys assigned to Malta during the interim tenure of Apostolic Nuncio Gaspare Visconte and replaced them with four galleys and 500 Spanish infantry under command of Don Juan Osorio which reached Malta on 10 January.[2] The Council of State requested of the Holy See by emissary Giovanni Giacomo Palio of Turin authority to fill vacancies among priory and bailiwick dignities and to proceed with ordinary day-to-day matters. In the meanwhile a sense developed the Holy See was awaiting return from France of Grand Commander Hugues de Loubenx de Verdalle who as Resident Ambassador at Rome had in the opinion of Pope Gregory XIII exhibited prudence, independence of thought, and dispassion concerning grave matters.[3] Perhaps above all else, Verdalle had remained neutral during recent differences. The morning after services for Grand Master Cassière the Council began re-asserting its authority. No future Grand Master should have power to create officers among the various law courts and inquisitor offices without approval of the Council. The Grand Master should not have authority to award Commanderies of Grace to anyone with less than ten years in the Habit or less than five years residence in the Convent, except to Brothers of the Langues of England and Germany. No Grand Master might take into his service more than eight Pages. And all future Grand Masters must pay four thousand scudos per annum for food service.[4]

Two days later on 12 January 1582 a General Assembly was convened by Apostolic Nuncio Visconte in the Great Hall of the Magistral Palace and then at Saint John's Co-Cathedral, its purpose election of a new Grand Master. The Assembly soon proceeded to selection of eight electors, one per langue, as follow: Grand Commander Hugues de Loubenx-Verdale for Provence, Lieutenant Marshal Jacques de Virieu-Pupetières for Auvergne, Claude de Ligny de Raray for France, Grand Conservator Francisco de Pomar for Aragon, Bailiff of Naples Niccolò Orsini di Rivalta for Italy, Bailiff of Eagle Oliver Starkey for England, Lieutenant Grand Bailiff Rudolph Radau for Germany, and Bailiff of Novaville Martín Duero Monroy for Castile. These eight appointed Verdalle as non-voting President or Preceptor of Elections, Juanito Torreglias of Aragon as Knight of Elections, Dominique de Courtade of Provence as Chaplain of Elections, and Serving Brother François Ha of France as Sergeant-at-Arms.

The last three, called the Triumvirate of Electors, selected a fourth elector from the Assembly, and the four selected a fifth, and the five a sixth, and so on in diminishing influence of individual electors to make up the Sixteen final electors at two per langue. These were: Dominique de Courtade and François de Puget for Provence; Jacques de Virieu-Pupetières and Pierre de la Porte for Auvergne; François Ha and Claude de Ligny de Raray for France; Juanito Torreglias and Don Geronimo Sagra for Aragon; Pirro Melzi and Centorio Cagnolo for Italy; Preceptor of Templecombe James Shelley and Emilio Pucci of Italy for England in the absence of another eligible Englishman (Oliver Starkey was subject to a long-standing prohibition preventing knights of the grand cross from voting in Magistral elections); Rudolph Radau and August Baron von Meersburg for Germany; and Hernando de Ovando and Rodrigo de Britto for Castile. These Sixteen retired in camera into the Sacristy where they found the Apostolic Nuncio waiting. He revealed to the Sixteen that by order of Pope Gregory XIII seeking to restore order among members of the Convent, there were only three acceptable candidates and the Preceptor of Elections was one of them. The second was Prior of Saint-Gilles and senior knight of the Langue of Provence François de Panisse, while the third was General of the Galleys and Pilier (in Verdalle's residential absence) of the Langue of Provence François de Moreton de Chabrillan who had been captured at 1552's disastrous assault on Zuara and enslaved for

12 years. Thus all three candidates were French from the Langue of Provence. Following four hours of deliberation Hugues de Loubenx de Verdalle was elected 52nd Grand Master of the Order of Jerusalem. At a Council meeting the following day four ambassadeurs extraordinaire were appointed to notify the Courts of Europe of the election, while Chabrillan was ordered to return the other three galleys from Civitavecchia to Malta as transport.[5]

Born at Loubenx in Gascony midway between Toulouse and Andorra the third son of Philippe de Loubenx de Verdalle and Anne de Montaut, Hugues de Loubenx de Verdalle was 51 years of age upon election, 29 years younger than his predecessor as Grand Master. He moreover came to the Magistracy by a most unconventional route. With no titled experience whatsoever except as Knight Commander of a succession of commanderies he was in 1579 appointed Resident Ambassador and Procurator-General to the Holy See. He even arrived at Rome wearing a Small Cross, the Small Cross there considered demeaning of the Vatican. Verdalle was consequently soon appointed Grand Commander entitled to the Grand Cross. The Grand Commander was a Conventual Bailiff resident at Malta, in fact the senior Conventual Bailiff resident at Malta, but at no time in the next three years did Verdalle appear at the Convent, and it was during those three years rebellion seethed at Malta ending with house arrest and eventual death of Grand Master Cassière. Equally unconventional, the Holy See for the only time in Hospitaller history limited the number of successor Magistral candidates to three pre-selected individuals only one of whom had impressed Pope Gregory XIII. Expecting a benevolent relationship with the Holy Father, the Sixteen Electors in less than four hours decided that candidate was their man.

The capitana, *San Pietro*, and *San Giovanni* reached Malta from Civitavecchia on 17 February 1582 following five months of absence, joining *San Iacomo* and returning deceased Grand Master Cassière to Malta for final interment. The galleys also brought with them Knights of the Grand Cross and many others honoring the deceased Grand Master. General Chabrillan reached the end of his term as Squadron Commander and was succeeded by newly appointed Bailiff of Santo Stefano Girolamo Avogadro of Vercelli. Upon Avogadro's nomination Giovanni Francesco Sanmartino was appointed flag-captain commanding the capitana in succession of Boniface de Puget

Chasteuil. Appointed to command of *San Iacomo* was Philippe de Tuilier de Hardemont succeeding Emilio Pucci. Tuilier de Hardemont immediately took *San Iacomo* to Naples transporting the Apostolic Nuncio on the first leg of his return to Rome. While returning to Malta *San Iacomo* seized at Stromboli a corsair brigantine with a crew of 30, liberating a somewhat larger number of Christians from the oars. She was towed to Malta.

Bishop of Malta Tomás Gargallo arrived with the capturing galley. General Avogadro having been appointed Bailiff of Santo Stefano early in the year succeeding Don Antonio di Bologna on the latter's death, was himself succeeded as Admiral by Federico Caccia of Novara. Caccia was shortly afterward elevated to the Bailiwick of Venosa where he succeeded Giuseppe Cambiano also of Novara and was himself succeeded as Admiral by Pompeo Soardo of Bergamo. Giuseppe Cambiano had authored during the 1543-1547 Magistracy of Claude de la Sengle a perceptive treatise on Hospitaller circumstances at the time. Entitled *The Maltese Dialogue* and translated into English it is available from some bookstores today.[6]

Early in April 1582 Avogadro took the four-galley squadron to Messina and Palermo to load Barcelona linen ordered earlier, Catalonia the first and at the time the leading Mediterranean producer of fine linen as well as a reliable source of other cloth. During the return voyage the galleys also transported two companies of soldiers dispatched by Viceroy Colonna to reinforce the Malta presidio. The day before return to Malta of the galleys there arrived in port a tender belonging to a large corsair galleon outfitted by new Viceroy of Naples and Duke of Osuna Pedro Téllez-Girón coming up from Cape Buonandrea on the far side of Libya's Gulf of Sidra where the galleon had run aground. The tender sought urgent oared-galley assistance in removing the galleon from shallows before she was discovered by the enemy. Departing Malta after filling water tanks the four galleys took course to the southeast 600 nautical miles distant but on arrival found no sign of the galleon, nor of debris suggesting her destruction. This mystery's resolution is not known to have been recorded, but loss of a Neapolitan galleon would have been recorded.

Returned to Malta there arrived in port a barque dispatched by Giovanni Giacomo Palio, then Procurator at Modica, Sicily, advising the Ottoman Armada was off Syracuse. On this advice the Order began taking defensive measures and dispatched Don Diego Brochero of Castile to investigate by frigate. Brochero returned to report there was no armada off Syracuse but rather six corsair galliots which had sacked Terranova (Gela), kidnapping 80 Christians, and which had since moved west toward North Africa. These were likely six of eleven galliots accompanying the aforementioned renegade Hassan Veneziano from Constantinople to Algiers for a second assignment as Beylerbey or Viceroy. Four of the eleven galliots were the personal property of Kiliç Ali, not embarked, which may have led to the Ottoman Armada identification. This disproportionate corsair strength in Christian waters vis-a-vis the four Malta galleys concerned the new Grand Master. Were the Malta galleys good only for logistics? Could the Convent be expected to staunch an overwhelming tide? Could it otherwise sustain its existence? Should it alternatively live at peace within the overwhelming tide it would no longer engender the financial and other support necessary to do so. It was an impossible conundrum.[7]

The Italian Langue's recurring search for equality vis-à-vis the French langues re-surfaced early in the Verdalle Magistracy in a contentious public squabble between the Grand Master and resident Italians concerning authority of the Admiral, a dignity of the Langue of Italy, over galleys and other vessels of the Religion as well as over their commanders. The Langue of Italy maintained the Admiral should be the ultimate maritime commander or the dignity of Admiral was a charade. The Grand Master maintained that authority over the lifelines of an island Republic was central to its survival and must be retained at the highest level of governance, that is, by Grand Master and Council of State. Pope Gregory XIII was forced to intervene with a Papal Brief dated 10 April forbidding innovation with pre-existing authority.[8] Any change to pre-existing authority must come from a Chapter General, and a Chapter General was accordingly scheduled for the first Sunday of January 1583.[9]

Quickly yielding to temptation, Grand Master Verdalle in the third month of his Magistracy purchased a galley hull at Messina, arming and equipping her at his own expense for service as a corsair or with the Malta squadron. She was to be commanded by Bernard de Roquelaure de Saint-Aubin. On arrival of the Magistral galley at Malta the Grand Master proposed to the Council she initially see service as a part of the galley squadron with seniority second to that of the capitana. With the matter further aired publicly, Federico Cortés commanding *San Pietro* as senior captain objected and refused to yield his position as Padrona or second in squadron command. Accused of an unwarranted disturbance, he was sentenced to spend the month of October at the feet of the Pope explaining himself under pain of deprivation of Habit. In the interim he was incarcerated in his own quarters and succeeded as captain of *San Pietro* by Hernando de Ovando. Ovando, however, refused the assignment while Cortés to placate the Grand Master decided to serve out his term. This incident was the beginning of Verdalle's own trial by rebellion.[10]

The four squadron galleys escorted to Valletta an English-flag sailing ship encountered in North African waters which had the effrontery when passing to fail to salute warships by dipping her flag to General of the Galleys Avogadro. Seeing the Maltese furl their sails and prepare to board, however, the English vessel had submitted. There were at this time similar ships preying upon Christian vessels and so Avogadro determined to escort her back to Malta for a proper search. This one, like merchantmen today, was guilty only of an absence of ordinary courtesy and/or knowledge of customs of the nautical road.[11]

Otherwise preying on the new Grand Master's mind was the failure so far to create a collachium, or city of Hospitallers, within the walls of Valletta. He prodded his architects and engineers to move collachium planning forward. In perennial suspicion of the Ottoman Armada, a suspicion wearing on all, the Order hired in Sicily a large number of soldiers most of whom were transported to Malta by the galleys, but 160 of whom were transported by the *Galleonetto of the Religion* commanded by Giulio Bandini of Florence. Sector Wardens were Commanders Don Lupe de Híjar of Aragon, Louis de Mailloc Sacquenville of France, and Bernardino Scaglia of Ivrea. Captain-at-Arms for Notabile (Mdina) was Arbogast von Andlau of Germany. And because the Grand Master had ordered a reinforced guard for Valletta, he ordered Marshal Antoine de Villars to make circuits of the walls without prejudice to Post commanders to ensure readiness.[12]

His Most Christian Majesty and Hospitaller King Henry III of France, by letter conveyed to Malta in the care of Hospitaller Anne de la Fontaine de Lesche of the Langue of France, requested as a matter of urgency the Priory of Toulouse be conferred on Antoine Scipion, carnal brother of Anne, Duke of Joyeuse, the King's brother-in-law by virtue of 1581 marriage to Queen Louise's sister Marguerite de Vaudémont (Marguerite de Navarre). Given his predecessor's unhappy history in yielding dignities to the powerful, Verdalle consulted with François de Puget, Grand Commander and Pilier of the Langue of Provence, that is, but for himself senior Provencal knight at Malta. Verdalle also consulted with other Provencal commanders and knights including Charles de Grasse-Briançon obtaining their agreement the Royal request could not be refused. The dignity of Prior of Toulouse had been vacant since the death of Mathurin Romegas in November. François de Puget was in June 1582 advanced to Prior of Toulouse while Briançon succeeded to Grand Commander, both dignities entitled to the Grand Cross. By prior agreement, Puget would yield the Priory of Toulouse to Scipion, retaining a right to wear the Grand Cross, on condition Scipion became a fully professed knight and paid the nominal admission fee. Antoine-Scipion de Joyeuse was at Royal request received into the Order of Malta, Langue of Provence, in 1581 and pursuant to the same Royal request was in 1582 appointed Prior of Toulouse. He was in 1589 released from his Hospitaller vows by Pope Sixtus V in order to succeed his deceased brother as head of family but continured as prior through 1593. During the entire period he was sustained in his unearned circumstances by priory income.[13]

During 1582 Bailiff of Manosque François de Moreton de Chabrillan passed away, cause of death unrecorded. Recently General of the Galleys, he was only 54 years of age. He would soon be succeeded as Bailiff by François de Puget-Chasteuil. Long-time Bailiff of the Morea Guillaume Malain-de-Lux reached the end of his 76 years at his Commandery of Bellecroix in Champagne. Having successfully avoided the Sieges of Rhodes and Malta as well as the Battle of Lepanto he left a son and a daughter and was succeeded as Bailiff by Louis de Bouteiller de Sainte-Geneviève. Antonio Maria Palio of Turin was appointed Prior of Pisa succeeding the deceased Giovanni di Ventimiglia, 25 years the incumbent, and Pedro Gonzales de Mendoza was appointed Prior of Ireland succeeding the deceased Romegas. Grand Conservator Francisco de Pomar was advanced to Castellan of Amposta and was succeeded as Grand Conservator by Don Lupe de Híjar. Bailiff of Noveville Martín Duero Monroy elected to move to Bailiff of Lora, and Grand Chancellor Antonio Maldonado succeeded to Bailiff of Noveville. Bailiff of Negroponte and acclaimed hero of the Great Siege of 1565 Francisco Guiral advanced to Grand Chancellor and was himself succeeded as Bailiff of Negroponte by Geronimo de Homedes.[14] During the year Bishop of Malta Tomás Gargallo became progressively deranged and violent and was confined under medical care for his own safety.[15]

The four galleys of the Religion escorted Viceroy of Sicily Marcantonio Colonna and Viceregal Court from Palermo to Messina reflecting perennially impassable roads if not banditry, and from Messina conducted an investigation of Sicily's uninhabited western islands. Their reward was a corsair brigantine with a crew of 26 and about the same number of liberated oarsmen. Three of the same galleys together with the new Magistral galley then proceeded into the Levant where they encountered and took a Greek vessel with Turks and considerable merchandise on board. Without thought of putting a prize crew on board and sending the ship to Malta, they off-loaded merchandise, Greeks, and Turks onto the galleys and sank their capture, their justification being the ship was Greek. The Council ordered they not be paid prize money. Two of these galleys, the capitana and *San Pietro*, detached themselves from the other two and proceeded once more into the Levant, left the plunder, and returned to Malta at end-September in company with five galleys of Sicily aboard which were Viceroy Colonna, his brother Prospero, Alonso de San Martín, and others of prominence, the Viceroy declaring his interest in seeing the new city of Valletta. This, however, was believed to be a pretext; his true interest was in clarifying several occult suspicions of the King such as inordinately close ties to France. The Viceroy satisfied himself in a single day, asking only that the two Malta galleys accompany his five galleys to Palermo. The other two galleys, that is the Magistral galley and *San Giovanni*, subsequently returned to Malta with two large caramussals and a good number of captives. In addition, a large sum of coin was found on one of the captures. Returning from the Levant to Malta at about the same time were the corsair galley and large galliot of, respectively, Ferrante Coiro of Milan and Pier Francesco Venturi of Florence. They, too, brought in rich hauls. Similarly returning from North Africa was Luis Davide's large armed galliot with a captured saettia, cargo of various merchandise and a Moorish crew. Thirty Christian slaves overcame the crew of a brigantine and sailed her from Djerba to Malta; they had reports from Tunis suggesting an excursion of galleys and galliots to sack Gozo. Three Malta galleys proceeded to Gozo with defensive supplies.[16]

During the year Bailiff of Lora Ernando Alarcón passed away. In the flush of pride washing across Christendom in the wake of 1522's loss of Rhodes, Alarcón was among the first to be inspired by his King's assessment: *Nothing in the world has ever been so well lost as*

Rhodes! He had been received into the Langue of Castile within weeks of his King's exclamation. At his death he was 78 years of age, 59 of them as an Hospitaller.

January 1583 was a month when the number of Hospitallers at the Convent increased almost daily, and Treasury resources were under strain clothing, housing, and feeding all of them. The Council of State wrote to the senior Hospitaller at each priory except priories of Germany and the Priory of England the latter of which no longer existed, asking that the stream of candidates coming to Malta be slowed to a manageable level.[17]

In February 1583 while at anchor in the bay of Saint Nicholas of Vlemona (Avelomona) at the Venetian island of Cerigo, modern Kithira, a Malta-flag corsair galleon owned and commanded by Hospitaller Diego de Brochero was seized by a squadron of Venetian galleys operating out of Candia Town (Iraklion). Seized with the galleon were two caramussals captured from Turks plus Turkish crews and associated plunder thus infringing Venetian neutrality. Brochero was seen earlier in this history when taken captive by Uluç Ali's Algerian Galley Squadron during the 1570 Battle of Cape Passero. He had soon been ransomed by his family at a price but a small fraction of his future value. The same undervaluation would occur on this occasion.

The four galleys of the Religion, having proceeded to Messina toward the end of 1582 to load even more cloth from Barcelona as well as to receive responsions and other items for the Common Treasury, returned to Malta on 23 February. A complaint was lodged with the Council of State by the Procurator of the Treasury against three of the four galley captains, Federico Cortés of *San Pietro*, Philippe de Tuilier de Hardemont of *San Iaccmo*, and Philibert de Mathay of *San Giovanni* alleging the Receiver at Messina had properly consigned responsions to the ships' scribes or keepers of the written records, but that the three captains had improperly expropriated several hundred scudos for their own use setting a terrible precedent. The three captains were summarily condemned to incarceration in Birgu's Castle Saint Angelo with restitution of the expropriated amounts. Because the three captains were also near the ends of their terms as captain, they were respectively succeeded by first officers Don Juan Enriquez of Castile, by Giovanni Battista Somaia of Florence, and by Paolo Camillo Casati of Milan. The Langue of Italy again protested at usurpation of the right to make maritime assignments, particularly in that the forthcoming Chapter General then convening on 14 July was scheduled to address the matter.[18]

Early in March the four galleys of the Religion under General Avogadro in company with the Grand Master's Magistral galley commanded by Bernard de Roquelaure Saint-Aubin took course toward southern Sicily. Sailing in company were the proprietary galley of Hospitaller Giovan Battista Guinucci and the frigate of non-Hospitaller Giacomo Rispolo They were on the track of two English vessels engaged in piratical operations in local waters against not only Infidels but Christians as well, pursuing both a sailing vessel of Malta and the *Galleonetto of the Religion* while interdicting traffic between Malta and Sicily. This undertaking, however, was turned back by punishing weather and succeeded only when the weather calmed. Then *San Giovanni* under Paolo Camillo Casati, the Magistral galley under Saint-Aubin, Guinucci's galley, the proprietary galliot of Pierre de Saint-Aubin, and the proprietary brigantine of Bailiff Chabrillan this time sailed off the wind toward the coast of North Africa where they encountered and took a large germa the crew of which put up an obstinate defense. Much Christian blood was spilled costing the life of *San Giovanni*'s skipper Paolo Camillo Casati and those of many other Knights of the Habit together with those of hired soldiers and seamen. Two hundred twenty Turks, Moors, and Black Africans were taken captive.[19]

Following return to Malta of the foregoing vessels together with germa and captives, the four galleys of the Religion again departed to North Africa on track of the English pirates. Days later the Grand Master was informed by Viceroy Colonna that Kiliç Ali had exited the Dardanelles with fifty galleys exclusive of those assigned to the Rhodes Guard, also known as the Archipelago Guard. There were fifteen additional Ottoman galleys waiting at Negroponte to join the Ottoman Admiral with all 65 moving to Sicilian or Maltese waters. Colonna accordingly sent five galleys of Sicily to Malta with 600 embarked Spanish infantry under their General Don Manuel Ponce de León. Concerned the Malta Squadron might encounter the Ottomans at sea, Grand Master Verdalle dispatched a frigate along the squadron's track under command of Pietro Fantone. But four days later the squadron returned to port with a small Moorish garbo and one of the English pirates in tow. Command of the Grand Master's Magistral galley meanwhile passed from Bernard de Saint-Aubin to Rostaing des Essards-Laudun de Goût. Laudun de Goût joined with the private galley of Hospitaller Giulio Bandini and they together departed for the Levant but were both summoned back to Malta on the Kılıç Ali report.[20]

Having duly thanked the Viceroy for his assistance, four more Sicilian galleys under command of Hospitaller Francesco Colonna reached Malta transporting war munitions and other supplies but did not remain after off-loading. The 600 Spanish also departed as, they reported, the threat of an Ottoman incursion in local waters had been lifted. Viceroy Colonna disagreed and returned the 600 to Malta aboard the four galleys of Francesco Colonna. Two days later the Magistral galley under command of Laudun de Goût sailing in company in the Levant with the galley of Giulio Bandini of Florence also returned to Malta but with little to show for their effort, not even news of the Ottoman Armada. With discretion the better part of valor, Grand Master Verdalle and Council appointed titular Bailiff (Prior of Toulouse) François de Puget as Captain-at-Arms for Notabile, while Commanders Guido Pagliaro of Alessandro (Milan) 42 years a Hospitaller, Francisco de Valencia of Aragon, and Jean de Castellane d'Aluis of Provence were appointed Sector Wardens. The garrison at Gozo was reinforced while a large number of barques were posted on patrol in the Malta Channel between Gozo and Sicily. The galley *San Giovanni* crossed the Malta Channel to Pozzallo but learned nothing of the enemy. Eventually the four galleys of Sicily came for the Spanish infantry, and this time they departed not to return. There was no news of Kılıç Ali, and Malta stood down to ready for the 1583 Chapter General and to ready for the many Hospitallers expected to attend.[21]

Because it was customary at times of Chapters General to deploy the galleys with Caravan knights embarked, thus removing from the premises boisterous youth not yet eligible to participate in Chapters General, three squadron galleys together with the Magistral galley readied for sea. The squadron galleys were the 28-bank capitana under Giovanni Francesco Sanmartino together with the two 25-bank galleys *San Iacomo* under an exonerated Philippe de Tuilier Hardemont and *San Giovanni* under Giovanni Battista Somaia. Two days prior to the first Chapter General of Grand Master Verdale's Magistracy all four departed Malta under General of the Galleys Girolamo Avogadro bound for the Levant. Once convened, the Sixteen *Capitolari* (Legislators) were selected, two per langue, to in-camera consider matters brought before the Chapter General not resolved by unanimous consent. These were Grand Commander Charles de Grasse-Briançon and Bailiff of Manosque François de Puget-Chasteuil for Provence, Lieutenant Marshal Claude de Tersac-Lambes and Jacques de Virieu-Pupetières for Auvergne, Bailiff of the Morea Louis de Bouteiller de Sainte-Geneviève and Lieutenant Treasurer Louis de Mailloc Sacquenville for France, Lieutenant Grand Conservator Lupe del Poio and Juan Otto Torreglias for Aragon, Admiral Giovan Francesco Langosco de Conti della Motta and Prior of Capua Bernardino Scaglia for Italy, Prior of Ireland Don Pedro Gonzales de Mendoza and Bailiff of Eagle Oliver Starkey for England, Lieutenant Grand Bailiff Auguste Baron von Meersburg and Wilhelm von Cronberg for Germany, and Bailiff of Lora Martín Duero Monroy and Gonzalo Porras for Castile. These Sixteen reviewed various statutes and orders of declining pertinence, amending or killing or leaving unaltered. Among other matters the Sixteen approved an imposition of 50,000 gold scudos assessed against wealth of individual entities (a property tax). There was a second imposition of 40,000 gold scudos against the general wealth or common assets of the Order. A third assessment of 30,000 gold scudos to prepare for an Ottoman siege brought the total to 120,000 gold scudos. Catalan Onofre Belver just returned from two years as resident ambassador to Vienna reported to Grand Master and Council on his findings concerning past-due German responsions and the state of Lutheran affairs. Niccolò Grimaldi of Genoa, 30 years an Hospitaller, was appointed Belver's successor. The *capitolari* reached no consensus to alter the privileges, duties, and other responsibilities of the Order's Admiral.[22]

The galley squadron capitana returned alone to Malta on 10 August 1583, two days short of a month since her departure, those visible on board exuding a great sadness and sense of injustice. Sailing in company with the Magistral galley and with squadron galleys *San Iacomo* and *San Giovanni* between Cerigotto (Antikithera) and Crete's Cape Spada, the Maltese had unexpectedly been set upon by seven Turkish galleys, and to save herself the capitana had abandoned her company. The Convent and people of Malta were confused and disturbed that three galleys and their crews should thus fall into the hands of Turks. But toward evening of the same day the Magistral galley entered port alone with an identical tale having had to abandon the two remaining galleys. The Grand Master in particular was deeply disturbed by the reports; he donated his 28-bank Magistral galley to the Order including armament, equipment, and oarsmen. But several days later a saettia of Scio (Chios) arrived at Malta and reported the two missing galleys to be lying in the port of Candia (Heraklion), captured off Cape Spada by seven galleys of the Duchy's Guard commanded by Filippo Pasqualigo. Pending further investigation by a commission of four knights who would, among other things, review Avogadro's sailing orders, General Avogadro and Captains San Martino and Laudun were removed from their positions and incarcerated in Fort Saint Elmo. Over the next month there arrived tales penned by captives of demeaning treatment as prisoners-of-war. In the meanwhile Infidel oarsmen, citizens of countries with which Venice had friendly relations, had been liberated.

The Council appointed Prior of Ireland Don Pedro Gonzales Mendoza ambassadeur extraordinaire to the Holy See and Venice. En route Rome he was to consult with the Viceroys of Sicily and Naples, complaining as he would at Rome of the illegal and unwarranted seizure at sea in a fury of artillery and musketry of two of the Order's galleys. The galleys had even been towed into Candia Town's harbor poop-first with the colors of Saint John trailing in the sea, a custom normally reserved for mortal enemies defeated in combat at sea. At Venice Mendoza's lamentations, however, were effectively countered by charges Venetian merchantmen were being waylaid at sea by Maltese corsairs and that Infidel and other passengers and merchandise were being summarily removed, the passengers imprisoned or held for ransom, the merchandise going the way of plunder.[23]

During this period the Grand Master's nephew Commander François d'Astorg de Ségreville was appointed Ambassadeur Extraordinaire to the Catholic Court at Madrid with orders to elicit sympathy for the Order of Hospitallers and pressure on Venice. He was to be accompanied by Giovan Otto Bosio, an experienced diplomat able to interpret right as wrong and vice-versa. Commander Juste de Fay Gerlande of Auvergne was similarly dispatched to the French Court of Hospitaller King Henry III. Malta was going to need all the assistance it could muster. The three ambassadors were transported to

Messina by the three galleys of the Religion, that is, by the 28-bank capitana *Santa Maria de la Vittoria* originally a Magistral capitana new in 1568, the 25-bank *San Pietro* laid down at Marseille in 1577 but not entering service until 1579, commanded at the time by Don Juan Enriquez, and a later 25-bank Magistral galley *La Speranza* new in 1582 donated to the Order by Grand Master Verdalle. These three galleys were now commanded by Regent of the Galleys Francisco de Valencia in succession of Girolamo Avogadro who had been charged with criminal conduct. Departing Messina on 18 October the galleys the following night heard several discharges of artillery from the castle at Gozo. Investigating, they discovered four galliots from Bizerta had put a party ashore and raided Rabat, the city surrounding the castle, carrying into slavery seventy of its citizens plus plunder. Adverse winds, however, prevented pursuit. Grand Master and Council were highly incensed by the obvious scorn with which the corsairs regarded Gozo Governor Jorge Fortugno and by his failure to maintain an adequate guard. A committee of inquiry was formed which severely censured Fortugno. It is often quipped that when it rains it pours, and carelessness and culpability had been raining on Malta under Cassière and Verdalle. On the other hand, indefensibility of Gozo had for some time been a matter of deep concern to Grand Master Verdalle given a Galley Squadron of only four galleys. In August he had asked Gozitans for voluntary contributions to a defense fund and had levied a tax on agricultural production. On 13 August the Pope had weighed in with a Papal Indulgence forgiving sins of those contributing to the defense fund.[24]

During the year the Convent had a large galleon built to its specifications able to securely transport grain from Sicily and other producing locales to Malta. Former Romegas protege René de Pins of Provence was appointed captain, serving well in his new capacity. Regent Valencia departed once more with the three galleys for Messina where the capitana *Santa Maria de la Vittoria* was exchanged for a new *Vittoria* constructed at Naples. On the return voyage the galleys transported to Malta Monsignor Pier Francesco Costa of Albenga, Apostolic Delegate to the Diocese of Malta and new Inquisitor in succession of Monsignor Federico Cefalotto. Also during 1583 a tithe on the plunder of every armed vessel flying the flag of Malta was levied in support of the Monastery of Saint Ursula quartered in the former

Magistral Palace at Birgu, the tithe varying with the number of resident nuns. Niccolò Orsini di Rivalta passed away in 1583. Received into the Order 55 years earlier during the few years between Rhodes and Malta, his historic perspective would be sorely missed. He was succeeded as Bailiff of Naples by Admiral Pompeo Soardo, Soardo in turn succeeded as Admiral by Commander Bernardino Scaglia who a few months later succeeded to the Priory of Capua and was in turn succeeded as Admiral by former Seneschal Giovan Francesco della Motta returning from ten years of retirement. Forty-two years a Hospitaller, Soardo of Bergamo also passed away during the year and was succeeded as Bailiff of Naples by Motta who was succeeded in turn as Admiral by Certorio Cagnolo. Similarly in the Langue of Castile Dom Vasco da Cunha was appointed Bailiff of Lango while Aragon's Grand Conservator Don Lupe de Híjar was appointed Bailiff of Caspe, Bailiff of Negroponte Geronimo de Homedes succeeding to Grand Conservator. Luis de Quintanilla who a bit later succeeded Homedes as Grand Conservator left the Bailiwick of Negroponte to Catalan Adrián de Maimon.[25]

The information-gathering phase of the proceedings against General of the Galleys Girolamo Avogadro was concluded following five months of investigation, and the facts of the matter were presented to a Board of Inquiry on 9 January 1584. Pozzo does not share all of those facts, but Avogadro must have believed the seven assailing galleys to be Turkish, a natural assumption under the circumstances. Had he known they were Venetian, he would also have known that fact would soon become public knowledge. Thus he was not guilty of falsehoods but rather guilty of command failures and poor judgment. The immediate background presented to the Board encompassed an earlier encounter with four Turkish sailing ships anchored under the island of Ialy (Yiali) between Lango (Kos) and Nisiros. Without consulting his captains Avogadro assailed the largest Turk, a galleon carrying 500 passengers as well as crew and marines. He was followed by the Magistral galley under Laudun de Goût. Not so *San Iacomo* under Hardemont and *San Giovanni* under Somaia which assailed a second Turkish ship which was taken with 60 Turks dead. The large galleon, however, fended off attack and was abandoned by the assailants as was the smaller ship taken earlier by the other two galleys. It was the judgment of the Board of Inquiry that had all four galleys assailed the galleon together, she would have been taken and the three smaller Turkish vessels, immobilized in the absence of wind, would have struck their colors. The Board's second finding dealt with failure to follow orders which specified the four galleys return from the Levant by way of the North African coast and not by way of Karpathos and Venetian waters in the passage north of Crete. This order seemed to stem from the February 1583 capture of Diego Brochero's galleon and prizes. There was no finding concerning Avogadro's failure to come to the defense of *San Iacomo* and *San Giovanni* when attacked by the Venetians. He was condemned to one year incarceration in Castle Saint Angelo and to three years loss of income from the Bailiwick of Santo Stefano which was diverted to the Common Treasury.[26]

Having concluded the case against Avogadro, Grand Master and Council appointed Charles de Grasse-Briançon General of the Galleys succeeding both Avogadro and Regent Francisco de Valencia. Upon Briançon's nomination Jean de Vassadel-Vaqueiras was appointed to command of the squadron capitana or flagship. The two Hospitaller galleys seized by Venetians in August 1583, *San Iacomo* and *San Giovanni*, reached Malta from Corfu on 26 February 1584 but in very poor condition. So, too, were the crews following six months captivity, this despite the Grand Master's frequent dispatch to Corfu of a frigate carrying fresh foods and fresh clothing as well as money with which to relieve prisoner circumstances. Senior of the two captains Philippe de Tuilier Hardemont of the Priory of Champagne, thought to be in his late-thirties, died at Syracuse en route to Malta. He was succeeded in command of *San Iacomo* by Don Hernando de Heredia. Pier Francesco Somaia of *San Giovanni* was placed under arrest for failing to take the smaller Turk at Ialy under tow and, additionally, as culpable in the loss of *San Giovanni*. Somaia was further accused of having killed one of his own soldiers, of having mistreated younger knights of the caravan, and other excesses. Don Hernando de Hinistrosa succeeded Somaia in command of *San Giovanni*.[27]

Ambassador Pedro Gonzales de Mendoza sped once again to Rome and Venice, this time in connection with the earlier detention of Diego Brochero. Having armed at Messina a large galleon for corsair activity against Infidels, and then having captured in combat two large Turkish sailing vessels, Diego Brochero, his galleon, and captures were seized in turn at an uninhabited cove in the Archipelago by the same Venetian squadron which later took two of the Malta galleys. Sent to oars of the capturing galleys, the prisoners were eventually taken to Venice. This time Mendoza demanded immediate release of Brochero, his officers, his crew, his galleon, and his Turkish captures as having been taken in Turkish waters under the rules of war.

During the month the *Galleon* and *Galleonetto of the Religion* were at the loading docks of Girgenti (Agrigento) when surprised by a furious storm which the galleonetto (a Maltese term meaning the smaller of two galleons) was unable to withstand. She broke loose of her moorings and was thrown up on the beach where crew, most appurtenances, and artillery were rescued but where the ship was lost. The larger galleon also broke loose of her moorings and went to the bottom of the harbor in spite of the best efforts of Captain René de Pins. Loss of these two vessels caused the Grand Master additional concern for two galliots raiding the North African coast. He dispatched the galley capitana under her skipper Jean de Vassadel-Vaqueiras to locate the galliots but Vaqueiras was unable to find anything. Thankfully, not even wreckage.[28]

Toward the end of April there arrived at Malta four galleys and a galliot of the Grand Duke of Tuscany's Order of Santo Stefano under command of their General Tommaso dei Medici. Arriving with them were Don Diego Brochero and other Hospitallers officering Brochero's galleon about whom the Grand Master over many months had been pleading for release from "illegal" detention. Brochero arrived at Malta to a mixture of sympathy and misguided anger at Venetians. Not released were his crew, his galleon, and his captures presumably returned to Turkish authorities. Medici had come in hope of a combined operation in the Levant with the five galleys of Malta. The operation was negotiated with a view to establishing the seniority of the Order of Jerusalem vis-a-vis the new Order of Santo Stefano to which Medici, an acclaimed veteran of the Battle of Lepanto, agreed.[29]

With command structure established and agreed, the nine galleys and single galliot departed Malta on 6 May 1584 bound directly to the Levant full of hope for fortuitous results. They were not long on the road, however, before forced to return by adverse weather. Eleven days following departure the capitana, *San Giovanni*, and *Buonaventura/ San Iacomo*, all three of Malta, returned to port without information concerning the other seven. Five additional days later the five oared Tuscan vessels also returned. Malta's *San Pietro* and Laudun de Goût's former Magistral galley called *La Speranza*, though, made it all the way to Cape Buonandrea in eastern Libya in expectation of a rendezvous with the others. With no rendezvous, they returned to Malta on 3 June. In the meanwhile the other eight oared vessels had again departed this time for Barbaria concerning which Grand Master and Council had ordered the route by way of the islands of Lampedusa, Pantelleria, Cimbalo (Zembra), and Galita 20 nautical miles off the coast of western Tunisia. From there the two squadrons were to take course for Cape Pula in southeastern Sardinia thence to Cape Carbonara on the far side of Cagliari, north to the Tuscan island of Montecristo and then south along the Roman coast past Mount Circe and finally to Sicily where the plunder was to be divided. There being no plunder to divide, the Malta galleys proceeded to Naples where there were various goods and coin waiting for transport to Malta.[30]

Claude de Lorraine, Knight of Aumale and Knight of Malta (cousin to Claude de Lorraine, Duke of Aumale), arrived at Malta from France in July 1584 aboard his own galley with a large number of gentlemen adventurers embarked. Also cousin to Henry I Prince of Joinville and Duke of Guise, he was received by the Grand Master and Council with all due honor. During the reception his captain, Hospitaller Philibert de Foissy-Chamesson, put to sea for several days and captured a garbo with merchandise and fifty Moorish crew. Aumale intended a corsair venture into the Levant and was thus spurred to an early departure. Grand Master Verdalle assigned the two remaining Hospitaller galleys *San Giovanni* under Don Hernando de Hinistrosa of Burgos and *Santa Maria* commanded by senior Captain Baldassar Marchetti of Messina as company with instructions to return in 20 days. They did. The other three Malta galleys under command of General Briançon waited at Licata for coin with which to purchase grain for the Università of Malta. While waiting these three took in the Gulf of Bendicari at Licata's doorstep a large brigantine and accompanying felucca commanded by a renegade called Benedetto. He would be burned at the stake at Malta by the Inquisition as an example to would-be renegades. Thirty-nine Turks and Moors were also taken captive while a near-equal number of Christian oarsmen were liberated.[31]

Gian Andrea Doria, Commander of the Catholic Armada or Spanish Mediterranean Galley Armada, returning from the Barbary Coast with 40 galleys at August-end visited Malta for four days, only ten of the galleys entering port, the others anchoring at Saint Paul's Bay. The visit was presumed by Verdalle to demonstrate Spanish Crown support for Malta in her dispute with Venice. Upon Doria's departure the Admiral was presented a gold goblet encrusted with jewels originally presented to Grand Master l'Isle-Adam by King Henry VIII during the former's 1528 visit to England.[32] In reality, Doria's visit was for the purpose of confirming or allaying a Vice-Regal suspicion Verdalle wished a closer relationship with the French Crown.

Pope Gregory XIII having located a galley hull at Naples in turn donated the hull to Malta. Laudun de Goût was ordered to Naples with his *La Speranza* where the latter's armament was transferred to the new galley to be called *Santa Marta*. She was described as ideal for corsair operations, probably meaning fast with a boarding rambade but no spur. As suggested by the foregoing, Verdalle spent considerable time dealing with or simply pondering the Venice matter, but without advancing Malta's interests. There had been no movement toward release of Brochero's galleon crew or return of the galleon. As importantly, the sense Venice had the upper hand and that the proud Order of Saint John was impotent weighed heavily on the Grand Master. There was a further sense of injustice stemming from the Order's aid to Venice in each of the Republic's wars with the Ottomans, while Venice had failed to come to the aid of Malta during any of the four Great Sieges of 1444, 1480, 1522, and 1565. A Venetian merchantman delivering materials to Malta ordered by Malta was seized. In retaliation each of the Order's commanderies in Venetian territory was seized while financial support of individual Venetian Hospitallers was terminated. In October Briançon with three Maltese galleys joined Aumale on the coast of North Africa, but all four galleys returned to Malta with only a handful of Moors taken from a garbo.[33]

During the year 1584 Admiral Centorio Cagnolo was promoted to Bailiff of Santa Eufemia upon death of incumbent Ubertino di Solaro, and was succeeded as Admiral by Pirro Melzi of Milan who a bit later was promoted to Bailiff of Naples upon the death of Giovan Francesco Langosco de Conti della Motta and who was succeeded as Admiral by Rinaldo Nari of Syracuse. Castile's Bailiff of Novaville Antonio Maldonado advanced to Bailiff of Lora upon death of Martín Duero Monroy. Antonio Maldonado was in turn succeeded as Bailiff of Novaville by Grand Chancellor Luis de Quintanilla. Francisco de

Valencia succeeded to the dignity of Grand Chancellor and was himself succeeded as Bailiff of Lango by Luís d'Alvarez de Távora of Portugal who would be content with this dignity for sixty years until his death in December 1643. The Grand Master on authority of the Chapter General appointed as Seneschal his nephew Jean François d'Astorg de Ségreville. *Népotisme*.[34]

Fifty-three years an Hospitaller, Monroy had been wedded to Donna Catalina Miranda and was survived by Hospitaller sons Clemente and Martín the Younger. He was also survived by a reputation as the finest *procurador* (attorney) and diplomat in living Hospitaller memory. Finally, he was additionally survived by the elaborate sarcophagus cited in Chapter IV upon which rests in repose his own detailed lifelike sculpture, armored with an Hospitaller Grand Cross on the breastplate.[35]

Early in 1585 Ségreville returned from his embassy to the Court of Spain. Initiated in the Autumn of 1583 in hope of persuading King Philip to weigh in on the Malta-Venice (Brochero) impasse, the King had recently directed his own ambassador to the Holy See to propose a face-saving compromise. Niccolò Grimaldi of Genoa, appointed Ambassadeur Extraordinaire to the courts of Germany only months earlier than Ségreville's appointment, had not proved so successful. His task had been to pry loose past-due responsions. Michele Cadamosto of Lodi was appointed Grimaldi's successor. He was in March escorted as far as Sicily by the Order's five galleys still under General Briançon. The five were the capitana *Santa Maria de la Vittoria* under Jean de Vassadel-Vaqueiras, *Santa Marta* under Laudun de Goût, *San Giovanni* under Don Hernando de Hinistrosa, *San Iacomo* under Don Hernando de Heredia, and *San Pietro* under Don Juan Enriquez. Departing Malta at the same time was former Inquisitor Monsignor Pier Francesco Costa who a bit earlier had been succeeded by Monsignor Ascanio Libertano of Castel Barchio in the Diocese of Fano.

The five galleys put their passengers ashore at Syracuse and took on provisions for an excursion into the Levant. In the Levant they were joined by the galley of Knight of Aumale and Knight of Malta Claude de Lorraine, aged 21 years and hoping to develop warrior credentials. Under Chios in the eastern Aegean the six galleys came upon a large germa which when assailed put up an obstinate defense. It is not clear whether the germa mounted her own artillery, but she took such a pounding from galley bow-chasers she was sent to the bottom. One hundred thirty-two crew between Turks and Moors were taken off as were about 300 black Africans destined for Ottoman slave markets. While a rich haul of general cargo and coin was taken off before the ship went under, there was also rampant disorder among victorious self-seekers which left little for the Common Treasury and which brought criminal charges against general and captains (none removed from command assignments).[36]

Pope Gregory XIII suddenly and unexpectedly reached the end of his life on 10 April 1585. Eighty-three years of age, he had governed the Church for 13 years, one month, and three days. He was succeeded on 24 April by Felice Peretti di Montalto who then took the name of Sixtus V. Ségreville was appointed Ambassador of Obedience to render the Order's obedience to the new Pope and to receive confirmation of pre-existing privileges. Giovan Battista Rondinelli of Florence was similarly appointed new Resident Ambassador to the Holy See in succession of Giulio Cesare Malvicino who undertook a special embassy to Turin to congratulate in the name of Grand Master and Religion Duke of Savoy Charles Emmanuel I on his marriage at Saragoza to Infanta Catherine Michelle of Spain, youngest surviving daughter of Philip II.[37]

The six galleys returned to Malta early in May, but rather than go through an extended pratique engendered by suspicion of peste infestation, five re-deployed almost immediately on 11 May. Left at Marsamuscietto was *Santa Marta* because skipper Laudun de Goût had been laid low. And because General Briançon and other knights were also under the weather, Grand Master and Council appointed Aumale General of the Galleys in succession of Briançon. Aumale would deploy and return within 35 days having removed 140 Turks and Moors from two rich germas. While sacking the second of the two germas, however, Aumale discovered 11 Turkish galleys in the vicinity and abandoned to slavery his boarding party among whom were twelve Knights of the Habit. No formal inquiry was convened, nor was there ever a report concerning any of those abandoned.[37]

The five galleys deploying in May under Aumale had hardly returned to port when in mid-June four Turkish galleys appeared in the Malta Channel between Sicily and Gozo. The Maltese exited in pursuit, but the Turkish vessels had an insurmountable lead and could not be overtaken. Continuing on orders of the Council by way of Trapani to

Palermo they encountered a heavily-laden ship of Venice, waylaid her, and forced her to take course for Malta where she was sequestered with crew and cargo pending satisfactory resolution of the impasse between Order and Republic as proposed by Enriquez de Guzman, 2nd Count of Olivares and the Catholic King's Ambassador to the Holy See.[38]

Also Count of Alba de Liste, Guzmán arrived at Naples en route Palermo to be crowned Viceroy of Sicily in succession of the deceased Marcantonio de Colonna and of interim Viceroy Juan Alfonso Bisbal. He was escorted from Naples to Palermo by eight galleys of Sicily under command of Don Pedro de Leyva, General of Sicilian Galleys. This was the same Pedro de Leyva who in 1560 was taken captive as a child during the disastrous Battle of Djerba. Also in escort were the five galleys of Malta under Aumale which returned to Malta at end-August 1585. There they were greeted by rumor that Beylerbey (Viceroy) Hassan Veneziano of Tripoli with a large squadron of galleys was moving against Valletta. At Malta in addition to the island's squadron were 17 galleys of Naples under General Pedro de Toledo with the announced intention of raiding North African corsair havens, meanwhile seeking pilots and others with practical experience among shallows off the coast. Jean-Philibert de Foissy-Chamesson was among early volunteers. With the Tripoli rumor scotched and dissuaded by contrary winds, the Naples squadron retired directly to Naples while the eight Sicilians retired directly to Sicily. Accompanying the latter was Hospitaller Commander Don Pietro la Rocca to congratulate the new Viceroy on his appointment.[39]

Claude de Lorraine, Knight of Aumale, was recalled to France in September 1585 by the Prince of his family on the occasion of a new league established against the King of Navarre called the Catholic League. He renounced his position as General of the Galleys four months following accession and was succeeded by Prior of Capua Bernardino Scaglia. Francesco Bondelmonte of Florence was appointed to command of *Santa Marta* succeeding the deceased Laudun de Goût, and upon Scaglia's nomination Vincenzo Anastagi of Perugia was appointed flag captain succeeding Jean de Vassadel-Vaqueiras.[40] Anastagi was an acclaimed veteran of 1565's Great Siege of Malta during which he had commanded a cavalry detachment of fewer than 250 based behind enemy lines at Mdina. His unit was adept at opportune harassment, and on 7 August of that year raided the camps of Ottoman units conducting a major assault on Senglea's Fort Saint Michael and on Birgu's proximate walls. His disturbance to the rear of the assault suggested the long-expected arrival from Sicily of a Christian relief force, and the assault dissipated in Ottoman panic.[41]

Anastagi returned to Malta in September 1585 following 18 years in Papal service as military commander of Rome's Castel Sant'Angelo connected by fortified passage to Saint Peter's Basilica. His presence was such that in 1575 it had been celebrated in a full length portrait by Doménikos Theotokópoulos known as El Greco, the portrait now a part of New York City's Frick Collection. Anastagi's nomination by Squadron Commander Bernardino Scaglia to command of the squadron capitana had been quickly approved by the Council of State. He had no known enemies, but within days of arrival at Malta he was "murdered" by two fellow knights whose identities remain undisclosed to this writing.

Aumale departed Malta aboard his own galley and was accompanied as far as Syracuse by four galleys of the Malta squadron. There the squadron was joined by Leyva's galleys of Sicily for a campaign in the Levant which was first postponed by bad weather and then aborted by the approach of winter. Together they made a circuit of Sicily during which two small corsair galliots were taken off Augusta yielding a good number of new oarsmen and a modestly greater number of Christians liberated from corsair oars.[41]

In November 1585 Bernardino Scaglia sped with four galleys to Messina and Palermo in response to a request from the Viceroy of Sicily sent to the Grand Master by fast courier advising that Beylerbey of Tripoli Hassan Aga (Hassan Veneziano by whom Miguel de Cervantes was for five years enslaved at Algiers) would be joined by other Barbary corsairs planning to come or rendezvous at the time of the new moon in January at the island of Pantelleria approximately midway between Sicily and Tunisia. Nothing came of the matter but the four galleys did not return to Malta until May.[42]

During 1585 Grand Commander Charles de Grasse-Briançon swapped dignities with Bailiff of Manosque François de Puget-Chasteuil. Grand Chancellor Francisco de Valencia was appointed Bailiff of Novaville succeeding the deceased Luis de Quintanilla, and was himself succeeded as Grand Chancellor by Don Martín de Nieto. Isuardo di Sanmartino was appointed Prior of Pisa succeeding the deceased Antonio Maria Palio. The Council at year-end confirmed the prior year's decree mandating a squadron of five armed galleys as a number consistent with the Order's reputation. But the number was reinterpreted to give effect to galleys in shipyards for modification or repair. War against French Huguenots was drawing down the number of qualified captains available.[40]

French King Henry III pled for and obtained from Pope Sixtus V indulgences or levies on Church entities within the Kingdom in the amount of 100,000 scudos to fund war against the Huguenots. Because the Order's properties within the Kingdom were subject to the levies, Grand Master and Council dispatched Jean-Philibert de Foissy-Chamesson as Ambassadeur Extraordinaire to Rome and France with orders to resist levies on grounds the Order of Malta was also at war with the unfaithful. At Paris Foissy-Chamesson coordinated with Resident Ambassador Pierre d'Esparbez de Lussan their position and posture before the Crown with emphasis on insufficient cash flow to fund any new levies. Perhaps also reflecting conferral of the Priory of Toulouse on Antoine-Scipion de. Joyeuse as requested in 1582, the Hospitaller King agreed to levies limited to 25,000 scudos, one-quarter the proposed amount.[43]

Putting to sea in April 1586 was a new Magistral galley outfitted and armed at the Grand Master's expense but for the hull which was contributed by the Order. Commanded by René de Pins, she in May and June made a 24-day excursion into the Levant in the company of *Santa Marta*, seizing a caramussal with a cargo of hats among other rich items as well as 117 captives.[44]

Having wintered at Messina and Palermo, the four galleys of the Religion returned to Malta in May 1586. The four were the capitana *Santa Maria de la Vittoria* commanded by General Bernardino Scaglia himself, *Santa Marta* commanded by Francesco Bondelmonte, *San Giovanni* under Don Hernando de Hinistrosa, and *San Iacomo* under Don Hernando de Heredia. As combined operations against Infidel corsairs were planned, these four were accompanied by nine galleys of Sicily under Don Pedro de Leyva. Departing Malta the thirteen galleys investigated Lampedusa and Pantelleria between Malta and Tunisia before falling upon Tunisia's Cape Bon and Porto Farina

(Ghar al Milh). From Porto Farina the galleys sailed north to Marettimo and Favignana west of Sicily, and thence up the east coast of Sardinia and down the Roman coast of mainland Italy, the latter to satisfy Pope Sixtus. During the entire expedition not a single enemy vessel was sighted. The four galleys of Malta and seven of Sicily reached Malta on 10 July transporting Monsieur Jeannot de Loubenx de Verdalle, brother of the Grand Master.[45]

Killed early in June 1586 was Henri d'Angouleme, Hospitaller Grand Prior of France and illegitimate son of King Henry II of France by Lady Janet Fleming, at Aix-en-Provence in a duel with Baron of Castellane Philippe Altoviti, also mortally wounded in the duel. Grand Hospitaller Charles de la Rama du Plessis-Hérault as senior Hospitaller succeeded to the Dignity despite the candidacy of Francis of Lorraine, Marquis de Chaussin, who was not a professed knight. By hand-delivered letter dated 23 July, however, King Henry III requested the Priory devolve on his nephew Charles Batard d'Orleans. The Grand Master politely observed and regretted the Grand Priory had already been awarded and that Charles Batard d'Orleans was (also) not a professed knight. The latter was accordingly received into the Langue of France in 1587 and Plessis-Hérault found it politic to step down.[46]

Duke of Savoy Charles Emmanuel I decided to solemnize baptism of his first born and heir-apparent in the presence of princes and ambassadors. Having regained his health, Bishop of Malta Tomás Gargallo offered to represent the Order and islands at his own expense, and his offer was accepted. The capitana and *La Speranza* were readied and departed Malta on 16 September 1586 transporting not just Bishop Gargallo but the Grand Master's brother, as well, both bound for Savona and thence overland, Monsieur Verdalle to France and Gargallo to Turin for a protracted ceremony which took place in May of 1587. Among many others Cardinal Paolo Emilio Sfondrati represented the Pope at the ceremony, Madame de Carnavalet (Kernevenoy in the Celtic language of Brittany; her Hotel Carnavalet would become today's Musée Carnavalet dedicated to the history of Paris) represented Queen Mother of France Catherine de' Medici, Prince Gian Andrea Doria and the Marquess de Los Garres represented Infante Felipe of Spain, while Agostino Nani as Ambassadeur Extraordinaire represented the Republic of Venice. By then the two Hospitaller galleys had long since returned to Malta by way of Genoa and Livorno.[47]

During 1586 Don Lupe del Poio was promoted to Castellan of Amposta succeeding Francisco de Pomar. Within the Langue of Italy Rinaldo Nari stepped down as Admiral and was succeeded by former Resident Ambassador to the Holy See Giulio Cesar Malvicino. Luigi Tana of Chieri, 39 years an Hospitaller, advanced to the dignity of Prior of Lombardia succeeding the deceased Girolamo Gravina. Cardinal Ferdinando dei Medici was appointed by the Church as Protector of the Order of Jerusalem, and beginning in the following year when successor to his older brother as Grand Duke of Tuscany he continued to keep a benevolent eye on Malta while bringing progressive rule to Tuscany.

Also during 1586 Grand Master and Council forbade the practice of galley salutes when entering and leaving port and for embarkation and debarkation of persons of rank, a practice not observed by the Ottomans and costly to Christians. As with many vanguards of reform, this initiative had to be revoked in 1589, particularly in Spanish ports. A prohibition against carrying and storing in private quarters arquebuses and pistols in the towns of Malta similarly met with popular resistance but more success. Not only failing to see the good in prohibiting fire arms in public places, Marshal Pierre de Sacconyn kept up such a public and unyielding resistance he was ultimately defrocked with loss of all income and perquisites, and was incarcerated in Fort Saint Elmo and on the island of Gozo. He was succeeded as Marshal by Commander François de Lange de la Chenault.[48]

Pierre de Sacconyn did not go meekly. For two years following his release from imprisonment he petitioned Popes Gregory XIV and successors until Pope Clement VIII in 1593 issued a Brief restoring his Dignity. It was too late for that as the Dignity of Marshal had changed hands several times, and so Pierre de Sacconyn was appointed Prior of Auvergne. Incumbent Prior of Auvergne Claude de Montmorillon, however, refused to step down from a position he had held for two years. This refusal begat additional Papal Briefs and insufficient sympathy from a Crown court. Eventually Montmorillon was forced out of office.[49] There were more than domestic disturbances within the Convent. Those from without were equally upsetting with major consequences. Pope Sixtus V did not hide his disgust both with the Grand Master and with the entire Religion, while Cardinal Girolamo

Rusticucci had made his displeasure clear in the matter of a Venetian ship detained earlier and of a saettia cargo vessel recently detained in Venetian waters of Zante (Zakinthos) almost certainly the property of citizens of the Republic. The ship detained earlier was presumably the Venetian merchantman seized at Valletta in October 1584. Pope Sixtus then ordered both ship and saettia returned together with all persons and property removed, and that thenceforth all vessels proceeding to the Levant transporting Christians with merchandise other than prohibited items should be left undisturbed. This edict, which appeared to have been drafted by Venice, threatened to put licensed piracy or corsairing out of business. Grand Master and Council appointed three ambassadors experienced in these matters to proceed to Rome to present alternative views and considerations. These three were Admiral and former Resident Ambassador to the Holy See Giulio Malvicino, Lieutenant Treasurer and corsair captain Jean-Philibert de Foissy-Chamesson, and veteran diplomat Catalan Onofre Belver, all three fully briefed concerning facts and consequences. They were reminded the Religion conducted a just war sanctioned not only by custom and precedent but sanctioned as well by the Holy See, by Christian emperors, kings, and princes, and one necessary to overcome Infidel power in Syria, in Rhodes, and in all the cities, fortresses, mainland, and islands occupied by an enemy with the strength to make war by sea or land until they should occupy all of Europe, Asia, and Africa. A somewhat more cogent thesis was that the Ottomans at the time maintained 60 to 70 galleys guarding their coasts and islands against corsair incursions which would otherwise be free to themselves raid Christian coasts and islands.[50]

The three ambassadors departed Malta on 6 April 1587 aboard the Magistral galley commanded by René de Pins. They were put ashore at Messina while the galley continued to Spain on advice a large sum of Hospitaller responsions en route Malta by way of Catalonia had been stolen. Also embarked aboard the Magistral galley were Grand Conservator Adrián de Maimon and Don Esteban de Claramonte ordered to inform themselves concerning the theft and to seek recovery of the money. His Most Christian Majesty King Henry III of France had meanwhile received the Grand Master's letter of the past August regretting the Order's inability to confer the Dignity of Prior of France on the King's nephew Charles Batard d'Orleans, earlier denied Francis of Lorraine, Marquis de Chaussin. The King had consequently obtained from Pope Sixtus V a Papal Brief annulling award of the Dignity to Charles de la Rama du Plessis-Hérault, withdrawing renunciation of the Marquis de Chaussin, and awarding the Dignity of Prior of France to Charles Batard d'Orleans. Plessis-Hérault was to receive the Commandery at Troyes he had before promotion to Grand Prior. Truly, it must have seemed to Grand Master Verdalle the pressures of his office were overwhelming. In consequence, the Grand Master's standing with the Holy See took yet another severe blow. On the other hand, he was able to present to the Council a resolution of the matter which had been taken out of his hands and for which he was not responsible.[51]

Compliance with the Brief so that it did not appear a dictat was placed in the hands of the Grand Master's nephew François de Ségreville who proceeding to France presented compliance merely as a formality among other matters and a resolution of the King's request which would have occurred in any event. One of the other matters was failure of Prior of Champagne Michel de Seurre de Lumigny to remit his Priory's share of the 50,000 scudo property tax authorized by the July 1583 Chapter General. Elevated to his Dignity only upon insistence of the Court, perhaps the Court could assist the Order in collecting the impost.[52]

The four galleys of the Religion returned from Messina and en route captured a vessel with thirty Turks on board. All four later proceeded to the Levant in company with the Grand Master's galley, the capitana, *Santa Marta*, and *Speranza*, however, soon returning with spar problems. The other two, *Santa Maria delle Vittoria* and the new Magistral galley, continued on and took a caramussal and a germa, and then during their return, near Pozzalo, Sicily, captured two enemy brigantines which had despoiled the Church of Santa Cruz at Crotone in Calabria. Forty captive church-goers were liberated together with 60 Christian oarsmen while increasing to 122 the total number of captives.[53]

Bernardino Scaglia completed his tour as General in September 1587 and was succeeded by Bailiff of the Morea Louis de Mailloc Sacquenville, and upon the latter's nomination Tiberio Campolo of Messina was elected captain of the flagship succeeding Scaglia himself.[54]

On 28 April Grand Master Verdalle had written to Pope Sixtus V declaring his wish to again visit Rome, and by return letter under date of 22 July the Pope invited him to do so during the month of November. The Sacred Council was informed Verdalle planned to leave Malta in late October. Some on the Council wished to attend his journey, among these Bishop Gargallo. Others expressed opposition, some out of low regard for the Grand Master, some in fear of a further strain in Papal relations. Among these were Bailiff of Santa Eufemia Centorio Cagnolo, Bailiff of Naples Pirro Melzi, and Bailiff of Novaville Francisco de Valencia. The solicited invitation, however, made the Grand Master's visit to Rome a foregone conclusion. While the Grand Master planned his visit to Rome his corsair galley commanded by René de Pins returned from a raid along the coast of North Africa in company with the brigantine and frigate of Commander Octave Castellane-Salernes of Provence and two other frigates. Together they had seized a caramussal yielding an unreported number of captives plus a londro with a crew of 30 Turks, two cargoes, and two hulls.[55]

Meanwhile a raid on the coast of Anatolia had been proposed to the Grand Master and Council utilizing the four galleys of the squadron as well as the Magistral galley. To be guided by Greeks familiar with the destination, the five galleys were to proceed under General Sacquenville by way of Sapienza Island off the Morea's Modone (Methoni), traversing at night the passage between Cerigo (Kythera) and Cerrigotto (Antikythera) before climbing the east coast of the Morea to Cape Skillaion. From Cape Skillaion the five galleys were to cross the Saronic Gulf to Cape Colonne (Cape Sounion) unobserved and thence north through the d'Oro Strait between the mainland and Andros before crossing the Aegean to Mitilini. Still unobserved the five galleys were to proceed south at night along the Kara Burun Peninsula of the Anatolian mainland to Casale Monsalada (the fortress at Cesme). There troops were to be put ashore two hours before daybreak under command of Claude de Montmorillon to sack the castle at first light. The plan was approved and the five galleys accompanied by the brigantine and frigate of Castellane-Salernes departed Malta on 15 August 1587. Led by Montmorillon, the unexpected break-in and sack were less than satisfying. While no details survive, it may be presumed Montmorillon found the fortress reinforced and impregnable. Fifteen hundred nautical miles and 25 days later the expeditionary force returned to Malta with 200 captives including women and children, some removed from caramussals encountered along the way. Because most male captives were not circumcised, but rather Orthodox Greeks and Genovese, they were liberated with wives and children. There was no report of dead and wounded and no report of plunder other than captives most of whom rightly petitioned the Order for means to return to their homes.[56]

El Greco's Hospitaller Vincenzo Anastagi

Chapter VI

1587–1595

As the Grand Master's departure for Rome approached he asked the Council to deputize Bishop Tomás Gargallo and Commander Giovanni Otto Bosio to put in writing those matters and considerations he should discuss with Pope Sixtus leading to an improved Papal understanding of the Order of Hospitallers and to an improved relationship between Pope and Grand Master. He also asked the Council to place 100 peace-keeping soldiers in the city of Valletta under command of Jean de Marsac-Saillac of Provence. Finally, on 5 November 1587 he convened the Council for a review of matters of good governance. He also appointed as his Lieutenant with full authority to act in his stead during his absence Lepanto veteran and Bailiff of Negroponte Alonso de Tejada of the Langue of Castile. Three days later seven galleys of Sicily under command of Don Pedro de Leyva arrived Malta bringing 600 Spanish infantry under command of Hospitaller Juan della Nucia of Aragon sent by Viceroy and Count of Alba de Liste Diego Enríquez de Guzmán. There was to be no rebellion during this Grand Master's absence.[1]

On 11 November the Grand Master embarked aboard the Malta capitana along with peg-legged Lepanto-veteran Tejada and Council, the capitana accompanied by the three other Malta galleys as well as by his own Magistral galley plus the seven galleys of Sicily, the latter with Leyva's command standard lowered as the Grand Master was in command. All departed Malta in fair weather bound for Messina. At Messina Tejada and Council as well as the seven galleys of Sicily were left behind and the five Malta galleys continued to Gaeta by way of Pozzuoli in the Bay of Naples. At Gaeta the Grand Master was greeted by Cardinal Alessandro Damasceni Peretti di Montalto, 16 year-old great nephew of the Pope, and by a mounted escort of 300 including cavalry as well as many Hospitallers eight of whom were Knights of the Grand Cross. Travelling by carriage from Gaeta he reached Rome on 8 December 1587 in time for breakfast at Villa Mattei

(Villa Celimontana) on the Caelian Hill in Rome, his host Ciriaco Mattei, owner of one of the more comprehensive art collections of his time on display at the villa. Later that day he met the Pope in a full consistory of Cardinals, as did those in his immediate entourage. Ten days later Hugues de Loubenx de Verdalle was made Cardinal-Deacon of Santa Maria in Portico Octaviae by Pope Sixtus V, again in full consistory. During the interim he had numerous private audiences with the Pope during which mutual understanding and respect was developed. This last was the sole reason the Grand Master had wished to visit Rome.[2]

The news of Grand Master Verdalle's elevation to the Cardinalate reached Malta on 20 January 1588 following which spontaneous celebrations took place among the populace and a three-day holiday was declared. The Council of State appointed three ambassadors to the Holy See to thank His Holiness for the honor of having promoted their Grand Master to the Cardinalate. They were also to solicit return to Malta of the Grand Master because of advice from several sources that at Constantinople there was heightened activity to ready the Ottoman Armada for an assault on Malta. The three ambassadors were Commanders Bertrand de Varadier-Saint-Andiol of Provence, Juan Zaportella of Valencia, and Luigi Mazzinghi of Florence. They were consigned two letters, one to His Holiness and the other to the Cardinal Grand Master. They met the Cardinal Grand Master at Messina where he had arrived with the four galleys of the Religion from a detour to Naples requested by Viceroy Juan de Zúñiga y Avellaneda in order that Neapolitans might render the new Cardinal appropriate honors, as did citizens of Messina. It was difficult to comprehend the Cardinal Grand Master was held in widespread disrepute only two months earlier, but such esteem would prove to be fleeting.[3]

Following a quick celebratory visit to Syracuse, the Cardinal Grand Master reached Malta on 10 February 1588 to a tumultuous welcome, but also to advice that at Constantinople the 1586 wedding of Murad III's daughter Ayse Sultan to Ibrahim Pasha, Hungarian *devsirme* and Palace School product formerly Beylerbey of Egypt, had resulted in the groom's transfer to Constantinople as Kapudan Pasha in succession of the deceased Kılıç Ali Pasha. Ibrahim had reportedly made 100 galleys ready for an excursion to the west. Accordingly there was speculation that any such excursion might bypass Malta for Tripoli where locals were restless at Turkish rule represented by Beylerbey Hassan Veneziano and assigned janissaries. Even if Tripoli and not Malta, Malta necessarily recognized the possibility of an incursion coming or going, and necessarily accumulated food and munition stocks.[4]

Cardinal Grand Master Verdalle's second Chapter General convened at Malta on 20 March 1588. Following ceremonial formalities, the eight langues proceeded to election of their own legislators at two per langue. These were Grand Commander François de Puget and François de Vintimille d'Ollières for Provence, Marshal François de Lange de la Chenault and Claude de Montmorillon for Auvergne, Grand Hospitaller Bertrand Pelloquin and Bailiff of the Morea Louis de Mailloc Sacquenville for France, Bishop of Malta Tomás Gargallo and Bailiff of Caspe Geronimo de Hcmedes for Aragon, Prior of Messina Rinaldo Nari and Bailiff of Naples Pirro Melzi for Italy, Andrew Wyse[5] and Gonzalo de Porras cf Écija, Castile, for England, Lieutenant Grand Bailiff Arbogast von Andlau and Romuald von Orsbach for Germany, and Grand Chancellor Martín de Nieto and Antonio de Sampaio for Castile. These Sixteen gathered in Conclave as a Tribunal to decide controversial issues, to attend to supplicants, to make various grants, to consider the state of the Religion, and to consider the current applicability of various aged statutes, reforms, and prohibitions. Among current issues were new rules and procedures for proofs of nobility, re-assignment of grand crosses by Dignity, and re-affirmation of existing rules and regulations. It was likely during or shortly after this Chapter General Andrew Wyse of Waterford, Munster, was appointed Bailiff of Eagle in succession of the sincerely mourned Oliver Starkey. Originally Flemish of the Spanish Netherlands with an English father, a Member of Parliament representing St Albans sitting at Westminster in 1554, veteran of the 1565 Siege of Malta, and learned scribe, poet, and Latin scholar, he was 65 years of age at his passing.[6]

Following the Chapter General, *Cardinal Grand Master Verdalle commissioned Giacomo Bosio to write the History of the Religion, Bosio a man of clear erudition and copious fecundity.*[7]

Since his return from Rome Cardinal Grand Master Verdalle had been outfitting a new Magistral galley called *La Negrilla* to be commanded by Jean de Marsac-Saillac. Marsac-Saillac was the eldest son of Brenguier de Marsac, Seigneur de Saillac 200 kilometers north of Toulouse, and of Jeanne Saunier. He had elected to forego his inheritance to become a soldier of God. The inheritance would go to second son Joye de Marsac. Still in his early thirties, Jean would become perhaps the most capable galley commander in Hospitaller history.[8]

From early April 1588 *La Negrilla* sailed in company with the Cardinal Grand Master's Magistral capitana commanded by Jean de Vassadel-Vaqueiras in succession of René de Pins. These two deployed to the Levant together with a frigate, but encountered no enemy and returned to Malta empty-handed. From 13 April the four galleys of the Religion transported back to Sicily the 600 Spanish infantry helping to keep the peace during the Cardinal Grand Master's absence at Rome. These had been recalled by the Viceroy. But as news of the Ottoman Armada heated up, even amid doubt Malta might be its objective, Cardinal Grand Master and Council believed it expedient to bring in outside soldiers. General Sacquenville was sent to Messina with orders to hire a number of infantry. At Malta four Sector Wardens were appointed with authority to do whatever was necessary to make individual sectors ready for siege. The wardens were Bertrand de Varadier-Saint-Andiol of Provence, Marcantonio Altavilla of Casale Monferrato, Dom Diogo de Souza of Portugal, and Martin von Lesch of Germany. Commander Don Rodrigo Cortés of Catalonia was appointed Captain-at-Arms for Citta Vecchia (Mdina). The four galleys returning from Messina at end-May included a new 28-bank capitana laid down and completed at that city and armed with artillery from the old capitana. They brought with them 200 hired infantry. They were also accompanied by 15 galleys of Naples and seven of Sicily under their respective generals Don Pedro de Toledo and Don Pedro de Leyva on reports Hassan Veneziano, Viceroy of Tripoli, having sacked the town of Patrica 70 kilometers east of Anzio, might appear in local waters with eight galleys and other vessels. But concluding such reports false, the 22 visiting galleys departed the day following their arrival.[9]

The galleys of the Religion rested at Malta for some time before again departing on 16 July 1588 with the Magistral capitana to scour proximate coasts of Calabria, Naples, and Rome in search of Infidel corsairs. General Sacquenville used the excursion to transport to

Civitavecchia 130 captive Turkish oarsmen *purchased from Malta by the Church* for the new Papal Galley Squadron commanded by Orazio Lercari of Genoa. From Civitavecchia the Maltese proceeded to Genoa and did not return to Malta until 27 October, at that time bringing to the Convent Grand Bailiff of Germany Philipp Riedesel zu Camberg, Bailiff of Mallorca Ramón de Veri, and Commander Michele Cadamosto of Lodi, each an ambassador to the Court of Holy Roman Emperor Rudolph II. The Magistral *capitana*, however, proceeded from Genoa to Spain transporting Grand Chancellor Don Martín de Nieto enroute Castile, and Commander Rodrigo Cortés embarked to take delivery of responsions receivable from both Aragon and Castile.

The Cardinal Grand Master's *Negrilla* commanded by Jean de Marsac-Saillac, accompanied by a Magistral brigantine, meanwhile seeking opportunity in the Levant encountered and was severely damaged by a ponderous vessel of Alexandria reinforced with extra artillery and combatants powerful enough to take on ten galleys. She was so powerful as to be stunned by the audacity of a single galley investing. And that's what Marsac-Saillac believed was *Negrilla*'s only chance of survival. Unfurling a Turkish flag as if a galley of the Rhodes Guard she confidently parked herself under the enemy's massive hull. Then her grappling hooks were used by her own desperate combatants to scramble on board the larger vessel and furiously assail the suddenly-stunned enemy while discharging arquebuses as rapidly as they were able to be re-loaded. Midships artillery, too. Enemy fallen mounted. The remainder yielded, 250 Turks, Moors, and Black Africans laid down their arms. The captive vessel was conducted to Malta.

While returning to Malta the four squadron galleys encountered a caramussal transporting janissaries to Tunis. She was bombarded from a distance with (new) explosive incendiaries and went to the bottom; only four Turks survived. In addition to this encounter, Philibert de Foissy-Chamesson had earlier in the year outfitted and armed a new proprietary corsair galley with which he early in June deployed to the Levant. There he successfully preyed on several Turkish caramussals taking 70 captives as well as plunder.[10]

The Cardinal Grand Master had for some time been in the habit of breaking away from his duties at Valletta to stroll in the Buskett Gardens of Malta, a wasteland on arrival of the Hospitallers in

1530 and a wasteland again following 1565's Great Siege of Malta. Twenty-odd years later, however, the 300,000 square meter parkland had revived. Verdalle in this year had constructed on the perimeter a so-called hunting lodge more nearly a palace and now called the Verdalla Palace used by the President of Malta as a summer residence. These strolls had recently been coincident with the undeclared Anglo-Spanish War (1585–1604) during which a Spanish Armada dispatched by King Philip II of Spain (and former King of England as husband of Queen Mary I) failed in a 1588 attempt to escort an allied ground force from France to England for the purpose of de-throning Elizabeth I and re-establishing Catholicism within the country.

Bailiff of Lango Luis d'Alvarez de Távora was given to understand he would be the next Prior of Crato succeeding Don Antonio of Portugal, then a refugee still pretending to the throne of Portugal while living in England under protection of the Crown. During 1588 former Prior of Auvergne Claude de Montmorillon, forced to vacate the Dignity to accommodate a Court designee, was appointed Resident Ambassador to the Court of France. The four galleys of the Religion having returned to Malta from Civitavecchia and Genoa at end-October were at end-November ordered back to Messina to stand by for escort duty in connection with the marriage of former Cardinal Protector and current Grand Duke of Tuscany Ferdinando I de' Medici to Princess Christina of Lorraine, daughter of Duke of Lorraine Charles III and Claude of Valois, and, moreover, niece of King Henry III of France and granddaughter of Queen Mother Catherine de' Medici. Alert to these developments, particularly to approbation approval of the wedding of a member of the Royal family to a former member of the Church, Prior of France Charles de Valois, Batard d'Orleans, petitioned Church and Court to be released from his vows and for similar approval to wed Charlotte, daughter of Henry, Marshal of Amville, afterwards Duke of Montmorency.[11]

From Messina the four Malta galleys were in January 1589 ordered to Livorno and thence to Marseille as were the new Papal Squadron, the Squadron of Tuscany, and that of Genoa, all bringing in the new year in the French port. Shortly afterward Princess Christina and immediate suite embarked aboard the capitana of Tuscany and were transported with all other galleys as company by way of Savona to Livorno.

Early in the year 1589 the Cardinal Grand Master had occasions to display forethought in his dealings with the Spanish. The first of these occasions involved a Venetian-flag cargo vessel which ended up in the port of Malta with a cargo of wine. A customs inspection revealed she was also carrying a large quantity of swords, bars of iron, crude steel, and other war materials originating at Candia and Zante for respective delivery to England and Lisbon. As this was the fourth year of an undeclared war between Spain and England, and as Dom Antonio of Portugal was said to be part of an English expedition under Francis Drake expected to descend on the coast of Spanish Portugal in the Spring or Summer, the Cardinal Grand Master with little forethought informed the Spanish Court of the ship and her cargo. Venetian irritation far outweighed Spanish gratitude. The second and more unworthy occasion involved exposure of a cabal originating among three Portuguese Hospitallers aspiring to restoration of a Portuguese crown. These three, Dom Diogo de Souza, Antonio de Vega, and Pedro de Queirós were detained, questioned by the Inquisition, and imprisoned at Guve on the island of Gozo until ordered released by a Papal Brief Of Pope Clement VIII in 1592. Spain may not have noticed. The Convent did.[12]

The Cardinal Grand Master exchanged his battle-damaged galley *Negrilla* for a new galley laid down and completed at Livorno, artillery and equipment moved from old to new hull. The new *Negrilla* also commanded by Jean de Marsac-Saillac joined the Magistral capitana commanded by Jean de Vassadel-Vaqueiras of Provence and the proprietary galley owned and commanded by Jean-Philibert de Foissy-Chamesson of the Priory of Champagne who had overall command of the three galleys. Embarked with the caravan aboard Foissy-Chamesson's galley was 17 year-old Henri de Saintrailles of the same priory received as a knight only months earlier. These departed Malta early in May for the Levant where they had considerable success above the Cross of Cyprus (vertical axis Alexandria to Karamania, horizontal axis Rhodes to Cyprus) traveled by laden convoys or caravans from Egypt and Cyprus to Constantinople depending on wind. Near Cyprus they encountered and pursued two galleys of the Rhodes Guard beaching on the coast of that island, Ottoman since 1570. While the crews thus avoided capture, they abandoned their ships intact, including 400 Christian oarsmen who were liberated. Rather than plunder and burn the Guard galleys Foissy-Chamesson had them crewed by the liberated oarsmen and detachments from the three Christian galleys. The expanded and strengthened squadron seized several other Turkish vessels from which 260 captives were removed, finding on one of these 4,000 gold sultanas and 90 pieces of valuable brocade.[13]

The four galleys of the Religion having passed the Winter at Marseille, Livorno, Naples, and Messina returned to Malta on 15 May 1589 where command of the galley squadron passed from Louis de Mailloc-Sacquenville to Bailiff of Caspe Geronimo de Homedes. Homedes soon fell ill, however, and senior captain Bertrand de Varadier de Saint-Andiol received into the Order in 1548 was appointed Regent during Homedes' incapacity.[13]

Three of the regular squadron's galleys departed Malta for the Barbary Coast on 2 July under Saint-Andiol. These sacked rather than seized a large germa laden with olive oil, camel-hair cloth, and other items of Barbary production in spite of no combat damage to the germa. The captains were brought before the Council and censured, their plunder seized. By 11 August Homedes had recovered and was back in command of the squadron.[14]

Uprisings of Moors of Barbary against Turks of Tripoli in 1589 had resulted in some astonishing developments. The earliest of these was a movement born in Syria and Egypt of three Marabout holy men who interpreted the Koran differently than traditional Sunni, Sufi, and Shia orthodoxy. One of these early Marabouts migrated with followers to the Mahgreb, or North Africa west of Egypt, so many followers both Arab and Moor as to cause Hassan Aga (Hassan Veneziano), Ottoman Beylerbey of Tripoli, to suspect a revolt of locals against Ottoman rule. He initiated repairs and improvements to the fortress at Tripoli and then took himself to Constantinople to request of the Porte reinforcements and assistance of a powerful armada. While Veneziano was assembling 3,000 men to reinforce Ottoman Tripoli, Marabout-led Moors and Arabs besieged his fortress. Without artillery and munitions and engineers, however, the besiegers sought assistance from Malta as a party with a similar interest in expelling Turks from North Africa.

General Homedes departed for Tripoli with the capitana on 11 August 1589 transporting arms and munitions and experts in their use. These were put ashore on a beach controlled by the besiegers not too distant from Tripoli with a promise of greater assistance to come. Meanwhile Hassan Aga had obtained from the Sultan an armada of 55 galleys, three mahons, and nine caramussals which soon appeared off Tripoli and also put men and munitions ashore, a lot of men and munitions. With such a relief force, besieging Arabs and Moors lifted the siege and withdrew into the surrounding area. Hassan Aga took his armada back to Constantinople for the Winter.[15]

Grand Bailiff Philipp Riedesel zu Camberg was appointed resident ambassador to the Imperial Court of Rudolph II, and was ordered to restore order to the Bailiwick of Brandenburg to the extent possible. Martin Graf von Hohenstein had been Bailiff of Brandenburg since 1569, and during his administration the Bailiwick had become increasingly Lutheran. En route Vienna the Grand Bailiff was to seek an audience with Pope Sixtus V and to obtain Papal advice and authority. While intolerant of heretics, Pope Sixtus had no advice but did ask for a report of Camberg's findings. Upon arrival at the Imperial court Camberg uncovered even less concern if a certain amount of fatalism. As Grand Prior of Germany and Prince of the Empire during the years 1594 to 1593, moreover, Camberg would be routinely able to call on the Bailiwick for services willingly rendered.[16]

Pursuant to earlier agreement between the langues of Germany and Italy, Johann Philipp Lesch as senior knight of the Priory of Germany was in 1589 appointed Prior of Hungary succeeding Italian Vincenzo Carafa, popular incumbent since 1581. Thus satisfying the earlier agreement, Lesch immediately resigned in favor of Carafa who would serve the Hungarian Priory another 11 years. It would not be until 1605 that the Langue of Germany nominated a candidate satisfactory to Hungarians. Upon the death of Bailiff of Santo Stefano Girolamo Avogadro, Admiral Francesco Bonajuto of Syracuse was appointed his successor. Marshal François de Lange de la Chenault was appointed Bailiff of Devesset or Bailiff of Saint George de Lyon upon the death of incumbent Marc de la Goutte, while Chenault was succeeded as Marshal by Claude de Montmorillon.[17]

Early in the year 1590 Bailiff of Mallorca Ramón de Veri personally established a fund of 3,000 Maltese scudos the major part of which was located in the County of Modica, Sicily, for the purpose of making available several pieces of artillery for hired-use by the Religion particularly in the city of Valletta. In validating and recognizing the fund in 1597 Grand Master and Council agreed that members of the Veri family wishing to take the Habit be permitted to borrow from the fund for periods of up to one year monies necessary to pay their passage to Malta and other necessary expenses associated with Reception.[17]

The Marabouts surrounding Tripoli in 1590 again took up their plan to besiege that walled port-city and again sought artillery and munitions assistance of Malta. The Cardinal Grand Master ordered General Homedes to put his three galleys in position, and General Foissy-Chamesson to put his two Magistral galleys in position to support a siege by the Marabouts. Commander Octave Castellane-Salernes who was practiced in blowing reinforced-gates with explosive petards was with several others readied to do the same at Tripoli. Overall command of the siege fell to Esteban de Claramonte. Claramonte detailed an elaborate plan beginning six days prior to siege onset, a surprise assault with individual and group assignments to which all agreed. Because the siege would have been impossible without Hospitaller assistance, the Marabouts voluntarily assigned all Turkish captives to the Maltese as oarsmen. With all agreed on the details the galleys departed Malta at end-March and on Day Minus-6 put Hospitallers and artillery ashore at Suaga (Zuwara 100 kilometers west of Tripoli) only to be told by Marabout commanders the siege would be the following year, not the extant year.[18]

The galleys wasted no time packing up and on 12 April 1590 returned to Malta where another combined excursion with four galleys and a galliot of the Order of Santo Stefano was planned. One day prior to departure a Turkish galley arrived Malta bound from Tripoli to Constantinople with a variety of valuable items and with 6,000 essentially-pure gold zecchins (or *ducato de zecca* or ducats) which the presidio commander at Tripoli was submitting in the way of annual tribute to the Sultan at Constantinople. The Turkish crew had been overcome by the galley's 244 Christian oarsmen and the galley conducted safely to Malta. The windfall of 6,000 zecchins was taken as a good omen and on 7 May the combined squadrons, eight galleys, one galliot, and two frigates all under command of Geronimo de Homedes headed directly for the Levant and the Cross of Cyprus, here called the Cross of Alexandria, in search of the annual caravan bound for Constantinople. Prior to reaching the Cross, the combined squadrons encountered several Turkish vessels from which 92 Turks were removed. The good omen represented by the Turkish galley which arrived at Malta with 6,000 zecchins, though, proved not such a good omen. Encountering the annual caravan they found it escorted by 16 Turkish galleys which pursued the Christian vessels almost all the way back to Malta, the two frigates abandoned but for crews. From Malta the Tuscan commander, Pier Luigi dei Rossi, took his squadron back to Livorno by way of Messina.[19]

On 27 April 1590 the Grand Master nominated as Prior of England his nephew Jean François d'Astorg de Segreville. While the nomination was approved by the Council and took effect, the nomination was opposed in Council by Bailiff of Eagle Andrew Wyse who appealed the award to the Church's Rota Romana and three years later himself obtained award of that dignity on grounds he was born within the territorial limits (including Wyse's Ireland) of the Langue of England while Segreville was born outside of those limits.[20]

In spite of their prudent months-earlier turn-about and flight from the Caravan escort, the galleys of the Religion as well as those of the Grand Master were forced in the summer by financial circumstances to continue with excursions to the Levant and to North Africa where from various vessels 124 captives were removed. Constantly in these years the Religion found itself short of one thing or another, particularly of credit because the exhaustive civil war with French Huguenots had inhibited French Church collections on the one hand and increased levies on the Church on the other hand, substantially reducing responsions to Malta from Hospitaller priories and commanderies in that country.

In recent years following the December 1588 assassination by royal bodyguards of Henry I, Prince of Joinville and Duke of Guise, and assassination the next day of his brother Louis II, Cardinal of Guise, (nephews of deceased Hospitaller Grand Prior of France and 1563 General of the Galleys Francis of Lorraine) following which the responsible Christian King Henry III watched his Kingdom sink from calamity to desolation and ruin until in 1589 he, too, was assassinated. And all the while reduced responsions fell even further until, among other consequences, one more of the five galleys was laid-up and the Hospitaller squadron was reduced to three, and for another, the Common Treasury in July was reduced to a mere 6,000 scudos, the amount of the Turkish galley windfall.

Another affliction worsening at the same time was the tendency of Viceroy of Sicily and Count of Alba de Liste Diego Enríquez de Guzmán to fail to live up to established agreements concerning allocations of grain and other food staples. As 1590 was the first of five years of grain shortage throughout Italy and beyond, normal Sicilian production was rushed to seller's markets where prices reached 40 crowns per salma, almost double the price a year earlier and headed higher. With market prices only modestly lower in Messina and Palermo, the people of Sicily itself could not afford anything near the asking price. Catalan Onofre Belver was dispatched to Palermo to plead the Order's need and circumstances, but this was a year in which Sicily was selling its output to the highest bidder, and the Order's Common Treasury was scratching the bottom of the barrel. The Viceroy's single coherent response was to order a population census taken in August. The Census count exceeded 27,000 between Malta and Gozo, but the Order's only recourse was to send remaining galleys out to waylay grain shipments which could be paid for not with cash but with promises.[21]

Yet an additional disturbance roiled these troubled waters, particularly those of the Langue of Italy. Upon the 1590 death of incumbent Prior of Lombardia Luigi Tana of Chieri, 43 years a Hospitaller, Duke of Savoy Charles Emmanuel I petitioned Pope Sixtus V seeking a Grand Cross and succession to the Priory of Lombardia for two-year-old third son Emmanuel Philibert. Pope Sixtus was inclined to favor the request and sought advice of Cardinal Grand Master Verdalle. On becoming aware of these matters the Langue of Italy immediately registered its opposition with the Sacred Council or Council of State as Prior of Lombardia was the langue's senior dignity and the incumbent sat on the Council itself. The Council immediately deputized two attorneys to the Pope to register the Order's objections, Procurator of Capua Niccolò Grimaldi and Procurator of Barletta Marcello Mastrillo, with additional instruction to plea not only that the petition not be granted but that His Eminence embrace protection of the Order from all such outside interference in its affairs. And they were to remind the Pope that at present the Priories of France, Champagne, Toulouse, Rome, Venice, Castile, Portugal, and Bohemia were already similarly encumbered.[22]

Pope Sixtus V passed away on 27 August 1590 and was succeeded on 15 September by Giovanni Battista Castagna as Pope Urban VII.

Twelve days later Pope Urban VII also passed away. On 5 December Niccolò Sfondrati was elected Urban's successor as Pope Gregory XIV. In a compromise solution to the Savoy petition fostered by the latter, Emmanuel Philibert was placed in line to succeed to the Priory of Armenia with attendant Grand Cross, to assume the position after reception as a Hospitaller.[23]

It is instructive that in these years the Papal Squadron maintained ten galleys ready for sea under Lieutenant General Orazio Lercari. In 1588 Lercari reported seizing a galliot in the same paragraph he reported having sighted Hassan Veneziano and galliot flotilla, and in 1590 he reported sighting three more enemy galliots too fast for his squadron. Malta as well rarely sighted the enemy in home waters and needed to deploy to the Levant for slim pickings. The same appeared true for the Knights of Santo Stefano as well as for the galley squadrons of Naples and Sicily. *Were it not for the cost of maintaining naval forces, it would seem there was little reason to have them.*[24]

Cardinal Grand Master Verdalle and Council dispatched Prior of Hungary Don Vincenzo Carafa to Naples and thence to Rome as Ambassador of Obedience to new Pope Gregory XIV seeking reaffirmation of Order privileges. He was also to seek 100,000 scudos in famine relief as well as 200 forzati or forced laborers as oarsmen for a fourth squadron galley. Before Carafa was able to depart, however, came an order from Rome to forego such embassies as Rome, too, was suffering from famine and a depleted treasury.[25]

During the night of 17 April 1590 a Turkish galley of 22 banks watering at the island of Comino between Malta and Gozo was caught by a severe storm and totally destroyed on nearby shoals. The captain, sixty other Turks, and about 100 chained Christian oarsmen drowned. Forty Christians and a similar number of Turks survived, straggling into Valletta two days later. These revealed the Turkish galley was traveling in company with a galliot thought to have been sheltering at Lampedusa. General Homedes and the three galleys were ordered out to investigate but found no trace of the second vessel.[26]

The assignment of Geronimo de Homedes as General of the Galleys ended, and it was Grand Master Hugues Loubenx de Verdalle's wish that Homedes be succeeded by the Grand Master's nephew François d'Astorg de Ségreville. Pursuant to a Brief of Pope Sixtus V dated 12 January 1588 this assignment required a Knight of the Grand

Cross. Pursuant to an earlier Papal Brief of Pope Gregory XIII placing dignities of the defunct Langue of England in the hands of the Grand Master, Segreville succeeded with approval of the Council to the Priory of England albeit over the earlier objection of Bailiff of Eagle Andrew Wyse who had filed his objection with the Rota Romana appeals court. Ségreville thereby succeeded to a Grand Cross enabling appointment as General of the Galleys. Cementing his service as General, he was immediately dispatched on a corsair voyage to the Levant with the squadron capitana, with *Vittoria*, and with the grand master's Magistral capitana then commnded by Jacques de Touges-Noaillan in succession of Jean de Vassadel-Vaqueiras. These returned with a handful of captives taken from a caramussal carrying a large quantity of rice and other foodstuffs.[27]

Arriving at Malta in June 1590 was a new Papal Brief over signature of Pope Sixtus V mandating at behest of King Philip II that Hospitaller Luis de Ayala (Basque: Aiara) of the Langue of Aragon be awarded the Grand Cross with Honors. There would arrive 12 months later an even more strange and insolent Brief under date of 25 June 1591 causing a current of dissatisfaction to run through the Langue of Italy and beyond; Pope Gregory XIV had given his Hospitaller Master of House Fabrizio Berzio of Pavia formal authority to award all dignities of the Langue of Italy including Admiral and to allocate vacant commanderies, as well.[28]

Pursuant to this latter authority Cesare Ferretti of Ancona in the Adriatic Marche had been awarded the Commandery of Chiusi near Siena in Tuscany. Grand Master and Council immediately dispatched Grand Hospitaller Philibert de Foissy-Chamesson, Admiral Marcantonio Altavilla, and Bailiff of Negroponte Alonso de Tejada as ambassadors to lay before the Pontiff the Order's concerns.[29]

In late Autumn of 1590 fifteen year-old Guillaume Gadagne Beauregard of Lyon two generations removed from Florence had arrived at Malta with proofs of forebears and had asked to be received as a Knight of Malta. He must have been asked his age and must have dissembled. He may have recounted his experience fleeing the Seminary of Tournon in 1587 during the Wars of Religion to fight in Burgundy and of being assigned to the staff of Jean de Grivel de Grossouvre, a brother-in-law. The Calvinist!!!, his interrogator may have exclaimed at this gross exaggeration. No, the Royalist, young Guillaume would have replied. And of course he was himself Catholic. Everyone from Florence was of the Mother Church, he might have added in impeccable Tuscan Italian to reinforce his history. A year ago, he almost certainly would have continued, he had served at the Siege of Orleans under Jean-François de La Guiche, Seigneur de Saint-Géran, another Royalist and another in-law, failing to add that he had served as a cornet player. And for a second time he would have produced proofs which identified a line of merchant-bankers as of the nobility, though there was some question about his maternal grandmother. One year later 16 year-old Guillaume Gadagne Beauregard departed Malta a chevalier of the Langue of Auvergne having served his novitiate. But he would return.[30]

With famine persisting in 1591, the three galleys of the Religion and two of the Grand Master continued to intercept infrequent shipments through local waters, among these a bulk carrier in the Strait of Messina bound for Naples with a cargo of Apulian grain. With Naples suffering its own grain shortage, Viceroy of Naples Juan de Zúñiga y Avellaneda immediately sequestered the Order's deposits with local banks and agents, and, moreover, threatened further action. Grand Master and Council were forced to dispatch Commander Ramón de Fortuyn not just to reimburse the grain's consignees but to explain to the Viceroy that absent the seized grain a great number of people at Malta would have perished. A similar embassy headed by Receiver Baldassar Marchetti, Commander Onofre Belver, and Bailiff of Santa Eufemia Centorio Cagnolo, with Doctor Ledovico Platamone representing the Università of Malta was dispatched to Palermo to plead with Viceroy of Sicily Diego Enríquez de Guzmán, Count of Alba de Liste, for compassion and at least a small share of Malta's normal allotment of Sicily's grain, arguing a complete cessation of shipments was demonstrably unfair in light of Sicily's normal wheat crop.

Meanwhile the dignity of Admiral was vacated by death of incumbent Marcantonio Altavilla who was succeeded by Commander Aleramo de Conti della Lengueglia. Soon Prior of Pisa Isuardo di Sanmartino exercised his right of seniority to the Priory of Lombardia vacated by death of incumbent Luigi Tana, and Lengueglia opted for the Priory of Pisa. The Council then assigned Marzio Abenante of Cosenza as Admiral. Resident Ambassador to Rome Giulio Beccaria passed away suddenly and the Grand Master believed his nephew Ségreville was best equipped to fulfill this important position.

Francesco Lanfreducci was accordingly at end-August elected Regent of the Galleys in Ségreville's stead. This was Lanfreducci's first appearance in history since taken captive to Algiers following 1565's fall of Malta's Fort Saint Elmo. Ségreville and the special ambassadors cited above were dispatched aboard the squadron's three galleys and the grand master's flagship to Messina, the re-enforced squadron then proceeding under the Regent to Sardinia to beg of new Viceroy Gastón de Moncada y Gralla-Despla, 2nd Marquis of Aitona, a share of that Regency's grain. Speeded at the same time was a dispatch to King Philip II protesting assignment by the Holy See of special powers to Fabrizio Berzio, an Hospitaller of little seniority and less merit, and asking the Crown to intercede.[31]

In October Pope Gregory XIV died at the age of 56 years following a Papacy of 315 days. He was succeeded by Giovanni Antonio Facchinetti under the name of Innocent IX. Sixty-two days later on 30 December Pope Innocent IX passed away at the age of 72 years. He was succeeded on 30 January 1592 by Ippolito Aldobrandini as Pope Clement VIII.[32]

The Order of Saint John of Jerusalem and the people of Malta confronted an apocalyptic year of devastation, famine, and plague in 1592. With starvation the alternative, Regent Lanfreducci early in February took the three active squadron galleys and the Magistral Padrona north to Cape Passero where patience was rewarded with a ship of Sicilian Ragusa transporting 2,200 salmas of grain from Girgenti (Agrigento) to Palermo. While the people of Sicily were also suffering from famine, it was a famine induced by high prices and not by local crop failure. The Ragusan was guided to Valletta. The four Malta galleys were also rewarded with a Genovese carrier of 1,800 salmas bound from the market at Messina. She, too, was guided to Valletta. With election by the Conclave of Cardinals of Ippolito Aldobrandini as Pope Clement VIII at end-January Prior of Hungary Don Vincenzo Carafa was appointed Ambassador of Obedience to render the Order's obedience to Papal authority and to obtain reaffirmation of historic privileges. A second embassy was appointed to pay the Order's respects to new Viceroy of Sicily Enrique de Guzmán y Ribera, 2nd Count of Olivares, in succession of Diego Enríquez de Guzmán. This all-important ambassador was Vice-Chancellor Don Diego de Ovando steeped in the Order's financial circumstances. Tragically, he died en route Sicily and was succeeded by Doctor and Hospitaller Chaplain Giorgio Giampieri of Malta descended from Rhodians transplanted with the Order. Of the Priory of Navarre, Giampieri was soon confirmed as successor Vice Chancellor. Prior of the Church Alfonso de Domenico also passed away in 1592, and Giampieri succeeded to that dignity, as well. At Rome the Order's three ambassadors Grand Hospitaller Philibert de Foissy-Chamesson, Don Vincenzo Carafa, and Bailiff of Negroponte Alonso de Tejada had no success pleading for revocation of the authority delegated to Fabrizio Berzio. Quite the opposite, the Order was directed to not only accept the Brief but by promulgation of letters patent under seal of Grand Master and Council to comply with the Brief. And there was more. Berzio was to be assigned the Commandery of Saints Guglielmo and Damiano of Pavia as well as an annual income of 1,350 gold scudos from the Bailiwick of Santo Stefano without a Bailiff since the recent death of Giulio Cesar Malvicino. Thought to have been no more than 62 years of age at death, Malvicino had been trained in the law and for that reason arrived late as an Hospitaller. He nevertheless had time for the entire 1565 Great Siege of Malta and later had been entrusted with the critical assignment of Resident Ambassador to the Holy See and Procurator-Receiver at Rome. His absence would be painful.

A Bull ratifying Berzio authority was issued on 26 March 1592 and confirmed by the Convent on 10 May of the same year. The conclusion to be drawn from these Papal directives must have been Papal dissatisfaction with the Order's Grand Master and Council. Further weighing on the discretion of Grand Master and Council was an expectation of appointment at Royal direction of a new Prior of Castile and León having royal blood in the manner of Archduke Wenceslaus's 1578 appointment. The Priory of Barletta having become vacant by the December death of Hospitaller Cardinal Giovanni Vincenzo Gonzaga, it was taken at option by Prior of Pisa Aleramo de Conti della Lengueglia, while Admiral Marzio d'Abenante succeeded to Prior of Pisa and Commander Francesco Cataneo of Novara succeeded to Admiral. Because, however, Pope Innocent IX had earlier promised the Priory of Barletta to Don Ferdinando Gonzaga, son of Duke of Mantua Vincenzo I Gonzaga and newly received into the Langue of Italy, and because Pope Clement VIII had transferred the same dignity to Cardinal Scipione Gonzaga, the latter at the same time as Grand

Master and Council acted, the Langue of Italy threatened to explode. These external appointments were sucking the lifeblood out of the Langue of Italy. Lengueglia reverted to Prior of Pisa, and Abenante reverted to Admiral. Cateneo got a Grand Cross in recompense. Abenante soon got Malvicino's Bailiwick of Santo Stefano, while Cateneo soon got the Bailiwick of Naples upon death of Pirro Melzi of Milan. Melzi had been a highly respected Hospitaller in part because his father Francesco had been one of the more prominent artists of the Renaissance as well as student, companion, and executor of Leonardo da Vinci.[33]

During these months the galleys of the Religion on the first of two voyages to Syracuse plundered a merchant vessel with a cargo of timber and several Turks embarked, and on the second voyage invested two Turkish brigantines beached on the shore from which a good number were removed and sent to the oars. And the two Magistral galleys under Captain Touges-Noaillan proceeded to the Levant where above Cape Gelidonia they sank a caramussal and took a galleon, cargo of rice, flax, sugar, and spices with 206 captives between Turks, Moors, and a handful of merchants for whom healthy ransoms were received. The galleon would be converted to a Magistral warship.[34]

On 7 May 1592 four galleys of the Grand Duke of Tuscany put into Malta looking for a pilot with experience in Levantine waters. The Cardinal Grand Master assigned Captain Petrachi Caloriti of Rhodean ancestry. In only fifteen days the four galleys took in waters of Alexandria a sailing vessel and a germa out of Constantinople with cargoes of rice, flax, and spices also yielding 150 Turkish captives. But Alexandria was infested with plague and these ships were exposed. They brought to Malta another of the Four Horsemen of the Apocalypse with grave consequences for Maltese. During the voyage from Cape Buonandrea to Malta 22 people died of the disease. Knight of Santo Stefano Cristoforo Bontalenti of Florence was the first to die at Malta. There were so many ill of the disease the Pratique Infirmary at Marsamuscietto could not handle the load and many were sent on to the Sacred Infirmary at Valletta. Bailiff of Santa Eufemia Centorio Cagnolo and Commanders Ramón de Veri of Aragon and Jean-Baptiste de Puget-Chasteuil of Provence were on 25 June appointed commissioners to investigate the nature of the disease. They were soon joined by Bernard Roquelaure de Saint-Aubin of Provence and by Augustin d'Amours of France. Despite state-of-the-art medical practice, Malta experienced three distinct plague assaults, the first from June through August, the second from 12 November through

January 1593, and the third from March 1593 through the following June. When it ended, 800 of the 27,000 residents of Malta and Gozo were dead. Among the dead were forty knights and others of the Habit, an alarming one in ten of those present attributable to close auberge quarters.[34]

Given a Brief of Pope Sixtus V of January 1588 empowering the Cardinal Grand Master to select six commanderies as commanderies of grace, the Cardinal Grand Master's nephew Ségreville was in 1592 awarded the Commandery of Sainte-Lucie of the Priory of Saint-Gilles, one of the wealthier commanderies of the wealthiest priory. During the year Commander Cesare Ferretti obtained by decision of Pope Clement VIII the expectation of being awarded the Priory of England with attendant Grand Cross; this award would never occur because Andrew Wyse would remain incumbent until 1631. At his own option Bailiff of Novaville Francisco de Valencia became Bailiff of Lora. Valencia was succeeded at Novaville by Grand Chancellor Martín de Nieto while Bailiff of Negroponte Alonso de Tejada advanced to Grand Chancellor and Commander Ramón de Fortuyn advanced to Bailiff of Negroponte. The Bailiwick of the Morea was vacated twice during the year. On the first occasion Commander Jean d'Anglure Bourlemont, received into the Langue of France 54 years earlier, succeeded Louis de Mailloc Sacquenville upon the latter's passing 52 years following his own reception. Anglure Bourlemont also passed away during the year and was succeeded by André de Soissons de Pothières received a mere 45 years earlier. At Rome Pope Clement VIII appointed Hospitaller Commander Emilio Pucci of Florence to command of the Papal Galley Squadron. Cardinal Grand Master Verdalle appointed at his prerogative Gabriel le Petit de la Vauguyon of Poitiers and the Priory of Aquitaine to command of the new 28-bank squadron capitana *Santa Anna*.[35]

The year 1592 ended amid prolonged agony and suffering, and the year 1593 commenced with the terror of war. The Ottoman-Safavid War of 1578-1590 had ended on relatively favorable terms for the Ottomans including control of the Caucasus. The other side of the coin, however, was that subsequently Constantinople swarmed with unpaid spahis and idle others. By the end of 1592 they were eager and able to turn their attention to the west and, in fact, in June 1592 had wrested Bihac in Bosnia from Emperor Rudolph II's Habsburg

Croatia. The cost to Bihac was said to be 5,000 dead and 800 children carried away as slaves. Raids by the Ottomans in greater Hungary over the next four months were reported to have netted 35,000 captives. Then there were rumors of an Ottoman naval build-up intended to divert Habsburg Spain from going to Holy Roman Empire assistance. Because every Ottoman naval build-up was a threat to Malta, a General Citation under date of 15 January was promulgated to all priories, bailiwicks, and commanderies summoning able-bodied Hospitallers to Malta by early April equipped for combat.[36]

Early in May 1593 advice reached Malta of 60 well-equipped galleys sailing from Constantinople which when joined by the Rhodes or Archipelago Guard and by North African corsair squadrons would constitute an Armada of more than 100 galleys. These were west bound and said to have designs on Gozo. In point of fact, though, the Ottoman Armada never exited the Archipelago and Malta was left to fight only its ongoing battles with famine, disease, and debt. The Order's warships were thus left to seek out opportune captures. The Grand Master's Magistral galleon, captured a year earlier above Cape Gelidonia and converted to warship, having prowled various parts of the Levant returned to Malta with a captured germa, cargo of rice and flax with some few captives, only to immediately turn around for a second search for opportunity, returning the second time with her own cargo of foodstuffs seized from several caramussals. The galley squadron returned from Sicily having seized in the waters of Licata an Infidel-corsair brigantine and the brigantine's prize, the latter a Messinese saettia with a cargo of grain. During the squadron's return a second Infidel-corsair brigantine was seized yielding 27 captives. Because the two laid-up squadron galleys were unlikely to see service in time to recover their value, these were put up for sale by the Common Treasury while the Grand Master contributed his two Magistral galleys to public service for the balance of the year.[37]

Senior Magistral captain Jacques de Touges-Noaillan reached the end of his life at the exceptionally young age of 30, cause not reported, and was succeeded by Jean de Marsac-Saillac, also of the Langue of Provence. Prior of England Ségreville in June reached the end of his tour as General of the Galleys and was succeeded by Esteban de Claramonte of the Langue of Aragon. Claramonte had a bit earlier succeeded the deceased Geronimo de Homedes as Bailiff of Caspe.

Because Claramonte had been laid low by plague, however, Onofre de Belver also of Aragon was elected Regent in his stead in which position he made several voyages. Bailiff of Eagle Andrew Wyse had two years earlier rebelled at appointment of the Grand Master's nephew as Grand Prior of England, and his conduct had been sufficiently mutinous that his case had been referred to the Holy See in Rome. By order of Pope Clement VIII, distinctly unimpressed with the Grand Master, the elevation of Ségreville to Grand Prior was declared null and void, and the Priory of England was awarded to Wyse, the declaratory Papal Brief dated 8 June 1593 recognized and executed by the Order's Council. The Bailiwick of Eagle thus becoming vacant, the Grand Master as of the same date conferred it on Ségreville, thus enabling his nephew to continue wearing the Grand Cross.[38]

The same two Magistral galleys among other voyages departed Malta at end-July transporting Bailiff of Negroponte Ramón de Fortuyn to Spain to take delivery of a large sum of responsions and returned safely to Malta within two months. Having vacated the dignity of Vice-Chancellor upon promotion to Prior of the Church, Giorgio Giampieri had before leaving office nominated Giovanni Ottone Bosio, brother of historian Giacomo Bosio, as Lieutenant Vice-Chancellor. Giovanni Ottone Bosio, an individual of belles lettres well acquainted with law, in 1593 succeeded to the dignity of Vice-Chancellor.[39]

Mindful of Papal admonitions, Grand Master and Council in August deputized three commissioners to ensure that statutes concerning reception of novitiates were observed. The three commissioners were Esteban de Claramonte, Jean de Vintimille d'Ollioules, and Cattaliano Casati of Milan, each a knight of integrity.[40]

Having sought for some time a successor Resident Ambassador at Rome in place of an ailing Alonso de Tejada, the Grand Master in 1593 selected Commander Don Pietro la Rocca of Messina. La Rocca was versed in the Order's awkward relationship with Venice. A second matter about which he was instructed was the ease with which malcontents, in the Grand Master's view, received an audience at the Holy See. An example of the latter, according to the Grand Master, was Bailiff of Eagle Andrew Wyse who had objected to the appointment of nephew Ségreville as Grand Prior of England causing Pope Clement VIII to declare the elevation of Ségreville to Grand Prior to be null and void, and to award the Priory of England to Wyse.[41] The Priory of Barletta had been vacated by death of Hospitaller Cardinal Giovanni Vincenzo Gonzaga in 1591, and by Papal mandate was in 1593 conferred on six year-old Hospitaller Prince and future Cardinal Duke of Mantua Ferdinando Gonzaga. The Bailiwick of Santo Stefano was vacated by death of incumbent Marzio Abenante. Bailiff of Naples Francesco Cataneo succeeded Abenante and was succeeded at Naples by Admiral Baldassar Marchetti who was succeeded as Admiral by Tiberio Campolo of Messina. Antoine Scipion de Joyeuse stepped down as Prior of Toulouse in 1593, albeit with right to nominate kin for successor as well as a pension funded by the Priory of 1,750 scudos per annum. In January 1594 Grand Commander Jean Soubiran d'Arifat was advanced to Prior of Toulouse succeeding Joyeyuse and was himself succeeded as Grand Commander by Pierre de Montauban de Voguedemar.[42]

The Priory of Messina was in January 1594 vacated by peaceful death of incumbent Rinaldo Nari who narrowly escaped violent death if not violence while commanding the Malta capitana at 1571's Battle of Lepanto. He was succeeded by Prior of Pisa Aleramo de Conti della Lengueglia in competition with Prior of Lombardia Isuardo di Sanmartino and Admiral Tiberio Campolo. Lengueglia was in turn succeeded as Prior of Pisa by Ambrogio di Gioeni of Catania. Not much later there arrived at Malta an emissary of Cardinal Ascanio Colonna, son of Marcantonio Colonna, Captain-General of the Church at the Battle of Lepanto. The emissary was carrying a Papal Brief mandating possession by the Cardinal of the Priory of Venice, nominally vacant since the 1589 death of Cardinal Alessandro Farnese but administered by Prior of Lombardia Isuardo di Sanmartino.[43]

There was during this period yet a second Alessandro Farnese, this one an Hospitaller received in 1566 at Parma's Cathedral of San Donnino. Born 21 years earlier, he was the son of Duke of Parma Ottavio Farnese and by his mother Anne of Austria was the grandson of Holy Roman Emperor Charles V and nephew of Don Juan of Austria. At the Battle of Lepanto he reportedly was first to board the Ottoman his galley grappled, sword in one hand, dagger in the other. Farnese had been assigned to Gian Andrea Doria's Flagship of Genoa situated two positions to the right of his uncle's *Real* in the seven-galley command center, his galley assailed by an unidentified Ottoman which failed in its assignment. In 1578 Farnese became successor to his deceased uncle as Spain's Captain-General of Flanders reporting directly to King Philip II. He is termed the "Captain of His Age" by John Keegan's *Who's Who in Military History*. Never assigned to Malta, he was never cited by the Order's historians.[44]

Meanwhile early fires of the Long War between Imperial Hungary and the Ottoman Empire burned fiercely. Six months earlier the Ottomans under Albanian Grand Vizier Koca Sinan Pasha had launched campaigns which in 1594 resulted in the capture of Hungarian Gyor (Giavarino) and Slovakian Komarum. There was soon a Papal call for a Holy League to go to the aid of Emperor Rudolf II's brother Archduke (of Austria) Matthias commanding Hungarian ground forces. Numerous entities responded including the Tuscan Knights of Santo Stefano. The Knights of Malta who were able to field only three galleys as it was, declined on the basis of lack of funds and lack of resources further exacerbating Papal-Hospitaller enmity, an enmity focused on Hugues Cardinal Loubenx de Verdalle.

Esteban de Claramonte took the three-galley Malta squadron to Messina in the Spring of 1594 to rendezvous with Gian Andrea Doria's Spanish squadron and other contingents. He was joined by Hospitaller Captain-General Emilio Pucci with the Papal Squadron and by Montauto's lieutenant Marcantonio Califati with Tuscan galleys, but Doria failed to appear and one by one the three squadrons departed on their own recognizance. The Maltese returned to Malta bringing with them a new galley, *San Placido*, built at Messina. Returning to Malta at the same time from the Levant were the two galleys belonging to Grand Master Verdalle. These brought with them two prizes, germas with cargos of rice, flax, and 87 captives. There was a second attempt to rendezvous at Messina, also a failure, after which Claramonte again returned to Malta and made his four galleys ready for any local appearance of the Turkish armada.[45]

Grand Vizier Koca Sinan in May 1594 ordered 4th Vizier and Kapudan Cigalazade Yusuf Sinan Pasha to create a naval diversion along the Italian coast. Born Scipione Cicala, son of Vincenzo Cicala of a noble Genovese family related to the Cibo, the Doria, and the Lomellini, Scipione Cicala had been captured with his father in March 1561 by the corsair Uluç Ali. Sent to Constantinople, the

16 year-old Cicala is said to have abjured his faith to save his father. He much later assumed the name and rank of Cigalazade Yusuf Sinan and rose from Aga of the Janissaries to Provincial Beylerbey and General to Commander of the Ottoman Fleet to, briefly, Grand Vizier of the Ottoman Empire.[46]

With *San Placido* not yet ready for sea, the three squadron galleys sailing in company with the two Magistral galleys passed the month of June on the North African coast but returned to Malta with a mere handful of captive Moors taken from a garbo. The month of August began with a fruitless search of Sicily's uninhabited western islands before Viceroy of Sicily Enrique de Guzmán y Ribera notified the Cardinal Grand Master of an assembly of the Catholic Armada at Messina under command of Prince Gian Andrea Doria to oppose any approach of the Ottoman Armada. By fast frigate General of the Galleys Esteban de Claramonte was ordered to take his four squadron galleys and the Magistral capitana to the assembly. Tarrying at Messina for some days without news of Doria, however, Claramonte and the galleys returned to Malta. Fortuitously, it turned out.[47]

There then appeared an armada of some 70 Turkish galleys commanded by Cigalazade Yusuf Sinan Pasha. Raising the Sicilian coast at Syracuse in late-August he worked north plundering as he went and ended by sacking the town of Reggio on the Neapolitan side of the Strait of Messina at the beginning of September. An attack on Malta's Gozo was expected and defensive preparations were initiated. Prior of Pisa Don Ambrogio di Gioeni was appointed Captain-at-Arms for Civita Vecchia (Mdina) while Don Federico Meca of Aragon, Francesco Lanfreducci of Pisa, Boniface de Puget-Chasteuil of Provence, and Catalan Juan Bernero de Raimat of Lleida were appointed sector wardens. Feeding suspicion of an assault, the squadron frigate on 8 September brought reports that Sinan's Armada was headed for Catania just north of Syracuse and Augusta with Gozo his next destination. The population of Gozo was immediately ordered to retire within the curtain wall surrounding the town of Rabat (Victoria) while the citadel garrison was substantially reinforced by a large number of knights and soldiers transferred from Malta under command of Prior of Santo Stefano Baldassar Marchetti. It was all for naught. Cigalazade Yusuf Sinan Pasha had turned his armada toward home.[47]

By the Autumn of 1594 the Religion had become deeply disturbed by the deterioration of its six priories, great number of commanderies, and other assets in the Kingdom of France brought about by the protracted war between Roman Catholics and Huguenots. Following assassination of King Henry III in 1589, King Henry IV of Navarre, a Protestant, was unable to wrest Paris from the Catholic League and was forced to renounce Calvinism in favor of Catholicism. Throughout this period the Order of Jerusalem had no ambassador or other representative at the French Court which had dominion over most of the Order's assets as Pope Clement VIII had expressly forbidden recognition of the Protestant King. By the same token priories and assets had been occupied by adherents of one side or another on the pretext of war with the other side. In this fashion the Priory of Aquitaine had been usurped by Hospitaller Commander Robert de Chazé, and the Priory of Auvergne by the secular Baron Roger II de Saint-Lary de Bellegarde. Because the Order's appointed Prior of Aquitaine Georges Régnier de Guerchy was determined to take possession of his priory, he was instructed to proceed by way of Rome to obtain license for his journey and to make known to the Holy See the Common Treasury had run up debt in the amount of 250,000 scudos during the absence or reduced remission of Aquitaine responsions. But before Prior Guerchy was able to obtain an audience he received news of his priory which caused him to depart Rome for France without Papal license. Whatever that news, return of King Henry IV to Catholicism, for example, and a consequent end to Catholic League resistance to his reign, Guerchy had replaced Chazé by 1594 year-end and had been succeeded at Rome by an Embassy of three seasoned knights of the Grand Cross, Marshal Jacques de Virieu-Pupetières, Bailiff of Negroponte Ramón de Fortuyn, and Bailiff of Santo Stefano Baldassar Marchetti. There is no report, however, of financial assistance from the Holy See. Neither is there further mention of Robert de Chazé.[48]

On 25 September with Cigalazade Yusuf Sinan Pasha returned to the east, Doria reached Messina where he gathered a fleet of 74 galleys including 12 of his own, seven of Genoa, 16 of Spain, 14 of Naples, eight of Sicily, three of Tuscany, two of Savoy, five of Malta, and seven of the Church. Gathered a month or more earlier as in the year's failed plan, citizens of Reggio would not have been sold into slavery. Five days after arrival Doria dismissed individual Armada components as it was too late in the sailing season to undertake a fleet action.[49]

The aforementioned embassy departed Malta on 8 October 1594, a time and point at which many senior Hospitallers were leveling charges of irregularities and worse against the Cardinal Grand Master. A late sixteenth century memorandum by a group of Grand Crosses addressed to Pope Clement VIII complained among other things about the way proceedings against knights were held by Grand Master Verdalle. The memorandum stated many trials were held in secret without the knowledge of the Venerable Council of the Order. This violated the Order's strictures and was not consistant with proper administration of justice. Among other irregularities the memorandum referred to deputy commissioners who were appointed to form a body of judges (a judiciary), but who were also asked to appear as witnesses. Grand Master Verdalle was accused of having called witnesses to his quarters, suggesting to them what they had to say. In reward he promised titles, positions, benefices, and other compensation. Among other accusations, Verdalle forced judges to issue sentences according to his wish. This earned the supreme knight of the Order of Hospitallers the undesirable reputation of a despot. Prior of Capua Bernardino Scaglia was among so-called malcontents unhappy with Grand Master Verdalle, others Bailiff of Santa Eufemia Centorio Cagnolo, Prior of Pisa Ambrogio di Gioeni, Bailiff of Naples Tiberio Campolo, and Grand Prior of England Andrew Wyss. An unrelated complaint dealt with the inordinate share of plunder going to the Grand Master's own galleys and galleon at the expense of the Order.

A Papal Brief dated 25 June 1594 urged Grand Master and dissidents to make amends for the good of the Religion. This was cause for three more Hospitallers to depart for Rome, each an avowed opponent of the Grand Master. These were Commander Antonio de Vega of Castile, Dom Diogo de Souza of Portugal, and Pedro de Queirós also of Portugal. Having made their case to Pope Clemente VIII, the Grand Master was forced to defend himself by letter addressed to the Pope.[50] Still additional representatives of both sides departed Malta for Rome on 7 November 1594. In the end, Bishop of Malta Tomás Gargallo's testimony was damning of the Cardinal Grand Master.[51]

During the year Grand Prior of Germany Philipp Flach von Schwarzenberg passed away following 21 years as senior dignity of the German Langue. He was succeeded by Grand Bailiff Philipp Riedesel zu Camberg who in turn was succeeded as Grand Bailiff by Prior of

Dacia Bernhard IV von Angelach-Angelach who was succeeded at Dacia by Commander of Basel Weiprecht von Rosenbach. Miguel Cruzat of the Langue of Aragon was appointed Prior of Navarre succeeding uncle Luis Cruzat.[52]

Early in 1595 advice was received at Malta from agents at Constantinople as well as from other qualified sources that the Ottomans wished to capitalize on successes in Hungary with a signal victory by sea, and that the preferred conquest was that of Malta. The galleys transported Hospitaller Commander Bernardo de Aldana to Messina to convey to Viceroy of Sicily Enrique de Guzmán y Ribera, 2nd Count of Olivares, the Order's condolences upon the death of Vicereina María Pimentel de Fonseca. During the month news reached Malta concerning death at mid-month of Sultan Murad III, and accession of his first born to the throne as Mehmed III. The Grand Master considered it necessary to write to Pope, Catholic King, and other Christian princes, and particularly to the same Viceroy and to Viceroy of Naples Juan de Zúñiga y Avellaneda concerning advices received and to plead for their aid and assistance.[52]

In March Grand Master Verdalle became feeble and appointed Grand Commander Pierre de Montauban de Voguedemar as his lieutenant with power to act during his absence or incapacity. In a letter addressed to the Sacred Council he listed marine assets as two new galleys (1590's *Negrilla* and 1592's *Santa Anna*), one large cargo ship (the Magistral galleon), three galleys of the Religion (1588's never-named 28-bank capitana, 1594's *San Placido*, and 1583's *Santa Maria de la Vittoria*), a galleonetto or smaller galleon, and lesser vessels. The Grand Master also valued his estate at 500 thousand scudos which presumably included the three squadron galleys.[53] (Pozzo I-368)

Cardinal Grand Master Hugues de Loubenx-Verdale died on 4 May 1595, laid in state for two days in the Great Hall of the Magistral Palace, and on the third day was transported in a cortège by eight Knights of the Grand Cross, followed by 170 other knights, to his final resting place within St. John's Co-Cathedral at Valletta. He was 64 years of age and had governed the Hospitaller Order of Saint John of Jerusalem for thirteen of those years. Inauspiciously.[54] (Pozzo I-366)

Chapter VII

1595–1601

Following funeral services for deceased Grand Master Verdalle the Sacred Council appointed Bailiff of Caspe and General of the Galleys Esteban de Claramonte as Magistral Lieutenant in succession of Grand Commander Pierre de Montauban de Voguedemar, Claramonte a second son of one of the oldest and more esteemed families of Huesca. The Council also ruled on certain other matters, such rulings having the same authority as rulings by Chapters General. Among these rulings was a return to public use of public areas set aside for Magistral use such as the Buskett Gardens, a wasteland on arrival of the Hospitallers in 1530 and a wasteland again following 1565's Great Siege of Malta. Thirty years later, however, the 300,000 square meter preserve was forested and flowered parkland. The Council further ruled that Knights of Grace received without proof of nobility, such as knights received into the Langue of England under Protestant monarchs, were denied the right of vote during General Assemblies convened for the purpose of electing Grand Masters. Lorenzo Raimondi, a Knight of Grace thought to be of the Priory of Venice protested but to no avail. Most importantly, though, the operation of warships in competition with the Order was prohibited, this an off-and-on practice furthered by Parisot de la Valette when he might have otherwise concerned himself with defense of Malta, and a practice carried on by Valette successors. Sacred Council Chairman Claramonte, a veteran of 1565's Great Siege, may well have considered the Order's bloody Siege losses a direct result of such extra-curricular operations.[1]

On 7 May a General Assembly of all ambulatory Hospitallers at Malta eligible to vote was convened in the Church of St. John for the purpose of electing a new Grand Master. The eight langues each selected an initial elector representing that langue. These eight selected Grand Commander Pierre de Montauban de Voguedemar as non-voting President of Elections, the remaining seven selecting the Triumvirate of Elections who were Bernardo Capece of Naples as

Knight of Elections, Juan Cetrillas of Aragon as Chaplain of Elections, and Serving Brother Michel Fonder of Auvergne as Sergeant-at-Arms of Elections. These latter three then retired in seclusion and from those assembled selected a fourth elector, and the four selected a fifth, and the five a sixth, and so on until there were Sixteen Electors at two per langue as follows: Pierre de Roquelaure-Saint-Aubin and Honoré de Puget-Chasteuil for Provence, Claude d'Igny d'Agnac and Michel Fonder for Auvergne, Simon Cheminée de Boisbenet and Claude de Louet for France, Geronimo de Fozes and Chaplain Juan Cetrillas for Aragon, Bernardo Capece and Girolamo Agliata for Italy, Luigi Vivaldo and Lorenzo de Godoy of Castile for England as England had no voting-eligible Hospitallers, Johannes Werner Reitmann and Hartmann von der Tann for Germany, and Hernando Ruiz de Corral and Don Antonio Gonzales de Torres for Castile. Following due deliberation the Sixteen elected to near-unanimous approbation Castellan of Amposta Martín Garzés 53rd Grand Master of the Order of Jerusalem.[2]

Martín Garzés first comes to the attention of Bosio readers in a single line entry, and to the attention of Pozzo readers no earlier than the General Assembly convened to elect a successor to deceased Grand Master Hugues de Loubens-Verdale. To Bosio he was introduced by a roster, his name appearing on a list of Hospitallers heeding a summons to Malta during the Great Siege of 1565, arriving from Spain in time to be a part of the September 1565 Relief Force breaking the back of the Siege. To Dal Pozzo he was introduced as Castellan of Amposta, the senior dignity of the Langue of Aragon, coincidentally at Malta at the time of the General Assembly. His peers patently knew more. They knew and subsequent history confirmed Martin Garzés was a man of character and morality as well as a natural leader. The corsair assets of his predecessor would be incorporated into the Order's marine ranks and employed for the benefit of island residents and not for the benefit of individual purses. And the Order's hospital would regain its stature as Europe's leading medical facility. While there would be military and naval setbacks during his tenure as Grand Master, there would be no self-made disasters. And strained relationships abroad would be repaired. His Magistracy would be a welcome change.

Two days after his election the 69 year-old Grand Master convened his first meeting of the Sacred Council. His opening remarks were an expression of his wish the Council employ all of its ability for the common weal. A principal item on the agenda supporting this goal was the need to improve the Order's image at home and abroad. A first measure in that regard was to maintain a galley squadron of five galleys as already called for by Chapters General, and as enabled by the estate of the deceased Grand Master which included two relatively new galleys willed to the Order. Several unnamed commissioners were deputized to ascertain those items and matters necessary to properly equip the five galleys to best further the Order's public image. Eight other unnamed commissioners, one per langue, were deputized to assist Procurators of the Treasury in the inventory of the deceased Grand Master's estate. Grand Prior of England Andrew Wyse was appointed Ambassador of Obedience to render the Order's obedience to, and to receive reaffirmation of recently-denied historic privileges from, Ippolito di Aldobrandini who had ascended the Papal throne as Pope Clement VIII three years earlier and who had since become critical of the Order of Saint John and of its deceased Grand Master. Beyond concessions, a pre-existing Papal Bull promised financial assistance in re-fortifying the island of Gozo so that local residents would no longer constantly fear for their lives. There was also an image matter with the Republic of Genoa's Cross of Saint George pretending to seniority over the Standard of the Religion, a matter which the Pope could help resolve. Bernardo de Spelletta of Navarre and the Langue of Aragon was appointed Ambassadeur Extraordinaire to the Spanish Court of Philip II. One of his assignments was to plead for relief of the people of Malta suffering from impoverishment and famine and who were abandoning the islands for the mainland. He was also to plead for further assistance in construction of the Fortress of Gozo, and that the Viceroys of Naples and Sicily be directed to assign four to six companies of infantry necessary to preserve the Maltese garrison *in service to His Majesty*. (The mere thought much less expression of his Hospitaller Order in service to any one flag had been anathema to Grand Master Philippe Villiers de l'Isle-Adam whether fear or fact. In his view it would prove the Order's un-doing.)[3]

Esteban de Claramonte was in June 1595 succeeded in command of the galleys by Lodovico (Luigi) Vivaldo. Vivaldo nominated Giacomo Palio of Turin to command of the flagship in succession of Lupe de Arbizu. Appointed to command of the galleys *Santa Croce* and *Santa*

Fede ceded to the Order by deceased Grand Master Verdalle were, respectively, Boniface de Puget-Chasteuil of Provence in succession of Jean de Marsac-Saillac, and Jean de Serocourt of the Priory of Champagne in succession of *Santa Anna*'s Gabriel le Petit de la Vauguyon, while Catalan Onofre de Copones was appointed to command of *San Placido* and Francesco Moleti of Messina remained in command of *Vittoria*. Appointed to command of the Verdalle Galleon was Pedro Vetriano of Aragon and to command of the Galleonetto was Francisco Barreto of Castile.

With change of squadron commanders yet to occur, but with new captains in place, the squadron was summoned to Messina by Prince of Melfi Gian Andrea Doria and departed Malta under Claramonte on 7 June. In company was new Prior of Messina Aleramo de Conti della Lengueglia proceeding to his new priory. Lengueglia expected to have problems with non-Hospitaller Vincenzo Beccadelli di Bologna, Marchese di Marineo and Stratigo or military commander of Messina. Beccadelli viewed the Hospitaller Priory as a squatter, a squatter with infirmary which had been there for three and a half centuries. For his part, Claramonte had orders to return to Malta should Doria or further orders fail to appear as on earlier occasions, as plans for an Infidel corsair raid on Gozo had been passed to Malta.

Pausing one year earlier with four large galliots for fresh water at Lampedusa, Morat of Algiers then the new Admiral of Algiers in succession of Memi Arnaut and the first native-born Admiral of Algiers, found signs in the island's chapel of recent Christian presence. As no Christians were encountered during Morat's passage east from Algiers, and as it was too early in the season to be returning to home ports at Malta or Sicily, the four corsair galliots headed south toward Secco di Palo where the border of modern Libya meets Tunisia. Off the island of Djerba Morat surprised two galleys of the Knights of Santo Stefano commanded by Baccio Delbene of Florence. He did so by the stratagem of lowering mast and sails to the deck of two galliots and hiding those two behind the other two. The stratagem proved a lure to Delbene who advanced to the attack and did not realize his error until much too late. Morat's capitana and the smallest of the four corsair galliots clasped to either side of the Tuscan padrona and with an overwhelming advantage in numbers made short work of her defense. The other two corsair galliots commanded by Morat's brother and by Cafer Reis, a renegade Genovese, similarly came up on the capitana which resisted more stubbornly, but seeing the padrona overrun lost heart and struck her colors. Florentines were sent to the oars and Muslim oarsmen became crew. The six oared vessels reached Algiers in July where the victors were accorded a celebratory welcome. During the year since the two captures Morat's reputation had blossomed while the truth of numbers had been lost in the telling.[4]

Again finding neither assembly at Messina nor awareness of an imminent assembly, Claramonte turned about and headed for home. Meanwhile Grand Master and Council had deployed to Gozo Hospitallers of all langues but England as well as several companies of soldiers to surprise corsairs expecting to surprise Gozo. Also meanwhile Lieutenant Marshal Claude d'Igny d'Agnac and new Castellan of Amposta Don Geronimo de Fozes had been ordered to inspect the arms and equipment of all Hospitallers at both Malta and Gozo for readiness.[5]

Claramonte reached Syracuse on 17 June 1595 where nine days later while still loading foodstuffs and other items for Malta he learned of three galliots of Algiers sighted off Syracuse's Cape Murro di Porco. These were judged to be those of the corsair and Admiral of Algiers Morat Reis. Having the advantage of numbers Claramonte could not let opportunity pass; he that day got underway and turned his five prows in pursuit. Finding nothing at the Cape he heeded advice of Royal Pilot Jacques de Vincheguerre and located the three galliots taking on fresh water from a stream ten miles to the south at Longina. It was a cloud-free night only five days past full-moon, however, and Morat's lookouts saw them coming. The three galliots were each underway on Hospitaller arrival. An engagement ensued following intercept but with new captains unfamiliar with the squadron commander there was undue confusion and little coordination. The Hospitaller galleys came up with the corsairs individually, and did not bring their numbers to bear. Morat's Algerians, on the other hand, operated together as they practiced together, the lead Algerian reversing course for bow-mounted cannon salvos as the trailing Algerians moved ahead. Jean de Serocourt's *Santa Anna* grappled Morat's fleeing galliot at the latter's midships mezzanine deck and cut down numerous enemy with her swivel cannon while suffering equally numerous casualties from arquebus fire, but when Serocourt himself went down his rescue became a withdrawal. The

Maltese capitana also reached Morat's galliot, grappling at the poop so as to not injure chained Christian oarsmen. Again there was carnage on both sides before grappling lines were severed. Puget-Chasteuil's *Santa Croce* and Moleti's *Vittoria* did some cannon damage to the three Algerians, but Onofre de Copones' *San Placido* was never able to close within cannon range. In the end the enemy escaped with damage to both sides considerable.[6] Christian dead included knights Jacques de Lestang du Breuil of France, Ottavio Dentice and Camillo Pisanelli of Naples, Vincenzo Valfredi of the Piedmont, Giacomo Upezzinghi of Pisa, and Vicente Saida of Aragon. Gravely wounded by an arquebus round to the head was *Santa Fede* skipper Jean de Serocourt. Morat's narrow escape did no damage to his new fame as the truth of numbers was in the telling.[7]

Claramonte and the galley squadron returned to Malta on 29 June followed the same day by eight galleys of Naples under their commander Don Pedro de Toledo. The Neapolitans brought with them the September 1594 embassy to Rome of three seasoned knights of the Grand Cross, Marshal Jacques de Virieu-Pupetières, Bailiff of Negroponte Ramón de Fortuyn, and Bailiff of Santo Stefano Baldassar Marchetti. The embassy had concerned itself with the loss of responsions attending the civil war in France and consequent indebtedness of the Religion. The embassy was reminded the civil war in France had ended, and was promised nothing in the way of financial relief. Don Pedro de Toledo was otherwise at Malta to solicit a capable pilot for an excursion to the Levant. Marco di Maria of the Cyclades island of Naxos was assigned, and Toledo departed two days following arrival. Arriving Malta at about the same time were three galleys of Santo Stefano under Francesco Montauto returning from the Levant with 60 captives removed from various vessels but without news of Morat. Montauto was followed by eight galleys of Sicily under Don Pedro de Leyva which had been similarly pursuing Infidel corsairs. Concurrently with these visits Claramonte was succeeded in command of the galleys by Luigi Vivaldo.[8]

In August of the same 1595 the Grand Master received yet another summons from Gian Andrea Doria requesting the galleys of the Religion rendezvous with the rest of the Catholic Armada at Messina. Vivaldo took the five-galley squadron to Messina as requested but there found the fleet commander believing the season too far advanced for an excursion into the Levant. Vivaldo therefore obtained license to return to Malta and did so.[9]

Reports placed the Ottoman Armada under command of Cigalazade Yusuf Sinan Pasha at Navarin on the west coast of the Morea 390 nautical miles ENE of Malta where it was an obvious threat to Gozo. Grand Master and Council ordered four of the galleys to be reinforced with crew and oarsmen from the fifth galley and that the four proceed to Stanfane Island (Nisis Strofadi) south of Zante and proximate to Navarin to obtain available information concerning Ottoman intentions. The four galleys departed Malta on 21 September and by way of Stanfane ascertained the Ottoman Armada was indeed at Navarin but was in no condition to undertake offensive operations. The four galleys then proceeded under the Morea and across the Aegean to the Seven Capes of Anatolia between Macri (Fethiye) and Kalamaki (Kalkan) and down to Kastellorizon, 450 additional nautical miles without encountering the Archipelago Guard or any other Ottoman combat vessel. They returned to Malta on 16 October in company with a Greek germa captured from a crew of 19 transporting a Turkish cargo. During the Maltese excursion Vivaldo was made aware Don Pedro de Toledo with 14 galleys of Naples and eight of Sicily had in September put troops ashore at the entrance to the Gulf of Corinth and had put the city of Patras to the sack, coming away from infinite damage to citizenry with rich plunder and a large number of ransomable Greek and Jewish non-combatants as well as Turks. During this same period Grand Master Garzés was re-establishing at Malta an administration based on forethought and concern for ordinary citizens as well as one of reasoned governance of the Convent and Republic. Bread, produce, and meats were readily available in marketplaces, health care was free and equally available, and festive celebrations were rather frequent. Participants and observers agreed it had been many years since a similar period of reason and well-being at Malta.[9]

With little love for Hospitallers having suffered the shortcomings of Grand Master Verdalle, Viceroy of Naples Juan de Zúñiga y Avellaneda, 1st Duke of Peñaranda de Duero and 6th Count of Miranda ordered the execution of Marino Pagani of Nocera, 25 years an Hospitaller, on the specious charge of plotting the Viceroy's assassination. No evidence was produced, no legal proceeding took place, no notice was given, but Marino Pagani was grotesquely decapitated in Naples' central marketplace. Aghast, Grand Master Garzés was able only to appoint an ambassadeur extraordinaire to the courts of Rome and Madrid. This individual, Commander Cassano Bernizzone of Genoa, was charged with seeking an explanation. Bernizzone obtained a *Moto Proprio* from Pope Clement VIII expressing Papal displeasure and a demand by King Philip II that his viceroys at Naples and Sicily restore relations with Hospitallers to the *status quo ante*. But neither Bernizzone nor the Order ever obtained an explanation.[10]

Upon occasion of the 17 September 1595 absolution of French King Henry IV by Pope Clement VIII, recognizing the King's formal return to Roman Catholicism, Segreville as Bailiff of Eagle together with Francesco Lanfreducci and Frederico de Brito were assigned to convey the Order's congratulations to the Court of France. Segreville's lesser birth on his father's side, however, prevented him from carrying out the assignment and he was replaced by Philibert de Foissy-Chamesson.[11]

During 1595 Foissy-Chamesson succeeded Michel de Seurre de Lumigny as Prior of Champagne upon the latter's death, and was in turn succeeded as Grand Hospitaller by Henri d'Appellevoisin de la Bodinalière. Girolamo di Agliata was dispatched to Palermo to congratulate Giovanni II Ventimiglia y Moncada, 6th Marchese of Geraci, upon his accession as President of Sicily, and to discuss several items of mutual interest. Prior of Pisa Ambrogio di Gioeni passed away and the vacant Priory was conferred by Apostolic Brief on Don Antonio de Medici, 19 year-old natural son of Grand Duke of Tuscany Francesco I de Medici and Bianca Cappello, received as an Hospitaller for the occasion. The Priory thereafter became a family heirloom passed from father to son to the great detriment and distress of the Langue of Italy.[12]

Luigi Vivaldo passed away in November following 25 days of storm-tossed sailing. Eldest of three Hospitaller brothers thought to still be in his fifties, there was no announced cause of death. He was the last General of the Galleys of the Small Cross. Upon his death he was succeeded in command of the galleys by Pierre de Roquelaure Saint-Aubin, renowned corsair and skilled mariner, who nominated Jean-Pierre de Ruynal of Provence to be his flag captain in succession of Giacomo Palio of Turin.[13]

Also passing away in November was Emilio Pucci commanding the Papal Galley Squadron. Received at Florence as an Hospitaller in

1565 he appeared within months with September's Grand Soccorso slamming the door on Ottoman expectations of conquering Malta. Only 50 years of age at death, Pucci was a victim of one of the several pandemics plaguing Europe during the late Sixteenth Century. He was succeeded as Papal Commander by Hospitaller Cesar Magalotti also of Florence.[14]

Early in 1596 Grand Prior of Germany Philipp Riedesel zu Camberg arrived at Malta to confer with the Grand Master upon request of non-Hospitaller Elector of Brandenburg John George who wished his non-Hospitaller son Frederick IX, Margrave of Brandenburg, to be awarded the dignity of Bailiff of Brandenburg. The Margrave would be awarded the dignity in 1610 upon promotion of incumbent Martin, Graf von Hohenstein. Then 22 years of age the Margrave died one year later. In the meanwhile Grand Master and Council dispatched yet another ambassador to protest outside meddling in the award of Hospitaller dignities. This latest ambassador was Don Girolamo di Guevara who in the Spring would be dispatched to the Court of Holy Roman Emperor Rudolf II not so much on the matter of the Bailiwick of Brandenburg but on the Emperor's habit of rewarding loyal lieutenants with Hospitaller commanderies in Bohemia. Guevara was not the first Hospitaller ambassador to take up this matter with the Emperor, but he may have been the most successful by obtaining positive commitments to be effected within two years.[15]

It had for some time been recognized that to obtain maximum benefit from employment of the galleys and other vessels of the Order, a Committee of Knights of Judgment and Experience formed to counsel ships officers could be beneficial. Such a Committee was formed in the Spring of 1596 comprised of Admiral Don Pietro la Rocca of Messina, Bailiff of Caspe Don Esteban de Claramonte, Lieutenant Grand Bailiff Arbogast von Andlau, and Lieutenant Treasurer Antoine de Mornay de Villarceaulx of Rouen. The Committee focused on maritime abuses and means of prevention. The foregoing Committee members were in rotation replaced by Grand Chancellor Don Juan de la Rocca Pereira, Bailiff of Santa Eufemia Centorio Cagnolo, and Bailiff of Aquila François de Segreville. These three counseled officers on the command status of the capitana's captain or flag captain vis-a-vis more senior captains in company.[16]

Reports reached the Grand Master in Spring 1596 of transit by the Ottoman Armada through the Dardanelles passing between the two castles at the mouth exiting into the Aegean. The same reports again asserted the Armada's destination was Gozo. Grand Master and Council ordered Saint-Aubin and the five galleys to proceed directly to the Morea said to be the Armada's interim destination, to assess the threat to Malta and Gozo, and to return immediately. Saint-Aubin departed Malta on 11 May and returned 27 June confirming the Armada had transited the Dardanelles but not in formidable strength. In the meanwhile the Grand Master had received a letter from Gian Andrea Doria requesting the same five galleys reinforced with additional Hospitaller complements join the Catholic Armada assembling at Messina, and toward July-end Saint-Aubin took course for Messina. Saint-Aubin's report to Doria of an under-strength Ottoman Armada, according to Anderson who elsewhere in his *Naval Wars in the Levant* is scathing in his indictment of the Genovese admiral, may have helped persuade Doria to in August venture out of Messina and into the Archipelago. Once there, however, Doria failed to seek out the under-strength enemy afloat or ashore, while the ships so employed could have been much better utilized under their own recognizance.[17]

Meanwhile the matter of succession to the Priory of Lombardia for Emmanuel Philibert of Savoy, first raised in August 1590, was again broached, this time upon death of incumbent Isuardo di Sanmartino. The Order and particularly the Langue of Italy remained vociferously opposed. Three ambassadors were selected to reason with Pope Clement VIII. These were Bailiff of Aquila Segreville and Commanders Bernardo de Aldana of Castile and Girolamo di Guevara of Italy, the latter having recently established his diplomatic credentials at the Imperial Court of Rudolf II. These three ambassadors in August accompanied the galleys to Messina.[18]

When the Maltese galley squadron returned to Malta, its dearth of employment by and under Doria caused immense displeasure on the part of Grand Master Martin Garzés and Council. A board of inquiry was convened at Malta consisting of Lieutenant Grand Hospitaller Henri d'Appellevoisin de la Bodinatiere, Lieutenant Grand Conservator Don Antic de Cabrera, and Commander Ascanio Cambiano. The mandate of the board, however, was not to examine shortcomings of the Catholic Armada's employment under Gian Andrea Doria, a political minefield involving the Crown's judgment, but rather to examine history and response to claims of seniority to the Order of Jerusalem by Doria's Genovese contingent at fleet gatherings.[19]

During the month of December 1596 Grand Master and Council appointed Commander Giulio Pasi of Faenza Resident Ambassador to the Court of Rome in succession of Admiral Don Pietro la Rocca, and promoted to the Priory of Toulouse Grand Commander Pierre de Montauban de Voguedemar in succession of the deceased Jean Soubiran d'Arifat. Pierre de Roquelaure Saint-Aubin advanced to Grand Commander. Commander Jacques du Blot Viviers was appointed Resident Ambassador to the Court of France. Commander Diogo de Brito of Castile was appointed to command of *Santa Croce* succeeding Boniface de Puget-Chasteuil, while Georges de Castellane d'Aluis of Provence was appointed to command of *Santa Fede* succeeding Jean de Marsac-Saillac. Bernardino Barba of Turin was appointed to command of the new 28-bank galley *San Filippo* succeeding Francesco Moleti and *Vittoria*. Toward year-end Grand Master and Council commenced taking measures to collect past-due responsions from the Kingdom of France. Prior of Aquitaine Georges Régnier de Guerchy and Bailiff of Aquila Segreville were to pass through France and either collect past-due amounts or commence legal proceedings in the name of the Common Treasury. Other commissioners were appointed to move against recalcitrants in Italy and Spain. Sixty-three thousand scudos were collected within the Duchy of Charles of Lorraine, Duke of Mayenne, and 55,000 scudos from other secular debtors.[20]

One of three ambassadors assigned in September 1595 to convey the Order's congratulations to the Court of France on King Henry IV's absolution by Pope Clement VIII, Dom Frederico de Brito returned to Malta in January 1597 bringing with him fifty forzati or petty-criminal oarsmen contributed by the King together with recognition of the Order's historic privileges within the Kingdom.[21] That was the good news. As in earlier years and years to follow much of the bad news stemmed from the Long Turkish War (1593-1606) between Habsburg Hungary and the Ottoman Empire. This year the Holy See planned sending its own troops into Hungary under command of the Pope's nephew Gian Francesco di Aldobrandini. Also this year a letter was received at Malta from Holy Roman Emperor Rudolf II seeking Hospitaller ground force support. The Sacred

Council favorably endorsed the request on a voluntary basis. There was also the annual concern about the Ottoman Armada. Cigalazade Yusuf Sinan Pasha had been with Ottoman ground forces in Hungary in the year just ended. He had also served as Grand Vizier upon his return to Istanbul, but was currently unemployed while the Armada appeared rudderless. Nevertheless, there were reports of new galleys being added and of intent to deploy to the West which could be ignored only at peril.[22]

Early in 1597 Commander Giovan Battista Rondinelli of Florence, 36 years an Hospitaller, received consent and approval of the Sacred Council to establish a commandery of *giuspadronato* within the Rondinelli estates at Florence, *giuspadronato* meaning the commandery was to remain under control of the Rondinelli family and, for example, could not be assigned at the whim of a prince and must devolve on an Italian Hospitaller.[23]

As eleven months earlier, General of the Galleys Saint-Aubin was sent into the Levant to put his ear to the wind and ascertain exactly what was what, this time with four galleys reinforced with the complement of the fifth galley. These departed Malta on 25 April and sailed the length of the Archipelago until confident no Ottoman Armada would threaten Malta during 1597. The four galleys then turned to preying on the weak, first overcoming two armed brigantines and then one after another Turkish germas and caramussals each sent to the bottom but for five escorted to Malta with cargoes of rice, flax, spices, and other Turkish merchandise. Removed from all captures were 271 Turks, Moors, and several merchants with wives and children. Some of the captures stubbornly defended themselves, and the Maltese suffered numerous dead and 140 wounded. Among the dead were three knights, Francesco Azzolini of Siena, Don Jeronimo de Carvajal of Castile, and a knight of Savoy and the Langue of Auvergne whose name has been lost to history. Plunder arriving safely at Malta was valued at 80,000 gold scudos.[22]

Upon return of the four galleys from the Archipelago, President of Sicily and Marchese of Geraci Giovanni II Ventimiglia y Moncada requested of the Grand Master galley protection of Sicily during the absence of Sicily's own galley squadron. The five Maltese galleys were to pursue Infidel corsairs infesting the Sicilian coast. Following more than a month without sighting the enemy, however, the Maltese were released to take possession of a new capitana constructed at Messina.

Yet another corsair cruise was undertaken with the galleys *San Filippo* and *Santa Croce* respectively commanded by Bernardino Barba and Dom Diogo de Brito, the first Padrone or second-in-command of the squadron. These two galleys departed Malta on 19 August and took course for the seas between Candia and the coast of North Africa, particularly scouring the waters of Alexandria and Damietta at the mouth of the Nile. Several small ships were intercepted, plundered, and sent to the bottom. Fifty-seven crew were removed along with bales of tapestry and cordovan leather.[22]

During the year Marshal Jacques de Virieu-Pupetières was appointed Bailiff of Lyon upon death of incumbent François de Lange de la Chenault. Resident Ambassador to the Court of France Jacques du Blot Viviers advanced to Marshal pending assignment of a replacement ambassador. Raymond de Gozon-Mélac, an Hospitaller absent from these pages since reception in 1557, advanced to the dignity of Prior of Toulouse upon the sudden death of incumbent Pierre de Montauban de Voguedemar. Like many other Gozon Hospitallers, Raymond de Gozon-Mélac was directly descended from Dieudonné de Gozon, father of the 27th Grand Master of the Order of Jerusalem (1346-1353) of the same name. *Draconis Extinctor*. Grand Chancellor Don Juan de la Rocca Pereira was appointed Bailiff of Novaville upon death of incumbent Martín de Nieto, while Don Antonio de Toledo advanced to Grand Chancellor. Bailiff of Negroponte Ramón Fortuyn advanced to Grand Conservator upon death of incumbent Adrián de Maimon, while Hernando Ruiz de Corral advanced to Bailiff of Negroponte. Don Blasco d'Aragona of Palermo was dispatched to the Savoyard Court at Turin to render the Order's condolences to Duke Charles Emmanuel I concerning the passing of Duchess consort Catherine Michelle of Spain. Together they had sired ten children. Born Catalina Micaela, she was only 30 years of age. Bailiff of Lora Francisco de Valencia was ordered to the Court of Spain to similarly render the Order's condolences to the Duchess' father King Philip II and to the Duchess' sister Isabella, Governess of the Netherlands.[24]

The first Chapter General of Grand Master Martín Garzés convened at Valletta on Sunday 4 January 1598 in the Great Hall of the Magistral Palace. Following reception and sermon the Sixteen *Capitolari* or Legislators were selected two per langue as follow:

Grand Commander Pierre de Roquelaure-Saint-Aubin and Prior of Toulouse Raymond de Gozcn-Mélac for Provence, Bailiff of Lyon Jacques de Virieu-Pupetières and Lieutenant Marshal Philibert de Mathay for Auvergne, Grand Hospitaller Henri d'Appellevoisin de la Bodinalière and Lieutenant Treasurer Antoine de Mornay de Villarceaux for France, Grand Conservator Ramón Fortuyn and Bailiff of Caspe Esteban de Claramonte for Aragon, Admiral Don Pietro la Rocca and Bailiff of Santa Eufemia Centorio Cagnolo for Italy, Prior of England Andrew Wyse and Procurator for Ireland Don Mendo Tignosa of Palermo for England, Lieutenant Grand Bailiff Arbogast von Andlau and Friedrich Sundt for Germany, and Lieutenant Grand Chancellor Gonzalo Porras and Antonio Vega for Castile. Prior to commencement of formal proceedings Bailiff Claramonte proposed establishment of a trust initially funded by an advance from the Regency Court of Sicily in the amount of 12,000 scudos to be subsequently funded by descendants of his nephew Alberto Claramonte. The capital of the trust was to be managed by the Grand Conservator or his lieutenant and employed in the construction of 28-bank capitana galley hulls at Sicily at the rate of one per year in eight separate years, the hulls to be contributed to the Malta squadron for outfitting and armament. Because these galleys were to be constructed of well-seasoned timber, the Grand Master was required to place orders four years in advance. Each capitana was to bear the arms of the Religion, of the Grand Master at the time of completion, and of the founding Bailiff of Caspe. Finally, each capitana was to be called *Santo Stefano*. Claramonte's proposal was approved. Among formal deliberations of the Sixteen was continuation of funding levies mandated by the Chapters General of 1583 and 1588. Concerning galleys, the Admiral and General of Galleys together with two other committee members selected by the Grand Master and Council were to report every six months on governance and condition of the galleys. Another galley matter concerned recognition of Generals and Captains of the Galleys with two or more years service in those positions approved by Grand Master and Council. Finally, the Commandery of Devesset was to be incorporated within the Priory of Lyon on relocation of the latter.[25]

Upon supplication and request of the knights of the Langue of Provence, the Commandery of Avignon was to be detached from the

Priory of Saint-Gilles upon the death of Prior François de Puget, and the Commandery of Cavalleria was similarly to be detached from the Priory of Toulouse following death of Raymond de Gozon-Melac. The two commanderies were then to become available to deserving Provencal knights irrespective of Priory.[26]

His normal tenure as General of the Galleys having been exceeded, Pierre de Saint-Aubin was succeeded by Bailiff of Negroponte Hernando Ruiz de Corral. Ruiz de Corral nominated and the Council appointed Sancho Briceño of Castile as flag-captain commanding the flagship. At 1597 year-end the Council had appointed Jean François de Puget-Chasteuil of Provence to command of the new galley *San Giorgio* and Francesco Staiti of Messina to command of *San Placido* succeeding Onofre Copones. *San Filippo* was commanded by Bernardino Barba, and *Santa Croce* by Dom Diogo de Brito.[27]

Bernardino de Cárdenas y Portugal, Duque de Maqueda, arrived Sicily in 1598 as new Viceroy in succession of interim Viceroy and President Giovanni II Ventimiglia y Moncada. Grand Master and Council appointed Commander Don Antonio de Vega of Castile to render the Order's compliments to the new Viceroy and its wish for mutually beneficial relations. General Ruiz de Corral was ordered to transport Vega to Messina with the entire galley squadron to reinforce Vega's presence. The squadron was also expected to return with grain and other foodstuffs necessary to feed the local population. Accompanying the galleys to Messina was François de Harlay of the Langue of France en route to the Court of French King Henry IV as Resident Ambassador. Harlay was intercepted at Rome, however, and enjoined from recognizing a Protestant King. The position remained vacant for five years. Also accompanying the galleys to Messina was a protégé of Hospitaller Receiver of Responsions Gaspar de Monreal by the name of Alonso de Contreras, at age 16 searching for a place in history.

Imperialist commander Adolf Graf von Schwarzenberg on 28 March suddenly appeared before Ottoman-occupied Raab (Gyor) in northwest Hungary and one day later stormed and took the fortress. Raab was the first in a string of 1598 Schwarzenberg conquests including Eisenstadt (Kismarton) in eastern Austria, Veszprém, Várpalota, and Pest (lower Budapest) leading to Christian optimism in the Long Turkish War and to Schwarzenberg in 1599 becoming a Knight of the Holy Roman Empire beholden only to the Emperor.

Adolf's eldest son Adam Graf von Schwarzenberg was received into the Order of Jerusalem and in 1625 was raised to the dignity of Herrenmeister (Protestant Bailiff) of Brandenburg entitled to wear the Grand Cross.[28]

During these years English and Irish Roman Catholic asylum-seekers appeared at Malta seeking a home and status, and professing nobility without proofs. Among these was Daniel Clancy carrying a letter of recommendation from King Philip II of Spain. Referred to the Holy See, Pope Clement VIII endorsed admission of Clancy. Because Clancy would in time promise to lay claim to the dignity of Lieutenant Turcopolier or senior knight of the Langue at Malta able to vote at General Assemblies where Grand Priors were forbidden the vote, thus threatening Wyse's position without ever proving his nobility, Andrew Wyse hastened to Rome, and with the tacit support of Grand Master and Order, succeeded in warding off the threatened danger. Clancy was not admitted to the Order of Jerusalem. To prevent similar tactics in the future Wyse obtained a Magisterial Bull confirming him in his possession of the Priory. According to established custom, he could not now be deprived of his possession before the lapse of ten years. In fact, Wyse remained Grand Prior of England for 33 more years before coming to the end of his time.[29]

Giulio Pasi of Faenza, the Order's Resident Ambassador at Rome who had quietly defused Papal support for Clancy, passed away in May 1598 and was temporarily succeeded by Giacomo Bosio, author of the forepart of the Order's History. Stirring at Malta was great suspicion fed by various sources the Turkish Armada would in 1598 finally appear in the West. With May the month Ottoman incursions had in the past been identified, and with nothing so far detected, Grand Master and Council dispatched General Ruiz de Corral and all five galleys to the Levant to ascertain Ottoman intentions or movements. Ruiz de Corral was under orders should there be no report of Armada activity to undertake raids along the Anatolian coast and among islands of the Archipelago while intercepting Ottoman shipping. Departing Malta on 25 May Corral took course for Karamania on the underbelly of Anatolia where in the waters of Phineka (modern Finike) the squadron disabled a large caramussal in the vanguard of a convoy bound from Alexandria to Constantinople. Within sight of another sixteen convoyed vessels and their escort of ten galleys, Corral even so hoped to plunder the disabled caramussal before help arrived. Emboldened by the proximity of help, however, the caramussal's crew of 85 put up a stout defense. Following two hours of combat with half the caramussal crew dead, the remainder yielded just in time for the Maltese to remove surviving crew and plunder and ensure the ship went to the bottom. The squadron avoided pursuit by ten galleys on escort duty, not pursuit duty, and got away with six dead and 70 wounded, returning to Malta along the coast of Africa.[30]

Because Ruiz de Corral returned to Malta with no news of the Ottoman Armada whatsoever, *San Placido* under Francesco Staiti was ordered to the Strofadi islands off the western Morea and thence to the Braccia di Maina or arm of the Maina Peninsula extending down from southern Morea, the southernmost point of Greece controlling or at least observing east-west shipping lanes around Greece. Staiti departed Malta on 12 July and returned ten days later with news the Armada 60 galleys strong had exited the Dardanelles and was en route Navarin (Pylos) on the west coast of the Morea 385 nautical miles ENE of Malta.[31]

While Staiti was absent three of the four remaining galleys were reinforced by the complement of the fourth and proceeded to Messina seeking information on Ottoman intentions while also collecting at Messina the new galley *San Giorgio* constructed at Messina's Arsenal. Accompanying the four galleys during their return to Malta was Ambassador to Spain Don Bernardo de Spelletta transporting 40,000 scudos in coin which King Philip II, said to be responding to poverty of the Religion, was contributing to the fortification of Gozo. The contribution also happened, however, to equal the Order's share of profit accumulated by the Priory of Castile and Leon under Archduke of Austria and Hospitaller Prior Wenceslaus who died at 17 years of age in September 1578 and which had been a matter of diplomatic discussion ever since.[32]

Toward the middle of August 1598 the Order learned from a ship of Marseille the Ottoman Armada had exited the Archipelago and was headed further west. Grand Master and Council were convinced the Armada's destination was Gozo. Women, children, and the aged at Gozo were ordered into fortresses of Malta while headed in the opposite direction was a squadron of knights and serving brothers together with hired soldiers. Commander Luis de Carvajal of Castile was appointed Captain-at-Arms for Notabile (Mdina) while Bailiff of Negroponte and General of the Galleys Ruiz de Corral was appointed Captain-at-Arms and Governor of Vittoriosa and Senglea. Commanders Ramón de Veri of Catalonia, Ascanio Cambiano of Turin, and Jean de Vintimille d'Ollioules of Provence were appointed Sector Wardens with authority to make their city sectors ready for siege.[33]

With as yet no sign of the Ottoman Armada, the galleys *San Placido* commanded by Francesco Staiti and *San Giorgio* commanded by Jean François de Puget-Chasteuil were on 4 September sent into the Levant to ascertain the Armada's whereabouts and intentions. In the event there was no Armada threat, the two galleys were to proceed on corsair operations in the waters from North Africa's Cape Buonandrea to Damietta. Having heard nothing of the two galleys toward month-end, they were presumed to have proceeded toward Damietta in belief there was no threat to Malta. At about this time a frigate arrived from Sicily with a report the Armada 40 galleys strong was at Sicily's Cape Passero bound for Gozo. The frigate also reported that Cigalazade Yusuf Sinan Pasha, again Kapudan Pasha, had arrived off Messina on 20 September with the same 40 galleys, sent in a sailing tender under a white flag carrying gifts for the Viceroy, and asked that his mother Lucrezia Cicala be ferried out to his capitana. The Viceroy had demanded and received hostages against the safety of Sicilians visiting the Armada, the hostages including a son of the Pasha. That day and the next the Ottoman admiral entertained his mother, friends, family, and a party of Messinese knights and noble ladies requiring sailing feluccas as ferry transport. The Pasha and his armada departed on 22 September, some reports said for Algiers. On Wednesday 30 September, however, the Armada appeared in the Freo Channel between Malta and Gozo just before sunset. At Malta Lieutenant Marshal Philibert de Mathay commanding cavalry, infantry, and militia took station at Citta Vecchia.

On 1 October 1598 Grand Commander Pierre de Saint-Aubin was appointed to command of all defensive forces on the two islands. He, too, was on the wrong side of the Freo Channel. That day while taking on fresh water at Gozo the Ottomans put 2,000 troops ashore to keep beached galleys safe. There was a report of Hospitallers and infantry exiting the Gozo Citadel to repel Ottomans, but it seemed more than unlikely. The Ottomans departed on 2 October, taking course for North Africa.[34]

That same day the galleys *San Placido* and *San Giorgio* returned to Malta having been on corsair operations exactly four weeks during which they had encountered, plundered, and sunk fourteen enemy vessels. They brought with them 202 captive Turks and Moors as well as a 15th vessel, cargo of rice, flax, and other bulk items. At about the same time notice arrived of the death in September at Escorial, Spain, of King Philip II. A devout Catholic, he had been a staunch friend and supporter of the Knights of Saint John of Jerusalem, so much so the entire Convent was aware of its loss. Grand Master Garzés penned on behalf of the Order a letter of condolence addressed to Don Philip III, 20 year-old son of the deceased King, to the deceased King's sister Archduchess of Austria and Holy Roman Empress Maria, and to Infanta Isabella, Governess of the Netherlands. The Grand Master at the same time ordered Grand Chancellor Don Antonio de Toledo resident at the Court to carry out the Order's business with the new King as with the old. With appropriate delay, Grand Conservator Don Ramón de Fortuyn was dispatched as Ambassadeur Extraordinaire to congratulate the new King on his accession to the throne and on his forthcoming marriage to cousin Margaret of Austria, daughter of Charles II Francis of Austria, an Archduke of Austria and ruler of Inner Austria (Styria, Carniola and Carinthia) from 1564.[35]

During 1598 Don Gonzalo de Porras of Castile was appointed by Grand Master and Council to succeed the deceased Giulio Pasi of Faenza as Resident Ambassador and Procurator to the Court of Rome. Likewise Don Antic de Cabrera of Aragon was appointed Resident Ambassador to the Vice Regal Court of Naples where Viceroy and Count of Olivares Enrique de Guzmán y Ribera harbored unwarranted irritation with the Order. Finally, Resident Ambassador to King Philip II of Spain Don Martín de Guzman was re-appointed Resident Ambassador to King Philip III as he had been privy to the decision of King Philip II some months before his death re-affirming the Standard of the Religion as senior to and having precedence over that of the Republic of Genoa.[36] The galleys transported the three new ambassadors to Sicily en route their assignments. At Sicily at November-end, Corral and three galleys were assigned to transport the official household of new Viceroy Enrique de Guzmán y Ribera from Messina to Palermo, thereafter returning to Malta. Of the other two galleys, *San Filippo* commanded by Bernardino Barba was assigned to transport Ramón Fortuyn to Barcelona from where the latter proceeded by carriage to Madrid, while *San Giorgio* under Jean François de Puget-Chasteuil was assigned to take the other two ambassadors, Porras and Cabrera, as far as Naples. Toward the end of the year Ambassador to the Imperial Court of Rudolf II, Don Girolamo di Guevara, returned to Malta following three years at Vienna where he had been negotiating the future of the Priory and Commanderies of Bohemia. The resolution of this matter, according to Pozzo, was communicated in secret to Grand Master and Council.[37]

Also during 1598 (Titular) Bailiff of Brandenburg Johann Philipp von Lesch was advanced to Grand Bailiff while incumbent Bernhard von Angelach-Angelach advanced to Grand Prior. Lesch was succeeded as Bailiff of Brandenburg by Alsace's Arbogast von Andlau. Admiral Pietro La Rocca advanced to Bailiff of Santo Stefano upon death of incumbent Baldassar Marchetti, and was in turn succeeded as Admiral by Michele Cadamosto of Lodi. The Priory of Rome was vacated by death of Cardinal Alessandrino (Michele Bonelli), and was assigned by Pope Clement VIII (Ippolito di Aldobrandini) to Silvestro Aldobrandino, a great-nephew. Hospitaller Fabrizio Sforza Colonna was appointed Coadjutor or heir apparent to the Priory of Venice, a dignity then held by Cardinal Ascanio Colonna. Grand Hospitaller Henri d'Appellevoisin advanced to Treasurer of the Religion upon death of incumbent Antoine des Hayes d'Espinay Saint-Luc. Appellevoisin was succeeded as Grand Hospitaller by Commander of Villedieu (en-Dreugesin) Alof de Wignacourt. Also at year-end Fabrizio Berzetto of Vercelli succeeded Bernardino Barba in command of *San Filippo*. The Priory of Castile and León was vacated by death of incumbent Don Fernando de Toledo; prior to his death King Philip II had nominated as successor his own nephew Prince Philibert of Savoy, 10 year-old third son of Charles Emmanuel I, Duke of Savoy, and Infanta Catherine Michelle of Spain.[38]

In April of 1599, exasperated with pretensions of Inquisitor Monsignor Hortensio, Carlo Valdina in the courtyard of the old Hospital several times slapped the prelate with his hand, thus provoking the Church which initiated a proceeding which could have led to Valdina's incarceration. The prelate was pacified by a visit from three knights of the Grand Cross.[39]

During late Spring and Summer the four galleys of the Religion under General Corral made several opportunity cruises including one circumnavigating Sicily and exploring its uninhabited islands from which it returned in early June with three Turkish brigantines as prizes. One of these was taken off Cape Passero and the other two while beached at Cefalu on Sicily's north shore 32 nautical miles east of Palermo. Captives taken and sent to Christian oars totaled 73 while a larger number of Christians were liberated from Turkish oars. Awaiting the galleys at Messina were several crates of artillery, muskets, and ammunition, sent under shipping order of Philip III's Duchy of Milan. Upon receiving a report the Padrona galley of the Religion, *San Filippo*, commanded by Bernardino Barba had reached Naples during her return from Barcelona, Corral took the other four galleys to a rendezvous at that city. Commander Juan Fernandez d'Inestrosa of the Langue of Castile was embarked conveying the Order's compliments to Count of Lemos Fernando Ruiz de Castro Andrade y Portugal on his accession as Viceroy of Naples. The five galleys returned together to Malta, *San Filippo* transporting coin, jewels, and silver together valued at 180,000 scudos much of it destined for the Common Treasury.[40]

With 1598 assignment of the Priory of Castile and León to Prince Philibert of Savoy, the Bailiwick of Armenia again became available and in 1599 was assigned to Giorgio Carretto, senior knight of the Langue of Italy without dignity. The Holy See ruled in September, however, the Bailiwick of Armenia was to be extinguished upon resignation of Carretto or upon his death. Upon Carretto's death in 1607, though, new Pope Paul V would award the same dignity to Silvio Gonzaga received as an Hospitaller for the occasion. An illegitimate son of Duke of Mantua Vincenzo Gonzaga, Silvio presumably was a *nipote* of one or another iteration.

During 1599 Viceroy of Sicily Bernardino de Cárdenas y Portugal, 3rd Duke of Maqueda, commissioned a new galliot built to his order and placed her in proprietary corsair service under command of Ruy Perez de Moncada. In addition to crew, voluntary soldiery was solicited from the Spanish tercio assigned to Sicily. Among the latter was Alonso de Contreras, like Miguel de Cervantes a native of Madrid who like Cervantes had fled the city following a street brawl in which a participant had been killed. Again like Cervantes, Contreras was destined for a military career before authoring a memorable work of literature, his a manuscript autobiography. Now in the possession of the Biblioteca Nacional de España, the English translation of the manuscript has come down to us as *The Life of Captain Alonso de Contreras: Knight of the Military Order of St. John.* When signing on to the Maqueda galliot, Contreras was in his 17th year. Two years earlier he had been a protégé of Hospitaller Gaspar de Monreal, Receiver of Responsions at Malta. It would take another 30 years before Contreras produced sufficient evidence of his own credentials to be knighted as an Hospitaller assigned to the Langue of Castile.

Contreras's first cruise as a soldier was notable for the surprise and capture at the island of Lampedusa of Caragiali and his large 26-bank galliot, Caragiali also known as Ali Pasha a renegade Greco-Albanian born at Lepanto, a veteran of 1560's Battle of Djerba, of 1565's Ottoman Siege of Malta, of 1570's Battle of Cape Passero, and of 1571's Battle of Lepanto who for most of forty years had been termed "the greatest corsair of his day." Alonso de Contreras at the conclusion of his thirty years as a corsair might well have been considered the greatest corsair of *his* day.[41]

Doubtful of any surprise from the Ottoman Armada, the galleys *San Giorgio* under Jean François de Puget-Chasteuil together with *San Filippo* under Fabrizio Berzetto were in September 1599 sent into the Levant under orders to plunder enemy shipping, paying particular heed to the advice of Royal Pilot Jacques de Vincheguerre, a consummate mariner later Commander of the Galleys of France and still later Lieutenant General of French Naval Armies. Galleys and pilot departed Malta on 8 September and passed into the Archipelago before turning south toward the Egyptian coast. Off Damietta they took a Turkish vessel, crew of 30, laden with bales of silk among other items. From Damietta the two galleys took a westerly heading toward Rashid (Rosetta), like Damietta in the Nile Delta. Off the latter port they encountered a large germa bound from Djerba by way of Tripoli to Alexandria, cargo of baracan or camel's hair cloth and a variety of other merchandise. Embarked were a large number of Moors, a number of merchants, and about 200 Black Africans. With ill-considered confidence the germa crew resisted, the two galleys invested, and much of the germa crew did not survive combat. Worse, the germa was accidentally holed at the waterline by cannon-fire and went under. Only 51 germa crew were rescued while 50 galley soldiers and seamen failed to survive as did nine Hospitallers. These were knights Gabriel de Vincens-Savoillan of Provence, Catalan Andreu de Meiran Baia, Jean-Baptiste Saffalin-Vacheres of Provence, François de la Tour dit Vernainet of Auvergne, Nicolas de la Fontaine d'Ognon of Oise north of Paris, Claudio Bandi of Rimini, a Knight of Germany whose name was not recorded plus serving brothers Diego Martin of Aragon and Andrés Martinez of Castile.[42]

At Malta Grand Master and Council recognized a need at the Court of Caesar for a minister involving himself in the many and diverse Court matters affecting the Convent. Catalan Don Luis de Moncada was appointed Resident Ambassador and Procurator General to the Imperial Court of Rudolf II at Vienna. He was ordered to first proceed to Rome to receive the blessing of Pope Clement VIII with a Brief and letter respectively recommending him to the Emperor and Papal Nuncio. He was to uphold with all of his ability Caesar's decree of a year ago declaring the Priory of Bohemia and all of its commanderies the property of the Order of Jerusalem, theretofore usurped by the electors of Brandenburg, John George until a year earlier and Joachim Frederick at the time. Moncada accordingly embarked aboard the assigned galley *San Placido* commanded by Francesco Staiti and departed Malta on 7 October bound for Naples where Staiti had additional business and from which Moncada would proceed overland to Rome.[43]

Two days later the Infidel corsair and Italian renegade Mami Reis of Rhodes appeared above Gozo's northwestern Cape San Dimitrio aboard his bastarda galley accompanied by three galliots. The corsair made known he had enslaved Ambassador Moncada, Francesco Staiti, and the entire crew of *San Placido*. Mami Reis had formerly served for several years as Counsel aboard this same *San Placido* under the name of Nicolò Rodiotto, but had eventually fled to the Barbary Coast in a small boat. He would in the future become Sancakbey or Ottoman Governor of Rhodes personally commanding the Rhodes Guard. During the corsair's stay of three days at Gozo his ships seized seven more vessels transporting grain and provisions to Malta, while at Malta the Order had only two galleys, the squadron capitana and padrona under Corral. Soon, however, the two galleys sent into the Levant returned to Malta and all four galleys went in pursuit. Departing Malta on 12 October, they went by way of Lampedusa to Bizerta. For eleven days they fought contrary winds without catching sight of the enemy, and then returned to Malta. Luis de Moncada would be ransomed, not by the Convent but rather by his brother the Marqués de Aitona. Because Pozzo never again mentioned Staiti, he presumably died in slavery. Neither was there further mention of *San Placido*. Nor of her crew of about 110 Christians. Nor of her complement of Hospitallers estimated at fifty including young caravan knights. One such knight never again to reappear was Gabriel de la Fontaine Malgenestre received two years earlier. Descended from a cadet branch of the l'Isle-Adam family, he was a part of the embarked Caravan. Another never to reappear was Henri de Saintrailles of Lorraine and the Priory of Champagne, a second son of Henry de Saintrailles de Rostellain, Vicomte et Seigneur de Rotton, and of Louise de Gournay, Saintrailles also a cadet branch of the l'Isle-Adam family. Ten years an Hospitaller and not of the Caravan, Henri de Saintrailles had volunteered for this his last cruise.[44]

At Malta the populace was suffering not only huge people losses but the loss of grain and provisions, and so the Grand Master arranged with authorities at Licata for the four galleys to load foodstuffs at Licata's loading docks without the delay of undergoing pratique, galley crews remaining aboard. The galleys were in October 1599 dispatched to Licata with orders to load foodstuffs with all due speed and without going ashore for any other purpose. These orders seemed strange to Ruiz de Corral, and he debarked without undergoing pratique.[45]

Upon discovery, Ruiz de Corral was immediately relieved of his responsibilities in a scandal of disobedience. At the time Sancho Briceño commanded the Capitana *San Martino*, Dom Diogo de Brito commanded the Padrona *Santa Croce*, Jean François de Puget-Chasteuil commanded *San Giorgio*, and Fabrizio Berzetto commanded *San Filippo*. By order of Grand Master and Council Brizenio was appointed Governor of *San Martino*, and Ramiro de Tordesillas Cuevas of Castile succeeded Brito in command of the Padrona *Santa Croce* aboard which the Order's standard was hoisted. The two other commands remained unchanged. These four carried out necessary excursions in adverse weather during which the Grand Master's justifiable angst waned. Ruiz de Corral was reinstated for the remainder of his two-year term ending in February.[46]

During 1599 Grand Chancellor Don Antonio de Toledo succeeded to the dignity of Bailiff of Novaville upon death of incumbent Don Juan de la Rocca Pereira, while Bailiff of Negroponte Don Fernando Ruiz de Corral advanced to Grand Chancellor. Don Antic de Cabrera advanced to Bailiff of Negroponte, though a bit later he was further advanced to Grand Conservator. Dom Diogo de Souza of Portugal was appointed to the dignity of Bailiff of Acre, the first incumbent since the Holy Land. Grand Bailiff Johann Philipp von Lesch advanced to Grand Prior of Germany, and was succeeded as Grand Bailiff by Prior of Dacia Weipert von Rosenbach while Rosenbach was succeeded as Prior of Dacia by Arbogast von Andlau and Andlau was succeeded as Titular Bailiff of Brandenberg by Valentin von Hess. Prior of Ireland Don Pedro Gonzales de Mendoza succeeded Don Fernando Ruiz de Corral as General of the Galleys effective in February 1600, and upon Mendoza nomination Don Luis de Cardona the Elder was appointed captain of the capitana *San Martino*. Upon Council nomination Guillaume Gadagni Beauregard of Auvergne was appointed to command of *San Giorgio* succeeding Jean François de Puget-Chasteuil.[47]

The year 1600 opened with possession of the Priory of Hungary again a matter of contention between the langues of Italy and Germany. Johann Philipp von Lesch as senior knight without a dignity of the Priory of Germany had been appointed Prior of Hungary in 1589 pursuant to an agreed transfer of the Priory from Italy to Germany. Lesch had, however, immediately renounced his right to the Priory[48] in favor of incumbent Italian Don Vincenzo Carafa who had been appointed Prior of Hungary in July 1581 and who would thus remain Prior until 1600. Carafa had meanwhile obtained a Brief from Clement VIII recognizing the Priory (it was actually a bailiwick with right to call itself a priory and with right to call its bailiff a prior) as a dignity of the Langue of Italy. In that the priory rightfully belonged to the Langue of Germany as determined by successive Chapters General, the Germans had protested. The matter had been resolved by agreement that upon the death of Carafa, the priory would revert to the Langue of Germany. Meanwhile Prior of Capua Bernardino Scaglia passed away in 1600 and was succeeded by Carafa. Also meanwhile Johann Philipp von Lesch had in 1599 been advanced to Grand Prior of Germany resulting in a dearth of German candidates. This did not alter the agreement, but because of the priory's limited Italian life, no Italian knight found it an attractive dignity. The Langue of Italy had been further appeased, moreover, by recognition of the Priory of Pavia (originally conceived and so-far only awarded to Papal factotum Fabrizio Berzio) as a permanent dignity of the Langue of Italy. Transfer of the Priory of Hungary from Italy to Germany would not take place until 1605.[49]

During this period the Convent was notified of the death in Hungary during combat with Ottoman forces of Hospitaller Lelio Frangipani of the Langue of Italy. The son of Muzio Frangipani and nephew of Hospitaller Leone Strozzi by sister Giulia, he was a knight of great heart and enterprise thought to have been about 60 years of age. He is remembered by a marble bust in Rome's Church of San Marcello al Corso, a remembrance at less than half that age.[50]

In July 1600 Viceroy of Naples and Count of Lemos Fernando Ruiz de Castro Andrade y Portugal together with Viceroy of Sicily and Duke of Maqueda Bernardino de Cárdenas y Portugal, mutually decided on a surprise assault against Ottoman Tripoli. Eight galleys under command of Don Garcia de Toledo, Castellan of Castel Sant'Elmo at Naples and son of Don Pedro de Toledo, together with four galleys and two galiots of Sicily under Don Cesare d'Aragona were accordingly dispatched to Malta. Embarked were a good number of Spanish infantry under Maestro di Campo or Chief of Staff Andrés Salazar. These sought participation of the five galleys of Malta together with an embarked Maltese ground force, a participation unanimously approved by Grand Master and Council. General of the Galleys Don Pedro Gonzales de Mendoza was assigned collateral responsibility as Maltese ground force commander supported by three Sergeants Major respectively speaking French, Italian, and Spanish. Philibert de Mathay was to carry the Order's Standard while Guillaume de Beauregard commanding *San Giorgio* would place the petard to blow the gate. A 322-Hospitaller ground force was embarked at Marsa Scirocco (Marsaxlokk) and departed Malta on 28 July headed directly to Tripoli. The assault force found, however, Tripolitans and Turks forewarned and at the ready. A clear case of loose lips and an absence of secrecy. Realizing that without surprise the expedition was doomed to failure, the assault force returned whence it had come without even debarking the ground force. Three days following arrival back at Malta the

Neapolitan and Sicilian contingents returned to their home ports. While the aborted assault on Tripoli was taking place the Viceroy of Sicily's own *Galeón d'Oro* was completing an highly successful assault on the port of Alexandretta (Iskenderun), at the time a Silk Road terminus. Alonso Contreras was embarked as an assistant pilot and cartographer. A Portolan or Sailing Directions to eventually ensue from Contreras's charts is now in the possession of the Biblioteca Nacional de Madrid.[51]

Having agreed to act with others in escorting Maria de' Medici from Livorno to Marseille following her proxy wedding to King Henry IV of France, the five galleys under Gonzales Mendoza departed Malta on 27 August 1599 and proceeded directly to Livorno. At Livorno new Prior of Saint-Gilles Pierre de Roquelaure Saint-Aubin hastened to Florence to present himself to the Queen Consort of France and to her uncle Ferdinando I, Grand Duke of Tuscany. The groom had not attended his own proxy wedding on 5 October in Florence but rather awaited his bride at Montmélian in the lower Alps where the French were contesting Savoyard occupation of Saluzzo. In addition to Saint-Aubin the Queen Consort departed Florence for Livorno in the company of her uncle's spouse Grand Duchess Christina of Lorraine, of her sister Eleonora Duchess of Mantua, and of many other ladies of the Grand Duchy. The squadron of galleys awaiting the Queen Consort included in addition to the five of Malta under Mendoza, five of the Pope under Hospitaller Cesare Magalotti, and seven of Tuscany under nominal command of the Grand Duke's illegitimate brother Giovanni de Medici normally commanded by Marcantonio Calefati who was also present. The Queen Consort and her immediate entourage were embarked aboard the Tuscan capitana fittingly decorated for the occasion and flying the flag of France just below that of the Grand Duchy. Two full days following departure from Livorno the 17 galleys were met off Marseille by a felucca requesting they await the French galley flagship *La Reale* exiting Marseille to welcome the Queen Consort who soon transferred to the larger galley with her ladies-in-waiting. Entering port the Maltese capitana was assigned the place of honor to the right of the French flagship, much to the displeasure of Giovanni de Medici. Once ashore the Queen Consort demanded transportation to the King, while Giovanni de Medici complained about positioning of the Tuscan capitana, both begetting the notorious rejoinder of Grand Chancellor Maximilien de Béthune, *The Queen had been summoned to France to make babies, not to give orders.* Marie de Medici was to make six babies including King Louis XIII of France.[52]

Ambassador Saint-Aubin, General Mendoza, and all five Malta captains had audiences with the King during which gifts were exchanged. It is not clear whether the same was true for Tuscan captains as Giovanni de Medici had continued to voice his displeasure. Upon departure from Marseille the Maltese proceeded initially to l'île de Pomègues just offshore to permit the Tuscan Squadron to proceed ahead back to Livorno. At Pomègues the five galleys beached stern to the shore, prow cannon covered but ready. The Tuscans chose not to make an issue of it so close to Marseille but rather proceeded on their way. On Maltese arrival at Livorno, however, the Fortezza Vecchia guarding the old port opened fire. The Malta Squadron withdrew without entering port and reached home on 26 December 1600.[52]

Having been deprived of the Commandery of Pazos de Reinteros of the Priory of Castile during his absence as General, and with the Commandery newly assigned to Don Lorenzo de Figueroa, Under-Master of the Grand Master's House, Mendoza at year-end 1600 renounced his command of the squadron and was succeeded by Bailiff of Lyon Jacques du Blot Viviers. Upon nomination by the latter, François Breschard le Pensur of Burgundy and the Langue of Auvergne was appointed flag captain succeeding Don Luis de Cardona the Elder. During the absence of the five Maltese galleys over the final four months of 1600, two galleys armed and equipped for corsair operations by Vicereina of Naples Teresa de la Cueva y Bobadilla ended up at Malta under command of Hospitaller Fernando Aragones de la Cuba of Aragon. These made two raids into the Levant and returned with several Infidel prizes.[53]

During 1600 the Council decreed that no knight or serving brother would be received into the Convent without arms, sword, musket, morion helmet, and corselet. Secondly, no novitiate would be permitted on caravan without attestations of readiness from three Commissioners of Novitiates. Also during the year Don Martín de Ferrera was appointed Castellan of Amposta succeeding Don Geronimo de Fozes upon the latter's death. Jacques du Blot-Viviers had been advanced from Marshal to Bailiff of Lyon upon demise of incumbent Bailiff

Jacques de Virieu-Pupetières, while Claude de la Salle de Colombière had advanced to Marshal. Admiral Michele Cadamosto advanced to Bailiff of Venosa upon the death of incumbent Federico Caccia and was succeeded as Admiral by Prior of Hungary Giorgio del Carretto, while Commander Lodovico Coconato was appointed Prior of Hungary.[53]

The outset of 1601 was marked by the saddening infirmity and death of Grand Master Martín Garzés, worn by age and responsibility as well as by weight and retention of urine capped by fever. In possession of his faculties until the end, he consigned his one-fifth share of liquid assets to construction of a defensive tower at Freo (Mgarr) on the island of Gozo to be called Garzez Tower, and appointed Grand Commander Pierre d'Esparbez de Lussan his Magistral Lieutenant with authority to act in his stead in the event of his incapacity or death. He passed away on 7 February at the age of 75 years having governed the Religion for five years and nine months, a period of relatively constructive developments. His remains were properly embalmed and with all due ceremony entombed within St. John's Co-Cathedral at Valletta with other Grand Masters.[54]

Chapter VIII

1601–1606

T he Hospital's Council of State convened on 9 February 1601 to receive a report concerning Magistral matters from Magistral Lieutenant Pierre d'Esparbez de Lussan. Following the report it was Lussan's duty as President of the Council to appoint his own successor, and he so appointed Jacques du Blot Viviers, Bailiff of Lyon and General of the Galleys. As Magistral Lieutenant Vivier convened a General Assembly for the purpose of electing a new Grand Master. The Council prior to the General Assembly confirmed the existing 6,000 Maltese scudo annual salary to be paid Grand Masters. The Council also permanently forgave payments amortizing the capitalized cost of public housing due from residents of Senglea. The modest wherewithal of these ordinary citizens had never been sufficient to fund both construction cost and recovery from Great Siege destruction.[1]

At dawn on 10 February a General Assembly of all voting Hospitallers at Malta convened with 353 knights, chaplains, and serving brothers in attendance. This total excluded Hospitallers yet to complete two annual caravans and five years residence at the Convent as well as those indebted to the Common Treasury. The first order of business was selection by langue of an elector to represent that langue. The Eight Electors selected were Grand Commander Lussan for Provence, Marshal Claude de la Salle de Colombière for Auvergne, Grand Hospitaller Alof de Wignacourt for France, Don Juan de Paternò y Aragona for Aragon, Bailiff of Santa Eufemia Centorio Cagnolo for Italy, Prior of Ireland Don Pedro Gonzales de Mendoza for England, Lieutenant Grand Bailiff Johann Friedrich Hund von Saulheim for Germany, and Bailiff of Negroponte Hernando de Ovando for Castile. By virtue of the rule denying the vote to those indebted to the Common Treasury, English Hospitallers present necessarily supported by the Common Treasury were thus ineligible to vote at General Assemblies. By dignity alone Don Pedro Gonzales was the sole representative of England.[2]

These Eight Electors in camera selected Prior of Toulouse Raymond de Gozon-Mélac as non-voting President of Elections, Ippolito Malaspina of the Marquisate of Fosdinova as Knight of Elections, Simon Viel of France as Chaplain of Elections, and Serving Brother Gabriel Rosset of Malta and the Langue of Auvergne as Sergeant-at-Arms of Elections. The Eight Electors retiring, these latter three, called *The Triumvirate*, then selected a fourth elector, and the four selected a fifth, and so on until there were Sixteen Electors at two per langue. The thirteen additional electors in order of selection were (1) Jean de Vintimille d'Ollioules for Provence, (2) Commander Don Girolamo di Guevara of Italy for England, (3) Commander Gaspar de Monreal for Aragon, (4) Konrad von Rosenbach for Germany, (5) Diogo de Brito for Castile, (6) Commander Jean de Vassadel-Vaqueiras for Provence, (7) Commander François Breschard le Ponsur for Auvergne, (8) Commander Simon d'Aubigné de Boismozé for France, (9) Commander Antonio Pucci for Italy, (10) Commander Bartolomé (Bartomeu in Catalan) del Brull for Aragon, (11) Afonso de Vila Seca of Portugal for England, (12) Andreas Sturmfeder von Oppenweiler for Germany, and (13) Commander Ramiro de Tordesillas Cuevas of Toro, Zamora, for Castile. Following three hours of debate and discussion considering the candidacies of Bailiff of Santa Eufemia Centorio Cagnolo and Grand Hospitaller Alof de Wignacourt, neither having had command at sea, both owning corsair vessels, some electors appear to have been persuaded to switch support from Attorney Cagnolo to the younger Wignacourt following the lead of Knight of Elections Ippolito Malaspina. Grand Hospitaller Alof de Wignacourt was elected 54th Grand Master of the Order of Jerusalem.[3]

Born at Picardy's Litz in 1547, Alof de Wignacourt or Aloph de Vignacourt was the fourth son of six sons and three daughters of Jean de Wignacourt, Gentilhomme de la Chambre and Seigneur de Litz et La Rue-Saint-Pierre, and of Marie de la Porte de Vézins wed in 1538. Older brothers Adrien and Joachim succeeded to their father's estates while brothers Philippe and Charles embarked upon military careers. There is little information concerning brother Jean and sisters Yolande, Claudine, and Marie. In 1565 Alof de Wignacourt was received into the Order of Jerusalem, Langue of France, Diocese of Beauvais 20 kilometers west of Litz, and early in 1566 appeared at Malta as a novitiate responding to a general summons to counter a perceived threat to the island. In 1570 Wignacourt was appointed Lieutenant to Governor Christophe le Boulleur de Montgaudry of the vacant city of Valletta, a significant assignment for a young knight not yet a commander. He remained at Malta for more than the five years required for an appointment as commander including two years of galley caravan duty before returning to the commandery at Beauvais-en-Gâtinais. In 1590 he was appointed Commander of La Villedieu-en-Dreugesin. There were at the time at least five La Villedieu commanderies, four of the Langue of France, one of the Langue of Auvergne, this one 105km west of Paris. Founded by Templars no later than 1163, La Villedieu-en-Dreugesin was essentially as old as La Villedieu-lès-Bailleul founded in 1130, the oldest Hospitaller commandery in France. La Villedieu-en-Dreugesin was also situated in one of the several theaters of Religious War which appear to have consumed much of Wignacourt's preoccupation. Wignacourt remained Commander at Dreugesin until his election as Grand Master. During those relatively quiet years at Malta he was notably to be found in service to the Monarchy at war with Huguenots. He was sufficiently prominent in the latter regard to be mentioned as serving under Charles de Lorraine, duc d'Aumale, a leader of the Catholic League captured at 1590's Battle of Ivry by future King Henry of Navarre, at that time a Huguenot. When appointed Grand Hospitaller at Malta in 1598 succession of Henri d'Appellevoisin, it was Wignacourt's first Hospitaller dignity following 33 years in the Habit, apparently a reflection of his preoccupation. As Grand Hospitaller he was expected to remain resident at the Convent and to do double duty as Pilier or senior knight of the Langue of France present. Awarded the Grand Cross attending the dignity, he was twenty-six months later elected by his peers Grand Master of the Hospitaller Knights of Saint John of Jerusalem. During those 26 months Alof de Wignacourt acquired two proprietary galleons and two frigates soon dedicated to corsair war.

At the Council meeting following election the new Grand Master warranted his intention to govern with justice and consideration, heeding the counsel of others. Ambassadors Extraordinary were appointed to notify kings, princes, and other heads of state of the passing of Grand Master Martin Garzés and the election of his successor. Commander Rodrigo de Brito of Portugal and the Langue of Castile was ordered to Rome, Commander Niccolò della Marra of

Naples to Vienna, Guillaume de Meaux Boisbaudran of Melun in the
Île-de-France to Paris, and Don Bernardo de Zuniga of Pamplona to
Madrid. Wherewithal of the impoverished Common Treasury was
addressed, as was the paucity of food supplies with which to feed the
resident population persisting for more than a year. In this latter
connection Ruiz de Corral as Grand Chancellor was dispatched on
13 January with the galley *San Filippo* to Palermo to solicit of Viceroy
and Duke of Maqueda Bernardino de Cárdenas y Portugal 2,000
salmas of grain above and beyond Malta's normal allotment, the 2,000
salmas for assignment to the Università of Malta. Ruiz Corral also
obtained replacement of 3,500 salmas lost to corsairs over the past two
years. Separately, General Viviers had taken the remaining four galleys
to sea in search of unescorted merchant prey and had been fortunate
enough to divert two cargoes of grain to Malta each of 2,000 salmas.
These acquisitions from Sicily and at sea were sufficient for the balance
of 1601.[4]

Ambassadors were readying to depart when an impasse developed
between the new Grand Master and Inquisitor of Malta Monsignor
Fabrizio Veralli stemming from the wounding by blade of an unarmed
Valletta artisan at the hand of Hospitaller Don Francisco Pantoja of
Ávila de los Caballeros, a city of Castile and León. The Grand Master
ordered imprisonment of Pantoja at Guve, Gozo, pending an inquiry
into the matter. But the Inquisitor objected. The artisan was a protege
of the Inquisitor, and the Inquisitor demanded Pantoja be tried in the
Court of God. There was widespread revolt among the Convent at
Inquisitor interference with Hospitaller governance. Entire auberges
threatened to desert Malta for their homelands. The impasse developed
to a degree Pope Clement VIII, a former canon lawyer, not only
refused to receive Ambassador Brito, but also threatened to revoke all
privileges of the Order normally granted by the Holy See. Caught
between Hospitaller and Papal intransigence, Wignacourt colluded
with the Inquisitor and reached a face-saving compromise. Pantoja
was eventually remanded to custody of the Church at Rome and not to
the Inquisition.[5]

A galley of Sicily arrived at Malta in April 1601 sent by the Viceroy
of Sicily conveying Hospitaller Juan Francisco Pacheco of Castile
representing the Viceroy's official household to congratulate Alof de
Wignacourt on his elevation to the Magistral throne. Toward the end

of the same month ten galleys of Naples arrived under command of their General Don Pedro de Toledo. Arriving in company with Toledo was Francisco Ruiz de Castro, son of Viceroy of Naples and Count of Lemos Fernando Ruiz de Castro Andrade y Portugal. The Neapolitans proposed a joint operation against enemies of the Holy Church. Following deliberation by Grand Master and Council both squadrons were authorized to proceed to the Levant on the trail of the annual caravan from Alexandria to Constantinople. Because the earlier arrived Sicilian galley wished to accompany Vivier's Malta Squadron under Vivier's command the Grand Master ordered that the Sicilian galley fly the padrona flag. The five Malta galleys were the capitana *San Martino* under François Ereschard le Ponsur of Moulins, *San Giorgio* under Guillaume Gadagne Beauregard of Lyon, *Santa Croce* under Ramiro de Cuevas of Tordesillas, *San Filippo* under Fabrizio Berzetto of Vercelli, and a replacement *San Placido* under Giuseppe di Guevara of Syracuse. Jacques de Vincheguerre of Marseille was the pilot. The sixteen galleys departed Malta on 9 May under the command of Toledo, their objective interception of the caravan. With this intent the combined squadrons proceeded under the Morea and across the Archipelago 700 nautical miles over six days to take a position near the Caravan waypoint of Macri (Fethiye) at the island of Carago (Karacaoren) in the vicinity of the Seven Capes of Karamania.[6]

In the deserted port they for several days cleaned and waxed underwater hulls, took on fresh water, and made preparations. Six Turkish fishing craft also put into the port and from them the squadrons learned the Alexandria caravan consisted of ten well-armed galleys escorting three sultana galleons, presumably with cargos of rich merchandise and coin sent by Yavuz Ali Pasha, Serbian Beylerbey or Viceroy of Egypt, to the Sultan in Constantinople. Toledo had five of the six fishing craft destroyed, ceding the sixth to Pilot Vincheguerre. Two days later the remaining fishing craft was dispatched to Malta, towed three miles out by two galleys to catch the wind. It was in doing this they were discovered by a Turkish galley in the vanguard of the caravan. The fishing craft took cover against the shore and during the night evaded the enemy. Toledo and his squadrons, with the element of surprise gone, did not assail the caravan but rather proceeded to Cyprus where they unsuccessfully attempted to surprise two local Turkish galleys at Paphos. Returning from Cyprus they encountered a Greek saiche by which they were informed the caravan carried not only wealth but plague as well, strewing the sea with corpses. The Maltese returned to Valletta on 29 June with six galleys of Naples and passed through pratique with a clean bill of health. Earlier at the foot of the Strait of Messina Don Pedro de Toledo and four galleys of Naples had turned north toward that city while the galley of Sicily had headed for Palermo. The six galleys of Naples at Malta were under command of Don Garcia de Toledo, son of Don Pedro.[7]

Meanwhile at Malta rumors of an Ottoman appearance in the west were rife as Cigalazade Yusuf Sinan Pasha was known to have exited the Dardanelles with the Ottoman Armada. Even so Spanish General of the Sea Gian Andrea Doria proposed an assault on Algiers rather than a defense of Italy. Doria claimed to have obtained secret intelligence by means of a French adventurer, Le Roux, who declared himself not only an expert concerning the territory, but also able to instigate an uprising in favor of the Spanish. Catholic Armada constituents were accordingly summoned to assemble at Messina in June. The new Grand Master and Council determined to comply with Doria's request and ordered General Viviers to quickly ready his five galleys to re-deploy. And because it was the intention of Doria to lay siege ashore, the Maltese also gathered a battalion of knights and soldiers under command of Bailiff of Mallorca Don Antic de Cabrera. Carrying the Standard of the Religion was Gabriel de Touges-Noaillan of Provence while Commanders Don Geronimo Rutinel of Aragon and Nicolas de la Fontaine d'Ognon of the Langue of France were appointed Sergeants-Major. With battalion embarked the five galleys departed Malta on 18 July arriving Messina the following evening. At Messina they found 32 galleys of Spain and Genoa under command of Doria and lieutenants, ten each of Naples and Sicily respectively commanded by Don Pedro de Toledo and Don Pedro de Leyva, five each of the Church and Tuscany under Hospitaller Cesare Magalotti and Marcantonio Calefati, and three of Savoy which with the five of Malta totaled 70 warships each with embarked ground force, one of the larger Christian armadas seen in recent years. By letter from Doria to Wignacourt dated 24 July, however, the five Maltese were detached to create a diversion for Sinan Pasha in the Archipelago, and soon returned to Malta. *"Now comes Doria's final failure,"* according to R.C. Anderson in his *Naval Wars in the Levant*.[8]

Doria sailed from Messina to Algiers by way of Mallorca, his 65 galleys arriving off Algiers on 24 August 1601. The five Tuscan galleys were sent ahead to reconnoiter and connect by signal with Le Roux and agents ashore. There was ground fog and visibility was poor. The Tuscan galley *Siena* almost rammed the flagship aboard which Virginio Orsini had command of embarked troops, Orsini the latest in an unbroken line of identically named Church commanders. Calefati nevertheless made the agreed signals before the port, but in the city, contrary to plan, no renegades rose in revolt. There was no sign whatsoever of local support. Informed, Doria did not assemble his captains and consider alternatives. Nor did he wait for the ground fog to clear. No, he promptly ordered a return to Mallorca where he dismissed the several squadrons. He later bowed to the storm of ridicule aroused and asked to be relieved of his command. His resignation was accepted.[9]

Earlier Wignacourt and Council ahead of these developments had been determined to comply with the fleet commander's wishes in spite of the out-size difference in Hospitaller force vis-a-vis the Ottoman Armada. Viviers was ordered to leave his padrona which had an antenna (sail spar) problem in port and to reinforce the other four galleys with armament and personnel from the crippled vessel. The four galleys departed Malta on 4 August bound directly for Venetian Zante 410 nautical miles distant, arriving on 8 August. Embarked were the usual caravans and soldiery plus at least one adventurer; he was Alonso de Contreras of Madrid, future cartographer and autobiographer as well as the stuff of adventure novels. At 19 years of age he was already a veteran of close-aboard combat at sea, and was already drawing nautical charts. At Zante Viviers interrogated the Venetian Governor and the Spanish Consul, learning Sinan Pasha had gone to Alexandria with 35 galleys to install his son as Sancakbey of Cairo, and that the other 15 left to guard the Archipelago were doing so from Scio (Chios) in the eastern Aegean.[10] These and others still at Constantinople were said to be afflicted with peste or plague, and therefore to represent little if any threat to the Maltese. Sinan, born Scipione Cicala at Messina, was in 1601 on his second tour of duty as Kapudan Pasha commanding the Ottoman Navy, his first tour from 1591 to 1595. In between he had served as an Army Field Commander during the Hungarian Campaign of 1596, as Ottoman Grand Vizier later the same year, and as Beylerbey of Damascus during the ensuing year until his 1598 re-appointment as Kapudan.[11]

Leaving Zante, Viviers proceeded by way of Stanfane (Strofades) and Prodano Island off the west coast of the Morea. From Prodano reconnoitering parties explored the feasibility of an assault on Ottoman Modone, but judged it too strongly defended. Thereafter the four galleys proceeded by way of Sapienza Island and Venetian Cerigo (Kithera) to Passava (Greek Neocastro, Italian Castelnuovo), a Turkish fortress on the eastern side of Cape Matapan. En route the Maltese seized a Turkish caramussal without cargo, leaving it on the beach for local Mainiots. During the night of 17 August 420 knights and soldiers were put ashore under command of François Breschard le Ponsur, flagship commander, and three sergeants-major, Don Francisco Ordognes, Temistocle Montiglio of the Counts of Gabbiano, and Guillaume de Beauregard commanding *San Giorgio*. Situated on top of a steep hill, Passava fortress was surrounded by 420 meters of crennalated and bastioned wall punctuated by several gates. One of the latter was blown by petard while ladders were used to surmount an inner castle wall. This was where the garrison of 800 made its stand but was overwhelmed by the sheer ferocity of assailants, most defenders fleeing by way of rear gates. The fortress was torched after which the Maltese returned to Valletta on 30 August bringing 180 captives and 18 pieces of bronze artillery. Left behind were twelve soldiers and three knights, Leonardo Fazale of Tropea on the Calabrian coast, Girolamo Corbera of Palermo, and novitiate Lucho Fuentes of Castile.[12]

Infanta Anne of Austria was born at Valladolid on 22 September 1601, eldest daughter of Habsburgh King Philip III of Spain and of Queen Consort Margaret of Austria. Five days later Dauphin Louis of France was born at Fontainebleau, eldest son of Bourbon King Henry IV of France and Queen Consort Marie de Medici. These two births were at the time cause for celebration throughout Spain and France and at the Convent of Malta. Two months short of 200 years later Dumas Davy de la Pailleterie would be born at a roadside inn in Picardy. Forty-two years still later he as Alexandre Dumas pere would celebrate the same September 1601 births by immortalizing King Louis XIII and his Queen Anne of Austria in *The Three Musketeers*. Don Pedro Gonzales de Mendoza was dispatched to Spain to pay the

Order's compliments to the Spanish Royal family while Aymar de Clermont-Chaste of the Langue of Auvergne resident in France paid the Order's compliments to the French Royal Family.[13]

Following the Squadron's return from Passava it made several runs to Sicily for the purpose of transporting needed food supplies to Malta. A request from Viceroy of Sicily Bernardino de Cárdenas y Portugal brought the Squadron to Sicily yet once more where siege of an unidentified locale was discussed. But because there was no plan to employ additional units beyond the Maltese, the Viceroy and his proposal both died a natural death and the Squadron passed the remainder of the year at Syracuse. At year-end Jorge de Cárdenas y Manrique de Lara succeeded his father as interim Viceroy.[14]

Prior of the Church Giorgio Giampieri passed away during 1601 and was succeeded by Pedro de Urrea y Camarasa, Chaplain of the Castellania of Amposta. Also during the year Grand Conservator Don Antic de Cabrera succeeded to the Bailiwick of Mallorca upon the death of incumbent Raimundo de Veri, and was succeeded as Grand Conservator by Don Federico Meca. Simon Cheminée de Boisbenet was promoted to Grand Hospitaller, succeeding Alof de Wignacourt, but soon opted for the dignity of Bailiff of the Morea upon death of incumbent André de Soissons de Pothières, while Simon d'Aubigné de Boismozé became Grand Hospitaller. Grand Bailiff Weipert von Rosenbach succeeded to Grand Prior of Germany upon death of incumbent Johann Philipp von Lesch and was himself succeeded as Grand Bailiff by Arbogast von Andlau who left the Priory of Dacia to Valentin von Hess who in turn left the Titular Bailiwick of Brandenburg to Johann Friedrich Hund von Saulheim. (From 1589 Titular or nominal Bailiffs of Brandenburg were Hospitaller Roman Catholics; active Bailiffs or Herrenmeisters of Brandenburg were Hospitaller Lutherans.) Admiral Giorgio del Carretto was appointed Bailiff of Naples upon death of incumbent Tiberio Campolo, while Prior of Hungary Federico Coconato succeeded to Admiral and Ippolito Malaspina succeeded to Prior of Hungary. A short while later Coconato advanced to Bailiff of Venosa, Malaspina to Admiral, and Ascanio Cambiano to Prior of Hungary. Signorino Gattinara the Younger was appointed to command of the galley *San Filippo* succeeding Fabrizio Berzetto in the squadron commanded by Jacques du Blot Viviers. Giuseppe di Guevara of Syracuse was appointed to command of the replacement *San Placido* while Commander Marin de Clinchamp de la Buzardière of the Langue of France was assigned command of the Treasury's large new square-rigged sailing ship *Il Cigno*. An only child, Clinchamp under the right of primogeniture had inherited his father's substantial estates in 1576 at the age of 13 and was Seigneur de Buzardière, du Val en Sonnois, de la Quentinière, de la Rousselière, et al, upon reception into the Order of Jerusalem at age 18 in 1581. Upon awakening to paternity he would at an unrecorded date obtain Papal and Hospitaller dispensation to leave the Order of Saint John, would marry, and would sire three children including Louis de Clinchamp who would also become Seigneur de Buzardière, et al, in his minority. In a somewhat similar vein, 10 year-old Alfonso III d'Este was in 1601 received into the Order as a page. He would in 1608 renounce his vows and wed Isabella of Savoy, daughter of Charles Emmanuel I. Following her death in 1626 he would abandon his secular duties as Duke of Modena to become a Capuchin monk, leaving four sons and three daughters.[15]

Early in January 1602 Alonso de Villaseca y Ulloa of Castile was dispatched to Palermo as the Order's Ambassador of Condolence concerning the death of Viceroy Bernardino de Cárdenas y Portugal. Bailiff of Eagle François d'Astorg de Segreville was appointed Resident Ambassador to the Holy See succeeding Commander Gonzalo de Porras of Castile. The five galleys returned to Malta from Syracuse still under command of Jacques du Blot Viviers intending to make ready for an opportunity cruise in the Levant. At Malta there also arrived a felucca from Naples with letters from Catholic King Philip III and from Viceroy of Naples Francisco Ruiz de Castro respectfully requesting the Malta Squadron's presence at Naples for its valued contribution to matters under consideration.[15]

Opportunity cruise plans were shelved and the Squadron in mid-April departed Malta for Naples from whence in undisclosed service to His Majesty the five galleys continued to Genoa. While fortuitously at Genoa the Squadron took delivery of two new galleys constructed at that city's arsenal on order of Malta's Common Treasury. Returning to Naples the Squadron embarked 12 year-old Carlo Tagliavia d'Aragona II, Duke of Terranova and Prince of Castelvetrano (at the western end of Sicily), for transport to Palermo where new Viceroy Lorenzo Suárez de Figueroa y Córdoba, Duke of Feria, had just arrived. Grand Master and Council dispatched Diogo de Brito of Castile to compliment the new Viceroy on elevation to the Vice Regal throne and to take up the matter of food supplies for Malta and Gozo. Feria warranted the people of Malta would not suffer under his rule, but quickly endorsed the Maltese practice of paying for grain shipments intercepted at sea.[16]

Five Papal galleys appeared at Malta in 1602 under the command of Emilio Delfini of Rome, Lieutenant General of the Papal Squadron in succession of Hospitaller Cesare Magalotti who succumbed to the attack of a knife-wielding Turkish slave in May. Magalotti was 39 years of age and had earned a longer life; he was interred at Rome in the Church of Santa Maria di Minerva to the right of the nave. The Papal galleys brought with them as prisoner Hospitaller Fabrizio Sforza, second son of Francesco I Sforza, Marchese of Caravaggio, and of Costanza Colonna Sforza. Imprisoned at Milan in 1601 for an unreported crime or crimes not including homicide, he had been transferred under arrest to Delfini at Finale Ligure and was delivered to Malta in August 1602 with an escort of five galleys for further interrogation by Alof de Wignacourt. Following interrogation he was again imprisoned albeit in comfortable quarters at Fort Saint Elmo for four more years until his release with restriction in August 1606. While the charges against him were never proven, the length of his detention is evidence of their seriousness. An acolyte of Michelangelo Merisi da Caravaggio, a notorious street brawler, the charges may well have involved witness to murder.[16]

Jacques de Saint-Tropez, a non-Hospitaller acquaintance of Alof de Wignacourt, had recent information concerning the town of Hammamet (Maometta) on Tunisia's east coast 190 nautical miles as the crow flies west of Malta. This information promised plunder and captives for an impoverished Common Treasury. The Frenchman proposed to the Grand Master a surprise assault predicated on his information in return for three percent of the value of all plunder, and the Grand Master laid before the Council a plan of operations which was approved. Lieutenant Marshal Philibert de Mathay was placed in command of a siege force of 500 infantry and 240 knights, totals which with shipboard complements left Malta dangerously short-handed. Born at a family castle guarding a pass between Burgundy and modern Switerland, Mathay had a superb military resumé. He was assisted by Sergeants-Major Marc Antonio Brancaccio of Naples, a veteran of the wars in Flanders, Juan de Salazar of Castile, and Nicolas de la Fontaine d'Ognon, while Guillaume de Beauregard would plant petards against town gates. This is the same Guillaume Gadagne Beauregard of Florentine roots received as an Hospitaller in 1590 at the age of fifteen. Viviers and the five galleys with siege force embarked departed Malta on 4 August 1602 bound for Lampedusa mid-way to Hammamet, the galleys accompanied by five frigates and five feluccas. Alonso de Contreras was again embarked as an adventurer. Reaching Lampedusa the following day the expeditionary force found three infidel brigantines present, capturing two crewed by 58 Moors. Return to Malta of these captures delayed the expeditionary force several days, but the Tunisian coast was sighted on 10 August. Galley masts were thereupon unstepped to present a lower profile, while the plan was to put troops ashore the following night. A storm, however, delayed debarcation 36 hours, while during the night of 12-13 August a reconnaissance party before dawn stumbled upon a Moorish garbo at anchor one mile from Hammamet. The garbo was subdued by frigates but Hammamet was alerted. Viviers and commanders nevertheless elected to proceed.[17]

Hammamet, Coast of Tunis.

The ground force was put ashore by frigate, felucca, and galley skiff in the face of mounted daylight opposition easily dispersed. Enemy within the fortress of Maometta, however, took the landing force under cannon fire. The galleys responded with a furious and more effective cannonade of their own enabling the ground force to approach the walls in relative safety. Proximate to the walls, though, galley cannon fire was necessarily discontinued and the assault force came under heavy musket fire punctuated with heaved assegai spears and large stones dropped from wall parapets. A petard was placed against each of the two fortress gates one of which was ineffective, but the landing party poured through the destroyed gate, Contreras prominent among them. Others scaled the walls. The assault was all but over; the number of Moorish dead in the end approached 800 with additional wounded. The Standard of the Religion flew from a minaret. Realizing, however, Moorish relief would soon be on its way, the assault force put the town within and beyond the fortress to flame and retired with 396 captives, mostly women and children, and all of the plunder it could carry. Re-embarked by early afternoon, the expeditonary force on 16 August brought back to Malta twenty wounded knights and 28 wounded soldiers. Left behind were 16 soldiers and four knights, Antonio Sinibaldi of Osimo, Pompeo Simoni of Siena, Don Antonio de Fuentes of Teruel, and Francisco de Pantoja of Ávila, Castile, who had escaped the Inquisition only a year earlier. Dying of wounds during the return voyage was Charles d'Espinay of Normandy called the Chevalier de Saint-Luc, brother of Hospitallers François, Artus, and Claude d'Espinay Saint-Luc, all four younger brothers of Thimoléon d'Espinay Saint-Luc, Seigneur de Saint Luc, Vice-Admiral and Marshal of France. *Eight hundred killed, 400 enslaved, commission paid.*[18]

While the galleys and their embarked ground force were away, and while the garrison at Malta was short-handed, reports had been received the Ottoman Armada was en route Navarin (Pylos) on the Morea's west coast 400 nautical miles ENE of Malta with intent to come west under Kapudan Cigalazade Yusuf Sinan Pasha. Among possible Armada destinations was Malta. Commander Francesco Lanfreducci was appointed Captain-at-Arms and Governor of the City of Notabile (Mdina) while Commanders Antonio Martelli of Florence, Boniface de Puget-Chasteuil of Provence, and Ramiro de Cuevas of Alburquerque were appointed Sector Wardens with full authority to prepare their sectors for protracted siege. Women, children, and the aged at Gozo were brought into the shelter of Malta's Castle Saint Angelo under protection of Hospitallers from seven langues commanded by René de Rivery-Potonville of the Langue of France, and into the old Infirmary at Birgu under the care of Prior of Navarre Bernardo de Spelletta. A plan was developed to tie together bow to stern ships found in the port as a chain across the mouth of Grand

Harbor. Two frigates were dispatched on 15 August 1602 to recall the galleys from Hammamet but located them only one day to the west of Malta.[19]

A subsequent report was received from agents asserting that a large number of galleys were being assembled at Constantinople for a descent on Gozo. Alonso de Contreras was appointed captain of a 12-bank Magistral frigate with 37 crew and soldiers, and was ordered into the Greek archipelago to ascertain whether such reports were based on fact or fiction. He proceeded to station near Scio (Chios) on reports a Turkish galley armada had already exited the Dardanelles which was then at Tenedos. Older than his 20 years, Contreras believed that were the armada proceeding only as far as Modon and Navarin, often armada termini, it would proceed directly to those ports from Tenedos. Were the armada alternatively headed further west it would first proceed to Negroponte to wax underwater hulls and reprovision from larger markets while doing so. Meanwhile at Malta each langue had been asked to contribute to a force of 20 knights and a company of soldiers to succor the Castle on Gozo. A bit later Contreras brought word the Turkish armada consisting of 70 galleys had in fact arrived at Negroponte and was likely to appear in local waters. He was ordered back whence he had come, and to remain at least one step ahead of the armada warning those in its path.[20]

Fear of an Ottoman assault on Malta increased somewhat further on alerts reporting the Armada off the southern coast of Calabria and then in the Strait of Messina where it paused in the anchorage for San Giovanni near Reggio effectively blockading the Papal Galley Squadron in the harbor at Messina. Reports of these developments were brought to Malta by Contreras who had also alerted Reggio in advance of the Ottoman arrival. A second company of 100 soldiers was assigned to join the first at Gozo, and both knights and soldiers were placed under the command of Hospitaller Captain René de Rivery-Potonville of the Langue of France. Bernardo de Spelletta was dispatched to Gozo as Inspector-General to ensure all was in readiness including food supplies. At Malta various other defensive assignments were made, and Toussaint de Ternes-Boisgirault of the Priory of Aquitaine was dispatched by felucca to obtain a fresh report on the Ottoman Armada. He returned on 26 August and reported the Turkish galleys were poised for further assault. Jacques du Blot Viviers was appointed General of Land Forces and directed to prevent an Ottoman landing. These forces stood by for all of September 1602 at the end of which, and given lateness of the season, they stood down.[21]

Whereabouts of the Sicilian Galley Squadron were unknown. Reports arrived though that Viceroy of Sicily and Duke of Feria Lorenzo Suárez de Figueroa y Córdoba had disappeared from the Viceregal palace at Palermo in the middle of the night. There was fear he had been kidnapped. Thus the reports were accompanied by requests the Grand Master send a galley to the Barbary Coast seeking further information. The Grand Master was likewise asked to send another galley into the Levant for the same reason. Signorino Gattinara the Younger and the galley *San Filippo* together with the frigate of Vincenzo Rispolo were sent to the Barbary Coast but learned nothing of the Viceroy. Two frigates sent into the Levant, however, returned with news the Kapudan Pasha and his Armada had returned to the Archipelago and were en route Constantinople. On this news many soon concluded Sinan had simply been creating a diversion inhibiting the ability of Habsburg King Philip III of Spain to go to the aid of Habsburg Emperor Rudolf II in Hungary. Viceroy of Sicily Lorenzo Suárez de Figueroa attracted little attention returning to the Viceregal palace.[22]

During 1602 Admiral Ippolito Malaspina was appointed Bailiff of Naples, and was succeeded as Admiral by Prior of Hungary Ascanio Cambiano. Girolamo Agliata of Palermo succeeded to the Priory of Hungary. Grand Conservator Federico Meca advanced to Prior of Catalonia, and was succeeded as Grand Conservator by Raimundo de Veri (Ramon de Verdú in Catalan) who a bit later succeeded to the Priory of Catalonia upon the sudden death of Meca, a veteran of 1565's Great Siege as a participant in September's Grand Soccorso. Onofre Copones succeeded to the dignity of Grand Conservator. The Priory of Saint-Gilles was vacated by the death of Pierre de Saint-Aubin, an inspiration for other Hospitallers since 1555; Grand Commander Pierre d'Esparbez de Lussan succeeded to that premier dignity of the Langue of Provence while himself being succeeded as Grand Commander by Jean de Vintimille d'Ollicules. Bailiff of Lyon Jacques du Blot Viviers having completed his two years as General of the Galleys was succeeded in December by Admiral Ascanio Cambiano who nominated and the Council appointed Gabriele Simeoni (the Younger) of Chieri to command of the Capitana. Philippe Soubiran Esquivias d'Arifat of

Provence was appointed to command of the new galley *San Giovanni*. Don Bernardo de Spelletta was appointed Prior of Navarre succeeding Miguel Cruzat upon the latter's death, Cruzat another veteran of 1565's Great Siege. As Prior of Navarre, Spelleta was in December dispatched as ambassadeur extraordinaire to Viceroy of Sicily Lorenzo Suárez de Figueroa y Córdoba to represent famine need of the Maltese population and imminent calamity without relief.[23]

Extreme famine reigned at Malta and Gozo early in 1603, unrelieved by succor from Sicily. The galley squadron and galleons were fully employed in the search for food supplies. Among other actions, a vessel bound from Terranova to Messina, cargo of foodstuffs, was seized between Cape Passero and Syracuse by an English corsair breton, but the breton was in turn overcome by the galley squadron costing many lives among which was that of Alcide Marescotti of Siena, a promising knight barely in his thirties. The cargo, much needed at Malta, was delivered with the carrier to Messina where both were embargoed, but upon protest by the Grand Master citing the cost to Malta in lives, much of the cargo was released back to the Malta Squadron. During this period three opportunistic Greeks from Patras approached the Grand Master with a plan to raid food stores at both Patras and nearby Lepanto. Grand Master and Council altered the plan and in total secrecy agreed to it.[24]

General of the Galleys Ascanio Cambiano sailed from Malta on 7 April 1603 commanding four galleys reinforced with caravan and complement of *San Giorgio* which remained at Malta with a skeleton crew to serve needs of the Convent. The galleys were accompanied by the *Galleon of the Religion* commanded by Simon de Cornu de la Courbe of the Priory of Aquitaine, the two Magistral galleons belonging to Grand Master Wignacourt, the larger commanded by Amador de la Porte and the smaller by François de Vaudricourt, the tartan commanded by Sigismond de Franay d'Anisy, all four of the Langue of France, two chartered sailing ships, and four frigates aboard all of which were embarked 200 knights and 800 infantry divided in two groups. One of the groups was under the command of Jacques du Blot Viviers also commanding all embarked forces. The other group was commanded by *San Filippo* skipper Signorino della Gattinara the Younger as senior sergeant-major. The other two sergeants-major were Spanish-speaking Don Juan de Salazar and French-speaking René de

Rivery-Potonville. Fifty miles out of Malta the flotilla fortuitously encountered and took a Turkish caramussal, cargo of much-needed wheat, which was escorted back to Malta.[25]

The flotilla again pointed toward the Curzolari Islands sheltering the mouth of the Gulf of Patras, six days later passing between Keffalonia and Santa Maura and reaching the Curzolaris the night of 17 April 1603. While the flotilla divided in two prearranged groups Greek-speaking navigator Jacques de Vincheguerre of Marseille and Hospitaller Richard de Nini-Claret of Avignon separately proceeded by small craft to assure themselves the enemy had not been forewarned. Viviers' group consisted of the capitana, *San Giovanni*, one sailing ship, and two frigates, while Gattinara's group consisted of the padrona, *San Filippo*, the tartana, and two frigates. Vincheguerre and Nini-Claret returned with reports of local famine but not of readiness. The next night each group entered the Gulf of Patras and debarked on opposite shores five miles distant from both Lepanto and Patras. Viviers' group reached and surprised the hilltop redoubt at Patras that same night of 19-20 April. Gattinara's group arrived in daylight before Lepanto as the approach proved more difficult. In spite of being spotted, the latter group succeeded in blowing the gate, placing scaling ladders against the walls, and in having the better of resistance. Both fortresses were razed including towers and castles into which the enemy withdrew. The flotilla departed following four days of continuous skirmish, taking with them 76 bronze cannons and 392 captives including the Aga of Patras and his two sons, but little in the way of food stores. The Aga of Lepanto did not survive. Neither did twelve assailants among whom were knights Alessandro di Conti Martinenghi of Brescia and Louis de Fay-Puisieux of Pas-de-Calais, the first only months out of his novitiate, the latter 30 years an Hospitaller. Almost 90 others were wounded. Notable among assailants was Alfonso Castelsanpietro commanding those scaling Lepanto walls, Aloigi Castiglioni, and Pier Francesco Croce each of the latter commanding companies of arquebusiers, all three of Milan. Upon departing the Gulf of Patras Cambiano sent on to Malta one ship and the auxilliary vessels carrying spoils and captives which arrived safely on 5 May. The others headed toward the Aegean in search of grain ships, grain the original objective of the assaults. Five caramussals were found beached within a mile of the Ottoman fortress at Modon (Methoni). Seeing the galleys approach, three were able to flee under the cover of fortress guns. The other two were too slow. In addition to food stores twenty additional bronze cannons were among the plunder. Remaining units returned to Malta on 7 May.[26]

News of the foregoing success spread rapidly, aided in no small measure by the Order's Resident Ambassador at the Court of Spain. Pedro Gonzales de Mendoza was able to artfully combine requests for food and financial assistance with anecdotal reports of the maritime exploits of the Order's sea forces under Jacques du Blot Viviers and Ascanio Cambiano. In March King Philip had written to Viceroy of Sicily and Duke of Feria Lorenzo Suárez de Figueroa commanding the viceregency to permit enlistment in Sicily by Malta of buonavoglie or paid galley oarsmen, a practice which had recently been denied. This was followed on 10 May by another letter to the Viceroy with the King's wish Malta and its università as well as Gozo all three receive this year their full treaty quantities of foodstuffs from Sicily. An earlier letter drafted by Mendoza had requested Pope Clement VIII's attention to certain Hospitaller matters. A similar letter had been addressed to Venetian Doge Marino Grimani requesting final compensation for Diego de Brochero's corsair galleon seized by Venice 19 years earlier (in 1584). Brochero at the time (1603) had become a Royal Navy Armada commander.[27]

With appreciative reception in most ports the squadron excepting *San Giovanni* departed Malta on 20 May 1603 for Villefranche in greater-Nice to embark the two older sons of Duke of Savoy Charles Emmanuel I to be transported to Barcelona from where they would continue to Valladolid to be received by their uncle King Philip III of Spain and where they would complete their education. Sadly, eldest son and heir apparent Philip Emmanuel, Hospitaller Prince of Piedmont, would die in 1604 of unreported cause while still in Spain. He was only 18 years of age. Second son Victor Amadeus I would succeed his father in 1630. Following this assignment the four galleys proceeded to Marseille where the flagship and Gattinara's *San Filippo* were exchanged for two new galleys built there at the Order's direction, the capitana at 28 banks and the new *San Filippo* at 25 banks. The four galleys would return to Malta by July-end. Meanwhile *San Giovanni* under Soubiran d'Arifat investigated the North African coast and captured a Moorish garbo, cargo of barley bound for Tripoli.[28]

In July there arrived at Malta a Monsieur Cherelles, one of French King Henry IV's Masters of House, with a letter from the King and a second similar letter from Pope Clement VIII requesting a Grand Cross and one of the French Langue's three priories in France for the King's 5 year-old son Alexandre by mistress Gabrielle d'Estrées. Alexandre, Chevalier de Vendôme. would be received into the Order of Jerusalem, Langue of France, in 1606 and would successively be appointed Prior of Toulouse with attendant Grand Cross and Grand Prior of France. He would also be appointed General of the Galleys in 1612 at the age of 14 years but would die in one of half-brother Louis XIII's chateau-prisons in 1629 at 31 years of age.[29]

The Grand Master not wishing the Autumn to pass without some attempt against the enemy, an assault on Tunisian Monastir was proposed. Lieutenant Marshal François Breschard le Ponsur of the Langue of Auvergne was placed in command of ground forces with Signorino della Gattinara the Younger, René de Rivery-Potonville of Amiens, and Juan de Salazar of Esquivias, Castile, as Sergeants-Major. Commander Sebastien de Saint-Julien dit Perudette of Haute Savoie and the Langue of Auvergne was appointed Standard Bearer. Embarked was a landing force about half that put ashore at Patras and Lepanto.[30]

Commanding a naval squadron of five galleys, four frigates, and four feluccas, but none of the galleons and sailing ships at Patras, Cambiano departed Malta on 6 October bound for Lampedusa where final preparations were made including orders for the surprise attack. Sailing on a favorable wind the squadron at night reached a point one mile southeast of Monastir's large Ribat or fortress (standing today in remarkable preservation). But while the ground force was approaching along the beach the fortress saluted their arrival with a cannonade. Discovered, Ponsur immediately ordered re-embarcation much to the disappointment of his plunder-hungry force. With daylight, however, numerous troops of Moorish cavalry were seen scouring the beach, and with a muster of the assault force it became clear a French soldier among the first to debark had either made his way to the city and warned the garrison of the Hospitaller presence, or had been captured upon landing to the same effect. The squadron returned to Malta on 29 October 1603.[31]

The Turkish armada did not attempt an assault on Gozo in 1603 because of virulent bubonic plague rampant among the crews and at

Constantinople among people high and low where in December it felled 37 year-old Sultan Mehmed III. He was succeeded by 13 year-old Ahmed I. Perhaps heeding the advice of his powerful grandmother Safiye Sultan, Venetian-born Sofia Baffo, Ahmed would early in 1604 appoint Cigalazade Yusuf Sinan Pasha to command his Army of the East at war with Persia's Safavid Empire, thus depriving his Armada in the west of experienced leadership.[31]

Following its return from Monastir the Galley Squadron paused only a few days before undertaking a circumnavigation of Sicily with close inspection of the uninhabited islands off Trapani. Passing through the Straight north-bound, the galleys put into Syracuse and Messina before turning west to Palermo. At Palermo the Squadron returned Don Francisco Canna earlier dispatched to Malta with the compliments of new Viceroy of Sicily and 2nd Duke of Feria Lorenzo Suárez de Figueroa y Dormer also presenting the Grand Master with a handsome gift. Arriving at Palermo with the Squadron was Hospitaller Commander Antonio Centeno Guiral of León returning the compliment.[31]

During 1603 Federico Cocconato of Casale Monferrato with consent of the Langue of Italy and of the Council renounced the Bailiwick of Venosa retaining in retirement some of the annual income. Ascanio Cambiano was promoted to Bailiff of Venosa in succession and was himself succeeded as Admiral by Girolamo Agliata. Agliata was succeeded as Prior of Hungary by Commander Francesco Lanfreducci. With similar consents the independently wealthy Ippolito Malaspina renounced the Bailiwick of Naples to become General of the Galleys of the Papal States in August. Lanfreducci was accordingly advanced a second time to Bailiff of Naples leaving the Priory of Hungary to Commander Antonio Martelli of Florence. Grand Commander Jean de Vintimille d'Ollioules was appointed Bailiff of Manosque in succession of the deceased Charles de Grasse-Briançon and was succeeded as Grand Commander by Claude de Thézan Vénàsque of Saint-Didier, Provence. Vintimille's path to the top was instructive of would-be Hospitallers. Seventh of ten sons (and three daughters) of Gaspard 1er de Vintimille, Seigneur d'Ollioules et d'Evenos, as well as Baron de Tourvès by marriage to Anne d'Arcussia, Dame de Tourvès, Jean de Vintimille was received as a Hospitaller in 1559 at the age of 17.

Six years later and one year before Alof de Wignacourt's own reception he survived the Great Siege of Malta crouched behind the ramparts of Birgu, those walls and ramparts but pale shadows of similar structures left behind at Rhodes. And just as every survivor at Rhodes was at various times walking wounded, so too was every survivor at Malta. From the Great Siege until Wignacourt's election as Grand Master 36 years later history mentions Jean de Vintimille only once, as Commander of the Commandery at Valence from 1588 to 1591. At Wignacourt's election ten years still later Vintimille had yet to be awarded the dignity and Grand Cross earned on the walls of Birgu and likely earned yet again and again, an omission belatedly rectified in 1602 with his appointment at 60 years of age as Grand Commander.[32]

Also during 1603 Commander Charles de Rouffignac of Rouffignac-de-Saint-Cernan-de-Reilhac was appointed Marshal succeeding incumbent Claude de la Salle de Colombière upon the latter's death. Auguste Baron von Meersburg was appointed Prior of Dacia upon death or renunciation by incumbent Valentin von Hess. Commander Charles de Gaillardbois-Marconville was appointed Resident Ambassador to the Court of France ending a five-year vacancy occasioned by the absence of a Catholic Majesty. Upon Ascanio Cambiano's nomination Geronimo del Pero was appointed flag-captain succeeding Gabriel Simeoni. Giovanni Battista d'Abenante of Cosenza succeeded to command of the new galley *San Michele* while Alessandro Orsi of Bologna was appointed to command of *San Filippo* succeeding Signorino Gattinara the Younger.[33]

The paucity of foodstuffs at Malta and Gozo continued in 1604, forcing Grand Master and Council to supplement available stocks by sending a small flotilla into the Levant to seize grain wherever they could find it. *Saint-Louis*, the larger Magistral galleon, and two other sailing vessels were armed and outfitted at public expense and placed under command of Royal Pilot Jacques de Vincheguerre who took them into the Archipelago. There they preyed on various Turkish ships, cargoes of grain and other merchandise, which were sent back to Malta, Messina, and Syracuse with prize crews. The two Maltese sailing vessels, however, were eventually separated from the galleon by bad weather following which they encountered two larger English bretones of 500 or more gross tons which took the Maltese under fire, seized them, and led them to Milos, nominally Ottoman but with a miniscule garrison. After a few days at Milos *Saint-Louis* also arrived and overwhelmed the English bretones in a bloody contest costing Vincheguerre 20 dead and 40 wounded.[34]

Appropriating artillery and munitions from the bretones, Vincheguerre departed with his original company taking course for mainland Volos 330 kilometers north of Athens and 16 nautical miles up its own inland gulf, Volos a major food depot for Ottomans ashore and afloat. There they rendezvoused with Malta-flag corsair galleons commanded by Amador de la Porte of the Langue of France and by non-Hospitaller corsair Antonio Buleggia (brother of Malta-flag corsair Simón Buleggia). All five vessels proceeded up the gulf in pursuit of nine caramussals with cargoes for the most part grain. These beached and attempted to defend themselves with off-loaded cannon, but the crews fled when the three Maltese and two corsairs took them from the flank with a ferocious cannonade. The three galleons appropriated all of the artillery while the two sailing vessels loaded food stores from the beached caramussals after which all five vessels returned to Malta, arriving at end-March. This success not only relieved hunger among the population of Malta and Gozo but compensated for a disaster at the port of Licata when the *Galleon of the Religion* and several smaller vessels loading allotments of grain from Sicily were surprised by a southerly which crushed the ships against loading wharves. Eventually beached, the ships were not salvageable. Meanwhile four galleys of the Religion commanded by senior captain Geronimo de Angulo of Burgos retrieved from the ports of Messina and Syracuse two caramussals Vincheguerre earlier dispatched with prize crews.[35]

Grand Master Alof de Wignacourt's first Chapter General, the fifteenth celebrated at Malta and seventh at Valletta, convened on Sunday 15 February 1604. Following ceremonies the Chapter General opened with a review of two Apostolic Briefs. The first such Brief dated 14 June 1603 was an attempt to end discord between the Holy See and the Convent by ending certain pre-existing authority for the Convent to act alone. The second Brief dated 12 December and only recently received largely reversed the first Brief by restoring the Convent's authority to act alone on most matters. The Sixteen *compromissari* or lawmakers elected two per langue were Grand Commander Claude de Thézan Vénàsque and Prior of Toulouse Raymond de Gozon-Mélac for

Provence; Bailiff of Lyon Jacques du Blot Viviers and Lieutenant
Marshal François Breschard le Ponsur for Auvergne; Grand Hospitaller
Simon d'Aubigné de Boismozé and Bailiff of the Morea Simon
Cheminée de Boisbenet for France; Bishop of Malta Tomás Gargallo
and Grand Conservator Onofre Copones for Aragon; Admiral
Girolamo Agliata and Bailiff of Venosa and General of the Galleys
Ascanio Cambiano for Italy; Prior of England Andrew Wyse and
Procurator for the Prior of Ireland Giovanni Lanfranco Cebà of Genoa
for England; Grand Bailiff Arbogast von Andlau and Prior of Dacia
Auguste Baron von Meersburg for Germany; and Grand Chancellor
Fernando Ruiz de Corral and Commander Rodrigo de Brito for Castile.
Among other actions, these Sixteen confirmed ordinary responsions as
well as ongoing supplementary appropriations of 40 and 50 thousand
Maltese (silver) scudos as theretofore mandated, authorized borrowings
of up to 122 thousand gold ducats at the going interest rate in the event
of siege, authorized construction of a parish for donats and brothers,
set aside 12,000 scudos for construction of a new Capitana to be called
San Lorenzo, and ordered the Order's statutes to be reduced to a single
volume. The Chapter General adjourned on 13 March.[36]

In May 1604 eleven galleys of Naples arrived at Malta under General
Alvaro de Bazan, 2nd Marqués de Santa Cruz. Santa Cruz was
accompanied by the son of Viceroy of Naples and Duke of Benavente
Juan Alonso Pimentel de Herrera and by the son of Don Garcia de
Toledo. The Grand Master and Council accorded these notables a
generous and splendid hospitality during which Santa Cruz proposed a
joint galley squadron expedition into the Levant under Santa Cruz
command. Ascanio Cambiano remained General of the Galleys and was
ordered to ready for departure under the Viceregal Standard with the
title of Lieutenant to the Grand Master commanding the embarked
Hospitaller landing force. On the advice of agents in the Levant Santa
Cruz determined on a raid of the fortified city of Lango (Kos Town) on
the island of the same name, one of only a few islands in the eastern
Aegean with sizeable Ottoman garrisons. The two squadrons put their
embarked Spanish and Hospitaller shore parties ashore to the east of the
double-enceinte fortress built more than a century earlier by the same
Hospitallers and promptly began their assault with a party of
50 Hospitaller knights present by placing the petard which blew the
single gate to the outer wall. Defenders were ill-prepared and yielded

almost before all assailants had passed through the gate. Hospitaller fatalities were limited to a single knight, Fabio Scala of Osimo in the Province of Ancona, and to a handful of hired soldiers, though more were wounded. Captives numbered 165 of whom a third part were assigned to the Order, while 17 Hungarian captives from the ongoing Long Turkish War in that country were liberated. There was a questionable report the adjacent Greek city of Lango was sacked and obliterated, but this may have referred to the Ottoman quarter or simply have been an exaggeration concerning dwellings immediately outside the wall. There was no sign of the Ottoman Armada under Bosnian Kapudan Dervis Pasha likely preoccupied with his proximate appointment as Grand Vizier. His successor Giaffer or Djafer Pasha would later in 1604 take the Armada into the Adriatic but leave almost no sign of his visit.[37]

Arriving at Malta in June were seven galleys of Sicily under command of Juan de Padilla y Acuña, 2nd Count of Santa Gadea and Adelantado of Castile. With him was the Marqués de Villalba, eldest son of Viceroy of Sicily and Duke of Feria Lorenzo Suárez de Figueroa y Córdoba. The Adelantado proposed a joint operation with the Malta Squadron laying siege to one or more Ottoman fortresses, but as the Malta Squadron had yet to return from the eastern Aegean nothing could be agreed. The Adelantado re-appeared at Malta following the Squadron's return, and the combined squadrons departed on 16 July for Trapani and Palermo and a circumnavigation of Sicily in search of Infidel corsairs which proved fruitless. The galleys were next engaged in transporting Vice Chancellor Giovanni Otto Bosio to Rome, leaving Regent Vice Chancellor and Hospitaller Manuel de Chebedo of Portugal to carry on at Malta. At about this time former Bailiff of Naples Ippolito Malaspina arrived at Malta with five Papal galleys, but merely to manage personal affairs including care of his palace (61 Marsamxett Street) in Valletta. Malaspina departed three days later bound for Civitavecchia.[38]

The Long Turkish War (1593-1606) was draining the resources of Emperor Rudolf II's Holy Roman Empire. During these months of 1604 Francesco, III Marchese di Castiglione, I Marchese di Medole, and the Empire's Resident Ambassador to the Holy See, solicited assistance from all parts of the Christian world, including from Malta's Order of Jerusalem. Grand Master and Council considered what was appropriate given the Order's support of a voluntary brigade of Hospitaller cavalry since war outset. An impoverished Order decided on a further contribution of 50,000 copper scudos. In this connection Lieutenant Prior of Bohemia Leopold von Pöpel and Ritter Georg (Jerzy) Ceika were dispatched to Germany with orders to ensure transfer of the funds to Castiglione.[39] Note: Copper scudos or scudi began to be issued following 1565's Ottoman Siege of Malta. For the first 80 years copper scudos were considered analogous to a promissary note having a redemption value in the same amount of silver scudos. Reflecting chronically imbalanced budgets, from about 1635 so many copper scudo notes were outstanding that hyper-inflation set in and they lost essentially all value. Like Biden dollars.

During the year the Order of Jerusalem was pleased to receive a number of members of able families, among them Virginio Orsini, son of the Duke of Bracciano of the same name and another in a seemingly unbroken succession of Virginio Orsinos in service to the Church. Don Girolamo (Jeronimo) Pimentel, son of Viceroy of Naples and Duke of Benavente Juan Alonso Pimentel de Herrera, and Don Vincenzo di Guevara, son of the Duke of Bovino were others.

Reflecting the Grand Master's wish to have a competent confidant concerning the Common Treasury, the Council approved re-creation of a position in the Grand Master's Household with the title of Treasury Secretary last used in 1574. Giocondo Accarigi of Siena would be the next to hold the title. Prior of Navarre Don Bernardo Spelletta was appointed General of the Galleys succeeding Ascanio Cambiano. On Spelletta's nomination Don Geronimo Larrea of Basque Álava was appointed to command of the capitana, succeeding Geronimo del Pero. Commander Claude de Ravenel of the Langue of France was appointed to command of *San Giovanni* succeeding Philippe Soubiran d'Arifat, while Commander Fausto Bulgarini of Siena was appointed to command of *San Giorgio* succeeding Guillaume Gadagne Beauregard. Likewise future Grand Master Dom Luís Mendez de Vasconcellos was appointed Resident Ambassador to the Holy See succeeding Bailiff of Eagle Jean François d'Astorg de Segreville. Segreville concurrently renounced the office of Seneschal to which the Grand Master assigned Conventual Conservator Laurent de Virieu-Pupetières of Auvergne. The Dignity of Conventual Conservator was another re-activation and addition to the Magistral

Household intended to assist in financial management. Bailiff of Naples Francesco Lanfreducci succeeded to Bailiff of Pavia upon death of incumbent Fabrizio Berzio, and was succeeded at Naples by Commander Francesco Moleti of Messina. The Langues of Italy and Germany re-confirmed earlier agreements that the Priory of Hungary would devolve at first convenience from Italy to Germany. Finally, Commander Louis d'Argilliers was appointed Grand Hospitaller in succession of deceased incumbent Simon d'Aubigné de Boismozé.[40]

Early in 1605 Grand Master Wignacourt visited Gozo for the purpose of assessing defenses at the Citadel and at Freo's Garzez Tower, giving orders for purchase of construction and repair materials. The galleys having served as ferries during this brief period of time then took course for Naples on several matters. During the return voyage they paused at Messina to embark Viceroy and Duke of Feria Lorenzo Suárez de Figueroa y Córdoba and his Court for transfer to Palermo, banditry and poor roads still the explanation.[41]

At Rome Pope Clement VIII died on 3 March 1605 probably of gout which had immobilized him over his final years. He was succeeded 28 days later by Alessandro Ottaviano de' Medici as Pope Leo XI who would survive in office only 26 days before also passing away. Pope Leo was succeeded on 16 May by Camillo Borghese of Rome as Pope Paul V. Prior of Capua Don Vincenzo Carafa was dispatched to Rome to render the Order's obedience and to obtain a reaffirmation of the Order's privileges. He did so and more, obtaining ordination of the Minutes of the last Chapter General as well as of the Compilation of Statutes which for the new Pope's convenience had been translated from Latin to Italian by Historian Giacomo Bosio. On 8 May the Infante Felipe, future King Philip IV, was born at Valladolid. Prior of Ireland Don Pedro Gonzalez Mendoza was dispatched to the Spanish Court at that city to convey the Order's congratulations and well wishes.[42]

Departing Malta on 25 April four galleys of the Squadron commanded by Bernardo Spelletta took course for the Levant on a voyage of opportunity. Reinforced with Caravan and oarsmen of *San Giorgio* remaining in port, the four galleys proceeded all the way to the Seven Capes of Anatolia between Makri (Fethiye) and Kalamaki (Kalkan) with little opportunity. The four galleys returned to Malta at mid-June bringing with them a captured germa, cargo of rice and other items. The galleys also brought 77 captives more than half of whom were removed from other vessels left to proceed on their way and some of whom were ransomable. Toward the end of May during the Squadron's absence two burdened Infidel corsair brigantines were forced by bad weather to take shelter within Malta's southern bay of Marsascirocco (Marsaxlokk) where they began to settle under load and shipped water. Fausto Bulgarini commanding *San Giorgio* manned his oars with crew, replaced crew with individuals at hand, and proceeded to the scene where he hoped to come away with replacement oarsmen. His galley attempted to grapple the larger brigantine which with insufficient freeboard in bad weather nevertheless went to the bottom with her Christian oarsmen chained to the benches. Divers would recover the oarsmen who would be properly interred. Thirty-two corsairs, meanwhile, were pulled alive from the sea. They would end up at Christian oars. The smaller brigantine was able to clear the anchorage and was pursued by a frigate and two caiques also exiting Valletta on the news; the brigantine had too much of a headstart, however, and avoided capture.[43]

Over a period of years Malta had become a sponsor of Christian corsairs to a degree Grand Master and Council believed called for better regulation. One concern was the sheer number of heavily armed vessels in port, especially vessels with concealed munitions, and the consequent threat to the general public of a munitions accident. Another concern was the need for uniform rules applicable to all Christian corsairs flying the flag of Malta, and for uniform consequences of rules violations and outright fraud. On 17 June a committee was formed consisting of three knights of the Grand Cross and one senior commander each of different langues supplemented by a secular member usually to be a Doctor of Law. Called the *Armamenti*, these Commissioners were charged with developing rules and regulations applying to all corsairs flying the flag of Malta. Related rules prohibited arming of corsair vessels flying the flag of a foreign prince. Such vessels wishing to sell their plunder at Malta must pay ten percent of the value sold to the Common Treasury. Individuals wishing to embark on corsair operations under the flag of Malta must obtain a license to do so from the Council of State. The quantity and quality of munitions carried by individual corsair vessels was to be regulated and inspected. No Christian vessel, Christian property, or Christian individual could be subjected to a Malta-flag corsair attack. Finally, the Grand Master and other Christian princes were to have an automatic safe-conduct in the presence of Malta corsairs.[44]

In July 1605 Pope Paul V proposed a permanent union of the Papal Galley Squadron and the Malta Galley Squadron, a proposal which found Hospitallers less than luke-warm. For that reason nothing came of it. In July 25 galleys arrived at Malta, 10 of Naples under the Marqués de Santa Cruz, 8 of Genoa under Don Carlo Doria (youngest son of Gian Andrea Doria), and 7 of Sicily under the Adelantado of Castile and Count of Santa Gadea Juan de Padilla y Acuña. Embarked was Pedro de Leyva, Prince of Ascoli and General of Ground Forces, with three sons of the Viceroy of Naples in company and one of his own. Intending to besiege unnamed locales, these lords requested of Grand Master Alof de Wignacourt assistance of the Order's galley squadron commanded by Bernardo de Spelletta in creating a mainland diversion relieving Ottoman pressure on Emperor Rudolf II in Hungary. Spelleta was ordered to ready five galleys. Lieutenant Marshal Pierre (Pons) de la Porte of Auvergne was given command of the Hospitaller Battalion with Commanders Niccolò della Marra of Naples, Claude d'Urré de Venterol of Provence, and Iñigo de Espejo of Cordoba as sergeants-major.

The expeditionary force departed Malta on 22 July with the squadrons of Naples and Malta forming the battle group when cruising, the squadron of Genoa in the vanguard, and the squadron of Sicily comprising the rearguard, all under Santa Cruz's royal standard. An attempt to take the Castle of Formica behind the Albanian (Epirote) coast opposite Santa Maura (Levkas) failed and the five Maltese returned home with intent to rejoin later. Instead the galleys were held at Malta for fear of another Ottoman siege, and later dispatched on non-combat missions. The rest of the expeditionary force having withdrawn to Otranto meanwhile assailed Durazzo (Durres) at the beginning of August with complete success. Located on the coast of northern Albania and situated on a peninsula extending into the sea, the city and castle were surrounded by towered wall on which 40 cannon were mounted. Future Doge of Venice Sebastiano Venier had in 1570 failed in an attempt to reduce the city. Assailed on two sides by land and on two sides by sea, Santa Cruz nevertheless made quick work of it. In the end the wall towers were untenable and the wall breached. The cannons were removed for use in the Spanish kingdoms and the city was sacked. Not long afterward an Ottoman

Armada of 60 Turkish galleys commanded by Giaffer Pasha paused at Venetian Corfu seeking information concerning the Spanish force which had destroyed Durazzo, and was dissuaded from entering the Adriatic with a report the Spanish were then at Taranto. Thus the intended diversion at a time the Ottoman Porte's Treasury had also been drained by the war in Hungary.[45]

With no summons from the Marqués de Santa Cruz the Maltese turned to matters other than siege. The new galley *San Giacomo* commanded by Don Gaspar de Monreal of Aragon accompanied by *San Michele* under Giovanni Battista d'Abenante proceeded to Genoa and Savonna to embark the Grand Master's brother Joachim de Wignacourt, and subsequently to the most remote parts of France to embark the brother's guests. In the meanwhile the other three galleys returned to Malta from Licata on the southern coast of Sicily escorting grain carriers. Doing this they encountered and took three Turkish brigantines with 74 crew made captive and a similar number of Christian oarsmen liberated, but lost Hospitaller Henri Gayant of Paris embarked on his final caravan.[46]

During the year Grand Conservator Onofre de Copones was appointed Bailiff of Mallorca succeeding deceased incumbent Antic de Cabrera, Cabrera a veteran of the Great Siege of Malta born on the small Ballearic island of Cabrera 10nm south of Mallorca. Copones was succeeded himself as Grand Conservator by Bailiff of Negroponte Cristóbal de Zanoguera who a bit later would be advanced to Bailiff of Caspe, while Don Gonzalo de Porras acceded to the Bailiwick of Negroponte. Admiral Girolamo Agliata received into the Order 58 years earlier was advanced to Prior of Lombardia succeeding Emmanuel Philibert of Savoy on the latter's renunciation, while Prior of Hungary Antonio Martelli advanced to Admiral. On the latter rotation the Priory of Hungary fell vacant and was finally transferred to the Langue of Germany as repetitively demanded by Chapters General. Prior of Dacia Wilhelm von Cronberg was appointed Prior of Hungary while Titular Bailiff of Brandenburg Johann Friedrich Hund von Saulheim succeeded to the Priory of Dacia and Georg Christoph von Wittenberg succeeded to the dignity of Titular Bailiff of Brandenburg. Boniface de Puget-Chasteuil was appointed Grand Commander succeeding Claude de Thézan-Vénàsque upon the latter's death following 45 years as a Hospitaller. Monsignor Fabrizio Veralli was succeeded as Inquisitor of Malta by appointment of Monsignor Ettore Diotallevi di Rimini. Diotallevi arrived with instructions from the Holy Office to implement a decree of deceased Pope Clement VIII which with the support and guidance of the Holy Office in the year 1600 sought to reverse the policy of Pope Gregory XIII concerning the Order's privileges with the Holy See. These privileges, according to the Holy Office, had promoted within the Order a sense of immunity from strictures of the Holy Office. Also during the year the Order received a Papal Bull of Protection applying to new Cardinal Scipione Borghese, born Scipione Caffarelli, at the time 28 year-old son of the Pope's sister. By the end of Pope Paul V's Pontificate in 1621 his nephew owned half of southern Italy as well as the most valuable art collection in the entire country.[47]

Early in 1606 the Convent was informed of the loss of three commanderies, not commanderies of the Curia but rather commanderies of the Langue of Italy vacated by death of Giovan Battista Rondinelli of Florence who had been commander for most of his 45 years as a Hospitaller. Loss of these commanderies meant loss of revenue streams enabling advancement of young knights completing five years or more of Hospitaller service. Two of these commanderies, Santa Maria di Perugia, di Bergamo, e Giansone, and Santa Maria Maddelena di Parma were re-assigned to Monsignor Alessandro Vittorio, a nephew by the Pope's sister. The third, Benevento, was assigned to new Cardinal Innocenzo Del Bufalo-Cancellieri.[48]

In desperation all Italian knights congregated in the great hall of their auberge and resolved to go on strike. By decree, no Italian knight would embark aboard the galleys for Caravan duty, and all Italian knights were free to refuse other assignments. Grand Master Wignacourt considered sending those knights refusing assignments to Rome to plead their case at the feet of the Pope but hoped passions would cool. Two days later he summoned Admiral Martelli and more responsible elders of the Italian Langue, but in the end decided on three ambassadors representing the entire Order of Jerusalem, and by proxy both the Catholic King of Spain and the Christian King of France. Wignacourt had other motives for this course involving pretensions of Monsignor Ettore Diotallevi di Rimini, on the one hand and on the other the Pope's annointment of François d'Espinay Saint-Luc the Younger, still a novitiate, as Turcopolier senior to a host of Bailiffs with decades of service. Meanwhile Duke of

Savoy Victor Amadeus I had as Grand Master of his Order of Saint Lazarus of Jerusalem made it his goal to either recover the Order's wealth lost in the past to other Orders or to have ceded to his Order all commanderies of other Orders in Savoy, principally those of the Order of Saint John of Jerusalem. The three ambassadors were Bailiff of Santo Stefano Pietro la Rocca, Bailiff of Caspe Cristóbal de Zanoguera, and Lieutenant Marshal Pons de la Porte. Several members of the Sacred Council were deputized to brief the three ambassadors on these issues.[49]

Reaching Rome, and having presented their credentials, the three ambassadors obtained a Papal audience and humbly beseeched the Pope to reverse his assignments of the Order's commanderies as a matter best left to the Grand Master and Convent. They further begged the Pope to revoke his appointment of François d'Espinay Saint-Luc the Younger as Turcopolier for reasons of seniority. Thirdly, they begged the Pope to support established privileges of the Order which had withstood the test of time and innumerable Papacies. Finally, they reminded the Pope the Order of Saint Lazarus had been extinct for more than a hundred years and that there were innumerable Hospitallers from Hospitaller commanderies in Savoy reluctant to change their Habit. In response the Pope refused to revoke his assignment of the three commanderies but did agree to redirect the revenue stream to the Order's Common Treasury. He agreed to revoke the assignment of Turcopolier for the reasons pled. Given a similar but opposite plea one year earlier by Carlo Filiberto I d'Este, nephew of Duke Victor Amadeus I and General of his galleys, the Pope recommended that Bailiff La Rocca proceed to Turin to discuss the Duke of Savoy's wishes with the Duke of Savoy. Finally, the Pope did not wish to make a statement on the Order's privileges but rather wished to let time further clarify the issues.[50]

At Malta there meanwhile arrived a French saettia bound from Alexandria which during the voyage became separated from a vessel with 200 Turks embarked bound for Tunis with arms and equipment for new galliots and brigantines. Given wind direction, the French captain believed the other vessel should be within 100 miles of Malta. Recognizing galley crews to be in need of rest following various re-provisioning runs to Sicily and ambassadorial runs to Naples, General of the Galleys Bernardo de Spelletta even so sortied from Malta early in April with all five galleys and two frigates bound initially for the island of Linosa 75 nautical miles to the west, and then another 70 nautical miles to Pantelleria, both without news. From Pantelleria the seven vessels took course for the Island of Cimbalo (Zembra) at the mouth of the Gulf of Tunis 12 miles off Cape Bon where from a cove of the island lookouts were posted. There the Maltese were joined by two brigantines of Sardinia with news of a Christian sailing ship, cargo of grain, captured by four galliots of Bizerta and run up on a sandbank three miles from La Goletta outside of Tunis. Spelletta decided to re-float the grounded ship 15 miles distant, but during the night of 8 April 1606 while still sheltered in their cove all were caught in a westerly and southwesterly gale forcing the larger galleys to get underway and clear the rocky island. Three of the galleys did not make it, the capitana commanded by Don Geronimo de Larrea, *San Michele* commanded by François de la Tour de Vernainet of Auvergne, and *San Giorgio* commanded by Fausto Bulgarini of Siena, the first thrown back on the second and the two thrown back on the third. These broke up on island shoals with most crew and unshackled oarsmen making it safely ashore. The other two galleys, the padrona *San Giacomo* commanded by Don Gaspar de Monreal of Aragon and *San Luigi* commanded by Hartmann von der Tann of Germany respectively escaped to Trapani and Malta. There was no report concerning the two Sardinian brigantines though both frigates in company survived within the cove, one soon dispatched to Palermo seeking succor, the other to Malta with the catastrophic news arriving 17 April.[51]

Spelletta and other survivors at Cimbalo encamped on high ground above the same cove with food stores and munitions saved from the three destroyed galleys. At Malta Tann's *San Luigi* was dispatched to Sicily to locate powers-that-be and to plead for assistance. Back at Cimbalo the first in a succession of assaults took place on 14 April 1606 when survivors were besieged by a Tunisian flotilla of seventeen oared vessels large and small putting 700 combatants ashore. The engagement persisted most of the day before assailants withdrew pursued to the shore by Spelletta and his crews. That day five knights were lost including Vernainet and Bulgarini in addition to eight soldiers. Others were severely wounded.[51]

Four days later the assailants returned, this time with 22 oared vessels including four large galliots and a galley putting 1,200 men ashore including palace janissaries commanded by the son of Ramadan, Georgian Bey of Tunis (under Uthman or Kara Othman, ruling Dey of Tunis). Under-attired Christians had survived this entire period from 8 to 18 April in unusually cold and windy weather sapping will to resist. Enemy assaults simply added to constant misery. For two days this second Tunisian assault persisted before the enemy again withdrew on 20 April when confronted by coordinated Christian sorties of soldiers, knights, and paid oarsmen. One hundred twenty enemy were left on the field including a principal enemy commander. The Viceroy of Sicily had meanwhile sent in aid the seven galleys of Sicily commanded by the Adelantado of Castile and a galleon built at Palermo called *L'Arca di Noé* belonging to the Viceroy's son, the Marqués de Villalba. A third enemy assault at Cimbalo ended almost before it began when Christian sails were sighted on 22 April, these the sails of both surviving Malta galleys and the Galleon of the Religion commanded by Simon Cheminée de Boisbenet of the Priory of Aquitaine. Remaining Christian sails were sighted the following day, 23 April, by which time the last of the enemy had withdrawn from Cimbalo. Five hundred thirty-five survivors were taken off on 23 April by the galleons as well as all of the artillery from the three destroyed galleys. By 27 April all were returned to Malta. Forty dead or severely wounded, and a single volunteer caring for the severely wounded were left behind. In addition to François de la Tour de Vernainet and Fausto Bulgarini the dead included Laurent de Virieu-Pupetières and François de Mandre while one of the wounded was Serving Brother Thomas Bousquet who was executed at Constantinople, all three of the Langue of Auvergne. The remainder of the living were enslaved. Hartmann von der Tann, it might be noted, would go on to become the longest serving German Hospitaller, reaching his end in 1647 as Grand Prior of Germany and Prince of the Holy Roman Empire following 60 years of service all of which commenced after a university education in Rome and Siena.[52]

Two galley hulls at Naples were donated to the Order by King Philip III which would be armed with artillery from *San Michele* and *San Giorgio*, while a new galley called *Vigilanza* was located at Palermo to restore the Malta squadron to full strength. A fourth galley was nearing construction completion at Naples for which *San Luigi* would be exchanged, while a fifth galley, *San Filippo*, new in 1603 but hauled in the Arsenal at Malta in 1604 could soon be made ready. It is this latter galley at 25 banks to which much of the destroyed 28-bank capitana's artillery and equipment was temporarily transferred and which would be exchanged for *Vigilanza*, the latter becoming the new capitana. The balance of the old capitana's armament went to *San Giacomo* new in 1605. Construction completions, re-equipments, and swaps were all consummated by mid July. At about this time the Ottoman Galley Armada reached Navarin (Pylos) on the western coast of the Morea 55 galleys strong still commanded by Kapudan Giaffer Pasha who had succeeded Cigalazade Yusuf Sinan Pasha in 1604. Rumor of an assault on Malta picked up speed at Malta, accelerating on suggestions from Naples that Malta was the Armada's objective even though Naples itself would have seemed more suspect given Santa Cruz's sack of Ottoman Durazzo ten months earlier. Perhaps wondering himself, Santa Cruz in mid-June 1606 put to sea with 26 Neapolitan and Sicilian galleys patrolling the coast of the Kingdom of Naples from Reggio Calabria to Otranto. Better prepared than not as the Ottoman Galley Armada moved up the coasts of the Morea and Albania (Epirus), numerous defensive assignments were made at Malta including Sector Wardens responsible for defensive preparation within assigned sectors. The three Wardens were Commanders Don Giuseppe di Guevara of Syracuse, François de Rascas-Bagaris of Provence, and Jorge Arturo de Torres of Aragon. Catalan Don Ramón de Berga was appointed Captain-at-Arms for Notabile (Mdina), while Bailiff of Mallorca Onofre de Copones was appointed Governor of Vittoriosa (Birgu) and Senglea. There were no reported defensive assignments at Gozo, and it was Gozo which was raided, not by the Armada but by three galliots of Bizerta. These arrived at night and put raiders ashore, whisking away 20 Gozitans setting out for fields at daybreak. No one knew until the victims failed to return home that night.[53]

At Rome on 29 May 1606 the artist Michelangelo Merisi known as Caravaggio killed, possibly unintentionally, a young man named Ranuccio Tomassoni from Terni in Umbria. The circumstances of the brawl and death of Tomassoni remain mysterious. Following the death of Tomassoni, Caravaggio fled first to the Colonna estates south of Rome, then on to Naples where Costanza Colonna Sforza maintained a palace, she the widow of Francesco Sforza in whose household Caravaggio's father had held a position. Costanza's brother Ascanio was Cardinal-Protector of the Kingdom of Naples, another brother, Marzio, was an advisor to the Spanish Viceroy of Naples, and a sister was married into the important Neapolitan Carafa family, connections which might help explain Caravaggio's destination.[54]

Released from guarding the Neapolitan coast by Álvaro de Bazán, the Adelantado of Castile and General of Sicilian Galleys Juan de Padilla y Acuña proceeded to Malta with seven galleys of Sicily, some towing Malta's *San Luigi* disarmed at Palermo and some towing the new *San Alfonso* for which the old *San Luigi* was to have been exchanged, the first now a gift from the Catholic King, the latter still the Order's property. Eager to prove himself absent the senior Santa Cruz, the Adelantado proposed another raid on the Barbary town of Maometta (Hammamet) on Tunisia's east coast 190 nautical miles west of Malta. The combined squadron was to be composed of ten galleys, seven of Sicily, three of Malta, both with embarked ground force. Because Santa Cruz was reported to have taken 14 galleys of Naples toward the Levant, this excursion appeared to deprive Italy and Malta of any galley defense at a time when Giaffer Pasha's intentions were unknown. Nevertheless, given the Adelantado's rescue of shipwrecked Hospitallers at Cimbalo three months earlier and Malta's own successful conduct of a similar raid on Maometta in 1602, Grand Master and Council agreed.

The ten galleys departed Malta on 2 August and by way of Favignana and Cimbalo took course for Maometta, making a landfall at night on 14 August, eve of the Ascension of the Virgin, three miles southwest of the town. The Spanish ground force 800 strong was put ashore immediately including Alonso de Contreras, the Maltese following with 300 more carrying petards and ladders hoping to surprise defenders. While the Adelantado advanced with his slow-moving troops, the Maltese moved quickly ahead, silently mounting the walls and catching the few defenders apparently napping. There was no need for petards; wall gates were open and the Christians soon controlled the town. Town premises, that is, as there were few people to be seen and those were heading for the mosque. Two hours into the raid the Christians had only 70 captives. The ten Christian galleys had been expected, and Maometta had been alerted.[55]

An onshore wind began to blow threatening the galleys, and a retreat was sounded, no one knew by whom or at whose order. The retreat was disorderly with those engaged in pillaging the town lugging their ill-gotten gains. The rains came. So, too, did a mounted squadron of Moorish cavalry, scimitars flashing. A confused withdrawal became a rout. Many Christians took to the sea hoping to reach the galleys now struggling to get away from the shore; many poor souls did not make it, including the Adelantado. Some five hundred Christians including seventy Hospitaller infantry and thirty-nine Hospitallers of the Habit were killed or captured. Among the French were Sergeant-Major Louis de Pontevez, François de Vintimille d'Ollières (enslaved), Hélion de Castellane-Claret (enslaved), René de Castellane-Mazaugues, Pierre de Roquelaure-Saint-Aubin the Younger (the Pierre de Saint-Aubin received in 1576), Constans de Glandevez-Peypin and Jacques de Cadillac-Violès of Provence; Claude de la Salle Colombière, François d'Annaval, François Faioles de Berton, Gilbert du Crocq d'Auterat, Serving Brother Pierre Bonaventure of Auvergne; Jean de Monceaux la Houssaye, Novitiate Bonaventure de la Chastaigneraye de Fourny, Novitiate Philippe de Roncherolles of Normandy, Novitiate Claude de Rouere and 25 year-old Guillaume de Rambures (both enslaved) of France. Rambures of Chateau Rambures 45km west of Vignacourt would be quickly ransomed in 1607 only to lose his life in 1608 combat, Rouere was never ransomed and died a slave. Also killed or captured were Torquato Puccini of Lucca, Emilio Bovio of Bologna, Don Diego de Nicuesa of Naples, Ottaviano Lisci of Volterra, Cesare Roma of Milan (enslaved), Francesco Antonio Sciabica of Sicily, Francesco Ferranti Caimo of Milan, Agostino Paci of Rimini, Asdrubale Vecchi of Siena (brutally murdered by enraged captors), Antonio Giovio of Como, Pompeo Rospigliosi of Pistoia (novitiate enslaved), and Serving Brother Antonio Manzana, all of Italy; Don Cristobal Abarca, Don Francisco Ariscon Baiamonte, and Guillermo Puidorfila (enslaved) of Aragon; Hans von Walpot, Piotr Koczynski, Johann Georg von Rumstal, and Ludwig von Preussen of Germany; and Don Juan Bernardo de Quirós of Asturias, Don Antonio Moretto Giron, Don Francisco de Paz, Don Jerónimo Carvajal, and Don Bartolomé Morales of Guadalajara. All dead or enslaved. A strong swimmer, Alonso de Contreras was not among them.[56]

Chapter IX

1606–1613

Returned to Malta in such catastrophic circumstances the Hospitallers were confronted by a summons for the Catholic Armada to assemble at Messina under command of the Marqués de Santa Cruz as lieutenant to Hospitaller Prince Emmanuel Philibert of Savoy, the latter having succeeded Gian Andrea Doria as Spain's General of the (Mediterranean) Sea (or General of the Galleys). The genesis of the summons was said to be sudden realization Kapudan Giaffer Pasha and the Ottoman Galley Armada remained at Navarin in the Morea within striking distance of Italy, Sicily, and Malta. Bernardo Spelletta hastily readied the three Hammamet galleys (the capitana *Vigilanza* commanded by Don Geronimo Larrea together with the new *San Michele* and new *San Giorgio* under unreported command) plus the new *San Alfonso* commanded by Don Diego de Loez of Castile plus a ground force largely re-constituted because of Hammamet losses. All departed Malta early in September 1606. At Messina the Maltese found four galleys of the Vatican under Knight of Santo Stefano Papirio Bussi anchored in the outer Lazzaretto or pratique port. Santa Cruz's 16 Neapolitan galleys were anchored in the inner port. Adjacent to the Neapolitans were four galleys of Genoa, the Genovese capitana anchored in the place of honor immediately to the right of the fleet commander. Also within the inner harbour were seven galleys of Sicily, seven of Genoa's Carlo Doria and seven Tuscans under Iacopo Inghirami, the latter a Knight and Admiral of Santo Stefano destined to make an indelible impression on Mediterranean naval history.[1]

Arriving at the mouth of the harbor Spelletta gave the appropriate salute announcing the Malta presence, but the Genovese capitana showed no sign of yielding her place, and Santa Cruz let it be known Genoa and Malta each with four galleys would share the vanguard when underway. Spelletta protested that under Charles V and Philip II the capitana of Malta in the absence of that of the Pope had always been accorded the place of honor to the right of the fleet commander, and when in the presence of the Papal capitana to the left of the fleet commander, and that position had been formally confirmed by both monarchs. Spelletta was effectively informed Philip III had yet to opine on the matter, and he consequently removed his four galleys to the Lazzaretto joining the four Vatican galleys, the Malta capitana anchoring to the right of the Papal capitana. Days later there being no plan of operations the Maltese requested and were granted permission to return to Malta.[2]

In the wake of the foregoing precedence issue, a critical matter of the continued slide of a republic on the front-line of the war against Islam at Rhodes to a modest arm of the Kingdom of Spain at present, the General of the Galleys of Genoa authored a manifesto supporting Genoa's relative importance to the Kingdom of Spain and at the same time denigrating Malta's stature. Grand Master and Council were compelled to produce an alternative view. Historian Giacomo Bosio was the author.[1]

In early 1594 during the Magistracy of Hugues de Loubens de Verdalle the Priory of Venice had been assigned by Papal Bull to Cardinal Ascanio Colonna, maternal uncle of Hospitaller Fabrizio Sforza Colonna. The Cardinal four years later appointed his nephew Coadjutor or heir apparent to the Priory of Venice. Imprisoned at Milan in 1601 for an unreported crime or crimes not including homicide, Coadjutor Sforza had been remanded to Papal custody and transferred to Malta in August 1602 with an escort of five galleys. At Malta he had been interrogated by Grand Master Wignacourt following which he was again imprisoned albeit in comfortable quarters at Fort Saint Elmo for four more years until, the charges against him never proven and his sins expiated, his release with restriction, the restriction being a ban on his return to Milan without Papal approval. It is in this period of freedom Sforza succeeded his aging uncle as Prior of Venice with the attendant Grand Cross prerequisite to appointment as General of the Galleys. Also in September Bernardo de Spelletta reached the end of his two-year term as General of the Galleys, and "Prior of Venice" (sic) Fabrizio Sforza was appointed Spelletta's successor. On Sforza's nomination Alessandro Pagani was appointed flag captain succeeding Don Geronimo Larrea.[2]

On Sforza's first voyage as General he at end-October proceeded with the four galleys all the way to Barcelona to take delivery of a new capitana constructed in that city's arsenal against an order from the Claramonte Foundation, a trust established in 1604 by the family of former General Esteban de Claramonte to commission construction of a succession of 28-bank capitanas to be christened *Santo Stefano*. From Barcelona the squadron proceeded to Marseille where it passed the winter waiting for construction completion of a second galley on order of the Common Treasury. This latter galley was to be the new capitana as *Santo Stefano* did not turn out as well as expected, a fitting postscript to the entire year. In the end the squadron departed Marseille with five galleys thanks to forzati contributed by the Kingdom, *forzati* petty criminals forced to serve at galley oars to earn their freedom.[2]

During 1606 Admiral Antonio Martelli was appointed Prior of Messina succeeding the deceased Aleramo de Conti della Lengueglia, and was in turn succeeded as Admiral by Francesco Moleti of Messina. Don Giuseppe di Guevara was appointed Prior of Lombardia succeeding Girolamo Agliata upon the latter's death. Gédéon Blondel-Joigny de Bellebrune was appointed Grand Hospitaller succeeding the deceased Louis d'Argilliers. Bailiff of Novaville Don Antonio de Toledo was appointed Bailiff of Lora succeeding the deceased Francisco de Valencia while Grand Chancellor Don Fernando Ruiz de Corral succeeded to Bailiff of Novaville. Bailiff of Negroponte Gonzalo de Porras was appointed Grand Chancellor and was succeeded as Bailiff of Negroponte by Don Ramón de Berga. Noël Bruslart de Sillery of the Langue of France was appointed the Order's Resident Ambassador to the Court of French King Henry IV succeeding Charles de Gaillardbois-Marconville who returned to his Commandery of Saint-Vaubourg Normandy. Francisco Martínez commanding the Villalba galleon *L'Arca di Noé* which took off most Cimbalo survivors and his first officer Bernabé Barreda were received into the Order as knights of grace.[3]

Famine at Malta in 1607 was attributable not only to abysmal harvests in Sicily but to similar harvests in all of Italy. Grand Master Wignacourt was able to obtain a bare-minimum in supplemental supply with a special allotment of 10,000 salmas of grain from western Provence and by arming and re-launching the galley *San Luigi* for corsair missions initially under command of Obizzo Guidotti and latterly under command of future Grand Master Antoine de Paule.

This galley together with the *Galleon of the Religion* commanded by Claude de Crèvecoeur captured off the Seven Capes of Anatolia two large Turkish caramussals with cargoes of rice and other foodstuffs not to mention 180 crew. In November and December treaties were signed ending the Long Turkish or Thirteen Years War between the Holy Roman and Ottoman Empires, thus freeing-up the latter's forces to better prosecute war with Persia. Commanding Ottoman forces in the east, former Ottoman Fleet Commander Cigalazade Yusuf Sinan Pasha born Scipione Cicala came to an undescribed end to his sixty-year life in December. At Constantinople 16 year-old Sultan Ahmed I turned his thoughts to the Mediterranean frontier.[3]

The *Galleon of the Religion* deployed to the Levant a second time in 1607, this time proceeding to and sending back foodstuffs from Ottoman food depots at Volos and elsewhere. On this same excursion Crèvecoeur's vessel overcame a large Turkish caramussal off the coast of Cyprus with a cargo of soap and rice also yielding a significant quantity of Venetian gold sequins (formerly gold ducats), several merchants, and a Sheik with four of his sons, each expected to be ransomable. Thirty years an Hospitaller, Abel du Crocq de Chennevières of the Ile de France lost his life in this brief engagement.[3]

Because at Malta poverty persisted not only of foodstuffs but also of the means to purchase foodstuffs, the Grand Master in his own name as well as that of the Religion purchased additional stocks of food from Flemish merchants acquiring grain and produce at lower northern prices. Distribution of Flemish foodstuffs among the resident population was possible, however, only when rationed by Distribution Bulletins. In the never-ending chronicle of food shortages at Malta, and absence of building materials, and imbalanced budgets, some may still need to be reminded the island produced nothing in the way of food, assembled nothing without elsewhere purchasing the components, and balanced its finances only by virtue of responsions, royal largess, plunder, and copper scudos.[4]

His Catholic Majesty's Resident Ambassador to the Holy See Don Juan Fernández Pacheco, 5th Duke of Escalona and 5th Marqués of Villena, was in 1607 re-assigned as Viceroy of Sicily succeeding Giovanni III Ventimiglia, 8th Marchese of Geraci and Prince of Castelbuono. The Grand Master dispatched his Spanish Secretary Commander Alfonso de Villaseca y Ulloa of Castile to pay his personal compliments as well as those of the Religion. Villaseca was also to discuss several matters stemming from a disagreement with merchants of Palermo resulting in impairment of the Order's privileges under the new Viceroy's predecessor. The Viceroy returned the courtesy by dispatch of a member of his official household, Hospitaller Commander Don Miguel Borgia, son of the Duke of Gandia (Valencia), with seven galleys of Sicily. This Hospitaller was personally most appreciative of the Grand Master for having earlier assigned him the Magistral Commandery of Aliaga of the Castellany of Amposta.[5]

Likewise welcomed at Malta was Hospitaller Francesco Antonio Bertucci of Lesina (Hvar), Croatia, received into the Order of Jerusalem through the Langue of Germany, a knight of spirit and enterprise who in 1595 with favor and support of Emperor Rudolf II prompted a rebellion of Bosnians against occupying Turks. Bertucci had similarly treated with Grand Master Verdalle and Pope Clement VIII to wrest from Ottoman occupation the fortified Dalmatian city of Clissa (Klis) a short distance from Spalato (Split). Absent a positive response in the latter instance, his group of conspirators had taken the city and castle on their own in April of 1596, but could not hold it against a subsequent Ottoman siege. He was in 1607 at Malta seeking support for re-possession of former Hospitaller Commanderies in Podolia (western Ukraine then Poland) occupied by secular forces. This undertaking was urged for the next decade before its death in 1617 from the pen of Hospitaller Commander and future Knight of the Grand Cross Siegmund Karl Radziwill (Zygmunt Karol Radziwill) of the Langue of Germany and Court of Poland.[6]

Fabrizio Sforza and the squadron's five galleys returned from Marseille by way of Genoa, where Sforza's aforementioned mother Costanza Colonna and Hospitaller Marchese of Fosdinovo Ippolito Malaspina embarked, and Naples where his mother debarked and Caravaggio embarked. The galleys arrived at Malta on 12 July with both Caravaggio and Malaspina. Over the next twelve months Caravaggio painted five masterpieces including *The Beheading of St John the Baptist* and *St Jerome Writing*, both of which are preserved in St John's Co-Cathedral at Malta. During the same twelve months Caravaggio also painted *Sleeping Cupid* and *Portrait of a Knight of Malta* (Hospitaller Antonio Martelli) both of which are today exhibited in Florence's Pitti Palace. Finally, Caravaggio painted

Portrait of Grand Master Alof de Wignacourt with Page displayed in the Louvre at Paris, the page thought to be future Prior of France Nicolas de Paris Boissy. Wignacourt was at the time 61 years of age. On 14 July 1608 twelve months following his arrival on the island Caravaggio was received into the Order of Jerusalem as a Knight of Grace, that is, a Knight appointed at Magistral prerogative absent the same strictures of nobility required of the overwhelming majority of knights (Knights of Justice). Three months later Caravaggio was imprisoned for gravely wounding a fellow Hospitaller. Imprisoned within Castle Saint Angelo he weeks later escaped, also escaping from the island itself. Two months still later he was defrocked *in absentia* under one of his own masterpieces and expelled from the Order of Jerusalem. With benefit of hindsight, the five masterpieces made the entire business more than worthwhile.[7]

Sforza's five galleys meanwhile consisted of an unnamed capitana new in 1607 commanded by Alessandro Pagano of Milan, the 28-bank *Santo Stefano* new in 1606 commanded by Ubertino Ricasoli of Florence, *San Giovanni* new in 1606 under François de Cremeaux of Chamoille, Savoy, *San Alfonso* new in 1606 under Don Diego de Loez of Castile, and *San Giacomo* new in 1605 under Don Gaspar de Monreal of Teruel, southern Aragon. Four of these dispatched into the Levant returned with a Turkish prize and a crew of 40, but on a second deployment to North Africa returned not only without a capture but with General Sforza seriously ill. The capitana and *San Giacomo*, moreover, had been severely damaged by successive storms. The remaining two galleys *San Giovanni* and *Santo Stefano* made a third deployment and second to the Levant under senior captain Cremeaux, taking course for Libya's Cape Buonandrea on the far side of the Gulf of Sidra and thence to Port Soliman, a fresh-water source on the modern Egypt-Libya border 660 nautical miles ESE of Malta and 250 nm west of Alexandria. From Port Soliman the two galleys continued on to the waters of Damietta and Alexandria where the pickings proved slim. At the southern Anatolia island of Cacamo (Kekova), however, the two galleys encountered a large saiche, cargo of grain, under command of corsair Hassan Amurat. She was invested by both galleys one to each side and defenders quickly despaired of any escape. Amurat elected to take the boarders with him and fired his magazine which only served to severely burn his own crew and did little or no injury to boarders. All but thirteen of the Turkish

Luigi Mayer's Cacamo (Kekova) Roads.

crew died immediately or within the next two days, including Amurat. The ship and much of her cargo were also lost.[7]

The Grand Master having in April personally surveyed all harbors and anchorages of the island of Malta for the purpose of assuring an adequate guard, in September did the same thing at Gozo, this time by sea aboard the galley capitana. Arriving at Malta in October were four galleys of Sicily transporting Don Antonio Sandoval of Castile dispatched by the Viceroy to pay his compliments, departing five days later.[8]

Returned to Malta from Cacamo without further incident, *San Giovanni* and *Santo Stefano* soon sailed for Licata in company with *San Alfonso* then commanded by senior captain Don Blasco di Giurato di Modica (of Sicily) and with *San Giacomo* under Don Francisco de Saavedra of Galicia to escort several merchant vessels transporting grain and other foodstuffs to Malta. One of these was also transporting coin to enable the Università of Malta to purchase yet additional foodstuffs. Of the four galleys, southerly Scirocco winds forced one far west to Trapani and the other three a bit further west to the island of Favignana, all passing the night at these locales. At daybreak on 16 October the latter three galleys en route Trapani encountered five large galliots of Bizerta in pursuit of a square-rigged marcigliana headed north toward Sicily's Cape San Vito, the galliots taking the three galleys under fire before the latter were able to enter the fortified port, but soon did enter the port with little damage and no casualties. Hours later all four Maltese exited Trapani and turned north toward Cape San Vito on the galliots' track, but the galliots perceiving the galleys as stronger as well as up-wind (that is, able to fire their bow cannons while moving with the wind while the downwind opponents must furl their sails and turn into the wind to fire their bow cannons) no longer had an interest in engaging.[9]

Pursuant to an Apostolic Brief the dignity of Bailiff of Armenia and accompanying Grand Cross with Honors were during the year awarded to Silvio Gonzaga, illegitimate 15 year-old son of Vincenzo I Gonzaga, Duke of Mantua. Francesco Lomellino of Genoa was appointed Resident Ambassador and Procurator General to the Court of Rome succeeding future Grand Master Luís Mendes de Vasconcellos. Monsignor Leonetto della Corbara of Rome arrived at Malta succeeding Ettore Diotallevi as Inquisitor of Malta.[10]

Arriving at Malta toward year-end 1607 was a young Genovese seaman by the name of Andrea Anfus. He had been a slave in one of two galleys of the Greek renegade Mustafa Pasha which had departed Tunis in April bound for Constantinople by way of the uninhabited island of Lampedusa. At Lampedusa Anfus had been able to flee ashore and hide until the two galleys resumed their voyage. He had expected in reasonable time to hail a Christian vessel arriving at Lampedusa for fresh drinking water. For a period of eight months, however, the Genovese seaman sighted no Christian vessel, only three Turkish galleys. Re-captured escapees from Turkish and corsair vessels were not treated kindly if not immediately hung, and so Anfus did not reveal his presence. Always desperately hungry, in the entire eight months he had no bread other than a modest amount of soggy biscuit discovered in the cove where most visiting vessels sheltered. He had otherwise survived on fish caught with a trap contrived from a morion helmet, on snails, and on tree greens and other foliage. One day he discovered a water-damaged small boat arriving on the tide, a pair of small oars, and shreds of a small sail. With these repaired as best he was able, he set sail on what is usually a northwest wind. Four days later on 21 December he reached Cape San Demetrio, the NW extremity of Gozo 85 nautical miles distant. Had he not made it ashore at Gozo, he was on course to sail another 340 nautical miles to Ottoman Santa Maura.[11]

Possessing letters of recommendation from his father Henry II, Duke of Lorraine, from his soon to be deceased grandfather Charles III, Duke of Lorraine, and from Ferdinando I, Grand Duke of Tuscany, as well as a letter from Cardinal Camillo Borghese, since elevated as Pope Paul V, endorsing the recommendations and declaring this to be the wish of Our Lord, Charles of Lorraine Count of Brie arrived at Malta in early 1608 and was received into the Order of Jerusalem, Langue of Germany. Not, however, without first encountering objections of the German Langue whose members wished to re-convene the last Chapter General to endorse such a bending of the rules. As the galleys of the Order were not available to transport attendees to a re-convened Chapter General, and in acute embarrassment at the affront to those recommending the Count to the German Langue, Grand Master Alof de Wignacourt obtained a favorable vote from a majority of the Council, but the Grand Prior of Germany Arbogast von Andlau and Lieutenant Grand Bailiff von Strohfeldt strongly protested, even threatening to remove the entire Langue of Germany from the Convent and actually replacing the standards flying at their Auberge with that of the Holy Roman Empire. In the end, Charles de Lorraine, Comte de Brie, batard du Duc de Bar was received into the Priory of Champagne, Langue of France. The reason he had been proposed to the Langue of Germany was not stated but may have had to do with his mother said to be a German noblewoman, or may have simply been a reflection of the fact his father was the Duke of Bar, a German Duchy, as well as Duke of Lorraine, or both.[12]

With arrival of Spring's calmer seas, General Sforza was ordered to take four galleys to Bizerta 20 nautical miles west of the Gulf of Tunis in search of those large galliots which had briefly threatened three of the Order's galleys in October 1607. Admonished to exercise considerable caution, utilizing, for example, an accompanying felucca for reconnaissance and location of enemy vessels, and for another example, consulting with squadron captains and other officers with pertinent experience. And, should there be no oared vessels at Bizerta which somewhat like Tunis is not situated on the open coast but rather on an enclosed gulf, Sforza was ordered to investigate Porto Farina (Ghar al Milh) in the Gulf of Tunis with its own enclosed gulf.

Sforza departed Malta on 17 April and reached Lampedusa 95 nm distant early the next morning where his galleys surprised an 18-bank galliot with a crew of 77 Turks and Moors. The galliot captain was a former captive at Malta released upon loss of three galleys at Cimbalo (Zembra) at the mouth of the Gulf of Tunis exactly two years earlier. A prize crew and liberated Christians took the galliot back to Malta with the captured crew at the oars while the Malta Squadron continued to Bizerta where it found neither galliots nor galleys.

The same was true at Porto Farina. Forced by intemperate weather on the north coast of Tunisia to find a more friendly clime, the galleys moved down the east coast into the Gulf of Gabes where off the shallows of Djerba's Cantara Channel they cornered an urca with a cargo of olive oil and barracan (camel-hair cloth). About 100 of the crew were able to swim and wade safely ashore, 22 others were taken captive. By mid-June the Squadron reached the coast of Egypt almost one thousand nautical miles to the east where it remained another two months, taking and after removing a crew of forty burning a vessel with a cargo of Turkish timber bound for Alexandria. During the same months the Galleon of the Religion commanded by Obizzo Guidotti of Bologna was in the same waters accompanied by a galliot commanded by friend Alessandro Zambeccari, also of Bologna. These two captains were received into the Order of Jerusalem at the same diocese in the same year, though at age 12 Guidotti was six years younger than Zambeccari. Their two ships together returned to Malta with 74 captives, two caramussals with cargoes of grain, and a single saiche laden with grain. It was in taking the saiche that the aforementioned and recently ransomed Guillaume de Rambures lost his life.[13]

During the evening of 25 July 1608 six galleys of France arrived at Malta under command of Philippe-Emmanuel de Gondi, 28 year-old Comte de Joigny and Général des Galères de France. He and the six galleys were escorts for embarked Prince Francis of Lorraine, termed the Chevalier de Guise on whom in an earlier year had been conferred the Grand Cross with Honors. This was François-Alexandre (1589-1614), 19 year-old seventh son of Henry I, Prince of Joinville, sometimes called Le Balafré (Scarface), and of Catherine de Nevers. As François de Lorraine de Guise he had been received into the Langue of France in 1601 but had not sooner made the acquaintance of Alof de Wignacourt. Following undo ceremony he and his escort departed for France six days following arrival.[14]

Some few days following the Squadron's return from the Levant in August the same four galleys with little respite were ordered to Palermo to transport food stocks to Malta. While the galleys were at Palermo, Grand Master Wignacourt at Malta learned two armed corsair bertones normally guarding the fortress at Porto Farina were hauled for maintenance. He immediately ordered Sforza to attempt the port's reduction. This venture, however, was nipped in the bud by early launching of the two bertones reported to Sforza by a French tartana outside of the Gulf of Tunis. Upon return to Malta in September Sforza's two-year term as General of the Galleys ended, and he was succeeded by Admiral Francesco Moleti who nominated Prospero Pugiades of Trapani as flag captain.[15]

Hospitaller Vice Chancellor Giovanni Otto Bosio returned to Malta from four years at Rome. And because Regent Chancellor and Hospitaller Emanuel de Chebedo of Portugal had been recalled by Cardinal Pietro Aldobrandini, Bosio resumed the duties of Vice Chancellor only to find matters left in extreme disorder, so much so he requested of the Grand Master a number of temporary assistants. These assistants died before matters could be set straight.[15]

Early in 1609 advisories from the Levant concerning the Turkish Armada sped their way to Malta so frequently the threat represented by the Armada again could not be ignored. Grand Master and Council felt compelled to make defensive assignments earlier than at any other time in the Order's history at Malta. Appointed Sector Wardens were Commanders Giovan Angelo Centorio of Vercelli, Antonio Centeno Guiral of León, and Jean de Vassadel-Vaqueiras of Provence. Artus de Glandevez-Peypin of Provence was appointed Governor and Captain-at-Arms for Notabile (Mdina). Prior of Catalonia Don Miguel de Alentorn was appointed Governor of Vittoriosa (Birgu) and Senglea. Meanwhile the Galley Squadron at Naples was summoned back to Malta. Under command of new General Francesco Moleti, the Malta galleys had been at Naples to take delivery of a galley constructed in that city's Arsenal against an order from the Common Treasury. The new galley had replaced *San Giovanni* acquired in 1606 and was equipped with the older galley's armament. The Grand Master received a report a fast galley-sottile was departing Tunis for Constantinople transporting as captive the eldest son of Viceroy of Sicily and Duke of Escalona Juan Fernandez Pacheco. This would have been 15 year-old Diego Antonio Pacheco y Bragança captured earlier by Barbary corsairs. Moleti was ordered to make haste and intercept the Tunis galley, but a fast galley departing even before the news was not going to be easily located if at all. Volunteering to participate in the search was the Count of Sommariva in the Piedmont who had taken passage with the galleys from Naples. Also volunteering was Charles of Lorraine Count of Brie who arrived at Malta 12 months earlier to be received into the Priory of Champagne. But the search for a needle in a haystack was in vain. Lamentably, the unfortunate young man died in 1616, still in captivity at Constantinople.[16]

Following search for the captors of Diego Antonio Pacheco, and well off the direct route from Tunis to Constantinople, a large urca was encountered near Seco di Palo, the extensive body of shallow water extending well out to sea off the corner of land as well as the land itself where modern Libya meets Tunisia. Crewed by sixty Turks and Moors, the flat-bottomed urca was bound from Alexandria to ports in Tunisia with a cargo of rice and flax when intercepted by the Malta galleys each with 150 to 160 combatants plus oarsmen. The contest persisted for two hours and left many on both sides dead or wounded before the over-matched urca yielded.[17]

As the weeks and months of 1609 passed there was from time to time news of major developments with the Turkish Armada which was uniformly forwarded to Viceroy of Naples and Duke of Benevente Juan Alonso Pimentel de Herrera by express felucca, the crew supplemented by fourteen knights at two per langue as well as by a number of soldiers from the Citadel garrison at Gozo. On many occasions such news was cause for un-evacuated population to retire into the Citadel with provisions, animal stock, and fodder, while an alert guard was posted along the island's coast. Occasionally the fast frigate of non-Hospitaller Vincenzo Rispolo commanded by Hospitaller linguist Pier Francesco Rizzolo Salvatico of Piacenza was sent into the Levant to learn what people were saying about the Armada. Salvatico was under order when at Corfu to meet with Giovan Andrea Lipravoti, and when at Zante with Giovan Leonardo Latino, the two agents on whom the Grand Master most relied for news of enemy movement. On occasion the frigate even proceeded into the Archipelago in search of information, but on this occasion Lipravoti's reports suggested it would not be necessary. The armada, he reported, which exited the Dardanelles earlier proceeded only as far as Tenedos (Bozcaada) fifteen miles to the south where it had made rendezvous with the Archipelago or Rhodes Guard bringing armada strength to 60 galleys and two mahons (galleasses). It was next expected in the Morea to embark 8,000 infantry. Salvatico was back at Malta on 11 August with the foregoing information.[18]

Somewhat later there arrived at Malta further news of the Turkish Armada suggesting it had been divided into smaller units, and on 8 October 1609 a squadron of nine Turkish galleys appeared off Valletta. Their mission unknown, Fort Saint Elmo nevertheless took them under fire and drove them off. With their departure fear at Malta of the Turkish Armada would ebb. For Winter months.[19]

Bailiff of Santa Eufemia Centorio Cagnolo had meanwhile armed and equipped a corsair galleon flying the flag of Savoy under the command of Hospitaller Sforza Santinelli of Pesaro. In Levantine waters Santinelli set upon a ship of Venice which submitted only following a sharp conflict and was thoroughly looted as though a sack of a resisting city in revenge for besieger dead. Savoy and Venice were not at war. This crime reached an end only after all corsair cannons overheated and only when there was nothing of value remaining on the Venetian vessel. Then Santinelli sped to Malta hoping for the sanctuary of a fraternity and to be able to sell his plunder. At Malta he was charged with piracy while the plunder was confiscated and returned to Venice. Found guilty of the charge Santinelli was stripped of his Habit and ordered to pay restitution and damages through Leonido Loschi of Vicenza, the Order's Receiver at Venice.[19]

In contrast with the action of Santinelli preying on a merchant vessel crewed by non-combatants of a non-combatant state, Hospitaller Guy de Pot de Rhodes of Berry and the Langue of Auvergne, also commanding a corsair galleon, during the year engaged off Karamania a Turkish galleon armed as a warship bound from Alexandria to Constantinople. The Turkish crew of 200 put up a valiant defense for three full days before the ship began to settle. When the ship went to the bottom only eight of those opposing the Christians survived. Sailing in company with Guy de Pot, Hospitaller Nicolas de Baillieu also of the Langue of Auvergne commanding a second corsair galleon engaged a second Turkish galleon with somewhat more success.

Her capture. While dividing the spoils in a safe harbor, however, Nicolas Baillieu died of wounds suffered during the engagement.[20]

The *Galleon of the Religion* commanded by Obizzo Guidotti of Bologna while sailing in company with the galleon of the Grand Master commanded by Henri de Lancry de Bains of Boulogne-la-Grass and the Langue of France, at age 21 not old enough to qualify for either a Hospital command or commandery but the Grand Master's nephew, together took a caramussal with a cargo of grain. The *Galleon of the Religion* immediately returned with the capture to Malta before re-deploying with new captain Philippe de Gouy-Campremy, the latter's own corsair galliot in company. Having prowled the Archipelago for some months without prey, Gouy decided to put troops ashore at Mitilini (Lesbos) where they succeeded in capturing several Turks together with two beautiful young ladies whom they ransomed for 1,000 Venetian gold zecchinos (sequins). Not content with Mitilini takings, however, Gouy would seek the company of others elsewhere.[20]

Sforza Santinelli was not the first Hospitaller to fall afoul of Venice, nor would he be the last. Among contemporaries were three English brothers made famous in the theater. Their wakes were dramatized for the English stage in 1607 as *The Travailes of the Three English Brothers*, "Travailes" perhaps the English word for "Travels," perhaps the Middle English word for "Travails" or Torments. The brothers were the sons of Sir Thomas Shirley of Wiston in Sussex, a member of Parliament and sometime Treasurer-At-War for Queen Elizabeth I. In the latter capacity the elder Shirley (s)peculated with the Queen's money and retired with a large IOU. The first born of three sons and six sisters was Thomas Shirley the Younger. Educated at Hart Hall, Oxford, this Shirley served with the English Army in the Low Countries and in Ireland, for which he was knighted in 1589 and after which was made an attendant to the queen at Hampton Court. There he met and secretly married Frances Vavasor, Maid of Honor to the Queen. For that transgression he spent 14 weeks in the Tower of London. For turning her back on suitor Robert Dudley, son of the Queen's lover of the same name, Frances Vavasor was also expelled from the Court. Irrespective of Tower time the younger Sir Thomas Shirley was subsequently chosen a member of Parliament representing the East Sussex town of Hastings, famous for its 1066 battle between Normans and Saxons. All the while he was unsuccessfully seeking to repay his father's considerable debts. While an MP he in 1601 outfitted three privateers, one a three-masted square-rigged *bretone* or *bertone* of 900 tons mounting 34 guns called *Dragon* which he commanded himself. Late the following year he appeared before Ferdinando de' Medici, Grand Duke of Tuscany, from whom he obtained *letters of marque* authorizing his ships to wage corsair war on all things Turkish. Immediately confusing his flags, Shirley captured two Flemish and a Venetian merchantman, thus incurring the Grand Duke's wrath and occasioning departure of the two accompanying privateers. Worse, he was captured in turn while raiding the Aegean island of Kythnos, was charged with piracy, and was taken in chains to Constantinople. Thus this Shirley became the first member of the British Parliament to occupy an Ottoman dungeon.

The second-born Shirley was Anthony, also of Hart Hall, Oxford. Knighted by Henry IV of France for military service in that country, Sir Anthony Shirley incurred his own sovereign's displeasure: *"I will not have my sheep marked with a strange brand nor suffer them to follow the pipe of a strange shepherd."* He was imprisoned in a Royal Navy brig. With intervention of the Earl of Essex, a cousin by marriage, he was released and dispatched in 1598 to the court of Persian Emperor Abbas the Great. Accompanied by his teenage brother Robert, he sailed across the Aegean and along the southern coast of Turkey to Alexandretta, and from there traveled by camel to the royal court at Qazvin. Anthony's assignment was to establish commercial relations with the Persian Empire, but while there he entered into an agreement with the shah to train the shah's army in the use of artillery. Robert, though, did the training, teaching his hosts gunnery principles recently developed in the west, principles then used by he and the Persians to thrash the Ottomans at the Battle of Yerevan in 1605. *"The mighty Ottoman, terror of the Christian world, quaketh of a Shirley fever."* Anthony, made a prince of the Persian Empire, had earlier returned to Europe as Persian ambassador seeking alliances against the Ottomans, but for reasons of being a French knight and a Persian prince was not permitted to return to Britain. Rather, he was imprisoned at Venice for pretending to Venetian credentials, and so became the first Persian prince to occupy a Venetian dungeon. Released in 1605 he made his way to Madrid where he received a commission as Captain-General of Sicilian Galleys from Philip III. As commander of a Sicilian Galley Squadron numbering seven galleys he entered the Aegean in 1608 with intent to besiege the island of Mitilini, but instead diddled and dawdled in contrary winds until losses in combat at Andros forced his return to Sicily. Relieved of his commission upon arrival, he passed the rest of his life out of favor and impoverished at Madrid.

Robert Shirley had meanwhile been dispatched by Shah Abbas on a similar mission to Europe, taking with him his Circassian bride. Reflecting Persian success at Yerevan, Robert was well received at the court of Rudolph II where in 1609 he was made Count Palatine and Knight of the Holy Roman Empire. Thus he became the third son of Sir Thomas Shirley the elder to be knighted, each by different royalty. But upon his arrival in Britain his ambassadorial credentials were questioned and he was forced to return to Persia where he for some years fell out of favor. After 35 months in Ottoman dungeons Thomas the younger had also returned to Britain where he was slapped into the Tower of London at behest of the Venetian ambassador for having taken the Venetian merchantman three years earlier. Later released he was in 1612 on the final leg of his journey from court to courthouse jailed a fourth time, on this occasion as a *primogeniture* debtor, that is, inheritor of his father's debts. Robert, though, was not finished. In 1615 he would be introduced by letter of Shah Abbas to Grand Master Alof de Wignacourt who in November 1609 initiated cooperation between the Order of Malta and the Persian Empire with a letter to Shah Abbas.[21]

Late in the year 1609 King of Spain Philip III requested by letter to the Grand Master that Don Diego de Brochero be thanked in the name of the King for his counsel on matters of war and for his service concerning other important matters, and that Brochero's service to the Crown be extended. Grand Master and Council accordingly appointed Brochero Resident Ambassador to the Court of Spain succeeding Grand Chancellor Don Gonzalo de Porras who had filled the position for eight years. This was the same Diego de Brochero enslaved for five years by the Ottomans following the 1570 Galley Battle of Cape Passero, and the same Diego de Brochero a galleon corsair imprisoned by Venice in 1583 for transgressing on Venetian neutrality. Brochero was just beginning to make the pages of history. There was a second Royal letter ordering Magistrates of the Viceregency of Sicily pending a Royal determination to suspend jurisdiction over all persons and property of the Order of Malta. A third letter from the King concerning the Priory of Portugal established the Royal expectation that upon resignation or death of incumbent Prince and heir apparent Victor Amadeus of Savoy the Priory would devolve on a minor of the King's family.[22]

During the year Gabriele Saluzzo di Montemar succeeded the deceased Antonio Martelli as Prior of Messina. Martelli will live forever, however, as the subject of a Caravaggio masterpiece. A member of the extended Caravaggio family, Martelli was at the time 68 years of age. Grand Conservator Don Miguel de Alentorn (Miquel d'Alentorn i de Salbà) was appointed Prior of Catalonia succeeding the deceased Raimundo de Veri (Ramon de Verdú), while Bailiff of Negroponte Ramón de Berga (Ramon de Berga) succeeded to Grand Conservator, and Prior of Ireland Don Pedro Gonzales de Mendoza succeeded to Bailiff of Negroponte. Upon the death of Alentorn a short while later Berga succeeded to Prior of Catalonia, and Jorge Fortuyn advanced to Grand Conservator. Arthur de Glandevès was appointed Grand Commander succeeding Boniface de Puget-Chasteuil upon the latter's death. Grand Chancellor Gonzalo de Porras was appointed Bailiff of Novaville succeeding the deceased Don Fernando Ruiz de Corral, while Bailiff of Negroponte Don Pedro Gonzales de Mendoza succeeded to Grand Chancellor and Miguel de Junient succeeded to Bailiff of Negroponte. Diego de Brochero meanwhile received a Papal Brief awarding him the dignity of Prior of Ireland and attendant Grand Cross greatly disturbing Don Pedro Urtado de Mencoza who did not wish to part with it. At Rome Pope Paul V awarded Hospitaller Ambassador to Vienna Don Luis de Moncada a Grand Cross with Honors at behest of Spain's Viceroy of Aragon the Marqués de Aitona. Aitona was Luis de Moncada's brother Gastón de Moncada y Gralla-Despla.[22]

Early in December 1609 the five galleys departed Malta for Messina under command of Admiral and General of the Galleys Francesco Moleti. Seriously ill, Moleti was put ashore and hospitalized at Messina. Command of the Squadron devolved on senior Captain Prospero Pugiades commanding the capitana. Moleti died eight days later of unreported cause. He was a native of Messina pre-deceased by Hospitaller brother Michele in 1560, struck down by peste during that year's tragic expedition to Djerba. Francesco Moleti is thought to have been 68 years of age. He was shortly afterward succeeded as Admiral by Gabriele di Saluzzo di Montemar of Genoa and as General of the Galleys by Pons de la Porte of Chaponnay 30 kilometers south of Lyon. The latter nominated and the Council appointed François de Cremeaux to command of the squadron capitana.[23]

New Admiral Gabriele di Saluzzo also became ill, and while he recovered, the Langue of Italy exercised its prerogative of nominating its senior knight Angelo Centorio of Vercelli received in 1562 and a veteran of 1565's Great Siege of Malta to act in Saluzzo's stead at the Galley Squadron change of command on 12 January 1610.[24] On 10 February the cornerstone for Fort Saint Paul was laid at Saint Paul's Bay.[25]

Early in March Pons de la Porte's five galleys proceeded to the coast of Africa where they were immediately incapacitated for fifteen days by a punishing storm, after which they took course for Palermo and then Trapani to procure foodstuffs for transport to Malta. At Trapani General La Porte was advised there were Barbary ships in the Malta Channel harassing and seizing merchantmen, including merchantmen transporting provisions from Sicily to Malta. On 5 April fifteen miles off Sicily's Gulf of Terranova the squadron encountered a ship of Tunis mounting 24 guns threatening a ship of Candia west-bound with a cargo of wine, both then immobilized in the absence of wind. After ninety minutes of resistance, the Barbary ship was abandoned by remaining crew and went to the bottom. She had departed Tunis twelve days earlier, armed and equipped by Kara Othman Pasha/Uthman Dey, an Anatolian Turk who had been ruler of Tunis since 1593. Wounded in the engagement, he and 118 of 170 other Infidels were taken off the foundering ship, the remainder dead or doomed. There were in addition a number of Englishmen and other adventurers taken off who would like Uthman be held for ransom. Eighteen of the squadron's embarked soldiery lost their lives in this engagement, most while plundering when the corsair vessel went to the bottom. Uthman Dey would die of his wounds in September 1610.[23]

Englishman Robert Elliot, a familiar of Robert Dudley bastard son of the Earl of Leicester and longtime favorite of former Queen Elizabeth, was at the time under house arrest at Tunis but in connection with the ransoms would become aware of and would appear at Malta in 1613.

Having conveyed captives to Malta the squadron re-deployed immediately, again scouring the Malta Channel. Absent further encounters with the enemy, General La Porte proceeded once more to the coast of Africa. There a brigantine and a garbo were overcome yielding 40 captives. Returning these captives to Malta, La Porte was informed of four Infidel galliots lurking in waters of the Sgarambi (Egadi) Islands west of Sicily, but found nothing on the Squadron's arrival. In ensuing weeks the squadron transported Juan Fernandez Pacheco, retiring Viceroy of Sicily, from Palermo to Barcelona and returned to Malta by way of Marseille and Naples with large sums of responsion coin, jewels, and other items for the account of the Common Treasury. Also transported to Malta was the Grand Master's brother Joaquim Wignacourt. Upon arrival Pons de la Porte resigned his command without stated reason.[26]

In the third attempt on his life, and much to the great sorrow of the Convent, French King Henry IV was felled on 14 May 1610 by Catholic assassin François Ravaillac. Grand Hospitaller Adrien de Brion was appointed Ambassador of Condolence and dispatched to the Court to profess his and the Order's sorrow. Before Brion was able to reach the Court, however, he, too, was felled, but by an unidentified medical problem. He was replaced as Ambassador of Condolence by the Master of the Grand Master's House Girolamo di Guevara. King Henry IV was succeeded by his nine year-old son Louis XIII for whom the latter's mother Marie de Medici served as Regent for the next seven years.[27]

In June 1610 Pons de la Porte was succeeded in command of the galley squadron by Grand Commander Jean de Vassadel-Vaqueiras, an experienced soldier and seaman who for many years had been engaged as a corsair, and on the latter's nomination Henri de Merles Beauchamp was appointed to command of the squadron flagship in succession of François de Cremeaux who had moved to the flagship from *San Giovanni*. The Grand Master in his discretion also appointed Simon le Petit de la Hacquinière, François du Mansel Saint-Léger, and Raphaël de Grave-Sérignan to respectively command *San Alfonso* in succession of Don Blasco di Giurato di Modica, *Santo Stefano* in succession of Ubertino Ricasoli, and *San Giovanni* in succession of an unidentified replacement for François de Cremeaux.[27] The cornerstone for Fort Saint Lucien was laid at Marsascirocco (Marsaxlokk).[28]

In August three corsair galleons flying the flag of Malta and commanded by Hospitaller Chevaliers Jean-Jacques d'Izarn de Fraissinet of Saint-Germain-des-Prés and the Langue of Provence, René Moreau du Feuillet of Tours and the Priory of Aquitaine, and Jean de Conti-Gaucourt of Paris in company with the *Galleon of the Religion* commanded by the aforementioned Philippe de Gouy-Campremy of Brie, surprised at night the Fortress of Lajazzo/Laiazzo on the NW shore of the Gulf of Alexandretta (Iskenderun), made their way into it by means of a petard which blew the gate, took great plunder, and having destroyed the fortifications, carried off above three hundred captives. Philippe de Longvilliers de Poincy of future Saint-Christophe fame is reported to have been a contributor to successful entry into the fortress.[29]

Kapudan Khalil Pasha's Turkish Armada of 60 galleys and two mahons was at Tenedos when news of this disaster reached him. Born Armenian in what was then Cilicia or Lower Armenia, he abandoned any plan he might have had of putting embarked troops ashore at Gozo or in southern Italy and instead took course for the underbelly of Anatolia. The galleons of the three corsairs together with a pinnace were in September intercepted off Cyprus by fifty-odd of Khalil's galleys. While the pinnace escaped in light air, the three galleons were taken, including Fraisinet's *Galion Rouge* (80) in what Turks call the Battle of Kara Djahannum, or Black Hell, suggesting the Turkish victory came at a stiff price. None of the three galleon commanders is believed to have survived the battle or captivity. Philippe de Guissencourt received into the Langue of France in 1603 was one among many taken captive to Constantinople where he would die of an infected arm wound while awaiting ransom.[30]

During 1610 Gédéon Blondel-Joigny de Bellebrune renounced the dignity of Grand Hospitaller with reservation of his seniority right to the Priory of France. One of seventeen siblings of deceased parents, he had little prospect of any other estate, and very little prospect of this one prospectively assigned to Alexandre de Vendôme, bastard offspring of King Henry IV and Gabrielle d'Estrées. He was succeeded as Grand Hospitaller by Adrien de Brion who soon succumbed to an unreported ailment. Brion was in turn succeeded by François de Myée-Guespray. Grand Commander Artus de Glandevès-Peypin was appointed Bailiff of Manosque succeeding Jean de Vintimille d'Ollioules who died in slavery following the 1606 Christian reversal at Hammamet, while Jean de Vassadel-Vaqueiras succeeded to Grand Commander. Heinrich Baron von Logau of the Priory of Bohemia was appointed Prior of Hungary succeeding Wilhelm von Cronberg of Frankfurt. Following on the 1609 heels of the Empire's relocation from Vienna to Prague, this appointment was a manifestation of a ten-year interlude during which the Priory of Bohemia attempted to achieve parity with the Priory of Germany. In 1620 Logau would be succeeded as Prior of Hungary by Hartmann von der Tann of the Priory of Dacia and would be appointed Prior of Bohemia, ending the attempted rebellion. During the interim the Sacred Council had ruled in favor of Bohemia, but Pope Paul V eventually and finally ruled otherwise.[31]

Commander Francesco Lomellino in 1611 completed his three-year term as Resident Ambassador and Procurator General at Rome and was succeeded by Niccolò della Marra, the only knight available having the requisite experience. Lomellino came away from the assignment with a Grand Cross said to have been suggested to the Pope by none other than Spanish Ambassador Gastón de Moncada y Gralla, Marqués de Aitona, who had similarly obtained a Grand Cross for his brother the Hospitaller Ambassador to Vienna. Because there were limits to the number of Grand Crosses per langue, and because the Langue of Italy had no available Grand Cross, Francesco Lomellino of Genoa had been awarded the Grand Cross attending Castile's Bailiwick of Novaville. Meanwhile Don Pedro Gonzales de Mendoza had lost his Priory of Ireland and attendant Grand Cross by its 1609 Crown requested re-assignment to Don Diego de Brochero of Castile. As Grand Chancellor from 1609 to 1611 Mendoza had disdained the attendant Grand Cross because it could not be worn outside of Malta and Gozo. Re-assigned in 1611 Mendoza found himself Bailiff of Novaville absent a Grand Cross months earlier assigned to Francesco Lomellino.[32]

Early in April Hospitaller Guillaume Gadagni Beauregard of the Langue of Auvergne, not seen at Malta since late-1604 when he took employment with Grand Duke of Tuscany Ferdinando I de Medici, returned in command of four Tuscan galleons en route Livorno at the end of a 17-month deployment into the Levant. While Pozzo reported that over the 17 months Beauregard had taken a large number of enemy vessels yielding considerable plunder and about 400 captives, and while it was true his four galleons took on the annual caravan from Alexandria to Constantinople, fought an indecisive action against 43 Turkish galleys, and carried out several raids ashore, he was coming home with only 250 captives against 400 killed or wounded capturing them. His ships were also in need of substantial and expensive repair. This would be the last Tuscan expedition with sailing ships for some years.[33]

During 1611 Vaqueiras's galley squadron and the *Galleon of the Religion* commanded by Philippe des Gouttes were selected to support an assault on a new (1572-73) Turkish fortress (Neokastro) located on the southwest coast of the Morea. Hexagonal in plan with six towers, the fortress was situated between the town of Pylos and the entrance to the Bay of Navarin, controlling both, while the bay was large enough to accommodate a fleet and frequently did host the Ottoman Armada close enough to Malta to cause concern. The undertaking was suggested to Grand Master Alof de Wignacourt by two Greeks long resident in the area, promising that a surprise attack with scaling ladders and petards for blowing gates would catch the garrison napping and be certain of success. Embarked troops were placed under the command of François de Cremeaux with Luigi Mazzinghi of Florence, Claude d'Urre de Venterol of Provence, and Spaniard Baltasar de Marcilla of Navarre as sergeants-major. Because of uncertain wind the Galleon was sent ahead under sail to take a position between Keffalinia and the Strofadi Islands, with oared galleys following four days later. The two rendezvoused at Prodano Island eight nautical miles north of Navarin, and from there proceeded at night to the bay's entrance where troops were put ashore.

Turkish defenders, however, proved too alert, welcoming the newcomers with a cannon salute and forcing General Vaqueiras to recall landed combatants but for Hospitaller Girolamo Corbera of Palermo who did not live to hear the recall. The squadron and galleon on advice of another local Greek, Yiorgos Stamatis, diverted to the Gulf of Aegina diagonally across and a part of northeastern Morea. Two hours before daylight on 23 May 1611 embarked troops were put ashore at the Isthmus of Corinth in sufficient number to form a large battalion. These marched on the city of Corinth on the far side of the Isthmus, and while the distance was greater than the expected two miles, succeeded in a surprise attack. There was little resistance, but the city was put to the sack anyway. During the sack a body of mounted militia attempted their own surprise, but alert reaction on the part of Hospitaller commanders succeeded in turning them away. The sack yielded a large amount of plunder and 300 captives. Two-thirds of the latter, however, proved to be Greek and were released at the island of Aegina. While enemy cavalry appeared during the Christian withdrawal, Hospitaller losses were limited to two soldiers. Among many deserving of praise, according to Pozzo writing years after the fact, was future Grand Master Don Martin de Redin on his first caravan. Pozzo only indirectly lets his readers know this was a contest between prepared combatants and unprepared noncombatants. The Hospitallers ignored the city's mighty fortress of Acrocorinth while any garrison at Acrocorinth ignored the Hospitallers. General Vaqueiras immediately returned to Malta following the raid on Corinth as he had been alerted two laden urcas had departed Alexandria bound for the Barbary Coast.[34]

Pausing no longer than necessary to debark the shore battalion, retaining caravan knights in addition to ships company, Vaqueiras took the squadron west to Lampedusa hoping to pick up urca tracks, and then to the shallows of Barbaria without encountering the enemy. In the Gulf of Gaps (Gabès), however, the galleys overhauled six Moorish londros bound from Djerba which yielded 130 crew in addition to cargoes of wool, camel's hair, and barley. Three of the londros were sent to the bottom while the other three were towed to Malta. Following this second voyage the galleys investigated the waters of Sicily from Trapani in the west to Palermo on the north coast to Messina in the east where at the latter port in September they were detained several days by a summons of Catholic Armada units. The summons was issued by new Viceroy of Sicily Pedro Téllez-Girón, 3rd Duke of Osuna, and the assembly was commanded by Álvaro de Bazán, 2nd Marqués de Santa Cruz. With 34 galleys (12 of Naples under Bazán, 10 of Genoa under Duke of Tursi Don Carlo Doria, 7 of Spain and Sicily under Don Ottavio d'Aragona, and 5 of Malta) Santa Cruz reached Valletta on 15 September where waited a company of notables including 26 year-old Duke of Terranova Carlos Tagliavia d'Aragona, the Duke of Nocera, the Duke of Cerce, the Marchese d'Anzi, all three of the latter young Carafas of Naples, the Marchese of Terracusa directly descended from Gonzalo Fernández de Córdoba, the Duke of Benavente

Antonio Alonso Pimentel, plus squads of other notable offspring, all seeking glory. Apropos of the early September 1606 entry above, et seq, at Malta by order of King Philip III of Spain it was established the Standard of Malta had precedence over that of Genoa and all others excepting the Royal Standard of Spain and the Holy Standard of the Papal Squadron. This determination on the part of the King was attributed by many to the negotiating skills of Hospitaller Prior of Ireland and Resident Ambassador Diego de Brochero.[35]

While at Malta Santa Cruz obtained agreement of Grand Master and Council for Maltese participation in a planned siege of Cherchene (Kerkennah Islands) in the Gulf of Gabès. There is no report of hesitation to such agreement. For this purpose the landing force battalion was re-embarked, its new Commander Philibert de Mathay of Auvergne assisted by sergeants-major Gabriele Simeoni of Chieri, Philippe de Gouy-Camprémy of Hauts-de-France, and Don Ñuño de Alvarado of Estramadura. Cherchene was comprised of two low-lying and unfortified islands opposite and ten or more miles from the Tunisian coastal city of Sfax. This was yet another instance of an overwhelming force of Christians falling on a largely helpless Muslim-Arab community and carrying away men, women, and children for slave labor, this time 480 men, women, and children. In spite of no organized opposition, numerous armed Christians were among numerous unarmed dead. These included Hospitallers Louis de Galéan des Issards of Provence commanding Sicilian Galley Militia, as well as Don Francisco de Sarmiento of Burgos and Don Juan de Herrera of Seville. Notables reaching their end were the Dukes of Cerce and Nocera.[36]

Having retired from Cherchene, Santa Cruz's galley armada en route home was buffeted by a fierce wind and sea storm, reaching the island of Lampedusa beginning 6 October. The five Maltese did not reach home until 21 October, arriving from Lampedusa by way of Syracuse. Arriving the following day at Malta accompanied by two French and four Sicilian galleys was 13 year-old Prince Alexandre de Bourbon, Chevalier de Vendôme and Hospitaller Prior of Toulouse. Natural son of King Henry IV and half-brother of King Louis XIII, he expected to be appointed General of the Galleys upon expiration of Vassadel-Vaqueiras's two-year term. As Prior of Toulouse he had been awarded the attendant Grand Cross without which he could not by Papal edict be appointed General of the Galleys.[37]

During 1611 Admiral Gabriele di Saluzzo de Montemar of Genoa was appointed Prior of Capua succeeding the deceased Don Vincenzo Carafa, and was himself succeeded as Admiral by Prior of Messina Francesco Saccano of Messina. Saccano was in turn succeeded as Prior of Messina by Attilio Mastrogiudice of Sorrento. A bit later the Bailiwick of Santo Stefano was vacated by death of incumbent Pietro la Rocca; Saccano moved to the vacant bailiwick while Mastrogiudice moved to Admiral. Bailiff of Novaville Don Gonzalo de Porras was appointed Bailiff of Lora in succession of the deceased Don Antonio de Toledo, while Grand Chancellor Don Pedro Gonzales de Mendoza succeeded to the Bailiwick of Novaville. Commander Antonio Centeno Guiral moved up to Grand Chancellor. Treasurer Henri d'Appelvoisin was appointed Prior of Aquitaine succeeding Bertrand Pelloquin who had lived to the age of 90, seventy of them as an Hospitaller. Grand Hospitaller François de Myée Guespray succeeded to the dignity of Treasurer, and Jacques de Gaillardbois-Marconville became Grand Hospitaller. Felipe de Bardaxi was appointed Grand Conservator succeeding the deceased Jorge Fortuyn. Pursuant to authority granted by Chapters General the Grand Master appointed as Seneschal his nephew by his sister Jacques du Chenu du Belloy of the Langue of France, thus filling a vacancy created three years earlier upon death of Laurent de Virieu-Pupetières. Commander Bartolomé de Brull of Catalonia was appointed to command of the galley *Santo Stefano* succeeding François du Mansel Saint-Léger, while Commander Giulio Falco of Capua was appointed to command of *Santa Maria* succeeding Francesco Marchetti. The Commandery of San Giacomo at Campo Carbolini vacated by death of Agostino Mego was assigned by Magistrale Grace to the Grand Master's Italian Secretary Francesco dell Antella of Florence. Henri de Lancry de Bains, a nephew of the Grand Master, believed Antella had taken advantage of his uncle and became hostile and insulting of Antella. Anger became sword-play, and Lancry de Bains was killed. Wignacourt reappointed Antella his Italian Secretary and re-confirmed assignment of the Commandery of San Giacomo at Campo Carbolini.[38]

At 14 years of age Alexandre de Vendôme was on 17 April 1612 appointed successor to General of the Galleys Jean de Vassadel-Vaqueiras. Upon Vendôme's nomination Amador de la Porte was appointed flag captain in succession of Henri de Merles Beauchamp in command of the squadron flagship. At the time the four other squadron galleys were *San Alfonso* commanded by Simon le Petit de la Hacquinière, *Santo Stefano* commanded by Catalan Bartolomé del Brull (Bartomeu del Brull), *San Giovanni* commanded by Raphaël de Grave-Sérignan, and *Santa Maria* commanded by Giulio Falco.[39]

On Sunday 29 April 1612 Grand Master Wignacourt's second Chapter General convened at Malta. Most attendees suspected the business of the Chapter General would primarily be concerned with the state of the Common Treasury. Following a ceremonial opening the agenda moved directly to selection of the sixteen legislators who in camera would make most of the Chapter's decisions. Elected by their peers within each langue were Lieutenant Grand Commander Hercule de Vintimille du Revest and Honoré de Castellane du Boise for Provence, Marshal Pons de la Porte and Pierre-Louis de Chantelot for Auvergne, Grand Hospitaller Jacques de Gaillardbois-Marconville and Treasurer François de Myée Guespray for France, Prior of Navarre Bernardo Spelletta and Lieutenant Grand Conservator Gaspar de Monreal for Aragon, Bailiff of Santo Stefano Francesco Saccano and Bailiff of Naples Ippolito Malaspina for Italy, Prior of England (Designate) Cesare Ferretti (Andrew Wyse was and would remain Prior of England until death at Malta in 1631) and Don Severo Rodriquez del Valle of Granada for England, Titular Bailiff of Brandenburg Theodor Rolman von Battenberg and Jakob Christoph von Andlau for Germany, and finally Bailiff of Lora Gonzalo de Porras and Conventual Conservator Luis Mendes de Vasconcellos for Castile. Insofar as the Common Treasury was concerned, and considering all Convent expense, that is, of the Church, of the Infirmary, for feeding, for Ambassadorial expense, for agents at Infidel locations, for maintenance of five galleys and one great galleon of 3,000 salma capacity, for munitions and soldiers, for the Arsenal, Foundry, and Armories, for maintenance of fortifications and public structures, and so forth, it was the judgement of the Sixteen *Capitolanti* that from responsions and other sources, in addition to two earlier and continuing levies of 50 and 40 thousand scudos, the Convent must raise a one-time amount of 122,000 scudos. At Chapter General-end, Grand Master Wignacourt's administration of the Common Treasury was re-confirmed.[40]

Giovanni Battista Nari of Rome was appointed to command of the new galley *San Lorenzo* in the galley squadron commanded by

Caravaggio's Grand Master Alof de Wignacourt and Page.

Alexandre de Vendome. Leandro Colloredo of Friuli was appointed at the same time to command of *San Alfonso*. The change-of-command ceremony took place at month-end administered by Lieutenant Admiral Ottavio Natta, and the four galleys other than the capitana departed immediately for corsair operations along the African coast under command of Padrone Bartolomé del Brull of Aragon commanding the 28-bench *Santo Stefano*.[41]

Former Grand Master Martin Garzés had in 1596 initiated design and construction of an aqueduct to bring water from springs at Dingli and Rabat near Civitta Vecchia (Mdina) to Valletta which at the time was supplementing cistern rainwater and a single spring with fresh-water hand-carried from outside of city walls. The project, however, had been suspended within months for lack of sufficient funds. There had been a subsequent start-stop in 1610, but in July 1612 the project was resumed for good with supplemental financing from Grand Master Wignacourt himself. The project would be completed in April 1615 at a cost of 434,605 gold scudos. Bringing so much water to Valletta, the aqueduct's completion would spur another expansion of the city's population.[42]

Six Sicilian galleys under Ottavio d'Aragona had in 1612 already carried out a raid on Kalibia, Tunisia, and in company with seven Neapolitan galleys commanded by the Marqués de Santa Cruz, had carried out a second raid on the Fortress of La Goletta guarding access to the city of Tunis. Late in July of 1612 Viceroy of Sicily and Duke of Osuna Pedro Téllez-Girón summoned constituents to an assembly of the Catholic Armada at Messina. Vendome was accordingly ordered to take his five galleys to Messina and on arrival to call on the Viceroy and offer the services of his squadron. The five galleys departed Malta on 29 July and late the following day joined the aforementioned squadrons at Messina. According to Pozzo the three squadrons deployed to the Levant for two and one-half months and accomplished nothing. On his return to Malta in mid-October the young Vendome was gravely ill. While he and the capitana remained at Malta, Padrone Bartolomé del Brull took the remaining four galleys south to the African Coast and then for a circumnavigation of Sicily, both undertakings fruitless. While the four galleys were away Vendome resigned his generalship on advice of those concerned for his health, according to some, or according to others, because Ottoman Sultan

Ahmed I considered it duplicitous for the brother of ally Louis XIII to be commanding the galleys of Malta.[43]

Grand Master and Council appointed Dom Luis Mendez de Vasconcellos of Evora, Portugal, General of the Galleys succeeding Alexandre de Vendome. By Apostolic Brief Vasconcellos was also appointed to the English dignity of Bailiff of Eagle, succeeding the deceased François d'Astorg de Segreville. On nomination by Vasconcellos, Antonio Pereira de Lima of Portugal was appointed to command of the capitana. The piety of Grand Chancellor Don Pedro Gonzales de Mendoza was notable as he completed at his own expense and adorned with carvings and gilt the Chapel and the major part of the Church of San Jacobo of the Priory of Castile. Grand Bailiff Johann Friedrich Hund von Saulheim was appointed Grand Prior of Germany succeeding the deceased Arbogast von Andlau, while Prior of Dacia Georg Christoph von Weitingen advanced to Grand Bailiff. Titular Bailiff of Brandenburg Theodor Rolman von Battenberg likewise advanced to Prior of Dacia. Commander of Marseille and of Sainte-Eulalie Antoine de Paule was appointed a Capitulary Bailiff on recommendation of Cardinal François de Joyeuse, Archbishop of Toulouse. Upon death of Cardinal Silvestro Aldobrandini, grand-nephew of Pope Clement VIII, the Hospitaller Priory of Rome passed to his brother Cardinal Ippolito Aldobrandini the Younger (same name as Pope Clement VIII). Expropriating Grand Master Verdalle's 1595 conveyance of the Order's Commandery of Reggio to Duke of Modena Cesare d'Este, Pope Paul V upon death of Duke Cesare re-conveyed the Commandery to his own heir Duke Francesco d'Este, thus symbolically evicting Hospitaller Niccolò Sciortino of Noto who was forced to renounce what had temporarily been his Commandery.[44]

Grand Master Wignacourt early in 1613 took four galleys and their officers to Gozo for detailed inspections of the Citadel above Rabat (Victoria), particularly of the 3,300 feet of curtain wall surrounding the Citadel. The Grand Master and ensemble were also ascertaining standing needs of the local population as well as of siege needs should the island's entire population be required to retreat within the walls.

Prior of Aquitaine Henri d'Appelvoisin reached the end of his life on 28 March 1613 at Changillon in Poitiers. A veteran of 1565's Great Siege of Malta, he was 70 years of age 53 of which were as an Hospitaller.

Meanwhile the habitual interference of and expropriation by Popes of Italian dignities and commanderies was again a matter of smoldering resentment within the Langue of Italy. Seeking to calm resentment a Statement of Expectations concerning dignities and commanderies assigned to knights of an advanced age was proposed and adopted. Two Papal Briefs addressed the same subject. Knights from three langues were selected as ambassadors to meet with Pope Paul V for the purpose of aligning Hospitaller and Papal intentions. These were Cattaliano Casati of Milan, an Hospitaller for forty years, Juste de Bron de la Liègue of Dauphiné and the Langue of Auvergne, 53 years an Hospitaller, and Don Antonio Saavedra Rocha y Ovando of Cáceres, Extremadura, and the Langue of Castile 25 years an Hospitaller. These three were transported to Messina by the Galley Squadron and in April 1613 continued from Messina to Rome where they were joined by fourth ambassador Orazio Capeche Minutolo of Naples who had secretly been enlisting the support of Hospitallers assigned to the Vice Regencies of Sicily and Naples as well as of Hospitallers assigned to Philip III's Duchy of Milan. At his own expense Minutolo had pleaded to the Court at Madrid and received a Royal decree disapproving of expropriation by suggesting limits. Minutolo was not well received at Rome.[45]

Vasconcellos and the five galleys of the Religion departed Malta on 8 April 1613 bound for Syracuse and Messina to take on provisions for an extended deployment to the Levant. The General's orders were to besiege several Ottoman shore facilities known to Yannis Neni, a Greek informant from Smyrna (Izmir). Neni was embarked aboard the capitana as was Ground Force Commander Louis de Sauzet d'Estigniéres of the Marche and Langue of Auvergne. On board other galleys were three sergeants-major: French-speaking Claude de Castillon de Castellet of Provence, Italian Giovan Battista Nari also commanding *San Lorenzo*, and Don Nuño d'Alvarado of Asturias and the Langue of Castile together with 150 caravan knights and 600 hired soldiers divided by language into three companies. Crossing the Ionian and then the Aegean a distance from Messina of 650 nautical miles to within sight of Rhodes, the Malta Squadron encountered that of the Knights of Santo Stefano each five galleys strong and each with an embarked ground force.[46]

The Santo Stefano Squadron was commanded by, and for eleven years had been commanded by, the highly-regarded veteran commander

Iacomo Inghirami. Twenty-four years junior in age and knightly seniority to Vasconcellos, Inghirami sought assistance in undertaking an assault on a fortified Turkish settlement on the Mycale Peninsula on the mainland side of the Samos Channel, likely Priene on the south side of the peninsula with an elevated fortress originally Byzantine but since improved, perhaps Priene's Panionium on the north side of the Mycale Peninsula near modern Guzelcamli. Only the latter was readily accessible from the sea, but uphill through forest and bramble, and its small garrison would hardly have warranted Maltese assistance. Whichever, Pozzo made no mention of this undertaking perhaps because the senior knight present was not in command, an affront to Maltese sensibilities. In the event, the Turkish position reportedly proved too well defended or the terrain too difficult, and the assault force was recalled. The Tuscans thereafter separated from the Maltese, the first heading south and the latter heading north up the Kara Burun Peninsula opposite Chios. Inside the peninsula was one of Neni's suggested targets, the formerly Genovese town of Phocaea (Eski Foca). Located on the NE shore of the Gulf of Smyrna about 25 nautical miles from Smyrna itself, Phocaea had one of the safer harbors on the coast of Asia Minor, and the town had a long maritime history. Seamen of Phocaea in the 6th Century BCE founded the western Mediterranean city of Massalia, modern Marseille, among others. The town was defended by two Genovese fortresses, one overlooking the town and its harbor only occasionally garrisoned as well as a waterside fortress within the town, both improved by resident Turks.[47]

At about the same time (April 2013) the *Galleon of the Religion* commanded by Philippe des Gouttes while prowling the Barbary Coast at mid-month took two large prizes, one a vessel, cargo of olive oil, bound from Tunis to Alexandria crewed by 35 Moors, and the other a patache equipped at Algiers which put up a fight damaging the galleon. Not more than 22 of the enemy remained alive at the end. Of the galleon's complement there were also many dead and wounded, Antoine de Beauclerc Frémigny of France among the former and future Grand Master Annet de Clermont-Gessans among the latter. Frémigny had but weeks until eligible for a commandery. Returning to Malta between captures Gouttes brought news obtained from the 35 Moors that corsairs of Bizerta had been forewarned of a forthcoming raid on that port by the Galley Squadron of Sicily and had assembled

4,000 cavalry and a large number of infantry with which to ambush Sicilians put ashore, while Bizertan galliots and other vessels had been moved to safety in the seawater lake behind Bizerta. Grand Master Wignacourt dispatched Don Gonzalo de Saavedra by felucca to Trapani on 16 April, the day this news reached Malta, with a verbal report for Sicily's galley commander Don Ottavio d'Aragona, and with a letter to Viceroy of Sicily and Duke of Osuna Pedro Téllez-Girón with the same information. Aragona had already sailed for Bizerta but had been forced back to Favignana by adverse weather, and that was where he was located by Saavedra on 19 April, halting a second departure on 20 April.[48]

Chapter X

1613–1617

Crossing the top of the Kara Burun Peninsula as well as the mouth of the Gulf of Smyrna, Luis Mendes de Vasconcello's five galleys of Malta put their Ground Force quietly ashore west of Phocaea the night of 30 April 1613, and all 750 knights and soldiers proceeded without conversation to their destination. Leading the way were soldiers Pedro Cimar of Valencia and Claude Roy, both of the garrison of Malta. With the assistance of others they carried several petards for blowing gates, Roy's normal assignment to instruct knight novitiates with the Ground Force in the proper use of explosives. Next came Claude de Lancry de Bains, brother of Henri de Lancry de Bains, both nephews of Grand Master Wignacourt from Boulogne-la-Grass and the Langue of France. Claude commanded ten knights and 40 soldiers who would secure the gate following petard blast. With him was the guide and conceptual planner Yannis Neni. Next came four groups of soldiers each commanded by a galley padrone or first officer, the soldiers carrying ladders should the petards fail. Last came the Battalion itself under its commander and sergeants-major.

All was proceeding as planned with no doubt of victory when of a sudden there was a misstep. Guide and petard unit veered off into gardens adjacent to the road to avoid detection by sentinels. Those units following behind, however, remained on the road and arrived at the seaside fortress before the petard unit. Defenders, moreover, were ready, alerted by a marine source of the presence of Christian galleys in the Gulf of Smyrna. A musket-fire greeting from defenders brought the petard unit in a hurry and the gate was soon blown while ladders were also placed against the walls and the walls surmounted. About 100 knights and soldiers entered the fortress by these two routes, Francesco Capponi of Florence and Padrone or #2 aboard *San Giovanni* among those who did not make it. Even so, Christian commanders no longer believed victory was within reach as defenders had retired within the inner keep and the petard to blow the keep's gate had failed. Sergeant-Major Giovanni Battista Nari also commanding *San Lorenzo* had received a musket ball in an arm following a head wound from the petard blowing the outer gate. The failed blast on the gate to the inner keep similarly disabled the two petard carriers, Cimar and Roy. Meanwhile the bulk of the battalion remained outside of the fortress and resisted entering given uninhibited musket fire from the inner keep. A second attempt to blow the inner keep was discussed, but petards could not be located with neither Cimar nor Roy totally conscious. The assault on Phocaea was ended with recall of the assailing force.[1]

Eighteen captives, women and children, were taken to the galleys. Twenty-five assailants were dead, another mortally wounded. The latter was Juste de Fay Gerlande (the Younger) of Velay and the Langue of Auvergne. The second son of Gabriel de Fay, Seigneur de Gerlande, and nephew of Juste de Fay (the Elder), the younger Juste de Fay would die of his wounds on 30 August. Third and last son Charles remained an Hospitaller. Eldest son Juste-François, destined to become Seigneur de Gerlande, would also see his second and third sons become Hospitallers. Two knights were among the dead: Pietro Spino of Bergamo and Pier Francesco Oscasale of Cremona, the latter barely out of his novitiate.

Malaspina brought the galleys into the harbor for the evacuation. The entire enterprise had been a costly failure. Taking course to turn the island of Mitilini (Lesbos) a very large enemy caramussal was encountered which had no chance of either escaping or of fending off five galleys. An explosive shell was fired which ignited her poop and a huge cargo of lead and munitions went to the bottom. 138 Turks and Moors were taken off the sinking ship some of whom would be ransomed returning one percent of value lost. This incidental enterprise had also been a costly failure.[1]

At about the same time Admiral of the Knights of Santa Stefano Iacopo Inghirami was sailing the south coast of Anatolia, at mid-May 1613 reaching across the Gulf of Antalya to assail the Karamanian fortress at Agha Liman (Taşucu Seka Harbor), the port for ancient Seleucia in Isauria (Selifke). He did this on information from a privateer who had plundered the area finding an enormous quantity of gold, on the order of 200,000 florins, transported in smaller amounts from the Cypriot Sancakbeylik of Girne for *safekeeping*. Moreover, two years earlier 40 Tuscan sailors from the ship *Prospera* had been stranded by error of the captain, captured, tortured by Turks, and their heads hung on the city gate. Defending Agha Liman was a garrison of four hundred. At night Inghirami disembarked his ground force under the orders of future Tuscan Galley Commander Giulio da Montauto. A sentinel noticed their approach. The Tuscans nevertheless propped ladders against the walls and the gate was blown; besiegers burst through the gate and over the walls while enemy cavalry took flight and 150 Turks repaired to a tower and waited for help. Inghirami took the tower under fire from the sea followed by a ground assault within the walls. With surrender of defenders came conquest of two galleys of the Cyprus Guard found in the port as well as eight merchant ships. There were 313 captives and 237 liberated Christians; these people were embarked in two galleys sent back to Livorno with 16 pieces of artillery and four captured flags. Between dead and wounded, Tuscan casualties amounted to 50 combatants. Coin found, however, was disappointingly little.[2]

Departing Palermo on 25 May, Don Ottavio d'Aragona took Sicily's galley squadron into the Aegean proceeding all the way to Chios opposite Anatolia's Kara Burun Peninsula and back without encountering the enemy, though he did encounter the five-galley Tuscan Squadron. For his part he had 8 galleys with 800 soldiers embarked. At Cape Spartivento on the Italian boot in the vicinity of Stampalia, he sighted at 15 miles a vessel of high board; the vessel proved to be Venetian and provided false papers asserting she was bound for Messina. In reality she was headed for Tripoli and Modone (Methoni) and had taken on board a number of Turks and Moors. The vessel was seized and escorted to Palermo. Re-provisioning, Aragona departed again eight days following his return, this time on the wind by way of Sardinia to the Algerian coast where he put his troops ashore and laid waste to the coastal city of Chicheri or Djidjelli (Jijel) 130 nautical miles east of Algiers, killing the governor and, he reported, 800 others while also destroying four vessels in the harbor. Upon his return to Palermo Aragona was accorded a Royal welcome.[2]

Seven galleys of Naples under Marqués de Santa Cruz Alvaro de Bazan arrived Malta on 21 May 1613, departing four days later accompanied to Syracuse by the five-galley Malta Squadron still commanded by Luis Mendes de Vasconcellos. After re-provisioning all twelve galleys departed Syracuse for an opportunity cruise consuming much of June with no notable success. Toward the end of June Neapolitan and Malta squadrons separated, Santa Cruz returning to Naples until August and the Maltese headed for Marseille to take delivery of a replacement galley for *San Alfonso* then seven years of age. Everything was swapped, sails, rigging, oars, cannon, munitions, food supplies, oarsmen, crew, caravan, and captain. The squadron departed Marseille bound for Cartagena towing the bare hull of the old *San Alfonso*.

At Cartagena the five galleys took delivery of 234 thousand scudos in Castilian responsions plus an additional four thousand scudos in gold, silver, and jewels, all for the account of the Common Treasury. A number of caballeros embarked taking passage to Malta by way of France and Italy where yet more Hospitallers embarked for Malta.[3]

The aforementioned Englishman Robert Elliot had been liberated by Yusuf Dey, new Ruler of Tunis, and appeared at Malta with a plan for galley skiffs and feluccas to enter the port of Algiers and with artificial fire to burn Barbary ships present. With too little cross-examination the Grand Master approved his plan and ordered Vasconcellos to put it into effect. By way of Mallorca and Ibiza the galleys proceeded to a position behind Cape Matafou (El Marsa) at the eastern extreme of the Bay of Algiers ten miles from the port. Elliot, though, proved too vague and unaware for the plan to be carried out, perhaps even confusing Algiers with the port of his detention. The five Malta galleys weighed anchor and took course for Cartagena, unsuccessfully pursuing a galliot of Bizerta en route, but successfully seizing a corsair tartan near Grenada's Cape Gato. Malta losses included Cavaliere Antonio Benedetto Mignanelli of Siena ending his fifth year since reception.[4]

Returning to the Pratique Station within Marsamxett Harbor by way of Malta's south coast, Mendes Vasconcellos's Galley Squadron sighted at first light before sunrise on 17 August 1613 eight regular Turkish galleys off Marsascirocco Bay gathered together as if readying to put troops ashore. Bound for Tunis, it turned out, the troops were commanded by Christian renegades intending to interrupt festivities scheduled the next day, Sunday 18 August, for the annual Feast of Saint Helen at Castle Bircharkara (Birkirkara) ten kilometers north of the anchorage at Marsascirocco. Such feasts were attended by ransomable notables while Church treasures were gathered together in one place. But the coastal guard was awake at the local tower constructed in 1610, Fort Saint Lucien, and the tower's cannon fire alerted islanders, Hospitallers, and intruders alike of the present danger. The intruders and their eight galleys withdrew. The renegades were aware of the annual fiesta but unaware of the relatively new fort defending their proposed anchorage.[4]

Departing Palermo six days earlier, Ottavio d'Aragona headed once more to the Levant. By August-end his eight reinforced galleys were at Venetian Cerigo (Kythira) where he was informed of the passage of an Ottoman fleet of 50 galleys commanded by new Kapudan Mehmed Pasha, said to be a man of little naval experience, bound from Alexandria to Constantinople. (This pasha was the Kara Mehmed who 14 months later would for the first of two incumbencies become Grand Vizier. He had formerly been a commander of the Palace Guard and had taken as a child-bride one of the Sultan's daughters, thus qualifying as both a sea commander and grand vizier.) Because of contrary "Meltemi" winds strongest in August, Aragona had to wait five days at Nio (Ios), but imagined his prey similarly windbound. With abatement of the wind, he moved north into the Samos Channel where he encountered a Greek fisherman and was informed a Turkish squadron had been sailing the same waters en route Constantinople from Egypt carrying tribute collected in that region; he learned, moreover, that two galleys had been detached from the squadron and that the other eight, having put into Segacich (Sigacik) east of Çesme, must soon be at Scio (Chios). Aragona headed for Cape Corvo to lie in wait for the enemy. Reaching it, he sent a felucca back; she sighted the Turks (10 galleys, five in the vanguard, two in the center of the formation, and three in the rear) heading north from Scio Town. Aragona put six galleys in his front line and behind them held two in reserve. His capitana pounced on the enemy capitana, a galley of 25 banks; the other seven Sicilian galleys took on as many of the enemy. The enemy flagship submitted in an hour, the same went for another five galleys of 26 banks each. Of the remainder, one, chased by Aragona's *Scalona*, ran onto a shoal; the other three had also taken flight. One of these shipping water sank while being pursued. The reis of the other two vessels made good their escape but lost their heads at Constantinople. Aragona towed the six prizes to the island of Nicaria

(Ikaria). There were 458 Turkish prisoners, among them the squadron commander Sinan Pasha who would die at Milazzo (Sicily) of his wounds, as well as Mahaceret, Bey of Alexandria. 1,300 other Turks were later estimated to have lost their lives. Two hundred twenty-six Christians lost their lives among even more wounded, but 1,200 Christians were liberated. The plunder was enormous, both in terms of coin and merchandise estimated at 600,000 florins. Thirty-three additional Ottoman galleys reacting to the disaster pursued Aragona fruitlessly. These were likely commanded by the aforementioned Mehmed Pasha, formerly Beylerbey or Viceroy of Egypt.[2]

Perhaps realizing his earlier error, Robert Elliot in the company of Robert Dudley appeared at Rome to submit to Pope Paul V a plan to capture Tunis with the help of galleasses designed by Dudley, son of the Earl of Leicester of the same name, and to extirpate that nest of pirates. This was the same Robert Dudley who in 1594 as nominee of the Queen had lost the aforementioned Frances Vavasor by marriage to Sir Thomas Shirley. Not long after the two had wed, Shirley had commissioned three privateers and sailed off to obtain letters-of-mark from the Grand Duke of Tuscany. And it was not long after Shirley's departure that Robert Dudley also commissioned three privateers and sailed off to obtain letters-of-mark from the Grand Duke of Tuscany. Though the Elliot project was influentially backed (Dudley had become a prominent fixture at the Tuscan Court), the pope refused to have anything to do with it, and both Elliot and Dudley were referred to Madrid by Don Francisco de Castro, then Spanish Ambassador to the Holy See. King Philip III also declined to fund Elliot's project.[5]

By Papal Bull dated 25 September Pope Paul V incorporated within the office of Grand Master the dignities of Grand Prior of England, Prior of Ireland, and Bailiff of Eagle, thus reversing the mostly ignored Bull of Pope Gregory XIII ruling these dignities could not be awarded until England returned to the mother church, while also legitimizing his own pending appointment.[6]

Seven Christian slaves at Tunis, five of them English and two Italian, surprised and overcame at night on 11 November 1613 the crew of a Turkish patache anchored in the harbor of La Goletta, cargo of artillery and munitions with which Yusuf Dey expected to arm a large sailing ship waiting at Susa. Unarmed but for a few clubs and an equal number of knives, the Christians approached the patache in a small boat and climbed aboard without being noticed by the sleeping crew and seized the ship following a clash in which five crew and two English were injured but after which the prognosis was not good for the Christians. More crew appeared, five at the poop, six at the prow, and eight from midships hatches. It was only by dint of crew apathy all were subdued, sails were hoisted, and the ship exited the port. Seven days later she reached Malta with the remaining 12 crew, 20 pieces of artillery, and quantities of munitions.[7]

On 6 December 1613 Procurators of the Langue of Italy placed before the Council a contract agreed between Bailiff of Santa Eufemia Centorio Cagnolo as Procurator representing Prince of Rocella Don Fabritio Carafa as party of the first part, and as parties of the second part, Deputies of the Langue of Italy, the contract concerning foundation of a Bailiwick of *juspadronato*, meaning the right of the party of the first part to appoint bailiffs in succession together with the right to wear the Grand Cross in return for financial support of the bailiwick including construction of a church capitalized at 40,000 scudos. Should the line of Rocella be extinguished, the bailiwick would revert to the Langue of Italy. The contract was approved by Grand Master and Council, and Don Francesco Carafa was appointed first Prior of Rocella at age 15.[8]

In December 1613 the Grand Master's nephew and Seneschal Jacques du Chenu du Belloy was appointed Bailiff of Armenia in succession of deceased Papal-appointee Silvio Gonzaga. Belloy would remain Bailiff of Armenia for the next 46 years. Grand Hospitaller Jacques de Gaillardbois-Marconville succeeded to the Bailiwick of the Morea upon advancement of incumbent Simon Cheminée de Boisbenet to Prior of Aquitaine, while Pierre de Beaujeu advanced to Grand Hospitaller succeeding Gaillardbois-Marconville. Within weeks, however, Beaujeu was further advanced to Treasurer where he succeeded François de Myée Guespray and was succeeded as Grand Hospitaller by Gilles de Vieuxpont. Passing away in December was Bailiff of Lora Gonzalo de Porras, a Castilian Caballero admired throughout the Religion not only for his piety, prudence, and splendor but rather for integrity as resident ambassador to Rome and Madrid, and for his saintly life. Porras was succeeded by Don Pedro Gonzales de Mendoza, thus leaving the Bailiwick of Santo Sepulcro de Toro at Zamora to Don Antonio Centeno Guiral. The latter's vacation of the dignity of Grand Chancellor opened the way for Don Diego de Brochero who vacated the Priory of Ireland to which Papal appointee and non-Hospitaller Don Michele Calderoni acceded. The Portuguese Priory of Crato was promised to General of the Galleys and Bailiff of Acre Mendes de Vasconcellos upon death or resignation of incumbent Prince Victor Amadeus of Savoy. Charles de Ligne, 2nd Prince of Arenberg, was provided with the Order's authority to acquire at his own expense for return to the Order commanderies expropriated by secular entities in Holland. Thirteen year-old seventh son Eugene de Ligne of Arenberg was coincidentally received into the Order of Jerusalem, Langue of France.[9]

Early in March 1614 three Maltese galleys proceeded to Syracuse, loaded provisions and supplies, and departed. While returning to Malta they encountered and seized a patache with a crew of 18 Turks. Arriving at Malta with the provisions and supplies were letters from King Philip III of Spain and from Viceroy of Sicily and Duke of Osuna Pedro Téllez-Girón requesting the galleys of Malta proceed into the Levant in company with those of the Vice Regencies of Sicily and Naples to impede and disturb provisioning and assembly of the Turkish Armada which without doubt planned some months later to come west under Kapudan Khalil (or Halil) Pasha.[10]

Galley Squadron General Mendes Vasconcellos was ordered to make preparations for a deployment of five weeks into the middle of May. A ground force was readied as in 1613 under command of Louis de Sauzet d'Estigniéres, senior knight of the Langue of Auvergne, likely consisting as in 1613 of 150 caravan knights and 600 hired soldiers. Sergeants-major were the three galley captains: Spanish-speaking Antonio Pereira de Lima of the capitana, French-speaking Claude d'Urre de Venterol of *Santa Maria*, and Italian-speaking Giovanni Battista Nari of *San Lorenzo*. It is not clear whether these three of five galleys were cited because their skippers were sergeants-major or whether there were only three Malta galleys participating in the deployment. If only three Malta galleys, the embarked ground force would have been proportionally smaller. If all five the others were *San Alfonso* commanded by Leandro Colloredo of Friuli and *Santo Stefano* commanded by Catalan Bartolomé del Brull. Standard-Bearer was Jean-Baptiste de Vy of Franche-Comté and the Langue of Auvergne.

Departing Malta on 9 April 1614 Hospitaller galleys rendezvoused with the squadrons of Naples and Sicily at Messina under their respective commanders Marqués de Santa Cruz Alvaro de Bezan and Pedro de Leyva replacing Ottavio d'Aragona who, given his long list of marine successes, had in May been appointed General of Sicilian Cavalry. Santa Cruz assumed overall command of the 26 galleys present in the absence of Hospitaller Grand Prior of Castile and Captain-General de la Mar Prince Emmanuel Philibert, enroute from Cadiz with additional squadrons. Those assembled at Messina were delayed in departure for the Levant but did so on or about 12 May with not a few accidents, unhappy encounters, and a maximum of nasty weather before and after. Said to have a vague plan to raid the Ottoman re-victualing depot at Volos north of Athens, any such plan was aborted for unreported reason even though the Christian force was sighted at Skyros 95 miles distant from Volos and was so reported to Khalil Pasha. During the return Santa Cruz took leave for Naples after transiting the Strait of Messina while the other two squadrons proceeded to Palermo, arriving toward end-May.[11]

At Palermo Mendes Vasconcellos concluded discussions with Viceroy Osuna which must have commenced before departure from Messina. He obtained from the Viceroy a secret authorization for Malta and Gozo to ferment wine from crushed grapes free of duty, secret only insofar as the absence of duty was concerned. The related matter agreed dealt with the need for a new population census of those living on Malta and Gozo which among other things would indicate how much wine was needed for local consumption. And how much Sicilian grain. Prior of Navarre Bernardo de Spelletta was assigned responsibility for the census. By count there were 38,429 residents of the island of Malta and 2,655 residents of Gozo, not much more than half the 5,000 residents removed by Dragut 65 years earlier. While Viceroy Osuna wished the Malta Squadron to remain at Messina until arrival of Emmanuel Philibert, General Mendes cited instructions from the Grand Master that he return to Malta in May, already an impossibility. The Malta galleys reached Malta at midnight on 3-4 June where returning Hospitallers were informed Khalil Pasha was already in the Morea (Peloponnesus).[12]

A 44 year-old native of Zeytun, Cilicia or Lower Armenia, this was Ottoman Admiral Khalil's second term as Kapudan Pasha or Commander of the Ottoman Armada and all other Ottoman marine entities. He had exited the Dardanelles in April with 45 galleys, and at

Scio had been joined by 20 more coming from Rhodes. Informed of Santa Cruz's presence at Skyros, Khalil had departed Scio to intercept the Christians but failed to do so and then took course for Coron at the foot of the Morea near Modon. At Coron he would represent a clear and present danger to Malta. Evidencing the danger, the Ottoman Admiral moved from Coron to Navarin amid overt discussion of intent to proceed against Malta.[12]

Departing Navarin on 19 June 1614 fifty-two galleys and six galliots appeared off Malta two hours before sunrise on Sunday 6 July. Seven galleys and a mahon had been stripped of crew and artillery at Navarin to reinforce those which did come. Nevertheless, without troop and support transports, this was a raiding armada and not a siege armada, payback for Vasconcellos's raid on Phocaea a year earlier. The Turkish landing force came ashore in two places, first at Marsascirocco Bay on the SE corner of Malta where advance planning had failed to disclose Fort Saint Lucian constructed in 1610, and nearly coincidentally at Marsascala or Cala Saint Thomas two kilometers up the coast as the crow flies. Proximate to both of these landing points was a Parish village called Castle Saint Catherine (modern Zejtun) which appeared the Ottoman destination, while kidnapping for slave labor or ransom appeared the purpose. The name of this village was a misnomer as there was no castle at Castle Saint Catherine. Intended victims, therefore, had all retreated within walled Vittoriosa (Castle Saint Angelo) and Senglea (Fort Saint Michael). In the event, Fort Saint Lucian had forced a withdrawal at Marsascirocco. The landing party at Marsascala had been somewhat more successful putting between four and five thousand troops ashore which had split into two columns, one headed for Castle Saint Catherine and the second headed for Fort Saint Lucian. Grand Master Wignacourt with a large number of Hospitallers, hired soldiers, and villagers was positioned at Valletta's Porta Reale, the city's fortified gate. Hospitallers of the seven langues could be found at each of seven posts along Valletta's walls. Similarly, seven companies of knights representing the seven langues were ready at command of piliers or senior knights of the same langues.[13]

Exiting Valletta was the cavalry squadron commanded by François de Gouy-Campremy of the Langue of France, 64 years an Hospitaller. These took the road for Castle Saint Catherine to confront an enemy which they found surrounding the Parish-village. Marching behind the cavalry were galley-squadron knights under General Mendes Vasconcellos as well as knights of France who had arrived at Malta with Alexandre de Vendome in October 1611. But the column was not joined by expected cavalry from Mdina. Gouy-Campremy was killed and succeeded in command by Squadron Cornet François de Castillon-Castellet of Provence. Castillon-Castellet was in turn mortally wounded by a crossbow bolt in the hip. Also wounded were mounted knights Clemente Malabaila of Asti, Francesco Maria Panciatichi of Pistoia, and Pietro Maria Turamini of Siena. Citizens on horse Clemente Tabone of Malta and Spaniard Andrés Marconval proved most courageous, the latter dying of wounds two days later. On reports of the Christian column's adversity the Council dispatched Bailiff of Armenia and Seneschal Jacques du Chenu du Belloy with 60 more mounted Hospitallers as well as a large company of musketeers and a battalion of selected individuals. The Ottomans were finally confronted inside the village and their forced withdrawal became increasingly frantic. The Ottoman galleys were beached prow-first, however, enabling cover fire, and most escaped leaving fifty captives behind.[14]

Once its shore force had re-embarked the Ottoman galleys headed for fresh water at Saint Paul Bay which had also been fortified since the Ottomans updated their portalans, and they were forced by cannon-fire to proceed to adjacent Old Saline to the SE of Saint Paul Bay and to Melecha adjacent on the NW for fresh water. At Melecha the Turkish shore party burned houses and destroyed the church before departing in haste, so much haste that several caiques overturned on the way back to the galleys, leaving eight of their number to be captured. Uncertain at Valletta of Ottoman intentions, the Council appointed Marshal Juste de Bron de la Liègue as Captain-General of the Countryside, and as his sergeants-major Commanders Signorino Gattinara the Younger of Pavia, Simon le Petit de la Hacquinière of Aquitaine, Don Gonzalo de Saavedra of Galicia, and Christoph von Andlau of Elsass (Alsace), with Louis de Sauzet d'Estiniéres, senior knight of Auvergne to carry the Order's Standard. Their command comprised of 150 knights from all langues, a hand-picked squadron of soldiers, and about 300 cavalry headed for Castle Nasciar near Malecha. A separate party of 75 soldiers under command of Don Giovanni Ventimiglia of Palermo was dispatched by fast frigate to Gozo which had so far escaped Ottoman attention. And there were other assignments to be as ready as possible for all contingencies. Arriving at Castle Nasciar, however, Juste de Bron discovered the Ottoman Armada had departed at two in the morning, it was said by locals, grabbing a north wind for Greece. By daybreak Monday, however, there was no wind while a heavy mist or fog had settled over Malta and nearby sea. At Valletta the mouth of Grand Harbor was only occasionally visible, and those looking for the Ottomans had no way of knowing who or what was out there. The 58 Ottoman vessels had inched their way clockwise around Malta that Monday to a rock called Pietra Nera off the southeast coast where they awaited visibility and then took course that same evening for Tripoli 190 nautical miles to the south. At Tripoli longtime commandant Safer Dey had elected a course of his own inconsistent with wishes of the Porte. He was replaced by Sherif Pasha and was lost to history. From Tripoli the armada returned to Greece, underlining the Ottoman purpose at Malta. It was pay-back in kind. Both raids were unsuccessful and both raids resulted in unnecessary death and destruction. The raid nevertheless appears in Ottoman history as a victory lifting Khalil Pasha to the first of his two terms as Grand Vizier.[15]

During the evening of 12 July 1614 the galley capitana of the Grand Duke of Tuscany arrived at Valletta with Tuscan Admiral and Knight of Santo Stefano Iacopo Inghirami commanding. The capitana was towing a caramussal seized in African waters bound from the Levant to La Goletta outside of Tunis. She was laden principally with four long-range culverin cannons and one heavy ship-busting cannon needed by La Goletta for longer-range defense. The capitana had become separated at sea from three others of Inghirami's squadron which not much later also appeared at Valletta. Eight days later on 20 July twenty additional galleys arrived, twelve of Naples commanded by Santa Cruz and eight of Sicily commanded by General of the Galleys Pedro de Leyva. Both squadrons were there to offer additional defense, embarked ground forces as well as galleys. Santa Cruz on behalf of Viceroy of Naples and Count of Lemos Pedro Fernández de Castro Andrade y Portugal offered Naples' embarked ground force on any occasion of threat to Malta. With expected arrival any day of Hospitaller Grand Prior of Castile and Captain-General de la Mar Prince Emanuel Philibert and the Catholic Armada, Wignacourt graciously declined the Viceroy's offer for the moment. Upon departure of the Ottoman Armada from Malta on 7 July the Grand Master had ordered the felucca commanded by Don Melchor de Lozorazo (Basque Lizarazu) of Navarre to proceed in the direction of Tripoli, and the frigate of Jean Baptiste d'Accolans of Auvergne to proceed in the direction of Cape Bon, Tunisia, for a sense of Ottoman intentions. On 23 July Lozorazo returned with news extracted from several captives taken off Djerba the Ottomans had been at Tripoli awaiting 40 additional galleys. On this advice Wignacourt accepted two companies of Spanish troops to reinforce the Malta presidio. In addition, he appointed 16 year-old Alexandre de Vendôme his lieutenant and Captain-General of all of the island of Malta during the period the Turkish Armada remained or was believed to have remained within striking distance. On 28 July Accolans returned having also been to the waters of Djerba (Cantera Channel) where locals had been expecting to re-provision the additional galleys, but there had been no additional galleys; the Ottomans had returned to Navarin. A caique was dispatched to Naples with this advice while Lozorazo was returned to Tripoli.[16]

A letter was received from the Marqués de Santa Cruz requesting the Malta Galley Squadron be put in readiness to join the Catholic Armada upon imminent arrival of Fleet Commander Prince Emanuel Philibert with 20 galleys of Spain and Genoa. Mendes Vasconcellos not only received instructions as General of the Galleys but also as embarked Ground Force Commander. His sergeants-major were *San Lorenzo* Captain Giovan Battista Nari, Antoine de Glandevez-Cuges of Provence, and Don Martín de Saavedra Torreblanca of Córdoba with Louis de Sauzet d'Estigniéres to again carry the Order's Standard. About the middle of August the five Malta galleys made rendezvous with the Catholic Armada at Messina. Following an exchange of salutes, the Standard of Malta was lowered on the Malta capitana and raised on the Spanish capitana in deference to the Prince as Hospitaller Prior of Castile. While the Catholic Armada was assembling at Messina four galleys of Naples and the Order's *Santo Stefano* proceeded to Malta to retrieve the two companies of Spanish soldiers on loan to the Malta presidio as well as fifty additional Hospitaller knights, ten to each of the five Hospitaller galleys, plus Bailiff of Mallorca Onofre Copones as Ambassadeur Extraordinaire to convey the Order's compliments to the fleet commander.

Emmanuel Philibert's Armada at this point was comprised of 60 galleys divided into three squadrons: left, right, and Battle. The latter included the capitana of Malta to the right of the Royal capitana with the four other Malta galleys proximate to their own capitana. To the left of the Royal capitana was the padrona of the four-galley Papal Squadron commanded by Camillo Nardi of Rome with his three other galleys nearby. Beyond the Papal padrona was the capitana of Federico Ghislieri also of Rome with a second galley nearby. Santa Cruz with his squadron (12) plus four galleys of Genoa were on the right wing, while Pedro de Leyva with his squadron (8) and the Tuscans of Iacomo Inghirami (4) were on the left wing. Astern of the Royal galley was Duke of Tursi Don Carlo Doria with eight of his galleys plus the Royal padrona and six other galleys of Spain. But it was a matter of little significance. Shades of his predecessor! When the Prince was assured the Ottoman Armada had returned to the Levant he released the various components of his own Armada and returned to Madrid. Savoy had meanwhile engaged Spanish Milan in war for control of the Marquisate of Monferrato, and Savoyard Emmanuel Philibert suddenly if temporarily became surplus to Spanish need. While Vasconcellos and his five galleys reached Malta on 9 October, they were in November summoned back to Sicily to transport Viceroy Osuna and his official and marital households from Messina to Palermo, finally returning to Malta on 20 November. Much ado about nothing.[17]

Also arriving Malta at this time was the *Galleon of the Religion* commanded by Geronimo de Ariscon of Navarre. While returning from the Levant 70 miles north of Cape Buonandrea on the far side of the Gulf of Sidra, Ariscon's galleon had encountered a large patache flying the flag of Tunis crewed by 90 Turks. This same patache had ten days earlier overcome a Venetian urca aboard which a prize crew had been transferred. The prize was sailing in company. Ariscon had assailed both patache and urca for two full days of bloody combat when the patache abandoned her prize and fled the scene. The urca was captured and found to be transporting merchandise valued at 130 thousand scudos. On arrival at Malta the urca in addition to cargo had 19 Turks on board, many wounded. Aboard the galleon there were 24 wounded and four dead including Ariscon's Basque lieutenant Don Melchor de Lozorazo.[18]

Nevertheless, within days Ariscon put back to sea again bound for the Levant, this time accompanied by the corsair galliot of Esteban Zapatero, and this time headed for Cacamo (Kekova Island) on the south coast of Lycia. He had been persuaded by a Greek seaman in his crew to attempt a surprise assault on a Turkish castle six miles from Cacamo. At midnight in the anchorage on the day of arrival Friday 19 December 1614 Ariscon left the galleon under care of his new lieutenant Don Juan de Amarian and put a shore party of 240 men aboard the galliot and galleon caique for transport to the mainland among whom were Caballero Don Vicente Pau Pertusa of Huesca and Galleon Chaplain Pierre Bouillet. Almost immediately the Greek guide lost his way, but eventually, having crossed a stream and bog, the assault party reached an area of three large castles (likely Sura, Myra, and Andriake) crawling with Turks mounted and on foot, and were themselves soon assailed. One hundred thirty-six of the 240 were killed or captured among whom were Ariscon and Bouillet. The remainder made their way back to the galliot and caique waiting opposite Cacamo Island. No post-mortem analysis of the causes of this frightening loss of life was ever reported, but an habitually unsupported attraction to ill-defined undertakings would seem a common denominator, while loose lips would seem yet another.[19]

Reaching the end of his 25-year life on 6 January 1614 was Hospitaller François-Alexandre de Lorraine, known as the Chevalier de Guise, at Château des Baux, Provence, while demonstrating operation of a piece of new artillery which exploded. He was survived by his mother Catherine de Clèves. Passing in June was Bishop of Malta Tomás Gargallo at the age of 78 having been Bishop of Malta for 37 of those years. Pursuant to established procedure the Grand Master nominated three candidates to succeed Bishop Gargallo. These were Chaplains Pedro (Pere) de Sitges of Catalonia transplanted to Gozo, Basque Agustin de Oñati, Lieutenant Prior of the Conventual Church of Amposta, and Baldassare Cagliaries, a Maltese received into the Priory of Portugal. King Philip III would nominate the latter who would be consecrated by Pope Paul V. At season-end Bailiff of Acre Dom Luis Mendes de Vasconcellos was succeeded as General of the Galleys by Admiral Giovanni Angelo Centorio of Vercelli. Upon Centorio's nomination Flaminio Provana of Carignano was appointed Flag Captain succeeding Antonio Pereira de Lima.[20]

Pursuant to authority delegated by the 1604 Chapter General, the Grand Master appointed Pompeo Rospigliosi of Pistoia to command of *San Giovanni* in succession of Raphaël de Grave-Sérignan, and appointed Nicolas Bretel de Grémonville of Normandy to command of *San Lorenzo* in succession of Giovan Battista Nari. Prior of Capua Gabriele di Saluzzo di Montemar renounced his Priory though retaining a right to some of the Priory's income; he was succeeded by former corsair Ferrante Coiro who not long afterward would succeed Ottavio Natta as Prior of Messina and would himself be succeeded as Prior of Capua by Bernardino Barba. Ottavio Natta meanwhile advanced to Bailiff of Pavia. Juste de Bron de la Lègue acceded to the dignity of Marshal succeeding the deceased Pons de la Porte 44 years a Hospitaller. Grand Chancellor and former Admiral-General of Spain's Ocean Armada Diego de Brochero succeeded the deceased Don Antonio Centeno Guiral as Bailiff of Toro while Don Diego de Guzmán y Toledo advanced to Grand Chancellor. Grand Master Wignacourt, recognizing the new forts at Marsascirocco and Saint Paul's Bay were instrumental in failure of the Ottoman raid, ordered construction of yet another at Marsascala which would be completed in August as Fort Saint Thomas Apostle, fort and artillery at his personal expense amounting to 13,450 scudos.[21]

At the prompting of a single French soldier called la Fleur, Grand Master Wignacourt early in 1615 decided with seemingly little consideration on a suspect undertaking at the Aegean island of Samos. A former slave belonging to the Bey of Rhodes, la Fleur was assertedly enamored of one of the Bey's daughters and dreamed of taking her for his wife. For this reason la Fleur wrote to the Grand Master proposing a plan he asserted would result in acquisition of a large treasure, his share turning his dream into reality. La Fleur asserted the Bey had secreted his treasure in a country house on the island of Samos against the possibility he might someday fall out of favor. The treasure consisted of coin and jewels in the custody of a Turkish individual charged with its safe-keeping who lived among a handful of others with no security detail.[22]

Perhaps for reason of the Order's impoverished circumstances, the Grand Master may have given credence to this far-fetched proposal even though la Fleur's underlying information seemed implausible. All of those prominent in the planning and execution of this undertaking must have assumed that absent la Fleur's treasure there might well have been other opportunity on a large Greek island without Turkish garrison. In the event, Wignacourt chartered a Flemish urca delivering to Malta a cargo of timber from Venice, and posted on board a good number of soldiers under the command of François de Bertaucourt, his Master-of-House and nephew from Villes d'Oyse in northern France, and of Bertaucourt's lieutenant Louis de Perrin du Bus, both of Wignacourt's Langue of France. Also embarked were a number of knight adventurers including Achille d'Estamp Valencay of Tours, later Cardinal-Deacon of the Church of Sant'Adriano at Rome, François de Rochechouart of Poitou and of one of the more distinguished families of France, François de Courcelle-Rouvray of a family prominent in establishment of New France in North America, and others of similar credentials.[23]

The urca made it to Samos without incident, approaching the island at night and putting ashore Bertaucourt, his knights, and 180 soldiers, who with la Fleur as guide advanced into the countryside. One hour before dawn the shore party arrived at an area resident to native Greek islanders. These poured out of their homes, armed, while the village priest also appeared. The latter was given to understand the shore party intended no harm to Christians but rather intended locating the treasure and departing, at which proposition the priest snorted in doubt. In the interest of collapsing this sparsely-detailed account to its anticipated conclusion, there was no country house occupied by a Turk, and there was no treasure. La Fleure was seized while attempting flight, and the shore party returned foolishly to its urca. Meanwhile the Bey of Rhodes, not the Beylerbey and Ottoman Kapudan or fleet commander, but rather the Sancakbey or local area commander, was at sea between Samos and Patmos, the next major Aegean island south of Samos and the jumping off point for westbound shipping such as an urca bound from Samos to Malta. The Bey had with him five galleys, more than sufficient to take a merchant urca, even a merchant urca armed with cannon and soldiers. Fortunately, the Ottomans were sighted by the French corsair Rigault flying the flag of Malta who hailed the urca with his information. Returning safely if foolishly to Malta, Bertaucourt turned la Fleur over to a summary court. The Frenchman failed to receive the hand of the Beylerbey's daughter he had been promised, but did obtain his just reward. As for the fool's errand, there was no one to blame but the Grand Master himself.[23]

The Galleys of the Religion in February 1615 attempted to compensate for the foolishness of the urca in January. They seized in the Strait of Messina a patache armed for war, among other things taking 63 Turkish crew captive. In this way Malta was re-exposed to rumors of a massive Ottoman naval build-up intended to speed the pace of Christian subjugation. In the waning weeks of the prior year both Malta and Spain had been overcome with a sense of the need for defensive preparation. Speeding at the time to Rome and Naples with license to hire help in those cities were Commanders Giovan Battista Nari of Rome and Don Gonzalo de Saavedra of Cáceres. each seeking 400 soldiers. Commander Giacomo Marchesi of Naples was already at Messina seeking 1,200 such soldiers for immediate transfer to Malta. Orders were dispatched to all priories of all seven langues to have able-bodied Hospitallers at Malta by the first of May prepared to remain at least thirty days. For the same month of May Bailiff of Lora Don Pedro Gonzales de Mendoza was to preside as Governor of Vittoriosa and Senglea, while Giovan Lanfranco Cebà of Genoa was to serve as Captain-at-Arms of Notabile and Prior of Toulouse Alexandre de Vendôme was to serve as Captain-General of all areas outside of Valletta, Vittoriosa, and Senglea.[24]

On 21 April 1615 the 26.5 kilometer Wignacourt Aqueduct (and Subterranean Pipe) was inaugurated, each day bringing 49,000 cubic feet of water from elevated springs near Dingli and Rabat to Valletta and consumers in between. The Grand Master's name was assigned because he commissioned the aqueduct's completion and paid many of the invoices from his personal estate. Future Grand Master Jean-Paul de Lascaris Castellar was assigned responsibility for regulation of flow and fair distribution, this new responsibility analogous to his responsibility for grain distribution.[25]

During the month of January 1615 the Grand Master had received a letter from King Philip III of Spain warning the aforementioned massive Ottoman force was expected to move west against the coast of Italy, and that Hospitaller Prince Emanuel Philibert of Savoy would again be taking command of the Catholic Armada which would be assembling at Messina during the month of March. The King formally requested participation of the galleys of the Religion. With everything in order Admiral and Captain-General Giovan Angelo Centorio departed Malta on 23 April 1615 for Messina under orders to report to and to serve under Prince Philibert against forces of the Ottoman Empire, and in the Prince's absence to similarly serve under Viceroy of Sicily and Duke of Osuna Pedro Téllez-Girón. But after waiting day after day feeding on rumors of an enemy which failed to appear and of a fleet commander who also failed to appear, the Malta Galley Squadron returned home in mid-June. In the meanwhile Grand Master and Council rescinded the May summons sent earlier to all priories.[26]

The Duke of Osuna even so craved specific information concerning Ottoman movement and intentions. He dispatched one of two proprietary galleys to Malta seeking company where his galley was joined by the squadron's padrona galley *Santa Maria* commanded by Claude d'Urre de Venterol. Both headed for the Levant looking for information departing Malta on 27 June. Thirteen days later they turned around at Venetian Cerigo (Kythera) with certain news some of the Ottomans were already at Navarin (Pylos) while others bringing the total to 70 galleys were presently enroute various assembly points. On reflection, however, this certain news appeared suspicious, and on inspection appeared unreliable. Meanwhile most of the soldiers hired earlier arrived at Malta in July, including the 400 from Rome. Hired and commanded by Giovan Battista Nari, these were transported from Civitavecchia by the Papal Squadron of Francesco Centurione, eldest son of future Doge of Genoa Giorgio Centurione (r1621-1623), and were drawing salaries upon arrival at Malta while squabbling over assignments, particularly by those assigned to Gozo. But as the season advanced suspicion of an Ottoman incursion receded, and hired soldiers were returned to their places of origin at cost.[27]

King Louis XIII of France had come of age (13 years) at September-end 1614 and dispensed with his mother's Regency. In 1615 the King appointed his half-brother the Chevalier Vendome resident at Malta since October 1611 as his Ambassador of Obedience to Pope Paul V. The King also sent three French galleys to Malta which arriving in mid-June were to convey the Prince to Rome escorted as far as Naples by the five galleys of Malta under Giovanni Angelo Centorio, a veteran of 1565's Great Siege of Malta. The Prince's personal galley was also in company. An Hospitaller since 1606 the Prince nevertheless chose to sail aboard the Maltese capitana and was himself accompanied by many chevaliers of the Habit including the Grand Master's nephew and Bailiff of Armenia Jacques du Chenu du Belloy. Only 17 years of age, the Prince was genuinely respected by those around him including Grand Master Wignacourt. He received a fitting send-off as he would be returning to France following his ambassadorial mission.[28]

From Naples the Malta Squadron returned to Messina in July where Pedro de Leyva's Galley Squadron of Sicily and Iacopo Inghirami's Tuscan Squadron had just arrived having only recently been released by truce from participation in the Milan-Savoy War. Neapolitan galleys also released by truce were being deployed along the Kingdom's coast to warn of any Ottoman threat. Ottavio d'Aragona was already at sea in the Ionian commanding six vessels the personal property of Viceroy of Sicily and Aragona mentor Duke of Osuna Pedro Téllez-Girón. Of the six at least two were galleys. Among the others was Osuna's 46-gun galleon commanded by corsair Jacques Pierre, the widely-admired Pierre called "The Last Viking" for his Norman roots and "The Captain" for his prowess combating Ottomans in the Levant. Also in company was a 20-gun galleon commanded by Vincent Robert. These two were returning from the Morea where they had supported Greek Maniots in rebellion against occupying Turks, principally delivering weapons and munitions. In the Ionian off the southern Calabrian coast pointing toward the Strait of Messina a 25-bank galliot was sighted which, pursued, elected to beach. The personal property of Hassan Mariolo, an Italian thought to be a native of nearby Calabria, the galliot had a crew of 200 including combatants taken captive as well as 150 Christian oarsmen who were liberated. Mariolo was not among the captives and could not be located ashore. His galliot was towed to Palermo.[29] Meanwhile Iacomo Inghirami, already chaffing at Messina delay and likely inspired by the Mariolo capture, put to sea with his five Tuscan galleys, the same Ionian Sea, where he came across two smaller 18-bank galliots which yielded to Inghirami's numbers without resistance. The two galliots were also the property of Hassan Mariolo and between them yielded 120 crew and combatants plus 216 liberated Christian oarsmen. These captures were towed to Tuscan Livorno.[30]

Alerted by earlier reports from corsair Vincent Robert of a ten-caramussal Ottoman caravan readying to depart Alexandria bound for Constantinople carrying one million ducats in coin, the three squadrons at Messina put to sea in September on a later report of actual departure from Alexandria. Five Maltese, five Tuscan, and ten Sicilian galleys under command of Pedro de Leyva took course for the Greek Archipelago. Also putting to sea on the same report and sailing in company were the six vessels the personal property of Viceroy Osuna under command of Ottavio d'Aragona. Somewhere along the Anatolian coast the caravan was intercepted and the 26 Christian vessels came away with four caramussals, cargoes of rice, flax, and miscellaneous items while seven other merchantmen were reportedly sent to the bottom. It appears the million ducats escaped Christian coffers, though the division of plunder at Messina in October was attended by the Viceroy himself.[30]

Rubens' Hospitaller Ferdinando I Gonzaga.

Duke of Mantova Vincenzo Gonzaga had died in January 1612 and had been succeeded by eldest son Francesco who reigned for only eleven months before also dying. The latter was succeeded by second son and Cardinal of the Roman Catholic Church Ferdinando who acceded to the Ducal throne as Ferdinando I and renounced the Cardinalate. At the time of accession Ferdinando Gonzaga was also Hospitaller Prior of Barletta, and was induced by Grand Master Wignacourt to renounce that dignity subject to certain conditions. During the year 1615 Hospitaller Commander Francesco Lomellino of Genoa had negotiated those conditions. The Duke's renunciation was subject to an annual pension of 4,000 Neapolitan ducats and the right to wear the Grand Cross on his ducal robes. The vacant priory was awarded to Commander Girolamo Carafa, a member of one of the leading families of Naples.[31]

In expectation Queen Mother of France Marie de' Medici would prevail upon Pope Paul V to mandate award of the Grand Cross to Noël Brûlart de Sillery of the Langue of France, for ten years the Order's Resident Ambassador at the French Court, Grand Master and Council in 1615 appointed Commander Signorino della Gattinara the Younger Resident Ambassador and Procurator General to the Holy See succeeding Niccolò della Marra for the purpose of dissuading the Pope from endorsing the Queen Mother's request. Bailiff of Acre Luis Mendes de Vasconcellos, an individual of vast experience in the courts of princes who was thoroughly familiar with the Order of Jerusalem, was appointed Ambassadeur Extraordinaire to the Court of France to quietly persuade the Queen Mother not to petition the Pope to award the Grand Cross to Brûlart de Sillery. Both Gattinara and Vasconcellos were unsuccessful as Brûlart in 1616 was advanced from Commander to Capitulary Bailiff entitled to wear the Grand Cross. An individual of considerable family wealth Brûlart would in 1632 petition the Pope to be relieved of his Hospitaller vows and to become a priest; in doing so he would donate much of his wealth to fund a mission in New France (Canada) which would eventually be named Sillery, now a neighbourhood of Quebec City where a bronze statue perpetuates his memory.[31]

More importantly, Vasconcellos appeared at the Court of France to proclaim the Order's neutrality in what might be called the Gonzaga Wars. French noble Charles Gonzaga, Duke of Nevers, was the grandson of Margaret Paleologus of the family of Byzantine rulers, and he conspired to reclaim the Byzantine throne by fomenting an uprising of Greek Maniots in the Morea. Gonzaga also had a claim on the Duchy of Mantua through his wife Maria Gonzaga, and in 1627 would himself separately become direct male heir on death of the aforementioned Ferdinando Gonzaga. Charles Duke of Nevers would then take possession of the Duchy. This latter development would give rise to the War of Mantuan Succession (1628–1631) pitting Nevers and allies France and Venice against alternative claimant Ferrante II Gonzaga and his allies the Habsburgs of Spain and Austria.[31]

Accompanied by the aforementioned Brûlart de Sillery, the Grand Master's elder brother Joachim returned to Malta for his health but died there in August 1615 at the age of 83 years. Highly respected at the Court of France, King Louis XIII made him a posthumous Knight of the Holy Spirit (Ordre des Chevaliers du Saint-Esprit).[32]

Arriving at Malta in February 1616 were Osuna's small galleon and two other vessels his personal property armed for corsair operations. Embarked was the Syrian Druze leader Fakhr-al-Din ibn Maan (Fakhreddine). Forty-five years of age, Fakhreddine had for the two years through June 1615 been living in voluntary exile at the Court of Grand Duke of Tuscany Cosimo II de' Medici with whom he had been in formal alliance since 1609 seeking to maintain the semi-independent Druze-Maronite Emirate of Mount Lebanon. His voluntary exile had been occasioned by loss of Lebanon's coastal cities of Beirut, Sidon, and Tripoli to the Ottoman Beylerbey of Damascus, while local resistance from mountain fastnesses had been continued during his exile under brother Yunus and son Ali. At the time Fakhreddine was the guest of Viceroy of Sicily and Duke of Osuna Pedro Téllez-Girón who since September 1615 had been appointed to but had yet to take up the Viceregency of Naples. Throughout his exile Fakhreddine had been seeking European support for his mini-state including a crusade against or other war with the Ottoman Empire. Precisely what he hoped to obtain from the Order of Jerusalem is unknown, but he was received with cannon salutes and attention befitting a head of state. Fakhreddine's visit was at least in part a farewell as he intended returning to Lebanon upon departing Malta.[33]

The day following Fakhreddine's departure, which was 7 March 1616, the *Galleon of the Religion* commanded by Augustin d'Amours of Paris and the Langue of France arrived Malta in company with two prize-crewed caramussals seized in the Levant with 95 Turkish captives exclusive of 17 lost in combat. Amours sadly brought with him Hospitaller Diego de Nicuesa of the Langue of Italy and Spanish Kingdom of Naples killed in the attendant combat. Nicuesa was the namesake and a direct descendant of the first European to explore Colombia, coming ashore in 1510 at what is now Cartagena.[34]

Meanwhile the Duke of Osuna had five galleons and one patache at sea including that in which Fakhreddine and family were embarked, all six under command of Osuna's corsair admiral Francisco de Ribera counseled by Jacques Pierre of Normandy. The six ships were headed for the Cross of Alexandria in search of an Ottoman caravan. At the same time Osuna had sent to Malta two proprietary galleys under command of Captain Pedro Sanchez-Almonte because in company with the galleys of the Religion they, too, were headed for the Cross of Alexandria.

There were, however, then at Malta only three galleys, the capitana, *Santo Stefano*, and *San Lorenzo*. *Santa Maria* and *San Giovanni* were absent having transported Ambassador Vasconcellos to Marseille enroute Paris. General Centorio was ordered to take the three available galleys and to sail in company with Sanchez-Almonte beyond Libya's Gulf of Sidra and around Cape Buonandrea (Cape Luko) to water at Porto Solimano (El Salloum just over the modern border with Egypt), and from there to proceed slowly toward Alexandria 250 nautical miles further east alert to reports concerning both Ribera and caravan. With these instructions Centorio departed Malta on 15 April. The five galleys reached the Egyptian coast at Porto Solimano without encountering Osuna's galleons or hearing of any caravan but did encounter two Turkish caramussals transporting soldiers which were seized after protracted and bloody combat. Two hundred fifty Turks were killed. Three hundred sixty-two additional soldiers and crew were taken captive, including 40 Christian Greeks, Russians, and Armenians who would be liberated at Malta. There was also a large number of Maltese dead including four Hospitallers, Nicolas de Grémonville of Haute Normandie commanding *San Lorenzo*, Alfonso Ugorgieri of Siena, François de Roquefeuil of Provence, and Serving Brother Abraam Vincena. Of the Sicilians 72 perished.[35]

Osuna's six galleons had meanwhile delivered Fakhreddine to the Syrian coast and were harassing the enemy around Ottoman Cyprus. Following Hospitaller return to Messina in July 1616, Osuna embarked aboard the three Malta galleys to take up his new duties as Viceroy of

Naples, while his predecessor at Naples, Pedro Fernández de Castro Andrade y Portugal, took passage on the same galleys to Messina as Viceroy of Sicily. Hospitaller Gaspar de Monreal of Navarre was dispatched from Malta to Palermo to pay the Order's compliments on accession of Castro Andrade.[36]

Francisco de Ribera's five galleons the property of the Duke of Osuna were the capitana *Nostra Senora de la Concepcion* (52), *Almiranta* (34), *Carretina* (34), *San Juan Bautista* (30), and *Santa Maria Buenaventura* (27), plus the shallow-draft patache *Santiago* (14). These warships also carried 1,000 soldiers. The squadron early in the deployment had patrolled Calabrian waters in search of Barbary corsairs, but fruitlessly. Off the Karamanian coast, though, the squadron seized 16 caramussals laden with a variety of merchandise which were returned to Italy with prize crews or sent to the bottom. The six Christian corsairs also pursued a renegade English corsair in Ottoman service en route Saline (Salinas, or Marina of Larnaca), Cyprus, and on 19 June surprised in that port ten defenseless vessels four of which were able to flee. From the crew of one vessel Ribera ascertained the English corsair had meanwhile repaired with four other corsairs behind a boom enclosing the port of Famagusta.[38]

The Christians then took up comings and goings hoping to lure the corsairs from Famagusta until, off Cape Gelidonia on 14 July 1616, they encountered 55 Ottoman galleys mounting upward of 250 guns commanded by the Beys of Karamania (Antalya) and Rhodes. The Turks arranged themselves in a half-moon formation with the two capitanas at each end and a third flagship in the center. The latter would almost certainly have been that of Kapudan Ali Pasha Güzeldje. The battle was initiated with reciprocal cannonades, and was ended with considerable damage to eight Ottoman galleys, one dismasted, and all purposely heeled to stem leaks to damaged hull timbers. Darkness separated the combatants, but combat was resumed the following morning by the Bey of Rhodes with 25 galleys assailing *Almiranta* (34) while most of the enemy assailed the capitana *Concepcion* (52) and nearby *Carretina* (34). At the end of the day both *Concepcion* and *Carretina* as well as another ten galleys were badly damaged, two of the latter dismasted. On the third day combat was again resumed but in increasing wind an aid to sailing vessels and troublesome for oared galleys in combat. After a failed attempt at boarding, the enemy capitanas led a withdrawal. In the end, following three days of combat, 19 Ottoman galleys were damaged, two of them disabled, and one had gone to the bottom. 3200 janissaries, seamen, and oarsmen were said by Christians to have been killed; Ribera's losses were reported as 34 dead and 93 wounded. He proceeded to Candia Town with his capitana under tow because of upper spar damage, paused there for urgent repairs, and proceeded to his new homeport of Naples in August by way of Messina. With the victory he was appointed an Admiral of Spain and awarded the Order of Santiago by a King theretofore and subsequently opposed to corsair operations.[38]

In governing Naples Viceroy Osuna wished to show his gratitude to the Religion with signs of benevolence. He sped an edict under date of 15 October 1616 reaffirming privileges granted Malta by Emperor Charles V under dates of February 1522 and April 1538 confirmed by King Philip II under date of March 1560. The final six months of 1616 were, however, a period of pacificity at Malta. Of western marine combatants, none were active after July, Osuna's galleons having suffered significant damage during the three days of July combat off Cape Gelidonia, Inghirami's Tuscan capitana and padrona damaged in a May tussle south of Negroponte (Evia), Centurione's Papal galleys ferrying supplies to the Papal canton of Avignon in France, and Sicily's galleys uncertain under new leadership.[40]

Aldobrandino Aldobrandini, grandnephew of Pope Clement VIII (r1592-1605), at age 23 obtained command of the Hospitaller galleys succeeding Giovanni Antonio Centorio. Upon Aldobrandini's nomination Obizzo Guidotti was appointed to command of the flagship succeeding Flaminio Provana, while Lodovico Castiglione of Milan was appointed to command of *San Lorenzo* succeeding the deceased Nicolas Brettel de Grémonville, and Denys de Polastron de la Hillière was appointed to command of *Santo Stefano* succeeding Claude d'Urre de Venterol. Prior of Messina Ferrante Coiro reached the end of his life. A veteran of the Great Siege of Malta of whom Historian Giacomo Bosio wrote at the time of studying the Siege, "a young man of great courage and great valor," he would be succeeded as Prior of Messina by Prior of Capua Francesco Bernardino Barba who was in turn succeeded as Prior of Capua by Signorino Gattinara the Younger. Bailiff of the Morea Jacques de Gaillardbois-Marconville succeeded to Prior of Champagne upon death of incumbent Philibert de Foissy-Chamesson, also a veteran of the Great Siege of Malta

56 years a Hospitaller, and was himself succeeded as Bailiff of the Morea by Grand Hospitaller Simon le Petit de la Hacquinière. Guillaume de Meaux Boisbaudran was appointed Grand Hospitaller. Yet an additional veteran of the Great Siege of Malta, Bailiff of Lyon Jacques du Blot Viviers died following 60 years as an Hospitaller, 16 of them as Bailiff of Lyon. He was succeeded by Marshal Juste de Bron de la Liègue who would in turn be succeeded as Marshal by Louis de Sauzet d'Estigniéres. Finally, in succession of Resident Ambassador to France Brûlart de Sillery, Grand Master and Council appointed Joachim de Montaigu-Fromigières, 44 years an Hospitaller.[41]

The new year of 1617 began with a rush of rumors concerning the Ottoman Armada which not only put the Grand Master on edge but similarly unnerved the Viceroys of Naples and Sicily. Osuna had been focused on Venice as hostile to Spain, even as Viceroy of Sicily. Now as Viceroy of Naples with his viceregency actually bordering on the Adriatic, termed a Venetian gulf by Venetians, his focus on Venice was even sharper. He had, moreover, brought with him from Sicily to Naples an ever-increasing proprietary armada centered on broadside-gunned galleons. And he brought with him to Naples his young galleon Admiral Francisco de Ribera, his galleon tactician Jacques Pierre, his galley commander Pedro de Leyva, and his mixed fleet specialist and protege Ottavio d'Aragona. By end-February Aragona was in the Adriatic with eleven ships; and he was not there to combat the Ottoman Armada. Nevertheless, according to Pozzo, both viceroys called for an assembly of the Catholic Armada in April, Viceroy of Sicily Francisco Ruiz de Castro specifying Palermo as the venue. Aldobrandini's Malta galleys responded to the summons as did Sicilian galleys under new commander Count of Elda Antonio Coloma y Saa, but it is not clear whether any other squadrons appeared, not even the Royal Neapolitan Squadron which was at Naples until 6 May. In June, two months after arrival at Palermo, without having embarked on any productive operation, the Sicilians joined Pedro de Leyva commanding Osuna's proprietary galleys in the Adriatic. Aldobrandini returned with his galleys to Malta as Grand Master and Council had rightly refused to take naval action threatening to any party other than the Infidel.[42]

Englishman Robert Elliot had been resident at Naples since his failure to organize an assault on Tunis in 1613, and early in 1617 had been given command of Viceregency brigantines and shallow-draft barques intended should push come to shove to strike Venetian lagoons. In April he had been sent into the Adriatic, his purpose to become familiar with that Venetian "gulf." During the deployment his galleon was observed taking soundings in Venetian ports from Ancona to Trieste. In addition to taking soundings the galleon flying Osuna's personal flag waylaid two Venetian merchantmen and removed cargo valued at 60,000 Venetian gold ducats. While the merchantmen were recovered, not so their cargo.[43]

Jacques Pierre had in May left Naples in the company of corsair compatriot Claude Langlade. An explosives expert, Langlade had been Pierre's first officer in the past and would again be his first officer in the future. With a letter of introduction from Venice's Ambassador to the Holy See and with sea transportation provided by Venice's Consul at Ancona, Pierre and Langlade reached Venice and met with Doge Giovanni Bembo. Why he would leave Naples for Venice is not recorded, but severance of employment most often has to do with compensation. He and Langlade arrived at Venice without a sou. There is also no record of what was discussed with Bembo but both were men of the sea, Bembo a wounded galley captain at 1571's Battle of Lepanto and later Venice's Provveditore of the Sea or senior naval officer. There must have been a degree of mutual respect. From subsequent developments it may also be assumed the two petitioners asked for positions in the republic's galleon armada, an armada historically dependent on foreigners and an armada likely to welcome an individual of Jacques Pierre's renown. Jacques Pierre's wife and children in Sicily had meanwhile been placed under house arrest while 6,000 gold ducats said to have been found there had been confiscated. Pierre would soon be accused of theft and treachery, and Viceroy Osuna would unsuccessfully seek his extradition. Instead, Jacques Pierre was referred to Provveditore of Terra Firma Pietro Barbarigo commanding military operations in Istria where he presented a promising solution to Venice's longstanding Uskok pirate insurgency. It may be germane that a Uskok problem of decades was solved within the next three months. Pierre was next referred to Provveditore of the Sea Lorenzo Venier and given command of Venice's galleon *Santa Giustina* with Langlade as lieutenant. Home-ported at Corfu, and with family in Sicily, it is not clear Jacques Pierre ever returned to Venice.[44]

In June 1617 more recent news of the Ottoman Armada reached Malta. The Armada was outside the Dardanelles with intent to proceed into the "Ponente," literally translating as "The West," most likely meaning an assault on either Italy or Malta as the closest enemy west of the Ottoman Morea. For more definitive news the Malta Squadron was dispatched to the Morea under orders to return to Malta should the enemy be sighted. But should no enemy be sighted, the squadron commander had flexibility to undertake a raid on enemy dispositions or return to Malta as locally determined appropriate. Reaching the waters of Modone and Corone with no sighting and no rumor of Armada intent, Aldobrandini decided on an excursion along the Karaman Coast of southern Anatolia where he preyed on several small vessels and drove a lanterned Turkish galley of 24 banks aground at Kaledran Creek (the border between modern Antalya and Mersin Provinces). Forty-eight Christians were liberated from the oars while 120 captive Turks commanded by Cypriot renegade Alber Bey of Rhodes were sent to the oars. The lone Hospitaller to not survive this engagement was Philibert-Tristan de Maignelay of Paris. According to Historian Mathieu de Goussancourt, Maignelay was the seventh of 17 successive sons born to Charles Tristan and Catherine de Morely, this one in 1591.[45]

Fed by Taurus Mountains ten miles distant, Kaledran Creek was a river which did not run dry in summer months. Squadron galleys were thoroughly washed with clean mountain water and water kegs refilled whether full or empty. At Kaledran Creek the Maltese were visited by locals known in Turkish as *Karamanli* and in Greek as *Karamanlidhes*, a Turkish-speaking population of Orthodox Christians descended from Byzantine rule. Their own descendants would in 1923 be among 1.1 million "Orthodox Greeks" swapped that year and the next for 380,000 Greek-speaking "Muslim Turks" then living in Greece. Advised there were eight poorly-armed Ottoman galleys at Famagusta no more than 150 nautical miles distant, and following counsel with his captains, Aldobrandini decided to proceed to Famagusta and seize the eight galleys. He put a crew of 100 plus 140 oarsmen aboard the captured galley under command of Pier Francesco Rizzolo Salvatico of Piacenza with Bernardino Tortelli of Arezzo as lieutenant. As the enlarged squadron of six galleys departed, however, a powder leak in a storage chamber at the bow of the captured galley ignited and the ship went up in flames, only personnel and artillery salvaged.[46]

Consequently avoiding Famagusta the squadron pointed toward the Egyptian coast, and then Crete, and then Calabria where the debris of two Turkish galleys and a mahon lost in a September storm was encountered before the squadron reached Malta 2,400 nautical miles under the keels since departure. Commanded by Kapudan Çelebi Ali Pasha Güzeldje (The Handsome), an Armenian native of Lango (Kos) whose forebears had been settled there in 1366 with Hospitaller assistance, the Ottoman Armada had indeed come west in 1617 as advertised, reaching the southern coast of Calabria without putting troops ashore before returning storm-damaged to the Morea.[47]

Chapter XI

1617–1622

Fear at Malta and elsewhere in Christianity of the Ottoman Armada eased on news of the November 1617 assassination of 27 year-old Ottoman Sultan Ahmed whose reign had become increasingly militant. He was succeeded as Sultan by half-brother Mustafa already at age 26 known as Mustafa the Mad. Surely there was enough turmoil within the Empire to ignore matters without.

Early in 1617 Alonso de Contreras had been assigned command of two munitions-laden 400-ton galleons lying at Sanlúcar on the Atlantic coast of Spain and had received orders to sail to the relief of San Juan, Puerto Rico, besieged, he was told, by England's Walter Raleigh. Forty-six days following departure he made initial landfall at the island of Martinique and subsequently reached San Juan without encountering English of any kind. Weeks later he was ordered by Governor Felipe de Biamonte y Navarra to escort two smaller vessels to Santo Domingo and once there to erect a small fort at the mouth of the city's Ozama River. Having erected yet another fort at Santiago de Cuba, he finally encountered one of Raleigh's corsairs, the smallest of five. She was discovered at Cuba's Island of Pines off the big island's SW coast where she put up little or no resistance to Contreras's two galleons and a smaller but well-armed Spanish vessel sailing in company. From captured English crew he learned that Raleigh had returned to England following the death in combat of second son and namesake "Wat" Raleigh killed in an assault on a Spanish outpost in Guiana. As Spain and England had not been at war since 1604, the elder Raleigh had been beheaded shortly after return in 1618. Contreras would return to Spain in 1619 wondering about his own fate.[1]

During 1617 Admiral Giovan Angelo Centorio was advanced to Bailiff of Santo Stefano upon death of incumbent Francesco Saccano of Messina, 64 years an Hospitaller and veteran of 1565's Great Siege of Malta who had been posted to the walls of Birgu with his brother Antonio, the latter not living to Siege-end. Centorio was succeeded as

Admiral by Prior of Messina Francesco Bernardino Barba. Signorino Gattinara the Younger moved to Prior of Messina ceding the Priory of Capua to Alessandro Benzi of Chieri. Hercule de Vintimille du Revest was appointed Bailiff of Manosque in succession of the deceased Arthur de Glandevès. Vice Chancellor Giovan Otto Bosio was appointed Bailiff of Pavia succeeding the deceased incumbent Ottavio Natta in spite of opposition on the part of Commander Giulio Cesare Santinelli as an heir apparent. Santinelli objected because Bosio had been appointed a knight of grace and not a knight of justice, and by the rules these dignities were available only to knights of justice. While Santinelli had right on his side, Bosio had seniority, 54 years an Hospitaller, as well as a degree of Convent respect Santinelli could not match. While Bosio remained Bailiff of Pavia, Santinelli was so obstreperous he was initially confined to quarters, then to Fort Saint Elmo, and finally banned from ever becoming a bailiff. Santinelli did not relent. His procurators demanded a public assembly of knights at which the Order's position was defended by Bailiff of Armenia and Seneschal to the Grand Master Jacques du Chenu du Belloy while the procurators accused the Order of bending the rules. Assembled Hospitallers as jurors found in the Order's and Bosio's favor. Bosio's incumbency begat an unrelated disagreement with Mendes Vasconcellos concerning which of the two was senior to the other, Bailiff of Pavia or Bailiff of Acre. Bosio won this one, as well, this time with the rules on his side.[2]

Upon presentation by Lieutenant Grand Chancellor Don Francisco de Saavedra, Don Eugenio Ramirez Maldonado of Valladolid was appointed Vice Chancellor in succession of Bosio. Maldonado was a Doctor of Letters who had been a member of the faculty at the University of Salamanca. Advancing to the Priory of Barletta in succession of Girolamo Carafa was Leonido Loschi of Vicenza. Henry II Duke of Lorraine by means of Secretary Jacques Seiur dispatched to Malta proposed his son the Count de Brie be awarded the Grand Cross. Grand Master and Council in consideration of the importance of the House of Lorraine appointed the Count a capitulary bailiff absent which, or equivalent, no Grand Cross could be awarded. The Grand Cross was duly awarded to Capitulary Bailiff Charles de Lorraine who was then assigned as lieutenant aboard the galley *Santa Maria* commanded by Pietro dei Medici, a knight of the Small Cross.[3]

On 11 July 1617 Hospitaller Lodovico Melzi of Milan died at Magenta, a municipality of greater Milan. He was 59 years of age. Received into the Order of Jerusalem at Milan in 1579, this was Pozzo's first entry citing his existence, not because he did not long remain a Hospitaller but rather because he remained a Hospitaller never posted to Malta, never completing a galley caravan, and never eligible for any position of Hospitaller authority. In August 1585 he had departed Milan for Flanders with Spanish-Italian forces of Hospitaller Duke of Parma Alessandro Farnese. Six years later he was a cavalry captain in service to Pope Gregory XIV fighting Huguenots in France. In 1592 he was in service to Duke of Savoy Charles Emmanuel I in combat with future French King Henry IV then a Protestant. By 1595 he was again in Flanders this time commanding two companies of cavalry in service to Archduke Albert VII of Austria. In 1605 he was promoted to Lieutenant-General in command of light cavalry in Flanders and Brabant. During the 1614 War of Mantuan Succession in service to Spain he commanded both cavalry and infantry. But all of this was merely school for his authorship of a military text on the maintenance and use of cavalry in combat entitled *Regole militari sopra il governo e servitio particolare della cavalleria* published in 1611 and subsequently translated into several languages as a cavalry handbook. He was survived by Hospitaller cousins Giovanni and Sforza Melzi. And, prompting this entry, by the written word.[3]

In late-July 1617 Neapolitan galley commander Pedro de Leyva on his own authority had removed his galleys from the Adriatic and had written to King Philip III warning that in spite of peace negotiations leading to the Treaty of Madrid which would be signed on 6 September in Paris ending hostilities between Spain and Austria on the one hand and Venice on the other, Neapolitan Viceroy Pedro Téllez-Girón, 3rd Duke of Osuna, was on the brink of a new war with Venice.

On 19 November Francisco de Ribera in the absence of Leyva commanding the Neapolitan Armada comprised of 15 sailing vessels, most of them galleons, but without Leyva's galleys, appeared off Ragusa (modern Dubrovnik). Venetian Provveditore of the Gulf Lorenzo Venier set out from the port of Santa Croce (Dubrovnik's port of Gruž, then a part of Venetian Dalmatia) with his sailing vessels under Captain of Ships Francesco Morosini towed by galleys. Venier had 18 sailing vessels, 16 of them galleons including Jacques Pierre's

Santa Giustina, some with Dutch crews, others with English crews. He also had 28 galleys, as well as 5 galleasses, and 7 Albanian barques. That night he made contact with the enemy by means of artillery. Ribera was heading NW along the Dalmatian coast on a light north-easterly wind trailed by the Venetians. While the odds seemed to favor the Venetians, most of Morosini's sailing vessels were armed merchantmen crewed by foreigners whereas Neapolitan vessels were warships many of which had battle-tested crews. At dawn, Venier in pursuit with the wind failing disposed his sailing ships in a semicircle within which he assembled all of his galleys with bow chasers bearing; Ribera chose a double line-abreast deployment the leading line turning to bring broadside guns to bear while the trailing line moved ahead to reverse the maneuver. The fighting lasted all day, though at a distance and with results in no way decisive. That night the Neapolitans disengaged with little damage to either side and bore away toward Manfredonia (25nm north of Barletta), Italy. While Lorenzo Venier followed, both antagonists were caught in a frigid northeasterly (bora) and the Venetians lost five galleys on shoals off the island of Melite (Mljet). Eventually Venier lost contact with the enemy and at Pelagosa (Palagruža, Croatia) gave up the chase. Casualties were few except in reports of the other side's losses.[4]

During the year 34 year-old Joachim Ernst von Brandenburg, Protestant Markgraf zu Brandenburg-Ansbach, together with several other nobles of his household, visited Malta incognito for seven days perhaps not coincidentally following stillborn birth of the Markgraf's second son Albrecht. They departed Malta for Sicily embarked aboard a felucca. Much to the Order's mortification and shame, the felucca was captured in the Malta Channel by two Barbary brigantines. The Markgraf and entourage were escorted to Tunis and enslaved pending ransom. Considering his own honor at risk with that of the Order, Grand Master Wignacourt footed the ransom, at 16,000 scudos very nearly three years of his salary. The Markgraf, however, reimbursed the Grand Master not only in kind but with an in-person thanks.[5]

Toward the end of December 1617 a new Grand Galleon arrived at Malta under command of Philippe de Gouttes, "the finest and most powerful in the Mediterranean" constructed at Amsterdam at a cost of 60,000 gold scudos sparing no expense. She transported from Marseille one of two pieces of field artillery, long-range culverins, contributed by Prior of Saint-Gilles Pierre d'Esparbez de Lussan.[6]

The Grand Galleon, fully reinforced with knights and soldiers, was sent to the Levant early in 1618 in company with both the Galleonetto or Smaller Galleon under François de la Trollière of Burgundy and the Langue of Auvergne and the Tartan under Pierre de Caruel de Merey of Évreux and the Langue of France, while Aldobrandini with four galleys departed Malta on 24 April with orders to locate the three vessels along the Cross of Alexandria and together intercept the caravan exiting from that city. Both vessels and galleys returned empty-handed as the caravan failed to materialize. The three vessels and four galleys then joined at Palermo a six-unit Sicilian Galley Squadron commanded by its General Antonio Coloma y Saa. They jointly planned an assault on Susa (Sousse), a fortified port on eastern Tunisia's Gulf of Hammamet harboring English renegade Sampson Denball. Denball was a protégé and Lieutenant of the infamous John Ward about whom a play had appeared on the London stage featuring a ballad entitled *The Famous Sea-Fight between Captain Ward and the Rainbow* of which the first lines go: *Come all you gallant seamen bold, // All you that march to drum, // Let's go and look for Captain Ward, // Far on the sea he roams. // He is the biggest robber // That ever you did hear, // There's not been such a robber found // For above this hundred year.* There are additional verses, and there are additional Ward ballads another of which goes: *Go tell the king of England, go tell him this from me // If he reign king of all the land, I will reign king at sea.*

Enroute Susa in June 1618 the Maltese and Sicilians together recovered a Christian vessel off the island of Pantelleria midway between Sicily and Susa taken earlier by galleys of Bizerta, plundered, and abandoned. Soon thereafter they also captured an urca bound from Susa to Tunis. Reaching Susa at night they found Denball's well-armed vessels sheltering under seaside fortress walls while a larger fortress crowning a rise in the center of Susa also threatened the newcomers. Denball, a renegade Englishman from Dartmouth calling himself Ali Reis and aware of their coming, had also reinforced his ships with infantry. Seeking to set the ships afire, Christians approached aboard 20-odd skiffs and caiques sproned for boarding. Under fortress walls, however and as must have been anticipated, they were subjected to a hail of arquebus and crossbow fire and were able to torch only a single ship. Forced to withdraw, Hospitallers sustained conspicuous losses among whom were the slain Antoine de Barras the Younger of Provence as well as wounded knights Rafael Cedeño of Aragon and Alessandro da Filicaia of Florence each commanding a caique. Other Hospitallers losing their lives included 21 year-old Charles de Saint-Priest of Forez one year short of completing five years at the Convent, 22 year-old Claude de Champestières, just completing five years at the Convent plus completing his final caravan, Meraud du Pelous received at the age of 14 in 1602, and 23 year-old César de Saint-Peryer Maupertuis, all but the latter of the Langue of Auvergne, Saint-Peryer of the Langue of France.[7]

The number of Barbary corsairs in this instance and during these years was daunting and increasing notwithstanding the number of Christian squadrons on the lookout for them. While the Duke of Osuna put seventeen new ships of varying capability into service during 1617, they were not sufficiently numerous to control local seas. No longer willing to suffer corsair depredations the Christian King of France, Louis XIII, intended a fleet which would sweep the seas of Barbary corsairs and had appointed as Admiral of the Levant with responsibility for the sweeping, Charles, Duke of Guise and Governor of Provence. Guise, hoping to have the *Grand Galleon* in his service, had written to the Grand Master concerning the matter and asking she be sent to Toulon. For this reason the *Grand Galleon* was recalled to Malta from corsair search along the southern coast of Sicily. During the return to Malta the *Grand Galleon* sailing alone encountered and was engaged by three large vessels under Denball's command in a contest which endured an entire day, Denball's ships obliged by cannon damage to retire. On 3 August the *Grand Galleon* reinforced with 35 additonal knights and with many additional soldiers was dispatched to Toulon under command of Philippe de Gouttes for a projected combined operation against Barbary corsairs. The French, however, were diverted by the Huguenot War and this expensive warship sat idle at Toulon for the better part of a year.[8]

Naples Brigantine Commander Robert Elliot had again been sent into the Adriatic, this time without an armed galleon but with orders to support overthrow at Venice of Doge and authorities orchestrated by scores of Neapolitan and other subversives infiltrated into the city for its annual Marriage of the Sea celebration on Ascension Day 14 May 1618. This undertaking would come to be known as the Spanish

Conspiracy. Elliot, however, instead of pushing straight for Venice loitered in the Adriatic south of Ancona looking for prizes of the type which a year earlier had yielded 60,000 Venetian gold ducats.[9]

Meanwhile the Spanish Conspiracy to overthrow the Republic of Venice and to incorporate its possessions into the Kingdom of Naples had been uncovered when confided to Baldassare Juven not long before May's Marriage of the Sea ceremony. A French Huguenot soldier of fortune and nephew of 74 year-old Duke of Lesdiguières and Marshal of France François de Bonne, both at Venice looking for employment, Juven dragged his informant before the Senate to reveal details of the plot as his informant knew them. It is not clear who this informant was, but in the ensuing investigation an individual by the name of Nicolas Regnault claiming to be secretary to Jacques Pierre came under suspicion. "Secretary" in translation from French to Venetian Italian may have meant no more than that Regnault had transcribed or executed some document for Pierre who was not otherwise known to have ever had a secretary. From then on, though, Pierre came to be cited as ringleader of the Spanish Conspiracy. Pierre was not at Venice to defend himself as he was still with the Venetian Armada off the coast of Dalmatia (Croatia), since early May under the command of Pietro Barbarigo in succession of Lorenzo Venier. Barbarigo then with the war-time rank of Captain-General was ordered to do away with Pierre and Langlade who went to the bottom of the Adriatic in weighted sacks off the island of Curzola (Korcula) without ever again seeing Venice. Six others identified as having had some contact with Jacques Pierre were separately executed at Venice. Eventually a total approximating 270 persons were executed, each without due process. Not among these was Spanish Ambassador Alfonso de la Cueva, Marqués de Bedmar, whose ambassadorial residence was found to be storage for arms and munitions to be used in overthrowing established authority. He had diplomatic immunity. Also not among these was Pedro Téllez-Girón, 3rd Duke of Osuna and Viceroy of Naples, who by any stretch of anyone's imagination had to be the ringleader. Finally, not among these was Robert Elliot whose non-arrival at the scene was, according to some survivors, cause of the Spanish Conspiracy's failure.[10]

Comprised of 18 ships including Jacques Pierre's former command plus 5 galleasses and 24 galleys, Barbarigo's Venetian Armada departed Curzola on 25 May 1618, and with advice Francisco de Ribera was at

Brindisi appeared off that port three days later. Given Venetian numbers, however, the Neapolitans refused to come out from under fortress cover. The war between Naples and Venice, if it could be called a war, was over.[11]

In the Spring of 1618 Hospitaller Commander Don Fernando Ruiz del Prado of Aragon was appointed Resident Ambassador and Procurator General to the Holy See, succeeding Admiral Signorino Gattinara the Younger. On the November biennial anniversary of his appointment as General of the Galleys Aldobrandino Aldobrandini was succeeded by the same Signorino Gattinara. Upon Gattinara's nomination Alfonso Castelsanpietro of Milan was appointed to command of the squadron capitana. Antonio Mastrillo of Nola in the Priory of Naples and Gaspard-Acton de Limons of Auvergne were respectively appointed to command of the galleys *San Lorenzo* and *San Giovanni*. Dispatched to the viceregal court of Francisco Ruiz de Castro at Palermo was ambassadeur extraordinaire and Grand Conservator Felipe de Bardaxi hoping to negotiate increased allotments of Sicilian grain.[12]

On 22 November three Neapolitan galleys disguised as Turks departed Naples under command of Simone Costa and proceeded as far as the mouth of the Dardanelles. On 17 December 1618 the three galleys engaged and captured the *Galleon of the Sultana* off Tenedos. She was said by Neapolitans to be a western-built galleon mounting 60 guns and displacing 1,000 tons with the Greek or Serbian mother of 14 year-old Sultan Osman II, Sultana or Valide Sultan Mahfiruz Hatun, embarked. Perhaps related, Mahfiruz Hatun was last reported alive in 1618, the year of Osman's accession. Similarly, from the middle of 1620 Osman's governess, the Daye Hatun, began to receive an extraordinarily large stipend, one thousand aspers a day rather than her usual two hundred aspers, an indication she had become the official stand-in for the Valide Sultan. The galleon was sent to Portugal by Osuna as a gift for King Philip III, and there is no report of the Valide Sultan following capture of the *Galleon of the Sultana*.[13]

On the brink of being replaced as Viceroy of Ottoman Algiers, Mustafa IV Pasha sent seven large broadside-gunned warships east toward Malta and Sicily perhaps hoping to change the course of events. Though Signorino Gattinara had been appointed General of the Galleys late in 1618, he had as yet not returned to Malta from Rome. Aldobrandini re-assumed command when the same seven

Algerian vessels appeared off Valletta on the morning of 18 January 1619. Readied in haste, the squadron had the advantage of mobility in little or no wind, but the Algerians clung together limiting the ability of the Maltese to do anything but cannonade from a distance. The wind freshened on the second day and the Algerians departed. The course of events at Algiers would remain unchanged as Kassan Qaid Kussa Pasha was already en route the Empire's western capital with a company of the Sultan's elite *Yeniçeri*. And with a black kaftan.[14]

Early in February 1619 Valletta was visited by Ludwig V, Landgraf of Hessen-Darmstadt, during his return from visiting Holy Places in Syria. Traveling incognito he was nevertheless soon recognized by members of the German Langue and therefore requested an audience with Grand Master Wignacourt. Wignacourt was absent from Valletta at Mount Verdala (Verdala Palace) in the Buskett Gardens re-created by Grand Master Verdalle following destruction during the 1565 Great Siege of Malta. There the Landgraf was cordially received by the Grand Master. The nature of their conversation was not reported but may have had to do with infestation by Infidel corsairs of local waters and the need for caution when traveling, or it may have had to do with the Landgraf's two year-old son Frederick of Hessen-Darmstadt who would in 1637 be received into the Order of Jerusalem. The conversation, however, certainly included the Grand Master's offer of transportation with the Galley Squadron scheduled to soon depart for Marseille.[15]

The squadron departed for Marseille under Signorino della Gattinara the Younger to take delivery of a new capitana and of a second new galley constructed in the local Arsenal. Ludwig of Hessen-Darmstadt and companions were embarked. At Marseille old hulls were exchanged for new galleys with one of the old hulls re-fitted and returned as a sixth stopgap galley. She was crewed by Hospitallers and adventurers enroute Marseille to Malta and by 200 captive oarsmen contributed by the Crown. The new 28-bank capitana had been constructed on order of the Lussan Foundation of Prior of Saint-Gilles Pierre de Lussan at a cost of 10,000 scudos with over-runs of 5,000 scudos paid by Lussan himself. The second new galley had 25-banks and was on order by the Common Treasury. There occurred during the return voyage an event a credit to the faith of Denys de Pelastron de la Hillière commanding the galley *Santo Stefano* also at 28-banks. Or a miracle. Sailing at night under full sail off Vado Ligure en route Livorno *Santo Stefano* ran up onto shoals which stopped her in her track, the Shallows of Vado, She hit with such force it was impossible to back off. Having tried everything else Hilliere asked that his crew kneel and pray to God. A sudden wind developed in opposition to the sea, raising swells, and swells lifted their galley free. Hauled out at Livorno, they found the hull ruptured by the shoal, but a piece of shoal remaining in the rupture had prevented the galley from sinking.[16]

Not long after the Squadron's return from Marseille and Livorno the five regular galleys departed Malta for a raid along the coast of North Africa where they seized two Moorish garbos with the capture of 106 Infidels. During this same period the Galleonetto of the Religion returning from another raid into the Levant took near Malta a Turkish patache which, equipped with a fine armament, was able to put up a stiff defense in which many Turks lost their lives, though

Anthony Van Dyck's Hospitaller Emmanuel Philibert.

87 remained alive when she struck her colors. The Tartan of the Religion in a separate but coincident engagement took a much smaller patache, 18 of the enemy surviving and made captive. On the other hand, two Barbary galliots had the audacity to enter Marsamuscetto under the guns of Fort Saint Elmo and snatch two tartans at anchor. Bound for Sicily with cargoes of Algerian timber; twelve watch-standers were enslaved.[17]

For the second time Savoyard Prince Emmanuel Philibert, Spanish Admiral and Hospitaller Prior of Castile, called for an assembly at Messina of the Catholic Armada, the first time in 1614, this time in 1619. His purpose was to remove Sampson Denball from Susa and to render Susa itself untenable for military purposes. According to Church historian Alberto Guglielmotti, Susa had been selected not by Philibert but by Viceroy of Naples and Duke of Osuna Pedro Téllez-Girón. In either event, Grand Master Wignacourt doubled up on the call for assembly by dispatching Savoyard Hospitaller Umberto di Saluzzo della Manta with the five galleys of Malta under Gattinara to Villefranche from where Saluzzo proceeded to the Savoyard Court of Charles Emmanuel I at Turin. There he congratulated Duke and eldest son Prince Victor Amadeus on the latter's marriage in February at Paris to Fille de France Christine, sister of King Louis XIII.

From Villefranche the Maltese then took course for Messina. Because Emmanuel Philibert harbored suspicion of the Ottoman Galley Armada not relieved by a May-June investigation on the part of Osuna's Santa Cruz, the five Maltese and one galley of Carlo Doria were dispatched to the Morea in July for sign of Ottoman presence. Proceeding as far as Modone at the western foot of the Morea, a distance of almost 400 nautical miles, the six galleys were back at Messina in little more than a week with a report the Ottoman Armada was off the coast of Syria and could not be considered a threat.[18]

When assembled in August 1619, Emmanuel Philibert had eight galleys of Sicily under command of its General Antonio Coloma y Saa, 19 galleys of Naples primarily under command of Marqués de Santa Cruz Alvaro de Bazan, six of Tuscany under Giulio da Montauto, five of Malta under Signorino della Gattinara, five of the Church under its General Francesco Centurione, three from Spain, and 14 from Genoa four of which flew the flag of the Republic with the remainder belonging to private owners, most to Carlo Doria. A dispute arose over precedence between Genoa and Malta, and when Philibert ruled in favor of Malta, the four regular Genovese left for home. Seven others fell by the wayside. The Armada sailed from Messina on 12 August with 49 galleys bound for Malta where three more were left behind as unfit for service, one belonging to Carlo Doria and two to Naples. At Malta the Malta Squadron embarked its landing force again commanded by Marshal Louis d'Estigniéres and composed of 150 Hospitaller knights, 18 adventurers, and 500 hired soldiers. Also at Malta the Armada was joined by four frigates and twelve other small craft to be used in putting troops ashore. The 46 remaining galleys and small craft sailed from Malta on 15 August and put the Maltese landing force as well as Spanish tercio units of Naples and Sicily ashore at Susa before dawn on 19 August. Antonio Mastrillo commanding the padrona *San Lorenzo* carried the petard for blowing the gate. He advanced on order of Maestro di Campo Don Diego de Pimentel with a large supporting cast and attached the petard. The gate successfully blew but there was a second gate on the inner face of the wall. Meanwhile both Spanish and Maltese advanced to the walls with scaling ladders on order of Gaspard-Acton de Limons, skipper of *San Giovanni* and one of three Hospitaller sergeants-major. The scaling ladders, however, did not reach the wall-top because a dry moat or fosse had been dug against the wall. Assailants instead suffered a continuous rain of musket shot and crossbow bolts from the wall-top to which boiling pitch was soon added.[19]

From the moment of first landing vigilant Moors had understood what was coming and where. Fire-lighting illuminated Christians at likely places of assault, including those bringing a second petard two of whom were killed while Mastrillo was mortally wounded. The Spanish commander Pimentel also fell, gravely wounded. Then came Moorish cavalry cutting down those on the flanks. The assault failed, the shore force was recalled, and the Catholic Armada by way of the Freo Channel between Malta and Gozo was back at Syracuse on 23 August, the Maltese having retrieved the three galleys left at Valletta. There were one hundred fifty dead and wounded Christians, all of them either Spanish or Hospitaller. Among Hospitaller dead were the knights Mérode de Pelons, and Novitiate Melchior de Gozon of Provence, François Juniet de la Meuse of the Langue of France, Bernardo de Camparolles of Aragon, Diego Bonal de Acevedo of Castile, and Hospitaller Knight of Grace and Captain of Infantry

Antoine André serving with the Spanish. The wounded included Alfonso Castelsanpietro commanding the squadron capitana, Jean de Saligny of Auvergne, Dom Diogo d'Azevado of Portugal, and Luis Mendes de Vasconcellos also of Portugal. It is likely this Vasconcellos is a related namesake of the former general of the galleys at the time said to be governor of Angola. These and all others of the 150 dead and wounded may be considered victims of loose lips and unprofessional military planning, so loose and so unprofessional Dartmouth's Sampson Denball had removed his corsair vessels to safety even before arrival of those intending to permanently eliminate the threat he and the vessels represented.[20]

At Syracuse Emmanuel Philibert decided to take the Catholic Armada south of the Morea seeking opportunity, and was further considering an assault on Ottoman Santa Maura (Levkas). He could not be seen, of course, to have failed to bring peace or at least a victory with such a powerful armada. Disappointingly, his squadron commanders told him they would need additional siege equipment and soldiers to even consider Santa Maura. Five days following their 30 August departure from Syracuse his 46 galleys reached Venetian Cerigo (Kythera) south of the Morea's Cape Saint Angelo (Cape Malo). Here in the anchorage opposite the town of Kapsala the Catholic Armada learned the Ottoman Armada 60 galleys strong was then at Negroponte (Evia) 135 nautical miles to the northeast. The Christians also learned the Ottomans were struggling against peste or plague, reason enough, some immediately suggested, to remain well clear and reason enough to remain on the western side of the Morea and Epirus whatever came next. At a council of war eleven of thirteen senior commanders counseled returning to Italy on grounds of numerical strength of the enemy and in consideration of the contagious disease the enemy carried. No further consideration of any action against Ottoman Santa Maura was reported. Reaching Venetian Zante (Zakinthos) during the return voyage the same thirteen senior commanders were told the Ottomans were then at Navarin 70 nautical miles to the south and seeking to confront the Catholic Armada. Any remaining thought of Santa Maura was now abandoned and the Christians took course for Venetian Corfu following which they crossed the Strait of Otranto with wind on their quarter and reached Messina on 21 September. The Ottoman Armada then 70 galleys strong reached Corfu on 19 September only two days behind the

Catholic Armada. Emmanuel Philibert released individual contingents to return home in mid-October, and the Malta Squadron was the first to depart. Ottoman Kapudan Ali Pasha Güzeldje (The Handsome) had reason for satisfaction, and it was not because he would in two months be advanced to Grand Vizier of the Ottoman Empire.[21]

Then came the single Christian success of 1619, albeit a small success. Ottavio d'Aragona exited Naples with six galleys on 13 November, took a small Tripolitan off the coast of Italy, ran before a storm to Venetian Corfu, and proceeded south. In the waters of Kefalonia (Kefallinia) and Zante his six galleys sighted the heavily-armed 26-bank capitana of the Sanjak of Santa Maura. The odds were prohibitive. The Ottoman was boarded and yielded in three quarters of an hour. 180 Christians were liberated from the oars and 60-odd Turks were sent to the oars, the crew and combatants abnormally short-handed. Neapolitan losses amounted to seven dead and eight wounded. The captured capitana was towed into Naples on 23 December.[22]

Sixty-one years an Hospitaller, Grand Prior of France Georges Régnier de Guerchy had died in November 1618 at The Temple in Paris. He was succeeded in 1619 by 21 year-old Prince Alexandre de Vendome who vacated the dignity of Prior of Toulouse to which Jean de Vassadel-Vaqueiras succeeded. Antoine de Paule succeeded Vaqueiras as Grand Commander. Soon thereafter, however, Vaqueiras also died and was succeeded as Prior of Toulouse by Jean de Mars Liviers. Upon death of incumbent Simon Cheminée de Boisbenet, Jacques de Gaillardbois-Marconville succeeded to the dignity of Prior of Aquitaine, vacating the Priory of Champagne which was assigned to brother Charles de Gaillardbois-Marconville. Signorino delle Gattinara succeeded the deceased incumbent Centorio Cagnolo as Bailiff of Santa Eufemia and was himself succeeded as Admiral by Alessandro Benzi. Cagnolo had been a go-to Hospitaller attorney for 69 years and Bailiff of Santa Eufemia for 35 of them. Benzi was almost immediately promoted to Bailiff of Venosa and was succeeded as Admiral by Giulio Cesare Santinelli, the same Santinelli who only two years earlier had been banned from ever becoming a bailiff had one year earlier succeeded Gattinara as Prior of Capua which he now left to Bongianni Gianfigliazzi of Florence, the same Bongianni Gianfigliazzi who had saved the galley squadron standard following 1570's rout of the galley squadron off Cape Passero. Louis de Sauzet d'Estigniéres was advanced to Prior of Auvergne upon the death of Claude de Montmorillon who had been Prior of Auvergne for 28 years, Estigniéres vacating the dignity of Marshal to which Juste de Fay Gerlande succeeded. The Grand Master appointed Girolamo di Guevara of Naples to succeed Fernando Ruiz del Prado as Resident Ambassador to the Holy See. He also appointed Jean-François de Vion-Tessencourt of Rouen to command of *Santo Stefano* succeeding Denys de Polastron de la Hillière, Jean de Glandevez-Cuges of Provence to command of *Santa Maria* in succession of Pietro dei Medici, and Roberto Strozzi of Florence to command of *San Lorenzo* succeeding the deceased Antonio Mastrillo. Commander Don Lorenzo de Figueroa was appointed Resident Ambassador to the Court of Spain succeeding Bailiff of Toro Don Diego de Brochero. Finally, Don Francesco Marchetti of Messina was appointed Ambassadeur Extraordinaire to the Imperial Court of Ferdinand II at Vienna.

Upon his 1619 return from Spanish America with that year's treasure armada Alonso de Contreras was immediately assigned to complete the overhaul and fitting out of six large galleons and two pataches at Borgo Shipyard on the Guadalquivir River of western Spain. All eight vessels were brought down to Sanlúcar by year-end, freshly caulked and ready for sea. At Sanlúcar command was assumed by a reluctant Knight of the Military Order of Santiago. His name was Lorenzo de Zuazola and his orders were to deliver the ships and their cargoes to the Philippines by way of the Cape of Good Hope or South America's Strait of Magellan. A brave soldier born of illustrious family, Lorenzo de Zuazola had no marine experience whatsoever. Promised a fleet command by King Philip III but not receiving this one, Alonso de Contreras could only swallow his apprehension. Underway on 21 December 1619, five of the six galleons were 13 days later lost in a storm. The dead Zuazola was merely the latest Spanish noble to meet with disaster at sea. The sixth galleon had run aground during the same storm and was salvageable. Her soldier-skipper, Garcia Álvarez de Figueroa, would become the next armada commander. Not a noble, Alonso de Contreras would refloat the sixth galleon, a vessel of more than 800 tons carrying 40 bronze cannons, but would never become an armada commander.[23]

New Inquisitor Monsignor Antonio Tornielli of Novara arrived at Malta in succession of Monsignor Fabio Delagonessa who departed with a letter of commendation from Grand Master Wignacourt. Arriving in the port with two vessels of France was that country's new Resident Ambassador to the Ottoman Porte Philippe Harlay de Sancy. Accompanied by wife and family, he was also accompanied by considerable curiosity. He succeeded his brother Achille who represented France at Constantinople for nine years before accusations of chicanery had him bastinadoed on order of Sultan Mustafa. Early in 1620 there also appeared at Malta Francesco Ottomano with papers identifying him as a son of Ottoman Sultan Ahmed. His papers, signed by former Inquisitor of Malta Cardinal Fabrizzio Veralli, also warranted his conversion to Christianity. Ahmed lived to the age of 27 years and seven months and in that time gave birth to nine recognized sons and six recognized daughters. Francesco Ottomano was not one of them. The eldest of the recognized sons, Sultan Osman II, was only 16 years of age at the time of Francesco Ottomano's visit to Malta. Thus there must be more or less to this story than meets the eye. Francesco Ottomano nevertheless was received as a visitor worthy of special attention. Upon his 6 April departure he was issued a passport as a citizen of Malta.[24]

On the 12th of April 1620 the five galleys departed under General Gattinara bound for Syracuse and Messina to load biscuit and other provisions before proceeding into the Greek Archipelago on a voyage of opportunity. Near Samos on the far side of the Aegean the five galleys encountered and seized a Turkish galleonetto bound from Constantinople to Alexandria with a cargo of timber especially valuable at Malta, but furnished with a complement of resolute crew and passengers. When the galleonetto was boarded these stalwarts resisted for two hours and submitted only because fifty of their number were dead or dying with no more than 62 remaining alive. The latter number included five wealthy merchants who went for healthy ransoms on top of carried coin. Among Christian dead was a single knight, Chevalier René de Sciattigny Rouere of the Langue of France. The galleonetto with prize crew was escorted to Kali Limenes in eastern Crete "where Paul came unto a place called The Fair Havens." (The Holy Bible, King James Version, Book of The Acts of The Apostles, Chapter 27) At Kali Limenes the Malta Squadron encountered the Galleonetto, the Patache, and the Tartan of the Religion bound for Malta. These took the captured galleonetto in company under command of the galley capitana's second officer Pier Francesco Pecchio of Milan.[25]

From Kali Limenes the Malta Squadron took course for Venetian Zante where it proceeded to an anchorage (Ormos Vroma) on the far west side of the island out of sight of most traffic to and from the Morea. Gattinara's intention was to raid the Ottoman arms depot at Castel Tornese (Chlermoutsi) nine miles across the channel between Zante and the Morean mainland. Near the anchorage was the house of a Greek goatherd formerly a long-time employee at Castel Tornesi where he had been unfairly treated by the Ottoman governor. Gattinara made contact.[26]

During the night of 3–4 June 1620 the five galleys rowed in silence the 28 miles from their west-side anchorage to the shore below Castel Tornese. Sixty knights were put ashore, 12 per galley, mostly young caravan knights, as well as 80 embarked soldiery and crew per galley for a total with knights of 460 combatants under the command of capitana skipper Alfonso Castelsanpietro still nursing a wound from the aborted assault on Susa ten months earlier. Under Castelsanpietro were the five galley padrones: Giovanni Battista Marliani (acting) of the capitana, Jean de Villeneuve-Chateauneuf of the padrona *Santa Maria*, Jacques de Goullard d'Invillier of *Santo Stefano*, Don Juan Franus of *San Giovanni*, and Nicolò Gianfigliazzi of *San Lorenzo*. Villeneuve-Chateauneuf carried petards to blow gates; he was accompanied by 20 knights and 40 soldiers guided by the aforementioned Greek goatherd. The Greek guided the Maltese not only up 700 feet from the shore in the dark, but through the curtain wall and into the central keep! One mile from the castle they surprised and silenced an outer patrol. With a single musket round they silenced a second guard; no alarm was sounded. They reached the wall without being discovered. Because there were houses outside of the wall Castelsanpietro ordered Invillier of *Santo Stefano* and Franus of *San Giovanni* with 60 men to watch these houses and to prevent inhabitants from disturbing the operation. Villeneuve-Chateauneuf meanwhile attached a shaped charge petard to the external wall gate which blew to perfection. So too did the inner wall gate. The Maltese poured into the fortress and onto the piazza. But standing tall at the far end of the piazza was the so-called keep, a fortified tower into which the garrison had withdrawn. A third petard was successful and the Maltese entered the keep but this time were engaged in hand to hand combat punctuated by musket fire and by stone blocks dropped from on high slowing the Maltese advance.[27]

It is not clear defenders ever yielded. In fact, there was simply an abrupt end to Pozzo's description of the confrontation within the keep, and immediately following in a new paragraph is a presentation on developments beyond the walls. Neither is there mention of the arms depot, the purpose of the raid. Within the houses beyond the walls were found large quantities of silk and other valuable merchandise of a quality so renowned most of it normally ended up at Constantinople. Some of it, however, was subject to Venetian prepayment, and in 1621 Venetian merchant Marco Morosini would appear at Malta seeking redress in the amount of 2,500 gold zecchins. Meanwhile, there was no report of captive combatants but there were 85 captives between men, women, and boys taken from housing outside of the walls, several of the men wealthy merchants. One of these shortly afterward attempted to buy his freedom at Zante on a promise of 10,000 gold zecchins but was refused. While admiring their plunder the Maltese were alerted to a relief column of 300 Ottoman cavalry four miles distant and so withdrew, but in good order without panic. Notably, and equally confusing, there was no interference with the plundering beyond the walls by the enemy last seen within the keep. Notable, in addition, was that the Maltese sustained only three fatalities, Louis de Bar-Buranlure of Auvergne and two soldiers, though there were many wounded. Anderson, though, described the outcome as capture and sack. The Squadron was back at Malta by 11 June where oarsmen were rested for fifteen days and new caravans were embarked for a third deployment, this time to the coast of North Africa.[28]

The Maltese in June 1620 had news of two vessels which one report indicated would be loading cargo bound by way of the Cantera Channel through shallows south and east of Tunisia's Djerba. On arrival outside of Djerba Island Gattinara found one of these ships loading while the other was careened. Because both were safely under fortress guns the Maltese could not do anything about them, fortress and guns in 1560 built and emplaced at great cost by Christians. In the shallows behind Djerba Island there were in addition three caiques one of which had waylaid a merchant garbo and detained its crew of ten. In the shallows these, too, were beyond reach.

During July news of the Ottoman Armada at Navarin spread like wildfire as this was early enough in the season for the Ottomans to make one or more thrusts against the West. The Armada, moreover, was again commanded by the competent and aggressive Ottoman-Armenian Khalil Pasha beginning his third assignment as Kapudan Pasha. The Catholic Armada was summoned by Viceroy of Sicily and Count of Lemos Francisco Ruiz de Castro to assemble at Messina, specifically the Royal Squadrons of Genoa, Naples, and Sicily as well as the Galley Squadron of Malta. These were later joined by squadrons of the Church and Tuscany respectively under new commander Alessandro Pallavicini of Genoa and Ottavio da Montauto of Florence. This was the first assembly in ten years not influenced by Duke of Osuna Pedro Téllez-Girón who had been succeeded by interim Viceroy of Naples Cardinal Gaspar de Borja y Velasco and recalled to Spain in June. In April of 1621 his arrest would be ordered by the State Council and he would remain under arrest for the remainder of his life, a victim of his own zeal as much as inattention to his royal mandate.[29]

Arriving Malta in July aboard a galley of France was the Grand Master's brother Adrien de Wignacourt, father of a 2 year-old son of the same name who would be received into the Order of Jerusalem at the age of 3 years and who would in 1690 be elected 63rd Grand Master. Brother Adrien had come for a visit and was accompanied by Hospitaller Noël Brûlart de Sillery, Malta's former Resident Ambassador to the French Court of Louis XIII and at the time France's Resident Ambassador to the Holy See. Sillery departed on the same galley 20 days later, and from France embarked on his new assignment at Rome. Adrien de Wignacourt remained at Malta for three months, visiting, before embarking aboard one of two of the Order's galleys bound for Marseille.[30]

Receiving the viceregal summons to Messina while off Djerba, the Squadron returned to Malta for the Grand Master's instructions, made essential personnel changes, and proceeded to Messina where it arrived on 22 August. Six days earlier the Ottoman Armada 55 galleys strong, seeking, it is said by historian Alberto Guglielmotti, revenge for the Catholic Armada's assault on Susa, had appeared off Manfredonia on the Adriatic coast of the Kingdom of Naples, and over the next three days destroyed the city of 2,000 residents, that is, at the end only the castle and a part of its walls were left standing and the population had been halved. The town surrounding the castle had been sacked for three days by 6,000 debarked Ottomans and obliterated, its magnificent Cathedral of San Lorenzo Maiorano leveled as were all other public buildings and most private homes, its fortunate residents repairing to the castle where the castle's castellan refused to deliver them up to Khalil Pasha. An accord was finally reached, however, whereby those in the castle obtained their freedom in return for a ransack of the castle during which everything of value was removed.[31]

At Messina the Catholic Armada numbered 40 galleys, and on learning of Manfredonia and departure of the Ottoman Armada on 18 August, assembled generals in consultation with the Viceroy decided to detach the fastest eighteen of Messina's 40 galleys to investigate and tail the departing Armada to deter or hinder any similar incursions ashore. Gattinara opposed the plan on the basis of numbers, suggesting the 18 would have no chance should the 55 turn on them. He suggested all 40 Christian galleys go in similar pursuit, confident the 40 could come out on top given existing reinforcement of oarsmen, embarked soldiery, and valiant galley commanders while the Turks labored under loads of plunder and captives. The proposal that 18 galleys go in pursuit was elected, of which three were Hospitaller galleys with the other two Hospitallers seeking news of the Ottomans. These two were told at Otranto the Turks had retired to the Levant. On that report the 18 returned to Messina and Gattinara's squadron returned to Malta.

Given the history of the Ottoman Armada, additional precautions were adopted at Malta. Ten knights and 100 soldiers were dispatched to reinforce the citadel at Gozo. Acting Prior of England Cesare Ferretti was appointed Governor of Vittoriosa and Senglea while Don Nicolás Cotoner, uncle of the brothers Cotoner who would each be elected Grand Master, was appointed Captain at Arms at Notabile. Don Niccolò della Marra of Naples, Balthazar d'Agoult of Provence, Baldassare Marsili of Siena and Maximilian Schliederer von Lachen of Germany were appointed Sector Wardens. All visiting adventurers were enrolled in a company placed under the command of Hospitaller Georges de Stainville of the Priory of Champagne. Marshal Juste de Fay Gerlande was appointed Commander of Ground Forces or militia beyond the walls with 40 Knights of whom Toussaint de Ternes-Boisgirault of the Priory of Aquitaine, Pietro dei

Medici of Florence, and Don Pedro de Puiades of Catalonia were sergeants-major.[32]

In November 1620 Grand Master Wignacourt accompanied by staff embarked aboard two galleys and visited Gozo for an inspection of fortresses and to show interest in the well-being of residents. While at Gozo he established 17 four-man patrols for nocturnal-warning duty. Also in November the cornerstone of the Church of Our Lady of Liesse was laid on the shore of Grand Harbor close to Lascaris Battery and the site of the fish market. Church construction was funded from a donation by the Grand Master's nephew, Seneschal and Bailiff of Armenia Jacques du Chenu du Belloy. In December Don Francesco Marchetti, Ambassadeur Extraordinaire to the Imperial Court in Vienna, returned to Malta. His principal task at Vienna had been to obtain confirmation the Priory of Bohemia (Czech Republic) and its commanderies remained a part of the Order of Jerusalem. The Emperor so confirmed by letter dated 6 August 1620, but in fact, at writing, the priory and its commanderies continued in large part to be occupied by Protestants locally called Hussites. Three months later on 8 November, unbeknownst to Marchetti and Malta Council members convened to hear his report, an Imperial army commanded by Duke Maximilian I of Bavaria defeated Reformation generals at the Battle of White Mountain. Two days later Prague opened its gates to the counter-reformation army, thus ending two centuries of Protestant rule in Bohemia.

In other 1620 developments, Grand Chancellor Don Diego de Guzman y Toledo was deprived of the dignity (for absenteeism) and succeeded by Bailiff of Negroponte Don Rodrigo Tello de Guzman who in turn was succeeded as Bailiff of Negroponte by Fernando Ruiz de Prado. Prior of Hungary Heinrich Baron von Logau was appointed Prior of Bohemia succeeding the deceased Leopold von Pöpel. Prior of Dacia Hartmann von der Tann succeeded to the Priory of Hungary and was himself succeeded as Prior of Dacia by Titular Bailiff of Brandenburg Theodor Rolman von Battenberg. Johann Conrad von Rosenbach succeeded to the Bailiwick of Brandenburg. At the same time Ernst Georg, Markgraf von Brandenburg, remained Protestant Herrenmeister recognized by the Hospital. Grand Conservator Felipe de Bardaxi advanced to Castellan of Amposta succeeding Don Martín de Ferrera upon the latter's death, and was himself succeeded as Grand

Conservator by Fernando Ruiz de Prado. The latter left the Bailiwick of Negroponte to Don Francisco de Saavedra. Bailiff of Lora Don Pedro Gonzales de Mendoza died during the year following an illustrious and meritorious career in Hospitaller ranks much of which was passed counseling His Most Catholic Majesty on matters of war, the viceregencies, and Malta. He was succeeded as Bailiff of Lora by Don Diego Brochero who ceded the Bailiwick of the Holy Sepulcher to Don Rodrigo Tello de Guzmán. Don Ottavio di Gioeni of Catania was appointed Prior of Barletta succeeding the deceased Leonida Loschi. And finally, Prince Victor Amadeus of Savoy in consequence of his marriage to Christine Marie of France renounced the Hospitaller Priory of Crato in Portugal to which King Philip III appointed his brother and former Prior of Barletta Cardinal Infante Ferdinando. His time as General of the Galleys ended, Signorino della Gattinara was succeeded in command by Charles de Lorraine, Comte de Brie. Upon the latter's nomination François de Faulcôn de Rys of the Languedoc was appointed flag captain succeeding Alfonso Castelsanpietro. The Grand Master separately notified the Council he had appointed Dom Pedro de Sousa of Portugal to command of *San Giovanni* succeeding Gaspard-Acton de Limons. Giovan Battista Abenante of Cosenza was appointed to command of the Grand Galleon succeeding Philippe de Gouttes upon the latter's reassignment. Similarly, Don Diego de Góngora y Pineda of Baena, Córdoba, had been appointed to command of the Galleonetto of the Religion in succession of François de la Trollière upon the latter's reassignment.[33]

Pope Paul V died on 28 January 1621 at the age of 68 having occupied the Papal throne for 15 years and 257 days. Following a Conclave of Cardinals he was succeeded on 9 February by Alessandro Ludovisi of Bologna who took the name of Gregory XV. Prior of Rome Aldobrandino Aldobrandini was appointed Ambassador of Obedience and proceeded to Rome to warrant the Order's obedience to Papal authority. The Pope elevated his nephew Ludovico Ludovisi, also of Bologna, to Cardinal six days after his own election as Pope. Ludovisi was then appointed Cardinal-Protector of the Order of Jerusalem. It was this habit of Popes to make nephews (*nipotes* in Italian) Cardinals that begat the Italian word "nepotismo" and the English word "nepotism." Not more than two months after the passing of Pope Paul V, King Philip III died on the final day of March 14 days short of 43 years of age. This latter death was a severe blow to Malta as Philip had always come down on the Order's side in times of conflict and matters of dispute, and as importantly, in terms of food supplies for Malta's population. The Order sped Bailiff of Lora Diego de Brochero to Madrid to convey condolences in the name of the Grand Master and the Religion to the deceased's eldest son King Philip IV as well as to Infantes and Infantas.[34]

At the beginning of the 1621 season early in April, the Count of Brie took advantage of the weather to shake-down his five galleys with an opportunity cruise along the coast of North Africa including through the Cantera (Cantara) Channel where recent advice again suggested Infidel merchant ships might be available for the taking. But in fact no opportunity presented itself to the Squadron, neither within the channel nor in nearby Secco di Palo, the extensive body of shallow water extending well out to sea off the corner of land where modern Libya meets Tunisia. Returning to Malta by way of Lampedusa, however, a sail was sighted in the distance and put to the chase. Sailing and rowing at the same time the galleys closed the gap as the sail was not an oared vessel but rather a flat-bottomed merchant urca, but an urca armed for combat with 25 mostly bronze cannons. Six hours after initiating an artillery exchange the urca lost her mainmast and three of her seven sails, prompting the Maltese to board. The going did not get any easier as there were more than a hundred janissaries, Moors, and renegades putting up a staunch defense under command of Hussein of Chios, a wealthy sea captain who included among his possessions 300 Christian slaves. Hence his capture would bring a large ransom in terms of returned Christians. When the urca yielded, 22 of her crew were dead and a larger number wounded. Malta lost 12 hired soldiers with more than 60 others wounded of whom nine were Hospitallers, the more seriously wounded Charles le Cat de Bazancourt of the Langue of France, Francesco Silos of Bitonto in Apulia, and Pietro Diottallevi of Rimini. The urca was towed safely the 95 nautical miles to Malta. Not so a prize taken 80 miles to the east of Malta by the Patache of the Religion. Laden with valuable cargo and with a crew of 47 remaining after combat, she went to the bottom while en route Malta. Caiques picked up the crew, but the ship and her cargo were lost.[35]

Offsetting successes of 1621, Resident Ambassador to the Holy See Girolamo di Guevara died at Rome, and Grand Master Wignacourt appointed as Guevara's successor Commander Giulio Falco of Capua. Upon Guevara's death four commanderies of the Langue of Italy were vacated, to wit, the Camera Magistral of Cicciano in greater Naples and the Commanderies of Milano, Monopoli in Apulia, and Bufalora in Lombardia. The Grand Master conferred the Magistral Commandery of Cicciano upon Carlo Valdina, his Receiver at Palermo, while the other three were assigned by the Langue of Italy to Ottavio Bottigella of Pavia, to Pompilio Fantone of Siena, and to Giocondo Accarigi of Siena. New Pope Gregory XV, however, vacated these assignments and instead assigned the Magistral commandery of Cicciano to Obizzo Guidotti of the Pope's own Bologna, the Commanderies of Milano and Bufalora to Francesco Sacrati, created Cardinal Priest in the consistory of 19 April, while the Commandery of Monopoli was assigned to Marco Antonio Gozadini, also a new Cardinal. This was not the first time a Pope had interfered in the assignment of commanderies and it would not be the last time. Neither was it the first time the Langue of Italy got hot under the collar at loss of revenue to deserving commanders. The Grand Master appointed Admiral Niccolò della Marra Ambassadeur Extraordinaire to Pope Gregory to protest against interference in the affairs of the Order, but there was no sympathy at the Holy See and no redress until death of those receiving the Papal largess.[36]

The first embassy to the Spanish Court upon death of King Philip III was followed by a second conveyed to Cartagena by the entire Galley Squadron departing Malta on 15 July. This second embassy consisted of Acting Prior of England Cesare Ferretti, Commander and Lieutenant Grand Hospitaller Michel de Pontailler de Thallemey, and Don Luis de Moncada, brother of Gastón de Moncada y Gralla, Marqués d'Aitona. They were to convey to King Philip IV the Order's congratulations on his accession and to seek confirmation of Philip III's ruling on seniority vis a vis Genoa. And there were to be critical discussions concerning a larger grain allotment for the people of Malta. Expected to return by 15 September, Thallemey and galleys did not return until 20 November, the galleys transporting in addition to Thallemey large quantities of responsions in coin, gold, and silver plus Hospitallers reporting for duty at the Convent.[37]

It became necessary for the Count of Brie to address matters of importance in Lorraine without having completed his two-year term as General of the Galleys. With approval of the Council he was released and succeeded by Bailiff of Mallorca Onofre de Copones, and upon the latter's nomination Don Diego de Góngora y Pineda of Castile was appointed flag-captain of the galley capitana succeeding François Faulcôn de Rys. Meanwhile the Grand Master appointed Antoine d'Isimieux of Auvergne to command of *Santo Stefano* succeeding Jean-François de Vion-Tessancourt, Francesco Antonio Solari of Turin was appointed to command of *San Lorenzo* succeeding Roberto Strozzi, and Don Tomás de Hoces of Córdoba was appointed to command of *Santa Maria* succeeding Jean de Glandevez-Cuges. Treasurer Pierre de Beaujeu de Montot of Langres was appointed Prior of Champagne succeeding the deceased Charles de Gaillardbois-Marconville, while Grand Hospitaller Guillaume de Meaux Boisbaudran moved up to Treasurer. Amador de la Porte was appointed Grand Hospitaller. Grand Commander Antoine de Paule was appointed Prior of Saint-Gilles upon conditional resignation of Pierre d'Esparbez de Lussan, the conditions having to do with pension and quarters. Balthazar d'Agoult Moriès advanced to Grand Commander. Fernando Ruiz del Prado was appointed Bailiff of Caspe, renouncing the dignity of Grand Conservator to which Bernardino Abarca was appointed. Diego de Brochero conceded his seniority and right to the Priory of Castile in view of the juspadronato incumbency of Emmanuel Philibert and was consequently appointed Bailiff of Lora succeeding the deceased Don Gonsalo de Porras. Received in 1563, Porras had been a part of 1565's Grand Soccorso breaking the back of the Great Siege of Malta. Teseo Cavagliati of Casale advanced to Prior of Capua succeeding the deceased Bongianni Gianfigliazzi. Giulio Cesare Santinelli became Prior of Messina, renouncing the dignity of Admiral to which Niccolò delle Marra succeeded. Prince Emmanuel Philibert arrived at Messina; he would in January 1621 succeed Count of Lemos Francisco Ruiz de Castro as Viceroy of Sicily. *Hospitaller Viceroy of Sicily*.[38]

Prince Karl, 23 year-old third son of Georg Friedrich, Margrave of Baden-Durlach, arrived for a visit during his world tour. In that Georg Friedrich had been a huge force for counter-revolution in Greater Germany, his son was royally received by Grand Master and Convent, and while at Malta endowed a House of Baden within the Langue of Germany. Prior of Aquitaine Jacques de Gaillardbois-Marconville expressed his affection and compassion for the Order by donating to the Common Treasury 8,482 scudos from his estate. By special request of King Louis XIII and of Charles, Duke of Guise, a request hand delivered to Malta by future Grand Master Annet de Clermont-Gessans of the Duke's staff, the Grand Galleon of the Religion was for a second time assigned to duty with the Kingdom of France. Claude de Castellane Montmeyan commanding the Grand Galleon was accordingly ordered to make her ready for sea.[39]

Because there was in the port of Malta a squadron of Marseille commanded by Théodore de Mantin, Seigneur de Manty, squadron and Grand Galleon departed in company on 24 May.[41] Both the Grand Galleon and the Seigneur de Manty took part in the Battle of Saint-Martin-de-Ré off La Rochelle on 27 October in which a Royal fleet under Charles, Duke of Guise, fought an inconclusive engagement with a smaller Huguenot fleet commanded by Jean Guiton. Lieutenant to Guise was Royal Pilot of Malta and Governor of the Tour de Marseille Jacques de Vincheguerre so often mentioned in Pozzo's *History*; he did not survive the battle. In his late fifties, Vincheguerre left a wife, four sons, and a daughter resident at Malta. Montmeyan and the Grand Galleon returned to Malta in October 1623.[40]

In May Prior of Bohemia Heinrich Baron von Logau was dispatched as Ambassadeur Extraordinaire to the Court of Holy Roman Emperor Ferdinand II at Vienna to congratulate the Emperor and Empress Eleonora Gonzaga, Princess of Mantua, on their February marriage. In an unrelated assignment, Logau took with him Pope Gregory XV's 1622 Bull. In grotesque contrast to the blessed event of matrimony, 17 year-old Ottoman Sultan Osman II was garroted on 20 May while imprisoned in Constantinople's Seven Towers Fortress. This ungodly event within months of the Sultan's own marriage was occasioned by the Sultan's failure at 1621's Siege of Khotyn (then Moldavia, now Ukraine) and subsequent withdrawal which he blamed on the Janissary Corps. The Janissary Corps proved more powerful than the young Sultan. But the Corps also placed the fate of the Empire in the hands of Mad Mustafa I who had preceded Osman as Sultan for three months and now succeeded Osman for 16 more months. Mustafa would spend the following 16 years in mental care.[41]

The foregoing instability brought about a measure of calm both at Malta as well as in the Kingdoms of Naples and Sicily, though it was a calm living with crop failure. Sicily, once the grain basket for ancient

Rome and as recently as 1621 exporting 40,000 tons, could not properly feed its own people in 1622. Drought was the culprit, and it hit Malta's meager grain production, as well. On the first day of June Grand Master and Council sped by the galley *San Giovanni* to Messina Conventual Conservator and Lieutenant Grand Hospitaller Michel de Pontailler de Thallemey recently returned from the Court of Philip IV in Madrid. From Messina Thallemey proceeded by horse to the Viceregal Court of Prince Emmanuel Philibert to represent the calamity and anguish of crop failure impacting the people of Malta and Gozo. Two days following Thallemey's return to Malta on 7 June, Titular Prior of England Cesare Ferretti and Don Luis de Moncada returned from Madrid and the embassy earlier shared with Thallemey. They brought with them a favorable determination on the matter of precedence continually disputed by Genoa. They had also engaged in discussions with the Crown concerning food supplies, and brought with them from the King a letter addressed to Emmanuel Philibert ordering an additional 2,000 salmas per year be added to the 10,000 salmas already allocated for a total equivalent to 3,492 metric tons.[42]

The usual combined Armada assembled at Messina between June and September, while an Ottoman Armada came as far as Navarin, but no meeting took place. In what had become an annual pattern the five Galleys of the Religion were summoned on short notice and departed Malta under General Onofre de Copones full of embarked enthusiasm. Don Diego Góngora y Pineda of Castile commanded the capitana, Dom Pedro de Sousa of Portugal commanded *San Giovanni*, Antoine d'Isimieux of Auvergne commanded *Santo Stefano*, Francesco Antonio Solari of Turin commanded *San Lorenzo*, and Don Tomás de Hoces of Córdoba commanded *Santa Maria*. Embarked were the normal quotas of 30 caravan knights and 120 hired soldiers. Viceroy of Sicily and Spanish Captain-General of the Sea Emmanuel Philibert as in 1621 ordered the Malta Squadron into the Levant in June to obtain news of the Ottomans. Copones reported back the Ottomans, still commanded by the formidable Khalil Pasha, were weak, tired, and beset by peste or plague. During both June and October three galleys of the squadron of Don Carlo Doria and four of Naples arrived Malta to make common cause during absence of the Malta Squadron. The Patache of the Religion commanded by Charles de Vaivre of Langres in the Priory of Champagne returned to Malta with 80 crew seized from a merchant germa which at the start of combat had 150 Turkish crew and quite a number of Christian slaves. The germa had been sent back to Malta under a prize crew but north of Gazi (Iraklion), Candia, went up on shoals and was lost with all on board rescued. Several Malta-flag corsairs also returned from the Levant with good plunder and numerous captives. Among these was the lateen-rigged single-mast corsair tartan belonging to Jean-Baptiste de Galéan-Chateauneuf of Provence with 65 captives and a variety of merchandise.[43]

Attempting to escape the heat of August 1622, Grand Master Alof de Wignacourt retired to the Verdala Palace in the Buskett Gardens where for diversion he engaged in the hunt. While pursuing a hare on 26 August he suffered a stroke, fell from his horse, and hit his head. The accident took place at very nearly the same spot at which Grand Master Parisot de la Valette had met his end in 1568. Suffering a high fever the Grand Master was on 27 August transported to the infirmary at Citta Vecchia or Notabile (modern Mdina) where the Council and others assembled. Admiral Niccolò della Marra of Naples was appointed Magistral Lieutenant with power to act in the Grand Master's stead in the event of the latter's absence or incapacity. On 11 September the Grand Master was administered extreme unction. He died three days later at the age of 75 having reigned as Grand Master 21 years, seven months, and four days, the longest tenure since that of Pierre d'Aubusson in 1503.[44]

Chapter XII

1622–1623

Deceased Grand Master Alof de Wignacourt lay in state in the Great Hall of the Magistral Palace before being transported to the Church of Saint John in a splendid cortege followed by a seemingly infinite number of Maltese most of whom necessarily remained outside of the Church for memorial services. The Grand Master was then moved to a dedicated chamber to await preparation of his place in the Church's Magistral Crypt. That same day of 16 September 1622 Magistral Lieutenant Niccolò della Marra convened in the Great Hall of the Magistral Palace a meeting of the Council of State at which Prior of the Church Pedro Urrea Camarasa of Aragon was appointed successor Magistral Lieutenant. Pursuant to statute Camarasa then dismissed Marra and summoned a General Assembly of eligible Hospitallers present and ambulatory at Malta for the following morning.[1]

The General Assembly convened at Malta on 17 September was attended by 365 knights, serving brothers, and chaplains eligible to vote. Selected in camera by each langue were the eight initial electors. These were Prior of Saint-Gilles Antoine de Paule for the Langue of Provence representing 60 votes, Marshal Juste de Fay Gerlande of the Langue of Auvergne with 34 knights, serving brothers, and chaplains present and voting, Lieutenant Grand Hospitaller and Conventual Conservator Michel de Pontailler de Thallemey for the Langue of France with 62 votes, Commander of La Spluga and Vallfogona (de Ripollès) Nicolás Cotoner for the Langue of Aragon with 41 votes, Commander of Orvieto Cattaliano Casati for the Langue of Italy with 130 votes, Titular Prior of England Cesare Ferretti for the Langue of England with one non-English vote, Lieutenant Grand Bailiff Jakob Christoph Andlau for the Langue of Germany with seven votes, and Bailiff of Acre Dom Luís Mendes de Vasconcellos for the Langue of Castile with 30 votes. These Eight Electors selected from the Assembly Grand Commander Balthazar d'Agout of Provence as non-voting

Preceptor of Elections, Commander of Marseille Honoré de Puget-Chasteuil of Provence as Knight of Elections, Pedro Sitges of Aragon's Commandery of Barcelona as Chaplain of Elections, and Serving Brother Gabriel Rosset of Auvergne's Commandery of Villejésus as Sergeant-at-Arms of Elections. These latter three as the Triumvirate next selected a fourth elector from the Assembly, and the four selected a fifth elector, and the five selected a sixth elector, and so forth, until there were Sixteen Electors at two per langue. The Sixteen Electors were Honoré de Puget-Chasteuil and Commander of Merlas and Corbin Jean-Paul de Lascaris-Castellar for Provence; Gabriel Rosset and Commander of Limoges Pierre-Louis de Chantelot for Auvergne; Lieutenant Grand Hospitaller Pontailler de Thallemey and Commander of Soummerols and Croix en Brie Pierre de Bertaucourt for France; Chaplain Pedro Sitges and Commander of Auñón and Alambra Baltasar de Marcilla for Aragon; Commander of Piazza (Noto) and Treasury Secretary Militello Giocondo Accarigi and Commander of Verona Don Francesco Marchetti for Italy; Commander of San Leonardo di Chieri Alfonso Castelsanpietro of Italy and Commander of Aliaga and Castellon Lupe de Arbizu of Navarre for England; Maximilian Schliederer and Wilhelm Heinrich Wasbergh for Germany; and for Castile Vice Chancellor Don Eugenio Ramirez and Lieutenant Grand Chancellor Dom Luís de Brito. These Sixteen retired in camera and for five hours considered the merits of announced and unannounced candidates for the Magistracy, including Bailiff of Acre Dom Luís Mendes de Vasconcellos and Prior of Saint-Gilles Antoine de Paule. One report termed latter stages of the session a horse race determined by age (Vasconcellos's final opportunity). Luís Mendes de Vasconcellos of Portugal and the Langue of Castile was elected 55th Grand Master of the Order of Jerusalem.[2]

At the time of his election Luís Mendes de Vasconcellos was 81 years of age a second son of Francisco Mendes de Vasconcelos and of Isabel Pais de Oliveira born in 1541 at Evora, then Portugal's second city. His grandparents on both sides were distinguished nobility of Evora. Nothing is known of Mendes's early years, but in 1559 at the age of 18 the University of Evora was established and opened its doors the same year. Because of Mendes's ultra-late reception into the Order of Jerusalem at the age of 30, because of the respect attending his election as Grand Master, and most importantly because of his family roots in Evora, it may be hypothesized he passed much of those intervening years prior to reception in pursuit of higher education at university, likely studying the Classics as well as Law, Latin, and Spanish. As Commander of Vera Cruz and Bailiff of Acre, Luis Mendes de Vasconcellos was from 1604 to 1607 assigned as Resident Ambassador and Procurator-General to the Holy See, the Order's most critical diplomatic post given the Order as an arm of the Church and particularly given the penchant for Papal interference in Order affairs. Mendes was appointed Titular Bailiff of Eagle in 1613, a dignity attended by the Grand Cross, and General of the Galleys in both 1613 and 1614 in spite of his advanced age. He was a highly-respected member of the Hospitaller fraternity said to have been endorsed by his predecessor as next Grand Master.

Five days following his election Vasconcellos convened the Sacred Council for the purpose of righting the ship of state. In so doing he graciously thanked members of the Council for the honor he had been accorded. One of the more mundane tasks facing the Council was an inventory of the deceased Grand Master's estate which several weeks later would be assessed at 204,607 gold scudos of which 71,576 scudos was in coin. The balance was mostly represented by various proprietary vessels engaged in corsair operations. Works of art in the Magistral Palace, however, brought the value of the entire estate to 434,605 scudos. A token amount of the coin had been willed to brother Adrien de Wignacourt. The balance of the estate had been left to the Common Treasury. Express wishes of the former Grand Master concerning maintenance of the sweet-water aqueduct and of the five fortresses constructed during his administration were adopted as policy. Pursuant to the former Grand Master's wishes, his nephew and Bailiff of Armenia Jacques du Chenu du Belloy was appointed a testamentary executor as were Commanders François de Vintimille d'Ollières and Don Eugenio Ramirez, his Secretary and Vice Chancellor. Finally, the Council appointed Niccolò della Marra to succeed the deceased Giulio Santinelli as Prior of Messina and moved Prior of Capua Teseo Cavagliati to Admiral making room at the latter priory for Luigi Mazzinghi.[3]

Early in November 1622 a Dutch warship arrived Valletta flying the flag of Algiers. She had been dispatched by prearrangement of Cornelis Pijnaker, Ambassador of the Dutch States-General at Algiers and Tunis, to recover thirteen Turks held as prisoners at Malta. Embarked was Cornelis Pauw, Consul-designate of the States-General at Aleppo and Dutch spokesman in the ensuing discussions. Because the Dutch warship had been seized by Algerians from the Dutch she was one side of a proposed swap. The thirteen Turks, the other side of the proposed swap, had once been the property of Alof de Wignacourt but had since been scattered among former Wignacourt staff. Grand Master Vasconcellos authorized purchase by the Common Treasury of the thirteen Turks who were returned to Pauw with a letter of friendship to the States-General. This was Malta's first sight of a square-rigged broadside-gunned Dutch warship. It would not be the last.

Wenceslaus Hollar's Dutch and Spanish Warships.

Responding to a petition by Mother Superior Charlotte de Cluys, Prioress of the Order's Abbaye Royale Notre-Dame du Lys, the Council of State by decree in December approved establishment at Fontainbleau of a new and replacement Convent for Sisters of the Malta Habit and, subject to oversight of the Grand Master, made Grand Prior of France Prince Alexandre de Vendome responsible for replacement and relocation.[4]

During the year Bailiff of Negroponte Don Luís de Moncada was appointed Grand Conservator succeeding the deceased Bernardino Abarca and was himself succeeded as Bailiff of Negroponte by Don Bernardino de Zuniga. Dom Pedro de Vargas de Azevedo advanced to

Titular Bailiff of Acre vacated by election of Grand Master Vasconcellos. Resident Ambassador to the Court of France Joachim de Montaigut-Fromigières of Provence was appointed Prior of Toulouse succeeding the deceased Jean de Mars Liviers. Prior of Messina Niccolò della Marra was appointed Captain-General of the Galleys succeeding Onofre de Copones, and on his nomination Alfonso Dura, a Neapolitan trained in the law, was appointed flag captain succeeding Don Diego Góngora of Navarre. Giorgio Ghislieri was appointed to command of *San Giovanni* succeeding Dom Pedro de Sousa. In December Grand Master Vasconcellos fell terribly ill, and by 19 December was unable to administer the Convent. On that date his Councilors were summoned in camera, and in their presence he appointed Prior of Capua Luigi Mazzinghi of Florence as his Lieutenant with power to act in his absence or incapacity.[5]

During the period of the Grand Master's incapacity Conventual Conservator Michel de Fontailler de Thallemey was appointed to the vacant dignity of Bailiff of Eagle with its attendant Grand Cross. Georges de Stainville-Bompierre was appointed to command of the galley *San Francesco* replacing *Santo Stefano* commanded by Antoine d'Isimieux. Hiérosme (Jerôme) de Feuquières-Beauvoisin of the Seigneurie de Feuquières at Thory in the Haute-de-France reached the end of a distinguished warrior's life at Malta, accumulated wounds the cause. He was about 80 years of age and had been an Hospitaller for more than sixty of those years, his reception into the Langue of France so long ago it pre-dated comprehensive records. With his death the Feuquières name and estates also came to an end.[6]

Luís Mendes de Vasconcellos was laid to rest on 7 March 1623 in the crypt of the Church of St. John at Valletta, ten days short of six months since his elevation. According to the Portuguese Historical Dictionary Luís Mendes de Vasconcellos was survived by son Joanne Mendes de Vasconcelos, a leading military figure in the War of Portuguese Restoration or independence from Spain. Given the latter's period of military service, he was more likely a great nephew than a son. A single source repeated additionally asserts that late in life Luis Mendes de Vasconcellos served as Colonial Governor of Angola. Given no such attestation by Pozzo as well as appearances at Malta immediately before and after, and a coincident appearance at Malta of someone with the same name, the governor may have actually been another member of the extended Mendes family.[7]

Glossary of Notable Figures

ALENTORN, MIGUEL (Miguel de Alentorn, Miquel d'Alentorn i de Salbà (in Catalan), Bosio's Michele di Lantorn, Pozzo's Michel d'Alentor). Catalan of Alentorn 140km NW of Barcelona. Knight of Malta, Langue of Aragon. Received (c1562). Loses hand and two companions in Messina brawl with minions of Sipione Doria as Caravan Knight (1562). Knight Commander of Mas-Deu (1579+). Grand Conservator (1605-1609), Knight of the Grand Cross. Prior of Catalonia (1609). (c1544-1609)

ALARCÓN, ERNANDO (Ernando Alarcón, Bosio's Ernando de Alarcon/ Fernando de Alarcon). Spanish of Alarcón 195km SE of Madrid. Knight of Jerusalem, Langue of Castile. Received (1523). Castellan of Milazzo (1552+). Knight Commander (1565). Lieutenant Grand Chancellor (1565-1569). Pilier Langue of Castile (1568). Grand Chancellor (1569-1574), Knight of the Grand Cross. Bailiff of Lora (1574-1582). (1504-1582)

ALDOBRANDINI, ALDOBRANDINO (Aldobrandino Aldobrandini, Pozzo's Aldobrandino Aldobrandini). Italian of Rome. Son of Gianfrancesco and of Olimpia di Pietro Aldobrandini. Grand nephew of Pope Clement VIII (Ippolito Aldobrandini) and of Gregory XV (Alessandro Ludovisi). Knight of Malta, Langue of Italy. Received (1612). Grand Prior of Rome (1612-1634), Knight of the Grand Cross. General of the Galleys (1616-1618). Lieutenant-General of Papal Galleys (1621-1623). Military Commander of the HRE during the 30 Years War (1628-1634). Killed Battle of Nördlingen (1634). (c1593-1634)

ALI PASHA GÜZELDJE (Ali Pasha Güzeldje, Celebi Ali Pasha, İstanköylü Ali Pasha, Pozzo Not Cited). Armenian of Kefalos, Lango (Kos). Son of İstanköylü Ahmed Pasha, Beylerbey of Tripoli (1589-1590). Kapudan Pasha (1614-1619). Vizier (1614-1621). Battle of Cape Gelidonia (1616). Grand Vizier (1619-1621).

AMOURS, AUGUSTIN (Augustin d'Amours, Pozzo's Agostino d'Amours) of Paris. Knight of Malta, Langue of France. Received (1598). Knight Commander. Commands Galleon of the Religion (1616). Galley Captain (1630-1631). Commander of Boncourt (1646-1654). Grand Hospitaller (1647-1649), Knight of the Grand Cross. Treasurer (1649-1651). Bailiff of the Morea (1651-1652). (+1652)

ANASTAGI, VINCENZO (Vincenzo Anastagi, Bosio's Vicenzo Anastagi, Pozzo's Vincenzo Anastagi). Italian of Perugia. Brother of Hospitaller Marcello Anastagi. Knight of Malta, Langue of Italy. Received (1563). Ottoman Siege of Malta - Mdina Cavalry Commander (1565). Military Commander Rome's Castel Sant'Angelo (1567-1585). Galley Captain designate – Murdered (1585). (1531-1585)

ANDLAU, ARBOGAST (Arbogast von Andlau, Pozzo's Arbogaffo Abandlau). German of Andlau in Elsass (Alsace) 40km SW of Strasbourg. A 2nd son of Imperial Governor Hans von Andlau and wife Ursula von Eptingen. Knight of Malta, Langue of Germany. Received (1571). Knight Commander of Tobel (Switzerland) and Feldkirch (Austria) (1577-1604). Lieutenant Grand Bailiff (1588-1603). Commander of Freiburg im Üechtland (1593+). Titular Bailiff of Brandenburg (1598-1599), Knight of the Grand Cross. Titular Prior of Dacia (1599-1601). Grand Bailiff (1601-1607). Commander of Zurich (1607-1612). Grand Prior of Germany and Prince of Heitersheim (1607-1612) (1550-1612)

ANDLAU, JAKOB CHRISTOPH (Jakob Christoph von Andlau, Pozzo's Giacomo Christoforo Abandlau). German of Andlau in Elsass (Alsace) 40km SW of Strasbourg. A 2nd son of Hans Ludwig III von Andlau and Veronika von Ramstein. Younger brother of Hans Ludwig IV von Andlau. Knight of Malta, Langue of Germany. Received (c1602). Knight Commander. Lieutenant Grand Bailiff (1623). Seneschal to Grand Master Antoine de Paule (1623), Knight of the Grand Cross. Commander of Schleusingen and Weißensee (1635-1638). Grand Bailiff (1635-1638). Commander of Burgsteinfurt, Lage, Villingen and Rottweil (1636-1637). (c1585-1638)

ANDRADE, GIL (Gil de Andrade, Bosio's and Pozzo's Gil d'Andrada). Spanish of San Martiño de Andrade in northern Galicia. One-eyed, according to Morgan 568. Younger brother of Hospitaller Fernando de Andrade. Knight of Malta, Langue of Castile. Received (1540) Knight Commander. Malta Galley Captain (1558-1564). Sultana Capture (1564). Ground Force Commander at capture of Penon de Velez de la Gomera (1564). In Spanish Service commanding eight galleys (1565). Gran Soccorso (1565). Commodore of Spanish Galleys at Lepanto (1571). As Lieutenant to Don Juan commands up to 22 Spanish galleys (1571-1575). (+)

ANGELACH-ANGELACH, BERNHARD (Bernhard von Angelach, Bernhard IV von Angelach-Angelach, Pozzo's Bernardo d'Angloch). German of Waldangelloch 70km NW of Stuttgart, Baden-Württemberg. Son of Bernhard III von Angelach-Angelach and Magdalena von Sternenfels. Knight of Malta, Langue of Germany. Received (1551). Lieutenant Grand Bailiff (1558). Knight Commander Breisach am Rhein (1561), and of Leuggern and Dorlisheim (1562). Lieutenant Grand Prior (1570). Prior of Dacia (1578-1594), Knight of the Grand Cross. Commander of Rottweil (1589-1599). Grand Bailiff (1594-1598). Grand Prior of Germany and Prince of Heitersheim (1598-1599). (1532-1599)

APPELLEVOISIN, HENRI (Henri d'Appellevoisin, Henri d'Appellevoisin de la Bodinatière, Bosio's Henry d'Apeleuoisin, Pozzo's Henrico d'Appelleuosin). French of La Bodinatière 75km NE of La Rochelle. May have been a bastard son of Hardy d'Appelvoisin and half-brother of Bertrand d'Appelvoisin, Seigneur de La Bodinatière. Knight of Malta, Langue of France. Received (1560). Commander of Auzon en Poitou (1566-1604). Lieutenant Treasurer (1593-1595). Lieutenant Hospitaller (1595). Grand Hospitaller (1595-1598), Knight of the Grand Cross. Treasurer (1598-1611). Commander of Corie (1600). Prior of Aquitaine (1611-1613). (+1613)

ARAGONA, OTTAVIO (Ottavio d'Aragona, Ottavio d'Aragona Tagliavia Ventimiglia). Italian of Palermo and of the Princes of Castelvetrano. Son of Carlo, Prince of Castelvetrano, and of his wife the noblewoman Margherita Ventimiglia Moncada. Veteran of Combat in Catalonia (1581), Milan (1583), Flanders (1587), France (1590), Piedmont (1593), and Flanders again (1596). Naval Service of Sicily (1604-1614). General of Sicilian Cavalry (1614-1615). Naval Service of Naples (1616-1623). (1565-1623)

ARIFAT, SOUBIRAN (Jean Soubiran d'Arifat, Bosio's Giovanni de Soubiran detto Arifat, Pozzo's Gio: de Soubiran d'Arifat). French of Arifat 105km ENE of Toulouse. Knight of Malta, Langue of Provence, Priory of Toulouse. Received (1555). Battle of Ierepetra (1557). General Assembly Elector (1572). Commander of Rayssac (1575-1582). Grand Commander (1591-1594), Knight of the Grand Cross. Prior of Toulouse (1594-1596). (+1596)

ARQUINVILLIER, JACQUES (Jacques d'Arquinvillier de Tourville, Jean de Arquinvilliers, Jean de Hargenvillier, Bosio's Iacomo d'Arquembourg). French perhaps of Tourville-sur-Arques, Normandy. A 2nd Son of Olivier d'Arquinvillier (†1520), Chevalier and Seigneur de Saint Rimault, and of Andrée d'Aymeret (†1519). Brother of Louis d'Arquinvillier 1503-1579 wed to Marthe Alleaumé (†1572). Knight of Malta, Langue of France. Received (1541). Knight Commander. Treasurer (1563). Bailiff of the Morea (1563-1564), Knight of the Grand Cross. Grand Hospitaller (1564-1571). Gran Soccorso (1565). Prior of Champagne (1571), appointment rescinded by Crown in favour of Michel de Seurre de Lumigny. Prior of Aquitaine (1577-1587). (+1587)

AUMALE (Claude de Lorraine, Chevalier d'Aumale). French of Saint-Denis (Paris). 4th Son of 11 children of Claude de Lorraine, Duke d'Aumale, and Louise de Brézé. Abbott of Bec in Normandy. Abbot of Saint-Martin d'Auchy near Aumale. Knight of Malta, Langue of France. General of the Galleys (May-Sep 1585). (1564-1591)

AVOGADRO, GIROLAMO (Girolamo Avogadro, Pozzo's Girolamo Auogadro). Brother of Hospitaller Paolo Avogadro. Italian of Vercelli in the

Piedmont. Knight of Malta, Langue of Italy. Received (1541). Ottoman Siege of Malta (1565). Brother killed Fort Saint Elmo (1565). Admiral (1582), Knight of the Grand Cross. General of the Galleys (1582-1583). Bailiff of Santo Stefano (1582-1590). (+1590)

BARDAXI, FELIPE (Felipe de Bardaxi, Pozzo's Filippo de Bardaxi.) Spanish of Valle de Bardaji (Bardaixi in Aragonese) 270km NW of Barcelona. Knight of Malta, Langue of Aragon. Knight Commander. Grand Conservator (1611-1620), Knight of the Grand Cross. Castellan of Amposta (1620-1631). (+1631)

BARRIENTOS, JUAN (Juan de Barrientos, Bosio's Giouanni de Barrientos). Spanish of Barrientos 50km SW of León. Knight of Jerusalem, Langue of Castile. Commander of Ciudad Rodrigo (1541). Siege of Algiers (1541). Lieutenant Chancellor (1557). Bailiff of Negroponte (1563), Knight of the Grand Cross. Bailiff of Lora (1563-1574). (+1574)

BATTENBERG, THEODOR ROLMAN (Theodor Rolman von Battenberg, Theodor Rolman von Battenberck, Dietrich Rollmann von Dattenberg, Pozzo's Theodorico Rolman de Tatemberg). German of Battenberg (now Stębark, Poland) 190km N of Warsaw. Knight of Malta, Langue of Germany. Knight Commander of Villingen (c1611-c1632). Statutory Bailiff of Brandenburg (1611-1620), Knight of the Grand Cross. Prior of Dacia (1620-c1632). (+c1632)

BAZAN, ALVARO (Álvaro de Bazán y Benavides, Pozzo's Santa Croce) of Naples. 2nd Marqués de Santa Cruz. Son of Alvaro de Bezan 1st Marqués de Santa Cruz. Grandson of Alvaro de Bazan the Elder, nephew of Alonso de Bazan. Admiral of Naples. Capitán General de las Galeras de Portugal, Nápoles y España. Lieutenant-General del Mar. (1571-1646)

BEAUCHAMP, HENRI (Henri de Merles-Beauchamp, Henri de Merles Belcampo, Pozzo's Henrico de Merles Beauchamps). French of the Comtat Venaissin. Son of Balthazar de Merles and Hélène de Petris. Brother of Hospitallers Jérôme and Pierre and eight others. Uncle of Hospitaller Thomas-Joseph. Knight of Malta, Langue of Provence. Received (1592). Flag Captain (1610-1612). Commander of Jales (1640-1654). Grand Commander (1644-1645), Knight of the Grand Cross. Prior of Toulouse (1646-1655). General of the Galleys (1647-1648). (1577-1655)

BELVER, ONOFRE (Onofre de Belver, Onofre de Bellver, Onofre de Beluer, Bosio's Onofrio de Beluer, Pozzo's Honofrio de Beluer). Catalan of Belver de Cinca 215km W of Barcelona. Knight of Malta, Langue of Aragon. Piccolo Soccorso (1565), assigned Mdina cavalry. Scouts Aegean aboard Rispolo frigate (1575). Knight Commander (1580). Resident Ambassador to HRE (1581-1583). Regent of the Galleys (1593). (+)

BERTUCCI, FRANCESCO (Francesco Bertucci, Francesco Antonio Bertucci, Franjo Antun Brtučević, Pozzo's Francesco Bertucci). Italian of Hvar in Venetian

Dalmatia. Capuchin Monk. Knight of Malta, Langue of Germany. Knight Commander and titular Prior of Vrana. Temporarily Captures Ottoman Klis (1596). (+1626)

BLONDEL. GÉDÉON (Gédéon Blondel de Joigny-Bellebrune, Pozzo's Gedeone de Bellebrune). French of Bellebrune, Pas de Calais, 45km W of Thérouanne. Fourth son among 17 children of Antoine de Blondel, Baron of Bellebronne, and of Catherine de Carüel. Knight of Malta, Langue of France. Received (1569). Knight Commander. Grand Hospitaller (1606-1610), Knight of the Grand Cross. Commander Saint-Etienne de Renneville (1610-1624). (+c1624)

BLOT-VIVIERS, JACQUES (Jacques du Blot-Viviers, Bosio's and Pozzo's Giacomo du Blot Viuiers or Uiuiers). French of Viviers. 13th of 13 children of Antoine de Chauvigny de Blot, Baron du Viviers, and Françoise du Gué. Brother of Hospitaller Claude du Blot Viviers. Knight of Malta, Langue of Auvergne. Received (1556). Grand Soccorso (1565). Commander of Tortebesse (1573-1594). Master of Grand Master Cassière's House (1574-1577). Marshal (1597-1600), Knight of the Grand Cross. Resident Ambassador to France (1597). General of the Galleys (1600-1602). Bailiff of Lyon (1600-1616). Magistral Lieutenant (1601). (1543-1616)

BOISBAUDRAN, GUILLAUME (Guillaume de Meaux Boisbaudran, Guillaume de Meaux de Boishaudran, Pozzo's Guglielmo de Meaux Boisboudran/Meaulx Boisboudrant). French of Melun. Uncle of Hospitaller Gabriel de Chambes de Boisbaudran. Knight of Malta, Langue of France. Received (1579). Commander of Boncourt (1603-1622). Commander of Saint-Étienne-de-Renneville (1619-1630). Grand Hospitaller (1616-1621), Knight of the Grand Cross. Treasurer (1621- 1626). Bailiff of the Morea (1626). Grand Prior of France (1626-1639). (c1562-1639)

BONINSEÑA, PEDRO (Pedro Boninseña, Bosio's Pietro Boninsegni, Balbi's Buoinsegna). Spanish of Vallodolid. Knight of Malta, Langue of Castile. Received (1537). Great Siege of Malta (1565). Captain of Reserves (1565). Resident Ambassador to the Spanish Court (1567-1568 and 1569-1570). Commander of Fuente la Peña and Receiver General (1581). (c1520-1581)

BOSIO, GIACOMO (Giacomo Bosio, Iacomo Bosio). Italian of Chivasso (metropolitan Turin). Son of Giovanni Bartolomeo Bosio, Commissioner General for French King Francis, and Anna Bosio. Younger Brother of Gianotto Bosio, Agent at Venice for the Hospitaller Order of Saint John, and of Giovanni Otho Bosio. Historian. (1544–1627)

BRIANÇON, CHARLES DE GRASSE (Charles de Grasse Briançon, Brianson, Biancon, Bosio's and Pozzo's Carlo de Graffe Brianfon). French of Briançon 185km NE of Manosque. Second son of Jean de Grasse Briançon, Seigneur de Briançon, Soleilhas, Gars, Montblanc et autres lieux, and of Catherine de Villemurs.

Brother of Hospitaller Jerome killed at Zuara. Knight of Malta, Langue of Provence. Received (1547). Zuara Raid (1552). Knight Commander of Saliers. Ottoman Siege of Malta (1565). Grand Commander (1582-1585), Knight of the Grand Cross. General of the Galleys (1584-1585). Bailiff of Manosque (1585-1603). Commander of Fézenas (1595-1603). (1526-1603)

BROCHERO, DIEGO (Diego de Brochero, Diego Brochero de la Paz y Anaya, Diego de Brocheu, Bosio's and Pozzo's Diego Brochero). Spanish of Salamanca 130km W of Anaya (NW Spain). Knight of Malta, Langue of Castile. Received (1567). Galley Battle Cape Passero (1570). Ottoman Slave (1570-1575). Knight Commander of Castronuño (Valladolid). Majordomo to Philip II's Anne of Austria (1575-157x). Corsair (157x-1582). Venetian Captive (1583). No Report (1584-1589). Spanish Service (1590-1608). Admiral-General of the Ocean Armada (1595). Admiral-General 2nd (Cape Finisterre) Spanish Armada (1596). Vice Admiral 3rd (Falmouth) Spanish Armada (1597). Twice escort for Treasure Fleets from Azores (1600). Kinsale Landing (1601). Compiles Navy Regulations (1606). Commander of Yébenes (Toledo). Prior of Ireland (1609-1613), Knight of the Grand Cross. Resident Ambassador Court of Spain (1609-1619). Grand Chancellor (1613-1614). Bailiff of Toro (1614-1620). Bailiff of Lora (1620-1624). Grand Prior of Castile and León (1624-1625). (c1545-1625)

BRÛLART, NOËL (Noël Brûlart, Noël Brûlart de Sillery, Noël Bruslart de Sillery, Pozzo's Natale de Brulart Sillery). French of Sillery, France, 15km SE of Reims. The youngest child of Lord Pierre Brûlart de Berni and Dame Marie Cauchon de Sillery. Knight of Malta, Langue of France. Received (1597). Resident Ambassador to France (1606-1616). Capitulary Bailiff (1616-1634), Knight of the Grand Cross. French Ambassador to Holy See (1620-1622). Commander of La Villedieu-en-Dreugesin (1627-1640). Funds foundation of a mission in New France (Canada) which will eventually be named Sillery (1632). Petitions Pope for dispensation to relinquish knighthood and become a priest (1632-1634). Priest (1634-1640). (1577-1640)

BRULL, BARTOLOMÉ (Bartolomé del Brull, Catalan Bartomeu del Brull, Pozzo's Bartolomeo de Brull). Catalan of El Brull 70km N of Barcelona. Knight of Malta, Langue of Aragon. Knight Commander. Elector (1601) General Assembly. Galley Captain (1612-1614). (+)

BRUNI, GASPARE (Malcolm's Gasparo Bruni, Bosio's Gaspare Bruni, Pozzo's Gasparo Bruni). Venetian of Dulcigno, Dalmatia (Ulcinj, Montenegro). Son of Matteo Bruni. Brother of Archbishop of Bar Giovanni Bruni and of Serofino Bruni. Knight of Malta, Langue of Italy, Diocese of Venice. Received as a prudent and practiced commander (1567). Agent at Ragusa/Dubrovnik (1567). Captain of Church Capitana #1 (1570). Captain of Church Capitana #2 (1571). Battle of Lepanto (1571). Avignon Garrison (1574-1575). Receiver at Venice (1589-1594). Knight Commander of Cosenza (1595-1598). (c1520-c1598)

CABRERA, ANTIC (Antic de Cabrera, Bosio's Anton de Cabrera, Pozzo's Antic de Cabrera). Spanish of Isla Cabrera, Islas Balearic, 11nm S of Mallorca. Eldest of two sons and two daughters of Antic de Cabrera and of Anna de Colom. Knight of Malta, Langue of Aragon. Ottoman Siege of Malta (1565). Knight Commander. Bailiff of Negroponte (1599), Knight of the Grand Cross. Grand Conservator (1599-1601). Bailiff of Mallorca (1601-1605). (+c1605)

CAGNOLO, CENTORIO (Centorio Cagnolo, Bosio's Centorio Cagnola, Pozzo's Centorio Cagnuolo). Italian of Vercelli. Knight of Malta, Langue of Italy. Received (1550). Procurator (Attorney) at Licata and Mazara, Sicily (1561). Receiver at Palermo (1565). Magistral Receiver at Malta (1565). Ottoman Siege of Malta (1565). Receiver at Palermo (1565-1573). Knight Commander (1573). Procurator Priory of Pisa (1574). Procurator at Rome (1575). General Assembly Elector (1582). Admiral (1583-1584), Knight of the Grand Cross. Bailiff of Santa Eufemia (1584-1619). Savoyard-Flag Corsair Galleon Owner (1600-1619). (c1533-1619)

CAMBERG, PHILIPP RIEDESEL (Philipp Riedesel zu Camberg, Pozzo's Filippo Reidefel). German of Bad Camberg, Hesse, 45km NW of Frankfurt. Son of Henrich Riedesel zu Camberg and Catherine von Sebolt. Knight of Malta, Langue of Germany. Received (1569). Knight Commander of Erlingen (1569-1598). Receiver Upper Germany (1569+). Malta Chapter General (1574). Grand Bailiff of Germany (1588-1594), Knight of the Grand Cross. Resident Ambassador HRE (1589+). General of the Imperial Danube Fleet (1594-1598). Grand Prior of Germany and Prince of the Empire (1594-1598). (+1598)

CAMBIANO, ASCANIO (Ascanio Cambiano, Ascanio Cambiani, Bosio's Commendatore Cambiano, Pozzo's Afcanio Cambiano). Piemontese of Ruffia. Third son of Giambattista Cambiano, Lord of Ruffia, and of Virginia Argentero. Knight of Malta, Langue of Italy. Received (1557). Grand Soccorso (1565). Commander of Murello. Prior of Hungary (1601-1602). Admiral (1602-1603), Knight of the Grand Cross. General of the Galleys (1602-1604). Lango Raid (1604). Bailiff of Venosa (1603-1619). (+c1619)

CAMBIANO, GIUSEPPE (Giuseppe Cambiano, Giuseppe Cambiani, Bosio's Giofeppe Cambiano). Piemontese of Ruffia. Law Studies. Knight of Malta, Langue of Italy. Received (1528). In Service to Holy See (1538). Knight Commander (NLT1551-1568) of Fossano. Defense Counsel Loss of Tripoli (1551). Author (1554-1556). Ambassador Extraordinary Court of Spain concerning Maduro Matter (1557). Receiver at Rome (NLT 1560). Ambassador to Council of Trent (1562). Ambassador/Receiver Holy See (1562-1569). Admiral (1569-1570), Knight of the Grand Cross. Bailiff of Venosa (1570-1572). (c1500-1572).

CARAFA, VINCENZO (Vincenzo Carafa, Bosio's Vicenzo Carrafa, Pozzo's Don Vincenzo Caraffa). Italian of Terra di Lavoro in the north of the Kingdom of Naples. Brother of Hospitaller Girolamo Carafa. Knight of Malta, Langue of Italy. Received (1535). Knight Commander. Ottoman Siege of Malta (1565). Prior of Hungary (1574-1575, 1581-1589, 1589-1600), Knight of the Grand Cross. Prior of Capua (1600-1611).(c1517-1611)

CARAGIALI (Caragiali, Ali Pasha, Karag Ali, Carag Alì, Cargiali, Voguedemar's Cargely, Bicheno's Kara Djaly, Contreras's Caradali, Bosio's Caragiali, Pozzo's Caragiali). Greco-Albanian Renegade of Lepanto. Godfather of Murat of Albania. Corsair of Algiers. Uluc Ali Lieutenant. Raids Milazzo (1563). Romegas and Gaspard de la Motte capture Caragiali lieutenant Memi Caragia and galliot (1563). Ottoman Siege of Malta (1565). Battle of Cape Passero (1570). Battle of Lepanto (1571). Escapes Lepanto with most of Algiers contingent (1571). Captured at Lampedusa by Viceregal (Sicily) Corsair Ruy Perez de Mercado (1599). (+)

CARRETTO, GIORGIO (Giorgio Carretto, Giovanni Giorgio del Carretto, Pozzo's Giorgio del Carretto). Italian of Turin. Received (1556). Battle of Djerba (1560). Knight Commander. Bailiff of Armenia (1599), Knight of the Grand Cross. Prior of Hungary (1599-1600), Admiral (1600-1601). Bailiff of Naples (1601-1601). Bailiff of Armenia (1601-1607). (+1607)

CASSIÈRE, JEAN L'EVÊSQUE (Jean l'Evêsque de La Cassière, Jean l'Eveque de la Cassière, Bosio and Pozzo's Giouanni le Vefque della Casfiera or Cafsiera). French of La Cassière near Clermont-Ferrand. Grandson of Jehan Levesque, Squire and Lord of La Cassiere, and of his wife Marie de Montfoulloux by their son Jehan and his wife Marie. Knight of Jerusalem, Langue of Auvergne. Received (c1520). Commander of La Racherie (1536+). Failed Raid on Zuara (1552). Bailiff of Lango (1567-1568), Knight of the Grand Cross. Marshal (1568-1572). 51st Grand Master of the Order of Jerusalem (1572-1581). (1502-1581)

CASTELSANPIETRO, ALFONSO (Alfonso Castelsanpietro, Pozzo's Alfonso Castel San Pietro). Italian of Milan. Knight of Malta, Langue of Italy. Received (1584). Knight Commander. Razing of Lepanto (1603). Flag Captain (1619-1620). Siege of Susa (1619). Castel Tornese Raid (1620). Procurator Lombardia (1631). (+)

CENTORIO, GIOVANNI ANGELO (Giovanni Angelo Centorio, Bosio's Giovan Angelo Centorio, Pozzo's Gio: Angelo Centorio). Italian of Vercelli. Knight of Malta, Langue of Italy. Received (1562). Ottoman Siege of Malta (1565). Knight Commander. Pilier (1610). Admiral (1614-1617), Knight of the Grand Cross. General of the Galleys (1615-1616). Bailiff of Santo Stefano (1617-1623). (+1623)

CERVANTES, MIGUEL (Miguel de Cervantes, Miguel de Cerbantes, Miguel de Cervantes Saavedra, El Manco de Lepanto, Pozzo Not Cited). Spanish of

Madrid. Second son of Rodrigo de Cervantes and Leonor de Cortinas. Wedded to Catalina de Salazar y Palacios. Spanish Marine (1570-1575). Battle of Lepanto (1571), wounded in two places. Siege of Tunis (1573). Captured at sea (1575). Captive at Algiers (1575-1580). Author (1580-1616). (1547-1616)

CHABRILLAN, FRANÇOIS DE MORETON (François de Moreton de Chabrillan, François de Chabrillan, Bosio's Francesco de Moreton Chabrillan, Pozzo's Francesco de Moretton Chabrillan). French of Chabrillan in Dauphiné. Fifth son of François de Moreton de Chabrillan, Seigneur de Chabrillan, and of Dauphine de Seytres. Brother of Hospitaller Christophe de Moreton de Chabrillan. Knight of Malta, Langue of Provence. Received (1546). Commander of Montpellier and Bordeaux, in order. Zuara Raid Ottoman Captive (1552-1566). Commander of Burgaud (1562-1577). Galley Commander (1570). Commander of Renneville (to 1580). Grand Commander (1576-1579), Knight of the Grand Cross. Commander of Caignac (to 1580). Bailiff of Manosque (1579-1582). General of the Galleys (1579-1581). (c1528-1582)

CIGALAZADE YUSUF SINAN PASHA (Cigalazade Yusuf Sinan Pasha, Sinan Pasha, Scipione Cicala, Setton's Cigalla, Pozzo's Capitan Bassa Cicala). Scipione Cicala son of Vincenzo Cicala of a noble Genovese family related to the Cibo, the Doria, and the Lomellini. Aga of Janissaries (1575-1578). Beylerbey of Van and Vizier (1583-1585). Beylerbey of Bayazit (1586). Beylerbey of Erzurum (1590) and Ottoman Field Commander (1590) during War with Persia. Kapudan Pasha (1591-1595). Hungarian Campaign (1596). Grand Vizier (1596). Beylerbey of Damascus (1596-1597). Kapudan Pasha (1598-1604). Army Field Commander (1604-1605). (1545-1605)

CLARAMONTE, ESTEBAN (Esteban/Estevan de Claramonte, Bosio's Stefano Claramunt, Pozzo's Stefano Claramonte). Spanish of Estadilla, Huesca, 220km NW of Barcelona. Second son of Jerónimo de Claramunt, Lord of Artasona (Huesca), and of Felipa de Castelblanc. Knight of Malta, Langue of Aragon. Received (1553). Knight Commander (1564). Ottoman Siege of Malta (1565). Succeeds the deceased Francisco Zanoguera at The Spur on the tip of Senglea (1565). Bailiff of Caspe (1593-1605), Knight of the Grand Cross. General of the Galleys (1593-1595). (+1605)

COCCONATO FEDERICO (Federico Cocconato, Federico Cocconati, Bosio's Federico Cocona, Pozzo's Federico Coconato). Italian of Casale Monferrato. Knight of Malta, Langue of Italy. Received (1550). Grand Soccorso (1565). Battle of Lepanto (1571). Prior of Hungary (1600-1601), Knight of the Grand Cross. Admiral (1601). Bailiff of Venosa (1601-1603). Retires (1603). (c1533-Unk)

COIRO, FERRANTE (Ferrante Coiro, Bosio's Ferrante Coyro, Pozzo's Ferrante or Ferdinando Coiro). Italian of Milan. Knight of Malta, Langue of

Italy. Received (1563). Piccolo Soccorso (1565). Corsair with Proprietary Galliot (1568). With Saint-Aubin Extraordinary Plunder (1569). Battle of Lepanto (1571). Knight Commander. Prior of Capua (1614), Knight of the Grand Cross. Prior of Messina (1614-1616). (+1616)

CONTRERAS, ALONSO (Alonso de Contreras, Alonso de Guillén y de Contreras). Spanish of the Parish of San Miguel in Madrid. Son of Don Gabriel Guillén and Doña Juana de Roa y Contreras. Toledo Sack of Patras (1595). Monreal Minion at Malta (1597). Viceregal soldier (1598-1599). Capture of Caragiali at Lampedusa (1599). Galion d'Oro (1600). Cartographer (1600-1605). Siege of Passava (1601). Siege of Hammamet (1602). Commands Magistral frigate (1602-1605). 2nd Siege of Hammamet (1605). Serving Brother, Langue of Castile (1611-1629). Voyage to the Indies (1617-1619). Governor of Pantelleria (1627-1628). Received Knight (of Grace) of Malta, Langue of Castile (1629). In Service to Count of Monterrey (1629-1633). Autobiographer (1630). Knight Commander of Puente de Órbigo (1633-1641). (1582–1641)

COPONES, ONOFRE (Onofre de Copones, Onofre de Copons, Bosio's Nofre Coppones, Pozzo's Honofric Copones). Catalan of Copons 80km WNW of Barcelona. Knight of Malta, Langue of Aragon. Ottoman Siege of Malta (1565). Knight Commander. Galey Commander (1595-1596).Longina Galley Battle (1595). Grand Conservator (1602-1605), Knight of the Grand Cross. Chapter General Legislator (1604). Bailiff of Mallorca (1605-1625). (+1625)

CORONADO, JUAN VASQUEZ (Juan Vasquez de Coronado, Juan Vasquez, Bichino's Juan Vazquez de Coronado, Bosio's Giovan Vafquez de Coronado, Pozzo's Gio: Vafquez di Coronado). Spanish of Salamanca. Knight of Malta, Langue of Castile. Knight Commander. Regent of Malta Galleys (1569). Warden Birgu (1569-1570). Spanish Commodore and Captain of *La Real* Battle of Lepanto (1571). Commands Squadron of seven Spanish galleys with 1,000 embarked infantry (1573). (+)

CREMEAUX, FRANÇOIS (François de Cremeaux de Chamoillet, Pozzo's Francesco de Cremeaulx). French of Chamoille, Savoy. Knight of Malta, Langue of Auvergne. Received (1581). Knight Commander. Flag Captain (1609-1610). Governor of Gozo (1613-1614). Marshal (1627-1639), Knight of the Grand Cross. General of the Galleys (1627-1629). Commander of Ormeteau (1637-1644). Prior of Auvergne (1639-1644). (+1644)

CRONBERG, WILHELM (Wilhelm von Cronberg, Pozzo's Guglielmo de Cromberg). German of Cronberg im Taunus, Frankfurt. The son of Kaspar von Cronberg and wife Margareta von Sötern. Knight of Malta, Langue of Germany. Received at Malta (1578). Knight Commander of Mainz and of Nieder-Weisel (1588-1609). Prior of Dacia (1605), Knight of the Grand Cross. Prior of

Hungary (1605-1607). Commander of Rotweil (1607-1609). Grand Bailiff of Germany (1607-1609). (+1609)

DENBALL, SAMPSON (Sampson Denball, Alì Reis, Anderson's Sansone, Pozzo's Sanfone). English of Dartmouth. Corsair. Renegade. Arrives Tunis with John Ward (1606). Vice-Admiral of Tunis Bretones (1610). Sails Under Flag of Algiers (1617). Sails in Company with John Ward (1622). Battle of Cape Zaphran (1624). Spanish Captive (1624). (+c1625)

DORIA, ANTONIO (Antonio Doria, Bosio's Gio. Antonio Doria). Italian of Genoa. Son of Battista Doria and Isotta (Isottina) Doria. Brother of Melchiorre Doria. Wed to Geronima Fieschi. Father of Cesare, Camilla, Giovanni Battista, Scipione, and Lelio Doria. Cousin of Andrea Doria, son-in-law of Brizio Giustiniani. Marquis of Santo Stefano, of Aveto, and of Ginosa. Knight of the Golden Fleece. Commander of Papal Galleys (1531-1533). Spanish Siege of Coron (1532). Spanish Siege of Tunis (1535) commanding 30 sailing vessels. Battle of Anti-Paxos (1537). Battle of Preveza (1538). Spanish Siege of Algiers (1541) with proprietary galleys. (c1495-1577)

DORIA, CARLO (Carlo Doria, Carlo I del Carretto, Pozzo's Carlo Doria). Italian of Genoa. Youngest son of Gian Andrea Doria. First Duke of Tursi, Prince of Avella, Knight of the Order of Saint James. Genovese Galley Squadron Commander (1605). (1576-1650)

DORIA, GIAN ANDREA (Gian Andrea Doria, Giovanni Andrea Doria, Bosio's Giovan' Andrea Doria, Pozzo's Gio: Andrea Doria) Italian of Genoa. Son of Giannettino Doria and great-nephew and adopted son of Andrea Doria. Father of Giovanni Doria called Giannettino. Spain's General of the (Mediterranean) Sea, that is, of Spain's Galleys (1557-1601). Battle of Djerba (1560). Gran Soccorso (1565). (1539-1606)

EMMANUEL PHILIBERT (Prince Emmanuel Philibert, Pozzo's Prince Filiberto). 3rd Son of Charles Emmanuel I, Duke of Savoy, and of Catherine Michelle of Spain, youngest surviving daughter of Philip II of Spain. Knight of Malta, Langue of Italy. Received (1591). Bailiff of Armenia (1591-1595), Knight of the Grand Cross. Prior of Lombardia (1595-1598). Prior of Castile (1598-1624). Spanish Captain-General of the Sea (Mediterranean) (1612-1624). Viceroy of Sicily (1622-1624). Dies of Plague (1624). (1588-1624)

ESPARBEZ, PIERRE (Pierre d'Esparbez de Lussan, Bosio's Pietro de Sparuiers Luffan, Pozzo's Pietro Defparuez Luffan). French of Lussan 55km NW of Avignon. Knight of Malta, Langue of Provence. Received (1556). Ottoman Siege of Malta (1565). Magistral Galliot Commander (1567). Commander of Argentens (1573+). Commander of Golfech (1583-1617). Grand Commander (1600-1602), Knight of the Grand Cross. Prior of Saint-Gilles (1602-1621). (+1621)

ESTIGNIÉRES, LOUIS (Louis d'Estigniéres, Louis de Sauzet d'Estigniéres, Pozzo's Luigi de Sofel Eftinieres). French of Estignieres, a village of the Marche in the Diocese of Limoges 360km W of Lyon. Knight of Malta, Langue of Auvergne. Received (1573). Knight Commander of Tortebesse (1604-1611). Failed Assault Phocaea or Eski Foca (1613). Marshal (1616-1619), Knight of the Grand Cross. Failed Assault Susa (1619). Prior of Auvergne (1619-1627). (+1627)

FERRETTI, CESARE (Cesare Ferretti, Pozzo's Cesare Ferretti). Italian of Ancona, 150km NE of Perugia on the Adriatic. Knight of Malta, Langue of Italy. Received (1567). Commander of Chiusa (1591). Knight of the Grand Cross (1592) with Expectation of Appointment as Prior of England (which never occurred). Chapter General Legislator (1612). General of the Galleys (1629-1631). Bailiff of Santo Stefano (1631-1634). (c1550-1634)

FLACH, PHILIPP (Philipp Flach, Philipp Flach von Schwarzenberg, Philippus Flach von Schwartzenberg, Eosio and Pozzo's Filippo Flach, not his lieutenant Engelbert Flach). Rhenish of the Saarland. Son of Eberhard Flach von Schwarzenberg and Amalia von Ellenbach. Knight of Malta, Langue of Germany. Received (1546). Galley Commander (1554-1555). Lieutenant Grand Bailiff (1555-1559). Captain-at-Arms and Governor of Notabile (1557). Knight Commander of Saint-Jean-de-Bassel and of Dorlisheim. Commander HRE Danube Armada (1566). Grand Bailiff of Germany (1571-1573), Knight of the Grand Cross. General of the Galleys (1572-1573). Commander of Ritterhaus Bubikon (1573-1594). Grand Prior of Germany and Imperial Prince of Heitersheim (1573-1594). (c1525-1594)

FOÇES, GERONIMO (Geronimo de Foçes, Bosio's Gironimo de Foçes). Catalan of Foçes, Catalonia. Knight of Malta, Langue of Aragon. Captain Galley Santa Anna (1570). Battle of Cape Passero (1570). (+1570)

FOISSY-CHAMESSON (Jean-Philibert de Foissy-Chamesson, Bosio's Filibert de Foissy Chamesson, Pozzo's Filiberto de Foissy Chamesson). French of Foissy in the Côte-d'Or 60km SW of Dijon. Knight of Malta, Langue of France, Priory of Champagne. Received (1560). Ottoman Siege of Malta (1565). Magistral Galley Captain (1573-1577). Commander of Romagne (1573-1616). Squadron Galley Commander (1578-1579). Lorraine Galley Commander (1584). Proprietary Galley Commander (1586-1589). Lieutenant Treasurer (1587+). Corsair (1588-1595). Commander of Nancy (1589+). Grand Hospitaller (1591-1595), Knight of the Grand Cross. Prior of Champagne (1595-1616). (c1542-1616)

FONTAINE, PIERRE (Pierre de la Fontaine, Bosio's Pietro della Fonteine, Pozzo's Pietro de la Fontaine). 3rd Son of Pierre de la Fontaine and Jeanne de Baudry, Dame de Ognon, Malgeneste, and Villiers le Bel. Uncle of Hospitaller Guillaume de la Fontaine. Knight of Jerusalem, Langue of France. Received (1512). Ottoman Siege of Rhodes (1522). Commander of Mont-de-Soissons

(1527-1533). Commander of La Villedieu-en-Dreugesin (1534-1548). Commander of Villedieu-Élancourt (1550-1567). Commander of Chantereine (1555-1573) and of Hainault-Cambrésis (1562-1572). Bailiff of Lango (1555-1557), Knight of the Grand Cross. Treasurer (1557-1558). Grand Hospitaller (1558-1562). General of the Galleys (1560-1561). Prior of Champagne (1562-1563). Grand Prior of France (1563-1573). (1490-1573)

FORTUYN, RAMÓN (Ramón de Fortuyn, Raimundo de Fortuyn, Bosio's Ramondo Fortuyn, Pozzo's Raimondo Fortuin). Catalan of Mallorca likely the product of a Dutch-Catalan union; child of Empire. Knight of Malta, Langue of Aragon. Wounded in jaw at Zuara where commended for bravery (1552). Brother of Jorge de Fortuyn. Ottoman Siege of Malta (1565) where described as born from the womb to be an Hospitaller; at Elmo until gravely wounded. Knight Commander of Aquaviva (1569-1599). Senior Commissioner of Valletta Construction (1569). General Assembly Elector (1572). Receiver General (1573). Bailiff of Negroponte (1592-1597), Knight of the Grand Cross. Grand Conservator (1597-1599). Chapter General Legislator (1598). (+1599)

FRAISINET, JEAN-JACQUES (Jean-Jacques de Fraisinet, Jean-Jacques d'Isnard de Fraisinet, Anderson's Chev de Fressinet, Pozzo's Freiffenet). French of Frayssinet 140km N of Toulouse. Knight of Malta, Langue of Provence. Received (1589). Owner 80-gun Corsair *Galion Rouge*. Destroys Fortress of Laiazzo (1609). Loses Life and Galleon at Battle of Kara Djahannum, or Black Hell. (+1609).

GADAGNE, GUILLAUME (Guillaume de Guadagne, Guillaume de Gadagni, Guillaume de Guadagne Beauregard, Pozzo's Guglielmo Guadagni Beauregard). French of Lyon. 4th Son of Thomas III de Gadagne (sic), Dauphin Francis' Gentleman of the Chamber, Bailiff of Beaujolais, and Lieutenant-General of the Bourbonnaise, and of Helene Marconnay of the Bourbonnaise. Knight of Malta, Langue of Auvergne. Received (1590). Hospitaller Galley Captain (1601-1604). Tuscan Warship Squadron Commander (1609-1611). (1575-1615)

GAILLARDBOIS-MARCONVILLE, CHARLES (Charles de Gaillardbois-Marconville, Charles de Gaillarbois-Marconville, Pozzo's Giacomo de Gaillarbois). French of Marconville 120km N of Paris. Likely a younger brother of Jacques, both unrecorded or out-of-wedlock sons of Philippe de Gaillardbois, Seigneur de Marconville. Knight of Malta, Langue of France. Received (1570). Commander of Villedieu-les-Bailleu (1594+), Bailleul, et Saint-Vaubourg Normandy (1598-1616). Resident Ambassador France (1603-1606). Commander of Ivry (1614-1619). Prior of Champagne (1619-1621). (+1621)

GAILLARDBOIS-MARCONVILLE, JACQUES (Jacques de Gaillardbois-Marconville, Jacques de Gaillarbois-Marconville, Jean-Jacques de Gaillarbois, Pozzo's Giacomo de Gaillarbois). French of Marconville 120km N of Paris. Likely an older brother of Charles, both unrecorded or out-of-wedlock sons of

Philippe de Gaillardbois, Seigneur de Marconville. Knight of Malta, Langue of France. Commander of Boncourt (1554). Lieutenant Hospitaller and Chatelain of Malta (1574). Treasurer (1576-1577), Knight of the Grand Cross. Commander of Sommereux (1608+). Bailiff of the Morea (1613-1616). Prior of Champagne (1616-1619). Prior of Aquitaine (1619-1640). Commander of Beauvais-sur-Matha (1633-1640). (+1640)

GALÉAN-CHATEAUNEUF (Jean-Baptiste de Galéan-Chateauneuf, Jean-Baptiste de Galéan-Castelnau, Pozzo's Gio: Battifa Gallean Caftelnouo). French of Utelle. 4th Son of Lazare Galléan, Seigneur d'Utelle, and of Lucrèce Gallian. Cousin of Hospitallers Jean-Jérôme and Lazare-Marcel Galéan-Chateauneuf. Knight of Malta, Langue of Provence. Received (1599). Corsair with fast lateen-rigged tartan (1604-1634). (+1634)

GARZÉS, MARTIN (Martin Garzés, Martin Garzez, Martin Garces, Don Martin Garsèz, Martin Garcès, Bosio's Martino Garzes, Pozzo's Martin Garzez, Funes' Martin Garzes). Spanish of Pamplona, Navarre. Knight of Malta, Langue of Aragon. Received (c1544). Emissary of Spanish Crown (1564). Grand Soccorso (1565). Knight Commander. Castellan of Amposta (1594-1595), Knight of the Grand Cross. 53rd Grand Master of the Order of Jerusalem (1595-1601). (1526-1601)

GATTINARA, SIGNORINO (Signorino della Gattinara, Signorino della Gattinara the Younger, Pozzo's Signorino della Gattinara). Italian of Pavia. Knight of Malta, Langue of Italy. Received (1567). Knight Commander. Galley Commander (1601-1602). Resident Ambassador to Holy See (1615-1618). Prior of Capua (1616-1617), Knight of the Grand Cross. Prior of Messina (1617-1619). Admiral (1618-1619). General of the Galleys (1619-1620). Capture and Sack of Castel Tornese (1620). Bailiff of Santa Eufemia (1619-1640). (+1640)

GIANFIGLIAZZI, BONGIANNI (Bongianni Gianfigliazzi, Bongianni Gianfiliazzi, Bosio's Bongianni Gianfigliacci, Pozzo's Bongianni Gianfigliazzi). Italian of Florence. Son of Piero di Bongianni di Gherardo and Maria di Ubertino Strozzi. Brother or Cousin of Hospitaller Nicolo Gianfigliazzi. Knight of Malta, Langue of Italy. Received (1568). Battle of Cape Passero (1570). Battle of Lepanto (1571). Captive at Constantinople (1571-c1576). Tuscan Ambassador to Constantinople (1578). Commander of Tuscan Prato (1583-1610). Resident Tuscan Ambassador to Spain (1583-1587). Debtors Prison (1593-1609). Commander of Hospitaller San Vitale at Verona (1610-1621). Prior of Capua (1619-1621), Knight of the Grand Cross. (1549-1621)

GIOÙ, PIERRE (Pierre de Gioù, Pierre de Joux, Bosio's Pietro de Gioù). French of Aveyron. Knight of Malta, Langue of Auvergne. Received (1534). Liaison to Andrea Doria at Siege of Mehedia (1550). Sengle Staff (1553-1557). Seneschal (1561-1563). Commander of La Marche (1563+), of Montchamp (1561-1575), and of Courtesserre (1563+). General of the Galleys (1563-1565). Capture of Sultana (1564). Siege of Penon de Velez de la Gomera (1564). Ottoman Siege of Malta (1565). Bailiff of Lango (1566), Knight of the Grand Cross. Marshal (1567-1568), Resident Ambassador Court of France (1568). (c1517-1568)

GIUSTINIANI, PIETRO (Pietro Giustiniani, Bosio's Pietro Giuftiniani; Pozzo's Pietro Giuftiniano). Italian of Venice. Son of Paolo Giustiniani of Candia and Rhodes. Knight of Jerusalem, Langue of Italy. Received as a minor (1523). Law School. Ottoman Siege of Malta (1565) where he is wounded defending fort Saint Michael. Admiral (1566), Knight of the Grand Cross. Prior of Messina (1567-1586). General of the Galleys (1570-1572). Battle of Lepanto (1571). Ambassador of Condolences (1579). (c1510-1586)

GLANDEVÈZ, JEAN-CLAUDE (Jean-Claude de Glandevèz, Claude de Glandeves, Bosio's Claudio de Glandeues). French of Haute-Provence. Knight of Malta, Langue of Provence. Knight Commander of Puimoisson (1548-1570). Grand Commander (1568), Knight of the Grand Cross. Prior of Saint-Gilles (1569-1571). (+1572)

GONZAGA, GIOVANNI VINCENZO (Giovanni Vincenzo Gonzaga, Gian Vincenzo Gonzaga, Bosio's Vicenzo Gonzaga). Fourth son of Don Ferrante Gonzaga, Prince of Molsetta and Viceroy of Sicily, and of Isabella di Capua. Younger brother of Hospitaller Andrea Gonzaga. Knight of Malta, Langue of Italy. Received at age two (1542). Commander. Prior of Barletta (1556-1591), Knight of the Grand Cross. General of the Galleys (1562-1563). Cardinal of the Roman Catholic Church (1578-1591). (1540-1591)

GONZAGA, FERDINANDO (Ferdinando Gonzaga, Ferdinand I Gonzaga, Pozzo's Ferdinando Gonzaga). Italian of Mantua (Mantova). The second son of Vincenzo I Gonzaga, Duke of Mantua and Montferrat, and of Eleonora de' Medici. A great grandson of Holy Roman Emperor Ferdinand I. Knight of Malta, Langue of Italy. Received at Age 5 (1592). Prior of Barletta (1593-1612), Knight of the Grand Cross. Cardinal of the Roman Church (1607-1612). Duke of Mantua and Montferrat (1612-1626). (1587-1626)

GOUTTE, MARC (Marc de la Goutte, Bosio's Marco della Goutte, Pozzo's Marco de la Goutte). French of La Goutte 210km WNW of Lyon. Knight of Malta, Langue of Auvergne. Commander of Les Salles (Auvergne-Rhone-Alps) 100km W of Lyon. Tripoli Garrison (1551). Commander of Selles (1561). Galley Captain (1561-1562). Receiver at Lyon (1565). Marshal (1572-1574), Knight of the Grand Cross. Bailiff of Lyon (1574-1589). Commander of Ormeteau (1576-1581). Commander of Montredon (1589). (+1589)

GOUTTES, PHILIPPE (Philippe des Gouttes, Philippe Raquin des Gouttes, Pozzo's Filippo de Gouttes). French of Thionne 160km NW of Lyon. Son of

Antoine Raquin, Seigneur des Gouttes, and of Renée d'Amanzé. Brother of (sister) Claude Raquin des Gouttes. Knight of Malta, Langue of Auvergne. Received (1599). Knight Commander (1611). Captain Galleon of the Religion (1611-1613). Captain Grand Galleon (1617-1620). Royal Navy (1620-1649). Marshal (1641-1644), Knight of the Grand Cross. Prior of Auvergne (1644-1649). Lieutenant Général des Armées Navales de France (1644-1649). Cardinal de Richelieu's Père de la Mer. (c1580-1649)

GOUY-CAMPREMY, FRANÇOIS (François de Gouy-Campremy, Bosio Not Cited, Pozzo's Com. de Campremy). French of Gouy 100km NE of Campremy, Campremy 120km N of Paris. Family unknown. Knight of Jerusalem, Langue of France. Received (1550). Knight Commander. Killed Ottoman Raid Malta (1614). (c1532-1614)

GOZON-MÉLAC, FRANÇOIS (François de Gozon-Mélac, François de Gozon, Bosio's Francesco de Gozon detto Melac). French of Chateau de Melac a Saint-Rome-de-Cernon 165km NE of Toulouse. Brother of Hospitaller Pierre de Gozon-Mélac. Knight of Jerusalem, Langue of Provence. Siege of Algiers (1541). Galley Captain (1549-1550). Commander of Argentens (1550-1563). Commander of Bordeaux (1558-1574). Bailiff of Manosque (1563-1578), Knight of the Grand Cross. (+1578)

GOZON-MÉLAC, RAYMOND (Raymond de Gozon-Mélac, Bosio's Ramon de Gozon Melac, Pozzo's Raimondo de Gozon Melac). French of Rouergue. Knight of Malta, Langue of Provence. Received (1557). Grand Soccorso (1565). Commander of Fajolles et de Burgaud (1594-1604). Commander of Le Bastit (1597-1604). Prior of Toulouse (1597-1604), Knight of the Grand Cross. (+1604)

GUADAGNI, PIETRO (Pietro Guadagni, Pierre de Gadagne, Bosio's Pietro Guadagni, Pozzo's Pietro Guadagni). Italian of Florence. Son of Filippo Guadagni, Magistrate of Florence. Knight of Malta, Langue of Italy. Received (1564). Ottoman Siege of Malta (1565). Captive at Algiers (1565-1568). Battle of Lepanto (1571). Captive at Constantinople (1571-1573). Knight Commander (1573). Receiver-General Tuscany (1573-1574). Galley Commander (1574-1576). (1545-1592)

GUETE, GERONIMO (Geronimo de Guete, Geronimo de Huete, Bosio's Girolamo de Guete/Guette, Funes's Ieronimo de Guete, Pozzo's Girolamo de Guette). Spanish of Huete 250km WNW of Valencia. Law School. Knight of Malta, Langue of Aragon. Knight Commander. Galley Captain (1545). Captain of Great Galleon (1558-1559). Ottoman Siege of Malta (1565). Grand Conservator (1570-1574), Knight of the Grand Cross. Resident Ambassador to Holy See (1573-1574). Castellan of Amposta (1573-1575). (+1575)

GUEVARA, GIROLAMO (Girolamo Guevara, Girolamo Guerrara, Pozzo's Don Girolamo di Gueuara). Italian of Naples originally Spanish Basque of Guevara. Brother of Giuseppe. Knight of Malta, Langue of Italy. Knight Commander. Special Ambassador Vienna (1595-1598). Final Elector General Assembly (1601). Master of the Horse (1605). Master of the House (1608-1610). Ambassador of Condolence (1610). Commander of Cicciano, Milano, Monopoli, and Bufalora. Resident Ambassador Holy See (1619-1621). (+1621)

GUEVARA, GIUSEPPE (Giuseppe Guevara, Giuseppe di Guevara, Joseba de Guevara (Basque), Pozzo's Don Giuseppe di Guevara). Italian of Syracuse originally Spanish Basque of Guevara. Brother of Girolamo. Knight of Malta, Langue of Italy. Received (1559). Knight Commander. Galley Captain (1601-1602). Prior of Lombardia (1606-1626), Knight of the Grand Cross. (+1626)

GUIDOTTI, OBIZZO (Obizzo Guidotti, Opizzio Guidotti, Pozzo's Obizzo Guidotti). Italian of Bologna. Knight of Malta, Langue of Italy. Received at Age 12 (1583). Commander of Parma. Galley Captain (1606, 1617-1618). Galleon Captain (1608). Two Caramussal Capture Seven Capes (1608). Admiral (1635-1637), Knight of the Grand Cross. Bailiff of Santo Stefano (1637-1638). (1571-1638)

GUIRAL, FRANCISCO (Francisco de Guiral, Bosio's Francesco de Guiral). Spanish. Knight of Malta, Langue of Castile. Received (1535). Knight Commander. Galley Captain (1564-1567). Siege of Malta (1565). Castellan of Castile (1570). Bailiff of Negroponte (1580-1582), Knight of the Grand Cross. Grand Chancellor (1582-1583). (c1517-1583)

HASSAN BARBAROSSA (Hassan/Hasan Pasha). Son of Kheir-ed-Din Barbarossa, son-in-law of Dragut (according to Haedo at Morgan I-432n but father-in-law of Dragut daughter according to Bosio III-624), son-in-law of the King of Kuku (according to Morgan). Father of Hassan Bey or Mohammad Reis (?). Battle of Preveza (1538). Beylerbey of Algiers (1545-1551), (1557-1561), and (1562-1567). Ottoman Siege of Malta (1565). Battle of Lepanto (1571). (1517-1571)

HAYES, ANTOINE (Antoine des Hayes, Antoine des Hayes d'Espinay Saint-Luc, Bosio's Antoine des Hayes Sainct Luc, Pozzo's Antonio des Hayes Saint Luc). French of Normandy's Saint-Luc 95 km W of Paris. Sixth son of Robert II d'Espinay des Hayes and Christine de Sains. Younger brother of Hospitaller Jean d'Espinay. Knight of Malta, Langue of France. Received (1536). Grand Soccorso (1565). Commander of Saint-Etienne-de-Renneville (1576-1601), Chantereine, and La Neuville (Flanders). Treasurer (1577-1598), Knight of the Grand Cross. Resident Ambassador Court of France (1580-1585). (1521-1598)

HÉRAIL-RIVIÈRE, PIERRE (Pierre d'Hérail-Rivière, Pierre Hérail dit Rivière, Bosio Not Cited, Pozzo's Pietro d'Hebrail la Ribera). Occitan of SW France. Knight of Malta, Langue of Provence. Commander of Durban

(1572-1575). Grand Commander (1573-1575), Knight of the Grand Cross. Chapter General (1574). Ground Force Lieutenant General (1574). Captain-at-Arms and Governor of Mdina (1575). (+1575)

HOCES, TOMÁS (Tomás de Hoces, Don Tomás de Hoces, Don Tomás de Hozes, Pozzo's D. Tomaso Hozes). Spanish of Córdoba. Knight of Malta, Langue of Castile. Received at age 15 (1597). Knight Commander. Galley Commander (1621-1623). Commander of Benevento and Rubiales (1623+). Lieutenant Chancellor (1629-1631). Grand Chancellor (1631-1634), Knight of the Grand Cross. Bailiff of Novaville (1634-1639). Bailiff of Toro (1639-1648). Commander of Tocina y Pazos de Arenteiro (1648-1661). Bailiff of Lora (1648-1661). (1582-1661)

HOMEDES, GERONIMO (Geronimo de Homedes, Bosio's Girolamo d'Omedes, Pozzo's Girolamo d'Homedes). Catalan of Zaragoza. Son of leading citizen of Zaragoza Don Miguel de Homedes. Nephew of Grand Master Juan de Homedes y Coscon. Brother of Hospitaller Miguel de Homedes. Knight of Malta, Langue of Aragon. Galley Captain (1560-1562). Grand Soccorso (1565). Bailiff of Negroponte (1582-1584), Knight of the Grand Cross. Grand Conservator (1584-1586). Bailiff of Caspe (1587-1593). General of the Galleys (1589-1591). (+1593)

INGHIRAMI, IACOPO (Iacopo Inghirami, Jacopo Inghirami, Fabio Inghirami, Stefaniana Iacopo Inghirami, Pozzo's Giacomo Inghirami). Italian of Volterra, Tuscany. Knight of Santo Stefano. Received (1581). French Catholic League (1588-1596). Galley Commander (1596-1601). Vice Admiral of Galleys (1601-1602). Admiral of Santo Stefano Galleys (1602-1616). Marchese of Montegiove (1616-1624). Civil and Military Governor of Livorno (1618-1620). Prior of Borgo San Sepulcro (1620-1624). Admiral of Santo Stefano Galleys (1622-1624). (1565-1624)

JUNIENT, PEDRO (Pedro de Junient, Pedro de Iunient, Pere de Junyent, Bosio's Pietro de Iunient). Catalan of Junyent 195km NNW of Barcelona. Knight of Jerusalem, Langue of Aragon. Commander of Orle and Bompas (1556+). Grand Conservator (1563-1569), Knight of the Grand Cross. Grand Soccorso (1565). Prior of Catalonia (1569-1578). (+1578)

KARA OGIA (Kara Ogia, Karagoz/Black Eye, Setton's Caracosa, Caracogia, Bicheno's Kara Khodja.) Italian of Chioggia (Venetian Lagoon). Devsirme draftee. Yeniceri or Janissary schools including the Naval School at Gallipoli. Captain of Janissaries. Ottoman Navy. Galley Commander. Squadron Commander. Ottoman Siege of Malta (1565). Invasion of Cyprus (1570). Bey of Valona (1571). Battle of Lepanto (1571). (+1571)

KHALIL PASHA (Khalil Pasha, Halil Pasha.) Armenian of Cilician Zeitun, Ottoman Empire, renamed Süleymanlı in 1915 and obliterated by earthquake in

2023. Son of Pirî His. Wed to Beyhan Sultan. Aga of Janissaries (1607-1609). Kapudan Pasha (1609-1611), (1613-1614), and (1619-1625). Battle of Kara Djahannum (1609). Vizier (1609-1629). Grand Vizier (1616-1619) and (1626-1628). (1570-1629)

KIZILAHMEDLI MUSTAFA PASHA (Kizilahmedli Mustafa Pasha, Mustafa Pasha, Bosio's Mostafa Bascia) Turkish of Sinop. Son of Mirza Mehmet Bey and Beyazid II's daughter Kamer Sultan. Serdar or Commander of Landed Forces at Siege of Malta (1565). Commander under Suleiman at the Siege of Hungarian Szigetvár (1566). Fourth Vizier. Retired (1566). (+)

LALA MUSTAFA PASHA (Lala Mustafa Pasha, Mustafa Pasha, Lala Kara Mustafa Pasha) Bosniac of Sokolac (Sarajevo). Younger brother of Deli Husrev Pasha. Topkapi Palace Education (Endurun Kolej). Janissary. Sancakbey of Damascus. Serdar or Commander of Landed Forces at Conquest of Venetian Cyprus (1570-1571) and in Campaign against Georgia and Persia (1578). Fifth Vizier. Grand Vizier (1580). (c1500-1580)

LANFREDUCCI, FRANCESCO (Francesco Lanfreducci, Francesco Lanfreducci il Vecchio, Bosio's Francesco Lanfreducci, Pozzo's Francesco Lanfreducci). Italian of Pisa. Knight of Malta, Langue of Italy. Received (1557). Ottoman Siege of Malta (1565). Captive at Algiers (1565-1591). Regent of the Galleys (1591-1592). Commander of Faenza (to 1614). Prior of Hungary (1603), Knight of the Grand Cross. Bailiff of Naples (1603-1604). Bailiff of Pavia (1604-1614). (c1540-1614)

LASTIC, LOUIS (Louis de Lastic, Bosio's Luis de Laftic). French of Lastic, Puy-de-Dome, Auvergne 230km W of Lyon. 4th son and 6th of at least nine children of Louis de Lastic, Baron de Lastic et de Rochegude, and of Anne Motier de La Fayette. Great Nephew of Grand Master Jean de Lastic. Knight of Jerusalem, Langue of Auvergne. Received (1523). Commander of Lavaufranche (1547). Commander of Bourganeuf (1547-1576). Marshal (1554-1557), Knight of the Grand Cross. Grand Prior of Auvergne (1557-1576). (1505-1576)

LAUDON DE GOÛT ((Rostaing des Essards-Laudun de Goût, Bosio's Roftan de Laudun, Pozzo's Roftan de Laudun). French. Knight of Malta, Langue of Provence. Received (1562). Lieutenant to Gaspard de la Motte (1563-1564). Sultana Capture (1564). Ottoman Siege of Malta (1565). Great Galleon First Officer (1565-1567). Commands Great Galleon (1567-1568). Commands Galleonetto (1569-1570). Battle of Lepanto (1571), Volunteer *San Pietro*. Commands at Storm Loss of Great Galleon (1573). Defrocked (1573). Galliot Corsair (1575). Commands Magistral Galley (1582-1583). Corsair (1584). Magistral Galley Command (1584-1585). Dies of Plague (1585). (c1545-1585)

LESCH, JOHANN PHILIPP (Johann Philipp Lesch, Johann Philipp Lesch von Mühlheim, Pozzo's Filippo Lefche). German of Wetzlar, Hesse, 75km N of Frankfurt. Knight of Malta, Langue of Germany. Received (1565). Knight Commander of Sulz-Soultz (1568-1599). Commander of Colmar (1570-1599). Lieutenant Grand Bailiff (1571). Battle of Lepanto (1571). General Assembly Elector (1572). Commander of Villingen (1576-1601). Titular Bailiff of Brandenburg (1589-1599), Knight of the Grand Cross. Grand Prior of Germany and Prince of Heitersheim (1599-1601). (c1545-1601)

LOGAU, HEINRICH (Heinrich von Logau und Olbersdorf, Pozzo's Henrico di Logau and Henrico de Logau). German of Prussian Silesia. Brother of David von Logau. University of Siena (1586-Unk). Knight of Malta, Langue of Germany. Received (Unk). Commander of Troppau and Fürstenfeld (Unk). Governor of County of Glatz (1601-1607). Diplomatic mission to Russian Grand Duke Boris Godunov (1604). Lieutenant Prior of Bohemia (1608-1610). Prior of Hungary (1610-1620). Prior of Bohemia and Austria (1620-1625). (+1625)

LOZORAZO, MELCHOR (Melchor de Lozarazo, Basque Melchor de Lizarazu, Pozzo's Melchor de Lizerazu). Basque of Navarre. Knight of Malta, Langue of Aragon. Felucca Commander Scouting Tripoli (1614). Lieutenant *Galleon of the Religion* (1614). Killed in Action during Urca Capture (1614). (+1614)

LUSSAN, PIERRE (Pierre d'Esparbez de Lussan, Bosio's Pietro de Sparvier detto Luffan). French of Lussan 55km NW of Avignon. Sixth son of Bertrand d'Esparbez and Louise de Sainte-Felix. Knight of Malta, Langue of Provence. Received (1560). Ottoman Siege of Malta (1565). Captain Magistral Galliot (1567-1568). Siege of Zuaga (1567). Commander of Golfech (1583-1617) and Argentens (1583-1617). Resident Ambassador to France (1585-1588), Knight of the Grand Cross. Grand Commander (1600-1602). Prior of Saint-Gilles (1602-1621). Retired (1621). (c1542-c1622)

MAGALOTTI, CESARE (Cesare Magalotti, Pozzo's No Mention). Tuscan of Florence. Knight of Malta, Langue of Italy. Received (1582). Knight Commander. Lieutenant General of Papal Galleys (1596-1602). Failed Siege of Algiers (1601). (1562-1602)

MAGNASCO, ANDREA (Andrea Magnasco, Giovanni Andrea Magnasco, Captain Fantone, Captain Fantoni, Bosio's Capitan Fantone or Gio. Andrea Magnafco). Italian of Genoa. Sea Captain owning a square-rigged sailing vessel. In irregular service to Hospitallers from 1550. Ottoman Siege of Malta (1565) commanding 150 soldiers. Knight of Malta, Langue of Italy. Received (September 1565). Lieutenant to Guion de Saugniac commanding the Grand Galleon (1565). Magistrale Capitana (1567). (+1567)

MAIMÓN, ADRIÀ (Adrià Maimón, Adrián de Maimón, Tuerto (One-Eye), Bosio's Adriano Maimon and Adrian Maymon, Pozzo's Adriano de Maimon). Catalan of Vélez Blanco 140km W of Cartagena. Knight of Malta, Langue of Aragon. Received (c1540). Loses eye in Combat at Sea (1542). Malta-flag Corsair (1554). Ottoman Siege of Malta (1565). Knight Commander. Bailiff of Negroponte (1584-1586), Knight of the Grand Cross. Grand Conservator (1586-1597). Prior of Catalonia (1587-1601). (+1601)

MALAIN, GUILLAUME (Guillaume de Malain, Malain de Lux, Guillaume de Malain de Lux, Bosio's Guglielmo de Malain, Pozzo's Guglielmo de Malin le Lux). French of Mâlain 25 km W of Dijon, 300 km SE of Paris, and 300 km SW of Bellecroix. Third son of Jacques de Malain, Seigneur de Lux, and Louise de Savoisy. Uncle of Prior of Champagne Humbert de Malain de Lux. Knight of Jerusalem, Langue of France, Priory of Champagne. Received (1524). Commander of Bellecroix (1565+). Treasurer (1565-1571), Knight of the Grand Cross. Bailiff of the Morea (1571-1582). Commander of Saint-Jean-du-Vieil-Aître (1578-1582). Commander of Nancy and Pontaubert (1578+). (+1582)

MALASPINA, IPPOLITO (Ippolito Malaspina, Pozzo's Ippolito Malaspina). Italian of Fosdinovo. Marquese of Fosdinovo. Eldest son of Giuseppe Malaspina, Marchese di Fosdinovo, and of Luigia Vittoria Doria. Cousin of Giovanni Andrea Doria. Knight of Malta, Langue of Italy. Received (1556). Grand Soccorso (1565). Galley Captain (1570). Prior of Hungary (1601), Knight of the Grand Cross. Admiral (1601-1602). Commander of Maruggio (c1603). Bailiff of Naples (1601-1603 and 1606-1625). Captain-General of Papal Galleys (1603-1605). (1540-1625)

MALDONADO, ANTONIO (Antonio Maldonado, Bosio's Antonio Maldonado). Spanish. Knight of Malta, Langue of Castile. Auditor of Accounts (1559). Galley Captain (1559-1560). Lieutenant Grand Chancellor (1560). Commander of La Bamba (1560-1573+). Regent of the Galleys (1560). Ottoman Siege of Malta (1565). Commander of Fresno (1566-1568+). Resident Ambassador Spain (1566-1567, 1568-1569, 1570-1573). Commander of Bamba (1569-1592). Grand Chancellor (1577-1582), Knight of the Grand Cross. General of the Galleys (1577-1579). Resident Ambassador Spain (1580). Bailiff of Novaville (1582-1584). Bailiff of Lora (1584-1592). (+1592)

MALVICINO, GIULIO CESAR (Giulio Cesar Malvicino, Bosio's Giulio Cesar Maluicino, Pozzo's Giulio Cesar Maluicino). Italian of Naples. Law student. Knight of Malta, Langue of Italy. Received (1552). Ottoman Siege of Malta (1565). Commander. Procurator-Receiver at Naples (1571). Resident Ambassador to Holy See (1584-1585). Admiral (1586-1587), Knight of the Grand Cross. Bailiff of Santo Stefano (1591-1592). (c1530-1592)

MAMI REIS OF RHODES (Mami Reis of Rhodes, Nicolò Rodiotto). Italian of Rhodes. Hospitaller deployment counsel assigned San Placido (1594). Ottoman Corsair. Ottoman Commander Rhodes galleys (1599). (+)

MARIOLO, HASSAN (Hassan Mariolo, Hasan Mariolo, Azan Mariol, Pozzo's Assan Maricolo). As Mariolo is the Italian word for rogue, it is likely Hassan Mariolo was an Italian renegade, and as his operating area was the Italian Ionian, it is equally like his origins were in Calabria where he made two miraculous escapes on foot. His home port, however, was necessarily in neighboring Ottoman Albania. Barbary corsair. Ottoman Sea Commander. Pursued by Inghirami, loses beached galliot near Crotone, saves himself (1602). Pursued by Ottavio d'Aragona, loses beached galliot near Crotone, saves himself (1615). Commands a Turkish Galley of the Santa Maura Guard (1624). Raids Ithaka (1624). (+c1630)

MARSAC-SAILLAC, JEAN (Jean de Marsac-Saillac, Jean de Marsac de Saillac, Jean de Marsac de Saulhac, Pozzo's Gio: de Marfa Saillac). French of Saillac 200km N of Toulouse. Eldest son of Brenguier de Marsac, Sieur de Saillac, and of Jeanne Saunier. Brother of 2nd son Joye de Marsac, successor Sieur de Saillac. Baron of La Chapelle-Livron. Knight of Malta, Langue of Provence. Received (1571). Battle of Lepanto (1571). Knight Commander. Magistral Galley Commander (1588-1593). Senior Magistral Galley Commander (1593). Squadron Galley Commander (1595-1596). (+)

MASSINBERT, OSWALD (Oswald Massinbert, Oswald Massingberd, Porter's Massingbert, Bosio's Vfuardo Mafimbert). English of Sutton, Lincolnshire. Second son of Sir Thomas Massinbert of Sutton (later himself an Hospitaller) and Joan Braytoft of Braytoft, Lincolnshire. Knight of Jerusalem, Langue of England. Preceptor of Yeaveley and Barrow (to1540). Prior of Ireland w/o Grand Cross (1547). Lieutenant Turcopolier (1548-1553+). (+c1573)

MECA, FEDERICO (Federico Meca, Frederic Meca, Bosio's Fadrique Mecca, Pozzo's Federico Mecca). Catalan. Brother or Cousin of Hospitallers Francisco (Francesc) and Luis (Lluís) Meca. Knight of Malta, Langue of Aragon. Knight Commander. Ottoman Siege of Malta – Grand Soccorso (1565). Flag Captain (1569-1570). Battle of Cape Passero (1570). Battle of Lepanto (1571). Galley Command (1580). Sector Warden (1594). Grand Conservator (1601-1602), Knight of the Grand Cross). Prior of Catalonia (1602). (+1602)

MEMI ARNAUD (Memi Arnaud, Arnaut Memi, Memi Arnaud, Mami Arnaud, Morgan's Memmi Rais, Morgan's Arnaud Memmi). Algiers Corsair. Uluc Ali Lieutenant (1563). Algiers Siege of Oran and Mers-el-Kébir (1563). Great Siege of Malta (1565). Admiral of Algiers (to 1572). Pilot (Navigator) for Kilic Ali (1572-1574). Admiral of Algiers (1574-1594). Captures El Sol and Cervantes (1575). Pilot for Kapudan Cigalazade Yusuf Sinan Pasha (1594-?) (+)

MELZI, PIRRO (Pirro Melzi, Pirro de Melzi, Bosio's Pirro Meltio, Pozzo's Pirro Melzi). Italian of Milan. Fifth son of eight children born to Francesco Melzi, Student, Companion, and Estate Executor of Leonardo da Vinci, and of Angiola Landriani. Uncle of Hospitaller Lodovico Melzi. Knight of Malta, Langue of Italy. Received (1550). Grand Soccorso (1565). Knight Commander. Galleon Commander (1570-1571). General Assembly Elector (1582). Admiral (1584), Knight of the Grand Cross. Bailiff of Naples (1584-1592). Chapter General Legislator (1588). (c1533-1592)

MENDOZA, PEDRO GONZALEZ (Pedro Gonzales de Mendoza, Pedro Gonzales de Mendoza the Younger. Bosio's Pietro de Mendozza. Pozzo's Pietro di Mendozza). Spanish of Guadalajara. Son of Viceroy of Naples (1575-1579) Inigo Lopez Mendoza y Mendoza and Maria de Mendoza. Knight of Malta, Langue of Castile. Turcopolier (1576-1578), Knight of the Grand Cross. Conventual Bailiff (1578-1582). Commander of Pazos de Reinteros (1576-1600). Prior of Ibernia/Ireland (1582-1609). General of the Galleys (1600). Superintendant of Novitiates (1605). Turcopolier (1606). Bailiff of Negroponte (1609). Grand Chancellor (1609-1611), Pilier of Castile. Bailiff of Novaville (1611-1613). Bailiff of Lora (1613-1620). (+1620)

MENDOZA, PEDRO HURTADO (Pedro Hurtado de Mendoza, Bosio's Pietro de Mendozza, Pozzo's Pietro Urtado/Vrtado de Mendozza). Spanish of Mondéjar, Guadalajara. University Educated in Law and Classics. Uncle of Hospitallers Don Garcia de Mendoza and Don Bernardino de Mendoza. Knight of Malta, Langue of Castile. Received (1566). Procurator Langue of Castile (1569). Knight Commander. Ambassadeur Extraordinaire (1576). Sector Warden (1581). (+)

MESQUITE, PEDRO (Pedro de Mesquite, Pedro de Mezquita, Bosio's Pietro de Mezquita and Pietro Mesquita, Pozzo's Pietro de Mesquita). Portuguese of Faro 280km SSE of Lisbon. Uncle of Hospitaller Bendo Mesquite. Knight of Malta, Langue of Castile. Knight Commander of Moura Morta (1565-1579). Ottoman Siege of Malta (1565) as Captain of Arms and Governor of Notabile. Commander of Algoz (1568-1579). Bailiff of Lango (1571-1579), Knight of the Grand Cross. (+c1579)

MONREAL, GASPAR (Gaspar de Monreal, Gaspard de Monreal, Pozzo's Gasparo de Monreal). Basque of Monreal (Basque *Elo*), Navarre, 20km SE of Pamplona. Knight of Malta, Langue of Aragon, Priory of Navarre. Receiver at Malta (1597). Corsair Galleon Owner and Contreras Mentor (1597). Knight Commander. General Assembly Elector (1601). Galley Captain (1605-1606). Lieutenant Grand Conservator (1612). Prior of Navarre (1625-1626), Knight of the Grand Cross. (+1626)

MONROY, MARTÍN DUERO (Martín Duero Monroy, Bosio's Martin de Duero, Pozzo's Martino Duero Monroi). Spanish of Valladolid. Son of Don Juan de Duero and of Donna Juana de Monroy. Wedded to Donna Catalina Miranda and father of Hospitallers Clemente and Martín Duero the Younger. Law degree Universidad de Valladolid. Knight of Malta, Langue of Castile. Received (1531). Knight Commander. Defense Attorney for the indicted at Tripoli (1551). Lieutenant Chancellor (1571). Bailiff of Negroponte (1575-1579), Knight of the Grand Cross. Procurador (Attorney) del Tesoro en Convent (1576). Bailiff of Novaville (1579-1582). Bailiff of Lora (1582-1584). (c1502-1584)

MONTALÈGRE, ANTOINE (Antoine de Montalègre, Antoine de Rodez dit Montalègre, Antoine de Rodez-Montalègre, Bosio's Antonio de Rodès Montalegre). French of Château de Montalègre 150km NE of Toulouse. Son of Bernard de Rodez-Montalègre and Catherine de Ricard. Knight of Jerusalem, Langue of Provence. Received (c1543). Commander of Espalion (1550-1551). Commander of Vaour (1566-1568). Grand Commander (1566-1568), Knight of the Grand Cross. (1526-1568)

MONTE, PIETRO DEL (Pietro del Monte, Pierino del Monte, Morgan's Monti, Bosio's Pietro di Monte). Italian of San Savino. First born of Margherita del Monte and of Checco di Cristofano Guidalotti at Monte San Savino, Tuscany. Cousin of Pope Julius III. Nephew of Cardinal Antonio Del Monte. Uncle of Hospitallers Carlo Sforza and Antonio del Monte. Knight of Jerusalem, Langue of Italy. Received (1516). Ottoman Siege of Rhodes (1522). Castellan of Rome's Castel Sant'Angelo (1550-1555). Admiral (1555-1565), Knight of the Grand Cross. General of the Galleys (1558). Prior of Capua (1565-1568). Ambassador to Holy See (1566-1568). 49th Grand Master of the Order of Jerusalem (1568-1572). (1495-1572)

MONTGAUDRY, CHRISTOPHE (Christophe le Boulleur de Montgaudry the Younger, Bosio's Chriftofano le Boulleur detto Montgauldri, Pozzo's Christoforo de Montgaudry). French of Normandy and Paris. Knight of Malta, Langue of France. Doria's Siege of Monastir (1550). Doria's Siege of Mehedia (1550). Commander of Saint-Étienne-de-Renneville (1553-1579). Sengle's Master of the House (1554). Procurator-General in France (1556). Bailiff of Lango (1569-1571), Knight of the Grand Cross. Treasurer (1571-1576). General of the Galleys (1573-1575). Grand Hospitaller (1576-1577), Pilier Langue of France. (+c1577)

MONTMORILLON, CLAUDE (Claude de Montmorillon, Pozzo's Claudio de Montmorillon). French of Montmorillon 400km WNW of Lyon. Likely a younger son out of wedlock of Claude de Montmorillon, Seigneur d'Essenlay. Knight of Malta, Langue of Auvergne. Received (1554). Grand Soccorso (1565). Knight Commander. Prior of Auvergne (1585-1587), Knight of the Grand Cross. Resident Ambassador Court of France (1588-1589). Marshal (1589-1591). Prior of Auvergne (1591-1619). (+1619)

MORAT REIS (Morat Reis, Morat Rais, Murat, Amurat, Morgan's Morat Rais of Algiers, Pozzo's Corsaro Morat di Biserta). Nephew of Amurat(I) Reis.

Corsair of Algiers. Admiral of Algiers (1594-1608). Sea Defeat ot Tuscans (1594). Sack of Regio Calabria (1594). Battle of Longina (1595). Clears Marseille of Tuscans (1597). Bey of Rhodes (1616). (+1616)

MOTTA, GIOVAN FRANCESCO DELLA (Giovan Francesco Langosco de Conti della Motta) of Vercelli. Uncle or Cousin of Hospitaller Girolamo Langosco della Motta. Knight of Malta, Langue of Italy. Received 1541. Receiver for Grand Master Valette (1565). Ottoman Siege of Malta (1565). Conventual Conservator (1565-1568), Knight of the Grand Cross. Seneschal to Grand Master Del Monte (1568). Commander of Polizzi Generosa (1568). Resident Ambassador to the Holy See (1568-1573). Admiral (1583). Bailiff of Naples (1583-1584). (+1584)

MUEZZINZADE ALI PASHA (Müezzinzade Ali Pasha, Sofu Ali Pasha, Sufi Ali Pasha, Meyzinoglu Ali Pasha, Bosio's Ali Bafcia). Turkish of Edirne. Son of a Dervish. Wed to a Granddaughter of Suleiman the Magnificent. Father of Mehmet and a younger son. Janissary. Aga of Janissaries (1563-1566). Beylerbey of Egypt (1563-1566). Vizier under Sokollu Mehmed Pasha (1566-1571). Kapudan Pasha (1568-1571). Invasion of Cyprus (1570). Battle of Lepanto (1571). (+1571)

NARO, RINALDO (Rinaldo Naro, Rinaldo Nari, Bosio's Rinaldo Naro, Pozzo's Rinaldo Naro). Italian of Syracuse. Knight of Malta, Langue of Italy. Received (Unknown). Knight Commander. Procurator at Syracuse (1566). Commander Galley Capitana (1570-1572). Battle of Lepanto (1571). Wounded (1571). Admiral (1584-1586), Knight of the Grand Cross. Prior of Messina (1586-1593). (+1593)

PANISSE, FRANÇOIS (François de Panisse, Jean-François de Panisse, Bosio's Francesco de Panisses, Pozzo's Francesco de Pannisses). French of Vedènes 12km E of Avignon. Fifth son of seven sons and a daughter of Jean de Panisse, Baron of Malijai and Seigneur de Vedènes, and of Alizette de Pazzi, both families originally of Tuscany. Knight of Malta, Langue of Provence. Receiver at Avignon (to 1570). Commander of Renneville (1570-1573). Grand Commander (1570-1573), Knight of the Grand Cross. Magistral Lieutenant (1572). Seneschal (1572-1573). Prior of Saint-Gilles (1573-1591). (c1520-1591)

PAULE, ANTOINE (Antoine de Paule, Pozzo's Antonio de Paula). French of Toulouse. Fifth son of Antoine de Paule, a Chief Magistrate-Parliament of Toulouse, and of Marie Binet. Uncle of Hospitaller Jean de Bernuy Villeneuve. Knight of Malta, Langue of Provence. Received (1571). Commander of Marseille and of Sainte-Eulalie. Galley Captain (1607). Capitulary Bailiff (1612), Knight of the Grand Cross. Commander of Lacapelle-Livron (1617-1619). Grand Commander (1619-1621). Prior of Saint-Gilles (1621-1623). 56th Grand Master of the Order of Jerusalem (1623-1636). (1551-1636)

PELLOQUIN, BERTRAND (Bertrand Pelloquin, Bertrand Pelloquin de la Plesse, Pozzo's Beltrando Pelloquin). French of La Plesse 135km N of Nantes. Knight of Malta, Langue of France, Priory of Aquitaine. Received (1540). Commander of Montgauger (1582). Grand Hospitaller (1587-1591), Knight of the Grand Cross. Grand Prior of France (1591-1602). Commander of Villedieu-Élancourt (1597-1603). Prior of Aquitaine (1602-1611). (c1521-1611)

PERTEV PASHA (Pertev Pasha, Pertev Paşa, Pertev Mehmed Pasha, Bosio's Portaù Bascià, Pozzo's Portau Generale). Herzegovinian. Devşirme Draftee. Enderun Kolej (Topkapi Palace). Yeniçeri. Aga of Janissaries (1554). Suleiman's Nakhchivan Campaign (1554). Vizier (1555-1571). Suleiman's Siege of Szigetvar (1566). Beylerbey of Rumelia (1569-1571). Area Fleet Commander (1570-1571). Battle of Lepanto (1571), wounded, escaped. (+1572)

PIALI PASHA (Piali Pasha, Pyali Paşa, Bosio's Pialì Bascià) Croatian from Viganj. Devşirme Draftee. Endurun Kolej (Topkapi Palace) Education. Husband of Sultana Gevher Han, daughter of Suleiman son Selim II. Father of Bey of Alexandria Mahaceret (or Mahomet). Sancakbey of Gallipoli (1554). Bahriye Beylerbeyi or First Lord of Admiralty (1554). Kapudan Pasha (1554-1567,1571). Battle of Djerba (1560). Naval Command Ottoman Siege of Malta (1565). Commands Naval Force supporting Invasion and Seizure of Cyprus (1570). Ottoman Fleet Commander (1572). (c1515-1578)

PIERRE, JACQUES (Jacques Pierre, The Last Viking, The Captain). French of Normandy. Corsair with letters of marque from the Grand Duke of Tuscany, from the Duke of Savoy, and from the Viceroy of Sicily. Tuscan Galleon Commander (1609-1611). Neapolitan Naval Commander (1614-1617). Captain Venetian Galleon (1617-1618). Executed (1618). (c1575-1618)

PINS, RENÉ (René de Pins, Pozzo's Renato de Pins). French of Chateau de Pins at Caucalières 80 kilometers east of Toulouse. Of the family of Odon de Pins, 23rd Grand Master of the Order of Jerusalem and of Roger de Pins, 29th Grand Master of the Order of Jerusalem. Knight of Jerusalem, Langue of Provence. Received (1571). Romegas Protégé (1581). Captain of Grand Galleon (1583). Captain of New 25-Bank Magistral Galley (1586-1588).

PONT, LOUIS (Louis du Pont. Louis Dupont, Bosio's Luigi Pont). French of the Haute-Garonne near Toulouse. Likely an older Brother of Hospitaller Charles du Pont. Knight of Jerusalem, Langue of Provence. Ottoman Siege of Rhodes (1522). Galley Captain (1541). Commander of Latronquière (1544-1550). Grand Commander (1560-1562). Prior of Saint-Gilles (1562-1568). Ottoman Siege of Malta (1565). (+1568)

PORRAS, GONZALO (Gonzalo de Porras, Pozzo's Gondisaluo de Porras). Spanish of Écija, Seville, 135km NNW of Malaga. Knight of Malta, Langue of

Castile. Received (1563). Grand Soccorso (1565). Lieutenant Grand Chancellor (1588). Resident Ambassador Rome (1598-1601). Resident Ambassador Madrid (1601-1609). Bailiff of Negroponte (1605-1606), Knight of the Grand Cross. Grand Chancellor (1606-1609). Bailiff of Novaville (1609-1611). Bailiff of Lora (1611-1613). (c1545-1613)

PORTE, AMADOR (Amador de la Porte, Pozzo's Amador de la Porte). French of Paris. 4th of four sons of François de la Porte, Seigneur de la Lunardière and Avocat, and of second wife Magdeleine Charles. Uncle of Armand Jean du Plessis, Cardinal Richelieu, by sister Suzanne de la Porte. Seigneur d'Issertieux (1568-1644). Weds Françoise de Culan (1616). Father of Jean de La Porte (1626). Knight of Malta, Langue of France. Received (1584). Wignacourt Galleon Commander (1603+). Commander of Clichy and of La Braque. Galley Capitana Commander (1612). Grand Hospitaller (1621-1623), Knight of the Grand Cross. Resident Ambassador France (1624-1626). Treasurer (1626-1629). Bailiff of the Morea (1629-1632). Prior of Champagne (1632-1639). Grand Prior of France (1639-1641). Pilier Langue of France (1641-1644). Governor of Le Havre, Intendant General de la Marine. (c1568-1644)

POZZO, BARTOLOMEO (Bartolomeo dal Pozzo, L'Italia Nobile's Bartolomeo Dalpozzo). Italian of Verona. Son of Vincenzo and Margherita Moscarda. Elder Brother of Hospitaller Vincenzo dal Pozzo. Uncle of Hospitaller Giacomo dal Pozzo. Battle of the Dardanelles (1619) as novitiate. Knight of Malta, Langue of Italy. Received (1619). Commander/Bailiff of San Giovanni a Mare di Napoli (1655), Knight of the Grand Cross. Historian (1702-1722). (1637-1722)

PROVANA, ANDREA (Andrea Provana, Andrea Provana Count of Leini, Andrea di Leiny, Bosio's Andrea Prouana Conte di Leini, Pozzo's Sig. di Leiny). Savoyard of Leinì. Count of Leinì, Count of Alpignano and Frossasco, Count of Castellata; Lord of Viù, of the Valley of Lemme, Usseglio, Balangero, San Secondo di Pinerolo e Beinette. Knight of the Most Holy Order of the Annunciation. Admiral of Savoy. Captain-General of Savoyard Galleys, Grand Admiral of the Order of Saints Maurice and Lazarus. Battle of Lepanto (1571). (1511-1592)

PUCCI, EMILIO (Emilio Pucci, Bosio's Emilio Pucci, Pozzo's Emilio Pucci). Italian of Florence. Son of Pandolfo Pucci and of Cassandra di Pierfilippo da Gagliano. Knight of Malta, Langue of Italy. Grand Soccorso (1565). Knnight Commander. Papal Galley Captain (1574+). Hospitaller Galley Captain (1581-1582). Captain-General of Papal Galley Squadron (1592-1595). 1545-1595

PUGET-CHASTEUIL, FRANÇOIS (François de Puget-Chasteuil, François de Puget-Chastuel, Bosio's Francesco de Puget. Pozzo's Francesco de Chestuel). French of the Seigneurie de Chasteuil 90km E of Manosque. Knight of Malta, Langue of Provence. Received (1541). Knight Commander of Tortebesse (1555-1559). Ottoman Siege of Malta (1565) assigned Fort Saint Michael. Galley Flag

Captain (1573). Grand Commander (1582 and 1585-1591), Knight of the Grand Cross. Commander of Curbans (1582-1600). Prior of Toulouse (1582-1585). Prior of Saint-Gilles (1591-1600). (c1524-1600)

RAMADAN PASHA (Ramadan Pasha, Cayto Ramadan Pasha, Ramadan Sardo, Morgan's Ramadam Sardo). Kidnapped as Sardinian Goatherd. Purchased in Slave Market. Learns to Speak and Write Arabic. Abjures Christianity. Sardinian Renegade. Weds Corsican Renegade. Lieutenant to Uluç Ali (1569). Governor of Tunis (1570-1573). Pasha of Algiers (1574-1577). Pasha of Tunis (1577-1579). Pasha of Tremizan (1579). (c1526-1584)

RAMBURES, GUILLAUME (Guillaume de Rambures, Pozzo's Guglielmo de Rambure). French of Rambures 80km WNW of Picardie. Appears to be a nephew of Jean IV de Rambures or of another cadet branch of the Rambures of Chateau Rambures. Knight of Malta, Langue of France. Received (1597). Ottoman Captive taken at Second Assault on Maometta (1606). Ransomed by Family (1607). Loses life in combat at sea (1608). (c1580-1608)

RENGIFO, LUIS (Luis Rengifo, Bosio's Luis Rangiffo/Rengiffo). Spanish. Knight of Malta, Langue of Castile. Received (1524). Commander of Rubiales (1552-1569). Assault on Zuara (1552). Bailiff of Negroponte (1568-1569), Knight of the Grand Cross. Grand Chancellor (1569). (+1569)

RÉGNIER DE GUERCHY, GEORGES (Georges Régnier de Guerchy, Georges Renier de Guerchy, Bosio's George de Reinier Guerchy, Pozzo's Giorgio de Renier Guerchy). French of Guerchy 155km SE of Paris. Knight of Malta, Langue of France. Received (1558). Gran d Soccorso (1565). Commander of Coulommiers (1583-1596). Commander of Villedieu-Élancourt (1603-1619). Prior of Aquitaine (1594-1602), Knight of the Grand Cross. Grand Prior of France (1602-1618). (+1619)

REQUESENS, DIMES (Dimes de Requesens, Dimes de Requesens i Joan de Soler, Bosio's Dimas de Requesens). Catalan. Son of Galcerán de Requesens i de Santacoloma and Doña Isabel Juana de Soler or next generation. Brother or nephew of Galceran de Requesens i Joan de Soler, of Hospitaller Bernat de Requesens i Joan de Soler, and of eleven other siblings. Knight of Jerusalem, Langue of Aragon, Catalonia, and Navarre. Ottoman Siege of Rhodes (1522). Commander of Orla, Bompas, and Collioure (1532+). Commander of Barcelona (1545-1562). Bailiff of Negroponte (1551-1563), Knight of the Grand Cross. Prior of Catalonia (1563-1569). (+1569)

RIBERA, FRANCISCO (Francisco de Ribera y Medina). Spaniard of Toledo. Son of Don Pedro Fernández de Ribera, nobleman of León, and of Isabel de Medina of Mascaraque, Toledo. Galleon Captain and Squadron Commander. Spanish Admiral. Knight of the Order of Santiago. Lord of Cuesta. Knight of the Military Order of Saint James of the Sword. (1582-1626)

RIVALTA, NICCOLÒ (Niccolò di Rivalta, Niccolò Orsini di Rivalta, Niccolò Orsini of the Lords of Rivalta, Bosio's and Pozzo's Nicolo Orsino di Riualta). Piemontese of Rivalta. Knight of Malta, Langue of Italy. Received (1528). Corsair. Captain-at-Arms for the Castle of Gozo (1553). Procurator/Attorney, then Receiver in Sicily (1554). Admiral (1567-1569), Knight of the Grand Cross. Prior of Naples (1569-1584). General of the Galleys (1584). (c1511-1584)

ROMEGAS, MATHURIN (Mathurin d'Aux de Lescout-Romegas, Maturino de Lescut, Bosio's Maturino de Lefcut de Romegasso, Pozzo's Romegasso or Romegas). Gascon of Mansonville 75km NW of Toulouse. Knight of Romegas, a cadet branch of the family d'Armagnac. 2nd son of Jean III d'Aux and Béraude de Beauville. Military Studies at Malta (1542-1546). Knight of Malta, Langue of Provence. Received (1547). Survives Overturned Galley (1555). Seizes two abandoned galleons (1557). Magistral Galliot Captain (1558). Capture of Sultana (1564). Commander of Rouergue. Ottoman Siege of Malta (1565). Defends Fort Saint Michael (1565). Prior of Ireland (1573-1582), Knight of the Grand Cross. Grand Commander (1575-1576). Commander of Cavalleria (1575+). Prior of Toulouse (1576-1581). Lieutenant to Grand Master Cassière (1577-1581). (1528-1581)

ROSENBACH WEIPERT (Weipert von Rosenbach, Wiprecht von Rosenbach, Pozzo's VVperto de Rofembach). German of Rosenbach Castle in the hamlet of Rosenbach near Hainstadt, Baden-Wurttemberg. Son of Konrad von Rosenbach zu Lindheim and Agnes von Buches zu Staden. Knight of Malta, Langue of Germany. Received (1567). Battle of Lepanto (1571). Commander of Freiberg in Switzerland (1573-1576). Commander of Hohenrain and Reiden (1577-1594). Commander of Basel and Rheinfelden (1577-1600). Lieutenant Grand Bailiff (1591-1594). Commander of Rohrdorf and Dätzinngen (1592-1600). Commander of Schwäbisch Hall (Affaltrach) and Prior of Dacia (1594-1598), Knight of the Grand Cross. Grand Bailiff (1599-1601). Grand Prior of Germany and Imperial Prince of Heitersheim (1601-1607). (1549-1607)

RUIZ DE CORRAL (Don Hernando Ruiz de Corral, Fernando Ruiz de Corral, Fernando Ruyz de Corral, Ferdinando, Hernán, Bosio's Fernando Ruiz de Corral, Pozzo's Ruiz de Corral). Spanish of Corral de Almaguer 100km SSE of Madrid. Knight of Malta, Langue of Castile. Received (1563). Sultana Capture (1564); one of two commended by name. Ottoman Siege of Malta (1565); one of two commended by name in defense of 15 July assault on Senglea. Lieutenant Grand Chancellor (1595). Bailiff of Negroponte (1597-1599), Knight of the Grand Cross. General of the Galleys (1598-1599). Grand Chancellor (1599-1606). Bailiff of Novaville (1606-1609). (c1545-1609).

RUIZ DEL PRADO, FERNANDO (Fernando Ruiz del Prado, Pozzo's Ferdinando Ruiz de Prado.) Spanish of Aragon. Knight of Malta, Langue of

Aragon. Knight Commander (bef 1618). Resident Ambassador and Procurator to Court of Rome (1618-1619). Bailiff of Negroponte (1620), Knight of the Grand Cross. Grand Conservator (1620-1621). Bailiff of Caspe (1621-1624). (+c1624)

SAAVEDRA, FRANCISCO (Francisco de Saavedra, Pozzo's Francesco de Saauedra). Spanish of Galicia. Knight of Jerusalem, Langue of Castile. Received (1577). Knight Commander. Counselor on Courtesy (1606 and 1613). Galley Captain (1607-1608). Spanish Court of Auditors (1614). Lieutenant Grand Chancellor (1614). Commissioner of Armaments (1615). Bailiff of Negroponte (1620-1621), Knight of the Grand Cross. (+1621)

SACCANO, FRANCESCO (Francesco Saccano, Bosio's Don Francesco Saccano.) Italian of Messina. Likely Younger Brother of Ottavio Saccano, Older Brother of Antonio Saccano. Knight of Malta, Langue of Italy. Received (1559). Ottoman Siege of Malta, Walls of Birgu (1565). Procurator at Messina (1598). Prior of Messina (1609-1611), Knight of the Grand Cross. Admiral (1611). Bailiff of Santa Stefano (1611-1617). (+1617)

SACQUENVILLE, MAILLOC (Louis de Mailloc Sacquenville, Louis de Mailloc-Sacquenville, Boissat's Commandeur de Sacquenuille, Bosio's Luis de Mailloc detto Sacquenuille/Saquenuille, Balbi's Saquavilla, Pozzo's Lodovico Mailloc Sacquenuille). French of Sacquenville (50 km south of Rouen), Normandy. Apparently a second son of Jehan de Mailloc, Seigneur de Sacquenville, and Perrine de Pardieu. Knight of Malta, Langue of France. Received (1540). Ottoman Siege of Malta (1565). Knight Commander of Sainte-Vaubourg Normandy (1565-1575). Master of House/Seneschal (1565-1568). Receiver in France (1568). Commander of La Croix-en-Brie (1569-1592). Commander of Saint-Maulvis (1570). Romegas Disciple (1581). Lieutenant Treasurer (1583). Bailiff of the Morea (1587-1592), Knight of the Grand Cross. General of the Galleys (1587-1589). (c1523-1592)

SAINT-AUBIN, BERNARD (Bernard de Roquelaure Saint-Aubin, Bosio's Bernardo de Roquelaure detto Sant'Aubin il Giouane, Pozzo's Bernardo de Roquelaure S. Aubin). French of Roquelaure (Gascony) 85km W of Toulouse. Younger brother of Pierre de Roquelaure Saint-Aubin (the Elder). Knight of Malta, Langue of Provence. Received (1565). Magistrale galliot commander (1569-1570+). Commands Magistrale Capitana (1582). (+)

SAINT-AUBIN, PIERRE (Pierre de Saint-Aubin, Pierre de Roquelaure-Saint-Aubin, Bosio's Pietro de Rocque Laure de Sant'Aubin/Aubino, Pozzo's Pietro de Roquelaure S. Aubin vecchio). Gascon of Roquelaure-Saint-Aubin 45km W of Toulouse. Brother of Hospitaller Bernard de Roquelaure-Saint-Aubin (the Younger). Knight of Malta, Langue of Provence. Magistral Galliot Captain (1562). Magistral Galley Captain, takes Corsair galliot (1562). Lieutenant to Romegas (1564). Sultana Capture (1564). Magistral Sultana Captain (1564). Captain

Magistral Padrona (1564). Captain Captured Galliot (1565). Gran Soccorso (1565). Grand Commander (1596), Knight of the Grand Cross. General of the Galleys (1595-1598). Prior of Saint-Gilles (1600-1602). (c1538-1602)

SALCEDO, LUIS (Luis de Salcedo, Luis de Salzedo, Bosio's Luigi Salzedo, Pozzo's Lodouico Salcedo). Basque of Salcedo 240km NW of Zaragoza. Knight of Jerusalem, Langue of Aragon. Ottoman Siege of Rhodes (1522) at Lindos and Rhodes Town. Knight Commander. Pilier Langue of Aragon (1553). Lieutenant Grand Conservator (1554-1561). Final Elector of Parisot de Valette (1557). Bailiff of Caspe (1561-1584), Knight of the Grand Cross. Ottoman Siege of Malta (1565). Chapter General Legislator (1566). Chapter General (1569). Chapter General Legislator (1574). (+1584)

SALVAGO, RAFFAELLO (Raffaello Salvago, Bosio's Raffaello Saluago). Italian of Genoa. Lyric poet. Historian. Knight of Jerusalem, Langue of Italy. Commander of Troia (in Apulia). Bailiff of Genoa. Ottoman Siege of Rhodes (1565).

SALVIATI, BERNARDO (Bernardo Salviati, Bosio's Saluiati) of Florence. Eighth of eleven children of Jacopo Salviati and Lucrezia de' Medici. Brother of Cardinal Giovanni Salviati. Nephew of Popes Leo X and Clement VII. Cousin once-removed of Queen Catherine of France. Cousin of Hospitaller Leone and Marshal of France Pietro Strozzi. Knight of Jerusalem, Langue of Italy. Prior of Rome (1525-1561), Knight of the Grand Cross. Resident Ambassador and Procurator-General to Holy See (1528-1538). Captain of Galleys (1531-1534). Siege of Modon (1531). Siege of Coron (1532). Captain-General of Papal Galley Squadron (1533-1534). Roman Catholic Cardinal (1561-1568). (1508-1568)

SALVIATI, FRANÇOIS (François de Salviati, Bosio Not Cited, Pozzo's Francesco Saluiati Fiorentino). French of Chateau de Talcy (170km SSW of Paris). Likely a second son of Bernard Salviati, Florentine banker and counselor to King Francis I (r1515-1547), and of Françoise Doulcet. If so, François de Salviati was a cousin of Queen and Regent Catherine de Medici. Knight of Malta, Langue of France. Received (1541). Commander of Fieffes. Resident Ambassador to France (1571-c1574). (c1523-c1574)

SAN CLEMENTE, FRANCISCO (Francisco de San Clemente, Francesc de Santcliment i de Santcliment in Catalan, Bosio's S. Clement and San Clement). Catalan. Son of Don Francisco de San Clemente of Barcelona and of Beatriu de Corbera i de Santacoloma. Knight of the Order of Malta, Langue of Aragon. Commander of Barcelona and Receiver in Catalonia (1567). Commander of Aquaviva. Grand Conservator and Pilier of Aragon (1669-1670), Knight of the Grand Cross. General of the Galleys (1569-1570). Battle of Cape Passero (1570). Found guilty of cowardice and executed (1570). (+1570)

SANDE, ÁLVARO (Álvaro de Sande, Álvaro de Sande y Golfín de Paredes, Bosio's Aluaro de Sande) Spanish of Cáceres in western Spain. Son of Don Juan de Sande, Second Señor de Valhondo. Spanish Military Commander. Siege of Tunis (1535). Monastir Garrison Commander (1540). Tercio of Lombardia Commander (1559). Lieutenant-General Commanding Landed Forces Battle of Djerba (1560). Ottoman Captive at Constantinople (1660-1662). Ransomed (1662). Commands Grand Soccorso Landing Force at Malta (1565). 1st Marqués de la Piovera (1573). (1489-1573)

SANDILANDS, JAMES (James Sandilands, Bosio's Iacomo de Sandeland). Scot. Second son of James Sandilands, Baron Calder. Knight of Malta, Langue of England. Received (1540). Preceptor of Torphichen (1547-1560). Valette Elector (1557). Lord Torphichen (1564-1579). Weds Janet Murray (1564). (c1511-1579)

SANGORRIN, JUAN (Juan de Sangorrin, Bosio's Giouanni de Sangorrin, Pozzo's Gio: de Sangorin). Spanish of El Sangorrin 80km ESE of Navarre. Knight of Malta, Langue of Aragon, Priory of Navarre. Knight Commander. Galley Captain (1547-1548). Dragut Captive (1548). Galleonetto Captain (1550). Grand Soccorso (1565). Grand Conservator (1574-1575), Knight of the Grand Cross. Castellan of Amposta (1575-1582). (+c1582)

SANMARTINO, ISUARDO (Isuardo Sanmartino, Isuardo San Martino, Isuardo di Signori di Sanmartino, Bosio's Isuardo Sanmartino, Pozzo's Isuardo Sanmartino, Isnardo di San Martin). Italian of Peio in the Trentino-Alto Adige/Südtiro 330km ENE of Turin. Knight of Malta, Langue of Italy. Received (1565). Ottoman Siege of Malta (1565). Prior of Pisa (1585-1591), Knight of the Grand Cross. Prior of Lombardia (1591-1596). (+1596)

SAUGNIAC, GUION (Guion de Saugniac de Belcastel, Guion de Saugniac the Elder, Bosio's Guion de Soniac Belcaftel). French of Belcastel, Aveyron, Rouergue 150km NE of Toulouse. Knight of Malta, Langue of Provence. Received (1550). Knight Commander. Grand Soccorso (1565). Captain of Great Galleon/Sultana (1565-1568). Captain of Galley *San Iacomo* (1569). Captain of former Capitana *San Giovanni* (1569). (+)

SAULHEIM, JOHANN (Johann von Saulheim, Johann Friedrich Hund von Saulheim, Pozzo's Federico Hundt de Saulheim). German of Saulheim, 55km SW of Frankfurt. Son of Friedrich II Hund von Saulheim and Regula Christophera von Affenstein. Knight of Malta, Langue of Germany. Received (c1572). Commander of Kleinerdlingen (1600). Lieutenant Grand Bailiff (1601-1605). Titular Bailiff of Brandenburg (1601-1605), Knight of the Grand Cross. Prior of Dacia (1605-1609). Grand Bailiff (1609-1612). Commander of Rottweil (1610-1612). Commander of Bubikon (1612-1635). Grand Prior of Germany and Prince of the Empire (1612-1635). (c1555-1635)

SCAGLIA, BERNARDINO (Bernardino Scaglia, Bosio's Bernardino Scaglia, Pozzo's Bernardino Scaglia). Piemontese of Ivria. Knight of Malta, Langue of Italy. Knight Commander (1541). Galley Commander (1552-1553). Galliot Commander (1553+). Lieutenant Prior of Capua (1553). Grand Soccorso (1565). Master of the House for Grand Master Pietro del Monte (1568). Lieutenant Ground Force Commander (1571). Diet of Ratisbon (1573-1577). Admiral (1583), Knight of the Grand Cross. Prior of Capua (1583-1600). Regent of the Galleys (1585-1587). (+1600)

SCHILLING, GEORG (Georg Schilling von Cannstatt, Jorge Schilling, Boissat's George Schiling, Bosio's Giorgio Schiling, Schilingh, Gran Bagliuo). German of Neuffen in Baden-Württemberg. Son of Heinrich Schilling von Cannstatt and Dorothea von Venningen. Knight of Jerusalem, Langue of Germany. Received (1502). Knight Commander of Sulz, Dorlisheim, Überlingen, Bubikon, Hall-Affaltrach (1531-1544), and Mergentheim. Lieutenant Grand Bailiff (1522-1525). Ottoman Siege of Rhodes (1522). Grand Bailiff of Germany (1534-1546). Governor of Tripoli (1535-1537). Captain of Galleys (1541-1543). Grand Prior of Germany and Prince of the Holy Roman Empire (1546-1554). (c1487-1554)

SCIROCCO, MEHMET (Mehmet Scirocco, Şuluk Bey, Mehmet Sirocco, Mahomet Sirocco, Shuluck Mehmet, Setton's Siroco, Bosio' Scirocco, Pozzo's Mehemet Scirocco). Ottoman from Eastern Europe. Corsair of Algiers. Sancakbey of Alexandria (1569-1571). Battle of Lepanto (1571). (+1571)

SCHÖNBORN, JOHANN GEORG (Johann Georg von Schönborn, Georg von Schönborn, Bosio Not Cited, Pozzo's Giorgio Schomborn). German of Hesse. Son of Johannes von Schönborn and Gutta von Mudersbach. Brother of two Teutonic knights. Partner of Elisabeth Marder. Knight of Malta, Langue of Germany. Received (1541). Receiver Upper Germany (1549+). Knight Commander of Worms (1549-1572). Commander of Rothenburg ob der Tauber (1557-1587). Grand Bailiff of Germany (1573-1587). Commander of Rottweil (1574-1587). (+1587)

SCHWALBACH, KONRAD (Konrad von Schwalbach, Conrad von Schwalbach, Bosio's Corrado Scuualbac/Schualbac). Hessian of Schwalbach, Rhine-Hesse. Partner of Buches von Staden. Father of Johann von Schwalbach. Knight of Jerusalem, Langue of Germany. Seneschal (1495). Commander of Tobel, Switzerland (1501-1528). Commander of Rottweil (1503) and Ueberlingen. Commander of Saint Gallen (1510). Grand Bailiff (1512-1534), Knight of the Grand Cross. General Assembly (1513). Missing and Thought Dead (1522). Re-confirmed as Grand Bailiff (1524). (+1534)

SÉGREVILLE, FRANÇOIS (François de Ségreville, Jean François d'Astorg de Ségreville, Pozzo's Francefco di Segreuille). French of Ségreville 30km SE of Toulouse. A second son of Jean d'Astorg, Chevalier and Seigneur de Ségreville er de Montbartier, and of Jeanne de Loubens de Verdalle. Nephew of Grand Master Hugues Loubens de Verdalle. Knight of Malta, Langue of Provence. Received (1572). Amb Extra Spain (1583-1584). Seneschal (1584-1604). Prior of England (1591-1593), Knight of the Grand Cross. General of the Galleys (1591). Resident Ambassador to the Holy See (1591). Commander of Sainte-Lucie (1592). Bailiff of Eagle (1593-1612). Resident Ambassador to the Holy See (1601-1604). (+1612)

SERBELLONE, GABRIELE (Gabriele Serbellone, Gabrio Serbellone, Serbelloni, il Grande Gabrio). Italian of Milan. Eldest son of Giovanni Pietro Serbellone and Isabella Rainoldi. Cousin of Pope Pius IV. Condottiero. Captain-General of the Papal Guard, Governor of the Vatican, and Superintendent of Vatican Fortresses (1562). Knight of Malta, Langue of Italy. Received (1562). Knight Commander of Ferrara and Montecchio (1562-1580). Prior of Hungary (1562-1574, 1575-1580), Knight of the Grand Cross. Arms two galleys for corsair employment (1565). Battle of Lepanto (1571). Viceroy of Tunis (1573-1574). Imprisoned Constantinople (1574-1575). Serves Don Juan in Flanders (1578). (1509-1580)

SEURRE, MICHEL (Michel de Seurre de Lumigny, Michel de Sevre, Bosio's Michel de Seure, Pozzo's Seurè). French of Lumigny en Brie. Son of Antoine de Seurre and of Louise de Verdelot. Knight of Malta, Langue of France. Extraction of Mary Queen of Scots (1548). Captain of French Galliot (1551). Gentilhomme Ordinaire de la Chambre du Roi, Chambellan du Roi, Conseiller (1560). French Ambassador to Court of Saint James (1560-1562). Commander of Flanders (1564). Bailiff of Bobigny (1565-1571), Knight of the Grand Cross. Prior of Champagne (1571-1595). (+1595)

SFORZA, FABRIZIO (Fabrizio Sforza, Fabrizio Sforza Colonna, Pozzo's Fabritio Sforza). Italian of Milan. Second son of Francesco I Sforza, Marchese of Caravaggio (a town in Bergamo Province, Lombardia), and of Costanza Colonna Sforza. Knight of Malta, Langue of Italy. Received (c1595). Lieutenant Prior or Coadjutor of Venice (1598-1608). House Arrest Milan-Malta (1601-1606) on unspecified charges excluding homicide never proven. Prior of Venice (1608-1626), Knight of the Grand Cross. General of the Galleys (1606-1608). (1579-1626)

SHELLEY, RICHARD (Richard Shelley, Bosio's Riccardo Scelei/Sceley). English of Michelgrove, Sussex. Son of Judge William Shelley. Brother of Hospitaller James Shelley. Nephew of Hospitaller John Shelley. Forebear of lyric poet Percy Bysshe Shelley. Member of Parliament (1547). Diplomat in Service to Crown of England (1549-1557). Knight of Malta, Langue of England. Received (1557). Preceptor of Sleibech and Helston (1557-1587). Turcopolier (1557-1566). Grand Prior of England (1566-1587). At Convent (1566-1569). Departs Malta never to return (1569). (c1513-1587)

SIN, SALVADOR (Salvador de Sin, Salvador de Sineu, Bosio's Saluador de Sin). Catalan of Sineu 40km ENE of Palma, Mallorca. Knight of Jerusalem, Langue of Aragon. Ottoman Siege of Malta (1565). Knight Commander (1569). Bailiff of Negropont (1569-1570), Knight of the Grand Cross. (+1570)

SPARR, JOACHIM (Joachim von Sparr, Joachim Sparr von Trampe, Bosio's Gioachino Spar). German of Trampe in Brandenburg. Son of Christoph von Sparr and a Frau von Schlieben. Brother of Hospitallers Christoph and Johann. Knight of Malta, Langue of Germany. Received (1547). Knight Commander of Herrenstrunden (1553-1571). Commander of Mainz and Nieder-Weisel (1555-1571). Commander of Nidda (1567-1571). Grand Bailiff of Germany (1568-1571), Knight of the Grand Cross. Killed Battle of Lepanto (1571). (+1571)

SPELLETTA, BERNARDO (Bernardo de Spelletta, Pozzo's Bernardo de Spelletta). Spanish of Navarre. Knight of Malta, Langue of Aragon. Knight Commander. Resident Ambassador to Spain (1595-1598). Prior of Navarre and Pilier Langue of Aragon (1602-1622), Knight of the Grand Cross. General of the Galleys (1604-1606). 3-Galley Storm Loss at Cimbalo (1606). Hammamet Disaster (1606). Chapter General Legislator (1612). Heads Census Commission (1614). (+1622)

STARKEY, OLIVER (Oliver Starkey, Bosio's and Pozzo's Oliviero Starquei). Flemish, then English. Member of Parliament for Saint Albans (1554). Knight of Malta, Langue of England. Received (1555). Preceptor of Quenyngton (1555). Lieutenant Turcopolier (1560-1569). Bailiff of Eagle (1569-1588), Knight of the Grand Cross. (1523-1588)

TANN, HARTMANN (Hartmann von der Tann, Hartmann von Than, Pozzo's Arthaman de Than). German of Rockenstuhl, Thuringia. Son of Würzburg Councilor Melchior Anhard von der Thann. Studied at Rome and Siena. Knight of Malta, Langue of Germany. Received (1587). General Assembly (1595). Knight Commander of Überlingen and Sulz (1596+). Lieutenant Grand Bailiff (1598-1612). Galley Captain (1606-1607). Prior of Dacia (1612-1620), Knight of the Grand Cross. Prior of Hungary (1620-1635). Commander of Utrecht, Cologne, Heimbach, Freiburg i.Br. and Bubikon (1635-1647). Grand Prior of Germany and Prince of Heitersheim (1635-1647). (1566-1647)

TEJADA, ALONSO (Alonso de Tejada, Bosio's Alonso de Texeda, Pozzo's Alonso de Texeda). Spanish of Zamora 65km N of Salamanca. Knight of Malta, Langue of Castile. Received (1544). Failed Raid on Zuara (1552). Gravely wounded in knee; loses a lower leg (1552). Sicily (1565). Captain of Infantry (1567 & 1570). Galley Captain (1571). Battle of Lepanto (1571). Receiver in Castile (1581+). Bailiff of Negroponte (1586-1592), Knight of the Grand Cross. Resident Ambassador to Rome (1592-1593). Grand Chancellor (1592-1594). (+1594)

THALLEMEY, PONTAILLER (Michel de Pontailler de Thallemey, Pozzo's Michele de Pontailler Thallemey). French of Talmay, Champagne, 60km NW of Besançon. Likely an unrecorded son of Louis de Pontailler seigneur de Talmay out-of-wedlock or by first wife Marguerite de Ray dame de Seveux. Knight of Malta, Langue of France, Priory of Champagne. Received (1584). Knight Commander (1621). Lieutenant Grand Hospitaller (1621-1622). Conventual Conservator (1622). Bailiff of Aquila (1622-1630), Knight of the Grand Cross. General of the Galleys (1624-1625). Capture of Santa Maura, Wounding of Thallemey (1625). (c1567-1630)

THÉZAN-VÉNÀSQUE, ANTOINE (Antoine de Thésan-Vénàsque, Bosio's Antonio de Tezan detto Venafque). French of Saint-Didier, Provence. Son of François de Thézan-Vénàsque, Lord of Saint-Didier, Vénàsque, and Méthamis, and Catherine de Tholon de Sainte-Jalle, daughter of Louis, Lord of Sainte-Jalle. Brother of Pierre, Jean, and Francois. Uncle of Hospitallers Antoine, Claude, Cathelin, and François. Knight of Malta, Langue of Provence. Received (1536). Commander of Garidech (1554-1560). Galley Captain (1554-1556). Survives Dockyard Creek Tragedy (1555). Corsair Galliot Owner (1557). Receiver Priory of Saint-Gilles (1561-1566). Commander of Avignon and Pézenas (1564-1572). (+)

TOUGES-NOAILLAN, JACQUES (Jacques de Touges-Noaillan, Pozzo's Commendator de Noilhan). French of Pouy-de-Touges 60km SW of Toulouse. Knight of Malta, Langue of Provence. Received (1580). Magistral Galley Captain (1591-1593). (1563-1593)

ULUÇ ALI (Uluç Ali, Occhiali, Uluch Alì, Giovanni Dionigi Galeni, Ulug'Alì el Fertas, Ali The Apostate, Il Tignoso, Kiliç Ali (Ali the Sword), Bosio's Vlucciali, Pozzo's Lucciali, Morgan's Cchali). Italian renegade of Le Castella (Licastella), Calabria, born Giovanni Dionigi. Son of a fisherman. Son-in-law of Chiafer Reis. Corsair. Dragut Lieutenant (1560-1565). Battle of Djerba (1560). Ottoman Siege of Malta (1565). Sancakbey or Governor of Tripoli (1565-1570). Beylerbey or Viceroy of Algiers (1568-1572). Battle of Cape Passero (1570). Battle of Lepanto (1571). Kapudan Pasha (1572-1587). (c1519-1587)

URRÈ, CLAUDE (Claude d'Urrè, Claude d'Urrè de Venterol, Pozzo's Claudio Durre Venterol). French of Venterol 75km NNE of Avignon. Third son of Georges d'Urrè, Seigneur de Venterol, and Marguerite de Broyes. Knight of Malta, Langue of Provence. Received (1577). Knight Commander of Peyries and Castelsarrasin. Grand Commander (1630-1631), Knight of the Grand Cross. Prior of Saint-Gilles (1631-1634). (c1561-c1637)

VALENCIA, FRANCISCO (Francisco de Valencia, Bosio's Francisco de Valentia, Pozzo's Francesco de Valentia). Spanish of Zamora 250km NW of Madrid. Knight of Malta, Langue of Castile. Received (1544). Grand Soccorso (1565). Galley Captive at Algiers (1577). Regent of the Galleys (1583-1584).

Lieutenant Grand Chancellor (1584). Grand Chancellor (1584-1585), Knight of the Grand Cross. Bailiff of Novaville (1585-1592). Bailiff of Lora (1591-1606). (+1606)

VALETTE, JEAN PARISOT (Jean Parisot de la Valette, Catalogue's's Jean de la Valette Parisot, Bosio's Giovanni di Valletta detto Parisot). French of Parisot. Son of Guillot de la Valette, Seigneur de Boismenon et de Cornusson, and of Jeanne de Castres. Brother of Bishop Francois de la Valette of Vabres and of Béatrix de La Valette-Parisot, Guillaume de La Valette-Parisot, Baron de Cornusson Guillot de La Valette, and of Antoinette de La Valette-Parisot. Partner of Catherine Grecque, father of Barthélemy de Valette (by Catherine Grecque) and of Isabella Buonaccorsi (by a Buonaccorsi mother). Knight of Jerusalem, Langue of Provence. Ottoman Siege of Rhodes (1522). Galley Captain (1534-1536). Spanish Siege of Tunis (1535). Galliot Corsair (1540-1541). Ottoman Galley Slave (1541-1542). Governor of Tripoli (1546-1549). Commander of Cagnac, Reneville, and Pézenas (1554-1564). Christian Raid on Zuara (1552). General of the Galleys (1554-1555). Bailiff of Lango (1555), Knight of the Grand Cross. Grand Commander (1555-1556). Prior of Saint-Gilles (1556-1557). Commander of Le (Bastit (1561-1563), Commander of Espalion (1563-1564). 48th Grand Master of the Order of Jerusalem (1557-1568). (1495-1568)

VASCONCELLOS, MENDES (Luís Mendes de Vasconcellos, Vasconcelos, Pozzo's Vafconcellos or Mendes). Portuguese of Evora. Son of Francisco Mendes de Vasconcelos and of Isabel Pais de Oliveira. Knight of Malta, Langue of Castile. Commander of Monsanto, later of Vera Cruz. Resident Ambassador to Holy See (1604-1607). Titular Bailiff of Eagle (Jan-Sep 1613), Knight of the Grand Cross. Titular Bailiff of Acre (1613-1622). General of the Galleys (1613-1614). Governor of Angola (1617-1621). 55th Grand Master of the Order of Jerusalem (1622-1623). (1542-1623)

VASSADEL-VAQUEIRAS (Jean de Vassadel-Vaqueiras, Pozzo's Giovanni Uaffadel Uaqueras). French of Vacqueyras in the Vaucluse. Brother of Hospitaller Guillaume de Vassadel-Vaqueiras. Knight of Malta, Langue of Provence. Received (1568). Battle of Lepanto (1571). Knight Commander. Galley Commander (1584-1585). Corsair (to 1610). Commander of Pézenas (1610). Grand Commander (1610-1619), Knight of the Grand Cross. General of the Galleys (1610-1612). Prior of Toulouse (1619). (c1550-1619)

VENEZIANO, HASSAN (Hassan Veneziano, Hassan Aga, Assan Basha, Morgan's Hassan Basha, Pozzo's Affan Agà). Italian of Venice. Venetian family name Andretta. Ragusan Galley Scribe. Dragut Captive (1556). Renegade. Algiers Treasurer (1568). Commander of Guard Galleys at Rhodes (1571). Battle of Lepanto (1571). Beylerbey and Pasha of Algiers (1577-1580) and (1582-1583). Nominal Pasha of Tunis (1581). Pasha of Tripoli (1583-1589). (1544-Unk)

VERDALLE, LOUBENS (Loubens Verdalle, Hugues de Loubens de Verdalle, Hugues Cardinal de Loubenx de Verdalle, Bosio's and Pozzo's Ugo de Loubenx or Leubenx Verdala). French of Loubens in Gascony midway between Toulouse and Andorra. Third of three sons and one daughter of Philippe de Loubens de Verdalle and Anne de Montaut. Brother of Seigneur and Baron Jacques de Loubens de Verdalle, of Jeannot de Loubens de Verdalle, and of Anne de Loubens de Verdalle. Uncle of Hospitaller François d'Astorg de Segreville. Knight of Malta, Langue of Provence. Received at Age 15 (1546). Knight Commander of Lacapelle-Livron (1560-1581). Commander of La Bastit (1567-1570). Commander of Pézenas (1577-1581), later of Castelsarrasin (1582-1595). Resident Ambassador Holy See (1579-1580). Grand Commander (1579-1582), Knight of the Grand Cross. 52nd Grand Master of the Order of Jerusalem (1582-1595). Cardinal-Deacon of Santa Maria in Portico Octaviae (1587-1595). (1531-1595)

VILLEGAGNON, NICOLAS DURAND (Nicolas Durand de Villegagnon, Bosio's Nicolo Villegagnon). Of Provins, France. Son of Jeanne de Fresne and Louis Durand, King's Prosecutor in the village of Meaux, ennobled by Francis I in 1516 then taking the name Villegagnon. One of eight(?) brothers to become Hospitallers including Noel, Pierre, and Rene, a ninth, Philippe, succeeding as Sieur de Villegagnon. Knight Commander of the Commanderie at Beauvais where he dies in January 1571. Vice Admiral of Bretagne. "The greatest seaman of his time." Hospitaller Ambassador to Court of France (1568-1570). (c1510-1571)

VINCHEGUERRE, JACQUES (Jacques de Vincheguerre, Pozzo's Giacomo Vinciguerra). French. Son of Vincens de Vincheguerre and Venture Vachier. Pilot and Corsair of Malta, Gentleman (Ordinary Nobleman) of the King, Captain of Ships, Governor of the Tower of Saint John of the City of Marseille (1611), Commander of the Galleys of France, Lieutenant General of French Naval Armies (1622). (c1565-1622)

VINTIMILLE, BALTHAZARD (Balthazard de Vintimille, Baltazar/Balthasar de Vintimille, Bosio's Baldassarre di Vintimiglia/Ventimiglia, Pozzo's Baldassar de Conti di Vintimiglia). French of Ollioules 60 km SE of Marseille. Fourth of six children of Bertrand VII de Vintimille (d1518), seigneur d'Ollioules, d'Evenos and du Revest, and of Yolande de Vintimille-Lascaris wed 1495. Brother of Gaspard I (c1496-1570), Pliette (ca1498), Louise (1500-1531), Jeanne (c1507), and Melchion (1511-1554). Uncle of Hospitaller Bertrand de Vintimille. Knight of Malta, Langue of Provence. Commander of Marseille (bef 1563). Ottoman Siege of Malta (1565). Bailiff of Lango (1568-1569), Knight of the Grand Cross. Grand Commander (1569-1570). Prior of Toulouse (1570-1576). (c1505-1576)

VINTIMILLE, BERTRAND (Bertrand de Vintimille des comtes de Marseilles d'Ollioules). French of Ollioules 60 km SE of Marseille. Tenth of ten children of Gaspard de Vintimille and Anne d'Arcussiak. Nephew of Hospitaller Balthazard de Vintimille. Knight of Malta, Langue of Provence. Received (1547). Commander of Marseille (1563-1568+). Ottoman Siege of Malta (1565). Comissioner of Valletta Housing (1571). Lieutenant-Governor of Valletta (1573). (+)

VIRIEU, JACQUES (Jacques de Virieu, Jacques de Virieu-Pupetières, Bosio's Iaques de Virieù, Pupetieres, Pozzo's Giacomo de' Virieu Pupetieres). Knight of Malta, Langue of Auvergne. Received (1556). Grand Soccorso (1565). Chapter General (1574). Resident Ambassador and Procurator at the Holy See (1575-1579). Chapter General (1578). Lieutenant Marshal (1582). Final Elector (1582). Chapter General (1583). Marshal (1591-1597), Knight of the Grand Cross. Bailiff of Devesset (Lyons) (1597-1600). (+1600)

VIVALDO, LODOVICO (Lodovico Vivaldo, Luigi Vivaldo, Bosio's Luigi Viualdo, Pozzo's Lodouico Uiualdo). Italian of the Piedmont's Mondovi. Brother of Hospitallers Giovan Battista and Costanzo. Knight of Malta, Langue of Italy. Received (1557). Grand Soccorso (1565). Knight Commander. Lieutenant Admiral (1595). General Assembly Elector (1595). General of the Galleys (1595). (+1595)

VOGUEDEMAR, PIERRE DE MONTAUBAN (Pierre de Montauban (was Montdragon) de Voguedemar, the Knight of Voguedemar, Bosio's and Pozzo's Pietro de Montauban Voguedemar). French of Montauban 50km N of Toulouse. Knight of Malta, Langue of Provence. Received (1549). Sergeant-Major Siege of Penon de la Velez Gomera (1563). Grand Soccorso (1565). Galley Captain Battle of Cape Passero (1570). Ottoman Captive (1570-1572). Governor Castle San Angelo (1581). Seigneur and Commander of Montsaunès (1583-1597). Grand Commander (1594-1596), Knight of the Grand Cross. Magistral Lieutenant (1595). Prior of Toulouse (1597). (c1530-1597)

WEITINGEN, GEORG (Georg Christoph von Weitingen, Pozzo's Giorgio Christoforo de VUitemberg). German of Weitingen, Baden-Württemberg. A younger son of Hans Volz von Weitingen and Agnes von Landenberg und Greifensee. Kept a concubine and fathered three children. Knight of Malta, Langue of Germany. Received (c1587). Knight Commander of Hohenrain und Reiden (1594-1611). Titular Bailiff of Brandenburg (1605-1609), Knight of the Grand Cross. Prior of Dacia (1609-1612). Commander of Rottweil, Würzburg, and Biebelried (1612-1634). Grand Bailiff of Germany (1612-1634). (c1570-1634)

WIGNACOURT, ALOF (Alof de Wignacourt, Alof de Vignacourt, Alophius Vignacourt, Bosio's Vuignacourt, Pozzo's VUignacourt). French of Picardy. One of six sons and three daughters of Jean de Vignacourt, Seigneur de Litz in

Beauvoisie, Oise Department, Picardy, 95km N of Paris, and of Marie de la Porte of Anjou. Uncle of future Grand Master Adrien de Wignacourt, of Hospitallers Jacques du Chenu du Belloy, Henri and Claude de Lancry de Bains, and of François de Bertaucourt. Knight of Malta, Langue of France. Received (1565). Commander of La Villedieu-en-Dreugesin (1590-1601). Grand Hospitaller (1598-1601), Knight of the Grand Cross. 54th Grand Master of the Order of Jerusalem (1601-1622). Prince of the Holy Roman Empire (c1538-1631). (1547-1622)

WYSE, ANDREW (Andrew Wyse, Andrew Wise, Mifsud's Wysse/Wisse/Wyse, Pozzo's Andrea UVisse, VVise, or Wiffe.) Irish of Waterford, Munster. Second son of James Wyse (Lord of the Manor of St. John) and Alisomme Finglas. Knight of Malta, Langue of England. Received (1582) at Malta. Bailiff of Eagle (1588-1593), Knight of the Grand Cross. Commander of Maruggio, Taranto, Italy (1593-1631). Grand Prior of England (1593-1631). Counselor to King Philip III of Spain (Philip II of Naples) in Kingdom of Naples (1602). Inactive at Malta (1604-1631). (c1560-1631)

Endnotes

Chapter I

[1](Bicheno 148). [2](Setton III-872). [3](Setton IV-870). [4](Bosio III-699). [5](Bosio III-714). [6](Balbi 187). [7](Bosio III-711). [8](Bosio III-706 et seq, Anderson 24). [9](Bosio III-709 et seq). [10](Bosio III-714). [11](Bosio III-623). [12](Bosio III-623, 722). [13](Bosio III-710 et seq). [14](Bosio III-721). [15](Bosio III-725). [16](Bosio III-726). [17](Bosio III-728 et seq). [18](Bosio III-733 et seq). [19](Bosio III-738 et seq). [20](Bosio III-741 et seq). [21](Bosio III-749 et seq, Setton IV-899 et seq). [22](Bosio III-768 et seq). [23](Bosio III-769 et seq, Setton IV-899 et seq). [24](Bosio III-766 et seq, Setton IV-903). [25](Bosio III-774). [26](Anderson 25). [27](Bosio III-778). [28](Bosio III-775 et seq). [29](Bosio III-781 et seq). [30](Bosio III-783 et seq). [31](Bosio III-789 et seq). [32](Bosio III-790). [33](Setton IV-907). [34](Bosio III-790 et seq). [35](Bosio III-792). [36](Bosio III-792 et seq). [37](Bosio III-793). [38](Bosio III-793). [39](Bosio III-793 et seq). [40](Bosio III-794 et seq). [41](Bosio III-795). [42](Bosio III-796, Goussancourt I-25). [43](Bosio III-797). [44](Bosio III-800). [45](Bosio III-802). [46](Anderson 26). [47](Bosio III-807). [48](Bosio III-802 et seq). [49](Bosio III-803 et seq). [50](Bosio III-804). [51](Bosio III-807 and 813, Setton IV-932). [52](Bosio III-812). [53](Bosio III-812 et seq). [54](Bosio III-813 et seq, Setton IV-919). [55](Bosio III-814). [56](Bosio III-814 et seq). [57](Bosio III-817). [58](Bosio III-818 to III-825).

Chapter II

[1](Bosio III-821 et seq). [2](Bosio III-822 et seq; Boissat 1007). [3](Bosio III-825). [4](Bosio III-826). [5](Bosio III-825 et seq, Setton IV-934 et seq). [6](Bosio III-826 et seq). [7](Bosio III-828). [8](Bosio III-828 et seq). [9](Bosio III-829). [10](Bosio III-829 et seq). [11](Setton IV-933). [12](Bosio III-832 et seq). [13](Bosio III-838 et seq). [14](Bosio III-839 et seq). [15](Bosio III-845). [16](Bosio III-840). [17](Bosio III-841 et seq). [18](Bosio III-842 et seq). [19](Bosio III-843). [20](Bosio III-845). [21](Bosio III-846 et seq; Morgan 492 et seq). [21](Bosio III-846 et seq; Morgan 492 et seq). [22](*Middle Sea* 311; Setton IV-954). [23](Bosio III-847 et seq, Anderson 26). [24](Bosio III-848; Martyrologe I-115, I-223). [25](Bosio III-848 et seq). [26](Bosio III-852). [27](Anderson 30). [28](Bosio III-854). [29](Bosio III-855). [30](Bosio III-856). [31](Bosio III-857). [32](Bosio III-858). [33](Bosio III-858, Morgan I-495, Pozzo I-27; http://www.projetgordes.fr/displayLettres[384][lettresGordes]). [34](Bosio III-860). [35](Bosio III-858 et seq). [36](Bosio III-857 et seq). [37](Bosio III-863). [38](Bosio III-864, Anderson 31). [39](Anderson 32, Setton IV-985, Norwich's *History of Venice* 471 et seq). [40](Bosio III-870). [41](Bosio III-864 et seq, Setton IV-985 et seq). [42](Bosio III-868). [43](Bosio III-871, Anderson 34, Setton IV-1007). [44](Bosio III-871; Bicheno 276). [45](Bosio III-871; Boissat 1037). [46](Pozzo I-9, Malcolm 153, Anderson 36). [47](Setton IV-1022n). [48](Pozzo I-13). [49](Malcolm 157). [50](Setton IV-1030 et seq). [51](Norwich 479, Setton IV-1039 et seq). [52](Pozzo I-10). [53](Pozzo I-11; Bicheno 208; Malcolm 158). [54](Pozzo I-26). [55](Pozzo I-25 et seq; Bicheno 253; Martyrologe I-171, I-230). [56](Pozzo I-24). [57](Bicheno various). [58](Pozzo I-30). [59](Pozzo I-31). [60](Pozzo I-33). [61](Pozzo I-34). [62](Pozzo I-35; Anderson 47). [63](Pozzo I-38).

Chapter III

[1](Pozzo I-40). [2](Pozzo I-42 et seq). [3](Pozzo I-41 et seq). [4](Pozzo I-46 et seq). [5](Pozzo I-49). [6](Pozzo I-49 et seq). [7](Anderson 47). [8](Pozzo I-52, Setton IV-1078). [9](Pozzo I-51, Anderson 49 et seq). [10](Pozzo I-51, Anderson 49 et seq). [11](Setton IV-1089). [12](Pozzo I-55 et seq). [13](Braudel 604). [14](Pozzo I-57, Anderson 53, Setton IV-1086, Morgan 475). [15](Pozzo I-58 et seq). [16](Pozzo I-61). [17](Pozzo I-61). [18](Pozzo I-61 et seq). [19](Anderson 54 et seq, Setton IV-1094n). [20](Pozzo I-69). [21](Pozzo I-62 et seq). [22](Pozzo I-66). [23](Pozzo I-66 et seq, Setton IV-1094n). [24](Anderson 55 et seq). [25](Pozzo I-75 et seq; Anderson 56). [26](Pozzo I-68). [27](Pozzo I-74). [28](Pozzo I-74). [29](Pozzo I-76). [30](Pozzo I-68 et seq). [31](Pozzo I-76 et seq). [32](Anderson 56). [33](Pozzo I-77 et seq). [34](Pozzo I-78; Anderson 56). [35](Pozzo I-13, I-78, Anderson 56). [36](Pozzo I-91). [37](Pozzo I-93). [38](Pozzo I-93). [39](Bosio III-573; Pozzo I-100). [40](Pozzo I-100). [41](Pozzo I-100 et seq). [42](Pozzo I-101 et seq). [44](Pozzo I-105 et seq, Braudel I-332). [45](Pozzo I-107 et seq). [46](Pozzo I-108 et seq). [47](Pozzo I-111 et seq).

Chapter IV

[1](Pozzo I-111 et seq). [2](Pozzo I-113 et seq). [3](Pozzo I-114 et seq). [4](Pozzo I-116 et seq). [5](Anderson 58). [6](Pozzo I-117 et seq). [7](http://www.san.beck.org/9-8-Italy.html, http://italycallingturkeyforculturalexchange.blogspot.com.tr/2012/04/our-town-trebisacce.html). [8](Pozzo I-120 et seq). [9](Pozzo I-124 et seq). [10](Pozzo I-127). [11](Pozzo I-127 et seq). [12](Pozzo I-128 et seq). [13](Pozzo I-130 et seq). [14](Pozzo I-130; Morgan 524). [15](Pozzo I-143 et seq). [16](Pozzo I-143 et seq, Bicheno 247). [17](Pozzo I-133 et seq). [18](Pozzo I-145 et seq). [19](Pozzo I-146 et seq). [20](Pozzo I-147 et seq). [21](Pozzo I-148). [22](Pozzo I-148 et seq). [23](Pozzo I-150 et seq). [24](Pozzo I-155 et seq). [25](Pozzo I-159 et seq). [26](Pozzo I-156 et seq). [27](Pozzo I-158). [28](Pozzo I-161 et seq). [29](Pozzo I-165). [30](Pozzo I-165 et seq). [31](Pozzo I-166, Anderson 59). [32](Pozzo I-167). [33](Pozzo I-166). [34](Pozzo I-168). [35](Pozzo I-166 et seq). [36](Pozzo I-161 et seq; Ambrogi). [37](Pozzo I-169). [38](Pozzo I-169 et seq). [39](Pozzo I-173 et seq, Boisgelen 314). [40](Pozzo I-171 et seq). [41](https://cvc.cervantes.es/literatura/cervantistas/coloquios/cl_XII/cl_XII_15.pdf). [42](Pozzo I-174). [43](Pozzo I-174). [44](Pozzo I-174 et seq, Morgan 524 et seq). [45](Pozzo I-176). [46](Pozzo I-178). [47](Pozzo I-176 et seq, Morgan 569 et seq). [48](Pozzo I-179 et seq, Anderson 59). [49](Pozzo I-186). [50](Pozzo I-189 et seq, TimesOfMalta@Romegas2).

Chapter V

[1](Pozzo I-212). [2](Pozzo I-213). [3](Pozzo I-215). [4](Pozzo I-216). [5](Pozzo I-218 et seq). [6](Pozzo I-220). [7](Pozzo I-220 et seq; Morgan 575). [8](Pozzo I-223). [9](Pozzo I-224). [10](Pozzo I-225). [11](Pozzo I-221). [12](Pozzo I-221 et seq). [13](Pozzo I-222). [14](Pozzo I-231). [15](Pozzo I-229). [16](Pozzo I-226 et seq). [17](Pozzo I-232). [18](Pozzo I-231). [19](Pozzo I-233). [20](Pozzo I-234). [21](Pozzo I-235 et seq). [22](Pozzo I-237). [23](Pozzo I-238 et seq). [24](Pozzo I-241 et seq). [25](Pozzo I-243 et seq). [26](Pozzo I-247 et seq). [27](Pozzo I-248). [28](Pozzo I-249 et seq). [29](Pozzo I-251). [30](Pozzo I-253 et seq). [31](Pozzo I-254 et seq). [32](Pozzo I-255; Anderson 60). [33](Pozzo I-256). [34](Pozzo I-260). [35](http://artevalladolid.blogspot.com/2015/07/monumentos-desaparecidos-la-casa-de-los.html). [36](Pozzo I-260 et seq). [37](Pozzo I-262). [38](Pozzo I-262 et seq). [39](Pozzo I-266). [40](Pozzo I-269). [41](Pozzo I-266 et seq). [42](Pozzo I-267). [43](Pozzo I-271 et seq). [44](Pozzo I-276). [45](Pozzo I-273). [46](Pozzo I-276 et seq). [47](Pozzo I-273 et seq). [48](Pozzo I-278 et seq). [49](Pozzo I-281 et seq). [50](Pozzo I-282 et seq). [51](Pozzo I-277). [52](Pozzo I-285 et seq). [53](Pozzo I-287; Martyrologe I-34). [54](Pozzo I-287). [55](Pozzo I-292 et seq). [56](Pozzo I-293 et seq).

Chapter VI

[1](Pozzo I-294 et seq). [2](Pozzo I-297 et seq). [3](Pozzo I-301 et seq). [4](Pozzo I-304). [5](Pozzo I-312). [6]Pozzo I-304 et seq; http://www.histparl.ac.uk/volume/1509-1558/member/starkey-oliver-1523-8386; Porter II-295; Mifsud 218. [7](Pozzo I-304). [8](Pozzo I-308). [9](Pozzo I-308 et seq; Guglielmotti (A2) 41). [10](Pozzo I-309 et seq). [11](Pozzo I-310 et seq). [12](Pozzo I-313 et seq). [13](Pozzo I-313). [14](Pozzo I-314 et seq). [15](Pozzo I-314-2 et seq). [16](Pozzo I-317). [17](Pozzo I-318). [18](Pozzo I-318 et seq). [19](Pozzo I-320 et seq). [20](Pozzo I-320 et seq, Mifsud 24). [21](Pozzo I-321 et seq, Braudel I-603 et seq). [22](Pozzo I-322). [23](Pozzo I-325). [24](Pozzo I-323 et seq). [25](Pozzo I-326). [26](Pozzo I-328). [27](Pozzo I-329). [28](Pozzo I-329 et seq). [29](Pozzo I-330). [30](Roque 94). [31](Pozzo I-327 et seq; Braudel 603 et seq). [32](Pozzo I-332). [33](Pozzo I-335 et seq). [34](Pozzo I-336 et seq). [35](Pozzo I-343). [36](Pozzo I-343 et seq, Braudel 1199, Setton 6). [37](Pozzo I-344). [38](Pozzo I-344). [39](Pozzo I-344 et seq). [40](Pozzo I-346). [41](Pozzo I-347 et seq). [42](Pozzo I-348). [43](Pozzo I-348 et seq). [44](Keegan). [45](Pozzo I-352, Anderson 63). [46](Bosio III-462, Pozzo I-351). [47](Pozzo I-352). [48](Pozzo I-351 et seq). [49](Pozzo I-352; Anderson 65; Guglielmotti (A2) 117 et seq). [50](Pozzo I-357). [51](Pozzo I-355 et seq; www.academia.edu/16198712/Justices_and_Injustices_the_Order_of_St_John_the_Holy_ See_and_the_ Appeals_Tribunal_in_Rome). [52](Pozzo I-359). [53](Pozzo I-368). [54](Pozzo I-366).

Chapter VII

[1](Pozzo I-366 et seq). [2](Pozzo I-368 et seq). [3](Pozzo I-369 et seq). [4](Morgan 607). [5](Pozzo I-371). [6](Pozzo I-372; Anderson 64). [7](Pozzo I-372 et seq; Morgan 609). [8](Pozzo I-374 et seq). [9](Pozzo I-375; Contreras 21). [10](Pozzo I-377). [11](Pozzo I-379). [12](Pozzo I-380). [13](Pozzo I-379 et seq). [14](Guglielmotti(A2) 126). [15](Pozzo I-381). [16](Pozzo I-381 et seq). [17](Pozzo I-382 et seq, Anderson 64). [18](Pozzo I-383). [19](Pozzo I-385 et seq). [20](Pozzo I-388). [21](Pozzo I-391). [22](Pozzo I-392). [23](Pozzo I-393 et seq). [24](Pozzo I-394). [25](Pozzo I-394 et seq). [26](Pozzo I-397). [27](Pozzo I-400). [28](Pozzo I-400; Setton V-14; Sire 201). [29](Pozzo I-400 et seq; Mifsud 36, 218). [30](Pozzo I-402 et seq). [31](Pozzo I-403). [32](Pozzo I-403 et seq). [33](Pozzo I-404 et seq). [34](Pozzo I-405 et seq). [35](Pozzo I-407 et seq). [36](Pozzo I-408). [37](Pozzo I-411). [38](Pozzo I-411 et seq). [39](Pozzo I-415). [40](Pozzo I-422). [41](Pozzo I-421 et seq). [42](Pozzo I-423). [43](Pozzo I-424). [44](Pozzo I-425 et seq; Goussancourt I-170, I-300). [45](Pozzo I-425 et seq). [46](Pozzo I-426). [47](Pozzo I-427). [48](Pozzo I-318). [49](Pozzo I-428). [50](Pozzo I-427 et seq; Pozzo I-425 et seq; Goussancourt I-307). [51](Pozzo I-432 et seq; Contreras 25). [52](Pozzo I-433 et seq). [53](Pozzo I-437). [54](Pozzo I-438 et seq).

Chapter VIII

[1](Pozzo I-440 et seq). [2](Pozzo I-441 et seq). [3](Pozzo I-442 et seq). [4](Pozzo I-443 et seq). [5](Pozzo I-445 et seq; Mifsud 134). [6](Pozzo I-447). [7](Pozzo I-447 et seq). [8](Pozzo I-449 et seq; Anderson 66; Guglielmotti(A2) 150 et seq). [9](Anderson 66). [10](Pozzo I-451). [11](Pozzo I-451; Contreras 39). [12](Pozzo I-450 et seq; *Contreras* 39). [13](Pozzo I-454). [14](Pozzo I-453). [15](Pozzo I-458). [16](Pozzo I-459 et seq). [17](Pozzo I-461 et seq; Contreras 39). [18](Pozzo I-462 et seq; Contreras 39 et seq). [19](Pozzo I-463). [20](Pozzo I-463; *Contreras* 41). [21](Pozzo I-464; Contreras 44). [22](Pozzo I-463 et seq; Anderson 68). [23](Pozzo I-460 et seq). [24](Pozzo I-470 et seq). [25](Pozzo I-472). [26](Pozzo I-472; Anderson 68). [27](Pozzo I-477). [28](Pozzo I-478; http://blog.peramuzesi.org.tr/en/haftanin-eseri/savoyali-filippo-emanuele/). [29](Pozzo I-479). [30](Pozzo I-480). [31](Pozzo I-481). [32](Pozzo I-481 et seq).

33(Pozzo I-482; Guglielmotti(A2) 165 et seq). 34(maltahistory.eu5.net /mh2/19752.html; Pozzo I-487 et seq;) 35(Pozzo I-437 et seq). 36(Pozzo I-485 et seq). 37(Pozzo I-488 et seq). 38(Pozzo I-489). 39(Pozzo I-490). 40(Pozzo I-491). 41(Pozzo I-492). 42(Pozzo I-493). 43(Pozzo I-492, Dubé 102). 44 Pozzo I-493 et seq). 45(Pozzo I-496 et seq; Anderson 70). 46(Pozzo I-497 et seq). 47(Pozzo I-498; Goussancourt I-320). 48(Pozzo I-499). 49(Pozzo I-499 et seq). 50(Pozzo I-503). 51(Pozzo I-507). 52(Pozzo I-507 et seq, Goussancourt I-117). 53(Pozzo I-515 et seq). 54(Pozzo I-483). 55(Pozzo I-516 et seq, Contreras 118 et seq). 56(Pozzo I-516 et seq; Contreras 118 et seq).

Chapter IX

1(Pozzo I-520). 2(Pozzo I-520 et seq). 3(Pozzo I-524). 4(Pozzo I-524 et seq). 5(Pozzo I-525). 6(Pozzo I-525, Malcolm 410 et seq). 7(Pozzo I-531). 8(Pozzo I-532 et seq). 9(Pozzo I-531 et seq). 10(Pozzo I-535 et seq). 11(Pozzo I-533). 12(Pozzo I-537 et seq). 13(Pozzo I-539 et seq). 14(Pozzo I-540 et seq). 15(Pozzo I-542). 16(Pozzo I-542 et seq). 17(Pozzo I-543). 18(Pozzo I-543 et seq). 19(Pozzo I-544). 20(Pozzo I-545). 21(Pozzo I-549). 22(Pozzo I-551 et seq). 23(Pozzo I-553). 24(Pozzo I-553 et seq). 25(Pozzo I-556). 26(Pozzo I-553 et seq). 27(Pozzo I-555). 28(Pozzo I-556). 29(Pozzo I-545; Dubé 265). 30(Anderson 75; Goussancourt 367; Imber). 31(Pozzo I-557). 32(Pozzo I-558). 33(Pozzo I-558; Anderson 76 et seq). 34(Pozzo I-558 et seq). 35(Pozzo I-560). 36(Pozzo I-560; Anderson 77). 37(Pozzo I-565 et seq). 38(Pozzo I-567 et seq). 39(Pozzo I-568 et seq). 40(Pozzo I-569 et seq). 41(Pozzo I-568, I-573). 42(Pozzo I-571). 43(Pozzo I-571; Anderson 78). 44(Pozzo I-572 et seq). 45(Pozzo I-574). 46(Pozzo I-573). 47(Pozzo I-573 et seq; Anderson 78; Bean 91). 48(Pozzo I-578; Anderson 79; Goussancourt I-51).

Chapter X

1(Pozzo I-575 et seq). 2(Anderson 79). 3(Pozzo I-578 et seq; Anderson 79). 4(Pozzo I-579 et seq). 5(https://www.british-history.ac.uk/cal-state-papers/venice/vol15/v-1). 6(Pozzo I-584). 7(Pozzo I-586 et seq; Guglielmotti(A2) 237). 8(Pozzo I-582). 9(Pozzo I-582 et seq). 10(Pozzo I-587). 11(Pozzo I-587 et seq; Anderson 80). 12(Pozzo I-588; Aydin). 13(Pozzo I-588 et seq; Anderson 81). 14(Pozzo I-589 et seq). 15(Pozzo I-591 et seq). 16(Pozzo I-593 et seq). 17(Pozzo I-595 et seq; Guglielmotti(A2) 240 et seq). 18(Pozzo I-598). 19(Pozzo I-598 et seq). 20(Pozzo I-599). 21(Pozzo I-599 et seq). 22(Pozzo I-601). 23(Pozzo I-601 et seq). 24(Pozzo I-603 et seq). 25(Pozzo I-605 et seq). 26(Pozzo I-604). 27(Pozzo I-604 et seq; GuglielmottiA2 193 & 245). 28(Pozzo I-610 et seq). 29(Treccani, Anderson 82). 30(Pozzo I-611; Anderson 84). 31(Pozzo I-613). 32(Pozzo I-613 et seq). 33(Pozzo I-622 et seq; Anderson 85). 34(Pozzo I-624; Goussancourt I-61; *An Universal History* Vol 61-502). 35(Pozzo I-624; Anderson 85). 36(Pozzo I-624 et seq; Anderson 85; Norwich 336). 37Deleted. 38(Anderson 86 et seq). 39Deleted. 40(Pozzo I-626 et seq). 41(Pozzo I-626 et seq). 42(Pozzo I-627 et seq; Anderson 90 et seq). 43(Anderson 96). 44(*History of Venice* 522 et seq; https://www.british-history.ac.uk/cal-state-papers/venice/vol15/v-1). 45(Goussancourt II-218; Pozzo I-628). 46(Pozzo I-628 et seq). 47(Pozzo I-629; Anderson 106).

Chapter XI

1(Contreras 196 et seq). 2(Pozzo I-632). 3(Pozzo I-634). 4(https://www.british-history.ac.uk/cal-state-papers/venice/vol15/v-1; Anderson 98 et seq). 5(Pozzo I-630). 6(Pozzo I-634). 7(Pozzo I-635 et seq; Anderson 106; Goussancourt I-46 et seq). 8(Pozzo I-636).

[9](www.british-history.ac.uk/cal-state-papers/venice/vol15/v-1; Anderson 102). [10](www.british-history.ac.uk/cal-state-papers/venice/vol15/v-1; Anderson 102). [11](Anderson 102). [12](Pozzo I-638 et seq). [13](Anderson 107). [14](Pozzo I-639). [15](Pozzo I-639). [16](Pozzo I-640 et seq). [17](Pozzo I-641). [18](Pozzo I-644 et seq; Anderson 108; Guglielmotti (A2)-251 et seq). [19](Pozzo I-644 et seq; Anderson 108). [20](Pozzo I-644 et seq; Anderson 108; Goussancourt I-13, I-258). [21](Pozzo I-649 et seq; Anderson 108; Guglielmotti(A2) 249). [22](Anderson 108). [23](Contreras 201 et seq). [24](Pozzo I-653). [25](Pozzo I-653 et seq). [26](Pozzo I-654). [27](Pozzo I-654 et seq). [28](Pozzo I-656 et seq; Anderson 109). [29](Pozzo I-657). [30](Pozzo I-659). [31](Pozzo I-658; Guglielmotti (A2) 252). [32](Pozzo I-657 et seq; www.statoquotidiano.it/26/01/2016/427899/427899/; Guglielmotti(A2) 252). [33](Pozzo I-659 et seq). [34](Pozzo I-669 et seq). [35](Pozzo I-670 et seq). [36](Pozzo I-680 et seq). [37](Pozzo I-673 et seq). [38](Pozzo I-683 et seq). [39](Pozzo I-685 et seq). [40](Pozzo I-718; Anderson 110). [41](Pozzo I-686). [42](Pozzo I-687 et seq). [43](Pozzo I-703; Anderson 110). [44](Pozzo I-691 et seq).

Chapter XII

[1](Pozzo I-691 et seq). [2](Pozzo I-695 et seq). [3](Pozzo I-700 et seq). [4](Pozzo I-702 et seq). [5](Pozzo I-705). [6](Pozzo I-706; Goussancourt I-393; Aubert de la Chesnaye's Dictionnaire de la noblesse VI-367). [7](Pozzo I-705; http://www.arqnet.pt/dicionario/vasconcelosjoannem.html)

Bibliography

Ambrogi P-R (2017) *Dictionnaire encyclopédique de Jeanne d'Arc*. Bilbao. Desclée De Brouwer

Anderson R (1952) *Naval Wars in the Levant 1559-1853*. Liverpool: University Press

Aprile F (1725) *Della cronologia universale della Sicilia*

Aydin M (2012) *Halil Paşa İbn Piri Vakfiyesi*. İstanbul. Kartal Türk Kızılayı Anadolu Lisesi Tarih Öğretmeni

Balbi F (2005) *The Siege of Malta, 1565*. Woodbridge, UK: The Boydell Press

Bean G (1989) *Aegean Turkey*. London. John Murray Publishers

Bicheno H (2004) *The Crescent and Cross*. London. Orion Books Ltd

Blackwood's Edinburgh Magazine No. 322 (1842)

Boisgelen L (1805), *Ancient and Modern History of Malta,* London, Richard Phillips

Boyssat (Boissat), P (1612) *Histoire des Chevaliers de l'Ordre de l'Hospital de S. Iean de Hiervsalem* Translated from the Italian by Guillaume Roville at Lyon

Bosio G (1601) *Della Terza Parte Dell'istoria della sacra religione ed ill.ma militia di San Giovanni Vol III*

Braudel F (1972) *The Mediterranean in the Age of Philip II*. New York: Harper Collins

Caird LH (1899) *The History of Corsica*. London: Unwin

Contreras A (Unk) *The life of Captain Alonso De Contreras*. Kessinger Publishing

Dubé J (2005) *The Chevalier de Montmagny (1601–1657)*. University of Ottawa Press

Funes J (c1650) *Coronica de la milicia y sagrada religion de San Juan Bautista ...,* Volume 2

Goussancourt M (1654) *Le Martyrologe de Chevaliers, Vol I & II*. Paris: Simeon Piget

Guglielmotti(A1) (1876) *La guerra dei pirati e la marina pontificia dal 1500 al 1560, vol. 2.* Florence Guglielmotti(A2) (1892) *Marina Pontificia: La Squadra Permanente Della Marina Romana, 1573-1644*

Imber C (2004) *Frontiers of Ottoman Studies*. I.B. Tauris, London

Inalcik H (2000) *The Ottoman Empire*. London. Phoenix Press

Keegan J (1996) *Who's Who in Military History*. London, Routledge

Lea H (1901) *The Moriscoes of Spain*. Philadelphia: Lea Brothers

Malcolm N (2015) *Agents of Empire*. New York City; Oxford University Press

Manfroni C (1895) *La Marine Militare del Granducato Mediceo Part 1*. Rome: Forzani

Mancing H (2003) *Cervantes Encyclopedia* Westport, Conn; Greenwood Publishing

Mifsud A (1914) *Knights Hospitallers of the Ven. Tongue of England in Malta*. Malta

Montluc B (1592) *Commentaires de Messire Blaise de Montluc*. Bordeaux

Morgan J (1731) *A Complete History of Algiers*. London. J Bettenham

Norwich J (1982) *History of Venice*. New York: Knopf Publishing

Norwich J (2006) *The Middle Sea: A History of the Mediterranean* New York: Doubleday

Porter W (1858) *History of the Knights of Malta Vols I & II*. London: Longman Brown

Pozzo B (1715) *Historia della Sacra Religione Militare di San Giovanni*. Venice: Gerolamo Albrizzi

Roque L (1891) *Catalogue des Chevaliers de Malte*. Paris. Alp. Desaide, Gravure Heraldique

Roncière (La) C (1906) *Histoire de la marine française*. Paris: Plon-Nourrit

Setton K (1976) *The Papacy and the Levant*, Philadelphia: The American Philosophical Society

Sire HJA (1996) *The Knights Of Malta*. New Haven: Yale University Press

Zimmerman P (1995) *Paolo Giovio and the Crisis of 16th Century Italy*. Princeton University Press

Index

Map of the Mediterranean.

www.ingramcontent.com/pod-product-compliance
Lightning Source LLC
Chambersburg PA
CBHW051219150426

42812CB00070BA/3371/J